DIABETIC
COOKBOOK FOR BEGINNERS

2000 Simple and Tasty Recipes for the Newly Diagnosed to Take Back Your Well-Being and Live Healthier

Lisa White

© **Copyright 2022 - All rights reserved.**

The content contained within this book may not be reproduced, duplicated or transmitted without direct written permission from the author or the publisher.

Under no circumstances will any blame or legal responsibility be held against the publisher, or author, for any damages, reparation, or monetary loss due to the information contained within this book. Either directly or indirectly.

Legal Notice:

This book is copyright protected. This book is only for personal use. You cannot amend, distribute, sell, use, quote or paraphrase any part, or the content within this book, without the consent of the author or publisher.

Disclaimer Notice:

Please note the information contained within this document is for educational and entertainment purposes only. All effort has been executed to present accurate, up to date, and reliable, complete information. No warranties of any kind are declared or implied. Readers acknowledge that the author is not engaging in the rendering of legal, financial, medical or professional advice. The content within this book has been derived from various sources. Please consult a licensed professional before attempting any techniques outlined in this book.

By reading this document, the reader agrees that under no circumstances is the author responsible for any losses, direct or indirect, which are incurred as a result of the use of information contained within this document, including, but not limited to, errors, omissions, or inaccuracies.

Table Of Contents

INTRODUCTION 18

ALL YOU NEED TO KNOW ABOUT DIABETES 19

   WHAT IS DIABETES? 19
   TYPES OF DIABETES 19
   WHAT IS HEALTHY EATING? 20
   FOODS THAT ARE GOOD FOR DIABETES 20
   FOODS WHICH ARE BAD FOR DIABETES 20

ESSENTIAL THINGS ABOUT SUGAR AND NUTRIENTS 21

   SHOULD I ELIMINATE SUGAR FROM MY DIET? 21
   DAILY CALORIE CONSUMPTION 21
   HOW MUCH OF SUGAR IS TOO MUCH? 21
   FOODS WITH HIGH SUGAR CONTENT 22

CHAPTER 3 BREAKFAST 23

   COCONUT AND BERRY SMOOTHIE 23
   WALNUT AND OAT GRANOLA 23
   CRISPY PITA WITH CANADIAN BACON 23
   COCONUT-BERRY SUNRISE SMOOTHIE 23
   AVOCADO AND GOAT CHEESE TOAST 24
   OAT AND WALNUT GRANOLA 24
   ZUCCHINI NOODLES WITH CREAMY AVOCADO PESTO 24
   AVOCADO CHICKEN SALAD 24
   PANCAKES WITH BERRIES 24
   OMELETTE À LA MARGHERITA 25
   SPANAKOPITA FRITTATA 25
   RATATOUILLE EGG BAKE 25
   COTTAGE PANCAKES 25
   GREEK YOGURT AND OAT PANCAKES 26
   SAVORY BREAKFAST EGG BITES 26
   SIMPLE GRAIN-FREE BISCUITS 26
   BRUSSELS SPROUT WITH FRIED EGGS 26
   VANILLA COCONUT PANCAKES 27
   CHEESY SPINACH AND EGG CASSEROLE 27
   CHOCOLATE-ZUCCHINI MUFFINS 27
   GLUTEN-FREE CARROT AND OAT PANCAKES 27
   BREAKFAST EGG BITES 28

   TACOS WITH PICO DE GALLO 28
   COCONUT AND CHIA PUDDING 28
   TOMATO WAFFLES 28
   BREAKFAST HOMEMADE POULTRY SAUSAGE 29
   SAUSAGE AND PEPPER BURRITO 29
   GOUDA EGG CASSEROLE 29
   BREAKFAST DIABETIC PANCAKES 30
   BLUEBERRY MUFFINS 30
   APPLE AND BRAN MUFFINS 30
   COCONUT AND BERRY OATMEAL 30
   CRISPY BREAKFAST PITA WITH EGG AND CANADIAN BACON 31
   APPLE AND PUMPKIN WAFFLES 31
   LAVENDER BLUEBERRY CHIA SEED PUDDING 31
   YOGURT WITH GRANOLA AND PERSIMMON 31
   SMOOTHIE BOWL WITH SPINACH, MANGO, AND MUESLI 32
   FRIED EGG WITH BACON 32
   BUCKWHEAT CRÊPES 32
   HAM AND CHEESE BREAKFAST BISCUITS 32
   HAM AND JICAMA HASH 32
   GREEK YOGURT SUNDAE 33
   MUSHROOM FRITTATA 33
   TROPICAL YOGURT KIWI BOWL 33
   BANANA CRÊPE CAKES 33
   BRUSSELS SPROUT HASH AND EGGS 33
   SPINACH, ARTICHOKE, AND GOAT CHEESE BREAKFAST BAKE 34
   HOMEMADE TURKEY BREAKFAST SAUSAGE 34
   CHEESY LOW-CARB OMELET 34
   ROASTED ONIONS AND GREEN BEANS 34
   DENVER OMELET 34
   HUNGARIAN PORRIDGE 35
   SCRAMBLED PESTO EGGS 35
   VANILLA HEMP DRINK 35
   PEPPERONI OMELET 35
   DELICIOUS NUT DREDGED PORRIDGE 35
   CRISPY TOFU 35
   COTTAGE CHEESE HOTCAKE 36
   MUSHROOM MUFFIN 36

Cinnamon And Coconut Porridge	36
Skillet-Based Kale And Avocado	36
Fat Burner Espresso	36
Blue Cheese Omelet	37
Hearty Chia Bowls	37
Pecan And Goat Cheese	37
Broccoli Egg Salad	37
Creamy Cheese Pancakes	37
Delicious Egg Muffins	37
Double Stuffed Cheese Peppers	37
Baked Stuffed Up Avocados	38
Colorful Vegetable Omelet	38
Simple Fried Eggs	38
Beef And Egg Early Morning Muffin	38
Spicy Chili Deviled Eggs	38
Classic Egg Porridge	38
Juicy Spanish Omelet	39
Delicious Breakfast Sausage Casserole	39
Excellent Scrambled Mug Eggs	39
Unique Salmon Omelet	39
Fine Spinach And Cheese Eggs	39
The Breakfast Margarita	39
Homely Honeydew Twist	40
The Sweet Melon Morning Kale	40
The Ultimate Morning Green	40
Fine Liquid Sunrise	40
Morning Aloha Smoothie	40
The Banana Delight	40
The Raspberry Minty Delight	40
The Rising Red Sun	41
Cinnamon And Beet Booster Dose	41
The Wisest Watermelon Glass	41
Cheery Charlie Checker	41
The Pom Drink	41
Bright Rainbow Health	41
Juicy Scotch Egg	42
Toasty Cauliflower And Avocado	42
Avocado Egg Crepes	42

Bacon And Shallots With Spinach	42
Mango And Pear Smoothie	42
Mesmerizing Artichoke Frittata	42
Egg In An Acorn	43
Barley Porridge	43
Tomato And Dill Frittata	43
Strawberry And Rhubarb Smoothie	43
Bacon Brie And Omelette Wedges	44
Greek Chicken And Penne Delight	44
Bacon And Chicken Pasta	44
Cocoa Pumpkin	44
Twisty Cucumber Honeydew	45
Berry-Licious Meta Booster	45
Healthy Potato Pie Glass	45
Vegetable And Green Tea Smoothie	45
Tropical Kiwi Pineapple	45
Greens And Herbs For All	45
Avocado And Edamame Drink	46
Peanut Butter And Cherry Delight	46
White Bean And Mango Delight	46
Cashew Apple Glass	46
Spicy Pear And Green Tea	46

CHAPTER 4 LUNCH 47

Warm Chicken and Spinach Salad	47
Stuffed Chicken	47
Chicken Sandwich	47
Buttermilk Fried Chicken	47
Zaatar Lamb Loin Chops	48
Vietnamese Grilled Pork	48
Provencal Ribs	48
Steak	48
Marinated Loin Potatoes	49
Beef with Mushrooms	49
Cheesy and Crunchy Russian Steaks	49
Chicken Nuggets	49
Pork Chops	50
Buffalo Chicken Hot Wings	50

Recipe	Page
Herb Chicken Thighs	50
Air Fryer Beef Steak Kabobs with Vegetables	51
Pork Liver	51
Air Fried Meatloaf	51
Pork Bondiola Chop	51
Air Fry Rib-Eye Steak	51
Asparagus And Lemon Salmon Dish	51
Walnut Encrusted Salmon	52
Especial Glazed Salmon	52
Lovely Molten Tuna Bites	52
Hearty Lemon And Butter Cod	52
A Broccoli And Tilapia Dish To Die For	52

CHAPTER 5 MEATLESS MAINS 54

Recipe	Page
Crispy Parmesan Cups with White Beans and Veggies	54
Lime Asparagus with Cashews	54
Cabbage Wedges	54
Black Pepper & Garlic Tofu	54
Watermelon & Arugula Salad	55
Broccoli & Mushroom Salad	55
French toast	55
Butter-orange Yams	56
Grilled Portobello & Zucchini Burger	56
Tarragon Spring Peas	56
Crust Less Broccoli Quiche	56
Potatoes with Provencal Herbs with Cheese	56
Spiced Potato Wedges	57
Roasted Delicata Squash with Thyme	57
Creamy Macaroni and Cheese	57
Creamy Pasta with Peas	57
Sesame Bok Choy with Almonds	57
Roasted Cauliflower with Tomatoes	58
Fried Avocado	58
Scrambled Eggs with Beans, Zucchini, Potatoes and Onions	58
Cantaloupe & Prosciutto Salad	58
Green Beans	59
Garden Vegetable Pasta	59
Teriyaki Tofu Burger	59
Tofu Curry	59
Faux Chow Mein	59
Roasted Tomato and Bell Pepper Soup	60
Festive Holiday Salad	60
Grilled Vegetable & Noodle Salad	60
Holiday Apple & Cranberry Salad	60
Zucchini "pasta" Salad	60
Homemade Vegetable Chili	61
Collard Greens with Tomato	61
Okra	61
Grilled Tofu & Veggie Skewers	61
Mushroom Cutlets with Creamy Sauce	62
Falafel with Creamy Garlic-Yogurt Sauce	62
Roasted Onions And Green Beans	62
Walnuts And Asparagus Delight	63
Hearty Roasted Cauliflower	63
Almond And Blistered Beans	63
Portobello Mushroom Risotto	63
Portobello Mushrooms And Cherry Tomatoes Mix	63
The Medi-Wrap	64
Garbanzo and Spinach Beans	64
Cilantro and Avocado Platter	64
Baby Potatoes Roast	64
Pineapple, Papaya, and Mango Delight	64
Grilled Eggplant Steaks	64
Everyday Traditional Chili	65
Cashew Mushroom Rice Risotto	65
Mediterranean Kale Dish	65
Authentic Zucchini Boats	65
Delicious Garlic Toast	65
Sesame Cucumber Mix	65
Lemon and Thyme Couscous	66
Roasted Sweet Potatoes And Brussels Sprouts	66
Curry Spiced Cauliflower with Toasted Pistachios	66
Mediterranean Zucchini Mushroom Pasta	66
Gentle Sweet Potato Curry	67

BROILED PORTOBELLO MUSHROOM BURGERS WITH GOAT CHEESE 67
GREEN BEAN STEW 67
ROASTED PARMESAN BROCCOLI 67
RED PEPPER HUMMUS WITH FRESH VEGGIES 67
MASHED CELERIAC 68
BAKED SPINACH AND FETA 68
FANTASTIC MEDITERRANEAN KALE 68

CHAPTER 6 GRAINS, BEANS AND LEGUMES 69

BLACK BEAN AND TOMATO SOUP WITH LIME YOGURT 69
CLASSIC TEXAS CAVIAR 69
LETTUCE TOMATO SALAD 69
CHICKEN CABBAGE SALAD 69
BELL PEPPER BLACK OLIVE SALAD 69
CHICKPEA WRAPS FOR QUESADILLAS 70
EGGS AND SNAP PEAS FRIED RICE 70
BAKED MARGARINE CHEESY FISH 70
THE BEST EVER VEGGIE FAJITAS 70
WEEKNIGHT CHICKPEA SPAGHETTI BOLOGNESE 70
FAT FREE SOFRITO DUMPLINGS 71
GARLIC ZUCCHINI CHICKEN SOUP 71
CHESTNUT LETTUCE WRAPS 71
CRISPY COWBOY BLACK BEAN FRITTERS 71
DANDELION AND BEET GREENS 72
BLACK BEAN, CORN, AND CHICKEN SOUP 72
KALE & CARROT VEGGIE SOUP 72
EGG PEA MIX WRAPPED IN KALE LEAVES 72
PEPPERONI CHEESED PITA 73
TOMATO GREEN CHILIES SOUP WITH LIME YOGURT 73
PERFECT CORN SALAD WITH PAPRIKA DRESSING 73
LOW SODIUM VEGGIE GREENS WITH BLACK BEANS 73
CLASSY CHICKEN BLACK BEAN SOUP 73
VEGETABLE BROTH KIDNEY BEANS VEGGIE BOWL 74
SPICY BROWN RICE WITH RED PEPPER & PAPRIKA 74
CHICKEN RICE WITH ALMOND CRANBERRY SALAD ...74
APPLE AND ALMOND BUTTER SPREAD PITA 75
BABY SPINACH WALNUT SALAD 75
RED KIDNEY BEANS WITH TOMATOES 75
BROWN RICE WITH CARROT, AND SCRAMBLED EGG 75
WILD RICE AND CRANBERRIES SALAD 75
MACARONI AND VEGETABLE PIE 76

CHAPTER 7 FISH AND SEAFOOD 77

SEA BASS AND RICE 77
SEA BASS AND CAULIFLOWER 77
CAJUN SALMON 77
TROUT AND ZUCCHINIS 77
CRAB CAKES 77
AIR FRIED CATFISH 77
GARLIC PARMESAN SHRIMP 78
ASIAN SESAME COD 78
EASY TUNA WRAPS 78
MUSTARD-CRUSTED SOLE 78
BAKED SALMON WITH GARLIC PARMESAN TOPPING 78
BLACKENED SHRIMP 79
CAJUN CATFISH 79
CAJUN FLOUNDER AND TOMATOES 79
CRISPY CALAMARI 79
CILANTRO SALMON 79
SESAME SALMON 79
OLD BAY CRAB STICKS WITH GARLIC MAYO 80
MANGO SHRIMP SKEWERS 80
SALMON WITH FENNEL AND CARROT 80
RANCH TILAPIA FILLETS 80
CILANTRO LIME GRILLED SHRIMP 80
CRAB FRITTATA 81
CRUNCHY LEMON SHRIMP 81
GRILLED TUNA STEAKS 81
CHILEAN SEA BASS WITH GREEN OLIVE RELISH 81
CILANTRO LIME SHRIMP 81
PANKO COCONUT SHRIMP 82
SHRIMP COLESLAW 82
EASY CREAMY SHRIMP NACHOS 82
ROASTED RED SNAPPER 82
SWORDFISH STEAKS AND TOMATOES 82

- Buttery Cod 83
- Lemon Scallops with Asparagus 83
- Honey Lemon Snapper with Fruit 83
- Fresh Rosemary Trout 83
- Asian-Inspired Swordfish Steaks 83
- Fish Tacos 84
- Lime Baked Salmon 84
- Lime Trout and Shallots 84
- Healthy Tuna Croquettes 84
- Generous Stuffed Salmon Avocado 84
- Baked Halibut Delight 84
- Hungry Tuna Bites 85
- Tilapia Broccoli Platter 85
- Simple Baked Shrimp With Béchamel Sauce 85
- Simple Sautéed Garlic And Parsley Scallops 85
- Mesmerizing Coconut Haddock 85
- "Salmon" Platter 86
- Feisty Bacon Scallops 86
- Grilled Lime Shrimp 86
- Mouthwatering Calamari 86
- Salmon And Zesty Cream Sauce 86
- Crisped Up Coconut Shrimp 87
- Spiced Up Tuna Avocado Balls 87
- Asian Glazed Salmon and Cauliflower 87
- Shrimp And Bacon Zoodles 87
- Baked Lobster Tails And Garlic Butter 87
- Spicy Sea Bass Hazelnuts 87
- Perfectly Marinated Grilled Salmon 88
- Salmon Fat Bombs 88
- Baked Cod And Tomato Capers Delight 88
- Perfect Tuna Salad And Pickle Boats 88
- Tuna And Spinach Salad 88
- Grilled Fish Salad Nicoise 88
- Broiled Chili Calamari 88
- Potato And Tuna Salad 89
- Three Citrus Sauce Scallops 89
- Heartthrob Mediterranean Tilapia 89
- Citrus Poached Lovely Salmon 89
- A Great Mediterranean Snapper 90
- Trout With Wilted Greens 90
- Garlic And Shrimp Pasta 90
- Cool Mediterranean Fish 90
- Pistachio Sole Fish 91

CHAPTER 8 VEGETABLES SIDES 92

- Delicious Golden Onion Rings 92
- Whole Wheat Bread Zucchini Bake 92
- Rainbow Vegetable Fritters 92
- Mediterranean Vegetable Skewers 92
- Roasted Veggies with Yogurt-Tahini Sauce 92
- Swiss cheese and Vegetable Casserole 93
- American-Style Brussels Sprout Salad 93
- Sundried Tomato with Brussels sprouts Roast 93
- Cardamom Spiced Swiss chard 93
- Japanese Tempura Bowl 94
- Balsamic Root Vegetables 94
- Winter Vegetable Braise 94
- Aromatic Thyme Spiced Button Mushrooms 94
- Peppery Bok Choy with Toasted Sliced Almonds 94
- Spicy Asparagus Cashews Bake 95
- Gingery Eggplant with Green Onions 95
- Peppery Egg Butternut Fritters 95
- The Best Cauliflower Tater Tots 95
- Three-Cheese Stuffed Mushrooms 95
- Sweet Corn Fritters with Avocado 96
- Greek-Style Vegetable Bake 96
- Grandma's Citrusy Broccoli Tofu 96
- One Pan Spiced Tofu with Spinach 96
- Chicken Broth Cauliflower Soup 96
- Cheese Coated Egg Muffins 97
- Cardamom spiced Kale and Chard 97
- Sautéed Peppery Mushrooms 97
- Low Sugar Bok Choy Bowl 97
- Easy Apple Porridge 97
- Vanilla and Flaxseed Meal 98
- Flaxseed Pancakes 98

Flaxseed Porridge	98
Tasty Vegetable Morning Hash	98
Hearty Walnut Porridge	98
Pumpkin Steel Cuts	98
Savory Oatmeal Delight	99
Apple and Cinnamon Oatmeal	99
Cinnamon and Spice Overnight Oats	99
Pecan and Pear Breakfast	99
Pitas and Broiled Grapefruits	99
Orange French Toast	100
Fruity-Licious Oatmeal	100
Roasted Hazelnut Bites	100
Delightful Mushroom Sauté	100
Kale and Carrot With Tahini Dressing	100
Cinnamon and Coconut Porridge	100
Banana and Buckwheat Porridge	101
Quinoa and Cinnamon Bowl	101
Cinnamon and Pumpkin Porridge	101
Quinoa and Date Mix	101
Quinoa Applesauce Muffins	101
Hearty Bran Muffins	102
A Wintry Fruit Sauce	102
Cinnamon Honey Baked Apple	102
Almond Carrot Cake	102
Mango Turmeric Chia Pudding	102
Spiced Apples and Raisins	103
Sweet Potato Brownie	103
Anti-Inflammatory Apricot Squares	103

CHAPTER 9 PORK, BEEF AND LAMB 104

Zucchini Lasagna	104
Roasted Duck Legs with Balsamic Mushrooms	104
Russian Steaks with Nuts and Cheese	104
Pork Paprika	105
Beef Goulash Soup	105
Beef-Vegetable Ragout	105
Fried Pork Chops	106
Pork on a Blanket	106
Greek Flat Iron Steaks	106
Spiced Burgers with Cilantro Cucumber Sauce	106
Sunday Brisket	106
Pork Rind	107
Ginger Chili Broccoli	107
Pork Tenderloin	107
Chestnut Stuffed Pork Roast	107
Beef, Tomato, and Pepper Tortillas	108
Salted Biscuit Pie Turkey Chops	108
Roasted Pork	108
Homemade Flamingos	108
Meatloaf Reboot	108
Turkey Enchiladas	108
Mexican Meat Loaf	109
Beef Daube Provencal	109
Boeuf Bourguignon	109
Pork and Pumpkin Stew	110
Crockpot Chipotle Steak	110
Chuck and Veggies	110
Southwest Turkey Lasagna	111
Balsamic Chicken & Vegetable Skillet	111
Deconstructed Philly Cheesesteaks	111
Ham & Brie Turnovers	111
Shredded Green Chili Beef	112
Chinese Pot Roast	112
Tuscan Pork Chops	112
Crockpot Flank Steak	112
Pot Roast Soup	113
Beef and Zucchini Meatballs	113
Meatballs with Spaghetti	113
Irish Beef Pot Pie	113
Spicy Beef Sloppy Joes	114
Roasted Steak and Tomato Salad	114
Lamb Fatteh with Asparagus	114
Oven-Baked Slow Baked Pork Shoulder	114
Onion And Bacon Pork Chops	115
The Classical Medi Pork	115
Awesome Asian Beef Steak	115

Recipe	Page
Healthy Avocado Beef Patties	115
The Fresh Thai Beef	115
Beef Zucchini Chips	116
Juicy Ground Beef Casserole	116
Majestic Beef And Tomato Squash	116
Tamari Steak Salad	116
Ravaging Beef Pot Roast	117
Juicy Glazed Beef Meatloaf	117
Zucchini Beef Sauté With Coriander Greens	117
Pure Broccoli Rib Eye	117
Mushroom And Olive "Mediterranean" Steak	118
Satisfying Low-Carb Beef Liver Salad	118
Perfect Aromatic Beef Roast	118
Beef Packed Zucchini Boats	118
Spicy Chipotle Steak	118
Beef Cheeseburger Wraps	119
Cheddar Jalapeno Meatloaf	119
Perfect Philly Cheesesteak Stuffed Peppers	119
Grilled Beef Short Loin	119
Hearty Beef Bourguignon	119
Zucchini And Cheddar Beef Mugs	119
Beef Stuffed Peppers	120
Fine Filet Mignon In Dijon Sauce	120
Shitake Butter Beef Dish	120
Crazy Beef Meatballs	120
Delicious Beef Casserole	120
Ground Beef Hamburger Patties	120
Ultimate Mediterranean Lamb Chops	121
Herbed Lamb Cutlets	121
Pork Chops And Wild Mushrooms	121
Herbed Pork Tenderloin	121
Mushroom Beef Risotto	122

CHAPTER 10 SOUPS AND STEWS 123

Recipe	Page
Asparagus and Chicken Soup	123
Mediterranean Fish and Quinoa Soup	123
Alkalizing Green Soup	123
Lentil, Ground Beef and Quinoa Soup	123
Hearty Lamb and Root Vegetables Soup	124
Spicy Red Pepper and Potato Soup	124
Creamy Brussels Sprout Soup	124
Tuscan Chicken Stew	124
Zucchini Vegetable Stew	124
Creamy Chicken Soup	125
Broccoli and Chicken Soup	125
Warm Chicken and Avocado Soup	125
Quick Clam Chowder	125
Beef Barley Soup	125
Seafood Stew	126
Potlikker Soup	126
Roasted Carrot Soup with Basil	126
Asparagus Carrot Soup	127
Meatball and Chickpea Soup	127
Beef Noodle Soup	127
Cabbage, Beef and Buckwheat Soup	127
Italian Wedding Soup	128
Italian Meatball Soup	128
Spicy Chick Pea Stew	128
Easy Salsa Chicken Stew	128
Moroccan Eggplant Stew	128
Cheeseburger Soup	129
Taco Soup	129
Lentil Vegetable Soup	129
Broccoli Soup	129
Chicken and Potato Stew	130
Mediterranean Spinach and Tomato Pasta	130
Butternut Squash Stew	130
Fish and Noodle Soup	130
Lime Chicken Tortilla Soup	131
Beef Barley Mushroom Soup	131
Split Pea Soup with Carrots	131
Buttercup Squash Soup	131
Creamy Sweet Potato Soup	132
Bean Soup with Lime-Yogurt Drizzle	132
Roasted Brussels sprouts and Cauliflower Soup	132
Beetroot and Carrot Soup	133

Recipe	Page
Baked Beet and Apple Soup	133
Vegetarian Borscht	133
Ingenious Eggplant Soup	133
Amazing Roasted Carrot Soup	134
The Brussels's Fever	134
Curious Roasted Garlic Soup	134
Beef And Onion Stew	134
Healthy Cucumber Soup	134
Dreamy Zucchini Bowl	134
Wild Mushroom Soup	135
Pumpkin And Coconut Cream Soup	135
Fish Packed White Chowder	135
Awesome Fish Curry	135
Honorable Mahi Mahi Stew	135
Hearty Crab Soup	136
Mexican Chicken Soup	136
Delicious Turkey Stew	136
Turkey, Kale, And Sausage Delight	136
Awesome Egg Drop Soup	136
Cheesy Broccoli Soup	136
Chicken Liver Stew	137
Chicken And Mushroom Stew	137
Garlic Chicken Soup	137
Spicy Fish Stew	137
Chilled Minty Avocado Soup	137
Original Guacamole Soup	137
Awesome Zucchini Soup	138
Spring Soup With Poached Egg	138
Spanish Soup	138
Butternut Garlic Soup	138
The Brussels's Fever	138
Dreamy Zucchini Bowl	138
Garlic Tomato Soup	139
Melon Soup	139
Healthy Ginger Soup	139
Cucumber Soup	139
Tasty Tofu and Mushroom Soup	139
Mushroom Cream Soup	140
Pumpkin, Coconut, and Sage Soup	140
Fine Black Bean Soup	140

CHAPTER 11 POULTRY 141

Recipe	Page
Stuffed Chicken Breasts Greek-style	141
Chicken & Tofu	141
Jerk Style Chicken Wings	141
Italian Chicken	142
Coconut Chicken	142
Spicy Lime Chicken	142
Chicken & Peanut Stir-Fry	142
Honey Mustard Chicken	142
Chicken Chili	143
Chicken with Chickpeas	143
Chicken, Oats & Chickpeas Meatloaf	143
Herbed Turkey Breast	144
Turkey with Lentils	144
Lemon Garlic Turkey	144
Crockpot Slow Cooker Ranch Chicken	144
Chicken Wings	145
Chicken Tenders	145
Chicken Meatballs	145
Chicken & Spinach	145
Balsamic Chicken	145
Mustard Chicken with Basil	146
Chicken with Cashew Nuts	146
Chicken & Broccoli Bake	146
Zucchini with Tomatoes	146
Chicken Liver Curry	147
Chicken Stuffed Potatoes	147
Greek Chicken Lettuce Wraps	147
Lemon Chicken with Kale	147
Amazing Buffalo Lettuce Wraps	147
Balsamic Chicken	148
Low-Carb Butternut Chicken	148
The Original Greek Chicken Breast	148
Chicken Ham And Turnip Pasta	148
Turkey Bacon Garlic Knots	148

Recipe	Page
Chinese Duck Breast	149
The Perfect Winter Turkey Goulash	149
Classic Teriyaki Chicken	149
Juicy Italian Chicken Basil Pizza	149
Cocktail-Styled Meatball	149
Zucchini And Duck Meal	150
Feisty Tikka Chicken And Butter	150
Creamy Chicken Cajun	150
Crispy Chicken Tenders	150
Easy-Going Chicken Lettuce Wraps	150
Beautiful Tarragon Chicken Roast	150
Cauliflower Rice And Chicken Curry	151
Juicy Chicken Blanket	151
The Duck Eye Ribeye	151
Everyone's Favorite Turkey Avocado Rolls	151
Sweet And Savory Grilled Chicken	151
The Perfect Mediterranean Turkey Cutlets	152
Burnt Fried Chicken	152
Crunched Up Chicken Taco Wings	152
Tarragon Creamy Chicken	152
Spicy And Sour Chicken Breast	152
Spicy Grilled Chicken	153
Michigan Turkey Meal	153
Bacon-Wrapped Chicken Breast With Spinach	153
Fancy Roast Chicken	153
Ravaging Oven Roasted Garlic Chicken Thigh	154
Loving Honey Lemon Chicken	154
Gnocchi Turkey Ham And Olives	154
Chicken And Parmesan Veggie	154
Awesome Chicken Cacciatore	155

CHAPTER 12 SALADS ... 156

Recipe	Page
Cabbage Slaw Salad	156
Green Salad with Blackberries, Goat Cheese, and Sweet Potatoes	156
Pomegranate & Brussels Sprouts Salad	156
Strawberry & Avocado Salad	156
Shrimp & Avocado Salad	156
Kale Salad with Avocado Dressing	157
Asian Noodle Salad	157
Avocado & Citrus Shrimp Salad	157
Healthy Taco Salad	157
Chicken Guacamole Salad	158
Warm Portobello Salad	158
Cucumber Salad	158
Green Power Salad	158
Spinach and Green Bean Salad	158
Mediterranean Spinach Salad	159
Arugula and Avocado Salad	159
Arugula, Radicchio and Pomegranate Salad	159
Roasted Beet Salad	159
Black Bean and Corn Salad	159
Perfect Quinoa Salad	160
Tropical Fruit Salad with Coconut Milk	160
Cucumber, Tomato, and Avocado Salad	160
Layered Salad	160
Baked "Potato" Salad	160
Caprese Salad	161
Chopped Veggie Salad	161
Tofu Salad Sandwiches	161
Lobster Roll Salad with Bacon Vinaigrette	161
Bean and Basil Salad	161
Tenderloin Grilled Salad	162
Barley Veggie Salad	162
Spinach Shrimp Salad	162
Sweet Potato and Roasted Beet Salad	162
Harvest Salad	163
Rainbow Black Bean Salad	163
Warm Barley and Squash Salad with Balsamic Vinaigrette	163
Winter Chicken and Citrus Salad	164
Hearty Brussels Salad	164
Broccoli Salad With Almond	164
Great Tomato Platter	164
Supreme Avocado and Cilantro Medley	164
Hearty Orange and Onion Salad	164

- Healthy Cauliflower Salad 165
- Lovely Japanese Cabbage Dish 165
- Southern Salad 165
- A Turtle Friend Salad 165
- Quinoa Been Salad 165
- Exceptional Watercress and Melon Salad 166
- Hearty and Quinoa and Fruit Salad 166
- Red Cabbage Coleslaw With Vinegar Dressing 166
- Balsamic Grilled Zucchini 166
- Fancy Eggplant Salad 166
- Great Pepper Soup 167
- Watermelon, Radish, And Beet Salad 167
- A Very "Medi" Tomato Soup 167
- Cucumber And Yogurt Salad 167
- Summer Veggie Chicken Wraps 168
- Chilled Chicken Artichoke And Zucchini Salad 168
- White Bean Soup And Swiss Chard 168
- Pure Kidney Beans And Cilantro Salad 168

CHAPTER 13 DINNER 169

- Cauliflower Mash 169
- French toast in Sticks 169
- Misto Quente 169
- Seared Tuna Steak 169
- Vegetable Soup 169
- Pork Chop Diane 170
- Autumn Pork Chops with Red Cabbage and Apples 170
- Chipotle Chili Pork Chops 170
- Orange-Marinated Pork Tenderloin 170
- Homestyle Herb Meatballs 171
- Lime-Parsley Lamb Cutlets 171
- Beef Chili 171
- Greek Broccoli Salad 171
- Mediterranean Steak Sandwiches 171
- Roasted Beef with Peppercorn Sauce 172
- Coffee-and-Herb-Marinated Steak 172
- Traditional Beef Stroganoff 172
- Chicken and Roasted Vegetable Wraps 173
- Spicy Chicken Cacciatore 173
- Scallion Sandwich 173
- Cheesy Cauliflower Gratin 173
- Strawberry Spinach Salad 173
- Garlic Bread 174
- Bruschetta 174
- Cream Buns with Strawberries 174
- Blueberry Buns 174
- Lean Lamb and Turkey Meatballs with Yogurt 175
- Air Fried Section and Tomato 175
- Cheesy Salmon Fillets 175
- Salmon with Asparagus 175
- Shrimp in Garlic Butter 175
- Cauliflower Mac and Cheese 176
- Easy Egg Salad 176
- Baked Chicken Legs 176
- Creamed Spinach 176
- Stuffed Mushrooms 176
- Cobb Salad 177
- Muffins Sandwich 177
- Bacon BBQ 177
- The All-Time Favorite Tomato And Basil Soup 177
- Healthy Lamb Stew 177
- Hearty Chicken Liver Stew 178
- Tender Slow Cooked Ham Stew 178
- Loving Cauliflower Soup 178
- Pork Sausage And Pepper Stew 178
- Simple Garlic And Lemon Soup 178
- Hearty Parmesan Baked Chicken 178
- The Almond Breaded Chicken Goodness 179
- Brown Butter Duck Breast 179
- Healthy Chicken Cream Salad 179
- BlackBerry Chicken Wings 179
- Hearty Chicken Keto Nuggets 180
- Zucchini Zoodles With Chicken and Basil 180
- Salsa Chicken 180
- Bacon And Chicken Garlic Wrap 180
- Cheesy Grilled Chicken Platter 180

Chicken Parmesan Fingers	180
Clean Parsley And Chicken Breast	181
Creative Lamb Chops	181
Crazy Lamb Salad	181
Healthy Slow-Cooker Lamb Leg	181
Spicy Paprika Lamb Chops	182
Simple Lamb Riblets And Mini Pesto	182
Terrific Jalapeno Bacon Bombs	182
Elegant Mushroom Pork Chops	182
Lemon And Garlic Pork Platter	182
The Herbal Buttery Pork Chops	183
Italian Pork Chops	183
Gentle Cheesy Pork Chops	183
Original Caramelized Pork Chops	183
Simple Pork Stuffed Bell Peppers	184
Parmesan Pork Steak	184
Curious Slow-Cooked Cranberry And Pork Roast	184
Satisfyingly Spicy Pork Chops	184

CHAPTER 14 SNACKS AND APPETIZERS 185

Crispy Parmesan Cauliflower	185
Cream Cheese Stuffed Jalapeños	185
Honeydew & Ginger Smoothies	185
Pea Soup	185
Potato Curry Soup	185
Asparagus Salad	186
Zucchini Salmon Salad	186
Cheesy Onion Dip	186
Almond Coconut Biscotti	186
Margarita Chicken Dip	186
Parmesan Truffle Chips	187
Filled Mushrooms	187
Mango and Avocado Salad	187
Salad with Strips of Ham	187
Pointed Cabbage Pot	188
Rustic Pear Pie with Nuts	188
Apricot Soufflé	188
Cinnamon Apple Popcorn	188

Blackberry Crostata	189
Ratatouille Salat	189
Brussels sprouts	189
Garlic and Herb Carrots	189
Mushroom and Leek Soup	190
Pistachio Cookies	190
Crispy Apple Chips	190
Chili Lime Tortilla Chips	190
Palm Trees Holder	190
Homemade Cheetos	191
Butternut Cream Soup	191
The Cheesy Mug	191
Cashew And Almond Butter	191
Crispy Walnut Crumbles	191
Keto Kohlslaw	191
Stuffed Mushrooms	192
Flax And Almond Crunchies	192
Juicy Salmon Fat Bombs	192
Roasted Herb Crackers	192
Crunchy Garlic Bread Stick	192
Magnificent Camembert Mushrooms	193
Golden Eggplant Fries	193
Cheesy Mozzarella Sticks	193
Salt And Rosemary Cracker	193
Premium Goat Cheese Salad	193
Grilled Avocado And Melted Cheese	194
Mozzarella And Bacon Bites	194
Brazilian Butter Macadamia	194
Tasty Roasted Broccoli	194
Spicy Pimento Cheese Dip	194
Bacon Smoky Doodles	194
Tantalizing Butter Beans	194
Walnuts And Asparagus Delight	195
Spicy Chili Crackers	195
Faux Mac And Cheese	195
Hearty Roasted Cauliflower	195
Sausage And Shrimp Skewers	195
Fancy Grilled Halloumi Bruschetta	196

Broccoli And Dill Salad	196
Cheddar Biscuits	196
The Faux Cinnamon Rice Pudding	196
Almond Flour English Cake	196
Bacon And Avocado Fat Bombs	196
Green Olives With Deviled Eggs	197
Spinach And Bacon Salad	197
Cool Bacon And Cheese Rolls	197
Roasted Brussels And Bacon	197
Parmesan Garlic Cauliflower	197
Flaxy Cheese Chips	197
Handy Baked Tortillas	197
Fine Jarlsberg Omelet	198
Asparagus And Baked Pork	198
Spicy Fired Up Jalapeno Poppers	198
Bacon And Chicken Patties	198
Juicy Grilled Ham And Cheese	198
Prosciutto Spinach Salad	199
Lasagna Spaghetti Squash	199
Blue Cheese Chicken Wedges	199
Feisty Bacon Snack	199
Bacon And Scallops Snack	199
Perfect Gluten-Free Gratin	200
Cheesed Up Bacon Butternut Squash	200
Great Nutty Lion	200
A Whole Melon Surprise	200
Muscular Macho Green	200
Buddha's Banana Berry	200
Brain Nutrition-Analyzer	201
Complete Banana Meal	201
Smoothie Vegetable Blast	201
Strawberry Banana Yogurt Smoothie	201
Cantaloupe Lettuce Smoothie	201
Powerful Alkaline Smoothie	201
Alkaline Breakfast Breaker	201
Mixed Berry Smoothie	202
Sweet Kale Smoothie	202
Almond Butter Berry Smoothie	202
Green Smoothie Bowl	202
The Flat Belly Smoothie	202
Mango And Blueberry Bean Smoothie	202
Pineapple Green Anti-Ager	203
Apple Cherry Pumpkin Tea	203
Beets And Berry Beauty Enhancer	203
Hot Buffalo Wings	203
A Jar Full Of Pecans	203
The Exquisite Spaghetti Squash	203
Worthy Bacon-Wrapped Drumsticks	204
Coconut Chocolate Cookie	204
Keto Shortbread	204
1 Minute Keto Muffin	204
Chilled No-Bake Lemon Cheesecake	204
Fancy Rutabaga Cakes	204
Eggplant Fries	205
Stuffed Parmesan Cheese Avocado	205
Orange And Coconut Creamsicles	205
Coffee Popsicles	205
Tantalizing Butter Beans	205
Healthy Carrot Chips	205
Hearty Brussels and Pistachio	206
Morning Peach	206
Sticky Mango Rice	206
Pecan and Blueberry Crumble	206
Oatmeal Cookies	206
Cherry Tomatoes and Linguine	207
Apple Slices	207
Vegetable and Red Pepper Hummus	207
Cocoa Mejdool Balls	207
Succulent Cheesy Cauliflowers	207
Creamy Leeks Platter	207
Tender Coconut And Cauliflower Rice With Chili	208
Perfect Smoked Peaches	208
Simple Apple Pie	208
Awesome Baba Ganoush	208
The Great Yellow Rice	208
Brown Rice	208

- Israeli Couscous Dish 209
- Roasted Cauliflower with Ginger and Mint 209
- Spicy Sautéed Kale and Chickpeas 209
- Roasted Fennel and Artichoke Hearts 209
- Lovely Japanese Cabbage Dish 209
- Herbal Roasted Baby Potatoes 209
- Brussels Sprouts And Pistachios 210
- Pesto Vegetable Pizza 210
- Chili Kale Chips 210
- Cherry Tomatoes And Linguine 210
- Caramelized Onion And Fennel Pizza 211
- Linguine Dredged In Tomato Clam Sauce 211
- A Honeydew And Cucumber Medley 211
- Natural Nectarine 211
- Fine Tea Toner 211
- The Grapefruit Glow 212
- The Anti-Aging Avocado 212
- A Green Grape Shake 212
- Berry-Licious Anti-Oxidant Banana Smoothie 212
- Protein-Packed Anti-Oxidizer 212
- Triple Berry Supreme 212
- A Green Grape Shake 213
- The Flaxseed Anti-Oxidizer 213
- Mixed Berry And Kiwi Medley 213
- Supreme Green Tea Glass 213
- Pomegranate Anti-Oxidizer 213
- Anti-Oxi Boosting Rolled Oats Smoothie 213
- Anti-Oxi Rich Almond Flavored Smoothie 214
- A Melon Cucumber Medley 214
- Kale And Beet 2021 Fusion 214
- Strawberry And Watermelon Medley 214
- Punch Watermelon 214
- Hearty Cucumber Quencher 214
- Dandelion Aloha 214
- Blueberry Detox Drink 215

CHAPTER 15 DESSERT 216

- Sticky Ginger Cake 216
- Tiramisu 216
- Toffee Apple Mini Pies 216
- Pineapple Frozen Yogurt 216
- Pomegranate Panna Cotta 217
- Coconutty Pudding Clouds 217
- Cream Cheese Pound Cake 217
- Dark Chocolate Coffee Cupcakes 217
- German Chocolate Cake Bars 217
- Gingerbread Soufflés 218
- Lemon Meringue Ice Cream 218
- Mini Bread Puddings 218
- Pumpkin Ice Cream with Candied Pecans 218
- Raspberry Almond Clafoutis 219
- Blackberry Soufflés 219
- Blueberry Lemon "Cup" Cakes 219
- Blueberry No-Bake Cheesecake 219
- Broiled Stone Fruit 220
- Café Mocha Torte 220
- Cappuccino Mousse 220
- Caramel Pecan Pie 220
- Carrot Cupcakes 221
- Raspberry and Dark Chocolate Mini Soufflés 221
- Tropical Fruit Tart 221
- Sweet Potato Crème Brule 221
- Raspberry Lemon Cheesecake Squares 222
- Mini Key Lime Tarts 222
- Moist Butter Cake 222
- No-Bake Chocolate Swirl Cheesecake 223
- No-Bake Lemon Tart 223
- Chocolate Cherry Cake Roll 223
- Chocolate Orange Bread Pudding 223
- Chocolate Torte 224
- Cinnamon Bread Pudding 224
- Coconut Cream Pie 224
- Coconut Milk Shakes 224
- Peach Custard Tart 225
- Peach Ice Cream 225
- Peanut Butter Pie 225

Raspberry Peach Cobbler	225
Deliciously Simple Brownie Muffin	226
The Avocado Day Stopper	226
Jalapeno Crisp	226
Easy Jalapeno Bread	226
Spicy Popper Mug Cake	226
Creamy Coffee Popsicles	227
The Most Elegant Parsley Soufflé Ever	227
Almond Butter Cup Cookies	227
Lovely Pumpkin Buns	227
Gingerbread Keto Muffins	228
Sensational Lemonade Fat Bomb	228
The Easy "No-Bake" Fudge	228
Elegant Poppyseed Muffins	228
Swirly Cinnamon Muffins	228
Mesmerizing Garlic Bagels	229
Ravaging Blueberry Muffin	229
No-Bake Cheesecake	229
Supreme Matcha Bomb	229
Hearty Almond Bread	229
Great Fudge Popsicles	230
Egg And Coconut Bread	230
The Beasty Green Glass	230
Spicy Bread Loaf	230
Clean Sugar-Free Lemon Curd	230
Fantastic Hollandaise Sauce	230
Chilled Cheesecake Cups	231
Raspberry Pudding Meal	231
Dreamy Vanilla Dessert	231
Coconut Pillow	231
The Brewed Coffee Surprise	231
Crusty Almond Roast	231
Cute Macaroon Bites	231
Simple Cinnamon Cocoa Almonds	232
Delightful Coconut Custard	232
Jalapeno And Bacon Fat Bomb	232
Poppy Seeds Fat Bomb	232
Creative Fudgsicles	232
Pink Yogurt Popsicles	232
Almond And Chocolate Butter Dip	233
Gentle Strawberry Greek Frozen Yogurt	233
Strawberry And Feta Delight	233
Cherry And Olive Bites	233
Amazing Tiramisu	233

CHAPTER 16 SAUCES DIPS AND DRESSING ... 235

Tangy Mexican Salad Dressing	235
Sriracha Dipping Sauce	235
Spaghetti Sauce	235
Pineapple Mango Hot Sauce	235
Pizza Sauce	235
Queso Verde	236
Cinnamon Blueberry Sauce	236
Citrus Vinaigrette	236
Cranberry Orange Compote	236
Creamy Poppy Seed Dressing	236
Dry Rub for Pork	237
Easy Cheesy Dipping Sauce	237
Raspberry & Basil Jam	237
Garlic Dipping Sauce	237
Herb Vinaigrette	237
Horseradish Mustard Sauce	237
Berry Dessert Sauce	238
Blackberry Spread	238
Blueberry Orange Dessert Sauce	238
Caramel Sauce	238
Cheesy Jalapeno Dip	238
Chinese Hot Mustard	238
Italian Salad Dressing	239
Italian Salsa	239
Alfredo Sauce	239
All Purpose Beef Marinade	239
All Purpose Chicken Marinade	239
Almond Vanilla Fruit Dip	239
Roasted Tomato Salsa	240
Spicy Asian Vinaigrette	240

Maple Mustard Salad Dressing	240
Maple Shallot Vinaigrette	240
Apple Cider Vinaigrette	240
Bacon Cheeseburger Dip	240
Basic Salsa	241
BBQ Sauce	241
Marinara Sauce	241
Orange Marmalade	241
Cashew And Almond Butter	242
Spinach Dip	242
Almond Milk	242
Whipped Coconut Cream	242
Nutty Butter	242
Standard Vegetable Stock	242
Mashed Celeriac	242
Spiced Oily Avocado	243
Hearty Cashew and Almond Butter	243
Black Bean Dip	243
Spicy Jerk Mayo	243
The Macadamia Dip	243
Tahini and Broccoli Slaw	243

CHAPTER 17 HEALTHY SMOOTHIES 244

Tropical Storm Glass	244
Cool Strawberry 365	244
Noteworthy Vitamin C	244
Hearty Papaya Drink	244
A Minty Drink	244
The Baked Apple	244
The Amazing Acai	245
Fine Yo "Mama" Matcha	245
The Pumpkin Eye	245
Great Green Garden	245
Generous Mango Surprise	245
Powerful Purple Smoothie	245
Banana Apple Blast	245
Energizing Pineapple Kicker	246
Dandelion And Carrot Booster	246
Green Skinny Energizer	246
Awesome Pineapple And Carrot Blend	246
Mango Energizer	246
Powerful Green Frenzy	246
The Minty Cucumber	247
Lemon Cilantro Delight	247
A Peachy Medley	247
Cilantro And Citrus Glass	247
The Deep Green Lagoon	247
The Wild Matcha Delight	247
The Green Potato Chai	247
Lemon Cilantro Delight	248
Lovely Green Gazpacho	248
Tropical Matcha Kale	248
The Glamorous Radiance	248
Mesmerizing Strawberry And Chocolate Shake	248
The Overloaded Berry Shake	248
Cool Coco-Loco Cream Shake	249
Healthy Chocolate Milkshake	249
The Cacao Super Smoothie	249
The Nutty Smoothie	249
The Strawberry Almond Smoothie	249
Mixed Fruit Madness	249
The Big Blue Delight	250
The Big Bomb Pop	250
The Pinky Swear	250
A Peachy Perfect Glass	250
Slim-Jim Vanilla Latte	250
Cauliflower Cold Glass	250
A Batch Of Slimming Berries	250
Fine Green Machine	251
The Summer Hearty Shake	251
The Mocha Built	251
Sweet Protein And Cherry Shake	251
Iron And Protein Shake	251
Creamy Peachy Shake	251
Protein-Packed Root Beer Shake	251
Peppermint And Dark Chocolate Shake Delight	252

Spiced Up Banana Shake 252

Mad Mocha Glass 252

Lemon And Cranberry Shake...252

Hearty Dandelion Smoothie 252

Apple And Zucchini Medley 252

Flax And Kiwi Spinach Smoothie 252

Cucumber Kale And Lime Apple Smoothie 253

28 DAYS MEAL PLAN... 254

Introduction

Do you know how to cook for a diabetic? Do you need to know? Well, chances are, if someone in your family is diabetic or you're just looking to be more conscious of what they're eating (or maybe you have diabetes yourself!), then the answer to both questions is yes!

There are several kinds of diabetes, each with its own set of peculiarities and limitations.

Type II Diabetes is caused by a problem with the body's production of insulin. The blood sugar level is regulated by the hormone insulin, w/c can lead to diabetes when it is too low. This means that to properly care for a diabetic, you need to make sure they get plenty of high-quality protein and fiber with every meal as well as controlling their blood sugar always levels.

High protein foods are extremely important because they give us the building blocks for everything else in our bodies. Protein is also thought to slow down digestion and thereby slow down the rate at which glucose enters the bloodstream - this is called The Glycemic Index (GI). Foods with a low GI are ideal for any diabetic.

The Glycemic Index can be roughly broken down into three groups: low, medium, and high. Low GI foods (55 or less) include foods like nuts, seeds, fish, vegetables, and fruit. Medium GI foods (56-69) include things like whole-grain bread, and anything made from white flour or enriched grains. High GI foods (70 or greater) include anything that contains refined sugar or high-fructose corn syrup. That's a lot of food! Foods that measure between are also important to check out, though.

You may be disappointed to find that many of our meals are "bad" for us, but taken moderately, may be very healthful. For example, an apple or orange can have a GI score of around 40 and still be considered low in carbohydrates. The same thing goes for other fruit, vegetables, and even certain types of meat like chicken breast or turkey. This is because the GI ratings are not very accurate for these kinds of foods - it's by weight rather than specifically by carbohydrate content or fiber content (which isn't included).

Fibers are the key to controlling blood sugar levels. Fibers are carbohydrates that we can't digest, and they help with a variety of other things like cholesterol levels and keeping us fuller for longer. Vegetables and fruits contain varying amounts of fiber, as do whole grains.

You can also determine how much fiber a food has in it by keeping track of the number of carbohydrates it contains. Fiber is present if the carbohydrate content is less than 5 grams.

So, what do you do with all this data? You need to make sure that your diabetic eats foods containing 5 grams or more of carbohydrate per portion. You may achieve this by selecting foods that are compatible with the information you've acquired. While the amount of carbohydrate in a serving may be 5 grams, serving sizes will vary between different food sources (e.g., one medium apple contains around 15 grams of carbohydrate while a half cup of raisins contains around 12 grams). When it comes to providing your diabetic with the proper nourishment, nutrition facts supplied by the US government (and other trustworthy sources) are the best way to go.

All You Need to Know About Diabetes

What Is Diabetes?

In modern society there is a huge increment of non-communicable diseases. The poor living standards and improper food consumption has led society towards this issue. There are several common diseases we can hear of nowadays. Out of them diabetes is one of the most common diseases we can experience. The number of instances is increasing every day all across the world.

Most people tend to think that diabetes is a blood born disease. That is a common myth. Actually, diabetes is a disease that has a relationship with a hormone called insulin. Insulin is an important hormone that is produced in our pancreas. The main duty of insulin is to help glucose (which comes from our food) to pass through our bloodstream to the cells in our body. Inside the cells the glucose is broken down into energy. Overall, we can say without insulin it is not possible for glucose to get into our cells.

"Important point: Sometimes the pancreas won't be able to produce insulin anymore. And in some people's bodies can't make good use of the insulin which is produced in their pancreas. As a result of that, the glucose level in the blood will be increased. If someone is experiencing one or both of these instances, we can diagnose him or her as a diabetic patient."

Types of Diabetes

When it comes to diabetes mainly, we can identify 3 types. They are as follows.
1. Type 1 Diabetes
2. Type 2 Diabetes
3. Gestational Diabetes

Type 1 Diabetes

This type of diabetes can develop at the age stage. But most of the time cases are being reported among children and young adults. Actually, it is caused by an autoimmune reaction of their bodies. Their own immune system begins to attack their insulin-producing cells in the pancreas. As a result of that, there won't be any insulin to work with glucose. So, the blood glucose result will climb sky-high within a short amount of time. Type 1 diabetes patients have only one last option for survival. That is to inject insulin every day for the rest of their lives. Still scientist is working on various researches to find the actual reason and cure for type 1 diabetes.

Type 2 Diabetes

This is the most common diabetes type. This type can be developed at any age as well. But it is mostly found in adult people. This is not an autoimmune-related issue like Type 1 diabetes. Most of the time patient's body is not making proper use of the insulin which is made by the pancreas. Sometimes with time the insulin production functionality of the pancreas may get reduced as well. Luckily this diabetes type is manageable. In extreme but rare instances insulin injections may require. Most of the time proper medications, physical activities and good eating habits will help you to manage Type 2 diabetes-like pro.

Gestational Diabetes

This is a special type of diabetes. Pregnant women who haven't had diabetes in their lifetime are the targeted category in this type. Most of the time this could happen as a result of irresponsible eating habits. This is a serious situation. Because the mother and the baby are at risk. The mother could develop Type 2 diabetes later in life. Also, the baby could become obese later in life, plus could develop Type 1 or Type 2 diabetes as well.

What Is Healthy Eating?

It is more about discipline than any other thing. Because most of the time people know what is good to eat and what is not good to eat. Most of the time they don't think twice to break a rule. The most common excuse they make is "I don't eat like this all the time". I do this only on special occasions. Well, a number of small occasions make a whole picture. So that is a weak argument. Always be honest to yourself. Your success is depending on the amount of discipline you carry.

With discipline you have to try these things.

1. Having meals on time
2. Keep the focus on a balanced diet
3. Carry on calorie and carb count
4. Staying hydrated throughout the day
5. Quit junk foods
6. Quit smoking
7. Avoid alcohol

I mentioned discipline. That is because if you have that, none of the above tips will be difficult for you to follow.

Foods That Are Good for Diabetes

1. Whole wheat bread
2. Brown rice
3. Lentils (Dhal)
4. Spinach
5. Almonds
6. Peanuts
7. Avocado
8. Onion
9. Cinnamon
10. Garlic
11. Oats
12. Tuna
13. Eggs
14. Zucchini
15. Carrots
16. Tofu
17. Pumpkin
18. Dark chocolate
19. Chickpeas
20. Cauliflower

Foods Which Are Bad for Diabetes

1. Sugar added drinks
2. Fruit juices with sweet flavor
3. Snacks with added preservatives
4. Honey
5. Sugar flavored cereals
6. White rice
7. White wheat products
8. Process Foods

Essential Things about Sugar and Nutrients

Should I Eliminate Sugar from My Diet?

So many people tend to believe that sugar consumption has a link with diabetes. It is not actually true. Especially for type 1 diabetes. It is not caused by sugar. It is caused by an autoimmune condition of the body. In type 2 diabetes the situation is not the same. There are few factors that could cause type 2 diabetes. High-calorie diet and obesity have a direct connection. If someone eliminates sugar and still consumes a high-calorie diet with proper exercises, there is a huge chance of increasing weight. In later life that could lead to developing diabetes. So having diabetes doesn't mean you should eliminate sugar completely from your diet. Make sure they are not artificial or processed sugars. I would highly recommend brown sugar as a healthy sugar source. You must cut off sugary drinks. Because liquids get absorbed by the body quicker than solid foods. Which can lead to a sudden increment of blood sugar levels. The other main point is that it is not practical to cut off sugar completely from your diet. When it comes to sugar there are two main ways we can identify. Direct sugars and indirect sugars.

Direct sugars can be considered as desserts, sugary drinks and some snacks. Indirect sugars can be considered as sugars from fruits and vegetables. Therefore, we cannot live without consuming sugar. We may cover our macronutrients from other sources. But most of our micronutrients come from fruits and vegetables. The main point is to manage high levels of calories. Then we can live a happy life while enjoying the foods we like.

Daily Calorie Consumption

For an adult person with diabetes the recommended calorie amount is 1400 to 1700 per day. Make sure that you cover that amount mainly from complex carbohydrates. As previously mentioned, you have to focus on 44% of total calories from carbohydrates. The rest of it should be covered with proteins and healthy fats. Consuming this many calories will help you to maintain a healthy weight and good blood sugar content. Please note that I have given the average measures. You may have to change the figures if you are on a weight loss journey or weight gaining journey. If you are following a certain task like that, please seek the advice of health professionals.

How Much of Sugar Is Too Much?

The standard sugar intake for an average man is 36g or 9 teaspoons per day. For average women it is 24g or 6 teaspoons per day. Children should not use more than 6 teaspoons of sugar per day. You have to focus well on hidden sugars. Because most of the time people do not pay attention to this area. So many brands use some shroud marketing strategies in order to hide the sugar quantity in the food. They use names like fructose, maltose and syrup. Consumers won't think twice about purchasing such an item.

Sometimes they might think that product is healthier than other products. The reality is those products do more harm than honest products which shows the sugar presence. Most of the time we tend to think that hidden sugars are present in drinks, cereals and jams. But sadly no. There are hidden sugars in foods that are famous for being healthier. Protein bars, Salad dressings, Chili sauces, Peanut butter and Soy milk are some of them. Those items may have almost the same or else more sugar levels than traditional sugary items. The main point I want to make is that never trust any food label saying low sugar. All most every brand is following some trick behind the scenes. I would prefer to use sugar-free versions of those foods.

Foods with High Sugar Content

In general, we know sweets, cookies, cakes, ice cream and soft drinks contain more sugar. So, it is easy for us to avoid them. But in the present market there are various types of food items that you don't even assume to contain huge amounts of sugars. It is always better to avoid other than taking a risk. By understanding the foods which are high in sugar, you can eliminate them or manage the consumption and move on towards a healthy lifestyle.

I have identified a list of special foods. The specialty of these foods is that they have other main priorities such as flavoring, color effect, enriched with vitamins, essential sauces, energy drinks, artificial sweeteners, iced teas & coffees, premade foods (soup) and canned food items can be identified under that category. Most of the time people focus only on the primary outcome of that certain product. That is not a good thing to do always you have to think outside the box and discover new things.

Chapter 3

Breakfast

Coconut and Berry Smoothie

Preparation time: 5 minutes
Cooking time: 0 minutes
Servings 2
Ingredients:
- ½ cup mixed berries (blueberries, strawberries, blackberries)
- 1 tablespoon ground flaxseed
- 2 tablespoons unsweetened coconut flakes
- ½ cup unsweetened plain coconut milk
- ½ cup leafy greens (kale, spinach)
- ¼ cup unsweetened vanilla nonfat yogurt
- ½ cup ice

Directions:
1. In a blender jar, combine the berries, flaxseed, coconut flakes, coconut milk, greens, yogurt, and ice.
2. Process until smooth. Serve.

Walnut and Oat Granola

Preparation time: 10 minutes
Cooking time: 30 minutes
Servings 16
Ingredients:
- 4 cups rolled oats
- 1 cup walnut pieces
- ½ cup pepitas
- ¼ teaspoon salt
- 1 teaspoon ground cinnamon
- 1 teaspoon ground ginger
- ½ cup coconut oil, melted
- ½ cup unsweetened applesauce
- 1 teaspoon vanilla extract
- ½ cup dried cherries

Directions:
1. Preheat the oven to 350°F (180°C). Line a baking sheet with parchment paper.
2. In a large bowl, toss the oats, walnuts, pepitas, salt, cinnamon, and ginger.
3. In a large measuring cup, combine the coconut oil, applesauce, and vanilla. Pour over the dry mixture and mix well.
4. Transfer the mixture to the prepared baking sheet. Cook for 30 minutes, stirring about halfway through. Remove from the oven and let the granola sit undisturbed until completely cool. Break the granola into pieces, and stir in the dried cherries.
5. Transfer to an airtight container, and store at room temperature for up to 2 weeks.

Crispy Pita with Canadian bacon

Preparation time: 5 minutes
Cooking time: 15 minutes
Servings 2
Ingredients:
- 1 (6-inch) whole-grain pita bread
- 3 teaspoons extra-virgin olive oil, divided
- 2 eggs
- 2 Canadian bacon slices
- Juice of ½ lemon
- 1 cup microgreens
- 2 tablespoons crumbled goat cheese
- Freshly ground black pepper, to taste

Directions:
1. Heat a large skillet over medium heat. Cut the pita bread in half and brush each side of both halves with ¼ teaspoon of olive oil (using a total of 1 teaspoon oil). Cook for 2 to 3 minutes on each side, then remove from the skillet.
2. In the same skillet, heat 1 teaspoon of oil over medium heat. Crack the eggs into the skillet and cook until the eggs are set, 2 to 3 minutes. Remove from the skillet.
3. In the same skillet, cook the Canadian bacon for 3 to 5 minutes, flipping once.
4. In a large bowl, whisk together the remaining 1 teaspoon of oil and the lemon juice. Add the microgreens and toss to combine.
5. Top each pita half with half of the microgreens, 1 piece of bacon, 1 egg, and 1 tablespoon of goat cheese. Season with pepper and serve.

Coconut-Berry Sunrise Smoothie

Preparation time: 5 minutes
Cooking time: 0 minute
Servings: 2
Ingredients:
- ½ cup mixed berries (blueberries, strawberries, blackberries)
- 1 tablespoon ground flaxseed
- 2 tablespoons unsweetened coconut flakes
- ½ cup unsweetened plain coconut milk
- ½ cup leafy greens (kale, spinach)
- ¼ cup unsweetened vanilla nonfat yogurt
- ½ cup ice

Directions:
1. In a blender jar, combine the berries, flaxseed, coconut flakes, coconut milk, greens, yogurt, and ice.
2. Process until smooth. Serve.

Avocado and Goat Cheese Toast

Preparation time: 5 minutes
Cooking time: 5 minutes
Servings: 2 (1 slice each)
Ingredients:
- 2 slices whole-wheat thin-sliced bread (I love Ezekiel sprouted bread and Dave's Killer Bread)
- ½ avocado
- 2 tablespoons crumbled goat cheese
- Salt

Directions:
1. In a toaster or broiler, toast the bread until browned.
2. Remove the flesh from the avocado. In a medium bowl, use a fork to mash the avocado flesh. Spread it onto the toast.
3. Sprinkle with the goat cheese and season lightly with salt.
4. Add any toppings and serve.

Oat and Walnut Granola

Preparation time: 10 minutes
Cooking time: 30 minutes
Servings: 16
Ingredients:
- 4 cups rolled oats
- 1 cup walnut pieces
- ½ cup pepitas
- ¼ teaspoon salt
- 1 teaspoon ground cinnamon
- 1 teaspoon ground ginger
- ½ cup coconut oil, melted
- ½ cup unsweetened applesauce
- 1 teaspoon vanilla extract
- ½ cup dried cherries

Directions:
1. Preheat the oven to 350°F. Line a baking sheet with parchment paper.
2. In a large bowl, toss the oats, walnuts, pepitas, salt, cinnamon, and ginger.
3. In a large measuring cup, combine the coconut oil, applesauce, and vanilla. Pour over the dry mixture and mix well.
4. Transfer the mixture to the prepared baking sheet. Cook for 30 minutes, stirring about halfway through. Remove from the oven and let the granola sit undisturbed until completely cool. Break the granola into pieces, and stir in the dried cherries.
5. Transfer to an airtight container, and store at room temperature for up to 2 weeks.

Zucchini Noodles with Creamy Avocado Pesto

Preparation Time: 10 minutes
Cooking Time: 20 minutes
Servings: 4
Ingredients:
- 6 c of spiralized zucchini
- 1 Tablespoon olive oil
- 6 oz. of avocado
- 1 basil leaf
- 3 garlic cloves
- 1/3 oz. pine nuts
- 2 Tablespoon lemon juice
- 1/2 teaspoon salt
- 1/4 teaspoon black pepper

Directions:
Spiralize the courgettis and set them aside on paper towels to absorb the surplus water.
In a kitchen appliance, put avocados, juice basil leaves, garlic, pine nuts, and sea salt and pulse until chopped. Then put vegetable oil in a slow stream till emulsified and creamy.
Drizzle vegetable oil in a skillet over medium-high heat and add zucchini noodles, cooking for about 2 minutes till tender.
Put zucchini noodles into a large bowl and toss with avocado pesto. Season with cracked pepper and a little Parmesan and serve.

Avocado Chicken Salad

Preparation Time: 5 minutes
Cooking Time: 10 minutes
Servings: 2
Ingredients:
- 10 oz. diced cooked chicken
- 1/2 cup 2% Plain Greek yogurt
- 3 oz. chopped avocado
- 12 teaspoon garlic powder
- 1/4 teaspoon salt
- 1/8 teaspoon pepper
- 1 tablespoon + 1 teaspoon lime juice
- 1/4 cup fresh cilantro, chopped

Directions:
Combine all Ingredients: in a medium-sized bowl. Refrigerate until able to serve.
Cut the salad in half and serve it together with your favorite greens.

Pancakes with Berries

Preparation Time: 5 minutes
Cooking Time: 20 minutes
Servings: 2
Ingredients:
Pancake:
- 1 egg
- 50 g spelled flour
- 50 g almond flour
- 15 g coconut flour 150 ml of water salt

Directions:
1. Put the flour, egg, and a few salts in a blender jar.
2. Add 150 ml of water.
3. Mix everything with a whisk.
4. Mix everything into a batter.
5. Heat a coated pan.
6. Put in half the batter.
7. Once the pancake is firm, turn it over.
8. Remove the pancake, add the last half of the batter to the pan, and repeat.
9. Melt chocolate over a water bath.
10. Let the pancakes cool.
11. Brush the pancakes with the yogurt.
12. Wash the berry and let it drain.
13. Put berries on the yogurt.
14. Roll up the pancakes.

15. Sprinkle them with granulated sugar.
16. Decorate the entire thing with the melted chocolate.

Omelette à la Margherita

Preparation Time: 10 minutes
Cooking Time: 20 minutes
Servings: 2
Ingredients:
- 3 eggs
- 50 g parmesan cheese
- 2 tablespoon heavy cream
- 1 tablespoon olive oil
- 1 teaspoon oregano
- Nutmeg
- Salt
- Pepper

For covering:
- 3 - 4 stalks of basil
- 1 tomato
- 100 g grated mozzarella

Directions:
1. Mix the cream and eggs in a medium bowl.
2. Add the grated parmesan, nutmeg, oregano, pepper, and salt and stir everything.
3. Heat the oil in a pan.
4. Add 1/2 of the egg and cream to the pan.
5. Let the omelet set over medium heat, turn it, then remove it.
6. Repeat with the last half of the egg mixture.
7. Cut the tomatoes into slices and place them on top of the omelets.
8. Scatter the mozzarella over the tomatoes.
9. Place the omelets on a baking sheet.
10. Cook at 180°C for five to 10 minutes.
11. Then, take the omelets out and decorate them with the basil leaves.

Spanakopita Frittata

Preparation time: 10 minutes
Cooking time: 15 minutes
Servings: 4
Ingredients:
- 2 tablespoons extra-virgin olive oil
- ½ sweet onion, chopped
- 1 red bell pepper, seeded and chopped
- ½ teaspoon minced garlic
- ¼ teaspoon sea salt
- ½ teaspoon freshly ground black pepper
- 8 egg whites
- 2 cups shredded spinach
- ½ cup crumbled low-sodium feta cheese
- 1 teaspoon chopped fresh parsley, for garnish

Directions:
1. Preheat the oven to 375°F (190°C). Place a heavy ovenproof skillet over medium-high heat and add the olive oil. Sauté the onion, bell pepper, and garlic until softened, about 5 minutes. Season with salt and pepper. Whisk together the egg whites in a medium bowl, then pour them into the skillet and lightly shake the pan to disburse.
2. Cook the vegetables and eggs for 3 minutes, without stirring. Scatter the spinach over the eggs and sprinkle the feta cheese evenly over the spinach.
3. Put the skillet in the oven and bake, uncovered, until cooked through and firm, about 10 minutes.
4. Loosen the edges of the frittata with a rubber spatula, then invert it onto a plate.
5. Garnish with the chopped parsley and serve.

Ratatouille Egg Bake

Preparation time: 20 minutes
Cooking time: 50 minutes
Servings: 4
Ingredients:
- 2 teaspoons extra-virgin olive oil
- ½ sweet onion, finely chopped
- 2 teaspoons minced garlic
- ½ small eggplant, peeled and diced
- 1 green zucchini, diced
- 1 yellow zucchini, diced
- 1 red bell pepper, seeded and diced
- 3 tomatoes, seeded and chopped
- 1 tablespoon chopped fresh oregano
- 1 tablespoon chopped fresh basil
- Pinch red pepper flakes
- Sea salt and freshly ground black pepper, to taste
- 4 large eggs

Directions:
1. Preheat the oven to 350°F (180°C). Place a large ovenproof skillet over medium heat and add the olive oil.
2. Sauté the onion and garlic until softened and translucent, about 3 minutes. Stir in the eggplant and sauté for about 10 minutes, stirring occasionally. Stir in the zucchini and pepper and sauté for 5 minutes.
3. Reduce the heat to low and cover. Cook until the vegetables are soft, about 15 minutes.
4. Stir in the tomatoes, oregano, basil, and red pepper flakes, and cook 10 minutes more. Season the ratatouille with salt and pepper. Use a spoon to create four wells in the mixture. Crack an egg into each well. Place the skillet in the oven and bake until the eggs are firm, about 5 minutes.
5. Remove from the oven. Serve the eggs with a generous scoop of vegetables.

Cottage Pancakes

Preparation time: 10 minutes
Cooking time: 20 minutes
Servings: 4
Ingredients:
- 2 cups low-fat cottage cheese
- 4 egg whites
- 2 eggs
- 1 tablespoon pure vanilla extract
- 1½ cups almond flour
- Nonstick cooking spray

Directions:

1. Place the cottage cheese, egg whites, eggs, and vanilla in a blender and pulse to combine.
2. Add the almond flour to the blender and blend until smooth.
3. Place a large nonstick skillet over medium heat and lightly coat it with cooking spray.
4. Spoon ¼ cup of batter per pancake, 4 at a time, into the skillet. Cook the pancakes until the bottoms are firm and golden, about 4 minutes.
5. Flip the pancakes over and cook the other side until they are cooked through, about 3 minutes.
6. Remove the pancakes to a plate and repeat with the remaining batter.
7. Serve with fresh fruit.

Greek Yogurt and Oat Pancakes

Preparation time: 5 minutes
Cooking time: 20 minutes
Servings: 4
Ingredients:
- 1 cup 2 percent plain Greek yogurt
- 3 eggs
- 1½ teaspoons pure vanilla extract
- 1 cup rolled oats
- 1 tablespoon granulated sweetener
- 1 teaspoon baking powder
- 1 teaspoon ground cinnamon
- Pinch ground cloves
- Nonstick cooking spray

Directions:
1. Place the yogurt, eggs, and vanilla in a blender and pulse to combine.
2. Add the oats, sweetener, baking powder, cinnamon, and cloves to the blender and blend until the batter is smooth.
3. Place a large nonstick skillet over medium heat and lightly coat it with cooking spray.
4. Spoon ¼ cup of batter per pancake, 4 at a time, into the skillet. Cook the pancakes until the bottoms are firm and golden, about 4 minutes.
5. Flip the pancakes over and cook the other side until they are cooked through, about 3 minutes.
6. Remove the pancakes to a plate and repeat with the remaining batter.
7. Serve with fresh fruit.

Savory Breakfast Egg Bites

Preparation Time: 10 minutes
Cooking Time: 20 to 25 minutes
Servings: 8
Ingredients:
- 6 eggs, beaten
- 1/4 cup unsweetened plain almond milk
- 1/4 cup crumbled goat cheese
- 1/2 cup sliced brown mushrooms
- 1 cup chopped spinach
- 1/4 cup sliced sun-dried tomatoes
- 1 red bell pepper, diced
- Salt and freshly ground black pepper, to taste
- Nonstick cooking spray
- Special Equipment:
- An 8-cup muffin tin

Directions:
1. Preheat the oven to 350°F (180°C). Grease an 8-cup muffin tin with nonstick cooking spray.
2. Make the egg bites: Mix the beaten eggs, almond milk, cheese, mushroom, spinach, tomatoes, bell pepper, salt, and pepper in a large bowl, and whisk to combine.
3. Spoon the mixture into the prepared muffin cups, filling each about three-quarters full.
4. Bake in the preheated oven for 20 to 25 minutes, or until the top is golden brown and a fork comes out clean.
5. Let the egg bites sit for 5 minutes until slightly cooled. Remove from the muffin tin and serve warm.
6. Tip: If you want to make a quick and easy breakfast, you can make these egg bites in single servings in the microwave.

Simple Grain-Free Biscuits

Preparation Time: 10 minutes
Cooking Time: 15 minutes
Servings: 4
Ingredients:
- 2 tablespoons unsalted butter
- 1/4 cup plain low-fat Greek yogurt
- Pinch salt
- 1 1/2 cups finely ground almond flour

Directions:
1. Preheat the oven to 375°F (190°C). Line a baking sheet with parchment paper and set aside.
2. Place the butter in a microwave-safe bowl and microwave for 15 to 20 seconds, or until it is just enough to soften.
3. Add the yogurt and salt to the bowl of butter and blend well.
4. Slowly pour in the almond flour and keep stirring until the mixture just comes together into a slightly sticky, shaggy dough.
5. Use a 1/4-cup measuring cup to mound balls of dough onto the parchment-lined baking sheet and flatten each into a rounded biscuit shape, about 1 inch thick.
6. Bake in the preheated oven for 13 to 15 minutes, or until the biscuits are lightly golden brown.
7. Let the biscuits cool for 5 minutes before serving.

Brussels Sprout with Fried Eggs

Preparation Time: 10 minutes
Cooking Time: 15 minutes
Servings: 4
Ingredients:
- 3 teaspoons extra-virgin olive oil, divided
- 1 pound (454 g) Brussels sprouts, sliced
- 2 garlic cloves, thinly sliced
- 1/4 teaspoon salt
- Juice of 1 lemon
- 4 eggs

Directions:
1. Heat 1 1/2 teaspoons of olive oil in a large skillet over medium heat.

2. Add the Brussels sprouts and sauté for 6 to 8 minutes until crispy and tender, stirring frequently.
3. Stir in the garlic and cook for about 1 minute until fragrant. Sprinkle with the salt and lemon juice.
4. Remove from the skillet to a plate and set aside.
5. Heat the remaining oil in the skillet over medium-high heat. Crack the eggs one at a time into the skillet and fry for about 3 minutes. Flip the eggs and continue cooking, or until the egg whites are set and the yolks are cooked to your liking.
6. Serve the fried eggs over the crispy Brussels sprouts.

Vanilla Coconut Pancakes

Preparation Time: 5 minutes
Cooking Time: 15 minutes
Servings: 4
Ingredients:
- 1/2 cup coconut flour
- 1 teaspoon baking powder
- 1/2 teaspoon ground cinnamon
- 1/8 teaspoon salt
- 8 large eggs
- 1/3 cup unsweetened almond milk
- 2 tablespoons avocado or coconut oil
- 1 teaspoon vanilla extract

Directions:
1. Stir together the flour, baking powder, cinnamon, and salt in a large bowl. Set aside.
2. Beat the eggs with the almond milk, oil, and vanilla in a medium bowl until fully mixed.
3. Heat a large nonstick skillet over medium-low heat.
4. Make the pancakes: Pour 1/3 cup of batter into the hot skillet, tilting the pan to spread it evenly. Cook for 3 to 4 minutes until bubbles form on the surface. Flip the pancake with a spatula and cook for about 3 minutes, or until the pancake is browned around the edges and cooked through. Repeat with the remaining batter.
5. Serve the pancakes on a plate while warm.

Cheesy Spinach and Egg Casserole

Preparation Time: 10 minutes
Cooking Time: 35 minutes
Servings: 8
Ingredients:
- 1 (10-ounce / 284-g) package frozen spinach, thawed and drained
- 1 (14-ounce / 397-g) can artichoke hearts, drained
- 1/4 cup finely chopped red bell pepper
- 8 eggs, lightly beaten
- 1/4 cup unsweetened plain almond milk
- 2 garlic cloves, minced
- 1/2 teaspoon salt
- 1/2 teaspoons freshly ground black pepper
- 1/2 cup crumbled goat cheese
- Nonstick cooking spray

Directions:
1. Preheat the oven to 375°F (190°C). Spray a baking dish with nonstick cooking spray and set aside.
2. Mix the spinach, artichoke hearts, bell peppers, beaten eggs, almond milk, garlic, salt, and pepper in a large bowl, and stir to incorporate.
3. Pour the mixture into the greased baking dish and scatter the goat cheese on top.
4. Bake in the preheated oven for 35 minutes, or until the top is lightly golden around the edges and eggs are set.
5. Remove from the oven and serve warm.

Chocolate-Zucchini Muffins

Preparation time: 15 minutes
Cooking time: 20 minutes
Servings: 12 (1 muffin each)
Ingredients:
- 1½ cups grated zucchini
- 1½ cups rolled oats
- 1 teaspoon ground cinnamon
- 2 teaspoons baking powder
- ¼ teaspoon salt
- 1 large egg
- 1 teaspoon vanilla extract
- ¼ cup coconut oil, melted
- ½ cup unsweetened applesauce
- ¼ cup honey
- ¼ cup dark chocolate chips

Directions:
1. Preheat the oven to 350°F. Grease the cups of a 12-cup muffin tin or line with paper baking liners. Set aside.
2. Place the zucchini in a colander over the sink to drain.
3. In a blender jar, process the oats until they resemble flour. Transfer to a medium mixing bowl and add the cinnamon, baking powder, and salt. Mix well.
4. In another large mixing bowl, combine the egg, vanilla, coconut oil, applesauce, and honey. Stir to combine.
5. Press the zucchini into the colander, draining any liquids, and add to the wet mixture.
6. Stir the dry mixture into the wet mixture and mix until no dry spots remain. Fold in the chocolate chips.
7. Transfer the batter to the muffin tin, filling each cup a little over halfway. Cook for 16 to 18 minutes until the muffins are lightly browned and a toothpick inserted in the center comes out clean.
8. Store in an airtight container, refrigerated, for up to 5 days.

Gluten-Free Carrot and Oat Pancakes

Preparation time: 10 minutes
Cooking time: 20 minutes
Servings: 4 (3 pancakes each)
Ingredients:
- 1 cup rolled oats
- 1 cup shredded carrots
- 1 cup low-fat cottage cheese
- 2 eggs
- ½ cup unsweetened plain almond milk
- 1 teaspoon baking powder
- ½ teaspoon ground cinnamon
- 2 tablespoons ground flaxseed

- ¼ cup plain nonfat Greek yogurt
- 1 tablespoon pure maple syrup
- 2 teaspoons canola oil, divided

Directions:
1. In a blender jar, process the oats until they resemble flour. Add the carrots, cottage cheese, eggs, almond milk, baking powder, cinnamon, and flaxseed to the jar. Process until smooth.
2. In a small bowl, combine the yogurt and maple syrup and stir well. Set aside.
3. In a large skillet, heat 1 teaspoon of oil over medium heat. Using a measuring cup, add ¼ cup of batter per pancake to the skillet. Cook for 1 to 2 minutes until bubbles form on the surface and flip the pancakes. Cook for another minute until the pancakes are browned and cooked through. Repeat with the remaining 1 teaspoon of oil and remaining batter.
4. Serve warm topped with the maple yogurt.

Breakfast Egg Bites

Preparation time: 10 minutes
Cooking time: 25 minutes
Servings: 8 (1 egg bite each)
Ingredients:
- Nonstick cooking spray
- 6 eggs, beaten
- ¼ cup unsweetened plain almond milk
- 1 red bell pepper, diced
- 1 cup chopped spinach
- ¼ cup crumbled goat cheese
- ½ cup sliced brown mushrooms
- ¼ cup sliced sun-dried tomatoes
- Salt
- Freshly ground black pepper

Directions:
1. Preheat the oven to 350°F. Spray 8 muffin cups of a 12-cup muffin tin with nonstick cooking spray. Set aside.
2. In a large mixing bowl, combine the eggs, almond milk, bell pepper, spinach, goat cheese, mushrooms, and tomatoes. Season with salt and pepper.
3. Fill the prepared muffin cups three-fourths full of the egg mixture. Bake for 20 to 25 minutes until the eggs are set. Let cool slightly and remove the egg bites from the muffin tin.
4. Serve warm, or store in an airtight container in the refrigerator for up to 5 days or in the freezer for up to 1 month.

Tacos with Pico De Gallo

Preparation time: 5 minutes
Cooking time: 10 minutes
Servings: 4
Ingredients:
For the Taco Filling:
- Avocado oil cooking spray
- 1 medium green bell pepper, chopped
- 8 large eggs
- ¼ cup shredded sharp Cheddar cheese
- 4 (6-inch) whole-wheat tortillas
- 1 cup fresh spinach leaves
- ½ cup Pico de Gallo
- Scallions, chopped, for garnish (optional)
- Avocado slices, for garnish (optional)

For the Pico De Gallo:
- 1 tomato, diced
- ½ large white onion, diced
- 2 tablespoons chopped fresh cilantro
- ½ jalapeño pepper, stemmed, seeded, and diced
- 1 tablespoon freshly squeezed lime juice
- 1/8 teaspoon salt

Directions:
To Make the Taco Filling
1. Heat a medium skillet over medium-low heat. When hot, coat the cooking surface with cooking spray and put the pepper in the skillet. Cook for 4 minutes.
2. Meanwhile, whisk the eggs in a medium bowl, then add the cheese and whisk to combine. Pour the eggs and cheese into the skillet with the green peppers and scramble until the eggs are fully cooked, about 5 minutes.
3. Microwave the tortillas very briefly, about 8 seconds.
4. For each serving, top a tortilla with one-quarter of the spinach, eggs, and Pico de gallo. Garnish with scallions and avocado slices (if using).

To Make the Pico De Gallo
1. In a medium bowl, combine the tomato, onion, cilantro, pepper, lime juice, and salt. Mix well and serve.

Coconut and Chia Pudding

Preparation time: 5 minutes
Cooking time: 0 minutes
Servings: 2
Ingredients:
- 7 ounces (198 g) light coconut milk
- ¼ cup chia seeds
- 3 to 4 drops liquid stevia
- 1 clementine
- 1 kiwi
- Shredded coconut (unsweetened)

Directions:
1. Start by taking a mixing bowl and adding in the light coconut milk. Add in the liquid stevia to sweeten the milk. Mix well.
2. Add the chia seeds to the milk and whisk until well-combined. Set aside.
3. Peel the clementine and carefully remove the skin from the wedges. Set aside.
4. Also, peel the kiwi and dice it into small pieces.
5. Take a glass jar and assemble the pudding. For this, place the fruits at the bottom of the jar; then add a dollop of chia pudding. Now spread the fruits and then add another layer of chia pudding.
6. Finish by garnishing with the remaining fruits and shredded coconut.

Tomato Waffles

Preparation Time: 15 minutes
Cooking Time: 40 minutes
Servings: 8
Ingredients:
- 2 cups low-fat buttermilk

- 1/2 cup crushed tomato
- 1 medium egg
- 2 medium egg whites
- 1 cup gluten-free all-purpose flour
- 1/2 cup almond flour
- 1/2 cup coconut flour
- 2 teaspoons baking powder
- 1/2 teaspoon baking soda
- 1/2 teaspoon dried chives
- Nonstick cooking spray

Directions:
1. Heat a waffle iron.
2. In a medium bowl, whisk the buttermilk, tomato, egg, and egg whites together.
3. In another bowl, whisk the all-purpose flour, almond flour, coconut flour, baking powder, baking soda, and chives together.
4. Add the wet Ingredients: to the dry ingredients.
5. Lightly spray the waffle iron with cooking spray.
6. Gently pour 1/4- to 1/2-cup portions of batter into the waffle iron. Cooking Time for waffles will vary depending on the kind of waffle iron you use, but it is usually 5 minutes per waffle. (Note: Once the waffle iron is hot, the cooking process is a bit faster.) Repeat until no batter remains.
7. Enjoy the waffles warm with Dandelion Greens with Sweet Onion.

Breakfast Homemade Poultry Sausage

Preparation Time: 15 minutes
Cooking Time: 15 minutes
Servings: 10
Ingredients:
- 1/2 red bell pepper, minced
- 1/2 orange bell pepper, minced
- 1/2 jalapeño pepper, minced
- 1 cup chopped tomatoes
- 1 garlic clove, minced
- 1 pound (454 g) ground chicken
- 1 pound (454 g) ground turkey
- 1/4 teaspoon smoked paprika
- 1/4 teaspoon ground cumin
- 1 tablespoon Worcestershire sauce

Directions:
1. Preheat the oven to 350°F (180°C).
2. In a large bowl, combine the red bell pepper, orange bell pepper, jalapeño pepper, tomatoes, garlic, chicken, turkey, paprika, cumin, and Worcestershire sauce. Gently fold together until well mixed.
3. With clean hands, take about 1/3-cup portions, and shape into balls about the size of a golf ball.
4. Gently press the balls into flat disks, and place on a rimmed baking sheet in a single layer at least 1 inch apart. Repeat with the remaining meat. You should have 10 patties.
5. Transfer the baking sheet to the oven and cook for 5 to 7 minutes.
6. Flip the patties and cook for 5 to 7 minutes, or until the juices run clear.
7. Serve with Not-So-Traditional Gravy and Veggie Hash.

Sausage and Pepper Burrito

Preparation Time: 10 minutes
Cooking Time: 15 minutes
Servings: 4
Ingredients:
- 8 ounces (227 g) bulk pork breakfast sausage
- 1/2 onion, chopped
- 1 green bell pepper, seeded and chopped
- 8 large eggs, beaten
- 4 (6-inch) low-carb tortillas
- 1 cup shredded pepper Jack cheese
- 1/2 cup sour cream (optional, for serving)
- 1/2 cup prepared salsa (optional, for serving)

Directions:
1. In a large nonstick skillet on medium-high heat, cook the sausage, crumbling it with a spoon, until browned, about 5 minutes. Add the onion and bell pepper. Cook, stirring, until the veggies are soft, about 3 minutes. Add the eggs and cook, stirring, until eggs are set, about 3 minutes more.
2. Spoon the egg mixture onto the 4 tortillas. Top each with the cheese and fold into a burrito shape.
3. Serve with sour cream and salsa, if desired.

Gouda Egg Casserole

Preparation Time: 12 minutes
Cooking Time: 20 minutes
Servings: 4
Ingredients:
- Nonstick cooking spray
- 1 slice whole grain bread, toasted
- 1/2 cup shredded smoked Gouda cheese
- 3 slices Canadian bacon, chopped
- 6 large eggs
- 1/4 cup half-and-half
- 1/4 teaspoon kosher salt
- 1/4 teaspoon freshly ground black pepper
- 1/4 teaspoon dry mustard

Directions:
1. Spray a cake pan with cooking spray, or if the pan is nonstick, skip this step. If you don't have a 6-inch cake pan, any bowl or pan that fits inside your pressure cooker should work.
2. Crumble the toast into the bottom of the pan. Sprinkle with the cheese and Canadian bacon.
3. In a medium bowl, whisk together the eggs, half-and-half, salt, pepper, and dry mustard.
4. Pour the egg mixture into the pan. Loosely cover the pan with aluminum foil.
5. Pour 1 1/2 cups water into the electric pressure cooker and insert a wire rack or trivet. Place the covered pan on top of the rack.
6. Close and lock the lid of the pressure cooker. Set the valve to sealing.
7. Cook on high pressure for 20 minutes.

8. When the cooking is complete, hit Cancel and quick release the pressure.
9. Once the pin drops, unlock and remove the lid.
10. Carefully transfer the pan from the pressure cooker to a cooling rack and let it sit for 5 minutes.
11. Cut into 4 wedges and serve.

Breakfast Diabetic Pancakes

Preparation Time: 5 minutes
Cooking Time: 5 minutes
Servings: 6
Ingredients:
- 1 cup Almond flour (blanched)
- 1/4 cup Coconut flour
- 2-3 tablespoons Erythritol
- 1 teaspoon baking powder (gluten-free)
- 5 large Eggs
- 1/3 cup Almond milk (unsweetened)
- 1/4 cup Avocado oil
- 1 1/2 teaspoons Vanilla extract
- 1/4 teaspoon Sea salt

Directions:
1. Begin by taking a mixing bowl and add in the blanched almond flour, coconut flour, erythritol, baking powder, eggs, almond milk, avocado oil, vanilla extract, and sea salt.
2. Use a whisk to mix all the ingredients: until smooth.
3. Take a nonstick pan and place it on a medium-low flame. Grease the pan with a cooking spray.
4. Once the pan is hot enough, drop 1/4 cup batter onto the pan and cook for about 2 minutes. Flip over and cook for another 2 minutes. Repeat the process with the remaining batter.
5. Transfer the cooked pancakes onto a serving platter and stack one over the other. Serve hot!

Blueberry Muffins

Preparation time: 10 minutes
Cooking time: 25 minutes
Servings: 18 muffins
Ingredients:
- 2 cups whole-wheat pastry flour
- 1 cup almond flour
- ½ cup granulated sweetener
- 1 tablespoon baking powder
- 2 teaspoons freshly grated lemon zest
- ¾ teaspoon baking soda
- ¾ teaspoon ground nutmeg
- Pinch sea salt
- 2 eggs
- 1 cup skim milk, at room temperature
- ¾ cup 2 percent plain Greek yogurt
- ½ cup melted coconut oil
- 1 tablespoon freshly squeezed lemon juice
- 1 teaspoon pure vanilla extract
- 1 cup fresh blueberries

Directions:
1. Preheat the oven to 350°F (180°C).
2. Line 18 muffin cups with paper liners and set the tray aside.
3. In a large bowl, stir together the flour, almond flour, sweetener, baking powder, lemon zest, baking soda, nutmeg, and salt.
4. In a small bowl, whisk together the eggs, milk, yogurt, coconut oil, lemon juice, and vanilla.
5. Add the wet Ingredients: to the dry Ingredients: and stir until just combined.
6. Fold in the blueberries without crushing them. Spoon the batter evenly into the muffin cups. Bake the muffins until a toothpick inserted in the middle comes out clean, about 25 minutes.
7. Cool the muffins completely and serve.
8. Store leftover muffins in a sealed container in the refrigerator for up to 3 days or in the freezer for up to 1 month.

Apple and Bran Muffins

Preparation time: 10 minutes
Cooking time: 20 minutes
Servings: 18
Ingredients:
- 2 cups whole-wheat flour
- 1 cup wheat bran
- 1/3 cup granulated sweetener
- 1 tablespoon baking powder
- 2 teaspoons ground cinnamon
- ½ teaspoon ground ginger
- ¼ teaspoon ground nutmeg
- Pinch sea salt
- 2 eggs
- 1½ cups skim milk, at room temperature
- ½ cup melted coconut oil
- 2 teaspoons pure vanilla extract
- 2 apples, peeled, cored, and diced

Directions:
1. Preheat the oven to 350°F (180°C). Line 18 muffin cups with paper liners and set the tray aside.
2. In a large bowl, stir together the flour, bran, sweetener, baking powder, cinnamon, ginger, nutmeg, and salt. In a small bowl, whisk the eggs, milk, coconut oil, and vanilla until blended.
3. Add the wet Ingredients: to the dry Ingredients, stirring until just blended. Stir in the apples and spoon equal amounts of batter into each muffin cup. Bake the muffins until a toothpick inserted in the center of a muffin comes out clean, about 20 minutes. Cool the muffins completely and serve.
4. Store leftover muffins in a sealed container in the refrigerator for up to 3 days or in the freezer for up to 1 month.

Coconut and Berry Oatmeal

Preparation time: 10 minutes
Cooking time: 35 minutes
Servings: 6
Ingredients:
- 2 cups rolled oats
- ¼ cup shredded unsweetened coconut

- 1 teaspoon baking powder
- ½ teaspoon ground cinnamon
- ¼ teaspoon sea salt
- 2 cups skim milk
- ¼ cup melted coconut oil, plus extra for greasing the baking dish
- 1 egg
- 1 teaspoon pure vanilla extract
- 2 cups fresh blueberries
- 1/8 cup chopped pecans, for garnish
- 1 teaspoon chopped fresh mint leaves, for garnish

Directions:
1. Preheat the oven to 350°F (180°C). Lightly oil a baking dish and set it aside.
2. In a medium bowl, stir together the oats, coconut, baking powder, cinnamon, and salt.
3. In a small bowl, whisk together the milk, oil, egg, and vanilla until well blended.
4. Layer half the dry Ingredients: in the baking dish, top with half the berries, then spoon the remaining half of the dry Ingredients: and the rest of the berries on top. Pour the wet Ingredients: evenly into the baking dish. Tap it lightly on the counter to disperse the wet Ingredients: throughout.
5. Bake the casserole, uncovered, until the oats are tender, about 35 minutes. Serve immediately, topped with the pecans and mint.

Crispy Breakfast Pita with Egg and Canadian bacon

Preparation time: 5 minutes
Cooking time: 15 minutes
Servings: 2
Ingredients:
- 1 (6-inch) whole-grain pita bread
- 3 teaspoons extra-virgin olive oil, divided
- 2 eggs
- 2 Canadian bacon slices
- Juice of ½ lemon
- 1 cup microgreens
- 2 tablespoons crumbled goat cheese
- Freshly ground black pepper

Directions:
1. Heat a large skillet over medium heat. Cut the pita bread in half and brush each side of both halves with ¼ teaspoon of olive oil (using a total of 1 teaspoon oil). Cook for 2 to 3 minutes on each side, then remove from the skillet.
2. In the same skillet, heat 1 teaspoon of oil over medium heat. Crack the eggs into the skillet and cook until the eggs are set, 2 to 3 minutes. Remove from the skillet.
3. In the same skillet, cook the Canadian bacon for 3 to 5 minutes, flipping once.
4. In a large bowl, whisk together the remaining 1 teaspoon of oil and the lemon juice. Add the microgreens and toss to combine.
5. Top each pita half with half of the microgreens, 1 piece of bacon, 1 egg, and 1 tablespoon of goat cheese. Season with pepper and serve.

Apple and Pumpkin Waffles

Preparation time: 10 minutes
Cooking time: 20 minutes
Servings: 6
Ingredients:
- 2¼ cups whole-wheat pastry flour
- 2 tablespoons granulated sweetener
- 1 tablespoon baking powder
- 1 teaspoon ground cinnamon
- 1 teaspoon ground nutmeg
- 4 eggs
- 1¼ cups pure pumpkin purée
- 1 apple, peeled, cored, and finely chopped
- Melted coconut oil, for cooking

Directions:
1. In a large bowl, stir together the flour, sweetener, baking powder, cinnamon, and nutmeg. In a small bowl, whisk together the eggs and pumpkin. Add the wet Ingredients: to the dry and whisk until smooth.
2. Stir the apple into the batter.
3. Cook the waffles according to the waffle maker manufacturer's directions, brushing your waffle iron with melted coconut oil, until all the batter is gone. Serve immediately.

Lavender Blueberry Chia Seed Pudding

Preparation Time: 1 hour 10 minutes
Cooking Time: 0 minutes
Servings: 4
Ingredients:
- 100 g blueberries
- 70 g organic quark
- 50 g soy yogurt
- 30 g hazelnuts
- 200 ml almond milk
- 2 tablespoon chia seeds
- 2 teaspoons agave syrup
- 2 teaspoons of lavender

Directions:
1. Bring the almond milk to a boil alongside the lavender.
2. Let the mixture simmer for 10 minutes at a reduced temperature.
3. Allow them to calm down afterward.
4. If the milk is cold, add the blueberries and puree everything.
5. Mix the entire thing with the chia seeds and agave syrup.
6. Let everything soak in the refrigerator for an hour.
7. Mix the yogurt and curd cheese.
8. Add both to the crowd.
9. Divide the pudding into glasses.
10. Finely chop the hazelnuts and sprinkle them on top.

Yogurt with Granola and Persimmon

Preparation Time: 5 minutes

Cooking Time: 5 minutes
Servings: 1
Ingredients:
- 150g Greek-style yogurt
- 20g oatmeal
- 60g fresh persimmons
- 30 ml of tap water

Directions:
1. Put the nonfat oatmeal in the pan.
2. Toast them, continually stirring, until golden brown.
3. Then, put them on a plate and allow them to calm down briefly.
4. Peel the persimmons and put it in a bowl with the water. Mix the entire thing into a fine puree.
5. Put the yogurt, the toasted oatmeal, and then puree in layers in a glass and serve.

Smoothie Bowl with Spinach, Mango, and Muesli

Preparation Time: 10 minutes
Cooking Time: 0 minutes
Servings: 1
Ingredients:
- 150g yogurt
- 30g apple
- 30g mango
- 30g low carb muesli
- 10g spinach
- 10g chia seeds

Directions:
1. Soak the spinach leaves and allow them to drain.
2. Peel the mango and cut it into strips.
3. Remove apple core and cut it into pieces.
4. Put everything except the mango alongside the yogurt in a blender and make a fine puree out of it.
5. Put the spinach smoothie in a bowl.
6. Add the muesli, chia seeds, and mango.
7. Serve the entire thing

Fried Egg with Bacon

Preparation Time: 5 minutes
Cooking Time: 10 minutes
Servings: 1
Ingredients:
- 2 eggs
- 30 grams of bacon
- 2 tablespoon olive oil
- Salt
- Pepper

Directions:
1. Heat oil in the pan and fry the bacon.
2. Reduce the heat and beat the eggs in the pan.
3. Cook the eggs and season with salt and pepper.
4. Serve the fried eggs hot with the bacon.

Buckwheat Crêpes

Preparation time: 20 minutes
Cooking time: 20 minutes
Servings: 5
Ingredients:
- 1½ cups skim milk
- 3 eggs
- 1 teaspoon extra-virgin olive oil, plus more for the skillet
- 1 cup buckwheat flour
- ½ cup whole-wheat flour
- ½ cup 2 percent plain Greek yogurt
- 1 cup sliced strawberries
- 1 cup blueberries

Directions:
1. In a large bowl, whisk together the milk, eggs, and 1 teaspoon of oil until well combined.
2. Into a medium bowl, sift together the buckwheat and whole-wheat flours. Add the dry Ingredients: to the wet Ingredients: and whisk until well combined and very smooth.
3. Allow the batter to rest for at least 2 hours before cooking.
4. Place a large skillet or crêpe pan over medium-high heat and lightly coat the bottom with oil.
5. Pour about ¼ cup of batter into the skillet. Swirl the pan until the batter completely coats the bottom.
6. Cook the crêpe for about 1 minute, then flip it over. Cook the other side of the crêpe for another minute, until lightly browned. Transfer the cooked crêpe to a plate and cover with a clean dish towel to keep warm. Repeat until the batter is used up; you should have about 10 crêpes.
7. Spoon 1 tablespoon of yogurt onto each crêpe and place two crêpes on each plate. Top with berries and serve.

Ham and Cheese Breakfast Biscuits

Preparation Time: 5 minutes
Cooking Time: 15 minutes
Servings: 4
Ingredients:
- 1 cup ham, diced
- 2 eggs
- 3/4 cup Mozzarella cheese, grated
- 1/2 cup low fat Cheddar cheese, grated
- 1/2 cup reduced fat grated Parmesan, grated

Directions:
1. Heat oven to 375°F (190°C). Line a baking sheet with parchment paper.
2. In a large bowl, combine the cheeses and eggs until fully combined. Stir in the ham.
3. Divide the mixture evenly into 8 parts and form into round rolls. Bake for 15 to 20 minutes or until cheese is completely melted and the rolls are nicely browned.

Ham and Jicama Hash

Preparation Time: 10 minutes
Cooking Time: 15 minutes
Servings: 4
Ingredients:
- 6 eggs, beaten
- 2 cups jicama, grated

- 1 cup low fat Cheddar cheese, grated
- 1 cup ham, diced
- From the Cupboard:
- Salt and ground black pepper, to taste
- Nonstick cooking spray

Directions:
1. Spray a large nonstick skillet with cooking spray and place over medium-high heat. Add jicama and cook, stirring occasionally, until it starts to brown, about 5 minutes.
2. Add remaining Ingredients: and reduce heat to medium. Cook for about 3 minutes, then flip over and cook until eggs are set, about 3 to 5 minutes more. Season with salt and pepper and serve.

Greek Yogurt Sundae

Preparation Time: 5 minutes
Cooking Time: 0 minutes
Servings: 1
Ingredients:
- 3/4 cup plain nonfat Greek yogurt
- 1/4 cup mixed berries (blueberries, strawberries, blackberries)
- 2 tablespoons cashew, walnut, or almond pieces
- 1 tablespoon ground flaxseed
- 2 fresh mint leaves, shredded

Directions:
1. Spoon the yogurt into a small bowl. Top with the berries, nuts, and flaxseed.
2. Garnish with the mint and serve.
3. Substitution tip: Use fresh or frozen berries in this sundae, as available. If using frozen, take the berries out of the freezer about 10 or 15 minutes before you make the sundae, so they can thaw.

Mushroom Frittata

Preparation time: 10 minutes
Cooking time: 15 minutes
Servings: 4
Ingredients:
- 8 large eggs
- ½ cup skim milk
- ¼ teaspoon ground nutmeg
- Sea salt and freshly ground black pepper, to taste
- 2 teaspoons extra-virgin olive oil
- 2 cups sliced wild mushrooms (cremini, oyster, shiitake, portobello, etc.)
- ½ red onion, chopped
- 1 teaspoon minced garlic
- ½ cup goat cheese, crumbled

Directions:
1. Preheat the broiler. In a medium bowl, whisk together the eggs, milk, and nutmeg until well combined. Season the egg mixture lightly with salt and pepper and set it aside.
2. Place an ovenproof skillet over medium heat and add the oil, coating the bottom completely by tilting the pan. Sauté the mushrooms, onion, and garlic until translucent, about 7 minutes.
3. Pour the egg mixture into the skillet and cook until the bottom of the frittata is set, lifting the edges of the cooked egg to allow the uncooked egg to seep under.
4. Place the skillet under the broiler until the top is set, about 1 minute.
5. Sprinkle the goat cheese on the frittata and broil until the cheese is melted, about 1 minute more. Remove from the oven.
6. Cut into 4 wedges to serve.

Tropical Yogurt Kiwi Bowl

Preparation time: 5 minutes
Cooking time: 0 minutes
Servings: 2
Ingredients:
- 1½ cups plain low-fat Greek yogurt
- 2 kiwis, peeled and sliced
- 2 tablespoons shredded unsweetened coconut flakes
- 2 tablespoons halved walnuts
- 1 tablespoon chia seeds
- 2 teaspoons honey, divided (optional)

Directions:
1. Divide the yogurt between two small bowls.
2. Top each serving of yogurt with half of the kiwi slices, coconut flakes, walnuts, chia seeds, and honey (if using).

Banana Crêpe Cakes

Preparation time: 5 minutes
Cooking time: 20 minutes
Servings: 4
Ingredients:
- Avocado oil cooking spray
- 4 ounces (113 g) reduced-fat plain cream cheese, softened
- 2 medium bananas
- 4 large eggs
- 1/2 teaspoon vanilla extract
- 1/8 teaspoon salt

Directions:
1. Heat a large skillet over low heat. Coat the cooking surface with cooking spray, and allow the pan to heat for another 2 to 3 minutes.
2. Meanwhile, in a medium bowl, mash the cream cheese and bananas together with a fork until combined. The bananas can be a little chunky.
3. Add the eggs, vanilla, and salt, and mix well.
4. For each cake, drop 2 tablespoons of the batter onto the warmed skillet and use the bottom of a large spoon or ladle to spread it thin. Let it cook for 7 to 9 minutes.
5. Flip the cake over and cook briefly, about 1 minute.

Brussels Sprout Hash and Eggs

Preparation Time: 15 Minutes
Cooking Time: 15 Minutes
Servings: 4
Ingredients:
- 3 teaspoons extra-virgin olive oil, divided
- 1 pound Brussels sprouts, sliced
- 2 garlic cloves, thinly sliced

- ¼ teaspoon salt
- Juice of 1 lemon
- 4 eggs

Directions:

1. In a large skillet, heat 1½ teaspoons of oil over medium heat. Add the Brussels sprouts and toss. Cook, stirring regularly, for 6 to 8 minutes until browned and softened. Add the garlic and continue to cook until fragrant, about 1 minute. Season with the salt and lemon juice. Transfer to a serving dish.

2. In the same pan, heat the remaining 1½ teaspoons of oil over medium-high heat. Crack the eggs into the pan. Fry for 2 to 4 minutes, flip, and continue cooking to desired doneness. Serve over the bed of hash.

Spinach, Artichoke, and Goat Cheese Breakfast Bake

Preparation time: 10 minutes
Cooking time: 35 minutes
Servings: 8
Ingredients:

- Nonstick cooking spray
- 1 (10-ounce) package frozen spinach, thawed and drained
- 1 (14-ounce) can artichoke hearts, drained
- ¼ cup finely chopped red bell pepper
- 2 garlic cloves, minced
- 8 eggs, lightly beaten
- ¼ cup unsweetened plain almond milk
- ½ teaspoon salt
- ½ teaspoon freshly ground black pepper
- ½ cup crumbled goat cheese

Directions:

1. Preheat the oven to 375°F. Spray an 8-by-8-inch baking dish with nonstick cooking spray.
2. In a large mixing bowl, combine the spinach, artichoke hearts, bell pepper, garlic, eggs, almond milk, salt, and pepper. Stir well to combine.
3. Transfer the mixture to the baking dish. Sprinkle with the goat cheese.
4. Bake for 35 minutes until the eggs are set. Serve warm.

Homemade Turkey Breakfast Sausage

Preparation time: 10 minutes
Cooking time: 10 minutes
Servings: 8 (1 patty each)
Ingredients:

- 1-pound lean ground turkey
- ½ teaspoon salt
- ½ teaspoon dried sage
- ½ teaspoon dried thyme
- ½ teaspoon freshly ground black pepper
- ¼ teaspoon ground fennel seeds
- 1 teaspoon extra-virgin olive oil

Directions:

1. In a large mixing bowl, combine the ground turkey, salt, sage, thyme, pepper, and fennel. Mix well.
2. Shape the meat into 8 small, round patties.
3. Heat the olive oil in a skillet over medium-high heat. Cook the patties in the skillet for 3 to 4 minutes on each side until browned and cooked through.
4. Serve warm, or store in an airtight container in the refrigerator for up to 3 days or in the freezer for up to 1 month.

Cheesy Low-Carb Omelet

Preparation Time: 5 minutes
Cooking Time: 5 minutes
Servings: 5
Ingredients:

- 2 whole eggs
- 1 tablespoon water
- 1 tablespoon butter
- 3 thin slices of salami
- 5 fresh basil leaves
- 5 thin slices of fresh ripe tomatoes
- 2 ounces fresh mozzarella cheese
- Salt and pepper as needed

Directions:

1. Take a small bowl and whisk in eggs and water
2. Take a non-stick Saute pan and place it over medium heat; add butter and let it melt
3. Pour egg mixture and cook for 30 seconds
4. Spread salami slices on half of the egg mix and top with cheese, tomatoes, and basil slices
5. Season with salt and pepper according to your taste
6. Cook for 2 minutes and fold the egg with the empty half
7. Cover and cook on LOW for 1 minute
8. Serve and enjoy!

Roasted Onions And Green Beans

Preparation Time: 10 minutes
Cooking Time: 15 minutes
Servings: 6
Ingredients:

- 1 yellow onion, sliced into rings
- ½ teaspoon onion powder
- 2 tablespoons coconut flour
- 1 and 1/3 pounds fresh green beans, trimmed and chopped
- ½ tablespoon salt

Directions:

1. Take a large bowl and mix salt with onion powder and coconut flour
2. Add onion rings
3. Mix well to coat
4. Spread the rings on the baking sheet lined with parchment paper
5. Drizzled with some oil
6. Bake for 10 minutes at 400 Fahrenheit
7. Parboil the green beans for 3 to 5 minutes in the boiling water
8. Drain it and serve the beans with baked onion rings
9. Serve warm, and enjoy

Denver Omelet

Preparation Time: 4 minutes
Cooking Time: 1 minute
Servings: 1
Ingredients:

- 2 tablespoons butter
- ¼ cup onion, chopped
- ¼ cup green bell pepper, diced
- ¼ cup grape tomatoes halved
- 2 whole eggs
- ¼ cup ham, chopped

Directions:
1. Take a skillet and place it over medium heat
2. Add butter and wait until the butter melts
3. Add onion and bell pepper and Sauté for a few minutes
4. Take a bowl and whip eggs
5. Add the remaining ingredients and stir
6. Add Sautéed onion and pepper, stir
7. Microwave the egg mix for 1 minute
8. Serve hot!

Hungarian Porridge

Preparation Time: 10 minutes
Cooking Time: 5-10 minutes
Servings: 2
Ingredients:
- 1 tablespoon chia seeds
- 1 tablespoon ground flaxseed
- 1/3 cup coconut cream
- ½ cup water
- 1 teaspoon vanilla extract
- 1 tablespoon butter

Directions:
1. Add chia seeds, coconut cream, flaxseed, water, and vanilla to a small pot
2. Stir and let it sit for 5 minutes
3. Add butter and place pot over low heat
4. Keep stirring as butter melts
5. Once the porridge is hot/not boiling, pour it into a bowl
6. Enjoy!
7. Add a few berries or a dash of cream for extra flavor

Scrambled Pesto Eggs

Preparation Time: 5 minutes
Cooking Time: 5 minutes
Servings: 4
Ingredients:
- 3 large whole eggs
- 1 tablespoon butter
- 1 tablespoon pesto
- 2 tablespoons creamed coconut milk
- Salt and pepper as needed

Directions:
1. Take a bowl and crack open your egg
2. Season with a pinch of salt and pepper
3. Pour eggs into a pan
4. Add butter and introduce heat
5. Cook on low heat and gently add pesto
6. Once the egg is cooked and scrambled, remove the heat
7. Spoon in coconut cream and mix well
8. Turn on the heat and cook on LOW for a while until you have a creamy texture
9. Serve and enjoy!

Vanilla Hemp Drink

Preparation Time: 10 minutes
Ingredients:
Servings: 1
- 1 cup water
- 1 cup unsweetened hemp milk, vanilla
- 1 and ½ tablespoons coconut oil, unrefined
- ½ cup frozen blueberries, mixed
- 4 cup leafy greens, kale, and spinach
- 1 tablespoons flaxseeds
- 1 tablespoon almond butter

Directions:
1. Add listed ingredients to a blender
2. Blend until you have a smooth and creamy texture
3. Serve chilled, and enjoy!

Pepperoni Omelet

Preparation Time: 5 minutes
Cooking Time: 20 minutes
Servings: 4
Ingredients:
- 6 eggs
- 15 pepperoni slices
- 2 teaspoons coconut cream
- Salt and freshly ground black pepper to taste
- 2 tablespoons butter

Directions:
1. Take a bowl and whisk eggs with all the remaining ingredients in it
2. Then take a skillet and heat the butter
3. Pour the ¼ of egg mixture into your skillet
4. After that, cook for 2 minutes per side
5. Repeat to use the entire batter
6. Serve warm, and enjoy!

Delicious Nut Dredged Porridge

Preparation Time: 10 minutes
Cooking Time: 15 minutes
Servings: 4
Ingredients:
- 1 cup cashew nuts, raw and unsalted
- 1 cup pecan, halved
- 2 tablespoons stevia
- 4 teaspoons coconut oil, melted
- 2 cups water

Directions:
1. Chop the nuts in a food processor and form a smooth paste
2. Add water, oil, and stevia to nuts paste and transfer the mix to a saucepan
3. Stir cook for 5 minutes on high heat
4. Lower heat to low and simmer for 10 minutes
5. Serve warm, and enjoy!

Crispy Tofu

Preparation Time: 5 minutes
Cooking Time: 20-30 minutes
Servings: 8
Ingredients:
- 1 pound extra-firm tofu, drained and sliced
- 2 tablespoons olive oil
- 1 cup almond meal

- 1 tablespoons yeast
- ½ teaspoon onion powder
- ½ teaspoon garlic powder
- ½ teaspoon oregano
- ¼ teaspoon salt

Directions:
1. Add all ingredients except tofu and olive oil to a shallow bowl
2. Mix well
3. Preheat your oven to 400 degrees F
4. In the wide bowl, add the almond meal and mix well
5. Brush tofu with olive oil, dip into the mix, and coat well
6. Line a baking sheet with parchment paper
7. Transfer coated tofu to the baking sheet
8. Bake for 20-30 minutes, making sure to flip once until golden brown
9. Serve and enjoy!

Cottage Cheese Hotcake

Preparation Time: 10 minutes
Cooking Time: 5-10 minutes
Servings: 2
Ingredients:
- 1 cup full–fat cottage cheese
- ½ cup full-fat ricotta cheese
- 2 whole eggs
- ¼ cup coconut cream
- ½ teaspoon baking powder
- 1 teaspoon vanilla extract
- Butter for frying
- 2 teaspoon almond butter

Directions:
1. Add cottage cheese, ricotta cheese, eggs, and coconut cream to a bowl and whisk well
2. Add ground almond, coconut flour, baking powder, vanilla extra, and whisk until smooth
3. Take a non-stick frying pan and place it over medium heat
4. Add a knob of butter
5. Once butter melts, add dollops of batter onto the hot pan
6. Once bubbles appear, flip the pancakes over
7. Serve with almond butter and some berries on top
8. Enjoy!

Mushroom Muffin

Preparation Time: 10 minutes
Cooking Time: 15 minutes
Servings: 12 muffins
Ingredients:
- 3 cups mushrooms, sliced
- 1 medium-large zucchini, sliced
- 1 cup baby spinach leaves
- 5 eggs, lightly beaten
- Salt and pepper to taste
- 5 ounces cream cheese, broken into little pieces

Directions:
1. Preheat your oven to 375 degrees F
2. Grease 12 hole-muffin tin
3. Place mushrooms, zucchini, spinach, eggs, salt, and pepper in a bowl
4. Mix well
5. Pour mix into muffin pan and transfer to oven
6. Bake for 12-15 minutes
7. Make cream cheese frosting by stirring cream cheese to loosen it and bring it to a spreadable consistency
8. Let the muffin cool and spread cream cheese
9. Enjoy!

Cinnamon And Coconut Porridge

Preparation Time: 5 minutes
Cook Time: 5 minutes
Servings: 4
Ingredients:
- 2 cups water
- 1 cup 36% heavy cream
- ½ cup unsweetened dried coconut, shredded
- 2 tablespoons flaxseed meal
- 1 tablespoon butter
- 1 and ½ teaspoon stevia
- 1 teaspoon cinnamon
- Salt to taste
- Toppings as blueberries

Directions:
1. Add the listed ingredients to a small pot, mix well
2. Transfer pot to stove and place it over medium-low heat
3. Bring to mix to a slow boil
4. Stir well and remove the heat
5. Divide the mix into equal servings and let them sit for 10 minutes
6. Top with your desired toppings, and enjoy!

Skillet-Based Kale And Avocado

Preparation Time: 5 minutes
Cooking Time: 10 minutes
Servings: 2
Ingredients:
- 2 tablespoons olive oil, divided
- 2 cups mushrooms, sliced
- 5 ounces fresh kale, stemmed and sliced into ribbons
- 1 avocado, sliced
- 4 large eggs
- Salt and pepper as needed

Directions:
1. Take a large skillet and place it over medium heat
2. Add a tablespoon of olive oil
3. Add mushrooms to the pan and Saute for 3 minutes
4. Take a medium bowl and massage kale with the remaining 1 tablespoon olive oil (for about 1-2 minutes)
5. Add kale to the skillet and place them on top of the mushrooms
6. Place slices of avocado on top of kale
7. Create 4 wells for eggs and crack each egg onto each hold
8. Season eggs with salt and pepper
9. Cover skillet and cook for 5 minutes
10. Serve hot!

Fat Burner Espresso

Preparation Time: 10 minutes
Servings: 2
Ingredients:
- 1 scoop Isopure Zero Carb protein powder
- 1 espresso shot

- ¼ cup Greek yogurt, full fat
- Liquid stevia, to sweeten
- Pinch of cinnamon
- 5 ice cubes

Directions:
1. Add listed ingredients to a blender
2. Blend until you have a smooth and creamy texture
3. Serve chilled, and enjoy!

Blue Cheese Omelet

Preparation Time: 10 minutes
Cooking Time: 15 minutes
Servings: 2
Ingredients:
- 4 eggs
- Salt, to taste
- 1 tbsp sesame oil
- ½ cup blue cheese, crumbled
- 1 tomato, thinly sliced

Directions:
1. In a mixing bowl, beat the eggs and season with salt.
2. Set a saute pan over medium heat and warm the oil. Add in the eggs and cook as you swirl the eggs around the pan using a spatula.
3. Cook eggs until partially set.
4. Top with cheese; fold the omelet in half to enclose the filling.
5. Decorate with tomato and serve while warm.

Hearty Chia Bowls

Preparation Time: 10 minutes
Cooking Time: Nil
Servings: 2
Ingredients:
- 1/4 cup walnuts, chopped
- 1 and 1/2 cups almond milk
- 2 tablespoons chia seeds
- 1 tablespoon stevia
- 1 teaspoon vanilla extract

Directions:
1. In a bowl, combine the almond milk with the chia seeds and the rest of the ingredients, toss, leave the mix aside for 10 minutes and serve for breakfast

Pecan And Goat Cheese

Preparation Time: 10 minutes
Cooking Time: 10 minutes
Servings: 4
Ingredients:
- 1 lb log goat cheese
- 1/3 cup pecans, chopped
- 3 tablespoons bacon syrup
- 2 teaspoons fresh basil, chopped
- 1 teaspoon fresh chives, chopped

Directions:
1. Add the chopped basil, bacon, and chives to a small saucepan. Cook for 1-2 minutes and set aside.
2. Finely chop the pecans and transfer them to a large plate. Then roll the goat cheese in the chopped pecans.
3. Drizzle with the bacon mixture and serve. Enjoy

Broccoli Egg Salad

Preparation Time: 10 minutes
Cooking Time: Nil
Servings: 4
Ingredients:
- 1 pound broccoli florets, steamed
- 4 eggs, hard-boiled, peeled, and cut into wedges
- 2 spring onions, chopped'/2 teaspoon chili powder
- 1 tablespoon olive oil
- 1 tablespoon lime juice
- Salt and black pepper to the taste

Directions:
1. In a bowl, combine the broccoli with the eggs and the other ingredients, toss and serve for breakfast.

Creamy Cheese Pancakes

Preparation Time: 10 minutes
Cook Time: 12 minutes
Servings: 4
Ingredients:
- 2 organic eggs
- 2 ounces cream cheese, softened 1/2 teaspoon ground cinnamon 1 packet stevia
- Olive oil nonstick cooking spray

Directions:
1. Place all the ingredients in a blender and pulse until smooth.
2. Transfer the mixture into a bowl and set aside for 2-3 minutes.
3. Grease a large nonstick skillet with cooking spray and heat over medium heat.
4. Add 1/4 of the mixture and tilt the pan to spread it in an even layer.
5. Cook for about 2 minutes or until golden brown.
6. Flip the side and cook for about 1 more minute.
7. Repeat with the remaining mixture.
8. Serve warm

Delicious Egg Muffins

Preparation Time: 10 minutes
Cooking Time: 20 minutes
Servings: 4
Ingredients:
- 6 tablespoons almond flour
- 2 tablespoons flaxseed meal
- 1/4 teaspoon baking soda
- 4 eggs
- 4 ounces cheddar cheese, shredded

Directions:
1. In a mixing bowl, thoroughly combine all the above ingredients until well incorporated.
2. Line a muffin tin with non-stick baking cups. Scrape the batter into the prepared baking cups.
3. Bake in the preheated oven at 350 degrees F for 15 to 17 minutes.
4. Transfer to a wire rack to cool slightly before unmolding and serving. Bon appetit!

Double Stuffed Cheese Peppers

Preparation Time: 10 minutes

Cooking Time: 25 minutes
Servings: 4
Ingredients:
- 4 summer bell peppers, divined and halved
- 1 clove of garlic, minced
- 4 ounces cream cheese
- 2 ounces mozzarella cheese, crumbled
- 2 tablespoons Greek-style yogurt

Directions:
1. Cook the peppers in boiling water in a Dutch oven until just tender or approximately 7 minutes.
2. Mix the garlic, cream cheese, mozzarella, and yogurt until well combined. Then, stuff the peppers with the cheese mixture.
3. Arrange the stuffed peppers on a til-lined baking pan.
4. Bake in the oven at 360 degrees F for 10 to 12 minutes. Serve at room temperature.

Baked Stuffed Up Avocados

Preparation Time: 10 minutes
Cooking Time: 15-20 minutes
Servings: 4
Ingredients:
- 3 avocados, halved and pitted, skin on
- 1/2 cup mozzarella, shredded
- 1/2 cup Swiss cheese, grated
- 2 eggs, beaten
- 1 tbsp fresh basil, chopped

Directions:
1. Set oven to 360 F. Lay avocado halves in an ovenproof dish. Mix cheese, pepper, eggs, and salt in a bowl. Split the mixture
2. into the avocado halves. Bake for 15 to 17 minutes. Decorate with basil before serving

Colorful Vegetable Omelet

Preparation Time: 10 minutes
Cooking Time: 5-10 minutes
Servings: 4
Ingredients:
- 2 tablespoons olive oil
- 1 cup Chanterelle mushrooms, chopped
- 2 bell peppers, chopped
- 1 white onion, chopped
- 6 eggs

Directions:
1. Heat the olive oil in a nonstick skillet over moderate heat. Now, cook the mushrooms, peppers, and onion until they have softened.
2. In a mixing bowl, whisk the eggs until frothy. Add the eggs to the skillet, reduce the heat to medium-low, and cook for approximately 5 minutes until the center starts to look dry. Do not overcook.
3. Taste and season with salt to taste.

Simple Fried Eggs

Preparation Time: 10 minutes
Cooking Time: 5-10 minutes
Servings: 4
Ingredients:
- 2 eggs
- 2 tbsp unsalted butter
- Seasoning:
- 1/4 tsp salt
- 1/8 tsp ground black pepper

Directions:
1. Take a skillet pan, place it over medium heat, add butter, and crack eggs in the pan when it has melted.
2. Cook eggs for 3 to 5 minutes until fried to the desired level, then transfer the eggs to serving plates and sprinkle with salt and black pepper.
3. Serve.

Beef And Egg Early Morning Muffin

Preparation Time: 10 minutes
Cooking Time: 15 minutes
Servings: 12
Ingredients:
- 2 lbs of ground beef (20% fat/80% lean meat ratio)
- 1 tbsp of mixed herbs
- 12 eggs
- 1 cup of shredded cheddar cheese
- 2 and 1/2 cups of spinach

Directions:
1. In a deep pan, saute the spinach with some olive oil for a few minutes until wilted. Remove from the heat and set aside.
2. In a 12-piece muffin, a tin dish begins lining each tin with around 1-2 tbsp of the ground beef to make a base cup. You should cover all sides of the tin and leave room for the spinach and eggs.
3. Top each meat cup with spinach, cheese, and one egg.
4. Cook in the oven for 15-18 minutes at 400F/200C

Spicy Chili Deviled Eggs

Preparation Time: 10 minutes
Cooking Time: 50 minutes
Servings: 4
Ingredients:
- 1/4 of lime, juiced
- 2 eggs, boiled
- 2 tsp chili garlic sauce
- 1/2 tsp paprika
- 1/8 tsp ground black pepper

Directions:
1. Peel the boiled eggs, then slice in half lengthwise and transfer egg yolks to a medium bowl using a spoon.
2. Mash the egg yolk, add the remaining ingredients and stir until well combined.
3. Spoon the egg yolk mixture into egg whites and then serve.

Classic Egg Porridge

Preparation Time: 10 minutes
Cooking Time: 15 minutes
Servings: 4
Ingredients:
- 2 organic free-range eggs
- 1/3 cup organic heavy cream without food additives

- 2 packages of your preferred sweetener
- 2 tbsp grass-fed butter ground organic cinnamon to taste

Directions:
1. Add the eggs, cream, and sweetener to a bowl, and mix.
2. Melt the butter in a saucepan over medium heat. Lower the heat once the butter is melted.
3. Combine together with the egg and cream mixture.
4. While Cooking, mix until it thickens and curdles.
5. When you see the first signs of curdling, remove the saucepan immediately from the heat.
6. Pour the porridge into a bowl. Sprinkle cinnamon on top and serve immediately.

Juicy Spanish Omelet

Preparation Time: 10 minutes
Cooking Time: 10 minutes
Servings: 4
Ingredients:
- 3 eggs
- Cayenne or black pepper
- 1/2 cup finely chopped vegetables of your choosing.

Directions:
1. In a pan, stir-fry the vegetables in extra virgin olive oil until lightly crispy.
2. Cook the eggs with one tablespoon of water and a pinch of pepper.
3. When almost cooked, top with the vegetables and flip to cook briefly.
4. Serve

Delicious Breakfast Sausage Casserole

Preparation Time: 10 minutes
Cooking Time: 45 minutes
Servings: 4
Ingredients:
- 8 eggs, beaten
- 1 head chopped cauliflower
- 1 lb sausage, cooked and crumbled
- 2 cups heavy whipping cream
- 1 cup sharp cheddar cheese, grated

Directions:
1. Cook the sausage as usual.
2. Mix the sausage, heavy whipping cream, chopped cauliflower, cheese, and eggs in a large bowl.
3. Pour into a greased casserole dish.
4. Cook for 45 minutes at 350°F/175°C, or until firm.
5. Top with cheese and serve.

Excellent Scrambled Mug Eggs

Preparation Time: 10 minutes
Cooking Time: 5 minutes
Servings: 4
Ingredients:
- 1 mug
- 2 eggs
- Salt and pepper
- Shredded cheese
- Your favorite buffalo wing sauce

Directions:
1. Crack the eggs into a mug and whisk until blended.
2. Put the mug into your microwave and cook for 1.5 - 2 minutes, depending on the power of your microwave.
3. Leave for a few minutes and remove from the microwave.
4. Sprinkle with salt and pepper. Add your desired amount of cheese on top.
5. Using a fork, mix everything together.
6. Then add your favorite buffalo or hot sauce and mix again.
7. Serve!

Unique Salmon Omelet

Preparation Time: 10 minutes
Cooking Time: 5-10 minutes
Servings: 4
Ingredients:
- 3 eggs
- 1 smoked salmon
- 3 links beef sausage
- 1/4 cup onions
- 1/4 cup provolone cheese

Directions:
1. Whisk the eggs and pour them into a skillet.
2. Follow the standard method for making an omelet.
3. Add the onions, salmon, and cheese before turning the omelet over.
4. Sprinkle the omelet with cheese and serve with the sausages on the side.
5. Serve!

Fine Spinach And Cheese Eggs

Preparation Time: 10 minutes
Cooking Time: 25-30 minutes
Servings: 4
Ingredients:
- 3 whole eggs
- 3 oz cottage cheese
- 3-4 oz chopped spinach, 1/4 cup parmesan cheese, 1/4 cup of milk

Directions:
1. Preheat your oven to 375°F/190°C.
2. Whisk the eggs, cottage cheese, parmesan, and milk in a large bowl.
3. Mix in the spinach.
4. Transfer to a small, greased oven dish.
5. Sprinkle the cheese on top.
6. Bake for 25-30 minutes.
7. Let cool for 5 minutes and serve.
8. Serve!

The Breakfast Margarita

Preparation Time: 5 minutes
Serving: 2
Ingredients:
- 1 tablespoon hemp seeds
- ½ a lime, juiced
- ¼ fresh avocado
- 2 mandarin oranges

- 1 cup of frozen strawberries
- 1 cup unsweetened coconut milk

Directions:
1. Add all the ingredients except vegetables/fruits first
2. Blend until smooth
3. Add the vegetable/fruits
4. Blend until smooth
5. Add a few ice cubes and serve the smoothie
6. Enjoy!

Homely Honeydew Twist

Preparation Time: 5 minutes
Serving: 2
Ingredients:
- 1 cup ice
- 1 tablespoon fresh mint
- 2 cucumbers, chopped
- 1 cup honeydew melon, peeled and seeded, chopped
- 1 cup of coconut water

Directions:
1. Add all the ingredients except vegetables/fruits first
2. Blend until smooth
3. Add the vegetable/fruits
4. Blend until smooth
5. Add a few ice cubes and serve the smoothie
6. Enjoy!

The Sweet Melon Morning Kale

Preparation Time: 5 minutes
Serving: 2
Ingredients:
- 1 tablespoon lemon juice
- 1 medium cucumber, diced
- 1 cup honeydew melon, peeled and chopped
- 4 cups kale, chopped

Directions:
1. Add all the ingredients except vegetables/fruits first
2. Blend until smooth
3. Add the vegetable/fruits
4. Blend until smooth
5. Add a few ice cubes and serve the smoothie
6. Add more toppings if needed
7. Enjoy!

The Ultimate Morning Green

Preparation Time: 5 minutes
Serving: 2
Ingredients:
- 1 medium whole tomato, diced
- 2 cups baby spinach, chopped
- 1 medium sweet green pepper, chopped
- 15 green grapes
- 1 cucumber, cubed
- 2 medium carrots, scrubbed and chopped
- 2 medium Granny Smith apples, quartered

Directions:
1. Add all the ingredients except vegetables/fruits first
2. Blend until smooth
3. Add the vegetable/fruits
4. Blend until smooth

5. Add a few ice cubes and serve the smoothie
6. Enjoy!

Fine Liquid Sunrise

Preparation Time: 5 minutes
Serving: 2
Ingredients:
- 1 cup ice
- 4 tablespoons protein powder
- 1 cup of frozen mango, sliced
- 1 cup of frozen strawberries
- 1 cup baby spinach
- 1 and ¾ cup unsweetened coconut milk drink

Directions
1. Add all the ingredients except vegetables/fruits first
2. Blend until smooth
3. Add the vegetable/fruits
4. Blend until smooth
5. Add a few ice cubes and serve the smoothie
6. Enjoy!

Morning Aloha Smoothie

Preparation Time: 5 minutes
Serving: 2
Ingredients:
- 1 cup ice
- 1 tablespoon coconut, shredded
- 1 cup of frozen mango, sliced
- ¾ cup pineapple sliced
- 1 and ½ cups unsweetened almond milk

Directions:
1. Add all the ingredients except vegetables/fruits first
2. Blend until smooth
3. Add the vegetable/fruits
4. Blend until smooth
5. Add a few ice cubes and serve the smoothie
6. Enjoy!

The Banana Delight

Preparation Time: 5 minutes
Serving: 2
Ingredients:
- 1 cup ice
- 2 tablespoons protein powder
- 1 tablespoon green superfood as preferred
- 1 frozen banana, cubed
- 1 cup baby spinach
- 1 cup unsweetened almond milk

Directions
1. Add all the ingredients except vegetables/fruits first
2. Blend until smooth
3. Add the vegetable/fruits
4. Blend until smooth
5. Add a few ice cubes and serve the smoothie
6. Enjoy!

The Raspberry Minty Delight

Preparation Time: 5 minutes
Serving: 2
Ingredients:
- 1 cup ice

- 1 teaspoon probiotics
- 1 tablespoon fresh mint
- ½ frozen banana, sliced
- 2 cups frozen raspberries
- 1 and ½ cups unsweetened almond milk

Directions:
1. Add all the ingredients except vegetables/fruits first
2. Blend until smooth
3. Add the vegetable/fruits
4. Blend until smooth
5. Add a few ice cubes and serve the smoothie
6. Enjoy!

The Rising Red Sun

Preparation Time: 5 minutes
Serving: 2
Ingredients:
- ¼ lemon, sliced
- ¼ Barlett pear, cored
- 1 medium beet, scrubbed and quartered
- 2 stalks celery
- 5 cups of baby spinach

Directions:
1. Add all the ingredients except vegetables/fruits first
2. Blend until smooth
3. Add the vegetable/fruits
4. Blend until smooth
5. Add a few ice cubes and serve the smoothie
6. Enjoy!

Cinnamon And Beet Booster Dose

Preparation Time: 5 minutes
Serving: 2
Ingredients:
- ¼ teaspoon cinnamon
- 1 medium cucumber, diced
- 1 medium beet, scrubbed and halved
- 1 cup kale, chopped
- 2 cups baby spinach, chopped

Directions:
1. Add all the ingredients except vegetables/fruits first
2. Blend until smooth
3. Add the vegetable/fruits
4. Blend until smooth
5. Add a few ice cubes and serve the smoothie
6. Enjoy!

The Wisest Watermelon Glass

Preparation Time: 5 minutes
Serving: 2
Ingredients:
- 1 tablespoon chia seeds
- 1 cup plain coconut yogurt
- 1 cup frozen cauliflower, riced
- 1 cup of frozen strawberries
- 1 cup coconut milk, unsweetened
- 1 and ½ cups watermelon, chopped

Directions:
1. Add all the ingredients except vegetables/fruits first
2. Blend until smooth
3. Add the vegetable/fruits
4. Blend until smooth
5. Add a few ice cubes and serve the smoothie
6. Enjoy!

Cheery Charlie Checker

Preparation Time: 5 minutes
Serving: 2
Ingredients:
- 1 cup skim milk
- 1 cup frozen blueberries
- 1 fresh banana
- ¾ cup plain low-fat Greek yogurt
- ½ cup frozen cherries
- ½ cup of frozen strawberries
- 1 tablespoon chia seeds

Directions:
1. Add all the ingredients except vegetables/fruits first
2. Blend until smooth
3. Add the vegetable/fruits
4. Blend until smooth
5. Add a few ice cubes and serve the smoothie
6. Enjoy!

The Pom Drink

Preparation Time: 5 minutes
Serving: 2
Ingredients:
- 1 cup plain coconut yogurt
- 1 cup baby spinach
- 1 cup frozen raspberries
- 1 cup frozen blackberries
- 1 cup unsweetened vanilla coconut milk

Directions:
1. Add all the ingredients except vegetables/fruits first
2. Blend until smooth
3. Add the vegetable/fruits
4. Blend until smooth
5. Add a few ice cubes
6. Add some berries if required
7. Add syrup if needed
8. Enjoy!

Bright Rainbow Health

Preparation Time: 5 minutes
Serving: 2
Ingredients:
- 1 tablespoon hemp seeds
- ¼ cup pomegranate arils
- 1 cup plain Low-Fat Greek Yogurt
- 1 cup frozen tropical fruit mix
- 1 cup of frozen strawberries
- 1 cup unsweetened vanilla almond milk

Directions:
1. Add all the ingredients except vegetables/fruits first
2. Blend until smooth
3. Add the vegetable/fruits
4. Blend until smooth
5. Add a few ice cubes and serve the smoothie
6. Enjoy!

Juicy Scotch Egg

Preparation Time: 10 minutes
Cooking Time: 25-30 minutes
Servings: 4
Ingredients:
- 4 large eggs
- 1 package of Beef Sausage (12 oz)
- 8 slices of thick-cut beef bacon
- 4 toothpicks

Directions:
1. Hard-boil the eggs, peel the shells and let them cool.
2. Slice the sausage into four parts and place each part into a large circle.
3. Put an egg into each circle and wrap it in the sausage.
4. Place inside your refrigerator for 1 hour.
5. Make a cross with two pieces of thick-cut bacon.
6. Place a wrapped egg in the center, fold the bacon over the top of the egg and secure with a toothpick.
7. Cook inside your oven at 450°F/230°C for 25 minutes.
8. Enjoy!

Toasty Cauliflower And Avocado

Preparation Time: 10 minutes
Cooking Time: 5-10 minutes
Servings: 4
Ingredients:
- 1 large egg
- 1 grated cauliflower head
- 1 chopped avocado
- 3/4 cup shredded mozzarella cheese
- Salt & Black pepper

Directions:
1. Set the oven to preheat at 420 F, then line the baking tray with a parchment paper
2. Cook the cauliflower in the microwave on high for 7 minutes
3. Allow the cauliflower to cool, then drain it on a paper towel.
4. Remove the excess moisture by pressing with a clean kitchen towel, then put them in a bowl.
5. Add the egg and mozzarella, then stir
6. Add the seasonings and mix evenly, then shape the mixture into medium squares
7. Arrange the squares on the prepared baking tray.
8. Allow baking until browned evenly, for about 20 minutes
9. In the meantime, puree the avocado with black pepper and salt.
10. Top with the pureed avocado.
11. Serve!

Avocado Egg Crepes

Preparation Time: 10 minutes
Cooking Time: 5 minutes
Servings: 4
Ingredients:
- 4 eggs
- 3/4 sliced avocado
- 2 teaspoons olive oil
- 1/2 cup alfalfa sprouts
- 4 slices of shredded turkey breast

Directions:
1. Pour the olive oil into a pan and heat over medium heat
2. Crush the eggs and cook for 3 minutes on each side of the pan as you spread to cook evenly.
3. Remove the eggs from heat, top with avocado, turkey breast, sprouts, and alfalfa, then roll up well.
4. Serve!

Bacon And Shallots With Spinach

Preparation Time: 10 minutes
Cooking Time: 20-25 minutes
Servings: 4
Ingredients:
- 16 oz raw spinach
- 1/2 cup chopped white onion
- 1/2 cup chopped shallot
- 1/2-pound raw bacon slices
- 2 tbsp butter

Directions:
1. Slice the bacon strips into small narrow pieces.
2. In a skillet, heat the butter and add the chopped onion, shallots, and bacon.
3. Sauté for 15-20 minutes or until the onions caramelize, and the bacon is cooked.
4. Add the spinach and sauté on medium heat. Stir frequently to ensure the leaves touch the skillet while cooking.
5. Cover and steam for around 5 minutes, stir and continue until wilted.
6. Serve!

Mango And Pear Smoothie

Preparation Time: 10 minutes
Cooking Time: nil
Serving: 1
Ingredients:
- 1 ripe mango, cored and chopped
- ½ mango, peeled, pitted, and chopped
- 1 cup kale, chopped
- ½ cup plain Greek yogurt
- 2 ice cubes

Directions:
1. Add pear, mango, yogurt, kale, and mango to a blender and puree
2. Add ice and blend until you have a smooth texture
3. Serve and enjoy!

Mesmerizing Artichoke Frittata

Serving: 4
Preparation Time: 5 minutes
Cooking Time: 10 minutes
Ingredients:
- 8 large eggs
- ¼ cup asiago cheese, grated
- 1 tablespoon fresh basil, chopped
- 1 teaspoon fresh oregano, chopped
- Pinch of salt

- 1 teaspoon extra virgin olive oil
- 1 teaspoon garlic, minced
- 1 cup canned artichokes, drained
- 1 tomato, chopped

Directions:
1. Preheat your oven to broil
2. Take a medium bowl and whisk in eggs, Asiago cheese, oregano, basil, sea salt, and pepper
3. Blend bowl
4. Place a large ovenproof skillet over medium-high heat and add olive oil
5. Add garlic and Saute for 1 minute
6. Remove skillet from heat and pour the egg mix
7. Return skillet to heat and sprinkle artichoke hearts, and tomato over eggs
8. Cook frittata without stirring for 8 minutes
9. Place skillet under the broiler for 1 minute, until the top is lightly browned
10. Cut frittata into 4 pieces and serve
11. Enjoy!

Egg In An Acorn

Preparation Time:10 minutes
Cooking Time: 20 minutes
Serving: 5
Ingredients:

- 2 acorn squash
- 6 whole eggs
- 2 tablespoons extra virgin olive oil
- Salt and pepper as needed
- 5-6 pitted dates
- 8 walnut halves
- A fresh bunch of parsley

Directions:
1. Preheat your oven to 375 degrees Fahrenheit
2. Slice squash crosswise and prepare 3 slices with holes
3. While slicing the squash, make sure that each slice has a measurement of ¾ inch thickness
4. Remove the seeds from the slices
5. Take a baking sheet and line it up with parchment paper
6. Transfer the slices to your baking sheet and season them with salt and pepper
7. Bake in your oven for 20 minutes
8. Chop the walnuts and dates on your cutting board
9. Take the baking dish out from the oven and drizzle slices with olive oil
10. Crack an egg into each of the holes in the slices and season with pepper and salt
11. Sprinkle the chopped walnuts on top
12. Bake for 10 minutes or more
13. Garnish with parsley and add maple syrup
14. Enjoy!

Barley Porridge

Preparation Time:5 minutes
Cooking Time: 25 minutes
Serving: 4
Ingredients:

- 1 cup barley
- 1 cup wheat berries
- 2 cups unsweetened almond milk
- 2 cups water
- ½ cup blueberries
- ½ cup pomegranate seeds
- ½ cup hazelnuts, toasted and chopped
- ¼ cup honey

Directions:
1. Take a medium saucepan and place it over medium-high heat
2. Place barley, almond milk, wheat berries, and water and bring to a boil
3. Lower the heat to low and simmer for 25 minutes
4. Divide amongst serving bowls and top each serving with 2 tablespoons blueberries, 2 tablespoons pomegranate seeds, 2 tablespoons hazelnuts, 1 tablespoon honey
5. Serve and enjoy!

Tomato And Dill Frittata

Serving: 4
Preparation Time:5 minutes
Cooking Time: 10 minutes
Ingredients:

- 2 tablespoons olive oil
- 1 medium onion, chopped
- 1 teaspoon garlic, minced
- 2 medium tomatoes, chopped
- 6 large eggs
- ½ cup half and half
- ½ cup feta cheese, crumbled
- ¼ cup dill weed
- Salt as needed
- Ground black pepper as needed

Directions:
1. Preheat your oven to a temperature of 400 degrees Fahrenheit
2. Take a large-sized oven-proof pan and heat up your olive oil over medium-high heat
3. Toss in the onion, garlic, and tomatoes and stir fry them for 4 minutes
4. While they are being cooked, take a bowl and beat together your eggs, half and half cream, and season the mix with some pepper and salt
5. Pour the mixture into the pan with your vegetables and top It up with crumbled feta cheese and dill weed
6. Cover it up with the lid and let it cook for 3 minutes
7. Place the pan inside your oven and let it bake for 10 minutes
8. Serve hot

Strawberry And Rhubarb Smoothie

Serving: 1
Preparation Time:5 minutes
Cooking Time: 3 minutes
Ingredients

- 1 rhubarb stalk, chopped
- 1 cup fresh strawberries, sliced
- ½ cup plain Greek strawberries
- Pinch of ground cinnamon
- 3 ice cubes

Directions:
1. Take a small saucepan and fill with water over high heat

2. Bring to boil and add rhubarb; boil for 3 minutes
3. Drain and transfer to a blender
4. Add strawberries, honey, yogurt, and cinnamon, and pulse the mixture until smooth
5. Add ice cubes and blend until thick and has no lumps
6. Pour into a glass and enjoy chilled
7. Add more berries if required

Bacon Brie And Omelette Wedges

Preparation Time:10 minutes
Cooking Time: 10 minutes
Serving: 6
Ingredients:
- 2 tablespoons olive oil
- 7 ounces smoked bacon
- 6 beaten eggs
- A small bunch of chives snipped
- 3 and ½ ounces brie, sliced
- 1 teaspoon red wine vinegar
- 1 teaspoon Dijon mustard
- 1 cucumber, halved, deseeded, and sliced diagonally
- 7 ounces radish, quartered

Directions:
1. Turn your grill on and set it to high
2. Take a small-sized pan and add 1 teaspoon of oil; allow the oil to heat up
3. Add lardons and fry until crisp
4. Drain the lardon on kitchen paper
5. Take another non-sticky cast iron frying pan and place it over the grill; heat 2 teaspoons of oil
6. Add lardons, eggs, chives, and ground pepper to the frying pan
7. Cook on LOW until they are semi-set
8. Carefully lay brie on top and grill until the Brie sets and shows a golden texture
9. Remove it from the pan and cut it up into wedges
10. Take a small bowl and create dressing by mixing olive oil, mustard, vinegar, and seasoning
11. Add cucumber to the bowl and mix;
12. Prepare a platter with the cucumber and wedges arranged together
13. Sprinkle some black pepper for additional taste
14. Add more fruits if desired
15. Enjoy!

Greek Chicken And Penne Delight

Preparation Time:20 minutes
Cooking Time: 20 minutes
Serving: 4
Ingredients:
- 16 ounces of penne pasta
- 1 and ½ tablespoons butter
- ½ cup red onion, chopped
- 2 garlic cloves, minced
- 1-pound boneless chicken breast, halved and cut into bite-sized portions
- 14 ounces artichoke hearts
- 1 tomato, chopped
- ½ cup feta cheese, crumbled
- 3 tablespoons fresh parsley, chopped
- 1 teaspoon dried oregano
- Salt and pepper to taste

Directions:
1. Take a large-sized pot and add salted water
2. Boil the pasta until Al-Dente
3. Drain the pasta and keep it on the side
4. Take a large skillet and place it over medium-high heat
5. Add butter and allow the butter to melt
6. Add garlic and onion and cook for 2 minutes
7. Add chopped chicken and keep them cooking for 5-6 minutes until you have a golden brown texture
8. Lower the heat to medium-low
9. Drain the chopped artichoke hearts and add them to the skillet alongside chopped tomato, fresh parsley, feta, lemon juice, oregano, drained pasta, and mix
10. Cook for 3 minutes
11. Season with pepper and salt
12. Serve and enjoy!

Bacon And Chicken Pasta

Preparation Time:15 minutes
Cooking Time: 20 minutes
Serving: 4
Ingredients:
- 8 ounces pack of linguine pasta
- 3 bacon, sliced
- 1 pound boneless chicken breast, halved, cooked, and diced
- Salt as needed
- 1 can 4.5 ounces tomatoes, peeled and diced (with juice)
- ¼ teaspoon dried rosemary
- 1/3 cup feta cheese, crumbled
- 2/3 cup pitted black olives
- 1 can (6 ounces) of artichoke hearts

Directions:
1. Take an l large-sized pot and fill it up with salted water
2. Bring the water to a boil and add linguine
3. Cook for 8-10 minutes until Al Dente
4. Take a large-sized deep skillet and cook the Bacon until brown
5. Crumble the bacon and keep it on the side
6. Season your chicken with salt
7. Stir the chicken and bacon into a large-sized skillet
8. Add tomatoes and rosemary and simmer the whole mixture for about 20 minutes
9. Stir in feta cheese, artichokes hearts, and olives and cook until thoroughly heated
10. Toss the freshly cooked pasta with the breast and serve immediately!
11. Garnish with some extra feta if your heart desires

Cocoa Pumpkin

Serving: 2
Preparation Time: 5 minutes
Ingredients:
- ¼ teaspoon pumpkin spice
- 1 tablespoon maple syrup
- 2 tablespoons organic unsweetened cocoa powder
- ¼ frozen banana, sliced

- ½ Barlett pear, cored
- 3 cups baby spinach
- 1 cup organic pumpkin puree
- 1 cup unsweetened almond milk

Directions:
1. Add all the ingredients except vegetables/fruits first
2. Blend until smooth
3. Add the vegetable/fruits
4. Blend until smooth
5. Add a few ice cubes and serve the smoothie
6. Enjoy!

Twisty Cucumber Honeydew

Preparation Time: 5 minutes
Serving: 2
Ingredients:
- 1 cup ice
- 1 tablespoon fresh mint
- 2 cucumbers, chopped
- 1 cup honeydew melon, peeled, seeded, and chopped
- 1 cup of coconut water

Directions:
1. Add all the ingredients except vegetables/fruits first
2. Blend until smooth
3. Add the vegetable/fruits
4. Blend until smooth
5. Add a few ice cubes and serve the smoothie
6. Enjoy!

Berry-Licious Meta Booster

Preparation Time: 5 minutes
Serving: 2
Ingredients:
- ¼ cup garbanzo bean
- 1 teaspoon flax oil
- ½ cup frozen blueberries
- ½ cup frozen broccoli florets
- 6 ounces Greek yogurt
- ¾ cup brewed and chilled green tea

Directions:
1. Add all the ingredients except vegetables/fruits first
2. Blend until smooth
3. Add the vegetable/fruits
4. Blend until smooth
5. Add a few ice cubes and serve the smoothie
6. Enjoy!

Healthy Potato Pie Glass

Serving: 2
Preparation Time: 5 minutes
Ingredients:
- 1 cup ice
- ¼ teaspoon cinnamon
- ¼ cup rolled oats
- ½ frozen banana
- 1 small orange, peeled
- ½ cup sweet potato, cooked and peeled
- 6 ounces Greek yogurt
- ½ cup untweeted almond milk

Directions:

1. Add all the ingredients except vegetables/fruits first
2. Blend until smooth
3. Add the vegetable/fruits
4. Blend until smooth
5. Add a few ice cubes and serve the smoothie
6. Enjoy!

Vegetable And Green Tea Smoothie

Serving: 2
Preparation Time: 5 minutes
Ingredients:
- 1 cup ice
- 2 tablespoons chia seeds
- ½ frozen bananas, diced
- ½ cup of frozen green peas
- ½ cup frozen cauliflower
- ½ cup frozen broccoli
- ¾ cup non-fat Greek yogurt
- 1 cup brewed and chilled green tea

Directions:
1. Add all the ingredients except vegetables/fruits first
2. Blend until smooth
3. Add the vegetable/fruits
4. Blend until smooth
5. Add a few ice cubes and serve the smoothie
6. Enjoy!

Tropical Kiwi Pineapple

Serving: 2
Preparation Time: 5 minutes
Ingredients:
- 1 cup ice
- 1 tablespoon ground flaxseed
- 1 tablespoon psyllium husk
- 6 almonds
- 2 tablespoons unsweetened coconut
- 1 medium kiwi, skin intact

Directions:
1. Add all the ingredients except vegetables/fruits first
2. Blend until smooth
3. Add the vegetable/fruits
4. Blend until smooth
5. Add a few ice cubes and serve the smoothie
6. Enjoy!

Greens And Herbs For All

Preparation Time: 5 minutes
Serving: 2
Ingredients:
- 1 cup ice
- 1 tablespoon ground flaxseed
- 1/3 cup fresh cilantro, chopped
- ½ lemon, juiced
- 1 pear, cored and chopped
- ½ frozen banana, sliced into rounds
- 2 cups baby spinach, chopped
- 2 stalks of celery, chopped
- 1 cup romaine lettuce, chopped

- ½ cup non-fat Greek yogurt
- 1 cup of water

Directions:
1. Add all the ingredients except vegetables/fruits first
2. Blend until smooth
3. Add the vegetable/fruits
4. Blend until smooth
5. Add a few ice cubes and serve the smoothie
6. Enjoy!

Avocado And Edamame Drink

Serving: 2
Preparation Time: 5 minutes
Ingredients:
- ¾ cup almond milk
- ½ cup edamame shelled
- ¼ cup avocado, diced
- ½ cup of frozen mango, diced
- 1 tablespoon coconut flour
- 1 cup ice

Directions:
1. Add all the ingredients except vegetables/fruits first
2. Blend until smooth
3. Add the vegetable/fruits
4. Blend until smooth
5. Add a few ice cubes and serve the smoothie
6. Enjoy!

Peanut Butter And Cherry Delight

Serving: 2
Preparation Time: 5 minutes
Ingredients:
- 1 tablespoon psyllium husk
- 1 tablespoon unsweetened peanut butter
- 2 tablespoons powdered peanut butter
- ¾ cup frozen cherries
- ½ cup silken tofu
- ¾ cup non-fat milk such as almond milk

Directions:
1. Add all the ingredients except vegetables/fruits first
2. Blend until smooth
3. Add the vegetable/fruits
4. Blend until smooth
5. Add a few ice cubes and serve the smoothie
6. Enjoy!

White Bean And Mango Delight

Serving: 2
Preparation Time: 5 minutes
Ingredients:
- 1 cup ice
- 2 tablespoons fresh mint leaves, chopped
- 1 tablespoon coconut flour
- 2 tablespoons hemp seeds
- ½ cup frozen spinach
- ½ cup of frozen mango
- 1/3 cup white beans, rinsed
- 1 cup cashew milk

Directions:
1. Add all the ingredients except vegetables/fruits first
2. Blend until smooth
3. Add the vegetable/fruits
4. Blend until smooth
5. Add a few ice cubes and serve the smoothie
6. Enjoy!

Cashew Apple Glass

Serving: 2
Preparation Time: 5 minutes
Ingredients:
- 1 cup ice
- 1 teaspoon apple pie spice
- 1 tablespoon cashew butter
- 1 medium apple, peeled and chopped
- ½ cup frozen peaches
- 1 serving of whey protein powder
- ¾ cup plain soymilk

Directions:
1. Add all the ingredients except vegetables/fruits first
2. Blend until smooth
3. Add the vegetable/fruits
4. Blend until smooth
5. Add a few ice cubes and serve the smoothie
6. Enjoy!

Spicy Pear And Green Tea

Serving: 2
Preparation Time: 5 minutes
Ingredients:
- 1 cup brewed and chilled green tea
- ½ cup silken tofu
- 1 small pear, skin on, cut into small pieces
- ½ frozen bananas, sliced into rounds
- 2 tablespoons ground flaxseed
- 1/8 teaspoon cayenne
- 2 tablespoons lemon juice
- ½ cup ice

Directions:
1. Add all the ingredients except vegetables/fruits first
2. Blend until smooth
3. Add the vegetable/fruits
4. Blend until smooth
5. Add a few ice cubes and serve the smoothie
6. Enjoy!

Chapter 4

Lunch

Warm Chicken and Spinach Salad
Preparation Time: 10 Minutes
Cooking Time: 16 - 20 Minutes
Servings: 4
Ingredients:
3 (5-ounce) low-sodium boneless, skinless chicken breasts, cut into 1-inch cubes
- 5 teaspoons olive oil
- 1/2 teaspoon dried thyme
- 1 medium red onion, sliced
- 1 red bell pepper, sliced
- 1 small zucchini, cut into strips
- 3 tablespoons freshly squeezed lemon juice
- 6 cups fresh baby spinach

Directions:
1. In a huge bowl, blend the chicken with the olive oil and thyme. Toss to coat. Transfer to a medium metal bowl and roast for 8 minutes in the air fryer.
2. Add the red onion, red bell pepper, and zucchini. Roast for 8 to 12 minutes more, stirring once during cooking, or until the chicken grasps an inner temperature of 165F on a meat thermometer.
3. Remove the bowl from the air fryer and stir in the lemon juice.
4. Lay the spinach in a serving bowl and top with the chicken mixture. Toss to combine and serve immediately.

Stuffed Chicken
Preparation Time: 15 Minutes
Cooking Time: 30 Minutes
Servings: 4
Ingredients:
- 2 chicken breasts
- 2 tomatoes
- 200 g basil
- 1 teaspoon black pepper
- 1 teaspoon cayenne pepper
- 100 g tomato juice
- 40 g goat's cheese

Directions:
1. Make a "pocket" from chicken breasts and rub it with black pepper and cayenne pepper.
2. Slice tomatoes and chop basil.
3. Chop the goat cheese.
4. Combine all the Ingredients:–it will be the filling for breasts.
5. Fill the chicken breasts with this mixture.
6. Take a needle and thread and sew "pockets".
7. Preheat the air fryer oven to 200 C. Put the chicken breasts in the tray and pour it with tomato juice.
8. Serve.

Chicken Sandwich
Preparation time: 40 minutes
Cooking time: 20 minutes
Servings: 6
Ingredients:
- 4 chicken breasts, pastured
- 1 cup almond flour
- ¾ teaspoon ground black pepper
- 1/2 teaspoon paprika
- 1 teaspoon salt
- 1/2 teaspoon celery seeds
- 1 teaspoon potato starch
- 1/4 cup milk, reduced-fat
- 4 cups dill pickle juice as needed
- 2 eggs, pastured
- 4 hamburger buns
- 1/8 teaspoon dry milk powder, nonfat
- ¼ teaspoon xanthan gum
- 1/8 teaspoon erythritol sweetener

Directions:
1. Place the chicken in a large plastic bag, seal the bag and then pound the chicken with a mallet until ½-inch thick.
2. Brine the chicken and for this, pour the dill pickle juice in the plastic bag containing chicken, then seal it and let the chicken soak for a minimum of 2 hours.
3. After 2 hours, remove the chicken from the brine, rinse it well, and pat dry with paper towels.
4. Place flour in a shallow dish, add black pepper, paprika, salt, celery, potato starch, milk powder, xanthan gum, and sweetener and stir until well mixed.
5. Crack eggs in another dish and then whisk until blended.
6. Switch on the air fryer, insert fryer basket, grease it with olive oil, then shut with its lid, set the fryer at 375 degrees F and preheat for 5 minutes.
7. Meanwhile, dip the chicken into the egg and then coat evenly with the flour mixture.
8. Open the fryer, add chicken breasts in it in a single layer, close with its lid, then cook for 10 minutes, flip the chickens and continue cooking for 5 minutes or until chicken is nicely golden and cooked.
9. When air fryer beeps, open its lid, transfer chicken into a plate and cook remaining chicken in the same manner.
10. Sandwich a chicken breast between toasted hamburger buns, top with favorite dressing and serve.

Buttermilk Fried Chicken
Preparation time: 20 minutes
Cooking time: 10 minutes

Servings: 4
Ingredients:
- 3 tablespoons cornmeal, ground
- 1-pound chicken breasts, pastured
- 6 tablespoons cornflakes
- 1 teaspoon garlic powder
- ¼ teaspoon ground black pepper
- 1 teaspoon paprika
- ¼ teaspoon salt
- ¼ teaspoon hot sauce
- 1/3 cup buttermilk, low-fat

Directions:
1. Pour milk in a bowl, add hot sauce and whisk until well mixed.
2. Cut the chicken in half lengthwise into four pieces, then add into buttermilk, toss well until well coated and let it sit for 15 minutes.
3. Place cornflakes in a blender or food processor, pulse until mixture resembles crumbs, then add remaining Ingredients, pulse until well mixed and then tip the mixture into a shallow dish.
4. After 15 minutes, remove chicken from the buttermilk, then coat with cornflakes mixture until evenly coated and place the chicken on a wire rack.
5. Switch on the air fryer, insert fryer basket, grease it with olive oil, then shut with its lid, set the fryer at 375 degrees F and preheat for 5 minutes.
6. Then open the fryer, add chicken in it in a single layer, spray with oil, close with its lid and cook for 10 minutes until nicely golden and cooked, turning the chicken halfway through the frying.
7. When air fryer beeps, open its lid, transfer chicken onto a serving plate and serve.

Zaatar Lamb Loin Chops

Preparation Time: 10 minutes
Cooking Time: 15-20 minutes
Servings: 4
Ingredients:
- 8: 3½-ounces bone-in lamb loin chops, trimmed
- 3 garlic cloves, crushed
- 1 tbsp. fresh lemon juice
- 1 tsp. olive oil
- 1 tbsp. Zaatar
- Salt and black pepper, to taste

Directions:
1. Preheat the Air fryer to 400°F and grease an Air fryer basket.
2. Mix the garlic, lemon juice, oil, Zaatar, salt, and black pepper in a large bowl.
3. Coat the chops generously with the herb mixture and arrange the chops in the air fryer basket.
4. Cook for about 15 minutes, flipping twice in between, and dish out the lamb chops to serve hot.

Vietnamese Grilled Pork

Preparation Time: 6 minutes
Cooking Time: 16 minutes
Servings: 6
Ingredients:
- 1-pound sliced pork shoulder, pastured, fat trimmed
- 2 tbsp. chopped parsley
- ¼ cup crushed roasted peanuts

For the Marinade:
- ¼ cup minced white onions
- 1 tbsp. minced garlic
- 1 tbsp. lemongrass paste
- 1 tbsp. erythritol sweetener
- ½ tsp. ground black pepper
- 1 tbsp. fish sauce
- 2 tsp. soy sauce
- 2 tbsp. olive oil

Directions:
1. Place all the Ingredients: for the marinade in a bowl, stir well until combined and add it into a large plastic bag.
2. Cut the pork into ½-inch slices, cut each slice into 1-inches pieces, then add them into the plastic bag containing marinade, seal the bag, turn it upside down to coat the pork pieces with the marinade, and marinate for a minimum of 1 hour.
3. Then switch on the air fryer, insert fryer basket, grease it with olive oil, then shut with its lid, set the fryer at 400°F, and preheat for 5 minutes.
4. Open the fryer, add marinated pork in it in a single layer, close with its lid and cook for 10 minutes until nicely golden and cooked, flipping the pork halfway through the frying.
5. When the air fryer beeps, open its lid, transfer pork onto a serving plate, and keep warm.
6. Air fryer the remaining pork pieces in the same manner and then serve.

Provencal Ribs

Preparation Time: 6 minutes
Cooking Time: 20-25 minutes
Servings: 4
Ingredients:
- 500 g pork ribs
- Provencal herbs
- Salt
- Ground pepper
- Oil

Directions:
1. Put the ribs in a bowl and add some oil, Provencal herbs, salt, and ground pepper.
2. Stir well and leave in the fridge for at least 1 hour.
3. Put the ribs in the basket of the air fryer and select 200°C for 20 minutes.
4. From time to time, shake the basket and remove the ribs.

Steak

Preparation Time: 6 minutes
Cooking Time: 18 minutes
Servings: 2
Ingredients:
2 steaks, grass-fed, each about 6 ounces and ¾ inch thick
- 1 tbsp. butter, unsalted
- ¾ tsp. ground black pepper
- ½ tsp. garlic powder
- ¾ tsp. salt
- 1 tsp. olive oil

Directions:

1. Switch on the air fryer, insert fryer basket, grease it with olive oil, then shut with its lid, set the fryer at 400°F, and preheat for 5 minutes.
2. Meanwhile, coat the steaks with oil and then season with black pepper, garlic, and salt.
3. Open the fryer, add steaks in it, close with its lid and cook 10 to 18 minutes at until nicely golden and steaks are cooked to desired doneness, flipping the steaks halfway through the frying.
4. When the air fryer beeps, open its lid and transfer steaks to a cutting board.
5. Take two large aluminum foil pieces, place a steak on each piece, top steak with ½ tbsp. butter, then cover with foil and let it rest for 5 minutes.
6. Serve straight away.

Marinated Loin Potatoes

Preparation Time: 8 minutes
Cooking Time: 40-50 minutes
Servings: 2
Ingredients:
- 2 medium potatoes
- 4 fillets marinated loin
- A little extra virgin olive oil
- Salt

Directions:
1. Peel the potatoes and cut. Cut with match-sized mandolin, potatoes with a cane but very thin.
2. Wash and immerse in water for 30 minutes.
3. Drain and dry well.
4. Add a little oil and stir so that the oil permeates well in all the potatoes.
5. Go to the basket of the air fryer and distribute well.
6. Cook at 160°C for 10 minutes.
7. Take out the basket, shake so that the potatoes take off. Let the potato tender. If it is not, leave 5 more minutes.
8. Place the steaks on top of the potatoes.
9. Select 10 minutes, and 180°C for 5 minutes again.

Beef with Mushrooms

Preparation Time: 8 minutes
Cooking Time: 41 minutes
Servings: 4
Ingredients:
- 300 g beef
- 150 g mushrooms
- 1 onion
- 1 tsp. olive oil
- 100 g vegetable broth
- 1 tsp. basil
- 1 tsp. chili
- 30 g tomato juice

Directions:
1. For this recipe, you should take a solid piece of beef. Take the beef and pierce the meat with a knife.
2. Rub it with olive oil, basil, chili, and lemon juice.
3. Chop the onion and mushrooms and pour it with vegetable broth.
4. Cook the vegetables for 5 minutes.
5. Take a big tray and put the meat in it. Add vegetable broth to the tray too. It will make the meat juicy.
6. Preheat the air fryer oven to 180°C and cook it for 35 minutes.

Cheesy and Crunchy Russian Steaks

Preparation Time: 6 minutes
Cooking Time: 22 minutes
Servings: 4
Ingredients:
- 800 g minced pork
- 200 g cream cheese
- 50g peeled walnuts
- 1 onion
- Salt
- Ground pepper
- 1 egg
- Breadcrumbs
- Extra virgin olive oil

Directions:
1. Put the onion cut into quarters in the Thermo mix glass and select 5 seconds speed 5.
2. Add the minced meat, cheese, egg, salt, and pepper.
3. Select 10 seconds, speed 5, turn left.
4. Add the chopped and peeled walnuts and select 4 seconds, turn left, speed 5.
5. Pass the dough to a bowl.
6. Make Russian steaks and go through breadcrumbs.
7. Paint the Russian fillets with extra virgin olive oil on both sides with a brush.
8. Put in the basket of the air fryer without stacking the Russian fillets.
9. Select 180°C for 15 minutes.

Chicken Nuggets

Preparation time: 10 minutes
Cooking time: 24 minutes
Servings: 4
Ingredients:
- 1-pound chicken breast, pastured
- 1/4 cup coconut flour
- 6 tablespoons toasted sesame seeds
- 1/2 teaspoon ginger powder
- 1/8 teaspoon sea salt
- 1 teaspoon sesame oil
- 4 egg whites, pastured

Directions:
1. Switch on the air fryer, insert fryer basket, grease it with olive oil, then shut with its lid, set the fryer at 400 degrees F and preheat for 10 minutes.
2. Meanwhile, cut the chicken breast into 1-inch pieces, pat them dry, place the chicken pieces in a bowl, sprinkle with salt and oil and toss until well coated.
3. Place flour in a large plastic bag, add ginger and chicken, seal the bag and turn it upside down to coat the chicken with flour evenly.
4. Place egg whites in a bowl, whisk well, then add coated chicken and toss until well coated.

5. Place sesame seeds in a large plastic bag, add chicken pieces in it, seal the bag and turn it upside down to coat the chicken with sesame seeds evenly.
6. Open the fryer, add chicken nuggets in it in a single layer, spray with oil, close with its lid and cook for 12 minutes until nicely golden and cooked, turning the chicken nuggets and spraying with oil halfway through.
7. When air fryer beeps, open its lid, transfer chicken nuggets onto a serving plate and fry the remaining chicken nuggets in the same manner.
8. Serve straight away.

Pork Chops

Preparation time: 5 minutes
Cooking time: 15 minutes
Servings: 5
Ingredients:
- 4 slices of almond bread
- 5 pork chops, bone-in, pastured
- 5 ounces coconut flour
- 1 teaspoon salt
- 3 tablespoons parsley
- ½ teaspoon ground black pepper
- 1 tablespoon pork seasoning
- 2 tablespoons olive oil
- 1/3 cup apple juice, unsweetened
- 1 egg, pastured

Directions:
1. Switch on the air fryer, insert fryer basket, grease it with olive oil, then shut with its lid, set the fryer at 350 degrees F and preheat for 5 minutes.
2. Meanwhile, place bread slices in a food processor and pulse until mixture resembles crumbs.
3. Tip the bread crumbs in a shallow dish, add parsley, ½ teaspoon salt, ¼ teaspoon ground black pepper and stir until mixed.
4. Place flour in another shallow dish, add remaining salt and black pepper, along with pork seasoning and stir until mixed.
5. Crack the egg in a bowl, pour in apple juice and whisk until combined.
6. Working on one pork chop at a time, first coat it into the flour mixture, then dip into egg and then evenly coat with breadcrumbs mixture.
7. Open the fryer, add coated pork chops in it in a single layer, close with its lid and cook for 10 minutes until nicely golden and cooked, flipping the pork chops halfway through the frying.
8. When air fryer beeps, open its lid, transfer pork chops onto a serving plate and serve.

Buffalo Chicken Hot Wings

Preparation time: 10 minutes
Cooking time: 45 minutes
Servings: 6
Ingredients:
- 16 chicken wings, pastured
- 1 teaspoon garlic powder
- 2 teaspoons chicken seasoning
- ¾ teaspoon ground black pepper
- 2 teaspoons soy sauce
- 1/4 cup buffalo sauce, reduced-fat

Directions:
1. Switch on the air fryer, insert fryer basket, grease it with olive oil, then shut with its lid, set the fryer at 400 degrees F and preheat for 5 minutes.
2. Meanwhile, place chicken wings in a bowl, drizzle with soy sauce, toss until well coated and then season with black pepper and garlic powder.
3. Open the fryer, stack chicken wings in it, then spray with oil and close with its lid.
4. Cook the chicken wings for 10 minutes, turning the wings halfway through, and then transfer them to a bowl, covering the bowl with a foil to keep the chicken wings warm.
5. Air fry the remaining chicken wings in the same manner, then transfer them to the bowl, add buffalo sauce and toss until well coated.
6. Return chicken wings into the fryer basket in a single layer and continue frying for 7 to 12 minutes or until chicken wings are glazed and crispy, shaking the chicken wings every 3 to 4 minutes. Serve straight away.

Herb Chicken Thighs

Preparation time: 6 hours and 25 minutes
Cooking time: 40 minutes
Servings: 6
Ingredients:
- 6 chicken thighs, skin-on, pastured
- 2 teaspoons garlic powder
- 1/2 teaspoon onion powder
- 1 teaspoon dried basil
- 1 teaspoon spike seasoning
- 1/2 teaspoon dried sage
- 1/4 teaspoon ground black pepper
- 1/2 teaspoon dried oregano
- 2 tablespoons lemon juice
- 1/4 cup olive oil

Directions:
1. Prepare the marinade and for this, place all the Ingredients: in a bowl, except for chicken, stir until well combined and then pour the marinade in a large plastic bag.
2. Add chicken thighs in the plastic bag, seal the bag, then turn in upside down until chicken thighs are coated with the marinade and let marinate in the refrigerator for minimum of 6 hours.
3. Then drain the chicken, arrange the chicken thighs on a wire rack and let them rest for 15 minutes at room temperature.
4. Meanwhile, switch on the air fryer, insert fryer basket, grease it with olive oil, then shut with its lid, set the fryer at 360 degrees F and preheat for 5 minutes.
5. Then open the fryer, add chicken thighs in it in a single layer top-side down, close with its lid, cook the chicken for 8 minutes, turn the chicken, and continue frying for 6 minutes.
6. Turn the chicken thighs and then continue cooking for another 6 minutes or until chicken is nicely browned and cooked.
7. When air fryer beeps, open its lid, transfer chicken onto a serving plate and cook the remaining chicken thighs in the same manner.
8. Serve straight away.

Air Fryer Beef Steak Kabobs with Vegetables

Preparation Time: 9 minutes
Cooking Time: 11 minutes
Servings: 4
Ingredients:
- Light soy sauce: 2 tbsp.
- Lean beef chuck ribs: 4 cups, cut into one-inch pieces
- Low-fat sour cream: 1/3 cup
- Half onion
- 8 skewers: 6 inches
- One bell pepper

Directions:
1. In a mixing bowl, add soy sauce and sour cream, mix well. Add the lean beef chunks, coat well, and let it marinate for half an hour or more.
2. Cut onion, bell pepper into one-inch pieces. In water, soak skewers for ten minutes.
3. Add onions, bell peppers, and beef on skewers; alternatively, sprinkle with black pepper.
4. Let it cook for 10 minutes in a preheated air fryer at 400°F, flip halfway through.
5. Serve with yogurt dipping sauce.

Pork Liver

Preparation Time: 9 minutes
Cooking Time: 16 minutes
Servings: 4
Ingredients:
- 500 g pork liver cut into steaks
- Breadcrumbs
- Salt
- Ground pepper
- 1 lemon
- Extra virgin olive oil

Directions:
1. Put the steaks on a plate or bowl.
2. Add the lemon juice, salt, and ground pepper.
3. Leave a few minutes to macerate the pork liver fillets.
4. Drain well and go through breadcrumbs; it is not necessary to pass the fillets through beaten egg because the liver is very moist, the breadcrumbs are perfectly glued.
5. Spray with extra virgin olive oil. If you don't have a sprayer, paint with a silicone brush.
6. Put the pork liver fillets in the air fryer basket.
7. Program 180°C, 10 minutes.
8. Take out if you see them golden to your liking and put another batch.
9. You should not pile the pork liver fillets, which are well extended so that the empanada is crispy on all sides.

Air Fried Meatloaf

Preparation Time: 6 minutes
Cooking Time: 25-30 minutes
Servings: 2
Ingredients:
- ½ lb. ground beef
- ½ lb. ground turkey
- 1 onion, chopped
- ¼ cup panko breadcrumbs
- 3 tbsp. ketchup
- ¼ cup brown sugar
- 1 egg, beaten
- Salt and pepper to taste

Directions:
1. Preheat the air fryer to 400°F.
2. Let the ground beef and ground turkey sit on the counter for 10 to 15 minutes, as it will be easier to hand mix without being chilled from the refrigerator.
3. Combine all the Ingredients.
4. Form into a loaf in a dish and place the dish in the frying basket. Spritz the top with a little olive oil.
5. Bake for 25 minutes, or until well browned. Let settle for about 10 minutes before serving.

Pork Bondiola Chop

Preparation Time: 8 minutes
Cooking Time: 22 minutes
Servings: 4
Ingredients:
- 1 kg bondiola in pieces
- Breadcrumbs
- 2 beaten eggs
- Seasoning to taste

Directions:
1. Cut the bondiola into small pieces
2. Add seasonings to taste.
3. Pour the beaten eggs on the seasoned bondiola.
4. Add the breadcrumbs.
5. Cook in the air fryer for 20 minutes while turning the food halfway.
6. Serve

Air Fry Rib-Eye Steak

Preparation Time: 11 minutes
Cooking Time: 18 minutes
Servings: 2
Ingredients:
- Lean rib eye steaks: 2 medium-sized
- Salt and freshly ground black pepper, to taste

Directions:
1. Let the air fry preheat at 400°F. Pat dry steaks with paper towels.
2. Use any spice blend or just salt and pepper on steaks.
3. Generously on both sides of the steak.
4. Put steaks in the air fryer basket. Cook according to the rareness you want. Or cook for 14 minutes and flip after halftime.
5. Take out from the air fryer and let it rest for about 5 minutes.
6. Serve.

Asparagus And Lemon Salmon Dish

Servings: 3
Preparation Time: 5 minutes
Cooking Time: 15 minutes
Ingredients:
- 2 salmon fillets, 6 ounces each, skin on
- Salt to taste

- 1 pound asparagus, trimmed
- 2 cloves garlic, minced
- 3 tablespoons butter
- ¼ cup parmesan cheese, grated

Directions:
1. Preheat your oven to 400 degrees F
2. Line a baking sheet with oil
3. Take a kitchen towel and pat your salmon dry; season as needed
4. Put salmon around a baking sheet and arrange asparagus around it
5. Place a pan over medium heat and melt butter
6. Add garlic and cook for 3 minutes until garlic browns slightly
7. Drizzle sauce over salmon
8. Sprinkle salmon with parmesan and bake for 12 minutes until salmon looks cooked all the way and is flaky
9. Serve and enjoy!

Walnut Encrusted Salmon

Servings: 3
Preparation Time: 10 minutes
Cooking Time: 14 minutes
Ingredients:
- ½ cup walnuts
- 2 tablespoons stevia
- ½ tablespoon Dijon mustard
- ¼ teaspoon dill
- 2 Salmon fillets (3 ounces each)
- 1 tablespoon olive oil
- Salt and pepper to taste

Directions:
1. Preheat your oven to 350 degrees F
2. Add walnuts, mustard, and stevia to a food processor and process until your desired consistency is achieved
3. Take a frying pan and place it over medium heat
4. Add oil and let it heat up
5. Add salmon and sear for 3 minutes
6. Add walnut mix and coat well
7. Transfer coated salmon to a baking sheet, bake in the oven for 8 minutes
8. Serve and enjoy!

Especial Glazed Salmon

Servings: 4
Preparation Time: 45 minutes
Cooking Time: 10 minutes
Ingredients:
- 4 pieces of salmon fillets, 5 ounces each
- 4 tablespoons coconut aminos
- 4 teaspoon olive oil
- 2 teaspoon ginger, minced
- 4 teaspoon garlic, minced
- 2 tablespoon sugar-free ketchup
- 4 tablespoons dry white wine
- 2 tablespoons red boat fish sauce

Directions:
1. Take a bowl and mix in coconut aminos, garlic, ginger, and fish sauce, and mix
2. Add salmon and let it marinate for 15-20 minutes
3. Take a skillet/pan and place it over medium heat
4. Add oil and let it heat up
5. Add salmon fillets and cook on HIGH for 3-4 minutes per side
6. Remove dish once crispy
7. Add sauce and wine
8. Simmer for 5 minutes on low heat
9. Return salmon to the glaze and flip until both sides are glazed
10. Serve and enjoy!

Lovely Molten Tuna Bites

Servings: 4
Preparation Time: 10 minutes
Cooking Time: 10 minutes
Ingredients:
- 10 ounces drained tuna
- ½ cup Keto-Friendly mayonnaise
- 1 medium avocado, cubed
- ¼ cup parmesan cheese
- ¼ cup almond flour
- ½ teaspoon garlic powder
- ¼ teaspoon onion powder
- Salt and pepper to taste
- ½ cup coconut oil

Directions:
1. Add the listed ingredients (except coconut oil) and avocado to a bowl and mix well
2. Take cubed avocados and fold them into tuna
3. Form balls from the mixture and dredge them in almond flour
4. Take a pan and place it over medium heat, add oil and let it heat up
5. Add tuna balls and fry until brown
6. Serve hot!

Hearty Lemon And Butter Cod

Servings: 3
Preparation Time: 5 minutes
Cooking Time: 20 minutes
Ingredients:
- 4 tablespoons salted butter, divided
- 4 thyme sprigs, fresh and divided
- 4 teaspoons lemon juice, fresh and divided
- 4 cod fillets, 6 ounces each
- Salt to taste

Directions:
1. Preheat your oven to 400 degrees F
2. Season cod fillets with salt on both sides
3. Take four pieces of foil; each foil should be 3 times bigger than the fillets
4. Divide fillets between the foils and top with butter, lemon juice, thyme
5. Fold to form a pouch and transfer pouches to a baking sheet
6. Bake for 20 minutes
7. Open and let the steam get out
8. Serve and enjoy!

A Broccoli And Tilapia Dish To Die For

Servings: 1
Preparation Time: 4 minutes

Cooking Time: 14 minutes
Ingredients:
- 6 ounces of tilapia, frozen
- 1 tablespoon of butter
- 1 tablespoon of garlic, minced
- 1 teaspoon of lemon pepper seasoning
- 1 cup of broccoli florets, fresh

Directions:
1. Preheat your oven to 350 degrees Fahrenheit
2. Add fish in aluminum foil packets
3. Arrange broccoli around fish
4. Sprinkle lemon pepper on top
5. Close the packets and seal
6. Bake for 14 minutes
7. Take a bowl and add garlic and butter, mix well and keep the mixture on the side
8. Remove the packet from the oven and transfer it to a platter
9. Place butter on top of the fish and broccoli, serve and enjoy!

Chapter 5

Meatless Mains

Crispy Parmesan Cups with White Beans and Veggies
Preparation time: 10 minutes
Cooking time: 5 minutes
Servings: 4 (2 cups each)
Ingredients:
- 1 cup grated Parmesan cheese, divided
- 1 (15-ounce) can low-sodium white beans, drained and rinsed
- 1 cucumber, peeled and finely diced
- ½ cup finely diced red onion
- ¼ cup thinly sliced fresh basil
- 1 garlic clove, minced
- ½ jalapeño pepper, diced
- 1 tablespoon extra-virgin olive oil
- 1 tablespoon balsamic vinegar
- ¼ teaspoon salt
- Freshly ground black pepper

Directions:
1. Heat a medium nonstick skillet over medium heat. Sprinkle 2 tablespoons of cheese in a thin circle in the center of the pan, flattening it with a spatula.
2. When the cheese melts, use a spatula to flip the cheese and lightly brown the other side.
3. Remove the cheese "pancake" from the pan and place into the cup of a muffin tin, bending it gently with your hands to fit in the muffin cup.
4. Repeat with the remaining cheese until you have 8 cups.
5. In a mixing bowl, combine the beans, cucumber, onion, basil, garlic, jalapeño, olive oil, and vinegar, and season with the salt and pepper.
6. Fill each cup with the bean mixture just before serving.

Lime Asparagus with Cashews
Preparation time: 10 minutes
Cooking Time: 15 To 20 minutes
Servings: 4
Ingredients:
- 2 pounds (907 g) asparagus, woody ends trimmed
- 1 tablespoon extra-virgin olive oil
- Sea salt and freshly ground black pepper, to taste
- ½ cup chopped cashews
- Zest and juice of 1 lime

Directions:
1. Preheat the oven to 400°F (205°C). Line a baking sheet with aluminum foil.
2. Toss the asparagus with the olive oil in a medium bowl. Sprinkle the salt and pepper to season.
3. Arrange the asparagus on the baking sheet and bake for 15 to 20 minutes, or until lightly browned and tender.
4. Remove the asparagus from the oven to a serving bowl. Add the cashews, lime zest and juice, and toss to coat well. Serve immediately.

Cabbage Wedges
Preparation time: 20 minutes
Cooking Time: 29 minutes
Servings: 6
Ingredients:
- 1 small head of green cabbage
- 6 strips of bacon, thick cut, pastured
- 1-teaspoon onion powder
- ½-teaspoon ground black pepper
- 1-teaspoon garlic powder
- ¾-teaspoon salt
- 1/4 teaspoon red chili flakes
- 1/2 teaspoon fennel seeds
- 3 tablespoons olive oil

Directions:
1. Switch on the air fryer, insert fryer basket, grease it with olive oil, then shut with its lid, set the fryer at 350 degrees F, and preheat for 5 minutes.
2. Open the fryer, add bacon strips in it, close with its lid and cook for 10 minutes until nicely golden and crispy, turning the bacon halfway through the frying.
3. Meanwhile, prepare the cabbage, for this, remove the outer leaves of the cabbage, and then cut it into eight wedges, keeping the core intact.
4. Prepare the spice mix and for this, place onion powder in a bowl, add black pepper, garlic powder, salt, red chili, and fennel and stir until mixed.
5. Drizzle cabbage wedges with oil and then sprinkle with spice mix until well coated.
6. When air fryer beeps, open its lid, transfer bacon strips to a cutting board and let it rest.
7. Add seasoned cabbage wedges into the fryer basket, close with its lid, then cook for 8 minutes at 400 degrees F, flip the cabbage, spray with oil, and continue air frying for 6 minutes until nicely golden and cooked.
8. When done, transfer cabbage wedges to a plate.
9. Chop the bacon, sprinkle it over cabbage and serve.

Black Pepper & Garlic Tofu
Preparation time: 20 minutes
Cooking Time: 40 minutes
Servings: 4
Ingredients:
- 14 oz. pkg. extra firm tofu
- 1 lb. asparagus, trim & cut in 1-inch pieces

- 8 oz. kale, remove stems & slice leaves
- 3 oz. Shiitake mushrooms, sliced
- 1 onion, halved & slice in thin wedges
- 1 green bell pepper, sliced
- What you'll need from store cupboard:
- ½ cup low sodium vegetable broth
- 8 cloves garlic, pressed, divided
- 2 ½ tbsp. light soy sauce, divided
- 2 -4 tbsp. water
- 2 tsp cornstarch
- 2 tsp black pepper, freshly ground, divided
- 1 tsp rice vinegar
- 1 tsp sriracha

Directions:
1. Heat oven to 400 degrees. Line a baking sheet with parchment paper.
2. Cut tofu in ½-inch slices and press between paper towels to remove excess moisture. Cut each slice into smaller rectangles.
3. In a Ziploc bag combine, 1 tablespoon soy sauce, water, 2 tablespoons garlic, rice vinegar, and 1 teaspoon pepper. Add tofu and turn to coat. Let marinate 15 minutes.
4. Place the tofu on the prepared pan and bake 15 minutes. Flip over and bake 15 minutes more. Remove from oven.
5. Place a large nonstick skillet over med-high heat. Add onion and cook until translucent, stirring frequently. Add bell pepper and cook 1 minute more.
6. Add garlic and mushrooms and cook 2 minutes, add a little water if the vegetables start to stick.
7. Stir in the kale and 2 tablespoons water and cover. Let cook 1 minutes, then stir and add more water if needed. Cover and cook another minute before adding asparagus and cook, stirring, until asparagus is tender crisp.
8. in a small bowl, stir together remaining soy sauce, broth, Sriracha, cornstarch, and pepper. Pour over vegetables and cook until heated through.
9. To serve plate the vegetables and place tofu on top.

Watermelon & Arugula Salad

Preparation time: 35 minutes
Cooking Time: 1 hour
Servings: 6
Ingredients:
- 4 cups watermelon, cut in 1-inch cubes
- 3 cup arugula
- 1 lemon, zested
- ½ cup feta cheese, crumbled
- ¼ cup fresh mint, chopped
- 1 tbsp. fresh lemon juice
- What you'll need from store cupboard:
- 3 tbsp. olive oil
- Fresh ground black pepper
- Salt to taste

Directions:
1. Combine oil, zest, juice, and mint in a large bowl. Stir together.
2. Add watermelon and gently toss to coat. Add remaining Ingredients: and toss to combine. Taste and adjust seasoning as desired.
3. Cover and chill at least 1 hour before serving.

Broccoli & Mushroom Salad

Preparation time: 10 minutes
Cooking Time: 10 minutes
Servings: 4
Ingredients:
- 4 sun-dried tomatoes, cut in half
- 3 cup torn leaf lettuce
- 1 ½ cup broccoli florets
- 1 cup mushrooms, sliced
- 1/3 cup radishes, sliced
- What you'll need from store cupboard:
- 2 tbsp. water
- 1 tbsp. balsamic vinegar
- 1 tsp vegetable oil
- ¼ tsp chicken bouillon granules
- ¼ tsp parsley - ¼ tsp dry mustard
- 1/8 tsp cayenne pepper

Directions:
1. Place tomatoes in a small bowl and pour boiling water over, just enough to cover. Let stand 5 minutes, drain.
2. Chop tomatoes and place in a large bowl. Add lettuce, broccoli, mushrooms, and radishes.
3. In a jar with a tight-fitting lid, add remaining Ingredients: and shake well. Pour over salad and toss to coat. Serve.

French toast

Preparation time: 10 minutes
Cooking Time: 15 minutes
Servings: 8
Ingredients:
- For the bread:
- 500g of flour
- 25g of oil - 300 g of water
- 25g of fresh bread yeast
- 12g of salt
- For French toast:
- Milk and cinnamon or milk and sweet wine
- Eggs - Honey

Directions:
1. The first thing is to make bread a day before. Put in the Master Chef Gourmet the Ingredients: of the bread and knead 1 minute at speed Let the dough rise 1 hour and knead 1 minute at speed 1 again. Remove the dough and divide into 4 portions. Make a ball and spread like a pizza. Roll up to make a small loaf of bread and let rise 1 hour or so.
2. Take to the oven and bake 40 minutes, 2000C. Let the bread cool on a rack and reserve for the next day. Cut the bread into slices and reserve.
3. Prepare the milk to wet the slices of bread.
4. To do so, put the milk to heat, like 500 ml or so with a cinnamon stick or the same milk with a glass of sweet wine, as you like.
5. When the milk has started to boil, remove from heat, and let cool.
6. Beat the eggs.
7. Place a rack on a plate and we dip the slices of bread in the cold milk, then in the beaten egg and pass to the rack with the plate underneath to release the excess liquid.

8. Put the slices of bread in the bucket of the air fryer, in batches, not piled up, and we take the air fryer, 180 degrees, 10 minutes each batch.
9. When you have all the slices passed through the air fryer, put the honey in a casserole, like 500g, next to 1 small glass of water and 4 tablespoons of sugar. When the honey starts to boil, lower the heat, and pass the bread slices through the honey.
10. Place in a fountain and the rest of the honey we put it on top, bathing again the French toast. Ready our French toast, when they cool, they can already be eaten.

Butter-orange Yams

Preparation time: 30 minutes
Cooking Time: 45 minutes
Servings: 8
Ingredients:
- 2 medium jewel yams, cut into 2-inch dices
- 2 tablespoons unsalted butter
- Juice of 1 large orange
- 1½ teaspoons ground cinnamon
- ¼ teaspoon ground ginger
- ¾ teaspoon ground nutmeg
- 1/8 teaspoon ground cloves

Directions:
1. Preheat the oven to 350°F (180°C).
2. Arrange the yam dices on a rimmed baking sheet in a single layer. Set aside.
3. Add the butter, orange juice, cinnamon, ginger, nutmeg, and garlic cloves to a medium saucepan over medium-low heat. Cook for 3 to 5 minutes, stirring continuously, or until the sauce begins to thicken and bubble.
4. Spoon the sauce over the yams and toss to coat well.
5. Bake in the preheated oven for 40 minutes until tender.
6. Let the yams cool for 8 minutes on the baking sheet before removing and serving.

Grilled Portobello & Zucchini Burger

Preparation time: 5 minutes
Cooking Time: 10 minutes
Servings: 2
Ingredients:
- 2 large portabella mushroom caps
- ½ small zucchini, sliced
- 2 slices low fat cheese
- Spinach
- What you'll need from store cupboard:
- 2 100% whole wheat sandwich thins
- 2 tsp roasted red bell peppers
- 2 tsp olive oil

Directions:
1. Heat grill, or charcoal, to med-high heat.
2. Lightly brush mushroom caps with olive oil. Grill mushroom caps and zucchini slices until tender, about 3-4 minutes per side.
3. Place on sandwich thin. Top with sliced cheese, roasted red bell pepper, and spinach. Serve.

Tarragon Spring Peas

Preparation time: 10 minutes
Cooking Time: 12 minutes
Servings: 6
Ingredients:
- 1 tablespoon unsalted butter
- ½ Vidalia onion, thinly sliced
- 1 cup low-sodium vegetable broth
- 3 cups fresh shelled peas
- 1 tablespoon minced fresh tarragon

Directions:
1. Melt the butter in a skillet over medium heat.
2. Sauté the onion in the melted butter for about 3 minutes until translucent, stirring occasionally.
3. Pour in the vegetable broth and whisk well. Add the peas and tarragon to the skillet and stir to combine.
4. Reduce the heat to low, cover, and cook for about 8 minutes more, or until the peas are tender.
5. Let the peas cool for 5 minutes and serve warm.

Crust Less Broccoli Quiche

Preparation time: 40 minutes
Cooking Time: 1 hour
Servings: 6
Ingredients:
- 3 large eggs
- 2 cups broccoli florets, chopped
- 1 small onion, diced
- 1 cup cheddar cheese, grated
- 2/3 cup unsweetened almond milk
- ½ cup feta cheese, crumbled
- What you'll need from store cupboard:
- 1 tbsp. extra virgin olive oil
- ½ tsp sea salt
- ¼ tsp black pepper
- Nonstick cooking spray

Directions:
1. Heat oven to 350 degrees. Spray a 9-inch baking dish with cooking spray.
2. Heat the oil in a large skillet over medium heat. Add onion and cook 4-5 minutes, until onions are translucent.
3. Add broccoli and stir to combine. Cook until broccoli turns a bright green, about 2 minutes. Transfer to a bowl.
4. In a small bowl, whisk together almond milk, egg, salt, and pepper. Pour over the broccoli. Add the cheddar cheese and stir the ingredients: together. Pour into the prepared baking dish.
5. Sprinkle the feta cheese over the top and bake 45 minutes to 1 hour, or until eggs are set in the middle and top is lightly browned. Serve.

Potatoes with Provencal Herbs with Cheese

Preparation time: 10 minutes
Cooking Time: 20 minutes
Servings: 4
Ingredients:
- 1kg of potatoes
- Provencal herbs
- Extra virgin olive oil
- Salt
- Grated cheese

Directions:
1. Peel the potatoes and cut the cane salt and sprinkle with Provencal herbs.
2. Put in the basket and add some strands of extra virgin olive oil.
3. Take the air fryer and select 1800C, 20 minutes.
4. Take out and move on to a large plate.
5. Cover cheese.
6. Gratin in the microwave or in the oven, a few minutes until the cheese is melted.

Spiced Potato Wedges

Preparation time: 20 minutes
Cooking Time: 40 minutes
Servings: 4
Ingredients:
- 8 medium potatoes
- Salt
- Ground pepper
- Garlic powder
- Aromatic herbs, the one we like the most
- 2 tbsp. extra virgin olive oil
- 4 tbsp. breadcrumbs or chickpea flour.

Directions:
1. Put the unpeeled potatoes in a pot with boiling water and a little salt.
2. Let cook 5 minutes. Drain and let cool. Cut into thick segments, without peeling.
3. Put the potatoes in a bowl and add salt, pepper, garlic powder, the aromatic herb that we have chosen oil and breadcrumbs or chickpea flour.
4. Stir well and leave 15 minutes. Pass to the basket of the air fryer and select 20 minutes, 1800C.
5. From time to time shake the basket so that the potatoes mix and change position. Check that they are tender.

Roasted Delicata Squash with Thyme

Preparation time: 10 minutes
Cooking Time: 20 Minutes
Servings: 4
Ingredients:
- 1 (1- to 1½-pound / 454- to 680-g) delicata squash, halved, seeded, and cut into ½-inch-thick strips
- 1 tablespoon extra-virgin olive oil
- ½ teaspoon dried thyme
- ¼ teaspoon salt
- ¼ teaspoon freshly ground black pepper

Directions:
1. Preheat the oven to 400°F (205°C). Line a baking sheet with parchment paper and set aside.
2. Add the squash strips, olive oil, thyme, salt, and pepper in a large bowl, and toss until the squash strips are fully coated.
3. Place the squash strips on the prepared baking sheet in a single layer. Roast for about 20 minutes until lightly browned, flipping the strips halfway through.
4. Remove from the oven and serve on plates.

Creamy Macaroni and Cheese

Preparation time: 15 minutes
Cooking Time: 25 minutes
Servings: 6
Ingredients:
- 1 cup fat-free evaporated milk
- ½ cup skim milk
- ½ cup low-fat Cheddar cheese
- ½ cup low-fat cottage cheese
- 1 teaspoon nutmeg
- Pinch cayenne pepper
- Sea salt and freshly ground black pepper, to taste
- 6 cups cooked whole-wheat elbow macaroni
- 2 tablespoons grated Parmesan cheese

Directions:
1. Preheat the oven to 350°F (180°C).
2. Heat the milk in a large saucepan over low heat until it steams.
3. Add the Cheddar cheese and cottage cheese to the milk, and keep whisking, or until the cheese is melted.
4. Add the nutmeg and cayenne pepper and stir well. Sprinkle the salt and pepper to season.
5. Remove from the heat. Add the cooked macaroni to the cheese mixture and stir until well combined. Transfer the macaroni and cheese to a large casserole dish and top with the grated Parmesan cheese.
6. Bake in the preheated oven for about 20 minutes, or until bubbly and lightly browned.
7. Divide the macaroni and cheese among six bowls and serve.

Creamy Pasta with Peas

Preparation time: 5 minutes
Cooking Time: 10 minutes
Servings: 4
Ingredients:
- 4 tomatoes, deseeded & diced
- 4 oz. fat free cream cheese, cut in cubes
- 1 cup peas, thawed
- ½ cup skim milk
- 4 tbsp. fresh parsley, diced
- What you'll need from store cupboard:
- ½ recipe Homemade Pasta, cook & drain
- 4 cloves garlic, diced fine
- 3 tbsp. olive oil
- 1 tsp oregano
- 1 tsp basil
- ½ tsp garlic salt

Directions:
1. Heat oil in a large skillet over medium heat. Add garlic and tomatoes, cook 3-4 minutes, stirring frequently.
2. Add peas, milk, cream cheese, and seasonings. Cook, stirring, 5 minutes, or until cream cheese has melted.
3. Add pasta and toss to coat. Serve garnished with parsley.

Sesame Bok Choy with Almonds

Preparation time: 5 minutes
Cooking Time: 7 minutes
Servings: 4
Ingredients:
2 teaspoons sesame oil
2 pounds (907 g) bok choy, cleaned and quartered

2 teaspoons low-sodium soy sauce
Pinch red pepper flakes
½ cup toasted sliced almonds
Directions:
1. Heat the sesame oil in a large skillet over medium heat until hot.
2. Sauté the bok choy in the hot oil for about 5 minutes, stirring occasionally, or until tender but still crisp.
3. Add the soy sauce and red pepper flakes and stir to combine. Continue sautéing for 2 minutes.
4. Transfer to a plate and serve topped with sliced almonds.

Roasted Cauliflower with Tomatoes
Preparation time: 30 minutes
Cooking Time: 45 Minutes
Servings: 4
Ingredients:
- 1 large head cauliflower, separated in florets
- 3 scallions, sliced
- 1 onion, diced fine
- What you'll need from store cupboard:
- 15 oz. can petite tomatoes, diced
- 4 cloves garlic, diced fine
- 4 tbsp. olive oil, divided
- 1 tbsp. red wine vinegar
- 1 tbsp. balsamic vinegar
- 3 tsp Splenda
- 1 tsp salt
- 1 tsp pepper
- ½ tsp chili powder

Directions:
1. Heat oven to 400 degrees.
2. Place cauliflower on a large baking sheet and drizzle with 2 tablespoons of oil. Sprinkle with salt and pepper, to taste. Use hands to rub oil and seasoning into florets then lay in single layer. Roast until fork tender.
3. Heat 1 tablespoon oil in a large skillet over med-low heat. Add onion and cook until soft.
4. Stir in tomatoes, with juice, Splenda, both vinegars, and the teaspoon of salt. Bring to a boil, reduce heat and simmer 20-25 minutes. For a smooth sauce, use an immersion blender to process until smooth, or leave it chunky.
5. In a separate skillet, heat remaining oil over med-low heat and sauté garlic 1-2 minutes. Stir in tomato sauce and increase heat to medium. Cook, stirring frequently, 5 minutes. Add chili powder and cauliflower and toss to coat. Serve garnished with scallions.

Fried Avocado
Preparation time: 5 minutes
Cooking Time: 10 minutes
Servings: 2
Ingredients:
- 2 avocados cut into wedges 25 mm thick
- 50g Pan crumbs bread
- 2g garlic powder
- 2g onion powder
- 1g smoked paprika
- 1g cayenne pepper
- Salt and pepper to taste
- 60g all-purpose flour
- 2 eggs, beaten
- Nonstick Spray Oil
- Tomato sauce or ranch sauce, to serve

Directions:
1. Cut the avocados into 25 mm thick pieces.
2. Combine the crumbs, garlic powder, onion powder, smoked paprika, cayenne pepper and salt in a bowl.
3. Separate each wedge of avocado in the flour, then dip the beaten eggs and stir in the breadcrumb mixture.
4. Preheat the air fryer.
5. Place the avocados in the preheated air fryer baskets, spray with oil spray and cook at 205°C for 10 minutes. Turn the fried avocado halfway through cooking and sprinkle with cooking oil.

Scrambled Eggs with Beans, Zucchini, Potatoes and Onions
Preparation time: 20 minutes
Cooking Time: 35 Minutes
Servings: 4
Ingredients:
- 300g of beans
- 2 onions
- 1 zucchini
- 4 potatoes
- 8 eggs
- Extra virgin olive oil
- Salt
- Ground pepper
- A splash of soy sauce

Directions:
1. Put the beans taken from their pod to cook in abundant saltwater. Drain when they are tender and reserve.
2. Peel the potatoes and cut into dice. Season and put some threads of oil. Mix and take to the air fryer. Select 1800C, 15 minutes.
3. After that time, add together with the potatoes, diced zucchini, and onion in julienne, mix and select 1800C, 20 minutes.
4. From time to time, mix and stir.
5. Pass the contents of the air fryer together with the beans to a pan.
6. Add a little soy sauce and salt to taste.
7. Sauté and peel the eggs.
8. Do the scrambled.

Cantaloupe & Prosciutto Salad
Preparation time: 10 minutes
Cooking Time: 15 minutes
Servings: 4
Ingredients:
- 6 mozzarella balls, quartered
- 1 medium cantaloupe, peeled and cut into small cubes
- 4 oz. prosciutto, chopped
- 1 tbsp. fresh lime juice
- 1 tbsp. fresh mint, chopped
- What you'll need from store cupboard
- 2 tbsp. extra virgin olive oil

- 1 tsp honey

Directions:
1. In a large bowl, whisk together oil, lime juice, honey, and mint. Season with salt and pepper to taste.
2. Add the cantaloupe and mozzarella and toss to combine. Arrange the mixture on a serving plate and add prosciutto. Serve.

Green Beans

Preparation time: 10 minutes
Cooking Time: 13 minutes
Servings: 4
Ingredients:
- 1-pound green beans
- ¾-teaspoon garlic powder
- ¾-teaspoon ground black pepper
- 1 ¼-teaspoon salt
- ½-teaspoon paprika

Directions:
1. Switch on the air fryer, insert fryer basket, grease it with olive oil, then shut with its lid, set the fryer at 400 degrees F, and preheat for 5 minutes.
2. Meanwhile, place beans in a bowl, spray generously with olive oil, sprinkle with garlic powder, black pepper, salt, and paprika and toss until well coated.
3. Open the fryer, add green beans in it, close with its lid and cook for 8 minutes until nicely golden and crispy, shaking halfway through the frying.
4. When air fryer beeps, open its lid, transfer green beans onto a serving plate and serve.

Garden Vegetable Pasta

Preparation time: 23 minutes
Cooking Time: 30 minutes
Servings: 6
Ingredients:
- 2 lbs. fresh cherry tomatoes, halved
- 2 zucchinis, chopped
- 2 ears corn, cut kernels off the cob
- 1 yellow squash, chopped
- ½ cup mozzarella cheese, grated
- ½ cup fresh basil, sliced thin
- What you'll need from store cupboard:
- Homemade Pasta, cook & drain
- 5 tbsp. olive oil, divided
- 2 cloves garlic crushed
- Crushed red pepper flakes, to taste
- Salt, to taste

Directions:
1. Heat 3 tablespoons oil in a large skillet over medium heat. Add garlic and tomatoes. Cover, reduce heat to low, and cook 15 minutes, stirring frequently.
2. In a separate skillet, heat remaining oil over med-high heat. Add zucchini, squash, and corn. Reduce heat to medium and cook until vegetables are tender. Sprinkle with salt.
3. Heat oven to 400 degrees.
4. In a large bowl combine tomato mixture, vegetables, and pasta, toss to mix. Pour into a 9x13-inch baking dish and top with cheese. Bake 10 minutes, or until cheese melts and begins to brown. Serve.

Teriyaki Tofu Burger

Preparation time: 10 minutes
Cooking Time: 15 minutes
Servings: 2
Ingredients:
- 2 3 oz. tofu portions, extra firm, pressed between paper towels 15 minutes
- ¼ red onion, sliced
- 2 tbsp. carrot, grated
- 1 tsp margarine
- Butter leaf lettuce
- What you'll need from store cupboard:
- 2 100% whole wheat sandwich thins
- 1 tbsp. teriyaki marinade
- 1 tbsp. Sriracha
- 1 tsp red chili flakes

Directions:
1. Heat grill, or charcoal, to a medium heat.
2. Marinate tofu in teriyaki marinade, red chili flakes and Sriracha.
3. Melt margarine in a small skillet over med-high heat. Add onions and cook until caramelized, about 5 minutes.
4. Grill tofu for 3-4 minutes per side.
5. To assemble, place tofu on bottom roll. Top with lettuce, carrot, and onion. Add top of the roll and serve.

Tofu Curry

Preparation time: 30 minutes
Cooking Time: 2 hours
Servings: 4
Ingredients:
- 2 cup green bell pepper, diced
- 1 cup firm tofu, cut into cubes
- 1 onion, peeled and diced
- What you'll need from store cupboard:
- 1 ½ cups canned coconut milk
- 1 cup tomato paste
- 2 cloves garlic, diced fine
- 2 tbsp. raw peanut butter
- 1 tbsp. garam masala
- 1 tbsp. curry powder
- 1 ½ tsp salt

Directions:
1. Add all Ingredients, except the tofu to a blender or food processor. Process until thoroughly combined.
2. Pour into a crock pot and add the tofu. Cover and cook on high 2 hours.
3. Stir well and serve over cauliflower rice.

Faux Chow Mein

Preparation time: 10 minutes
Cooking Time: 20 minutes
Servings: 4
Ingredients:
- 1 large spaghetti squash, halved and seeds removed
- 3 stalks celery, sliced diagonally
- 1 onion, diced fine
- 2 cup Cole slaw mix

- 2 tsp fresh ginger, grated
- What you'll need from store cupboard:
- ¼ cup Tamari
- 3 cloves garlic, diced fine
- 3-4 tbsp. water
- 2 tbsp. olive oil
- 1 tbsp. Splenda - ¼ tsp pepper

Directions:
1. Place squash, cut side down, in shallow glass dish and add water. Microwave on high 8-10 minutes, or until squash is soft. Use a fork to scoop out the squash into a bowl.
2. In a small bowl, whisk together Tamari, garlic, sugar, ginger, and pepper.
3. Heat oil in large skillet over med-high heat. Add onion and celery and cook, stirring frequently, 3-4 minutes. Add Cole slaw and cook until heated through, about 1 minute.
4. Add the squash and sauce mixture and stir well. Cook 2 minutes, stirring frequently. Serve.

Roasted Tomato and Bell Pepper Soup

Preparation time: 20 minutes
Cooking Time: 35 Minutes
Servings: 6
Ingredients:
- 2 tablespoons extra-virgin olive oil, plus more for coating the baking dish
- 16 plum tomatoes, cored and halved
- 4 celery stalks, coarsely chopped
- 4 red bell peppers, seeded, halved
- 4 garlic cloves, lightly crushed
- 1 sweet onion, cut into eighths
- Sea salt and freshly ground black pepper, to taste
- 6 cups low-sodium chicken broth
- 2 tablespoons chopped fresh basil
- 2 ounces (57 g) goat cheese, grated

Directions:
1. Preheat the oven to 400°F (205°C). Coat a large baking dish lightly with olive oil.
2. Put the tomatoes in the oiled dish, cut side down. Scatter the celery, bell peppers, garlic, and onion on top of the tomatoes. Drizzle with 2 tablespoons of olive oil and season with salt and pepper.
3. Roast in the preheated oven for about 30 minutes, or until the vegetables are fork-tender and slightly charred.
4. Remove the vegetables from the oven. Let them rest for a few minutes until cooled slightly.
5. Transfer to a food processor, along with the chicken broth, and purée until fully mixed and smooth.
6. Pour the purée soup into a medium saucepan and bring it to a simmer over medium-high heat.
7. Sprinkle the basil and grated cheese on top before serving.

Festive Holiday Salad

Preparation time: 30 minutes
Cooking Time: 1 hour
Servings: 8
Ingredients:
- 1 head broccoli, separated into florets
- 1 head cauliflower, separated into florets
- 1 red onion, sliced thin
- 2 cup cherry tomatoes, halved
- ½ cup fat free sour cream
- What you'll need from store cupboard:
- 1 cup lite mayonnaise
- 1 tbsp. Splenda

Directions:
1. In a large bowl combine vegetable.
2. In a small bowl, whisk together mayonnaise, sour cream, and Splenda. Pour over vegetables and toss to mix.
3. Cover and refrigerate at least 1 hour before serving.

Grilled Vegetable & Noodle Salad

Preparation time: 10 minutes
Cooking Time: 10 minutes
Servings: 4
Ingredients:
- 2 ears corn-on-the-cob, husked
- 1 red onion, cut in ½-inch thick slices
- 1 tomato, diced fine
- 1/3 cup fresh basil, diced
- 1/3 cup feta cheese, crumbled
- What you'll need from store cupboard:
- 1 recipe Homemade Noodles, cook & drain - 4 tbsp. Herb Vinaigrette
- Nonstick cooking spray

Directions:
1. Heat grill to medium heat. Spray rack with cooking spray.
2. Place corn and onions on the grill and cook, turning when needed, until lightly charred and tender, about 10 minutes.
3. Cut corn off the cob and place in a medium bowl. Chop the onion and add to the corn.
4. Stir in noodles, tomatoes, basil, and vinaigrette, toss to mix. Sprinkle cheese over top and serve.

Holiday Apple & Cranberry Salad

Preparation time: 10 minutes
Cooking Time: 15 minutes
Servings: 10
Ingredients:
- 12 oz. salad greens
- 3 Honeycrisp apples, sliced thin
- 1/2 lemon
- ½ cup blue cheese, crumbled
- What you'll need from store cupboard:
- Apple Cider Vinaigrette
- 1 cup pecan halves, toasted
- ¾ cup dried cranberries

Directions:
1. Put the apple slices in a large plastic bag and squeeze the half lemon over them. Close the bag and shake to coat.
2. In a large bowl, layer greens, apples, pecans, cranberries, and blue cheese. Just before serving, drizzle with enough vinaigrette to dress the salad. Toss to coat all Ingredients: evenly.

Zucchini "pasta" Salad

Preparation time: 35 minutes
Cooking Time: 1 Hour
Servings: 5

Ingredients:
- 5 oz. zucchini, spiralized
- 1 avocado, peeled and sliced
- 1/3 cup feta cheese, crumbled
- ¼ cup tomatoes, diced
- ¼ cup black olives, diced
- What you'll need from the store cupboard
- 1/3 cup Green Goddess Salad Dressing
- 1 tsp olive oil
- 1 tsp basil
- Salt and pepper to taste

Directions:
1. Place zucchini on paper towel lined cutting board. Sprinkle with a little bit of salt and let sit for 30 minutes to remove excess water. Squeeze gently.
2. Add oil to medium skillet and heat over med-high heat. Add zucchini and cook, stirring frequently, until soft, about 3 – 4 minutes.
3. Transfer zucchini to a large bowl and add remaining Ingredients, except for the avocado. Cover and chill for 1 hour.
4. Serve topped with avocado.

Homemade Vegetable Chili

Preparation time: 10 minutes
Cooking Time: 15 minutes
Servings: 4
Ingredients:
- 2 tablespoons extra-virgin olive oil
- 1 onion, finely chopped
- 1 green bell pepper, deseeded and chopped
- 1 (14-ounce / 397-g) can kidney beans, drained and rinsed
- 2 (14-ounce / 397-g) cans crushed tomatoes
- 2 cups veggie crumbles
- 1 teaspoon garlic powder
- 1 tablespoon chili powder
- ½ teaspoon sea salt

Directions:
1. Heat the olive oil in a large skillet over medium-high heat until shimmering.
2. Add the onion and bell pepper and sauté for 5 minutes, stirring occasionally.
3. Fold in the beans, tomatoes, veggie crumbles, garlic powder, chili powder, and salt. Stir to incorporate and bring them to a simmer.
4. Reduce the heat and cook for an additional 5 minutes, stirring occasionally, or until the mixture is heated through.
5. Allow the mixture to cool for 5 minutes and serve warm.

Collard Greens with Tomato

Preparation time: 10 minutes
Cooking Time: 20 minutes
Servings: 4
Ingredients:
- 1 cup low-sodium vegetable broth, divided
- ½ onion, thinly sliced
- 2 garlic cloves, thinly sliced
- 1 medium tomato, chopped
- 1 large bunch collard greens including stems, roughly chopped
- 1 teaspoon ground cumin
- ½ teaspoon freshly ground black pepper

Directions:
1. Add ½ cup of vegetable broth to a Dutch oven over medium heat and bring to a simmer.
2. Stir in the onion and garlic and cook for about 4 minutes until tender.
3. Add the remaining broth, tomato, greens, cumin, and pepper, and gently stir to combine.
4. Reduce the heat to low and simmer uncovered for 15 minutes. Serve warm.

Okra

Preparation time: 5 minutes
Cooking Time: 10 minutes
Servings: 4
Ingredients:
- 1-cup almond flour
- 8 ounces fresh okra
- 1/2 teaspoon sea salt
- 1-cup milk, reduced-fat
- 1 egg, pastured

Directions:
1. Crack the egg in a bowl, pour in the milk and whisk until blended.
2. Cut the stem from each okra, then cut it into ½-inch pieces, add them into egg and stir until well coated.
3. Mix flour and salt and add it into a large plastic bag.
4. Working on one okra piece at a time, drain the okra well by letting excess egg drip off, add it to the flour mixture, then seal the bag and shake well until okra is well coated.
5. Place the coated okra on a grease air fryer basket, coat remaining okra pieces in the same manner and place them into the basket.
6. Switch on the air fryer, insert fryer basket, spray okra with oil, then shut with its lid, set the fryer at 390 degrees F and cook for 10 minutes until nicely golden and cooked, stirring okra halfway through the frying.

Grilled Tofu & Veggie Skewers

Preparation time: 10 minutes
Cooking Time: 15 minutes
Servings: 6
Ingredients:
- 1 block tofu
- 2 small zucchinis, sliced
- 1 red bell pepper, cut into 1-inch cubes
- 1 yellow bell pepper, cut into 1-inch cubes
- 1 red onion, cut into 1-inch cubes
- 2 cups cherry tomatoes
- What you'll need from store cupboard:
- 2 tbsp. lite soy sauce
- 3 tsp barbecue sauce
- 2 tsp sesame seeds
- Salt & pepper, to taste
- Nonstick cooking spray

Directions:

1. Press tofu to extract liquid, for about half an hour. Then, cut tofu into cubes and marinate in soy sauce for at least 15 minutes.
2. Heat the grill to med-high heat. Spray the grill rack with cooking spray.
3. Assemble skewers with tofu alternating with vegetables.
4. Grill 2-3 minutes per side until vegetables start to soften, and tofu is golden brown. At the very end of cooking time, season with salt and pepper and brush with barbecue sauce. Serve garnished with sesame seeds.

Mushroom Cutlets with Creamy Sauce

Preparation time: 15 minutes
Cooking time: 20 minutes
Servings: 4
Ingredients:
For the sauce
- 1 tablespoon extra-virgin olive oil
- 2 tablespoons whole-wheat flour
- 1½ cups unsweetened plain almond milk
- ¼ teaspoon salt
- Dash Worcestershire sauce
- Pinch cayenne pepper
- ¼ cup shredded cheddar cheese

For the cutlets
- 2 eggs
- 2 cups chopped mushrooms
- 1 cup quick oats
- 2 scallions, both white and green parts, chopped
- ¼ cup shredded cheddar cheese
- ½ teaspoon salt
- ¼ teaspoon freshly ground black pepper
- 1 tablespoon extra-virgin olive oil

Directions:
To Make the Sauce
1. In a medium saucepan, heat the oil over medium heat. Add the flour and stir constantly for about 2 minutes until browned.
2. Slowly whisk in the almond milk and bring to a boil. Reduce the heat to low and simmer for 6 to 8 minutes until the sauce thickens.
3. Season with the salt, Worcestershire sauce, and cayenne. Add the cheese and stir until melted. Turn off the heat and cover to keep warm while you make the cutlets.
To Make the Cutlets
1. In a large mixing bowl, beat the eggs. Add the mushrooms, oats, scallions, cheese, salt, and pepper. Stir to combine.
2. using your hands, form the mixture into 8 patties, each about ½ inch thick.
3. In a large skillet, heat the oil over medium-high heat. Cook the patties, in batches, if necessary, for 3 minutes per side until crisp and brown.
4. Serve the cutlets warm with sauce drizzled over the top.

Falafel with Creamy Garlic-Yogurt Sauce

Preparation time: 15 minutes
Cooking time: 10 minutes
Servings: 4
Ingredients:
For the sauce
- ¾ cup plain nonfat Greek yogurt
- 3 garlic cloves, minced
- Juice of 1 lemon
- 1 tablespoon extra-virgin olive oil
- ¼ teaspoon salt

For the falafel
- 1 (15-ounce) can low-sodium chickpeas, drained and rinsed
- 2 garlic cloves, roughly chopped
- 2 tablespoons whole-wheat flour
- 2 tablespoons chopped fresh parsley
- ½ teaspoon ground cumin
- ¼ teaspoon salt
- 2 teaspoons canola oil, divided
- 8 large lettuce leaves, chopped
- 1 cucumber, chopped - 1 tomato, diced

Directions:
To Make the Sauce
1. In a small bowl, combine the yogurt, garlic, lemon juice, olive oil, and salt, and mix well. Cover and refrigerate until ready to serve.
To Make the Falafel
1. In a food processor or blender, combine the chickpeas and garlic, and pulse until chopped well but not creamy. Add the flour, parsley, cumin, and salt. Pulse several more times until incorporated.
2. Using your hands, form the mixture into balls, using about 1 tablespoon of mixture for each ball.
3. In a medium skillet, heat 1 teaspoon of canola oil over medium-high heat. Working in batches, add the falafel to the skillet, cooking on each side for 2 to 3 minutes until browned and crisp. Remove the falafel from the skillet, and repeat with the remaining oil and falafel until all are cooked.
4. Divide the lettuce, cucumber, and tomato among 4 plates. Top each plate with 2 falafel and 2 tablespoons of sauce. Serve immediately.

Roasted Onions And Green Beans

Serving: 6
Preparation Time: 10 minutes
Cooking Time: 15 minutes
Ingredients
- 1 yellow onion, sliced into rings
- ½ teaspoon onion powder
- 2 tablespoons coconut flour
- 1 and 1/3 pounds fresh green beans, trimmed and chopped
- ½ tablespoon salt

Directions:
1. Take a large bowl and mix salt with onion powder and coconut flour
2. Add onion rings
3. Mix well to coat
4. Spread the rings on the baking sheet lined with parchment paper
5. Drizzled with some oil
6. Bake for 10 minutes at 400 Fahrenheit

7. Parboil the green beans for 3 to 5 minutes in the boiling water
8. Drain it and serve the beans with baked onion rings
9. Serve warm, and enjoy!

Walnuts And Asparagus Delight

Serving: 4
Preparation Time: 5 minutes
Cooking Time: 5 minutes
Ingredients
- 1 and ½ tablespoons olive oil
- ¾ pound asparagus, trimmed
- ¼ cup walnuts, chopped
- Salt and pepper to taste

Directions:
1. Place a skillet over medium heat, add olive oil and let it heat up
2. Add asparagus; saute for 5 minutes until browned
3. Season with salt and pepper
4. Remove heat
5. Add walnuts and toss
6. Serve warm!

Hearty Roasted Cauliflower

Serving: 8
Preparation Time: 5 minutes
Cooking Time: 25 minutes
Ingredients
- 1 large cauliflower head
- 2 tablespoons melted coconut oil
- 2 tablespoons fresh thyme
- 1 teaspoon Celtic sea salt
- 1 teaspoon fresh ground pepper
- 1 head of roasted garlic
- 2 tablespoons fresh thyme for garnish

Directions:
1. Preheat your oven to 425 degrees F
2. Rinse cauliflower and trim, core, and slice
3. Lay cauliflower evenly on a rimmed baking tray
4. Drizzle coconut oil evenly over cauliflower, sprinkle thyme leaves
5. Season with a pinch of salt and pepper
6. Squeeze roasted garlic
7. Roast cauliflower until slightly caramelize for about 25 minutes, making sure to turn once
8. Garnish with fresh thyme leaves
9. Enjoy!

Almond And Blistered Beans

Serving: 4
Preparation Time: 10 minutes
Cooking Time: 20 minutes
Ingredients
- 1-pound fresh green beans, ends trimmed
- 1 and ½ tablespoon olive oil
- ¼ teaspoon salt
- 1 and ½ tablespoons fresh dill, minced
- Juice of 1 lemon
- ¼ cup crushed almonds
- Salt as needed

Directions:
1. Preheat your oven to 400 degrees F
2. Add in the green beans with your olive oil and also with salt
3. Then spread them in one single layer on a large-sized sheet pan
4. Roast it up for 10 minutes and stir it nicely, then roast for another 8-10 minutes
5. Remove it from the oven and keep stirring in the lemon juice alongside the dill
6. Top it up with crushed almonds and some flaky sea salt, and serve

Portobello Mushroom Risotto

Serving: 4
Preparation Time: 5 minutes
Cooking Time: 15 minutes
Ingredients
- 4 and ½ cups cauliflower, riced
- 3 tablespoons coconut oil
- 1 pound Portobello mushrooms, thinly sliced
- 1 pound white mushrooms, thinly sliced
- 2 shallots, diced
- ¼ cup organic vegetable broth
- Salt and pepper to taste
- 3 tablespoons chives, chopped
- 4 tablespoons butter
- ½ cup parmesan cheese, grated

Directions:
1. Use a food processor and pulse cauliflower florets until riced
2. Take a large saucepan and heat up 2 tablespoons of oil over medium-high flame
3. Add mushrooms and Saute for 3 minutes until mushrooms are tender
4. Clear the saucepan of mushrooms and liquid and keep them on the side
5. Add the rest of the 1 tablespoons oil to the skillet
6. Toss shallots and cook for 60 seconds
7. Add cauliflower rice, and stir for 2 minutes until coated with oil
8. Add broth to riced cauliflower and stir for 5 minutes
9. Remove pot from heat and mix in mushrooms and liquid
10. Add chives, butter, parmesan cheese
11. Season with salt and pepper
12. Serve and enjoy!

Portobello Mushrooms And Cherry Tomatoes Mix

Serving: 4
Preparation Time: 10 minutes
Cooking Time: 10 minutes
Ingredients
- 12 cherry tomatoes
- 2 ounces scallions
- 4 portobello mushrooms
- 4 and ¼ ounces of butter
- Salt and pepper to taste

Directions:
1. Take a large skillet and melt butter over medium heat
2. Add mushrooms and Sauté for 3 minutes
3. Stir in cherry tomatoes and scallions

4. Sauté for 5 minutes
5. Season accordingly
6. Sauté until veggies are tender
7. Enjoy!

The Medi-Wrap
Serving: 6
Preparation Time: 5 minutes
Cooking Time: Nil
Ingredients
- ¼ cup crispy chickpeas
- ¼ cup cherry tomatoes halved
- Handful baby spinach
- 2 romaine lettuce leaves, wrapping
- 2 tablespoons lemon juice, fresh
- ¼ cup hummus
- 2 tablespoons kalamata olives, quartered

Directions:
1. Take a bowl and mix in all ingredients except hummus and lettuce leaves; stir well
2. Put hummus over lettuce leaves, topping with the chickpea mixture
3. Wrap it up and serve
4. Enjoy!

Garbanzo and Spinach Beans
Serving: 4
Preparation Time: 5-10 minutes
Cooking Time: Nil
Ingredients
- 1 tablespoon olive oil
- ½ onion, diced
- 10 ounces spinach, chopped
- 12 ounces of garbanzo beans
- ½ teaspoon cumin

Directions:
1. Take a skillet and add olive oil; let it warm over medium-low heat
2. Add onions, garbanzo and cook for 5 minutes
3. Stir in spinach, cumin, and garbanzo beans, and season with sunflower seeds
4. Use a spoon to smash gently
5. Cook thoroughly until heated; enjoy!

Cilantro and Avocado Platter
Serving: 6
Preparation Time: 10 minutes
Cooking Time: nil
Ingredients
- 2 avocados, peeled, pitted, and diced
- 1 sweet onion, chopped
- 1 green bell pepper, chopped
- 1 large ripe tomato, chopped
- ¼ cup of fresh cilantro, chopped
- ½ a lime, juiced
- Salt and pepper as needed

Directions:
1. Take a medium-sized bowl and add onion, bell pepper, tomato, avocados, lime, and cilantro
2. Mix well and give it a toss
3. Season with salt and pepper according to your taste
4. Serve and enjoy!

Baby Potatoes Roast
Serving: 4
Preparation Time: 5 minutes
Cooking Time: 25 minutes
Ingredients
- 2 pounds of new yellow potatoes, scrubbed and cut into wedges
- 2 tablespoons extra virgin olive oil
- 2 teaspoons fresh rosemary, chopped
- 1 teaspoon garlic powder
- ½ teaspoon freshly ground black pepper and sunflower seeds

Directions:
1. Preheat your oven to 400 degrees Fahrenheit
2. Line the baking sheet with aluminum foil and set it aside
3. Take a large bowl and add potatoes, olive oil, garlic, rosemary, sea sunflower seeds, and pepper
4. Spread potatoes in a single layer on a baking sheet and bake for 25 minutes
5. Serve and enjoy!

Pineapple, Papaya, and Mango Delight
Serving: 2
Preparation Time: 20 minutes
Cooking Time: nil
Ingredients
- 1-pound fresh pineapple, peeled and cut into chunks
- 1 mango, peeled, pitted, and cubed
- 2 papayas, peeled, seeded, and cubed
- 3 tablespoons fresh lime juice
- ¼ cup fresh mint leaves, chopped

Directions:
1. Take a large bowl and add the listed Ingredients
2. Toss well to coat
3. Put in fridge and let it chill
4. Serve and enjoy!

Grilled Eggplant Steaks
Serving: 4
Preparation Time: 10 minutes
Cooking Time: 10 minutes
Ingredients
- 4 Roma tomatoes, diced
- 8 ounces cashew cream
- 2 eggplants
- 1 tablespoon olive oil
- 1 cup parsley, chopped
- 1 cucumber, diced
- Salt and pepper t taste

Directions:
1. Slice eggplants into three shtick steaks, drizzle with oil, and season with salt and pepper
2. Grill in a pan for 4 minutes per side
3. Top with remaining ingredients
4. Serve and enjoy!

Everyday Traditional Chili

Serving: 4
Preparation Time: 10 minutes
Cooking Time:15-20 minutes
Ingredients
- 1 onion, diced
- 1 teaspoon olive oil
- 3 garlic cloves, minced
- 28 ounces tomatoes, canned
- ¼ cup tomato paste
- 14 ounces kidney beans, canned, rinsed, and dried
- 2-3 teaspoons chili powder
- ¼ cup cilantro, fresh
- ¼ teaspoons salt

Directions:
1. Take a large-sized pot and place it over medium heat, add oil and let it heat up
2. Add onion and garlic; sauté for 5 minutes
3. Add tomato paste, tomatoes, beans, and chili powder, and season with salt
4. Lower heat and let it simmer for 10-20 minutes
5. Garnish with cilantro and parsley
6. Enjoy!

Cashew Mushroom Rice Risotto

Serving: 4
Preparation Time: 5 minutes
Cooking Time:15 minutes
Ingredients
- 4 and ½ cups cauliflower, riced
- 3 tablespoons coconut oil
- 1 pound Portobello mushrooms, thinly sliced
- 1 pound white mushrooms, thinly sliced
- 2 shallots, diced
- ¼ cup organic vegetable broth
- Salt and pepper to taste
- 3 tablespoons chives, chopped
- 4 tablespoons almond butter
- ½ cup cashew cream, grated

Directions:
1. Use a food processor and pulse cauliflower florets until riced
2. Take a large saucepan and heat up 2 tablespoons of oil over medium-high flame
3. Add mushrooms and Saute for 3 minutes until mushrooms are tender
4. Clear the saucepan of mushrooms and liquid and keep them on the side
5. Add the rest of the 1 tablespoons oil to the skillet
6. Toss shallots and cook for 60 seconds
7. Add cauliflower rice, and stir for 2 minutes until coated with oil
8. Add broth to riced cauliflower and stir for 5 minutes
9. Remove pot from heat and mix in mushrooms and liquid
10. Add chives, butter, cashew cream
11. Season with salt and pepper
12. Serve and enjoy!

Mediterranean Kale Dish

Serving: 4
Preparation Time: 10 minutes
Cooking Time:10 minutes
Ingredients
- 12 cups kale, chopped
- 2 tablespoons lemon juice
- 1 tablespoon olive oil
- 1 teaspoon coconut aminos
- Sunflower seeds and pepper as needed

Directions:
1. Add a steamer insert to your Saucepan
2. Fill the saucepan with water up to the bottom of the steamer
3. Cover and bring water to boil (medium-high heat)
4. Add kale to the insert and steam for 7-8 minutes
5. Take a large bowl and add lemon juice, olive oil, sunflower seeds, coconut aminos, and pepper
6. Mix well and add the steamed kale to the bowl
7. Toss and serve
8. Enjoy!

Authentic Zucchini Boats

Serving: 4
Preparation Time: 5 minutes
Cooking Time:25 minutes
Ingredients
- 4 medium zucchinis
- ½ cup marinara sauce
- ¼ red onion, sliced
- ¼ cup kalamata olives, chopped
- ½ cup cherry tomatoes, sliced
- 2 tablespoons fresh basil

Directions:
1. Preheat your oven to 400 degrees Fahrenheit
2. Cut the zucchini half-lengthwise and shape them into boats
3. Take a bowl and add tomato sauce; spread 1 layer of sauce on top of each the boat
4. Top with onion, olives, and tomatoes
5. Bake for 20-25 minutes
6. Top with basil, and enjoy!

Delicious Garlic Toast

Serving: 2
Preparation Time: 5 minutes
Cooking Time:5 minutes
Ingredients
- 1 teaspoon coconut oil
- Pinch of salt
- 1-2 teaspoons nutritional yeast
- 1 small garlic clove, pressed
- 1 slice of whole-grain bread

Directions:
1. Take a small-sized bowl and add all ingredients except bread; mix well
2. Toast your bread with seasoned oil or using a toaster; it should take about 5 minutes
3. Once done, spread garlic mix all over toast and serve
4. Enjoy!

Sesame Cucumber Mix

Serving: 4
Preparation Time: 15 minutes

Cooking Time: Nil
Ingredients
- 2 medium English cucumbers, peeled and cut into ¼-inch slices
- 2 tablespoons fresh parsley, chopped
- 3 tablespoons toasted sesame oil
- 2 tablespoons soy sauce
- 1 tablespoon mirin
- 2 teaspoons rice vinegar
- 1 teaspoon brown sugar
- 2 tablespoons toasted sesame seeds

Directions:
1. Take a small-sized bowl and add cucumbers and parsley; keep it on the side
2. Take another bowl and add oil, soy sauce, mirin, vinegar, and sugar and stir well; pour dressing over cucumbers
3. Let it sit for 10 minutes
4. Spoon cucumber salad into small bowls, sprinkle with sesame seeds, and serve
5. Enjoy!

Lemon and Thyme Couscous

Serving: 4
Preparation Time: 5 minutes
Cooking Time: 5 minutes
Ingredients
- 2 and ¾ cups vegetable stock
- Juice and zest of 1 lemon
- 2 tablespoons fresh thyme, chopped
- ¼ cup fresh parsley, chopped
- Salt and pepper to taste

Directions:
1. Take a pot and add the stock, lemon juice, thyme, and boil
2. Stir in couscous and cover; remove heat
3. Let it sit for 5 minutes; fluff with a fork
4. Stir in lemon zest and parsley, and season with salt and pepper
5. Enjoy!

Roasted Sweet Potatoes And Brussels Sprouts

Serving: 6
Preparation Time: 10 minutes
Cooking Time: 20 minutes
Ingredients
- 1 large sweet potato, peeled and sliced
- 1-pound Brussels sprouts, trimmed
- 1 tablespoon red wine vinegar
- 2 cloves garlic, minced
- 1/3 cup olive oil
- 1 teaspoon cumin
- ¼ teaspoon salt
- ¼ teaspoon black pepper

Directions:
1. Preheat your oven to 400 degrees F
2. Take a bowl and place all ingredients
3. Toss to coat well
4. Take a baking pan and transfer it
5. Lined with aluminum foil
6. Roast for 20 minutes
7. Serve and enjoy!

Curry Spiced Cauliflower with Toasted Pistachios

Serving: 2
Preparation Time: 5 minutes
Cooking Time: 20 minutes
Ingredients
- 7 ounces cauliflower, thinly sliced
- 2 tablespoons extra virgin coconut oil
- A handful of pistachios, crushed
- 1 tablespoon mustard seed
- ½ red onion, thinly sliced
- 1 teaspoon curry powder
- Salt to taste

Directions:
1. Preheat your oven to 350 degrees F
2. Take a pan and combine everything to coat the cauliflower with seasoning
3. Place the cauliflower on a baking dish
4. Lined with aluminum foil
5. Roast in the oven for 20 minutes
6. Serve and enjoy!

Mediterranean Zucchini Mushroom Pasta

Serving: 4
Preparation Time: 10 minutes
Cooking Time: 10 minutes
Ingredients
- ½ pound pasta
- 2 tablespoons olive oil
- 6 garlic cloves, crushed
- 1 teaspoon red chile
- 2 spring onions, sliced
- 3 teaspoons rosemary, chopped
- 1 large zucchini, cut in half lengthwise and sliced
- 5 large portabella mushrooms
- 1 can tomatoes
- 4 tablespoon parmesan cheese
- Fresh ground black pepper

Directions:
1. Cook the pasta in boiling water until Al Dente
2. Take a large-sized frying pan and place it over medium heat
3. Add oil and allow the oil to heat up
4. Add garlic, onion, and chili, and Saute for a few minutes until golden
5. Add zucchini, rosemary, and mushroom, and Saute for a few minutes
6. Increase the heat to medium-high and add tinned tomatoes and sauce until thick
7. Drain your boiled pasta and transfer it to the serving platter
8. Pour the tomato mix on top and mix using a tong
9. Garnish with parmesan and freshly ground black pepper
10. Enjoy!

Gentle Sweet Potato Curry

Serving: 4
Preparation Time: 15 minutes
Cooking Time: 25 minutes
Ingredients

- 1 teaspoon extra virgin olive oil
- 1 sweet onion, peeled and chopped
- 2 teaspoon garlic, minced
- 2 teaspoon ginger, peeled and grated
- 1 cup sodium-free vegetable stock
- 3 sweet potatoes, peeled and diced
- 1 large carrot, peeled and diced
- 1 tablespoon curry powder
- 1 teaspoon ground cumin
- ½ teaspoon ground coriander
- ½ teaspoon turmeric
- 1 zucchini, diced
- 1 yellow squash, diced
- 1 red bell pepper, thinly sliced
- ¼ cup water
- 1 tablespoon cornstarch

Directions:
1. Take a large saucepan and place it over medium-high heat
2. Add olive oil and heat it up
3. Add onion, ginger, and garlic, and Saute for 3 minutes
4. Stir in broth, sweet potatoes, carrot, curry powder, coriander, cumin, turmeric, and bring to a boil
5. Lower heat to low and simmer for 15 minutes
6. Add zucchini, squash, and red bell pepper and simmer for 5 minutes
7. Take a small bowl and stir in water and cornstarch until smooth
8. Adjust seasoning accordingly and serve
9. Enjoy!

Broiled Portobello Mushroom Burgers With Goat Cheese

Serving: 4
Preparation Time: 15 minutes
Cooking Time: 5 minutes
Ingredients

- 4 large Portobello mushroom caps
- 1 red onion, cut into ¼-inch thick slices
- 2 tablespoons extra virgin olive oil
- 2 tablespoons balsamic vinegar
- Pinch of salt
- ¼ cup goat cheese
- ¼ cup sun-dried tomatoes, chopped
- 4 ciabatta buns
- 1 cup kale, shredded

Directions:
1. Preheat your oven to broil
2. Take a large bowl and add mushrooms caps, onion slices, olive oil, balsamic vinegar, and salt
3. Mix well
4. Place mushroom caps (bottom side up) and onion slices on your baking sheet
5. Take a small bowl and stir in goat cheese and sun-dried tomatoes
6. Toast the buns under broiler for 30 seconds until golden
7. Spread goat cheese mixture on top of each bun
8. Place mushroom cap and onion slice on each bun bottom and cover with shredded kale
9. Put everything together and serve
10. Enjoy!

Green Bean Stew

Serving: 4
Preparation Time: 10 minutes
Cooking Time: 40 minutes
Ingredients

- ¼ cup extra virgin olive oil
- 3 garlic cloves, chopped
- 1 sweet onion, chopped
- Sea salt
- Freshly ground black pepper
- 1 pound fresh green beans, ends snipped and cut into 2-inch pieces
- 1 (8 ounces) can of tomato sauce
- ½ cup water

Directions:
1. Take a small skillet and place it over medium heat
2. Add olive oil and heat it up
3. Add garlic and onion and Saute for 3 minutes until the garlic is fragrant
4. Season with salt and pepper
5. Add beans to the skillet and stir gently with a spoon; cover and cook for 10 minutes
6. Stir in tomato sauce and water
7. Cover and cook for 25 minutes more
8. Serve and enjoy!

Roasted Parmesan Broccoli

Serving: 4
Preparation Time: 10 minutes
Cooking Time: 10 minutes
Ingredients

- 2 head broccoli, cut into florets
- 2 tablespoon extra-virgin olive oil
- 2 teaspoon garlic, minced
- Zest of 1 lemon
- Pinch of salt
- ½ cup parmesan cheese, grated

Directions:
1. Preheat your oven to 400 degrees F
2. Lightly grease the baking sheet with olive oil and keep it on the side
3. Take a large bowl and add broccoli with 2 tablespoons olive oil, lemon zest, garlic, lemon juice, and salt
4. Spread mix on the baking sheet in a single layer and sprinkle parmesan cheese
5. Bake for 10 minutes until tender
6. Transfer broccoli to serving the dish
7. Serve and enjoy!

Red Pepper Hummus With Fresh Veggies

Serving: 4
Preparation Time: 5 minutes
Cooking Time: nil
Ingredients
- 1 can (15 ounces) of chickpeas
- ¼ cup tahini
- 2 tablespoons extra virgin olive oil
- ¼ cup fresh squeezed lemon juice
- 2 garlic cloves, minced
- 2 tablespoons extra virgin olive oil
- ½ teaspoon ground cumin
- ¾ cup fire-roasted red peppers
- Pinch of cayenne pepper
- Assorted selection of veggies such as cauliflower, broccoli florets, carrot sticks, snow peas, celery)

Directions:
1. Add all of the listed ingredients (except veggies) and blend until you have a nice consistency
2. Serve the hummus with raw veggies
3. Enjoy!

Mashed Celeriac

Serving: 4
Preparation Time: 10 minutes
Cooking Time: 20 minutes
Ingredients
- 2 celeriac, washed, peeled, and diced
- 2 teaspoons extra-virgin olive oil
- 1 tablespoon honey
- ½ teaspoon ground nutmeg
- Sea salt
- Freshly ground black pepper

Directions:
1. Preheat your oven to 400 degrees Fahrenheit
2. Line a baking sheet with aluminum foil and keep it on the side
3. Take a large bowl and toss celeriac and olive oil
4. Spread celeriac evenly on a baking sheet
5. Roast for 20 minutes until tender
6. Transfer to a large bowl
7. Add honey and nutmeg
8. Use a potato masher to mash the mixture until fluffy
9. Season with salt and pepper
10. Serve and enjoy!

Baked Spinach And Feta

Serving: 6
Preparation Time: 10 minutes
Cooking Time: 12 minutes
Ingredients
- 6 ounces sun-dried tomato pesto
- 6 (6 inches) whole wheat pita bread
- 2 Roma plum tomatoes, chopped
- 1 bunch rinsed spinach, chopped
- 4 fresh mushrooms, sliced
- ½ cup feta cheese, crumbled
- 2 tablespoon parmesan cheese, crumbled
- 3 tablespoons olive oil
- Ground black pepper

Directions:
1. Preheat your oven to a temperature of 350 degrees Fahrenheit
2. Spread your tomato pesto onto one side of your pita bread and place them on your baking sheet (with the pesto side up)
3. Top up the pitas with spinach, tomatoes, feta cheese, mushrooms, and Parmesan cheese
4. Drizzle with some olive oil and season nicely with pepper
5. Bake in your oven for about 12 minutes until the bread are crispy
6. Cut up the pita into quarters and serve!

Fantastic Mediterranean Kale

Serving: 6
Preparation Time: 15 minutes
Cooking Time: 10 minutes
Ingredients
- 12 cups kale, chopped
- 2 tablespoons lemon juice
- 1 tablespoon olive oil
- 1 tablespoon garlic, minced
- 1 teaspoon soy sauce
- Salt and pepper as needed

Directions:
1. Add a steamer insert to your Saucepan
2. Fill the saucepan with water up to the bottom of the steamer
3. Cover and bring water to boil (medium-high heat)
4. Add kale to the insert and steam for 7-8 minutes
5. Take a large bowl and add lemon juice, garlic, olive oil, salt, soy sauce, and pepper
6. Mix well and add the steamed kale to the bowl
7. Toss and serve
8. Enjoy!

Chapter 6

Grains, Beans and Legumes

Black Bean and Tomato Soup with Lime Yogurt
Preparation time: 8 hours 10 minutes
Cooking time: 1 hour 33 minutes
Servings: 8
Ingredients:
- 2 tablespoons avocado oil
- 1 medium onion, chopped
- 1 (10-ounce / 284-g) can diced tomatoes and green chilies
- 1 pound (454 g) dried black beans, soaked in water for at least 8 hours, rinsed
- 1 teaspoon ground cumin
- 3 garlic cloves, minced
- 6 cups chicken bone broth, vegetable broth, or water - Kosher salt, to taste
- 1 tablespoon freshly squeezed lime juice
- ¼ cup plain Greek yogurt

Directions:
1. Heat the avocado oil in a nonstick skillet over medium heat until shimmering.
2. Add the onion and sauté for 3 minutes or until translucent.
3. Transfer the onion to a pot, then add the tomatoes and green chilies and their juices, black beans, cumin, garlic, broth, and salt. Stir to combine well. Bring to a boil over medium-high heat, then reduce the heat to low. Simmer for 1 hour and 30 minutes or until the beans are soft. Meanwhile, combine the lime juice with Greek yogurt in a small bowl. Stir to mix well. Pour the soup in a large serving bowl, then drizzle with lime yogurt before serving.

Tip: If you want to make a thicker soup, remove 1 cup of beans from the pot after the simmering, then pour the remaining soup in a food processor. Process to purée the soup until smooth, then move 1 cup of beans back to the soup and serve.

Classic Texas Caviar
Preparation time: 10 minutes
Cooking time: 0 minutes
Servings: 6
Ingredients:
For the Salad:
- 1 ear fresh corn, kernels removed
- 1 cup cooked lima beans
- 1 cup cooked black-eyed peas
- 1 red bell pepper, chopped
- 2 celery stalks, chopped
- ½ red onion, chopped

For the Dressing:
- 3 tablespoons apple cider vinegar
- 1 teaspoon paprika
- 2 tablespoons extra-virgin olive oil

Directions:
1. Combine the corn, beans, peas, bell pepper, celery, and onion in a large bowl. Stir to mix well.
2. Combine the vinegar, paprika, and olive oil in a small bowl. Stir to combine well.
3. Pour the dressing into the salad and toss to mix well. Let sit for 20 minutes to infuse before serving.

Tip: You can replace the lima beans with the same amount of pinto beans for a distinct flavor.

Lettuce Tomato Salad
Preparation time: 15 minutes
Cooking time: 0 minutes
Servings: 4
Ingredients:
- 4 cups chopped iceberg lettuce
- 1 cucumber, chopped
- 10 cherry tomatoes, halved
- 1 cup crumbled feta cheese
- 1 cup pitted black olives
- ½ red onion, thinly sliced
- ½ cup Greek Vinaigrette

Directions:
1. In a large bowl, combine the lettuce, cucumber, tomatoes, feta, olives, and onion. Toss to combine.
2. Toss with the dressing just before serving.

Chicken Cabbage Salad
Preparation time: 10 minutes
Cooking time: 0 minutes
Servings: 1
Ingredients:
- 1 cup shredded cooked rotisserie chicken meat
- 1 cup shredded cabbage or coleslaw mix
- 1 Asian pear, cored, peeled, and julienned
- 2 scallions, white and green parts, sliced on the bias (cut diagonally into thin slices)
- ¼ cup Asian Vinaigrette

Directions:
1. In a large bowl, combine the chicken, cabbage, pear, and scallions.
2. Toss with the vinaigrette just before serving.

Bell Pepper Black Olive Salad
Preparation time: 10 minutes
Cooking time: 0 minutes
Servings: 2

Ingredients:
- 2 cups chopped iceberg lettuce
- 10 cherry tomatoes, halved
- 1 cup pitted black olives, chopped
- 6 ounces ham, chopped
- ½ red onion, chopped
- 1 red bell pepper, seeded and chopped
- 10 basil leaves, torn
- ¼ cup Italian Vinaigrette

Directions:
1. In a large bowl, combine the lettuce, tomatoes, olives, ham, onion, bell pepper, and basil leaves.
2. Toss with the vinaigrette just before serving.

Chickpea Wraps for Quesadillas

Preparation time: 5 minutes
Cooking time: 10 minutes
Servings: 4
Ingredients:
- 1 cup chickpea flour
- 1 cup water
- ¼ teaspoon salt
- Nonstick cooking spray

Directions:
1. In a large bowl, whisk all together until no lumps remain.
2. Spray a skillet with cooking spray and place over medium-high heat.
3. Pour batter in, ¼ cup at a time, and tilt pan to spread thinly.
4. Cook until golden brown on each side, about 2 minutes per side.
5. Use for taco shells, enchiladas, quesadillas or whatever you desire.

Eggs and Snap Peas Fried Rice

Preparation time: 5 minutes
Cooking time: 15 minutes
Servings: 8
Ingredients:
- 2 cups sugar snap peas
- 2 egg whites
- 1 egg
- 1 cup instant brown rice, cooked according to directions
- 2 tablespoons lite soy sauce

Directions:
1. Add the peas to the cooked rice and mix to combine.
2. In a small skillet, scramble the egg and egg whites.
3. Add the rice and peas to the skillet and stir in soy sauce. Cook, stirring frequently, about 2 to 3 minutes, or until heated through. Serve.

Baked Margarine Cheesy Fish

Preparation time: 10 minutes
Cooking time: 20 minutes
Servings: 4
Ingredients:
- 1 pound (454 g) flounder
- 2 cups green beans
- 4 tablespoons margarine
- 8 basil leaves
- ounces (50 g) pork rinds
- ½ cup reduced fat Parmesan cheese
- 3 cloves garlic
- Salt and ground black pepper, to taste
- Nonstick cooking spray

Directions:
1. Heat oven to 350°F (180°C). Spray a baking dish with cooking spray.
2. Steam green beans until they are almost tender, about 15 minutes, less if you use frozen or canned beans. Lay green beans in the prepared dish.
3. Place the fish filets over the green beans and season with salt and pepper.
4. Place the garlic, basil, pork rinds, and Parmesan in a food processor and pulse until mixture resembles crumbs. Sprinkle over fish. Cut margarine into small pieces and place on top.
5. Bake 15 to 20 minutes or until fish flakes easily with a fork. Serve.

The Best Ever Veggie Fajitas

Preparation time: 10 minutes
Cooking time: 15 minutes
Servings: 4
Ingredients:
Guacamole:
- 2 small avocados pitted and peeled
- 1 teaspoon freshly squeezed lime juice
- ¼ teaspoon salt
- 9 cherry tomatoes, halved

Fajitas:
- 1 red bell pepper
- 1 green bell pepper
- 1 small white onion
- Avocado oil cooking spray
- 1 cup canned low-sodium black beans, drained and rinsed
- ½ teaspoon ground cumin
- ¼ teaspoon chili powder
- ¼ teaspoon garlic powder
- 4 (6-inch) yellow corn tortillas

Directions:
Make the Guacamole:
1. In a medium bowl, use a fork to mash the avocados with the lime juice and salt.
2. Gently stir in the cherry tomatoes.
Make the Fajitas:
3. Cut the red bell pepper, green bell pepper, and onion into ½-inch slices.
4. Heat a large skillet over medium heat. When hot, coat the cooking surface with cooking spray. Put the peppers, onion, and beans into the skillet.
5. Add the cumin, chili powder, and garlic powder, and stir.
6. Cover and cook for 15 minutes, stirring halfway through.
7. Divide the fajita mixture equally between the tortillas, and top with guacamole and any preferred garnishes.

Weeknight Chickpea Spaghetti Bolognese

Preparation time: 5 minutes

Cooking time: 25 minutes
Servings: 4
Ingredients:
- 1 (3- to 4-pound / 1.4- to 1.8-kg) spaghetti squash
- ½ teaspoon ground cumin
- 1 cup no-sugar-added spaghetti sauce
- 1 (15-ounce / 425-g) can low-sodium chickpeas, drained and rinsed
- 6 ounces (170 g) extra-firm tofu

Directions:
1. Preheat the oven to 400°F (205°C).
2. Cut the squash in half lengthwise. Scoop out the seeds and discard.
3. Season both halves of the squash with the cumin, and place them on a baking sheet cut-side down. Roast for 25 minutes.
4. Meanwhile, heat a medium saucepan over low heat, and pour in the spaghetti sauce and chickpeas.
5. Press the tofu between two layers of paper towels, and gently squeeze out any excess water.
6. Crumble the tofu into the sauce and cook for 15 minutes.
7. Remove the squash from the oven, and comb through the flesh of each half with a fork to make thin strands.
8. Divide the "spaghetti" into four portions, and top each portion with one-quarter of the sauce.

Fat free Sofrito Dumplings

Preparation time: 20 minutes
Cooking time: 15 minutes
Servings: 8 to 10
Ingredients:
- 4 cups water
- 4 cups low-sodium vegetable broth
- 1 cup cassava flour
- 1 cup gluten-free all-purpose flour
- 2 teaspoons baking powder
- 1 teaspoon salt
- 1 cup fat-free milk
- 2 tablespoons bottled chimichurri or sofrito

Directions:
1. In a large pot, bring the water and the broth to a slow boil over medium-high heat.
2. In a large mixing bowl, whisk the cassava flour, all-purpose flour, baking powder, and salt together.
3. In a small bowl, whisk the milk and chimichurri together until combined.
4. Stir the wet Ingredients: into the dry Ingredients: a little at a time to create a firm dough.
5. With clean hands, pinch offs a small piece of dough. Roll into a ball, and gently flatten in the palm of your hand, forming a disk. Repeat until no dough remains.
6. Carefully drop the dumplings one at a time into the boiling liquid. Cover and simmer for 15 minutes, or until the dumplings are cooked through. You can test by inserting a fork into the dumpling; it should come out clean.
7. Serve warm.

Garlic Zucchini Chicken Soup

Preparation time: 10 minutes
Cooking time: 15 minutes
Servings: 4
Ingredients:
- 2 tablespoons extra-virgin olive oil
- 12 ounces (336 g) chicken breast, chopped
- 1 onion, chopped
- 2 carrots, chopped
- 2 celery stalks, chopped
- 2 garlic cloves
- 6 cups unsalted chicken broth
- 1 teaspoon dried thyme
- 1 teaspoon sea salt
- 2 medium zucchinis cut into noodles (or store-bought zucchini noodles)

Directions:
1. In a large pot over medium-high heat, heat the olive oil until it shimmers.
2. Add the chicken and cook until it is opaque, about 5 minutes. With a slotted spoon, remove the chicken from the pot and set aside on a plate.
3. Add the onion, carrots, and celery to the pot. Cook, stirring occasionally, until the vegetables are soft, about 5 minutes.
4. Add the garlic and cook, stirring constantly, for 30 seconds. Add the chicken broth, thyme, and salt. Bring to a boil, and reduce the heat to medium.
5. Add the zucchini and return the chicken to the pan, adding any juices that have collected on the plate.
6. Cook, stirring occasionally, until the zucchini noodles are soft, 1 to 2 minutes more.

Chestnut Lettuce Wraps

Preparation time: 10 minutes
Cooking time: 0 minutes
Servings: 2
Ingredients:
- 1 tablespoon freshly squeezed lemon juice
- 1 teaspoon curry powder
- 1 teaspoon reduced-sodium soy sauce
- ½ teaspoon sriracha (or to taste)
- ½ cup canned water chestnuts, drained and chopped
- 2 (2.6-ounce/73.7 g) package tuna packed in water, drained
- 2 large butter lettuce leaves

Directions:
1. In a medium bowl, whisk together lemon juice; curry powder, soy sauce, and sriracha.
2. Add the water chestnuts and tuna. Stir to combine.
3. Serve wrapped in the lettuce leaves.

Crispy Cowboy Black Bean Fritters

Preparation time: 10 minutes
Cooking time: 25 minutes
Servings: 20 Fritters
Ingredients:
- 1¾ cups all-purpose flour
- ½ teaspoon cumin
- 2 teaspoons baking powder
- 2 teaspoons salt
- ½ teaspoon black pepper
- 4 egg whites, lightly beaten
- 1 cup salsa

- 2 (16-ounce / 454-g) cans no-salt-added black beans, rinsed and drained
- 1 tablespoon canola oil, plus extra if needed

Directions:
1. Combine the flour, cumin, baking powder, salt, and pepper in a large bowl, then mix in the egg whites and salsa. Add the black beans and stir to mix well.
2. Heat the canola oil in a nonstick skillet over medium-high heat.
3. Spoon 1 teaspoon of the mixture into the skillet to make a fritter. Make more fritters to coat the bottom of the skillet. Keep a little space between each two fritters. You may need to work in batches to avoid overcrowding.
4. Cook for 3 minutes or until the fritters are golden brown on both sides. Flip the fritters and flatten with a spatula halfway through the cooking time. Repeat with the remaining mixture. Add more oil as needed.
5. Serve immediately.

Dandelion and Beet Greens

Preparation time: 10 minutes
Cooking time: 15 minutes
Servings: 4
Ingredients:
- 1 tablespoon olive oil
- ½ Vidalia onion, thinly sliced
- 1 bunch dandelion greens, cut into ribbons
- 1 bunch beet greens, cut into ribbons
- ½ cup low-sodium vegetable broth
- 1 (15-ounce / 425-g) can no-salt-added black beans
- Salt and freshly ground black pepper, to taste

Directions:
1. Heat the olive oil in a nonstick skillet over low heat until shimmering.
2. Add the onion and sauté for 3 minutes or until translucent.
3. Add the dandelion and beet greens, and broth to the skillet. Cover and cook for 8 minutes or until wilted.
4. Add the black beans and cook for 4 minutes or until soft. Sprinkle with salt and pepper. Stir to mix well.
5. Serve immediately.

Tip: You can use collard greens, spinach, arugula, or Swiss chard to replace the beet greens or dandelion greens.

Black Bean, Corn, and Chicken Soup

Preparation time: 10 minutes
Cooking time: 25 minutes
Servings: 7
Ingredients:
- 2 tablespoons olive oil
- ½ onion, diced
- 1 pound (454 g) boneless and skinless chicken breast, cut into ½-inch cubes
- ½ teaspoon Adobo seasoning, divided
- ¼ teaspoon black pepper
- 1 (15-ounce / 425-g) can no-salt-added black beans, rinsed and drained
- 1 (14.5-ounce / 411-g) can fire-roasted tomatoes
- ½ cup frozen corn
- ½ teaspoon cumin
- 1 tablespoon chili powder
- 5 cups low-sodium chicken broth

Directions:
1. Grease a stockpot with olive oil and heat over medium-high heat until shimmering.
2. Add the onion and sauté for 3 minutes or until translucent.
3. Add the chicken breast and sprinkle with Adobo seasoning and pepper. Put the lid on and cook for 6 minutes or until lightly browned. Shake the pot halfway through the cooking time.
4. Add the remaining Ingredients. Reduce the heat to low and simmer for 15 minutes or until the black beans are soft.
5. Serve immediately.

Tip: You can use paprika, black pepper, onion powder, dried oregano, cumin, garlic powder, chili powder, and salt to make your own Adobo seasoning.

Kale & Carrot Veggie Soup

Preparation time: 10 minutes
Cooking time: 15 minutes
Servings: 2
Ingredients:
- 2 tablespoons extra-virgin olive oil
- 1 onion, finely chopped
- 1 carrot, chopped
- 1 cup chopped kale (stems removed)
- 3 garlic cloves, minced
- 1 cup canned lentils, drained and rinsed
- 1 cup unsalted vegetable broth
- 2 teaspoons dried rosemary (or 1 tablespoon chopped fresh rosemary)
- ½ teaspoon sea salt
- ¼ teaspoons freshly ground black pepper

Directions:
1. In a large pot over medium-high heat, heat the olive oil until it shimmers.
2. Add the onion and carrot and cook, stirring, until the vegetables begin to soften, about 3 minutes.
3. Add the kale and cook for 3 minutes more. Add the garlic and cook, stirring constantly, for 30 seconds.
4. Stir in the lentils, vegetable broth, rosemary, salt, and pepper. Bring to a simmer. Simmer, stirring occasionally, for 5 minutes more.

Egg Pea Mix wrapped in Kale Leaves

Preparation time: 10 minutes
Cooking time: 0 minutes
Servings: 2
Ingredients:
- 1 teaspoon Dijon mustard
- 1 tablespoon chopped fresh dill
- ½ teaspoon sea salt
- ¼ teaspoon paprika
- 4 hard-boiled large eggs, chopped
- 1 cup shelled fresh peas
- 2 tablespoons finely chopped red onion
- 2 large kale leaves

Directions:
1. In a medium bowl, whisk together mustard, dill, salt, and paprika.
2. Stir in the eggs, peas, and onion.
3. Serve wrapped in kale leaves.

Pepperoni Cheesed Pita

Preparation time: 10 minutes
Cooking time: 0 minutes
Servings: 2
Ingredients:
- ½ cup tomato sauce
- ½ teaspoon oregano
- ½ teaspoon garlic powder
- ½ cup chopped black olives
- 2 canned artichoke hearts, drained and chopped
- 2 ounces pepperoni, chopped
- ½ cup shredded mozzarella cheese
- 1 whole-wheat pita, halved

Directions:
1. In a medium bowl, stir together the tomato sauce, oregano, and garlic powder.
2. Add the olives, artichoke hearts, pepperoni, and cheese. Stir to mix.
3. Spoon the mixture into the pita halves.

Tomato Green Chilies Soup with Lime Yogurt

Preparation time: 8 hours 10 minutes
Cooking time: 1 hour 33 minutes
Servings: 8
Ingredients:
- 2 tablespoons avocado oil
- 1 medium onion, chopped
- 1 (10-ounce / 284-g) can diced tomatoes and green chillies
- 1 pound (454 g) dried black beans, soaked in water for at least 8 hours, rinsed
- 1 teaspoon ground cumin
- 3 garlic cloves, minced
- 6 cup chicken bone broth, vegetable broth, or water
- Kosher salt, to taste
- 1 tablespoon freshly squeezed lime juice
- ¼ cup Low-fat Greek yogurt

Directions:
1. Heat the avocado oil in a nonstick skillet over medium heat until shimmering.
2. Add the onion and sauté for 3 minutes or until translucent.
3. Transfer the onion to a pot, then add the tomatoes and green chilies and their juices, black beans, cumin, garlic, broth, and salt. Stir to combine well.
4. Bring to a boil over medium-high heat, and then reduce the heat to low. Simmer for 1 hour and 30 minutes or until the beans are soft.
5. Meanwhile, combine the lime juice with Greek yogurt in a small bowl. Stir to mix well.
6. Pour the soup in a large serving bowl, and then drizzle with lime yogurt before serving.

Perfect Corn Salad with Paprika Dressing

Preparation time: 10 minutes
Cooking time: 0 minutes
Servings: 6
Ingredients:
Salad:
- 1 ear fresh corn, kernels removed
- 1 cup cooked lima beans
- 1 cup cooked black-eyed peas
- 1 red bell pepper, chopped
- 2 celery stalks, chopped
- ½ red onion, chopped

Dressing:
- 3 tablespoons apple cider vinegar
- 1 teaspoon paprika
- 2 tablespoons extra-virgin olive oil

Directions:
1. Combine the corn, beans, peas, bell pepper, celery, and onion in a large bowl. Stir to mix well.
2. Combine the vinegar, paprika, and olive oil in a small bowl. Stir to combine well.
3. Pour the dressing into the salad and toss to mix well. Let sit for 20 minutes to infuse before serving.

Low Sodium Veggie Greens with Black Beans

Preparation time: 10 minutes
Cooking time: 15 minutes
Servings: 4
Ingredients:
- 1 tablespoon olive oil
- ½ Vidalia onion, thinly sliced
- 1 bunch dandelion greens cut into ribbons
- 1 bunch beet greens, cut into ribbons
- ½ cup low-sodium vegetable broth
- 1 (15-ounce / 425-g) can no-salt-added black beans
- Salt and freshly ground black pepper, to taste

Directions:
1. Heat the olive oil in a nonstick skillet over low heat until shimmering.
2. Add the onion and sauté for 3 minutes or until translucent.
3. Add the dandelion and beet greens, and broth to the skillet. Cover and cook for 8 minutes or until wilted.
4. Add the black beans and cook for 4 minutes or until soft. Sprinkle with salt and pepper. Stir to mix well.
5. Serve immediately.

Classy Chicken Black Bean Soup

Preparation time: 10 minutes
Cooking time: 25 minutes
Servings: 7
Ingredients:
- 2 tablespoons olive oil
- ½ onion, diced
- 1 pound (454 g) boneless and skinless chicken breast, cut into ½-inch cubes
- ½ teaspoon Adobo seasoning, divided

- ¼ teaspoon black pepper
- 1 (15-ounce / 425-g) can no-salt-added black beans, rinsed, and drained
- 1 (14.5-ounce / 411-g) can fire-roasted tomatoes
- ½ cup frozen corn
- ½ teaspoon cumin
- 1 tablespoon chili powder
- 5 cups low-sodium chicken broth

Directions:
1. Grease a stockpot with olive oil and heat over medium-high heat until shimmering.
2. Add the onion and sauté for 3 minutes or until translucent.
3. Add the chicken breast and sprinkle with Adobo seasoning and pepper. Put the lid on and cook for 6 minutes or until lightly browned. Shake the pot halfway through the cooking time.
4. Add the remaining Ingredients. Reduce the heat to low and simmer for 15 minutes or until the black beans are soft.
5. Serve immediately.

Vegetable Broth Kidney Beans Veggie Bowl

Preparation time: 10 minutes
Cooking time: 8 to 12 minutes
Servings: 8
Ingredients:
- 2 tablespoons olive oil
- 1 medium yellow onion, chopped
- 1 cup crushed tomatoes
- 2 garlic cloves, minced
- 2 cups low sodium canned red kidney beans, rinsed
- 1 cup chopped green beans
- ¼ cup low-sodium vegetable broth
- 1 teaspoon smoked paprika
- Salt, to taste

Directions:
1. Heat the olive oil in a nonstick skillet over medium heat until shimmering.
2. Add the onion, tomatoes, and garlic. Sauté for 3 to 5 minutes or until fragrant and the onion is translucent.
3. Add the kidney beans, green beans, and broth to the skillet. Sprinkle with paprika and salt, then sauté to combine well.
4. Cover the skillet and cook for 5 to 7 minutes or until the vegetables are tender. Serve immediately.

Spicy Brown Rice with Red Pepper & Paprika

Preparation time: 15 minutes
Cooking time: 20 minutes
Servings: 4
Ingredients:
- 1 tablespoon extra-virgin olive oil
- 1 bunch collard greens, stemmed and cut into chiffonade
- 1 carrot, cut into 2-inch matchsticks
- 1 red onion, thinly sliced
- ½ cup low-sodium vegetable broth
- 2 tablespoons coconut amino
- 1 garlic clove, minced
- 1 cup cooked brown rice
- 1 large egg
- 1 teaspoon red pepper flakes
- 1 teaspoon paprika
- Salt, to taste

Directions:
1. Heat the olive oil in a Dutch oven or a nonstick skillet over medium heat until shimmering.
2. Add the collard greens and sauté for 4 minutes or until wilted.
3. Add the carrot, onion, broth, coconut amino, and garlic to the Dutch oven, then cover and cook 6 minutes or until the carrot is tender.
4. Add the brown rice and cook for 4 minutes. Keep stirring during the cooking.
5. Break the egg over them, and then cook and scramble the egg for 4 minutes or until the egg is set.
6. Turn off the heat and sprinkle with red pepper flakes, paprika, and salt before serving.

Chicken Rice with Almond Cranberry Salad

Preparation time: 10 minutes
Cooking time: 45 minutes
Servings: 6 Cups
Ingredients:
Rice:
- 2½ cups chicken bone broth, vegetable broth, or water
- 2 cups wild rice blend, rinsed
- 1 teaspoon kosher salt

Dressing:
- Juice of 1 medium orange (about ¼ cup)
- 1½ teaspoons grated orange zest
- ¼ cup white wine vinegar
- 1 teaspoon pure maple syrup
- ¼ cup extra-virgin olive oil

Salad:
- ½ cup sliced almonds, toasted
- ¾ cup unsweetened dried cranberries
- Freshly ground black pepper, to taste

Directions:
Make the Rice:
1. Pour the broth in a pot, then add the rice and sprinkle with salt. Bring to a boil over medium-high heat.
2. Reduce the heat to low. Cover the pot, and then simmer for 45 minutes.
3. Turn off the heat and fluff the rice with a fork. Set aside until ready to use.
Make the Dressing:
4. When cooking the rice, make the dressing: Combine the Ingredients: for the dressing in a small bowl. Stir to combine well. Set aside until ready to use.
Make the Salad:
5. Put the cooked rice, almonds, and cranberries in a bowl, and then sprinkle with black pepper. Add the dressing, then toss to combine well.
6. Serve immediately.

Apple and Almond Butter Spread Pita

Preparation time: 10 minutes
Cooking time: 0 minutes
Servings: 2
Ingredients:
- ½ apple, cored and chopped
- ¼ cup almond butter
- ½ teaspoon cinnamon
- 1 whole-wheat pita, halved

Directions:
1. In a medium bowl, stir together the apple, almond butter, and cinnamon.
2. Spread with a spoon into the pita pocket halves.

Baby Spinach Walnut Salad

Preparation time: 10 minutes
Cooking time: 0 minutes
Servings: 2
Ingredients:
- 4 cups baby spinach
- ½ pear, cored, peeled, and chopped
- ¼ cup whole walnuts, chopped
- 2 tablespoons apple cider vinegar
- 2 tablespoons extra-virgin olive oil
- 1 teaspoon peeled and grated fresh ginger
- ½ teaspoon Dijon mustard
- ½ teaspoon sea salt

Directions:
1. Layer the spinach on the bottom of two mason jars. Top with the pear and walnuts.
2. In a small bowl, whisk together the vinegar, oil, ginger, mustard, and salt. Put in another lidded container. Shake the dressing before serving and add it to the mason jars. Close the jars and shake to distribute the dressing.

Red Kidney Beans with Tomatoes

Preparation time: 10 minutes
Cooking time: 8 to 12 minutes
Servings: 8
Ingredients:
- 2 tablespoons olive oil
- 1 medium yellow onion, chopped
- 1 cup crushed tomatoes
- 2 garlic cloves, minced
- 2 cups low sodium canned red kidney beans, rinsed
- 1 cup chopped green beans
- ¼ cup low-sodium vegetable broth
- 1 teaspoon smoked paprika
- Salt, to taste

Directions:
1. Heat the olive oil in a nonstick skillet over medium heat until shimmering.
2. Add the onion, tomatoes, and garlic. Sauté for 3 to 5 minutes or until fragrant and the onion is translucent.
3. Add the kidney beans, green beans, and broth to the skillet. Sprinkle with paprika and salt, then sauté to combine well.
4. Cover the skillet and cook for 5 to 7 minutes or until the vegetables are tender. Serve immediately.

Tip: You can use the same amount of water to replace the vegetable broth.

Brown Rice with Carrot, and Scrambled Egg

Preparation time: 15 minutes
Cooking time: 20 minutes
Servings: 4
Ingredients:
- 1 tablespoon extra-virgin olive oil
- 1 bunch collard greens, stemmed and cut into chiffonade
- 1 carrot, cut into 2-inch matchsticks
- 1 red onion, thinly sliced
- ½ cup low-sodium vegetable broth
- 2 tablespoons coconut aminos
- 1 garlic clove, minced
- 1 cup cooked brown rice
- 1 large egg
- 1 teaspoon red pepper flakes
- 1 teaspoon paprika
- Salt, to taste

Directions:
1. Heat the olive oil in a Dutch oven or a nonstick skillet over medium heat until shimmering.
2. Add the collard greens and sauté for 4 minutes or until wilted.
3. Add the carrot, onion, broth, coconut aminos, and garlic to the Dutch oven, then cover and cook 6 minutes or until the carrot is tender.
4. Add the brown rice and cook for 4 minutes. Keep stirring during the cooking.
5. Break the egg over them, then cook and scramble the egg for 4 minutes or until the egg is set.
6. Turn off the heat and sprinkle with red pepper flakes, paprika, and salt before serving.

Tip: You can use low-sodium soy sauce to replace the coconut aminos.

Wild Rice and Cranberries Salad

Preparation time: 10 minutes
Cooking time: 45 minutes
Servings: 6 Cups
Ingredients:
For the Rice:
- 2½ cups chicken bone broth, vegetable broth, or water
- 2 cups wild rice blend, rinsed
- 1 teaspoon kosher salt

For the Dressing:
- Juice of 1 medium orange (about ¼ cup)
- 1½ teaspoons grated orange zest
- ¼ cup white wine vinegar
- 1 teaspoon pure maple syrup
- ¼ cup extra-virgin olive oil

For the Salad:
- ½ cup sliced almonds, toasted
- ¾ cup unsweetened dried cranberries

- Freshly ground black pepper, to taste

Directions:

For the Rice

1. Pour the broth in a pot, then add the rice and sprinkle with salt. Bring to a boil over medium-high heat.
2. Reduce the heat to low. Cover the pot, then simmer for 45 minutes.
3. Turn off the heat and fluff the rice with a fork. Set aside until ready to use.

For the Dressing

1. When cooking the rice, make the dressing: Combine the Ingredients: for the dressing in a small bowl. Stir to combine well. Set aside until ready to use.

For the Salad

1. Put the cooked rice, almonds, and cranberries in a bowl, then sprinkle with black pepper. Add the dressing, then toss to combine well.
2. Serve immediately.

Tip: You can combine the Ingredients: for the dressing in a jar and shake to combine. So, you can keep the dressing and undressed salad in the refrigerate for future enjoyment.

Macaroni and Vegetable Pie

Preparation time: 15 minutes
Cooking time: 30 minutes
Servings: 6
Ingredients:

- 1 (1-pound / 454-g) package whole-wheat macaroni
- 2 celery stalks, thinly sliced
- 1 small yellow onion, chopped
- 2 garlic cloves, minced
- Salt, to taste
- ¼ teaspoon freshly ground black pepper
- 2 tablespoons chickpea flour
- 2 cups grated reduced-fat sharp Cheddar cheese
- 1 cup fat-free milk
- 2 large zucchinis, finely grated and squeezed dry
- 2 roasted red peppers, chopped into ¼-inch pieces

Directions:

1. Preheat the oven to 350°F (180°C).
2. Bring a pot of water to a boil, then add the macaroni and cook for 4 minutes or until al dente.
3. Drain the macaroni and transfer to a large bowl. Reserve 1 cup of the macaroni water.
4. Pour the macaroni water in an oven-safe skillet and heat over medium heat.
5. Add the celery, onion, garlic, salt, and black pepper to the skillet and sauté for 4 minutes or until tender.
6. Gently mix in the chickpea flour, then fold in the cheese and milk. Keep stirring until the mixture is thick and smooth.
7. Add the cooked macaroni, zucchini, and red peppers. Stir to combine well.
8. Cover the skillet with aluminum foil and transfer it to the preheated oven.
9. Bake for 15 minutes or until the cheese melts, then remove the foil and bake for 5 more minutes or until lightly browned.
10. Remove the pie from the oven and serve immediately.

Tip: You can use the organic quinoa pasta to replace the macaroni to make this recipe gluten-free.

Chapter 7

Fish and Seafood

Sea Bass and Rice
Preparation time: 10 minutes
Cooking time: 20 minutes
Servings: 4
Ingredients:
- 1pound sea bass fillets, boneless, skinless and cubed 1cup wild rice - 2cups chicken stock - 2scallions, chopped
- 1red bell pepper, chopped
- 1teaspoon turmeric powder
- 1tablespoon chives, chopped
- Salt and black pepper to the taste
- A drizzle of olive oil

Directions:
1. Grease the air fryer's pan with the oil, add the fish, rice, stock and the other Ingredients, toss gently and cook at 380 degrees F and cook for 20 minutes, stirring halfway.
2. Divide between plates and serve.

Sea Bass and Cauliflower
Preparation time: 5 minutes
Cooking time: 20 minutes
Servings: 4
Ingredients:
- 1pound sea bass fillets, boneless and cubed
- 1cup cauliflower florets
- 2tablespoons butter, melted
- 1teaspoon garam masala
- 1/2cup chicken stock
- 1tablespoon parsley, chopped
- Salt and black pepper to the taste

Directions:
1. In your air fryer, combine the fish with the cauliflower and the other Ingredients, toss gently and cook at 380 degrees F for 20 minutes.
2. Divide everything between plates and serve.

Cajun Salmon
Preparation Time: 12 minutes
Cooking Time: 0
Servings: 2
Ingredients:
- 2(4-oz. salmon fillets, skin removed
- 2tbsp. unsalted butter; melted.
- 1tsp. paprika
- 1/4tsp. ground black pepper
- 1/8tsp. ground cayenne pepper
- 1/2tsp. garlic powder.

Directions:
1. Brush each fillet with butter. Combine remaining Ingredients: in a small bowl and then rub onto fish. Place fillets into the air fryer basket
2. Bring the temperature to 390 Degrees F and set the timer for 7 minutes. When fully cooked, internal temperature will be 145 Degrees F. Serve immediately.

Trout and Zucchinis
Preparation Time: 20 minutes
Cooking Time: 0
Servings: 4
Ingredients:
- 3zucchinis, cut in medium chunks
- 4trout fillets; boneless
- 1/4cup tomato sauce
- 1garlic clove; minced
- 1/2cup cilantro; chopped.
- 1tbsp. lemon juice
- 2tbsp. olive oil
- Salt and black pepper to taste.

Directions:
1. In a pan that fits your air fryer, mix the fish with the other Ingredients, toss, introduce in the fryer and cook at 380F for 15 minutes. Divide everything between plates and serve right away

Crab Cakes
Preparation Time: 20 minutes
Cooking Time: 0
Servings: 4
Ingredients:
- 1/2medium green bell pepper; seeded and chopped
- 1/4cup chopped green onion
- 1large egg.
- 2(6-oz. cans lump crabmeat
- 1/4cup blanched finely ground almond flour.
- 1/2tbsp. lemon juice
- 2tbsp. full-fat mayonnaise
- 1/2tsp. Old Bay seasoning
- 1/2tsp. Dijon mustard

Directions:
1. Take a large bowl, merge all Ingredients. Set into four balls and flatten into patties. Place patties into the air fryer basket
2. Adjust the temperature to 350 Degrees F and set the timer for 10 minutes.
3. Flip patties halfway through the cooking time. Serve warm.

Air Fried Catfish
Preparation time: 5 minutes
Cooking time: 20 minutes
Servings: 4

Ingredients:
- 4 catfish fillets
- 1 tbsp. olive oil
- 1/4 cup fish seasoning
- 1 tbsp. fresh parsley, chopped

Directions:
1. Preheat the air fryer to 400 F.
2. Spray air fryer basket with cooking spray.
3. Seasoned fish with seasoning and place into the air fryer basket.
4. Drizzle fish fillets with oil and cook for 10 minutes.
5. Turn fish to another side and cook for 10 minutes more.
6. Garnish with parsley and serve.

Garlic Parmesan Shrimp

Preparation time: 5 minutes
Cooking time: 20 minutes
Servings: 2
Ingredients:
- 1 pound shrimp, deveined and peeled
- 1/2 cup parmesan cheese, grated
- 1/4 cup cilantro, diced
- 1 tablespoon olive oil
- 1 teaspoon salt
- 1 teaspoon fresh cracked pepper
- 1 tablespoon lemon juice
- 6 garlic cloves, diced

Directions:
1. Warmth the Air fryer to 350 F and grease an Air fryer basket.
2. Drizzle shrimp with olive oil and lemon juice and season with garlic, salt and cracked pepper.
3. Secure the bowl with plastic wrap and refrigerate for about hours.
4. Stir in the parmesan cheese and cilantro to the bowl and transfer to the Air fryer basket.
5. Cook for about 10 minutes and serve immediately.

Asian Sesame Cod

Preparation Time: 5 Minutes
Cooking Time: 7 to 9 Minutes
Servings: 1
Ingredients:
- 1 Tbsp. reduced-sodium soy sauce
- 2 tsps. Honey
- 1 tsp. sesame seeds
- 6 oz. (170 g.) cod fillet

Directions:
1. In a lesser bowl, put the soy sauce and honey.
2. Sprig the air fryer basket with nonstick cooking spray, then place the cod in the basket, brush with the soy mixture, and sprinkle sesame seeds on top. Roast at 360°F (182°C) for 7 to 9 minutes or until opaque.
3. Remove the fish and allow cooling on a wire rack for 5 minutes before serving.

Easy Tuna Wraps

Preparation Time: 10 Minutes
Cooking Time: 4 to 7 Minutes
Servings: 4
Ingredients:
- 1 lb. (454 g.) fresh tuna steak, cut into 1-inch cubes
- 1 Tbsp. grated fresh ginger
- 2 Garlic cloves, minced
- ½ tsp. toasted sesame oil
- 4 Low-sodium whole-wheat tortillas
- ¼ C. low-fat mayonnaise
- 2 C. shredded romaine lettuce
- 1 Red bell pepper, thinly sliced

Directions:
1. In a medium bowl, mix the tuna, ginger, garlic, and sesame oil. Let it stand for 10 minutes, and then transfer it to the air fryer basket.
2. Air fry at 390°F (199°C) for 4 to 7 minutes, or until done to your liking and lightly browned.
3. Make wraps with tuna, tortillas, mayonnaise, lettuce, and bell pepper. Serve immediately.

Mustard-Crusted Sole

Preparation Time: 5 Minutes
Cooking Time: 8 to 11 Minutes
Servings: 4
Ingredients:
5 tsps. Low-sodium yellow mustard
- 1 Tbsp. freshly squeezed lemon juice
- 4 (3 1/2-oz./99-g.) Sole fillets
- ½ tsp. dried thyme
- ½ tsp. dried marjoram
- 1/8 tsp. freshly ground black pepper
- 1 Slice low-sodium whole-wheat bread, crumbled
- 2 tsps. Olive oil

Directions:
1. In a small bowl, blend the mustard and lemon juice. Spread this evenly over the fillets. Place them in the air fryer basket.
2. In another small bowl, mix the thyme, marjoram, pepper, bread crumbs, and olive oil. Mix until combined.
3. Gently but firmly press the spice mixture onto each fish fillet's top.
4. Bake at 320°F (160°C) for 8 to 11 minutes, or until the fish grasps an inner temperature of at least 145°F (63°C) on a meat thermometer and the topping is browned and crisp. Serve immediately.

Baked Salmon with Garlic Parmesan Topping

Preparation Time: 5 Minutes
Cooking Time: 20 Minutes
Servings: 4
Ingredients:
- 1 lb. Wild-caught salmon filets
- 2 Tbsps. margarine
- ¼ C. reduced-fat parmesan cheese, grated
- ¼ C. light mayonnaise
- 2-3 Garlic cloves, diced
- 2 Tbsps. parsley
- Salt and pepper

Directions:
1. Heat the oven to 350°F and line a baking pan with parchment paper.
2. Place the salmon on the pan and season with salt and pepper.

3. In a medium skillet, over medium heat, melt butter. Add garlic and cook, stirring 1 minute.
4. Reduce heat to low and add the remaining Ingredients. Stir until everything is melted and combined.
5. Spread all evenly over the salmon and bake 15 minutes for thawed fish or 20 for frozen. Salmon is done when it flakes easily with a fork.

Blackened Shrimp

Preparation Time: 5 Minutes
Cooking Time: 5 Minutes
Servings: 4
Ingredients:
- 1 ½ lb. Shrimps, peeled and deveined
- 4 Lime wedges
- 4 Tbsps. cilantro, chopped
- 4 Garlic cloves, diced
- 1 Tbsp. chili powder
- 1 Tbsp. paprika
- 1 Tbsp. olive oil
- 2 tsps. Splenda brown sugar
- 1 tsp. cumin
- 1 tsp. oregano
- 1 tsp. garlic powder
- 1 tsp. salt
- ½ tsp. pepper

Directions:
1. In a small bowl, combine seasonings and Splenda brown sugar.
2. Heat oil in a skillet over med-high heat. Add the shrimps in a single layer, and cook 1 to 2 minutes per side.
3. Add seasonings, and cook, stirring, 30 seconds. Serve garnished with cilantro and lime wedges.

Cajun Catfish

Preparation Time: 5 Minutes
Cooking Time: 15 Minutes
Servings: 4
Ingredients:
- 4 (8 oz.) Catfish fillets
- 2 Tbsps. olive oil
- 2 tsps. Garlic salt
- 2 tsps. Thyme
- 2 tsps. Paprika
- ½ tsp. cayenne pepper
- ½ tsp. red hot sauce
- ¼ tsp. black pepper
- Nonstick cooking spray

Directions:
1. Heat the oven to 450°F. Spray a 9x13-inch baking dish with cooking spray.
2. In a small bowl, whisk everything together but the catfish. Brush both sides of fillets, using all the spices mixed.
3. Bake 10 to 13 minutes or until fish flakes easily with a fork.

Cajun Flounder and Tomatoes

Preparation Time: 10 Minutes
Cooking Time: 15 Minutes
Servings: 4
Ingredients:
- 4 Flounder fillets
- 2 ½ C. tomatoes, diced
- ¾ C. onion, diced
- ¾ C. green bell pepper, diced
- 2 Garlic cloves, finely diced
- 1 Tbsp. Cajun seasoning
- 1 tsp. olive oil

Directions:
1. Heat oil in a large skillet over med-high heat. Add onion and garlic and cook 2 minutes, or until soft. Add tomatoes, peppers, and spices. Cook 2 to 3 or minutes until tomatoes soften.
2. Lay fish over the top. Cover, reduce the heat to medium, and cook, 5 to 8 minutes, or until fish flakes easily with a fork—transfer the fish to serving plates and top with sauce.

Crispy Calamari

Preparation time: 5 minutes
Cooking time: 15 minutes
Servings: 4
Ingredients:
- 1lb. fresh squid
- Salt and pepper
- 2cups flour
- 1cup water
- 2cloves garlic, minced
- 1/2cup mayonnaise

Directions:
1. Detach the skin from the squid and discard any ink. Slice the squid into rings and season with some salt and pepper.
2. Put the flour and water in separate bowls. Dip the squid firstly in the flour, then into the water, then into the flour again, ensuring that it is entirely covered with flour.
3. Pre-heat the air fryer at 400F. Put the squid inside and cook for six minutes.
4. In the meantime, prepare the aioli by combining the garlic with the mayonnaise in a bowl.
5. Once the squid is ready, plate up and serve with the aioli.

Cilantro Salmon

Preparation time: 5 minutes
Cooking time: 15 minutes
Servings: 4
- Ingredients:
- 4salmon fillets, boneless
- Juice of 1/2 lemon
- 1/4cup chives, chopped
- 4cilantro springs, chopped
- 3tablespoons olive oil
- Salt and black pepper to the taste

Directions:
1. In a bowl, mix the salmon with all the other Ingredients: and toss. Put the fillets in your air fryer's basket and cook at 370 degrees F for minutes, flipping the fish halfway. Divide everything between plates and serve with a side salad.

Sesame Salmon

Preparation time: 5 minutes
Cooking time: 15 minutes
Servings: 6
Ingredients:

- 18oz. salmon fillet
- 2 tablespoons swerve
- 1 tablespoon apple cider vinegar
- 6 teaspoons liquid aminos
- 1 teaspoon minced ginger
- 1 tablespoon sesame seeds
- 2 tablespoons lemon juice
- 1/2 teaspoon minced garlic
- 1 tablespoon avocado oil

Directions:
1. Cut the salmon fillet on 8 servings and sprinkle with apple cider vinegar, minced ginger, lemon juice, minced garlic, and liquid aminos. Leave the fish for -15 minutes to marinate. After this, sprinkle the fish with avocado oil and put in the preheated to 380F air fryer in one layer. Cook the fish fillets for 7 minutes. Then sprinkle them with swerve and sesame seeds and cook for 2 minutes more at 400F.

Old Bay Crab Sticks with Garlic Mayo

Preparation time: 5 minutes
Cooking time: 20 minutes
Servings: 4
Ingredients:
- 1 tbsp. old bay seasoning
- 1/3 cup panko breadcrumbs
- 1 egg
- 1/4 cup mayonnaise
- 2 garlic cloves, minced
- 1 lime, juiced
- 1 tsp. flour

Directions:
1. Warmth your Air Fryer to 390 F. Spray the air fryer basket with cooking spray.
2. Beat the eggs in a bowl. In a separate bowl, merge panko breadcrumbs with old bay seasoning. In a third bowl, pour the flour.
3. Dip the crab sticks in the flour and then in the eggs, and finally in the breadcrumb mixture. Spray with cooking spray and arrange on the cooking basket. Cook for 12 minutes, flipping halfway through.
4. Meanwhile, mix well all the mayonnaise with garlic and lime juice. Serve with crab sticks.

Mango Shrimp Skewers

Preparation time: 5 minutes
Cooking time: 20 minutes
Servings: 2
Ingredients:
- 2 tbsp. olive oil
- 1/2 tsp. garlic powder
- 1 tsp. dry mango powder
- 2 tbsp. fresh lime juice
- Salt and black pepper to taste

Directions:
1. In a bowl, mix well the garlic powder, mango powder, lime juice, salt, and pepper. Add the shrimp and toss to coat. Cover and allow to marinate for minutes.
2. Warmth your Air Fryer to 390 F. Spray the air fryer basket with cooking spray. Transfer the marinated shrimp to the cooking basket and drizzle the olive oil.
3. Cook for 5 minutes, slide out the fryer basket and shake the shrimp; cook for 5 minutes. Leave to cool and serve.

Salmon with Fennel and Carrot

Preparation Time: 15 Minutes
Cooking Time: 13 to 14 Minutes
Servings: 2
Ingredients:
- 1 Fennel bulb, thinly sliced
- 1 large carrot, peeled and sliced
- 1 Small onion, thinly sliced
- ¼ C. low-fat sour cream
- ¼ tsp. coarsely ground pepper
- 2 (5-oz. /142-g.) salmon fillets

Directions:
1. Combine the fennel, carrot, and onion in a bowl and toss.
2. Put the vegetable mixture into a baking pan. Prepare in the air fryer at 400°F (204°C) for 4 minutes or until the vegetables are crisp-tender.
3. Remove the pan from the air fryer. Stir in the sour cream and sprinkle the vegetables with the pepper.
4. Top with the salmon fillets.
5. Return the pan to the air fryer. Roast for another 9 to 10 minutes or until the salmon just barely flakes when tested with a fork.

Ranch Tilapia Fillets

Preparation Time: 7 Minutes
Cooking Time: 17 Minutes
Servings: 2 fillets
Ingredients:
- 2 Tbsps. flour
- 1 Egg, lightly beaten
- 1 C. crushed cornflakes
- 2 Tbsps. ranch seasoning
- 2 Tilapia fillets
- Olive oil spray

Directions:
1. Place a parchment liner in the air fryer basket.
2. Scoop the flour out onto a plate; set it aside.
3. Put the beaten egg in a medium shallow bowl.
4. Place the cornflakes in a zip-top bag and crush them with a rolling pin or another small, blunt object.
5. on another plate, mix to combine the crushed cereal and ranch seasoning.
6. Dredge the tilapia fillets in the flour, then dip in the egg, and then press into the cornflake mixture.
7. Place the prepared fillets on the liner in the air fryer in a single layer.
8. Spray lightly with olive oil and air fry at 400°F (204°C) for 8 minutes. Carefully flip the fillets and spray with more oil. Air fry for an additional 9 minutes, until golden and crispy, and serve.

Cilantro Lime Grilled Shrimp

Preparation Time: 5 Minutes
Cooking Time: 5 Minutes

Servings: 6
Ingredients:
- 1 1/2 lbs. large shrimp raw, peeled, deveined with tails on
- Juice and zest of 1 lime
- 2 Tbsps. fresh cilantro chopped
- ¼ C. olive oil
- 2 Cloves garlic, diced fine
- 1 tsp. smoked paprika
- ¼ tsp. cumin
- ½ tsp. salt
- ¼ tsp. cayenne pepper

Directions:
1. Place the shrimps in a large Ziploc bag.
2. Mix the remaining Ingredients: in a small bowl and pour over the shrimps. Let them marinate for 20-30 minutes.
3. Heat up the grill. Skewer the shrimps and cook 2 to 3 minutes, per side, just until they turn pink. Be careful not to overcook them. Serve garnished with cilantro.

Crab Frittata

Preparation Time: 10 Minutes
Cooking Time: 50 Minutes
Servings: 4
Ingredients:
- 4 Eggs
- 2 C.s lump crabmeat
- 1 C. half-n-half
- 1 C. green onions, diced
- 1 C. reduced fat parmesan cheese, grated
- 1 tsp. salt
- 1 tsp. pepper
- 1 tsp. smoked paprika
- 1 tsp. Italian seasoning
- Nonstick cooking spray

Directions:
1. Heat the oven to 350°F. Spray an 8-inch springform pan or pie plate with cooking spray.
2. In a large bowl, whisk together the eggs and half-n-half. Add seasonings and parmesan cheese, stir to mix.
3. Stir in the onions and the crabmeat. Pour into the prepared pan and bake 35 to 40 minutes, or until the eggs are set and the top is lightly browned.
4. Let cool for 10 minutes, then slice and serve warm or at room temperature.

Crunchy Lemon Shrimp

Preparation Time: 5 Minutes
Cooking Time: 10 Minutes
Servings: 4
Ingredients:
- 1 lb. raw shrimps, peeled and deveined
- 2 Tbsps. Italian parsley, roughly chopped
- 2 Tbsps. lemon juice, divided
- 2/3 C. panko bread crumbs
- 2 ½ Tbsp. olive oil, divided
- Salt and pepper, to taste

Directions:
1. Heat the oven to 400°F.
2. Place the shrimps evenly in a baking dish and sprinkle with salt and pepper. Drizzle on one Tbsp. lemon juice and one Tbsp. of olive oil. Set aside.
3. In a medium bowl, combine parsley, the remaining lemon juice, bread crumbs, the remaining olive oil, and ¼ tsp. each of salt and pepper. Layer the panko mixture evenly on top of the shrimps.
4. Bake for 8 to 10 minutes or until the shrimps are cooked through and the panko is golden brown.

Grilled Tuna Steaks

Preparation Time: 5 Minutes
Cooking Time: 10 Minutes
Servings: 6
Ingredients:
- 6 (6 oz.) Tuna steaks
- 3 Tbsps. fresh basil, diced
- 4 ½ Tsps. olive oil
- ¾ tsp. salt
- ¼ tsp. pepper
- Nonstick cooking spray

Directions:
1. Place a grill on medium heat. Apply cooking spray.
2. Drizzle both sides of the tuna with oil. Sprinkle with basil, salt, and pepper.
3. Place the tuna on the grill and cook 5 minutes per side; the tuna should be slightly pink in the center.

Chilean Sea Bass with Green Olive Relish

Preparation Time: 10 Minutes
Cooking Time: 16 to 20 Minutes
Servings: 4
Ingredients:
- Olive oil spray
- 2 (6-oz. /170-g.) Chilean sea bass fillets or other firm-fleshed white fish
- 3 Tbsps. extra-virgin olive oil
- ½ tsp. ground cumin
- ½ tsp. kosher salt
- ½ tsp. black pepper
- 1/3 C. pitted green olives, diced
- ¼ C. finely diced onion
- 1 tsp. chopped capers

Directions:
1. Spray the air fryer basket with olive oil spray. Drizzle the fillets with olive oil and sprinkle with cumin, salt, and pepper. Place the fish in the air fryer basket. Bake at 325°F (163°C) for 10 minutes or until the fish flakes easily with a fork.
2. In the meantime, in a lesser bowl, stir together the olives, onion, and capers.
3. Serve the fish topped with the relish.

Cilantro Lime Shrimp

Preparation Time: 15 Minutes
Cooking Time: 8 Minutes
Servings: 4
Ingredients:
- 1 tsp. extra virgin olive oil
- ½ tsp. garlic clove, minced

- 1 lb. (454 g.) large shrimps, peeled and deveined
- ¼ C. chopped fresh cilantro or more to taste
- 1 Lime, zested and juiced
- ¼ tsp. salt
- 1/8 tsp. black pepper

Directions:
1. In a large, heavy skillet, heat the olive oil over medium-high heat.
2. Add the minced garlic and cook for 30 seconds until fragrant.
3. Toss in the shrimps and cook for about 5 to 6 minutes, stirring occasionally, or until they turn pink and opaque.
4. Remove from the heat to a bowl. Add the cilantro, lime zest and juice, salt, and pepper to the shrimps, and toss to combine. Serve immediately.

Panko Coconut Shrimp

Preparation Time: 12 Minutes
Cooking Time: 8 Minutes
Servings: 4
Ingredients:
- 2 Egg whites
- 1 Tbsp. water
- ½ C. whole-wheat panko bread crumbs
- ¼ C. unsweetened coconut flakes
- ½ tsp. turmeric
- ½ tsp. ground coriander
- ½ tsp. ground cumin
- 1/8 tsp. salt
- 1 lb. (454 g.) large raw shrimps, peeled, deveined, and patted dry
- Nonstick cooking spray

Directions:
1. Preheat the air fry to 400°F (205°C).
2. In a shallow dish, beat the egg whites and water until slightly foamy. Set aside.
3. In a separate shallow dish, mix the bread crumbs, coconut flakes, turmeric, coriander, cumin, and salt, and stir until well combined.
4. Dredge the shrimps in the egg mixture, shaking off any excess, then coat them in the crumb-coconut mixture. Spritz the air fryer basket with nonstick cooking spray and arrange the coated shrimps in the basket. Air fry the shrimps for 6 to 8 minutes, flipping once during cooking, or until golden brown and cooked through.

Shrimp Coleslaw

Preparation Time: 10 Minutes
Cooking Time: 0 Minutes
Servings: 4
Ingredients:
- 1 lb. (454 g.) frozen cooked shrimps, thawed
- 1 (8-oz. /227-g.) package shredded cabbage
- 3 Tangerines, peeled and sectioned
- 3 Scallions, sliced
- 3 Tbsps. olive oil
- 2 tsps. Grated fresh ginger root
- 2 Tbsps. white rice vinegar
- 1/8 tsp. red pepper flakes
- 1 Avocado, peeled, pitted, and sliced
- ¼ C. toasted slivered almonds (optional)
- 3 Tbsps. chopped fresh cilantro

Directions:
1. Stir together the shrimps, cabbage, tangerines, scallions, olive oil, ginger root, vinegar, and red pepper flakes in a large bowl.
2. Transfer to the refrigerator to chill for at least 30 minutes.
3. When ready to serve, sprinkle the avocado slices, almonds (if desired), and cilantro on top. Serve immediately.

Easy Creamy Shrimp Nachos

Preparation time: 5 minutes
Cooking time: 15 minutes
Servings: 4
Ingredients:
- 1 pound shrimp, cleaned and deveined
- 1 tablespoon olive oil
- 2 tablespoons fresh lemon juice
- 1 teaspoon paprika
- 1/4 teaspoon cumin powder
- 1/2 teaspoon shallot powder
- 1/2 teaspoon garlic powder
- Coarse sea salt and black pepper, to flavor
- 1 (9-ounce bag corn tortilla chips
- 1/4 cup pickled jalapeño, minced
- 1 cup Pepper Jack cheese, grated
- 1/2 cup sour cream

Directions:
1. Set the shrimp with the olive oil, lemon juice, paprika, cumin powder, shallot powder, garlic powder, salt, and black pepper.
2. Cook in the preheated Air Fryer at 390 degrees F for 5 minutes.
3. Place the tortilla chips on the aluminum foil-lined cooking basket. Top with the shrimp mixture, jalapeño and cheese. Cook another 2 minutes or until cheese has melted.
4. Serve garnished with sour cream and enjoy

Roasted Red Snapper

Preparation Time: 20 minutes
Cooking Time: 0
Servings: 4
Ingredients:
- 4 red snapper fillets; boneless
- 2 garlic cloves; minced
- 1 tbsp. hot chili paste
- 2 tbsp. olive oil
- 2 tbsp. coconut aminos
- 2 tbsp. lime juice
- A pinch of salt and black pepper

Directions:
1. Take a bowl and merge all the Ingredients: except the fish and whisk well
2. Rub the fish with this mix, place it in your air fryer's basket and cook at 380°F for 15 minutes
3. Serve with a side salad.

Swordfish Steaks and Tomatoes

Preparation Time: 15 minutes
Cooking Time: 0
Servings: 2
Ingredients:

- 30oz. canned tomatoes; chopped.
- 2 1-inch-thick swordfish steaks
- 2tbsp. capers, drained
- 1tbsp. red vinegar
- 2tbsp. oregano; chopped.
- Pinch of salt and black pepper

Directions:
1. In a pan that fits the air fryer, combine all the Ingredients, toss, put the pan in the fryer and cook at 390F for 10 minutes, flipping the fish halfway
2. Divide the mix between plates and serve

Buttery Cod

Preparation Time: 13 minutes
Cooking Time: 0
Servings: 2
Ingredients:
- 2 (4-oz.cod fillets
- 1/2 medium lemon, sliced
- 2 tbsp. salted butter; melted.
- 1tsp. Old Bay seasoning

Directions:
1. Place cod fillets into a 6-inch round baking dish. Brush each fillet with butter and sprinkle with Old Bay seasoning. Lay two lemon slices on each fillet
2. Secure the dish with foil and place into the air fryer basket. Adjust the temperature to 350 Degrees F and set the timer for 8 minutes
3. Flip halfway through the cooking time. When cooked, internal temperature should be at least 145 Degrees F. serve warm.

Lemon Scallops with Asparagus

Preparation Time: 10 Minutes
Cooking Time: 7 to 10 Minutes
Servings: 4
Ingredients:
- ½ lb. (227 g.) asparagus, ends trimmed and cut into 2-inch pieces
- 1 C. sugar snap peas
- 1 lb. (454 g.) sea scallops
- 1 Tbsp. lemon juice
- 2 tsps. Olive oil
- ½ tsp. dried thyme
- Pinch salt
- Freshly ground black pepper, to taste

Directions:
1. Place the asparagus and sugar snap peas in the air fryer basket. Air fry at 400°F (204°C) for 2 to 3 minutes or until the vegetables are just getting tender.
2. Meanwhile, check the scallops for a small muscle Added to the side, pull it off, and discard.
3. In a medium bowl, toss the scallops with lemon juice, olive oil, thyme, salt, and pepper. Place into the air fryer basket on top of the vegetables.
4. Air fry for 5 to 7 minutes, tossing the basket once during the cooking time, and the vegetables are tender. Serve immediately.

Honey Lemon Snapper with Fruit

Preparation Time: 15 Minutes
Cooking Time: 9 to 13 Minutes
Servings: 4
Ingredients:
- 4 (4-oz. /113-g.) Red snapper fillets
- 2 tsps. Olive oil
- 3 Nectarines, halved and pitted
- 3 Plums, halved and pitted
- 1 C. red grapes
- 1 Tbsp. freshly squeezed lemon juice
- 1 Tbsp. honey
- ½ tsp. dried thyme

Directions:
1. Put the red snapper in the air fryer basket and drizzle with the olive oil. Air fry at 390°F (199°C) for 4 minutes.
2. Remove the basket and add the nectarines and plums. Scatter the grapes overall.
3. Drizzle with the lemon juice and honey and sprinkle with thyme.
4. Return the basket to the air fryer and air fry for 5 to 9 more minutes, or till the fish flakes when tested with a fork and the fruit is tender. Serve immediately.

Fresh Rosemary Trout

Preparation Time: 5 Minutes
Cooking Time: 8 Minutes
Servings: 2
Ingredients:
- 4 to 6 Fresh rosemary sprigs
- 8 oz. (227 g.) trout fillets, about ¼ inch thick; rinsed and patted dry
- ½ tsp. olive oil
- 1/8 tsp. salt - 1/8 tsp. pepper
- 1 tsp. fresh lemon juice

Directions:
1. Preheat the oven to 350°F (180°C).
2. Put the rosemary sprigs in a small baking pan in a single row. Spread the fillets on the top of the rosemary sprigs.
3. Brush both sides of each piece of fish with olive oil. Sprinkle with salt, pepper, and lemon juice.
4. Bake in the preheated oven for 7 to 8 minutes, or until the fish is opaque and flakes easily.
5. Divide the fillets between two plates and serve hot.

Asian-Inspired Swordfish Steaks

Preparation Time: 10 Minutes
Cooking Time: 6 to 11 Minutes
Servings: 4
Ingredients:
- 4 (4-oz. /113-g.) Swordfish steaks
- ½ tsp. toasted sesame oil
- 1 Jalapeño pepper, finely minced
- 2 Garlic cloves, grated
- 1 Tbsp. grated fresh ginger
- ½ tsp. Chinese five-spice powder
- 1/8 tsp. freshly ground black pepper
- 2 Tbsps. freshly squeezed lemon juice

Directions:
1. Place the swordfish steaks on a work surface and drizzle with the sesame oil.

2. In a small bowl, mix the jalapeño, garlic, ginger, five-spice powder, pepper, and lemon juice. Rub this mixture into the fish and let it stand for 10 minutes. Put in the air fryer basket.
3. Roast at 380°F (193°C) for 6 to 11 minutes, or until the swordfish reaches an inner temperature of at least 140°F (60°C) on a meat thermometer. Serve immediately.

Fish Tacos

Preparation Time: 15 Minutes
Cooking Time: 9 to 12 Minutes
Servings: 4
Ingredients:
- 1 lb. (454 g.) white fish fillets, such as snapper
- 1 Tbsp. olive oil
- 3 Tbsps. freshly squeezed lemon juice, divided
- 1½ C. chopped red cabbage
- ½ C. of salsa
- 1/3 C. sour cream
- 6 Whole-wheat tortillas
- 2 Avocados, peeled and chopped

Directions:
1. Skirmish the fish with olive oil and sprinkle with one Tbsp. of lemon juice. Set in the air fryer basket and air fry at 400°F (204°C) meant for 9 to 12 minutes.
2. Meanwhile, combine the remaining two Tbsps. of lemon juice, cabbage, salsa, and sour cream in a medium bowl.
3. As soon as the fish is cooked, remove it from the air fryer basket and break it into large pieces.
4. Let everyone assemble their taco combining the fish, tortillas, cabbage mixture, and avocados.

Lime Baked Salmon

Preparation Time: 22 minutes
Cooking Time: 0
Servings: 2
Ingredients:
- 2(3-oz. salmon fillets, skin removed
- 1/4cup sliced pickled jalapeños
- 1/2medium lime, juiced
- 2tbsp. chopped cilantro
- 1tbsp. salted butter; melted.
- 1/2tsp. finely minced garlic
- 1tsp. chili powder

Directions:
1. Place salmon fillets into a 6-inch round baking pan. Brush each with butter and sprinkle with chili powder and garlic
2. Place jalapeño slices on top and around salmon. Pour half of the lime juice over the salmon and cover with foil. Place pan into the air fryer basket. Adjust the temperature to 370 Degrees F and set the timer for 12 minutes
3. When fully cooked, salmon should flake easily with a fork and reach an internal temperature of at least 145 Degrees F.
4. To serve, spritz with remaining lime juice and garnish with cilantro.

Lime Trout and Shallots

Preparation Time: 17 minutes
Cooking Time: 0
Servings: 4
Ingredients:
- 4 trout fillets; boneless
- 3garlic cloves; minced
- 6shallots; chopped.
- 1/2cup butter; melted
- 1/2cup olive oil
- Juice of 1 lime
- A pinch of salt and black pepper

Directions:
1. In a pan that fits the air fryer, combine the fish with the shallots and the rest of the Ingredients, toss gently
2. Put the pan in the machine and cook at 390F for 12 minutes, flipping the fish halfway.
3. Cut between plates and serve with a side salad.

Healthy Tuna Croquettes

Servings: 4
Preparation Time: 4 minutes
Cooking Time: 9 minutes
Ingredients:
- 1 can tuna, drained
- 1 whole large egg
- 8 tablespoons parmesan cheese, grated
- 2 tablespoons flax meal
- Salt and pepper to taste
- 1 tablespoons onion, minced

Directions:
1. Add all of the ingredients to a blender (except flax meal) and pulse the mixture into a crunchy texture
2. Form patties using the mixture
3. Dip both sides of the patties in flax meals and fry them in hot oil until both sides are browned well

Generous Stuffed Salmon Avocado

Servings: 2
Preparation Time: 10 minutes
Cooking Time: 30 minutes
Ingredients:
- 1 ripe organic avocado
- 2 ounces wild-caught smoked salmon
- 1-ounce fresh goat cheese
- 2 tablespoons extra virgin olive oil
- Salt as needed

Directions:
1. Cut avocado in half and deseed
2. Add rest of the ingredients to a food processor and process until coarsely chopped
3. Place mixture into avocado
4. Serve and enjoy!

Baked Halibut Delight

Servings: 8
Preparation Time: 15 minutes
Cooking Time: 30 minute
Ingredients:
- 6 ounces halibut fillets
- 1 tablespoon Greek seasoning
- 1 large tomato, chopped
- 1 onion, chopped
- 5 ounces kalamata olives, pitted

- ¼ cup capers
- ¼ cup olive oil
- 1 tablespoon lemon juice
- Salt and pepper as needed

Directions:
1. Preheat your oven to 350 degrees Fahrenheit
2. Transfer the halibut fillets to a large aluminum foil
3. Season with Greek seasoning
4. Take a bowl and add tomato, onion, olives, olive oil, capers, pepper, lemon juice, and salt
5. Mix well and spoon the tomato mix over the halibut
6. Seal the edges and fold to make a packet
7. Place the packet on a baking sheet and bake in your oven for 30-40 minutes
8. Serve once the fish flakes off, and enjoy!

Hungry Tuna Bites

Servings: 2
Preparation Time: 10 minutes
Cooking Time: 10 minutes
Ingredients:

- 10 ounces of Canned Tuna, drained
- ¼ cup Keto-Friendly mayonnaise
- 1 medium avocado, cubed
- ¼ cup parmesan cheese
- 1/3 cup almond flour
- ½ teaspoon garlic powder
- ¼ teaspoon onion powder
- Salt and pepper as needed
- ½ cup coconut oil

Directions:
1. Take a mixing bowl and add the listed ingredients except for coconut oil and avocado
2. Take the cubed avocado and carefully fold them in the tuna mix
3. Mix well and turn the mixture into balls
4. Roll the balls into almond flour
5. Take a pan over medium heat and add coconut oil
6. Allow the oil to heat up
7. Add tuna balls and cook them well until you have a brown texture
8. Serve and enjoy!

Tilapia Broccoli Platter

Servings: 2
Preparation Time: 4 minutes
Cooking Time: 14 minutes
Ingredients:

- 6 ounces of tilapia, frozen
- 1 tablespoon of butter
- 1 tablespoon of garlic, minced
- 1 teaspoon of lemon pepper seasoning
- 1 cup of broccoli florets, fresh

Directions:
1. Preheat your oven to 350 degrees F
2. Add fish in aluminum foil packets
3. Arrange broccoli around fish
4. Sprinkle lemon pepper on top
5. Close the packets and seal
6. Bake for 14 minutes

7. Take a bowl and add garlic and butter, mix well and keep the mixture on the side
8. Remove the packet from the oven and transfer it to a platter
9. Place butter on top of the fish and broccoli, serve and enjoy!

Simple Baked Shrimp With Béchamel Sauce

Servings: 4
Preparation Time: 10 minutes
Cooking Time: 5-7 minutes
Ingredients:

- 6-7 ounces of shrimp
- 1-ounce mozzarella
- 4 ounces béchamel sauce (recipe provided)
- 1 tablespoons ghee

Directions:
1. Cut boiled shrimp and transfer them to a baking dish
2. Pour sauce on top
3. Bake for 5-7 minutes
4. Serve and enjoy!

Simple Sautéed Garlic And Parsley Scallops

Servings: 4
Preparation Time: 5 minutes
Cooking Time: 25 minutes
Ingredients:

- 8 tablespoons butter
- 2 garlic cloves, minced
- 16 large sea scallops
- Salt and pepper to taste
- 1 and ½ tablespoons olive oil

Directions:
1. Seasons scallops with salt and pepper
2. Take a skillet and place it over medium heat, add oil and let it heat up
3. Saute scallops for 2 minutes per side; repeat until all Scallops are cooked
4. Add butter to the skillet and let it melt
5. Stir in garlic and cook for 15 minutes
6. Return scallops to skillet and stir to coat
7. Serve and enjoy!

Mesmerizing Coconut Haddock

Servings: 3
Preparation Time: 10 minutes
Cooking Time: 12 minutes
Ingredients:

- 4 haddock fillets, 5 ounces each, boneless
- 2 tablespoons coconut oil, melted
- 1 cup coconut, shredded and unsweetened
- ¼ cup hazelnuts, ground
- Salt to taste

Directions:
1. Preheat your oven to 400-degree F
2. Line a baking sheet with parchment paper
3. Keep it on the side
4. Pat fish fillets with a paper towel and season with salt
5. Take a bowl and stir in hazelnuts and shredded coconut

6. Drag fish fillets through the coconut mix until both sides are coated well
7. Transfer to baking dish
8. Brush with coconut oil
9. Bake for about 12 minutes until flaky
10. Serve and enjoy!

"Salmon" Platter

Servings: 3
Preparation Time: 5 minutes
Cooking Time: 6 minutes
Ingredients
- ¾ cup of water
- Few sprigs of parsley, basil, tarragon, basil
- 1 pound of salmon, skin on
- 3 teaspoons of ghee
- ¼ teaspoon of salt
- ½ teaspoon of pepper
- ½ of lemon, thinly sliced
- 1 whole carrot, julienned

Directions:
1. Set your pot to Saute mode, and water and herbs
2. Place a steamer rack inside your pot and place salmon
3. Drizzle Ghee on top of the salmon and season with salt and pepper
4. Cover lemon slices
5. Lock up the lid and cook on HIGH pressure for 3 minutes
6. Release the pressure naturally over 10 minutes
7. Transfer the salmon to a serving platter
8. Set your pot to Saute mode and add vegetables
9. Cook for 1-2 minutes
10. Serve with vegetables and salmon
11. Enjoy!

Feisty Bacon Scallops

Servings: 4
Preparation Time: 10 minutes
Cooking Time: 23 minutes
Ingredients:
- 1 pound bacon, uncured
- 2 pounds sea scallops, fresh and patted dry
- Lemon wedges
- 3 tablespoon golden ghee
- ¼ cup dry white wine

Directions:
1. Line two baking sheets with parchment paper
2. Preheat your oven to 400-degree F
3. Put bacon strips on a sheet evenly, bake for 15 minutes
4. Crumbled once cooked and cooled
5. Take a skillet and place it over high heat
6. Pour the grease and heat it up
7. Brown scallops in oil, cook for 3 minutes on each side
8. Set scallops on the side and add wine to the skillet
9. Use wine to deglaze the pan, scrape brown bits
10. Add ghee and make a wine sauce
11. Add scallops and bacon
12. Toss and cook for 1 minute more
13. Enjoy!

Grilled Lime Shrimp

Servings: 8
Preparation Time: 25 minutes
Cooking Time: 5 minutes
Ingredients:
- 1 pound medium shrimp, peeled and deveined
- 1 lime, juiced
- ½ cup olive oil
- 3 tablespoons Cajun seasoning

Directions:
1. Take a re-sealable zip bag and add lime juice, Cajun seasoning, olive oil
2. Add shrimp and shake it well; let it marinate for 20 minutes
3. Preheat your outdoor grill to medium heat
4. Lightly grease the grate
5. Remove shrimp from marinade and cook for 2 minutes per side
6. Serve and enjoy!

Mouthwatering Calamari

Servings: 4
Preparation Time: 10 minutes +1-hour marinating
Cooking Time: 8 minutes
Ingredients:
- 2 tablespoons extra virgin olive oil
- 1 teaspoon chili powder
- ½ teaspoon ground cumin
- Zest of 1 lime
- Juice of 1 lime
- Dash of sea salt
- 1 and ½ pounds squid, cleaned and split open, with tentacles cut into ½-inch rounds
- 2 tablespoons cilantro, chopped
- 2 tablespoons red bell pepper, minced

Directions:
1. Take a medium bowl and stir in olive oil, chili powder, cumin, lime zest, sea salt, lime juice, and pepper
2. Add squid and let it marinade and stir to coat, coat and let it refrigerate for 1 hour
3. Preheat your oven to broil
4. Arrange squid on a baking sheet, broil for 8 minutes turn once until tender
5. Garnish the broiled calamari with cilantro and red bell pepper
6. Serve and enjoy!

Salmon And Zesty Cream Sauce

Servings: 4
Preparation Time: 10 minutes
Cooking Time: 5-7 minutes
Ingredients:
- 2 boneless salmon or trout fillets
- 1/3 cup sour cream
- 2 tsp mustard
- 1 tbsp lemon juice
- 1/2 tsp dill
- 1 tsp lemon zest

Directions:
1. Mix all the cream ingredients and spices together in a small bowl.
2. Season with salt and pepper to taste and set aside.

3. Lightly grease a shallow pan and cook the fillets for 2-3 minutes on each side (for a medium to well-done result).
4. Serve on a dish and pour the sauce on top or side. You can serve it also with some broccoli or asparagus for an extra kick of taste and nutrients

Crisped Up Coconut Shrimp
Servings: 4
Preparation Time: 10 minutes
Cooking Time: 20 minutes
Ingredients:
- 1 pound of large shrimp (peeled and deveined)
- ½ cup coconut flour
- 1 tsp cayenne seasoning (salt included)
- 3 eggs beaten
- 1/2 cup unsweetened coconut flakes

Directions:
1. Keep the coconut flour with the seasoning, coconut flakes, and beaten eggs in separate bowls.
2. Dip and roll in the shrimps (one by one) into the coconut flour mixture, shake off the excess flour, dip in the eggs and then roll in last to the unsweetened coconut flakes.
3. Heat one cup of oil and fry the shrimps for 4-5 minutes or until golden brown.
4. Serve in a shallow dish with absorbing paper and serve with hot mayo (mayo with cayenne seasoning)

Spiced Up Tuna Avocado Balls
Servings: 4
Preparation Time: 10 minutes
Cooking Time: Nil
Ingredients:
- 2 avocados halved
- 1/2 lb of sushi-grade ahi tuna (or smoked tuna if you can't find any)
- 2 tbsp of mayo
- 1-2 sriracha sauce
- 1 tsp of toasted sesame seeds

Directions:
1. Mix the tuna with the mayo, sriracha sauce, and toasted sesame seeds in a small bowl.
2. Scoop and distribute the mixture onto the avocado halves.
3. Add some extra sriracha sauce optionally on top

Asian Glazed Salmon and Cauliflower
Servings: 4
Preparation Time: 10 minutes
Cooking Time: 5 minutes
Ingredients:
- 4 boneless fillets of salmon
- 2 cups (around 550 grams) of frozen cauliflower rice (or freshly ground cauliflower rice using a food processor)
- 4 tbsp of liquid aminos or soy sauce
- 2 tbsp of shallots, chopped finely
- 2 tbsp of sesame oil

Directions:
1. Make a marinade of the liquid aminos, shallots, and sesame oil and combine them into a bowl.
2. Soak the salmon fillets in the marinade and optionally refrigerate for at least an hour before cooking.
3. Pop these into the oven and bake for 10-12 minutes.
4. While the salmon cooks, heat and prepare the frozen cauliflower rice according to package instructions.
5. Serve the salmon over the cauliflower rice hot

Shrimp And Bacon Zoodles
Servings: 4
Preparation Time: 10 minutes
Cooking Time: 12 minutes
Ingredients:
- 1 lb of fresh peeled and deveined shrimp
- 5/4 cup of salted butter
- 2 cloves of garlic mashed
- 2-3 stripes of beef bacon, chopped
- 1 zucchini, made into zoodles using a spiralizer or mandolin slicer

Directions:
1. Heat a skillet, add the butter and shrimp and cook for 2 minutes on each side.
2. Add the garlic and cook for another minute.
3. Remove the shrimps from the heat and add the bacon and the zucchini noodles in the garlic oil. Cook tossing for 4-5 minutes.
4. Return the shrimps to the bacon zoodles, toss, and transfer to a deep dish.
5. Sprinkle optionally with some freshly grated parmesan

Baked Lobster Tails And Garlic Butter
Servings: 4
Preparation Time: 10 minutes
Cooking Time: 15 minutes
Ingredients:
- 4 lobster tails
- 1 lemon juiced
- 5 cloves of garlic
- 1/4 cup grated parmesan
- 4 tbsp of salted butter

Directions:
1. Preheat oven to 375F/180C. In a small bowl, combine the lemon juice, garlic, and grated parmesan.
2. Cut the clear skin, remove the lobster, and brush the tails with the garlic butter mix using kitchen shears.
3. Place on a baking sheet with parchment paper on top and bake in the oven for 15 minutes

Spicy Sea Bass Hazelnuts
Servings: 4
Preparation Time: 10 minutes
Cooking Time: 15-20 minutes
Ingredients:
- 2 sea bass fillets
- 2 tbsp butter
- 1/3 cup roasted hazelnuts
- A pinch of cayenne pepper

Directions:
1. Preheat your oven to 425·5F.

2. Line a baking dish with waxed paper. Melt the butter and brush it over the fish.
3. Process the cayenne pepper and hazelnuts in a food processor to achieve a smooth consistency. Coat the sea bass with the hazelnut mixture.
4. Place in the oven and bake for about 15 minutes

Perfectly Marinated Grilled Salmon

Servings: 4
Preparation Time: 10-50 minutes
Cooking Time: 10-20 minutes
Ingredients:
- 4 5-ounce salmon steaks
- 2 cloves garlic, pressed
- 4 tablespoons olive oil
- 1 tablespoon taco seasoning mix
- 2 tablespoons fresh lemon juice

Directions:
1. Place all the above ingredients in a ceramic dish; cover and let it marinate for 40 minutes in your refrigerator.
2. Place the salmon steaks onto a lightly oiled grill pan; place under the grill for 6 minutes.
3. Turn them over and cook for 5 to 6 minutes, basting with the reserved marinade; remove from the grill.
4. Serve immediately and enjoy

Salmon Fat Bombs

Servings: 4
Preparation Time: 10 minutes
Cooking Time: Nil
Ingredients:
- 2 tbsp cream cheese, softened
- 1 ounce smoked salmon
- 2 tsp bagel seasoning

Directions:
1. Take a medium bowl, place cream cheese and salmon, and stir until well combined.
2. Shape the mixture into balls, roll them into bagel seasoning and then serve

Baked Cod And Tomato Capers Delight

Servings: 4
Preparation Time: 10 minutes
Cooking Time: 25 minutes
Ingredients:
- 4 cod fillets, boneless
- 2 tablespoons avocado oil
- 1 cup tomato passata
- 2 tablespoons capers, drained
- 2 tablespoons parsley, chopped

Directions:
1. In a roasting pan, combine the cod with the oil and the other ingredients, toss gently, introduce in the oven at 370 degrees F and bake for 25 minutes.
2. Divide between plates and serve

Perfect Tuna Salad And Pickle Boats

Servings: 4
Preparation Time: 10 minutes + 30 minutes chill time
Cooking Time: Nil
Ingredients:
- 18 oz canned and drained tuna
- 6 large dill pickles
- 1/a tsp garlic powder
- 1/4 cup sugar-free mayonnaise
- 1 tsp onion powder

Directions:
1. Mix the mayo, tuna, onion, and garlic powders in a bowl. Cut the pickles in half, lengthwise. Top each half with a tuna mixture.
2. Place in the fridge for 30 minutes and serve

Tuna And Spinach Salad

Servings: 4
Preparation Time: 10 minutes
Cooking Time: Nil
Ingredients:
- 2 oz of spinach leaves
- 2 oz tuna, packed in water
- 1/4 tsp ground black pepper
- 1/4 tsp sea salt
- 2 tbsp coconut oil, melted

Directions:
1. Take a salad bowl, place spinach leaves in it, drizzle with 1 tbsp oil, sprinkle with 1/8 tsp of salt and black pepper, and then toss until mixed.
2. Top with tuna, sprinkle with remaining salt and black pepper, drizzle with oil and then serve

Grilled Fish Salad Nicoise

Servings: 4
Preparation Time: 10 minutes
Cooking Time: 10-15 minutes
Ingredients:
- 3/4 pound tuna fillet, skinless
- 1 white onion, sliced
- 1 teaspoon Dijon mustard
- 8 Nicoise olives, pitted and sliced
- 1/2 teaspoon anchovy paste

Directions:
1. Brush the tuna with nonstick cooking oil; season with salt and freshly cracked black pepper. Then, grill your tuna on a lightly oiled rack for approximately 7 minutes, turning over once or twice.
2. Let the fish stand for 3 to 4 minutes and break into bite-sized pieces. Transfer to a nice salad bowl.
3. Toss the tuna pieces with the white onion, Dijon mustard, Nicoise olives, and anchovy paste. Serve well chilled, and enjoy!

Broiled Chili Calamari

Serving: 4
Preparation Time: 10 minutes +1-hour marinating
Cooking Time: 8 minutes
Ingredients
- 2 tablespoons extra virgin olive oil
- 1 teaspoon chili powder

- ½ teaspoon ground cumin
- Zest of 1 lime
- Juice of 1 lime
- Dash of sea salt
- 1 and ½ pounds squid, cleaned and split open, with tentacles cut into ½-inch rounds
- 2 tablespoons cilantro, chopped
- 2 tablespoons red bell pepper, minced

Directions:
1. Take a medium bowl and stir in olive oil, chili powder, cumin, lime zest, sea salt, lime juice, and pepper
2. Add squid and let it marinade and stir to coat, coat and let it refrigerate for 1 hour
3. Preheat your oven to broil
4. Arrange squid on a baking sheet, broil for 8 minutes turn once until tender
5. Garnish the broiled calamari with cilantro and red bell pepper
6. Serve and enjoy!

Potato And Tuna Salad

Serving: 4
Preparation Time:10 minutes
Cooking Time: nil
Ingredients
- 1 pound of baby potatoes, scrubbed, boiled
- 1 cup tuna chunks, drained
- 1 cup cherry tomatoes, halved
- 1 cup medium onion, thinly sliced
- 8 pitted black olives
- 2 medium hard-boiled eggs, sliced
- 1 head of Romaine lettuce
- Honey lemon mustard dressing
- ¼ cup olive oil
- 2 tablespoons lemon juice
- 1 tablespoon Dijon mustard
- 1 teaspoon dill weed, chopped
- Salt as needed
- Pepper as needed

Directions:
1. Take a small glass bowl and mix in your olive oil, honey, lemon juice, Dijon mustard, and dill
2. Season the mix with pepper and salt
3. Add in the tuna, baby potatoes, cherry tomatoes, red onion, green beans, and black olives, and toss everything nicely
4. Arrange your lettuce leaves on a beautiful serving dish to make the base of your salad
5. Top them up with your salad mixture, and place the egg slices
6. Drizzle it with the previously prepared Salad Dressing
7. Serve hot

Three Citrus Sauce Scallops

Serving: 4
Preparation Time:10 minutes
Cooking Time: 15 minutes
Ingredients
- 2 teaspoons extra virgin olive oil
- 1 shallot, minced
- 20 sea scallops, cleaned
- 1 tablespoon lemon zest
- 2 teaspoons orange zest
- 1 teaspoon lime zest
- 1 tablespoon fresh basil, chopped
- ½ cup freshly squeezed lemon juice
- 2 tablespoons honey
- 1 tablespoon plain Greek yogurt
- Pinch of sea salt

Directions:
1. Take a large skillet and place it over medium-high heat
2. Add olive oil and heat it up
3. Add shallots and Saute for 1 minute
4. Add scallops to the skillet and sear for 5 minutes, turning once
5. Move scallops to the edge and stir in lemon, orange, lime zest, basil, orange juice, and lemon juice
6. Simmer the sauce for 3 minutes
7. Whisk in honey, yogurt, and salt
8. Cook for 4 minutes and coat the scallops in the sauce
9. Serve and enjoy!

Heartthrob Mediterranean Tilapia

Serving: 4
Preparation Time:15 minutes
Cooking Time: 15 minute
Ingredients
- 3 tablespoons sun-dried tomatoes, packed in oil, drained, and chopped
- 1 tablespoon capers, drained
- 2 tilapia fillets
- 1 tablespoon oil from sun-dried tomatoes
- 1 tablespoon lemon juice
- 2 tablespoons kalamata olives, chopped and pitted

Directions:
1. Preheat your oven to 372 degrees Fahrenheit
2. Take a small-sized bowl and add sun-dried tomatoes, olives, and capers and stir well
3. Keep the mixture on the side
4. Take a baking sheet and transfer the tilapia fillets and arrange them side by side
5. Drizzle olive oil all over them
6. Drizzle lemon juice
7. Bake in your oven for 10-15 minutes
8. After 10 minutes, check the fish for a "Flaky" texture
9. Once cooked properly, top the fish with tomato mixture and serve!

Citrus Poached Lovely Salmon

Serving: 4
Preparation Time:10 minutes
Cooking Time: 40 minutes
Ingredients
- 6 cups water
- ½ cup freshly squeezed lemon juice
- Juice of 1 lime
- Zest of 1 lime
- 1 sweet onion, thinly sliced
- 1 cup celery leaves, coarsely chopped
- 1 tablespoon fresh dill, chopped

- 1 tablespoon fresh thyme, chopped
- 2 dried bay leaves
- ½ teaspoon black peppercorns
- ½ teaspoon sea salt
- 1 (24 ounces) salmon side, skinned and deboned, cut into 4 pieces

Directions:
1. Take a large saucepan and place it over medium-high heat
2. Stir water, lemon, lime juice, lem0on juice, lime zest, onion, celery, greens, thyme, dill, and bay leaves
3. Strain the liquid through a fine-mesh sieve, discard any solids
4. Pour strained poaching liquid into a large skillet over low heat
5. Bring to a simmer
6. Add fish and cover skillet; poach for 10 minutes until opaque
7. Remove salmon from liquid and serve
8. Enjoy!

A Great Mediterranean Snapper

Serving: 2
Preparation Time:20 minutes
Cooking Time: 10 minute
Ingredients

- 2 tablespoons extra virgin olive oil
- 1 medium onion, chopped
- 2 garlic cloves, minced
- 1 teaspoon oregano
- 1 can (14 ounces) tomatoes, diced with juice
- ½ cup black olives, sliced
- 4 red snapper fillets (every 4 ounces)
- Salt and pepper as needed

Garnish
- ¼ cup feta cheese, crumbled
- ¼ cup parsley, minced

Directions:
1. Preheat your oven to a temperature of 425 degrees Fahrenheit
2. Take a 13x9 inch baking dish and grease it up with non-stick cooking spray
3. Take a large-sized skillet and place it over medium heat
4. Add oil and heat it up
5. Add onion, oregano, and garlic
6. Saute for 2 minutes
7. Add diced tomatoes with juice alongside black olives
8. Bring the mix to a boil
9. Remove the heat
10. Place the fish on the prepped baking dish
11. Season both sides with salt and pepper
12. Spoon the tomato mix over the fish
13. Bake for 10 minutes
14. Remove the oven and sprinkle a bit of parsley and feta
15. Enjoy!

Trout With Wilted Greens

Serving: 4
Preparation Time:5 minutes
Cooking Time: 15 minutes
Ingredients

- 2 teaspoons extra virgin olive oil
- 2 cups kale, chopped
- 2 cups Swiss chard, chopped
- ½ sweet onion, thinly sliced
- 4 (5 ounces) boneless skin-on trout fillets
- Juice of 1 lemon
- Sea salt
- Freshly ground pepper
- Zest of 1 lemon

Directions:
1. Preheat your oven to 375 degrees Fahrenheit
2. Lightly grease a 9 by a 13-inch baking dish with olive oil
3. Arrange the kale, Swiss chard, and onion in a dish
4. Top greens with fish, skin side up, and drizzle with olive oil and lemon juice
5. Season fish with salt and pepper
6. Bake for 15 minutes until fish flakes
7. Sprinkle zest
8. Serve and enjoy!

Garlic And Shrimp Pasta

Serving: 4
Preparation Time:5 minutes
Cooking Time: 15 minute
Ingredients

- 6 ounces whole-wheat spaghetti
- 12 ounces raw shrimp, peeled and deveined, cut into 1-inch pieces
- 1 bunch asparagus, trimmed
- 1 large bell pepper, thinly sliced
- 1 cup of fresh peas
- 3 garlic cloves, chopped
- 1 and ¼ teaspoons kosher salt
- ½ and ½ cups non-fat plain yogurt
- 3 tablespoon lemon juice
- 1 tablespoon extra-virgin olive oil
- ½ teaspoon fresh ground black pepper
- ¼ cup pine nuts, toasted

Directions:
1. Take a large-sized pot and bring water to a boil
2. Add your spaghetti and cook them for about 2 minutes less than the directed package instruction
3. Add shrimp, bell pepper, and asparagus and cook for about 2- 4 minutes until the shrimp are tender
4. Drain the pasta and the contents well
5. Take a large bowl and mash garlic until a paste forms
6. Whisk in yogurt, parsley, oil, pepper, and lemon juice into the garlic paste
7. Add pasta mixture and toss well
8. Serve by sprinkling some pine nuts!
9. Enjoy!

Cool Mediterranean Fish

Serving: 8
Preparation Time:15 minutes
Cooking Time: 30 minute
Ingredients

- 6 ounces halibut fillets
- 1 tablespoon Greek seasoning
- 1 large tomato, chopped
- 1 onion, chopped

- 5 ounces kalamata olives, pitted
- ¼ cup capers
- ¼ cup olive oil
- 1 tablespoon lemon juice
- Salt and pepper as needed

Directions:
1. Preheat your oven to 350 degrees Fahrenheit
2. Transfer the halibut fillets to a large aluminum foil
3. Season with Greek seasoning
4. Take a bowl and add tomato, onion, olives, olive oil, capers, pepper, lemon juice, and salt
5. Mix well and spoon the tomato mix over the halibut
6. Seal the edges and fold to make a packet
7. Place the packet on a baking sheet and bake in your oven for 30-40 minutes
8. Serve once the fish flakes off, and enjoy!

Pistachio Sole Fish

Serving: 4
Preparation Time: 5 minutes
Cooking Time: 10 minutes

Ingredients
- 4 (5 ounces) boneless sole fillets
- Salt and pepper as needed
- ½ cup pistachios, finely chopped
- Zest of 1 lemon
- Juice of 1 lemon
- 1 teaspoon extra virgin olive oil

Directions:
1. Preheat your oven to 350 degrees Fahrenheit
2. Line a baking sheet with parchment paper and keep it on the side
3. Pat fish dry with kitchen towels and lightly season with salt and pepper
4. Take a small bowl and stir in pistachios and lemon zest
5. Place sol on the prepped sheet and press 2 tablespoons of pistachio mixture on top of each fillet
6. Drizzle fish with lemon juice and olive oil
7. Bake for 10 minutes until the top is golden and fish flakes with a fork
8. Serve and enjoy!

Chapter 8

Vegetables Sides

Delicious Golden Onion Rings
Preparation time: 5 minutes
Cooking time: 15 minutes
Servings: 4
Ingredients:
- 1 large onion, slice ½-inch thick
- 1 egg
- ¼ cup sunflower oil
- 2 tablespoons coconut flour
- 2 tablespoons reduced fat Parmesan cheese
- 1/4 teaspoon parsley flakes
- 1/8 teaspoon garlic powder
- 1/8 teaspoon cayenne pepper
- Salt, to taste
- Ketchup, for serving

Directions:
1. Heat oil in a large skillet over medium-high heat.
2. In a shallow bowl, combine flour, Parmesan, and seasonings.
3. Beat the egg.
4. Separate onion slices into individual rings and place in large bowl, adds beaten egg and toss to coat well. Let rest 1 to 2 minutes.
5. In small batches, coat onion in flour mixture and add to skillet. Cook 1 to 2 minutes per side, or until golden brown. Transfer to paper towel lined cookie sheet.
6. Serve with ketchup.

Whole Wheat Bread Zucchini Bake
Preparation time: 5 minutes
Cooking time: 10 minutes
Servings: 6
Ingredients:
- 1 large zucchini, sliced into ¼-inch circle
- ¼ cup reduced fat, Parmesan cheese, grated fine - 3 tablespoons low-fat milk
- 1/3 cup whole wheat breadcrumbs
- ½ teaspoon garlic powder
- 1/8 Teaspoon cayenne pepper
- Nonstick cooking spray

Directions:
1. After slicing zucchini pat dry with paper towels. Let sit for 60 minutes before using. Then pat dry again.
2. Heat oven to 425°F (220°C). Spray a wire rack with cooking spray and place on cookie sheet.
3. In a medium bowl combine all except milk and zucchini. Pour milk into a shallow bowl.
4. Dip zucchini into milk the coat with bread crumb mixture. Place on wire rack and bake 10 to 15 minutes or until browned and crisp. Serve immediately.

Rainbow Vegetable Fritters
Preparation Time: 20 Minutes
Cooking Time: 10 Minutes
Servings: 2
Ingredients:
- 1 Zucchini, grated and squeezed
- 1 C. corn kernels
- ½ C. canned green peas
- 4 Tbsps. all-purpose flour
- 2 Tbsps. fresh shallots, minced
- 1 tsp. fresh garlic, minced
- 1 Tbsp. peanut oil
- Sea salt and pepper, to taste
- 1 tsp. cayenne pepper

Directions:
1. In a mixing bowl, thoroughly combine all Ingredients: until everything is well incorporated.
2. Shape the mixture into patties. Spritz the Air Fryer carrier with cooking spray.
3. Cook in the preheated Air Fryer at 365°F for 6 minutes. Place on top and cook for another 6 minutes. Serve immediately and enjoy!

Mediterranean Vegetable Skewers
Preparation Time: 30 Minutes
Cooking Time: 10 Minutes
Servings: 4
Ingredients:
- 2 Medium-sized zucchinis, cut into 1-inch pieces
- 2 Red bell peppers, cut into 1-inch pieces
- 1 Green bell pepper, cut into 1-inch pieces
- 1 Red onion, cut into 1-inch pieces
- 2 Tbsps. olive oil
- Sea salt, to taste
- ½ tsp. black pepper, preferably freshly cracked
- ½ tsp. red pepper flakes

Directions:
1. Soak the wooden skewers in water for 15 minutes.
2. Thread the vegetables on skewers; drizzle olive oil all over the vegetable skewers; sprinkle with spices. 3. Cook in the preheated Air Fryer at 400°F for 13 minutes. Serve warm and enjoy!

Roasted Veggies with Yogurt-Tahini Sauce
Preparation Time: 20 Minutes
Cooking Time: 10 Minutes
Servings: 4
Ingredients:

- 1 lb. Brussels sprouts
- 1 lb. button mushrooms
- 2 Tbsps. olive oil
- ½ tsp. white pepper
- ½ tsp. dried dill weed
- ½ tsp. cayenne pepper
- ½ tsp. celery seeds
- ½ Tsp. mustard seeds
- Salt, to taste

For the yogurt tahini sauce:
- 1 C. plain yogurt
- 2 Heaping Tbsps. tahini paste
- 1 Tbsp. lemon juice
- 1 Tbsp. extra-virgin olive oil
- ½ tsp. Aleppo pepper, minced

Directions:
1. Toss the Brussels sprouts and mushrooms with olive oil and spices. Preheat your Air Fryer to 380°F.
2. Add the Brussels sprouts to the cooking basket and cook for 10 minutes.
3. Add the mushrooms, turn the temperature to 390°F and cook for six more minutes.
4. While the vegetables are cooking, make the sauce by whisking all Ingredients. Serve the warm vegetables with the sauce on the side. Bon appétit!

Swiss cheese and Vegetable Casserole

Preparation Time: 50 Minutes
Cooking Time: 10 Minutes
Servings: 4
Ingredients:
- 1 lb. Potatoes, peeled and sliced (¼-inch thick
- 2 Tbsps. olive oil
- ½ tsp. red pepper flakes, crushed
- ½ tsp. freshly ground black pepper
- Salt, to taste
- 3 Bell peppers, thinly sliced
- 1 Serrano pepper, thinly sliced
- 2 Medium-sized tomatoes, sliced
- 1 Leek, thinly sliced
- 2 Garlic cloves, minced
- 1 C. Swiss cheese, shredded

Directions:
1. Start by warming your Air Fryer to 350°F. Spritz a casserole dish with cooking oil.
2. Place the potatoes in the casserole dish in an even layer; drizzle one Tbsp. of olive oil over the top. Then swell the red pepper, black pepper, and salt.
3. Add two bell peppers and half of the leeks. Add the tomatoes and the remaining Tbsp. of olive oil.
4. Add the remaining peppers, leeks, and minced garlic. Top with the cheese.
5. Cover the casserole with foil and bake for 32 minutes. Remove the foil and increase the temperature to 400°F; bake an additional 16 minutes. Bon appétit!

American-Style Brussels Sprout Salad

Preparation Time: 35 Minutes
Cooking Time: 10 Minutes
Servings: 4
Ingredients:
- 1 lb. Brussels sprouts
- 1 Apple, cored and diced
- ½ C. mozzarella cheese, crumbled
- ½ C. pomegranate seeds
- 1 Small-sized red onion, chopped
- 4 Eggs, hardboiled and sliced

For the dressing:
- ¼ C. olive oil - 2 Tbsps. champagne vinegar
- 1 tsp. Dijon mustard
- 1 tsp. honey
- Sea salt and ground black pepper, to taste

Directions:
1. Start by preheating your Air Fryer to 380°F.
2. Add the Brussels sprouts to the cooking basket. Spritz with cooking spray and cook for 15 minutes. Let it cool to room temperature for about 15 minutes.
3. Toss the Brussels sprouts with apple, cheese, pomegranate seeds, and red onion.
4. Mix all Ingredients: for the dressing and toss to combine well. Serve topped with the hardboiled eggs. Bon appétit!

Sundried Tomato with Brussels sprouts Roast

Preparation time: 15 minutes
Cooking time: 20 minutes
Servings: 4
Ingredients:
- 1 pound (454 g) Brussels sprouts, trimmed and halved
- 1 tablespoon extra-virgin olive oil
- Sea salt and freshly ground black pepper, to taste
- ½ cup sun-dried tomatoes, chopped
- 2 tablespoons freshly squeezed lemon juice
- 1 teaspoon lemon zest

Directions:
1. Preheat the oven to 400°F (205°C). Line a large baking sheet with aluminum foil.
2. Toss the Brussels sprouts in the olive oil in a large bowl until well coated. Sprinkle with salt and pepper.
3. Spread out the seasoned Brussels sprouts on the prepared baking sheet in a single layer.
4. Roast in the preheated oven for 20 minutes, shaking the pan halfway through, or until the Brussels sprouts are crispy and browned on the outside. Remove from the oven to a serving bowl.
6. Add the tomatoes, lemon juice, and lemon zest, and stir to incorporate. Serve immediately.

Cardamom Spiced Swiss chard

Preparation time: 10 minutes
Cooking time: 10 minutes
Servings: 4
Ingredients:

- 2 tablespoons extra-virgin olive oil
- 1 pound (454 g) Swiss chard, coarse stems removed and leaves chopped
- 1 pound (454 g) kale, coarse stems removed and leaves chopped
- ½ teaspoon ground cardamom
- 1 tablespoon freshly squeezed lemon juice
- Sea salt and freshly ground black pepper, to taste

Directions:
1. Heat the olive oil in a large skillet over medium-high heat.
2. Add the Swiss chard, kale, cardamom, and lemon juice to the skillet, and stir to combine. Cook for about 10 minutes, stirring continuously, or until the greens are wilted. Sprinkle with the salt and pepper and stir well. Serve the greens on a plate while warm.

Japanese Tempura Bowl

Preparation Time: 20 Minutes
Cooking Time: 10 Minutes
Servings: 3
Ingredients:
- 1 C. all-purpose flour
- Kosher salt and ground black pepper, to taste
- ½ tsp. paprika
- 2 Eggs
- 3 Tbsps. soda water
- 1 C. panko crumbs
- 2 Tbsps. olive oil
- 1 C. green beans
- 1 Onion, cut into rings
- 1 Zucchini, cut into slices
- 2 Tbsps. soy sauce
- 1 Tbsp. mirin
- 1 tsp. dashi granules

Directions:
1. In a shallow bowl, mix the flour, salt, black pepper, and paprika. In a separate bowl, whisk the eggs and soda water. In a third shallow bowl, combine the panko crumbs with olive oil.
2. Dip the vegetables in the flour mixture, then in the egg mixture; lastly, roll over the panko mixture to coat evenly.
3. Cook in the preheated Air Fryer at 400°F for 10 minutes, shaking the basket halfway through the cooking time. Work in batches until the vegetables are crispy and golden brown.
4. Then, make the sauce by whisking the soy sauce, mirin, and dashi granules. Bon appétit!

Balsamic Root Vegetables

Preparation Time: 25 Minutes
Cooking Time: 10 Minutes
Servings: 3
Ingredients:
- 2 Potatoes, cut into 1 ½-inch piece
- 2 Carrots, cut into 1 ½-inch piece
- 2 Parsnips, cut into 1 ½-inch piece
- 1 Onion, cut into 1 ½-inch piece
- Pink Himalayan salt and ground black pepper, to taste
- ¼ tsp. smoked paprika
- 1 tsp. garlic powder
- ½ tsp. dried thyme
- ½ tsp. dried marjoram
- 2 Tbsps. olive oil
- 2 Tbsps. balsamic vinegar

Directions:
1. Toss all Ingredients: in a large mixing dish.
2. Roast in the preheated Air Fryer at 400°F for 10 minutes. Shake the basket and cook for 7 more minutes.
3. Serve with some extra fresh herbs if desired. Bon appétit!

Winter Vegetable Braise

Preparation Time: 25 Minutes
Cooking Time: 10 Minutes
Servings: 2
Ingredients:
- 4 Potatoes, peeled and cut into 1-inch pieces
- 1 Celery root, peeled and cut into 1-inch pieces
- 1 C. winter squash
- 2 Tbsps. unsalted butter, melted
- ½ C. chicken broth
- ¼ C. tomato sauce
- 1 tsp. parsley
- 1 tsp. rosemary
- 1 tsp. thyme

Directions:
1. Start by preheating your Air Fryer to 370°F. Add all Ingredients: to a lightly greased casserole dish. Stir to combine well.
2. Bake in the preheated Air Fryer for 10 minutes. Gently stir the vegetables with a large spoon and increase the temperature to 400°F; cook for 10 more minutes.
3. Serve in individual bowls with a few drizzles of lemon juice. Bon appétit!

Aromatic Thyme Spiced Button Mushrooms

Preparation time: 10 minutes
Cooking time: 12 minutes
Servings: 4
Ingredients:
- 1 tablespoon butter
- 2 teaspoons extra-virgin olive oil
- 2 pounds (907 g) button mushrooms, halved
- 2 teaspoons minced fresh garlic
- 1 teaspoon chopped fresh thyme
- Sea salt and freshly ground black pepper, to taste

Directions:
1. Heat the butter and olive oil in a large skillet over medium-high heat.
2. Add the mushrooms and sauté for 10 minutes, stirring occasionally, or until the mushrooms are lightly browned and cooked though.
3. Stir in the garlic and thyme and cook for an additional 2 minutes.
4. Season with salt and pepper and serve on a plate.

Peppery Bok Choy with Toasted Sliced Almonds

Preparation time: 15 minutes
Cooking time: 7 minutes

Servings: 4
Ingredients:
- 2 teaspoons sesame oil
- 2 pounds (907 g) bok choy, cleaned and quartered
- 2 teaspoons low-sodium soy sauce
- Pinch red pepper flakes
- ½ cup toasted sliced almonds

Directions:
1. Heat the sesame oil in a large skillet over medium heat until hot.
2. Sauté the bok choy in the hot oil for about 5 minutes, stirring occasionally, or until tender but still crisp.
3. Add the soy sauce and red pepper flakes and stir to combine. Continue sautéing for 2 minutes.
4. Transfer to a plate and serve topped with sliced almonds.

Spicy Asparagus Cashews Bake

Preparation time: 10 minutes
Cooking time: 15 to 20 minutes
Servings: 4
Ingredients:
- 2 pounds (907 g) asparagus, woody ends trimmed
- 1 tablespoon extra-virgin olive oil
- Sea salt and freshly ground black pepper, to taste
- ½ cup chopped cashews
- Zest and juice of 1 lime

Directions:
1. Preheat the oven to 400ºF (205ºC). Line a baking sheet with aluminum foil.
2. Toss the asparagus with the olive oil in a medium bowl. Sprinkle the salt and pepper to season.
3. Arrange the asparagus on the baking sheet and bake for 15 to 20 minutes, or until lightly browned and tender.
4. Remove the asparagus from the oven to a serving bowl.
5. Add the cashews, lime zest and juice, and toss to coat well. Serve immediately.

Gingery Eggplant with Green Onions

Preparation time: 10 minutes
Cooking time: 40 minutes
Servings: 4
Ingredients:
- 1 large eggplant, sliced into fourths
- 3 green onions, diced, green tips only
- 1 teaspoon fresh ginger, peeled and diced fine
- ¼ cup plus 1 teaspoon cornstarch
- 1½ tablespoons soy sauce
- 1½ tablespoons sesame oil
- 1 tablespoon vegetable oil
- 1 tablespoon fish sauce
- 2 teaspoons Splenda
- ¼ teaspoon salt

Directions:
1. Place eggplant on paper towels and sprinkle both sides with salt. Let for 1 hour to remove excess moisture. Pat dry with more paper towels.
2. In a small bowl, whisk together soy sauce, sesame oil, fish sauce, Splenda, and 1 teaspoon cornstarch.
3. Coat both sides of the eggplant with the ¼ cup cornstarch, use more if needed.
4. Heat oil in a large skillet, over medium-high heat.
5. Add ½ the ginger and 1 green onion, then lay 2 slices of eggplant on top. Use ½ the sauce mixture to lightly coat both sides of the eggplant. Cook 8 to 10 minutes per side. Repeat.
6. Serve garnished with remaining green onions.

Peppery Egg Butternut Fritters

Preparation time: 15 minutes
Cooking time: 15 minutes
Servings: 6
Ingredients:
- 5 cup butternut squash, grated
- 2 large eggs
- 1 tablespoon fresh sage, diced fine
- 2/3 cup flour - 2 tablespoons olive oil
- Salt and pepper, to taste

Directions:
1. Heat oil in a large skillet over medium-high heat.
2. In a large bowl, combine squash, eggs, sage and salt and pepper to taste. Fold in flour.
3. Drop ¼ cup mixture into skillet, keeping fritters at least 1 inch apart. Cook till golden brown on both sides, about 2 minutes per side.
4. Transfer to paper towel lined plate. Repeat. Serve immediately with your favorite dipping sauce.

The Best Cauliflower Tater Tots

Preparation Time: 25 Minutes
Cooking Time: 10 Minutes
Servings: 4
Ingredients:
- 1 lb. cauliflower florets
- 2 Eggs
- 1 Tbsp. olive oil
- 2 Tbsps. scallions, chopped
- 1 Garlic clove, minced
- 1 C. Colby cheese, shredded
- ½ C. breadcrumbs
- Sea salt and ground black pepper, to taste
- ¼ tsp. dried dill weed
- 1 tsp. paprika

Directions:
1. Blanch the cauliflower in salted boiling water for about 3 to 4 minutes until al dente. Drain well and pulse in a food processor.
2. Add the remaining Ingredients; mix to combine well. Shape the cauliflower mixture into bite-sized tots.
3. Spritz the Air Fryer basket with cooking spray.
4. Cook in the preheated Air Fryer at 375°F for 16 minutes, shaking halfway through the cooking time. Serve with your favorite sauce for dipping Bon appétit!

Three-Cheese Stuffed Mushrooms

Preparation Time: 15 Minutes
Cooking Time: 10 Minutes
Servings: 3
Ingredients:
- 9 large button mushrooms, stems removed

- 1 Tbsp. olive oil
- Salt and ground black pepper, to taste
- ½ tsp. dried rosemary
- 6 Tbsps. Swiss cheeses shredded
- 6 Tbsps. Romano cheese, shredded
- 6 Tbsps. cream cheese
- 1 tsp. soy sauce
- 1 tsp. garlic, minced
- 3 Tbsps. green onion, minced

Directions:
1. Brush the mushroom caps with olive oil; sprinkle with salt, pepper, and rosemary.
2. In a mixing bowl, thoroughly combine the remaining Ingredients, combine them well, and divide the filling mixture among the mushroom caps.
3. Cook in the preheated Air Fryer at 390°F for 7 minutes.
4. Let the mushrooms cool slightly before serving Bon appétit!

Sweet Corn Fritters with Avocado

Preparation Time: 20 Minutes
Cooking Time: 10 Minutes
Servings: 3
Ingredients:
- 2 C. sweet corn kernels
- 1 Small-sized onion, chopped
- 1 Garlic clove, minced
- 2 Eggs, whisked
- 1 tsp. baking powder
- 2 Tbsps. fresh cilantro, chopped
- Sea salt and ground black pepper, to taste
- 1 Avocado, peeled, pitted, and diced
- 2 Tbsps. sweet chili sauce

Directions:
1. In a mixing bowl, thoroughly combine the corn, onion, garlic, eggs, baking powder, cilantro, salt, and black pepper.
2. Shape the corn mixture into six patties and transfer them to the lightly greased Air Fryer basket.
3. Cook in the preheated Air Fry at 370°F for 8 minutes; turn them over and cook for 7 minutes longer.
4. Serve the cakes with avocado and chili sauce.

Greek-Style Vegetable Bake

Preparation Time: 35 Minutes
Cooking Time: 10 Minutes
Servings: 4
Ingredients:
- 1 Eggplant, peeled and sliced
- 2 Bell peppers, seeded and sliced
- 1 Red onion, sliced
- 1 tsp. fresh garlic, minced
- 4 Tbsps. olive oil
- 1 tsp. mustard
- 1 tsp. dried oregano
- 1 tsp. smoked paprika
- Salt and ground black pepper, to taste
- 1 Tomato, sliced
- 6 oz. halloumi cheese, sliced lengthways

Directions:
1. Start by preheating your Air Fryer to 370°F. Spritz a baking pan with non-stick cooking spray.
2. Place the eggplant, peppers, onion, and garlic on the baking pan's bottom. Add the olive oil, mustard, and spices. Transfer to the cooking basket and cook for 14 minutes.
3. Top with the tomatoes and cheese; increase the temperature to 390°F and cook for five more minutes until bubbling. Let it sit on a cooling rack for 10 minutes before serving.
4. Bon appétit!

Grandma's Citrusy Broccoli Tofu

Preparation time: 15 minutes
Cooking time: 2 hours
Servings: 4
Ingredients:
- 1 package extra firm tofu, pressed for at least 15 minutes, cut into cubes
- 2 cups broccoli florets, fresh
- 1 tablespoon margarine
- ¼ cup orange juice
- ¼ cup reduced sodium soy sauce
- ¼ cup honey
- 2 cloves garlic, diced fine

Directions:
1. Melt butter in a medium skillet, over medium high heat. Add tofu and garlic and cook, stirring occasionally until tofu starts to brown, about 5 to 10 minutes. Transfer to crock pot.
2. Whisk the wet together in a small bowl. Pour over tofu and add the broccoli.
3. Cover and cook on high 90 minutes, or on low 2 hours.
4. Serve warm.

One Pan Spiced Tofu with Spinach

Preparation time: 15 minutes
Cooking time: 1 hour 25 minutes
Servings: 4
Ingredients:
- 1 package extra firm tofu, pressed 15 minutes and cut into cubes
- 1 package fresh baby spinach
- 2 limes
- 1 tablespoon margarine
- ½ cup raw peanut butter
- 2 tablespoons lite soy sauce
- 3 cloves garlic, chopped fine
- ½ teaspoon ginger
- ¼ teaspoon red pepper flakes

Directions:
1. Melt margarine in a large saucepan. Add tofu and garlic and cook, stirring occasionally, 5 to 10 minutes, or until tofu starts to brown.
2. Add remaining, except spinach and bring to simmer. Reduce heat, cover and cook, stirring occasionally 30 to 35 minutes.
3. Stir in the spinach and cook 15 minutes more. Serve.

Chicken Broth Cauliflower Soup

Preparation time: 10 minutes
Cooking time: 15 minutes
Servings: 6
Ingredients:

- 2½ pounds (1.1 kg) cauliflower florets
- ½ leek, white and pale green part, halved
- 4 tablespoons butter
- 2 teaspoons fresh parsley, diced
- 2 tablespoons low sodium chicken broth
- 2 teaspoons extra virgin olive oil
- 4 cloves garlic, diced fine
- ¼ teaspoon salt - ¼ teaspoon pepper

Directions:
1. Place the cauliflower in a steamer basket over boiling water. Cover and steam 10 to 15 minutes or until fork tender.
2. Rinse the leek under water and pat dry. Chop into thin slices.
3. Heat oil in a large skillet over medium-low heat. Add the leek and cook 2 to 3 minutes, or until soft. Add the garlic and cook 1 minute more.
4. Add all to a food processor and pulse until almost smooth. Serve warm, or refrigerate for a later use.

Cheese Coated Egg Muffins

Preparation time: 10 minutes
Cooking time: 20 minutes
Servings: 4
Ingredients:
- 4 egg whites
- ½ teaspoon fresh parsley, diced fine
- 3 tablespoons reduced fat Parmesan cheese, divided
- 2 teaspoons water
- ½ teaspoon salt
- Truffle oil to taste
- Nonstick cooking spray

Directions:
1. Heat oven to 400°F (205°C). Spray two muffin pans with cooking spray.
2. In a small bowl, whisk together egg whites, water, and salt until combined.
3. Spoon just enough egg white mixture into each muffin cup to barely cover the bottom. Sprinkle a small pinch of Parmesan on each egg white.
4. Bake 10 to 15 minutes or until the edges are dark brown, be careful not to burn them.
5. Let cool in the pans 3 to 4 minutes then transfer to a small bowl and drizzle lightly with truffle oil.
6. Add parsley and ½ tablespoon Parmesan and toss to coat. Serve.

Cardamom spiced Kale and Chard

Preparation time: 10 minutes
Cooking time: 10 minutes
Servings: 4
Ingredients:
- 2 tablespoons extra-virgin olive oil
- 1 pound (454 g) kale, coarse stems removed and leaves chopped
- 1 pound (454 g) Swiss chard, coarse stems removed and leaves chopped
- 1 tablespoon freshly squeezed lemon juice
- ½ teaspoon ground cardamom
- Sea salt to taste
- Freshly ground black pepper

Directions:
1. Place a large skillet over medium-high heat and add the olive oil.
2. Add the kale, chard, lemon juice, and cardamom to the skillet. Use tongs to toss the greens continuously until they are wilted, about 10 minutes or less.
3. Season the greens with salt and pepper. Serve immediately.

Sautéed Peppery Mushrooms

Preparation time: 10 minutes
Cooking time: 12 minutes
Servings: 4
Ingredients:
- 1 tablespoon butter
- 2 teaspoons extra-virgin olive oil
- 2 pounds button mushrooms, halved
- 2 teaspoons minced fresh garlic
- 1 teaspoon chopped fresh thyme
- Sea salt to taste
- Freshly ground black pepper

Directions:
1. Place a large skillet over medium-high heat and add the butter and olive oil.
2. Sauté the mushrooms, stirring occasionally, until they are lightly caramelized and tender, about 10 minutes.
3. Add the garlic and thyme and sauté for 2 more minutes.
4. Season the mushrooms with salt and pepper before serving.

Low Sugar Bok Choy Bowl

Preparation time: 15 minutes
Cooking time: 7 minutes
Servings: 4
Ingredients:
- 2 teaspoons sesame oil
- 2 pounds (907 g) bok choy, cleaned and quartered
- 2 teaspoons low-sodium soy sauce
- Pinch red pepper flakes
- ½ cup toasted sliced almonds

Directions:
1. Place a large skillet over medium heat and add the oil.
2. When the oil is hot, sauté the bok choy until tender-crisp, about 5 minutes.
3. Stir in the soy sauce and red pepper flakes and sauté 2 minutes more.
4. Remove the bok choy to a serving bowl and top with the sliced almonds.

Easy Apple Porridge

Serving: 2
Preparation Time: 10 minutes
Cooking Time: 5 minutes
Ingredients
- 1 large apple, peeled, cored, and grated
- 1 cup unsweetened almond milk
- 1 and a ½ tablespoon of sunflower seeds
- 1/8 cup of fresh blueberries
- ¼ teaspoon of fresh vanilla bean extract

Directions:
1. Take a large pan and add sunflower seeds, vanilla extract, almond milk, apples, and stir

2. Place it over medium-low heat
3. Cook for 5 minutes, making sure to keep the mixture stirring
4. Transfer to a serving bowl
5. Serve and enjoy!

Vanilla and Flaxseed Meal

Serving: 4
Preparation Time: 10 minutes
Cooking Time: 5-10 minutes
Ingredients
- 1 cup almond milk
- ¼ cup coconut flour
- 1 teaspoon cinnamon
- ¼ cup flaxseed, ground
- 1 teaspoon vanilla extract
- 10 drops stevia
- Pinch of salt

Directions:
1. Heat almond milk in a saucepan over low heat, whisk in coconut flour, salt, cinnamon, flaxseed
2. Stir well; once it bubbles, adds vanilla and stevia
3. Remove heat and add some garnish and berries as a topping
4. Enjoy!

Flaxseed Pancakes

Serving: 2
Preparation Time: 10 minutes
Cooking Time: 5-10 minutes
Ingredients
- 3 tablespoons water
- 2 tablespoons flaxseed
- Pinch of salt
- 1 and ½ tablespoons coconut oil
- ½ scoop vanilla vegan powder
- ¼ teaspoon baking powder

Directions:
1. Take a bowl and mix in flaxseeds and water, and mix in the oil
2. Mix in baking powder, protein powder, and salt
3. Stir well
4. Add wet ingredients to dry ingredients and mix properly
5. Take a non-stick pan and place it over medium heat
6. Scoop batter into your pan and cook for 5 minutes; flip and cook for 2 minutes more
7. Repeat until all batter has been used up
8. Enjoy!

Flaxseed Porridge

Serving: 2
Preparation Time: 10 minutes
Cooking Time: 5-10 minutes
Ingredients
- 1 cup almond milk
- 1 teaspoon cinnamon
- ¼ cup coconut flour
- ¼ cup ground flaxseed
- 10 drops stevia
- 1 teaspoon vanilla extract
- Pinch of salt
- 1 ounce's coconut, shaved for garnish
- 2 ounces blueberries for garnish
- 2 tablespoons almond butter, garnish
- 2 tablespoons pumpkin seeds, garnish

Directions:
1. Take a saucepan and place it over low heat
2. Whisk in coconut flour, salt, cinnamon, flaxseed, and stir
3. Add stevia, vanilla, and heat until bubbling
4. Remove from heat
5. Mix in remaining ingredients and stir
6. Garnish with blueberries, pumpkin seeds, or almonds, and serve
7. Enjoy!

Tasty Vegetable Morning Hash

Serving: 4
Preparation Time: 5 minutes
Cooking Time: 23 minutes
Ingredients
- 1 tablespoon sage leaves, chopped
- 1 bell pepper, diced
- 3 garlic cloves, minced
- 1 onion, diced
- 3 tablespoon olive oil
- 3 red potatoes, diced
- 15 ounces black beans, canned
- 1 tablespoon parsley, chopped
- 2 cups swiss chard, chopped
- Salt and pepper

Directions:
1. Take a skillet and place it over medium heat, add oil and let it heat up
2. Add potato, garlic and onion cook them for about 20 minutes
3. Add Swiss Chard and beans, and cook for 3 minutes
4. Season well with salt and pepper, and serve with parsley
5. Enjoy!

Hearty Walnut Porridge

Serving: 4
Preparation Time: 10 minutes
Cooking Time: 20 minutes
Ingredients
- 1 and ½ cups of water
- ½ cup coconut milk, unsweetened
- 1 cup Teff, whole grain
- ½ teaspoon cardamom, ground
- 1 teaspoon salt, fine
- ¼ cup walnuts, chopped
- 1 tablespoon maple syrup, pure

Directions:
1. Take a large bowl and place it over medium heat, add coconut oil and water, bring to a boil and stir in your Teff
2. Add cardamom, lower heat and simmer for 20 minutes
3. Mix in walnuts and maple syrup, and serve
4. Enjoy!

Pumpkin Steel Cuts

Serving: 4
Preparation Time: 5 minutes
Cooking Time: 20-25 minutes

Ingredients
- 3 cups of water
- 1 cup steel-cut oats
- ½ cup pumpkin puree, canned
- ¼ cup pumpkin seeds
- 2 tablespoons maple syrup
- Pinch of salt

Directions:
1. Take a large saucepan and place it over high heat; add water and let it boil
2. Add oats, stir and lower heat, simmer for 20-25 minutes
3. Stir in pumpkin puree and keep cooking for 3-5 minutes
4. Stir in pumpkin seeds and maple syrup, and season with salt
5. Serve and enjoy!

Savory Oatmeal Delight

Serving: 4
Preparation Time: 2 minutes
Cooking Time: 25 minutes
Ingredients
- 2 and ½ cups vegetable broth
- 2 and ½ cups unsweetened almond milk
- ½ cup steel-cut oats
- 1 tablespoon farro
- ½ cup almonds, slivered
- ¼ cup nutritional yeast
- 2 cups old-fashioned rolled oats
- ½ teaspoon salt

Directions:
1. Take a large saucepan and place it over medium heat, add broth and milk, and bring to a boil
2. Add oats, farro, almonds, and yeast, and cook over medium-high heat for 20 minutes
3. Add rolled oats and cook for 5 minutes more
4. Stir in salt, top with some berries
5. Serve and enjoy!

Apple and Cinnamon Oatmeal

Serving: 2
Preparation Time: 10 minutes
Cooking Time: 10 minutes
Ingredients
- 1 and ¼ cups apple cider
- 1 apple, peeled, cored, and chopped
- 2/3 cup rolled oats
- 1 teaspoon ground cinnamon
- 1 tablespoon pure maple syrup

Directions:
1. Take a medium-sized saucepan, bring apple cider to boil over medium-high heat
2. Stir in apples, oats, cinnamon
3. Bring cereal to a boil and lower heat to lower, simmer for 3-4 minutes until thickened
4. Spoon between two bowls and serve with maple syrup; enjoy!

Cinnamon and Spice Overnight Oats

Serving: 4
Preparation Time: 10 minutes (Overnight soak)
Cooking Time: nil
Ingredients
- 2 and ½ cups old-fashioned rolled oats
- 5 tablespoons pumpkin seeds
- 5 tablespoons pecans, chopped
- 5 cups unsweetened plant-based milk
- 2 and ½ teaspoons maple syrup
- ½ teaspoon salt
- ½ teaspoon cinnamon, ground
- ½ teaspoon ground ginger
- Fresh fruit as needed

Directions:
1. Take 5 wide-mouthed pint jars; in each jar, add ½ cup oats, 1 tablespoon pumpkin, 1 tablespoon pecans, 1 cup milk, ½ teaspoon maple syrup, 1 pinch salt, 1 pinch cinnamon, 1 pinch ginger
2. Stir well
3. Close lids tightly and store overnight
4. Serve with a topping of fresh fruit
5. Serve and enjoy!

Pecan and Pear Breakfast

Serving: 4
Preparation Time: 5 minutes
Cooking Time: 15 minutes
Ingredients
- 2 cups of water
- ½ teaspoon salt
- 1 cup medium bulgur
- 1 tablespoon vegan margarine
- 2 ripe pears, peeled, cored, and chopped
- ¼ cup pecans, chopped

Directions:
1. Take a large saucepan, bring water to a boil over high heat
2. Add salt, stir in bulgar
3. Lower heat to low and simmer for 15 minutes
4. Remove heat and stir in margarine, pears, pecans
5. Cover and let it sit for 12-15 minutes more
6. Serve and enjoy!

Pitas and Broiled Grapefruits

Serving: 4
Preparation Time: 10 minutes
Cooking Time: 15 minutes
Ingredients
- 2 whole-wheat pitas, cut into wedges
- 2 tablespoons coconut oil, melted
- 1 tablespoon ground cinnamon
- 2 tablespoons brown sugar
- 1 grapefruit, halved
- 2 tablespoons pure maple syrup

Directions:
1. Preheat your oven to 375 degrees F
2. Line the baking sheet with parchment paper and spread pita wedges in a single layer on the baking sheet
3. Brush melted coconut oil
4. Take a small bowl, add brown cinnamon sugar, and sprinkle over pita wedges
5. Bake for 8 minutes

6. Transfer pita to plates
7. Turn the oven to broil, place grapefruit halves on a baking sheet, and drizzle maple syrup over the top
8. Broil until syrup bubbles for 5 minutes
9. Serve with pita
10. Enjoy!

Orange French Toast

Serving: 4
Preparation Time: 15 minutes
Cooking Time: 10 minutes
Ingredients
- 3 bananas, ripe
- 1 cup unsweetened almond milk
- Zest of 1 orange
- 1 teaspoon ground cinnamon
- ¼ teaspoon nutmeg, grated
- 4 French bread slices
- 1 tablespoon coconut oil

Directions:
1. Take a blender and add banana, milk, orange juice, zest, cinnamon, and nutmeg; blend well until smooth
2. Pour mixture into 9 by 13-inch baking dish, soak bread in mixture for 5 minutes on each side
3. While the bread soaks, heat the griddle over medium heat and melt coconut oil; swirl well to coat
4. Cook bread slices until golden brown, 5 minutes on each side
5. Serve and enjoy!

Fruity-Licious Oatmeal

Serving: 3
Preparation Time: 10 minutes
Cooking Time: 10 minutes
Ingredients
- ½ cup apple juice, fresh and frozen
- ½ cup oatmeal
- ½ cup of water
- 3 prunes, dried
- 1 apple, small, diced
- 4 pecans, diced
- 3 apricots, dehydrated, dried, diced
- ¼ teaspoon cinnamon

Directions:
1. Take a small-sized saucepan and mix in apple juice and water; bring the mixture to a boil
2. Add half a cup of oatmeal, cook for 1 minute
3. Add pecans, cinnamon, and fruit pieces
4. Stir well, and add your desired fruit as a topping
5. Enjoy!

Roasted Hazelnut Bites

Serving: 4
Preparation Time: 30 minutes
Cooking Time: nil
Ingredients
- 10 hazelnuts, roasted
- 1 cup hazelnuts, toasted and chopped
- 1 teaspoon vanilla extract
- 2 tablespoons raw cocoa powder
- ¼ cup maple syrup

Directions:
1. Add ½ cup of chopped hazelnuts to a food processor and blend
2. Add vanilla extract, cocoa powder, and maple syrup and blend again
3. Roll 10 hazelnuts in cocoa powder mix and dip in the chopped hazelnut mixture
4. Roll the dough and make 10 balls
5. Freeze them for 20 minutes and serve!

Delightful Mushroom Sauté

Serving: 4
Preparation Time: 4 minutes
Cooking Time: 9 minutes
Ingredients
- 2 tablespoons clarified butter
- 1 tablespoon olive oil
- 1 and 1/2 pound gourmet mushrooms
- 4 garlic cloves, diced
- 1/3 cup white wine vinegar
- Salt as needed

Directions:
1. Take a heavy pan and place it over medium heat
2. Add olive oil and ½ butter
3. When smoking, add mushrooms and keep stirring until browned
4. Add another ½ butter and garlic
5. Stir everything well
6. Add white wine vinegar and cook until the liquid is absorbed
7. Season with salt, and enjoy!

Kale and Carrot With Tahini Dressing

Serving: 1
Preparation Time: 15 minutes
Cooking Time: nil
Ingredients
- Handful of kale
- 1 tablespoon tahini
- ½ head of lettuce
- Pinch of garlic powder
- 1 tablespoon olive oil
- Juice of ½ lime
- 1 carrot, julienned

Directions:
1. Add kale and roughly chopped lettuce to a bowl
2. Add grated carrots to the greens and mix
3. Take a small bowl and add the remaining ingredients; mix well
4. Pour dressing on top of greens and toss
5. Enjoy!

Cinnamon and Coconut Porridge

Serving: 4
Preparation Time: 5 minutes
Cooking Time: 5 minutes
Ingredients
- 2 cups of water
- 1 cup cashew cream
- ½ cup unsweetened dried coconut, shredded

- 2 tablespoons flaxseed meal
- 1 tablespoon almond butter
- 1 and ½ teaspoon stevia
- 1 teaspoon cinnamon
- Salt to taste
- Toppings as blueberries

Directions:
1. Add the listed ingredients to a small pot, mix well
2. Transfer pot to stove and place it over medium-low heat
3. Bring to mix to a slow boil
4. Stir well and remove the heat
5. Divide the mix into equal servings and let them sit for 10 minutes
6. Top with your desired toppings, and enjoy!

Banana and Buckwheat Porridge

Serving: 2
Preparation Time: 10 minutes
Cooking Time:15 minutes
Ingredients
- 1 cup of water
- 1 cup buckwheat groats
- 2 big grapefruits, peeled and sliced
- 1 tablespoon ground cinnamon
- 3-4 cups almond milk
- 2 tablespoon natural almond butter

Directions:
1. Take a medium-sized saucepan and add buckwheat and water
2. Place the pan over medium heat and bring to a boil
3. Keep cooking until the buckwheat absorbs the water
4. Lower heat to low and add almond milk; stir gently
5. Add rest of the ingredients (except grapefruits)
6. Stir and remove heat
7. Transfer into cereal bowls and add grapefruit chunks
8. Serve and enjoy!

Quinoa and Cinnamon Bowl

Serving: 4
Preparation Time: 10 minutes
Cooking Time:15 minutes
Ingredients
- 1 cup uncooked quinoa
- 1 and ½ cups of water
- ½ teaspoon ground cinnamon
- Pinch of salt
- A drizzle of almond/coconut milk for serving

Directions:
1. Rinse quinoa thoroughly underwater
2. Take a medium-sized saucepan and add quinoa, water, cinnamon, and salt
3. Stir and place it over medium-high heat
4. Bring the mix to a boil
5. Lower heat to low and simmer for 10 minutes
6. Once cooked, remove the heat and let it cool
7. Serve with a drizzle of almond or coconut milk
8. Enjoy!

Cinnamon and Pumpkin Porridge

Serving: 4
Preparation Time: 10 minutes
Cooking Time:15 minutes
Ingredients
- 1 cup unsweetened almond/coconut milk
- 1 cup of water
- 1 cup uncooked quinoa
- ½ cup pumpkin puree
- 1 teaspoon ground cinnamon
- 2 tablespoon ground flaxseed meal
- Juice of 1 lemon

Directions:
1. Take a pot and place it over medium-high heat
2. Whisk in water and almond milk and bring the mix to a boil
3. Stir in quinoa, cinnamon, and pumpkin
4. Lower heat to low and simmer for 10 minutes until the liquid has been evaporated
5. Remove heat and stir in flaxseed meal
6. Transfer porridge to small bowls
7. Sprinkle lemon juice and add pumpkin seeds on top
8. Serve and enjoy!

Quinoa and Date Mix

Serving: 2
Preparation Time: 10 minutes
Cooking Time:15 minutes
Ingredients
- 1 date, pitted and chopped finely
- ½ a cup of red quinoa, dried
- 1 cup of unsweetened almond milk
- 1/8 teaspoon of vanilla extract
- ¼ cup of fresh strawberries, hulled and sliced
- 1/8 teaspoon of ground cinnamon

Directions:
1. Take a pan and place it over low heat
2. Add quinoa, almond milk, cinnamon, vanilla, and cook for about 15 minutes, making sure to keep stirring it from time to time
3. Garnish with strawberries, and enjoy!

Quinoa Applesauce Muffins

Serving: 2
Preparation Time: 10 minutes
Cooking Time:15 minutes
Ingredients
- 2 tablespoons coconut oil
- ¼ cup ground flaxseed
- ½ cup of water
- 2 cups unsweetened apple sauce
- ½ cup brown sugar
- 1 teaspoon apple cider vinegar
- 2 and ½ cups whole wheat flour
- 1 and ½ cups cooked quinoa
- 2 teaspoons baking soda
- Pinch of salt
- ½ cup dried cranberries

Directions:
1. Preheat your oven to 400 degrees F
2. Coat muffin tin with liners
3. Take a large-sized bowl and stir in flaxseed and water; add apple sauce, sugar, coconut oil, and vinegar, and stir well

4. Add flour, quinoa, baking soda, and salt, and stir well until just combined
5. Gently fold in cranberries without stirring too much
6. Add 1/3 cup of batter to each muffin tin
7. Bake for 15-20 minutes until the top is lightly brown; let them cool for 10 minutes
8. Serve and enjoy!

Hearty Bran Muffins

Serving: 6
Preparation Time: 5 minutes
Cooking Time: 20 minutes
Ingredients

- 3 cups bran flake cereal
- 1 and ½ cups whole wheat flour
- ½ cup raisins
- 3 teaspoons baking powder
- ½ teaspoon cinnamon, ground
- ½ teaspoon salt
- 1/3 cup brown sugar
- ¾ cup fresh orange juice

Directions:
1. Preheat your oven to 400 degrees F
2. Take 12 muffin tins and lightly grease them
3. Add paper liners
4. Take a large bowl and add bran flakes, flour, raisins, baking powder, cinnamon, salt
5. Take another medium-sized bowl and add orange juice, oil, and sugar, and mix well
6. Pour wet ingredients into dry ingredients and mix until moist
7. Fill cups about 2/3rd full
8. Bake until golden brown; it should take about 20 minutes
9. Serve and enjoy!

A Wintry Fruit Sauce

Serving: 2 cups
Preparation Time: 5 minutes
Cooking Time: 20 minutes
Ingredients

- 1 cup of water
- 1 cup dried mixed fruit
- 1 teaspoon fresh lemon juice
- ½ teaspoon ground cinnamon
- ¼ cup apple juice

Directions:
1. Take a large-sized saucepan and add water, dried fruit, lemon juice, cinnamon
2. Boil over high heat, lower heat and simmer for 20 minutes
3. Remove heat and let it cool for 10 minutes
4. Transfer to food processor and process until smooth
5. Add apple juice and process again
6. Return sauce to saucepan and heat on low heat
7. Serve and enjoy when needed!

Cinnamon Honey Baked Apple

Serving: 4
Preparation Time: 5 minutes
Cooking Time: 25 minutes
Ingredients

- 1 cup apple juice
- ¼ cup of liquid honey
- 4 apples
- ¼ teaspoon ground cloves
- ½ teaspoon nutmeg
- 1 teaspoon cinnamon
- 1 teaspoon fresh ginger root, grated
- 2 dates, pitted and chopped
- ¼ cup dried cranberries
- ½ cup nuts and seeds

Directions:
1. Preheat your oven to 325-degree Fahrenheit
2. Take a bowl and add ginger roots, spices, dates, nuts, cranberries, seeds, and mix
3. Core apples and stuff each apple with seed and nut mix
4. Drizzle honey
5. Take an 8 x 8-inch square baking dish and add stuffed apples
6. Pour cider around apples
7. Bake for 25 minutes
8. Remove from the oven and enjoy
9. Serve!

Almond Carrot Cake

Serving: 12
Preparation Time: 10 minutes
Cooking Time: 0 minute
Ingredients

- 6 cups grated carrot, water removed
- 1 and ½ cups raisins, soaked in water removed
- 1 teaspoon cinnamon, grounded
- 1 cup almonds, soaked overnight and drained
- 1 teaspoon nutmeg, grated
- 1 cup dates, pitted and soaked in water for 1 hour
- 1 lemon zest
- 1 orange zest
- 1 teaspoon cardamom, grounded

Directions:
1. Place all ingredients in your food processor
2. Pulse until finely ground
3. Take a baking dish and place it firmly
4. Allow setting in the fridge before slicing
5. Serve and enjoy!

Mango Turmeric Chia Pudding

Serving: 2
Preparation Time: 8 hour
Cooking Time: 0 minute
Ingredients

- 1 cup coconut milk, unsweetened
- 1 medium mango
- 1 tablespoon shredded coconut
- 3 tablespoons chia seeds
- ½ teaspoon vanilla extract
- 1/8 teaspoon turmeric, grounded

Directions:
1. Take a bowl and combine coconut milk, vanilla, chia seeds, and turmeric into it
2. Whisk until well combined
3. Let it cool in your refrigerator overnight
4. Top with mango and coconut
5. Serve and enjoy!

Spiced Apples and Raisins

Serving: 6
Preparation Time: 10 minutes
Cooking Time: 15 minute
Ingredients
- ¾ teaspoon pumpkin pie sliced
- 2 apples, cored and sliced
- ½ cup walnuts, chopped
- ½ cup sultana raisins, soaked in water overnight
- 1 tablespoon coconut butter
- 1 orange juice

Directions:
1. Preheat the oven to 400 degrees F
2. Take a bowl and add all ingredients
3. Toss to combine everything
4. Arrange apples and the rest of the ingredients in a baking dish
5. Bake for 15 minutes in your oven
6. Serve and enjoy!

Sweet Potato Brownie

Serving: 6
Preparation Time: 1 hour
Cooking Time: 0 minute
Ingredients
- 1 whole medium sweet potato, boiled then peeled
- 5 tablespoons raw cacao powder
- ¼ cup rice malt syrup
- ¼ cup coconut oil, melted
- 2 cups almond nuts
- A pinch of salt

Directions:
1. Take a bowl and mash sweet potatoes into the bowl
2. Add in the rest of the ingredients
3. Mix thoroughly until well-combined
4. Take a baking dish and transfer it, then spread evenly
5. Let it cool in the refrigerator
6. Slice them into 12 squares
7. Serve and enjoy!

Anti-Inflammatory Apricot Squares

Serving: 8
Preparation Time: 60 minutes
Cooking Time: 0 minute
Ingredients
- 1 cup shredded coconut, dried
- 1 teaspoon vanilla extract
- 1 cup apricot, dried
- 1 cup macadamia nuts, chopped
- 1 cup apricot, chopped
- 1/3 cup turmeric powder

Directions:
1. Place all ingredients in your food processor
1. Pulse until smooth
2. Pour mixture into a square pan and press evenly
3. Serve chilled, and enjoy!

Chapter 9

Pork, Beef and Lamb

Zucchini Lasagna

Preparation time: 30 minutes
Cooking Time: 1 Hour
Servings: 4
Ingredients:
- 1 lb. lean ground beef
- 2 medium zucchinis, julienned
- 3 tomatoes, blanch in hot water, remove skins and dice
- 1 onion, diced
- 1 serrano chili, remove seeds and dice
- 1 cup mushrooms, remove stems and dice
- ½ cup low-fat mozzarella, grated
- What you'll need from store cupboard:
- 2 cloves garlic, diced fine
- ½ cube chicken bouillon
- 1 tsp. paprika
- 1 tsp. dried thyme
- 1 tsp. dried basil
- Salt and pepper
- Nonstick cooking spray

Directions:
1. Lay zucchini on paper towel lined cutting board and sprinkle lightly with salt. Let sit for 10 minutes.
2. Heat oven to broil. Blot zucchini with paper towels and place on baking sheet. Broil 3 minutes. Transfer to paper towels again to remove excess moisture.
3. Lightly coat a deep skillet with cooking spray and place over med-high heat. Add garlic, onion, and chili and cook 1 minute.
4. Add the tomatoes and mushrooms and cook, stirring frequently, about 4 minutes. Transfer vegetables to a bowl.
5. Add the beef to the skillet with the paprika and cook until no longer pink. Add the vegetables and bouillon to the beef along with remaining spices and let simmer over low heat 25 minutes.
6. Heat oven to 375 degrees. Line a small baking dish with parchment paper and place 1/3 of the zucchini in an even layer on the bottom. Top with 1/3 of the meat mixture. Repeat layers.
7. Sprinkle cheese over top and bake 35 minutes. Let rest 10 minutes before serving.

Roasted Duck Legs with Balsamic Mushrooms

Preparation time: 45 minutes
Cooking Time: 1 Hour
Servings: 4
Ingredients:
- 4 bone-in, skin-on duck legs
- 1/2 lb. cremini mushrooms, remove stems and cut caps into thick slices
- 1 green onion, sliced thin
- 1 small shallot, sliced thin
- 3-4 fresh thyme sprigs, crushed lightly
- What you'll need from store cupboard:
- 5 Tbs. extra-virgin olive oil
- 5 Tbs. balsamic vinegar
- 2 cloves garlic, sliced thin
- ½ tsp fresh thyme, chopped
- Kosher salt and freshly ground pepper

Directions:
1. Rinse duck and pat dry with paper towels.
2. In a shallow glass bowl, large enough to hold the duck, combine 3 tablespoons oil, 3 tablespoons vinegar, garlic, shallot, thyme sprigs, ½ teaspoon salt and some pepper. Add the duck, turning to coat. Cover and chill 3-4 hours turning legs once or twice.
3. Remove the duck from the marinade. Pour the marinade into a saucepan and bring to a boil over high heat. Remove from heat.
4. Place a footed rack on the bottom of a large pot, tall enough that the duck legs can stand 2 inches from the bottom. Add about 1 inch of water. Place the duck, skin side up on the rack. Cover and bring to a boil over med-high heat. Let steam until the skin is translucent, about 20 minutes.
5. While duck is steaming, heat the oven to 450 degrees. Line a roasting pan large enough to hold the duck with foil. Place a flat rack in the pan.
6. When the duck is ready, transfer it skin side up to the prepared rack. Brush the skin with the glaze and roast, until skin is brown and crisp, about 20 minutes. Remove from oven and glaze the duck again. Let rest for 5 minutes.
7. In a large skillet, over med-high heat, heat the remaining oil. Add mushrooms, green onions, and cook, stirring frequently about 2 minutes. Add the remaining vinegar, chopped thyme, salt and pepper to taste. Cook until mushrooms are soft and most of the liquid has evaporated.
8. To serve, place duck leg on a plate and spoon mushrooms over.

Russian Steaks with Nuts and Cheese

Preparation time: 30 minutes
Cooking Time: 20 Minutes
Servings: 4
Ingredients:
- 800g of minced pork
- 200g of cream cheese

- 50g peeled walnuts
- 1 onion
- Salt
- Ground pepper
- 1 egg
- Breadcrumbs
- Extra virgin olive oil

Directions:
1. Put the onion cut into quarters in the Thermo mix glass and select 5 seconds speed 5.
2. Add the minced meat, cheese, egg, salt, and pepper.
3. Select 10 seconds, speed 5, turn left.
4. Add the chopped and peeled walnuts and select 4 seconds, turn left, speed 5.
5. Pass the dough to a bowl.
6. Make Russian steaks and go through breadcrumbs.
7. Paint the Russian fillets with extra virgin olive oil on both sides with a brush.
8. Put in the basket of the air fryer, without stacking the Russian fillets.
9. Select 1800C, 15 minutes.

Pork Paprika

Preparation time: 1 hour, plus 20 minutes soaking
Cooking Time: 40 Minutes
Servings: 6
Ingredients:
- 1 lb. pork loin, trim fat and cut into 1-inch cubes
- 1 onion, diced fine
- 1 cup mushrooms, sliced thick
- 2/3 cup fat free sour cream
- What you'll need from store cupboard:
- 1 can petite tomatoes, diced
- ½ cup low sodium chicken broth
- 2 tbsp. olive oil
- 2 tbsp. sweet paprika, divided
- 1 tbsp. garlic, diced fine
- ½ tsp thyme
- ½ tsp caraway seeds, ground
- Salt & pepper to taste

Directions:
1. Place pork in large bowl and sprinkle 1 tablespoon paprika, salt and pepper over meat, toss to coat.
2. Heat 1 tablespoon oil in a large, deep skillet over med-high heat. Add pork and cook, stirring frequently until brown on all sides, about 5-6 minutes. Transfer to a plate.
3. Add remaining tablespoon of oil to skillet and the mushrooms. Cook, stirring, till browned and no more liquid remains in the pan, about 5 minutes. Add the mushrooms to the pork.
4. Add more oil if needed and the onion. Cook about 3-5 minutes, or they just start to brown. Add garlic and spices and cook another 1-2 minutes. Add tomatoes with juice and broth, cook, stirring frequently, until mixture starts to thicken, about 5 minutes.
5. Stir the pork and mushrooms into the sauce. Reduce heat, cover, and simmer 15 minutes, or until pork is tender. Serve.

Beef Goulash Soup

Preparation time: 30 minutes
Cooking time: 20 minutes
Servings: 4
Ingredients:
- Boneless beef top sirloin steak – 6 oz.
- Olive oil – 1 tsp.
- Chopped onion – ½ cup
- Water – 2 cups
- Beef broth – 1 (14.5 oz.) can
- No-salt-added diced tomatoes – 1 (14.5 oz.) can, undrained
- Thinly sliced carrot – ½ cup
- Unsweetened cocoa powder – 1 tsp.
- Garlic – 1 clove, minced
- Thinly sliced cabbage – 1 cup
- Dried wide noodles – ½ cup
- Paprika – 2 tsps.
- Light sour cream – ¼ cup
- Snipped fresh parsley

Directions:
1. Cut meat into ½-inch cubes. In a saucepan, cook and stir meat in hot oil until browned, for about 6 minutes. Add onion, cook and stir until onion softens, about 3 minutes.
2. Stir in the next six Ingredients: (through garlic). Bring to a boil. Reduce heat. Simmer, uncovered, for about 15 minutes or until meat is tender.
3. Stir in paprika, noodles, and cabbage. Simmer, uncovered, until noodles are tender but still firm, for about 5 to 7 minutes. Remove from heat.
4. Top each serving with sour cream.
5. Sprinkle with parsley and additional paprika.
6. Serve.

Beef-Vegetable Ragout

Preparation time: 30 minutes
Cooking time: 8 hours
Servings: 8
Ingredients:
- Beef chuck roast – 1 ½ lb.
- Sliced fresh button or cremini mushrooms – 3 cups
- Chopped onion – 1 cup
- Garlic – 4 cloves, minced
- Salt – ½ tsp.
- Black pepper – ½ tsp.
- Quick-cooking tapioca -1/4 cup, crushed
- 50% less-sodium beef broth – 2 (14.5 oz.) cans
- Dry sherry – ½ cup
- Sugar snap pea pods – 4 cups
- Cherry tomatoes – 2 cups, halved
- Hot cooked multigrain noodles – 4 cups

Directions:
1. Cut meat into ¾-inch pieces.
2. Coat a skillet with cooking spray. Cook meat, half at a time, in the hot skillet until browned.
3. Combine the next five Ingredients: (through pepper) in a slow cooker. Sprinkle with tapioca. Add meat and pour in broth and dry sherry.
4. Cover and cook on low for 8 to 10 hours or high for 4 to 5 hours. If slow cooker is on low, turn to high. Stir in sugar snap

peas. Cover and cook for 5 minutes. Stir in cherry tomatoes. Serve meat mixture over hot cooked noodles.

Fried Pork Chops

Preparation time: 10 minutes
Cooking Time: 35 Minutes
Servings: 2
Ingredients:
- 3 cloves of ground garlic
- 2 tbsp. olive oil - 1 tbsp. of marinade
- 4 thawed pork chops

Directions:
1. Mix the cloves of ground garlic, marinade, and oil. Then apply this mixture on the chops.
2. Put the chops in the air fryer at 3600C for 35 minutes

Pork on a Blanket

Preparation time: 10 minutes
Cooking Time: 10 Minutes
Servings: 4
Ingredients:
- ½ puff pastry sheet, defrosted
- 16 thick smoked sausages
- 15 ml of milk

Directions:
1. Preheat la air fryer to 200°C and set the timer to 5 minutes.
2. Cut the puff pastry into 64 x 38 mm strips.
3. Place a cocktail sausage at the end of the puff pastry and roll around the sausage, sealing the dough with some water.
4. Brush the top (with the seam facing down) of the sausages wrapped in milk and place them in the preheated air fryer.
5. Cook at 200°C for 10 minutes or until golden brown.

Greek Flat Iron Steaks

Preparation time: 10 minutes
Cooking time: 15 minutes
Servings: 4
Ingredients:
- Lemon – 1 - Boneless beef shoulder top blade steaks (flat iron) – 2 (6 to 8 oz.)
- Salt – ¼ tsp.
- Black pepper – ¼ tsp.
- Dried rosemary – 1 tsp. crushed
- Olive oil – 4 tsp.
- Grape tomatoes – 2 cups, halved
- Garlic – 2 cloves, minced
- Pitted green olives – 1/3 cup, halved
- Crumbled feta cheese – ¼ cup
- Lemon wedges

Directions:
1. Remove 1 tsp. zest from the lemon. Set zest aside. Cut steaks in half and season with salt and pepper. Sprinkle rosemary on both sides of the steaks.
2. Heat 2 tsps. Oil in a skillet. Add steaks and cook until medium rare, about 8 to 10 minutes. Turning once. Remove and set aside.
3. Add remaining 2 tsps. Oil to the skillet. Add garlic and tomatoes. Cook until tomatoes are soft and burst, for about 3 minutes. Remove from heat. Stir in the lemon zest and olives.

Serve steaks with tomato relish. Sprinkle with cheese and serve with the reserved lemon wedges.

Spiced Burgers with Cilantro Cucumber Sauce

Preparation time: 25 minutes
Cooking time: 15 minutes
Servings: 4
Ingredients:
- Plain fat-free Greek yogurt – 1 (5.3 to 6 oz.) container
- Finely chopped cucumber – 2/3 cup
- Snipped fresh cilantro – ¼ cup
- Garlic – 2 cloves, minced
- Salt – 1/8 tsp.
- Black pepper – 1/8 tsp.
- Canned garbanzo beans – ½ cup, rinsed and drained
- Lean ground beef – 1 lb.
- Finely chopped red onion – ¼ cup
- Chopped jalapeno pepper – 2 Tbsps.
- Salt – ½ tsp.
- Ground cumin – ¼ tsp.
- Ground coriander – ¼ tsp.
- Cinnamon – 1/8 tsp.
- Black pepper – 1/8 tsp.
- Radicchio – 1 head, shredded

Directions:
1. To make the sauce: in a bowl, stir together the first six Ingredients: (through black pepper). Cover and keep in the refrigerator.
2. In a bowl, mash garbanzo beans with a fork. Add the next eight Ingredients: (through black pepper), mix well. Form meat mixture into four ¾ inch thick patties.
3. Grill burgers, covered, over medium 14 to 13 minutes or until done (160F). Turning once.
4. Toss radicchio with additional fresh cilantro leaves.
5. Serve burgers on radicchio, top with sauce.

Sunday Brisket

Preparation time: 4 hours
Cooking time: 8 hours
Servings: 10
Ingredients:
- 1 teaspoon coarsely ground pepper
- 2 tablespoons cold water
- 3 tablespoons olive oil, divided
- 1 tablespoon tapioca flour
- 4 cups onions, sliced
- 1/2 teaspoon paprika
- 4 garlic cloves, minced
- 1 teaspoon Worcestershire sauce
- 1 tablespoon brown sugar
- 2 teaspoons Italian seasoning
- 1 fresh beef brisket (4 to 5 lbs.)
- 2 tablespoons tomato paste
- 1/3 cup all-purpose flour
- 1 can (14-1/2 ounces) reduced-sodium beef broth
- 1 teaspoon salt

- 4 tablespoons balsamic vinegar

Directions:
1. Preheat a tablespoon of oil in a skillet over medium heat; add and sauté sliced onions until softened. Then sprinkle with a 1 tablespoon of brown sugar and garlic.
2. Turn the heat down and cook until onions become brown, with occasional stirring, for about 10 minutes.
3. Transfer cooked onions to a slow cooker. Cut brisket into half and sprinkle with 1/3 cup all-purpose flour.
4. Preheat leftover oil in a skillet and then add brisket; cook both sides until browned and sprinkle with pepper and salt.
5. Transfer cooked brisket to the cooker over onions. Now add 4 tablespoons balsamic vinegar and cook over high heat.
6. Then stir in 2 tablespoons tomato paste, 1 can (14-1/2 ounces) broth, 1 teaspoon Worcestershire sauce, 2 teaspoons Italian seasoning and 1/2 teaspoon paprika until blended; pour this mixture over brisket.
7. Cover the cooker and cook for about 8-10 hours on low, until meat is completely cooked through.
8. Then take the brisket out from the cooker. Transfer cooking juices from the cooker to the pan; skim fat if any and boil it lightly.
9. Take a bowl and add 1 tablespoon tapioca flour and 2 tablespoons cold water; mix well until smooth and transfer to cooking juices with stirring. Cook for about 1-2 minutes until thickened.
10. Cut the brisket into thin slices. Serve the brisket with sauce and enjoy!

Pork Rind

Preparation time: 10 minutes
Cooking Time: 1h
Servings: 4
Ingredients:
- 1kg of pork rinds
- Salt
- ½ tsp. black pepper coffee

Directions:
1. Preheat the air fryer. Set the time of 5 minutes and the temperature to 2000C.
2. Cut the bacon into cubes - 1 finger wide.
3. Season with salt and a pinch of pepper.
4. Place in the basket of the air fryer. Set the time of 45 minutes and press the power button.
5. Shake the basket every 10 minutes so that the pork rinds stay golden brown equally.
6. Once they are ready, drain a little on the paper towel so they stay dry. Transfer to a plate and serve.

Ginger Chili Broccoli

Preparation time: 10 minutes
Cooking Time: 25 Minutes
Servings: 5
Ingredients:
- 8 cups broccoli florets
- 1/2 cup olive oil
- 2 fresh lime juice
- 2 tbsp. fresh ginger, grated
- 2 tsp chili pepper, chopped

Directions:
1. Add broccoli florets into the steamer and steam for 8 minutes.
2. Meanwhile, for dressing in a small bowl, combine lime juice, oil, ginger, and chili pepper.
3. Add steamed broccoli in a large bowl then pour dressing over broccoli. Toss well.

Pork Tenderloin

Preparation time: 10 minutes
Cooking time: 45 minutes
Servings: 2-4
Ingredients:
- 2 large eggs
- ¼ cup milk
- 2 cups seasoned breadcrumbs
- Salt and pepper to taste
- Nonstick cooking spray

Directions:
1. Slice the tenderloin into ½-inch slices.
2. Place the slices between two plastic sheets and tap them until each piece is ¼ inch thick.
3. In a large container, mix the eggs and milk.
4. In a separate container or dish, pour the breadcrumbs.
5. Introduce each piece of pork in the mixture of eggs and milk, letting the excess drain.
6. Then introduce the pork in the breadcrumbs, covering each side.
7. Place the covered pork on a wire rack for 30 minutes to make sure the cover adheres.
8. Preheat the air fryer to 400°F (204 °C).
9. Spray the basket of the air fryer with nonstick cooking spray. Place the covered sirloin in the basket in a single layer.
10. Cook the sirloin for 10 minutes, then take it out, turn it over and sprinkle with more nonstick spray.
11. Cook for 5-minutes more or until both sides are crispy and golden brown.

Chestnut Stuffed Pork Roast

Preparation time: 1 hour 30 minutes
Cooking time: 1 hour 35 minutes
Servings: 15
Ingredients:
- 5 lb. pork loin roast, boneless, double tied
- ½ lb. ground pork
- ½ cup celery, diced fine
- ½ cup onion, diced fine
- 2 tbsp. fresh parsley, diced, divided
- 1 tbsp. margarine
- What you'll need from store cupboard:
- 15 oz. can chestnuts, drained
- 2 cup low sodium chicken broth
- 3 tbsp. flour
- 2 tbsp. brandy, divided
- ½ tsp salt
- ½ tsp pepper
- 1/8 tsp allspice
- Salt & black pepper, to taste

Directions:
1. Heat oven to 350 degrees.
2. Untie roast, open and pound lightly to even thickness.

3. Melt margarine in a skillet over med-high heat. Add celery and onion and cook until soft.
4. In a large bowl, combine ground pork, 1 tablespoon parsley, 1 tablespoon brandy and seasonings. Mix in celery and onion. Spread over roast.
5. Lay a row of chestnuts down the center. Roll meat around filling and tie securely with butcher string. Roast in oven 1 ½ hours or until meat thermometer reaches 145 degrees. Remove and let rest 10 minutes.
6. Measure out 2 tablespoons of drippings, discard the rest, into a saucepan. Place over medium heat and whisk in flour until smooth. Add broth and cook, stirring, until mixture thickens. Chop remaining chestnuts and add to gravy along with remaining brandy and parsley. Season with salt and pepper if desired. Slice the roast and serve topped with gravy.

Beef, Tomato, and Pepper Tortillas

Preparation time: 20 minutes
Cooking time: 0 minutes
Servings: 6
Ingredients:
- 6 whole wheat flour tortillas (10-inch)
- 6 large romaine lettuce leaves
- 12 ounces (340 g) cooked deli roast beef, thinly sliced
- 1 cup diced red bell peppers
- 1 cup diced tomatoes
- 1 tablespoon red wine vinegar
- 1 teaspoon cumin
- 1/4 teaspoon freshly ground black pepper
- 1 tablespoon olive oil

Directions:
1. Unfold the tortillas on a clean work surface, then top each tortilla with a lettuce leaf. Divide the roast beef over the leaf.
2. Combine the remaining Ingredients: in a bowl. Stir to mix well. Pour the mixture over the beef.
3. Fold the tortillas over the fillings, then roll them up. Serve immediately.

Salted Biscuit Pie Turkey Chops

Preparation time: 15 minutes
Cooking time: 20 minutes
Servings: 4
Ingredients:
- 8 large turkey chops
- 300 gr of crackers
- 2 eggs
- Extra virgin olive oil
- Salt
- Ground pepper

Directions:
1. Put the turkey chops on the worktable, and salt and pepper.
2. Beat the eggs in a bowl.
3. Crush the cookies in the Thermo mix with a few turbo strokes until they are made grit, or you can crush them with the blender.
4. Put the cookies in a bowl.
5. Pass the chops through the beaten egg and then passed them through the crushed cookies. Press well so that the empanada is perfect.
6. Paint the empanada with a silicone brush and extra virgin olive oil.
7. Put the chops in the basket of the air fryer, not all will enter. They will be done in batches.
8. Select 200 degrees, 15 minutes.
9. When you have all the chops made, serve.

Roasted Pork

Preparation time: 10 minutes
Cooking Time: 30 Minutes
Servings: 2-4
Ingredients:
- 500-2000g Pork meat (To roast)
- Salt
- Oil

Directions:
1. Join the cuts in an orderly manner.
2. Place the meat on the plate
3. Varnish with a little oil.
4. Place the roasts with the fat side down.
5. Cook in air fryer at 1800C for 30 minutes.
6. Turn when you hear the beep.
7. Remove from the oven. Drain excess juice.
8. Let stand for 10 minutes on aluminum foil before serving.

Homemade Flamingos

Preparation time: 30 minutes
Cooking Time: 20 Minutes
Servings: 4
Ingredients:
1. 400g of very thin sliced pork fillets c / n
2. 2 boiled and chopped eggs
3. 100g chopped Serrano ham
4. 1 beaten egg
5. Breadcrumbs

Directions:
1. Make a roll with the pork fillets. Introduce half-cooked egg and Serrano ham. So that the roll does not lose its shape, fasten with a string or chopsticks. Pass the rolls through beaten egg and then through the breadcrumbs until it forms a good layer. Preheat the air fryer a few minutes at 180° C.
2. Insert the rolls in the basket and set the timer for about 8 minutes at 180o C.

Meatloaf Reboot

Preparation time: 20 minutes
Cooking Time: 9 Minutes
Servings: 2
Ingredients:
- 4 slices of leftover meatloaf, cut about 1-inch thick.

Directions:
1. Preheat your air fryer to 350 degrees.
2. Spray each side of the meatloaf slices with cooking spray. Add the slices to the air fryer and cook for about 9 to 10 minutes. Don't turn the slices halfway through the cooking cycle, because they may break apart. Instead, keep them on one side to cook to ensure they stay together

Turkey Enchiladas

Preparation time: 45 minutes
Cooking time: 35 minutes
Servings: 8

Ingredients:
- 3 cup turkey, cooked and cut in pieces
- 1 onion, diced
- 1 bell pepper, diced
- 1 cup fat free sour cream
- 1 cup reduced fat cheddar cheese, grated
- What you'll need from store cupboard:
- 8 6-inch flour tortillas
- 14 ½ oz. low sodium chicken broth
- ¾ cup salsa
- 3 tbsp. flour
- 2 tsp olive oil
- 1 ¼ tsp coriander
- ¼ tsp pepper
- Nonstick cooking spray

Directions:
1. Spray a large saucepan with cooking spray and heat oil over med-high heat. Add onion and bell pepper and cook until tender.
2. Sprinkle with flour, coriander and pepper and stir until blended. Slowly stir in broth. Bring to a boil and cook, stirring, 2 minutes or until thickened.
3. Remove from heat and stir in sour cream and ¾ cup cheese.
4. Heat oven to 350 degrees. Spray a 13x9-inch pan with cooking spray.
5. In a large bowl, combine turkey, salsa, and 1 cup of cheese mixture. Spoon 1/3 cup mixture down middle of each tortilla and roll up. Place seam side down in prepared dish.
6. Pour remaining cheese mixture over top of enchiladas. Cover and bake 20 minutes. Uncover and sprinkle with remaining cheese. Bake another 5-10 minutes until cheese is melted and starts to brown.

Mexican Meat Loaf

Preparation time: 30 minutes
Cooking time: 4 hours
Servings: 8
Ingredients:
- 6 garlic cloves, minced
- 2 pounds lean ground beef (90% lean)
- 6 tablespoons ketchup, divided
- 1/8 teaspoon cayenne pepper
- 2 tablespoons Worcestershire sauce
- 1/2 teaspoon pepper
- 12 saltines, crushed
- 1/2 teaspoon salt
- 1 medium onion, finely chopped
- 1 teaspoon paprika

Directions:
1. Make 3 strips of foil; crisscross the strips. Place these strips into a slow cooker at the bottom.
2. Now spray the strips with cooking spray. Take a bowl and add 2 tablespoons Worcestershire sauce, 12 crushed saltines, 2 tablespoons of ketchup, 1 finely chopped onion, 1/2 teaspoon salt, 1 teaspoon paprika, 1/8 teaspoon cayenne pepper, 1/2 teaspoon pepper and 6 minced cloves of garlic; combine well.
3. Add beef into the mixture and toss well until coated. Shape into a loaf. Place this round loaf over strips in the center.
4. Cover the cooker and cook for about 4-5 hours on low. Once done, take the meat out and transfer to a serving platter. Spread ketchup over Mexican meatloaf and enjoy!

Beef Daube Provencal

Preparation time: 1 hour 30 minutes
Cooking time: 5 hours
Servings: 8
Ingredients:
- 2 teaspoons olive oil
- 1 cup dry red wine
- Hot cooked pasta or mashed potatoes
- 1 (about 2 pounds) boneless beef chuck roast or venison roast, cut into 1-inch cubes
- 1-1/2 teaspoons salt, divided
- 1 bay leaf
- 1/2 teaspoon coarsely ground pepper, divided
- 1 teaspoon fresh thyme, chopped
- 2 cups carrots, chopped
- 1 teaspoon fresh rosemary, chopped
- 1-1/2 cups onion, chopped
- 1/2 cup beef broth
- 12 garlic cloves, crushed
- 1 can (14-1/2 ounces) diced tomatoes
- 1 tablespoon tomato paste
- Fresh thyme leaves (optional)
- Dash ground cloves

Directions:
1. Preheat oil in a skillet over medium heat; sprinkle meat with ¼ teaspoon of pepper and ½ teaspoon of salt.
2. Transfer meat to a skillet and cook both sides until browned; then transfer to a slow cooker.
3. Add 1-1/2 cups chopped onion, 12 crushed cloves of garlic, 2 cups of chopped carrots and remaining pepper and salt into the skillet; cook for about 4-6 minutes until golden brown.
4. Add 1 tablespoon of tomato paste; cook for about a minute until fragrant. Then add 1 cup dry red wine and boil it lightly.
5. Transfer the mixture into the slow cooker. Cover the cooker and cook for about 5-7 hours, until tender. Serve beef daube Provencal with mashed potatoes and cooked pasta. Sprinkle fresh thyme over top and enjoy!

Boeuf Bourguignon

Preparation time: 15 minutes
Cooking time: 8 hours
Servings: 12 servings (2/3 cup each)
Ingredients:
- 3 pounds beef stew meat
- 1 teaspoon salt
- 1-3/4 cups dry red wine
- 1/3 cup all-purpose flour
- 3 tablespoons olive oil
- 2 garlic cloves, minced
- 1/4 teaspoon pepper
- 3 tablespoons dried onion, minced
- 24 (about 2 cups) pearl onions, peeled
- 2 tablespoons dried parsley flakes
- 1-pound whole fresh mushrooms, quartered

- 8 bay leaves
- 8 bacon strips, chopped
- 1 teaspoon dried thyme

Directions:
1. Add 3 lbs. beef stew meat into a large plastic bag; then add 3 tablespoons olive oil, 1-3/4 cups dry red wine and all the seasonings. Seal this bag and shake lightly to coat the meat, refrigerate for 12 hours or overnight.
2. Cook bacon in a skillet over medium heat with occasional stirring until crisp. Drain on a plate cover with paper towels.
3. Discard dripping, if any. (Reserve only a tablespoon in the pan).
4. Add 1-pound whole fresh quartered mushrooms and 3 tablespoons of dried minced onion; cook over medium heat with stirring for a minute.
5. Now drain the marinade and reserve it. Transfer beef to a slow cooker.
6. Sprinkle with 1/3 cup all-purpose flour and 1 teaspoon salt; toss well until coated.
7. Top with the mixture of mushrooms and bacon along with reserved marinade.
8. Cover the cooker and cook for about 8-10 hours on low, until tender. Remove the bay leaf.
9. Serve Boeuf Bourguignon with noodles!

Pork and Pumpkin Stew

Preparation time: 30 minutes
Cooking time: 4 hours
Servings: 8
Ingredients:
- 1 onion, diced
- 1 (14.5-ounce) can black beans, drained and rinsed
- 16 oz. pork shoulder, trimmed of all visible fat, and cut into cubes of 1-inch
- 1 bay leave
- ½ teaspoon black pepper
- 4 sprig fresh thyme
- 1 teaspoon seasoning (salt-free, such as Mrs. Dash)
- 4 clove garlic, minced
- 1 tablespoon olive oil
- 1 small sugar/pie pumpkin, peeled, seeded, and diced
- 2 tablespoons tomato paste
- 3 carrots, peeled and diced
- 1 cup beef broth
- 4 celery stalks, diced
- 1/4 teaspoon ground cinnamon

Directions:
1. Season pork with salt, seasoning and pepper.
2. Preheat oil to a skillet over medium heat; cook pork for about 8 minutes until browned. Once browned, take it out and keep it aside.
3. Add 2 tablespoons tomato paste, 1/4 teaspoon ground cinnamon and 1 cup beef broth to a pan; whisk well.
4. Now add cooked browned meat along with leftover Ingredients: and liquid into slow cooker; stir well. Add to the slow cooker.
5. Cook for about 7 hours and 40 minutes on low or for 3 hours and 40 minutes on high.
6. Stir in 1 (14.5-ounce) can black beans and cook further for 20 minutes.
7. Before serving, remove bay leaf.

Crockpot Chipotle Steak

Preparation time: 15 minutes
Cooking time: 2 hours
Servings: 6
Ingredients:
- 2 cups canned crushed tomatoes
- 1 teaspoon garlic, finely minced
- 1 1/2 lbs. London broil, cubed
- 1 1/2 cup poblano pepper, cut into 1-inch squares
- ½ teaspoon salt free Mexican seasoning
- 1 1/2 cup red onion, cut into 1-inch squares
- 1/4 teaspoon kosher salt
- 3 teaspoons olive oil, divided
- 2 peppers chipotle chili in adobo
- 1 tablespoon light or dark brown sugar, packed
- ½ tablespoon adobo sauce from chipotle pepper can
- 1 tablespoon Worcestershire sauce

Directions:
1. In a bowl, mix steak cubes with salt and seasoning; toss well until coated and keep it aside.
2. Take out 2 chipotle peppers from the can and chop them finely. Transfer them to a bowl. Add 2 cups crushed tomatoes, 1 tablespoon Worcestershire sauce, 1 tablespoon brown sugar and 1/2 tablespoon of the sauce from can; stir well and keep it aside.
3. Preheat a teaspoon of oil in a nonstick pan; then add 1 1/2 cup red onion, 1 1/2 cup poblano pepper, and 1 teaspoon of finely minced garlic. Spread all these Ingredients: evenly in a pan and cook with stirring occasionally until crisp-tender. Once cooked, transfer into a Crockpot.
4. Again, preheat a teaspoon of oil in a pan. Then add half seasoned cubes of beef and cook each side for a minute, until browned. Once cooked, transfer these cubes into Crockpot.
5. Then stir in the adobo and crushed tomato mixture. Simmer in the crockpot on low for about 2-4 hours.
6. Serve right away!

Chuck and Veggies

Preparation time: 15 minutes
Cooking time: 9 hours
Servings: 2
Ingredients:
- ¼ cup dry red wine - ¼ teaspoon salt
- 8 oz. boneless lean chuck roast
- ¼ teaspoon black pepper
- 8 oz. frozen pepper stir-fry
- 1 teaspoon Worcestershire sauce
- 8 oz. whole mushrooms
- 1 teaspoon instant coffee granules
- 1 1/4 cups fresh green beans, trimmed
- 1 dried bay leaf

Directions:
1. Mix all the Ingredients: except salt in a bowl; combine well and then transfer to a slow cooker.

2. Cover the cooker and cook for about 9 hours on low and 4 1/2 hours on high, until beef is completely cooked through and tender.
3. Stir in ¼ teaspoon salt gently. Take out the vegetables and beef and transfer to 2 shallow bowls.
4. Pour liquid into the skillet; boil it lightly and cook until liquid reduces to ¼ cup, for about 1 1/2 minutes.
5. Pour over veggies and beef. Discard bay leaf and serve.

Southwest Turkey Lasagna

Preparation time: 50 minutes
Servings: 8
Cooking Time: 20 Minutes
Ingredients:
- 1 lb. lean ground turkey
- 1 onion, diced
- 1 green bell pepper, diced
- 1 red pepper, diced
- 8 oz. fat free cream cheese
- 1 cup Mexican cheese blend, grated
- ½ cup fat free sour cream
- What you'll need from store cupboard:
- 6 8-inch low carb whole wheat tortillas
- 10 oz. enchilada sauce
- ½ cup salsa
- 1 tsp chili powder
- Nonstick cooking spray

Directions:
1. Heat oven to 400 degrees. Spray a 13x9-inch baking dish with cooking spray.
2. In a large skillet, over medium heat, cook turkey, onion, and peppers until turkey is no longer pink. Drain fat.
3. Stir in cream cheese and chili powder.
4. Pour enchilada sauce into a shallow dish. Dip tortillas in sauce to coat. Place two tortillas in prepared dish. Spread with ½ the turkey mixture and sprinkle 1/3 of the cheese over turkey. Repeat layer. Top with remaining tortillas and cheese.
5. Cover with foil and bake 20-25 minutes, or until heated through. This can also be frozen up to 3 months.
6. Let rest 10 minutes before cutting. Serve topped with salsa and sour cream.

Balsamic Chicken & Vegetable Skillet

Preparation time: 10 minutes
Cooking time: 20 minutes
Servings: 4
Ingredients:
- 1 lb. chicken breasts, cut in 1-inch cubes
- 1 cup cherry tomatoes, halved
- 1 cup broccoli florets
- 1 cup baby Bella mushrooms, sliced
- 1 tbsp. fresh basil, diced
- What you'll need from store cupboard:
- 1/2 recipe homemade pasta, cooked and drain well
- ½ cup low sodium chicken broth
- 3 tbsp. balsamic vinegar
- 2 tbsp. olive oil, divided
- 1 tsp pepper
- ½ tsp garlic powder
- ½ tsp salt
- ½ tsp red pepper flakes

Directions:
1. Heat oil in a large, deep skillet over med-high heat. Add chicken and cook until browned on all sides, 8-10 minutes.
2. Add vegetables, basil, broth, and seasonings. Cover, reduce heat to medium and cook 5 minutes, or vegetables are tender.
3. Uncover and stir in cooked pasta and vinegar. Cook until heated through, 3-4 minutes. Serve.

Deconstructed Philly Cheesesteaks

Preparation time: 10 minutes
Cooking Time: 20 Minutes
Servings: 4
Ingredients:
- 1 lb. lean ground beef
- 5-6 mushrooms, halved
- 4 slices provolone cheese
- 3 green bell peppers, quartered
- 2 medium onions, quartered
- What you'll need from store cupboard:
- ½ cup low sodium beef broth
- 1-2 tbsp. Worcestershire sauce
- 1 tsp olive oil
- Salt & pepper, to taste

Directions:
1. Heat oven to 400 degrees.
2. Place vegetables in a large bowl and add oil. Toss to coat. Dump out onto a large baking sheet and bake 10-15 minutes, or until tender-crisp.
3. Place beef in a large skillet and cook over med-high heat until no longer pink. Drain off fat.
4. Add broth and Worcestershire. Cook, stirring occasionally, until liquid is absorbed, about 5 minutes. Salt and pepper beef if desired. Top with sliced cheese, remove from heat and cover until cheese melts.
5. Divide vegetables evenly between 4 bowls. Top with beef and serve.

Ham & Brie Turnovers

Preparation time: 30 minutes
Cooking Time: 25 Minutes
Servings: 8
Ingredients:
- 8 slices ham, diced
- 3 oz. brie cheese
- 1 egg
- What you'll need from store cupboard:
- 2 9-inch pie crusts, unbaked
- 2 tbsp. sugar free fig pre servings
- 2 tbsp. stone ground mustard
- 1 tbsp. water
- 1/8 tsp salt
- 1/8 tsp pepper

Directions:
1. Heat oven to 400 degrees. Line two cookie sheets with parchment paper.

2. On a lightly floured surface unroll one pie crust and cut 4 4-inch circles and place on prepared pan.
3. Gather up remaining dough, roll out and cut 4 more 4-inch circles and set aside
4. In a small bowl, combine fig preserves, mustard, salt, and pepper. Place a heaping teaspoon of fig mustard mixture in the center of dough on the pan and shape into a half dollar size
5. Use your hands to make a smaller circle of the brie and place on top of fig mixture. Place ham on top of the cheese, leaving ¼-inch edge.
6. In another small bowl, beat egg and water together. Brush around edge and top with 4-inch circle of dough. Repeat. Use a fork to seal the edges and cut a small X in the top. Brush with remaining egg wash.
7. Bake 25 minutes, or until golden brown. Remove from oven and cool on wire rack at least 5 minutes before serving. Repeat these steps with the second pie crust.

Shredded Green Chili Beef

Preparation time: 10 minutes
Cooking time: 7 hours
Servings: 12
Ingredients:
- 1 teaspoon chili powder
- 2 large sweet onions, halved and thinly sliced
- 1 can (28 ounces) green enchilada sauce
- 4 tablespoons packed brown sugar, divided
- 2 tablespoons canola oil
- 1 tablespoon paprika
- 1 (about 3 lbs.) boneless beef chuck roast
- 1-1/2 teaspoons salt
- 1/2 teaspoon pepper
- 1 teaspoon cayenne pepper
- 1 teaspoon garlic powder

Directions:
1. Add 3 tablespoons brown sugar along with thinly sliced onion into a slow cooker.
2. Combine leftover sugar with 1 teaspoon cayenne pepper, 1 tablespoon paprika, 1-1/2 teaspoons salt, 1 teaspoon chili powder, 1/2 teaspoon pepper and 1 teaspoon garlic powder; coat beef with this mixture completely.
3. Preheat some oil in a skillet and add beef; cook each side for about 1-2 minutes, until browned. Once cooked, transfer to the cooker.
4. Pour 1 can (28 ounces) green enchilada sauce over beef. Cover the cooker and cook for about 7-9 hours on low, until completely cooked through.
5. Once cooked, take the beef out and shred it with forks; transfer shredded beef back to the cooker and heat through.
6. Serve over potatoes, if needed and enjoy!

Chinese Pot Roast

Preparation time: 3 hours
Cooking time: 9 hours
Servings: 6
Ingredients:
- 2 onions, chopped
- 1/2 teaspoon ground ginger
- 3 pounds boneless pot roast
- 4 tablespoons cup water
- 2 tablespoons flour
- 4 tablespoons light soy sauce
- 1 tablespoon canola oil

Directions:
1. Fill the small bowl with 2 tablespoons flour; dip roast into it.
2. Preheat oil in a pan and cook the roast until browned. Then transfer it to a slow cooker followed by 2 large chopped onions on top.
3. Now combine 4 tablespoons cup water, 4 tablespoons light soy sauce and 1/2 teaspoon ground ginger; mix well and pour over roast in the cooker.
4. Cover the cooker and cook for about 10 minutes on high. Turn the heat down and cook for about 8-10 hours on low.
5. Slice the beef and serve along with rice. Enjoy the meal!

Tuscan Pork Chops

Preparation time: 30 minutes
Cooking time: 8 hours
Servings: 6
Ingredients:
- 6 (about 2-1/2 lbs.) bone-in pork chops, cut 1/2-inch think
- 4 ounces cooked orzo, kept warm
- 2 teaspoons Italian seasoning
- 2 tablespoons cold water
- 4 cloves garlic, minced
- 2 tablespoons cornstarch
- 1/2 teaspoon salt
- 2 zucchinis, cut into 1-inch pieces
- 1/4 teaspoon pepper
- 2 tablespoons balsamic vinegar
- 1 onion, chopped
- 2 (14-1/2-ounce) cans no-salt-added diced tomatoes, undrained

Directions:
1. Take a bowl and mix 1/4 teaspoon pepper, 1/2 teaspoon salt, 2 teaspoons Italian seasoning and garlic in it; stir well.
2. Add chopped onion to a slow cooker along with half of pork chops. Sprinkle half of the mixture of seasoning over pork chops.
3. Again, layer pork chops followed by remaining seasoning mixture on top.
5. Top last layer of seasoning with 2 tablespoons balsamic vinegar and undrained tomatoes. Then add pieces of zucchini.
6. Cover the cooker and cook for about 4-5 hours on high or for 8-9 hours on low.
7. Once cooked, transfer veggies along with meat to a platter.
8. Add 2 tablespoons cornstarch and 2 tablespoons cold water to a saucepan; cook well with stirring. Then add juices present from cooker into the pan slowly and gradually. Cook until thickened for about 2-3 minutes.
9. Serve Tuscan pork chops over veggies and meat. You can also serve it with orzo!

Crockpot Flank Steak

Preparation time: 10 minutes
Cooking time: 4 hours
Servings: 6
Ingredients:
- 2 tablespoons vinegar

- 1/8 teaspoon pepper
- 1 flank steak (about 1-1/2 lbs.), cut in half
- 1/2 teaspoon salt
- 1 tablespoon canola oil
- 1/2 teaspoon sugar
- 1 large onion, sliced
- 1 teaspoon garlic powder
- 1/3 cup water
- 1-1/4 teaspoons chili powder
- 1 can (4 oz.) green chiles, chopped

Directions:
1. Preheat some oil in a skillet and brown steak in it. Transfer browned steak into a slow cooker.
2. Add and sauté onion in the same skillet for about a minute. Start adding 1/3 cups of water gradually.
3. Add leftover Ingredients: and boil lightly. Pour this mixture over steak in cooker.
4. Cover the cooker and cook for about 4-5 hours on low, until meat is tender.
5. Before serving, slice the steak and serve along with pan juices and onion!

Pot Roast Soup

Preparation time: 10 minutes
Cooking Time: 7 hours
Servings: 6
Ingredients:
- Beef shoulder roast boneless 2 ½ pounds (1 kg 134 g)
- Onions, chopped 2 cups
- Diced tomatoes 15 oz. (425 g)
- Hash brown potatoes, cubed 1 cup
- Beef broth 1 cup
- Minced garlic 1 tbsp.
- Dried thyme leaves 1 tsp
- Pepper ¼ tsp
- Broccoli slaw 2 cups
- Frozen peas ½ cup

Directions:
1. Cut roast into equal pieces.
2. Place in a slow cooker and add onions, tomatoes, broth, thyme, garlic, and pepper.
3. Cover and cook for 5 to 6 hours on high until beef is tender.
4. Add in broccoli and potatoes, and cook for half an hour.
5. Add in peas and cook for 20 more minutes or until the peas are done.
6. Serve after done.

Beef and Zucchini Meatballs

Preparation time: 5 minutes
Cooking Time: 25 minutes
Servings: 4
Ingredients:
- Ground beef 1 pound (454 g)
- Grated zucchini 1 cup
- Salt ¼ tsp
- Pepper ¼ tsp

Directions:
1. Preheat oven to 400 F (204 °C).
2. In a bowl, mix all Ingredients: and shape them into 20 meatballs.
3. Place on a baking sheet and bake for 23-25 minutes.
4. Serve hot.

Meatballs with Spaghetti

Preparation time: 15 minutes
Cooking Time: 30 minutes
Servings: 6
Ingredients:
- Grounded turkey breast 1 pound (454 g)
- Chopped onion ½ cup
- Egg, beaten 1
- Plain bread crumbs ¼ cup
- Garlic powder 1 tsp
- Salt ½ tsp
- Black pepper ½ tsp
- Canola oil 1 tbsp.
- Sliced mushrooms 8 oz. (227 g)
- Marinara sauce 26 oz. (737 g)
- Spaghetti, cooked 12 oz. (340 g) - dried
- Dried basil leaves ½ tsp

Directions:
1. Combine turkey with onions, breadcrumbs, eggs, salt, pepper, and garlic powder. Mix well and form in meatballs.
2. In a skillet, brown meatballs on all sides for about 5-8 minutes and remove them. Then cook mushrooms for about 5-8 minutes. Add in meatballs, then cover with marinara sauce and basil. Cook for 11-12 minutes.
3. Serve with spaghetti.

Irish Beef Pot Pie

Preparation time: 10 minutes
Cooking Time: 30 minutes
Servings: 6
Ingredients:
- Beef flat iron steaks 1 ½ pound (680 g)
- Cremini mushrooms, sliced 8 oz. (227 g)
- Frozen sliced carrots 1 ½ cups
- Frozen peas 1 ½ cups
- Fresh thyme, chopped 2 tsp, divided
- Minced garlic 1 tsp, divided
- Salt and pepper to taste
- Cornstarch 3 tbsp.
- Beef broth 14 oz. (397 g)
- Refrigerated pie crust 7 oz. (198 g)

Directions:
1. Preheat oven to 425 F (218 °C).
2. Cut the steaks into strips.
3. In a skillet, add the mushrooms and cook for 3 minutes.
4. Add in carrots, peas, thyme, and garlic, and cook for another 4-5 minutes. Remove from skillet.
5. Add beef to the skillet and cook for 2 minutes. Season with salt and pepper and take out.
6. Take an empty skillet, mix cornstarch into the broth and cook until slightly thick. Add in beef and veggies.
7. Place defrosted pie crust into the pie plate, fill in the beef mixture and bake for 19-20 minutes. You can cover the pie with the remaining crust if you want.

8. Serve when done.

Spicy Beef Sloppy Joes

Preparation time: 20 minutes
Cooking time: 8 hours
Servings: 12
Ingredients:
- Lean ground beef – 2 lb.
- Lower-sodium salsa – 2 ½ cups
- Coarsely chopped fresh mushrooms – 3 cups
- Shredded carrots – 1 ¼ cups
- Finely chopped red and green sweet peppers – 1 ¼ cups
- No-salt added tomato paste – ½ (6-oz.) can
- Garlic – 4 cloves, minced
- Dried basil – 1 tsp. crushed
- Salt – ¾ tsp.
- Dried oregano – ½ tsp. crushed
- Cayenne pepper – ¼ tsp.
- Whole wheat hamburger buns – 12, split and toasted

Directions:
1. Cook ground beef in a skillet until browned. Drain off fat.
2. In a slow cooker, add the meat and combine the next 10 Ingredients: (through cayenne pepper).
3. Cover and cook on low for 8 to 10 hours or on high for 4 to 5 hours.
4. Spoon ½-cup of the meat mixture onto each bun.
5. Serve.

Roasted Steak and Tomato Salad

Preparation time: 20 minutes
Cooking time: 20 minutes
Servings: 4
Ingredients:
- Beef tenderloin steaks – 2 (8 oz.), trimmed
- Cracked black pepper – 1 tsp.
- Kosher salt – ¼ tsp.
- Small tomatoes – 6, halved
- Olive oil – 2 tsps.
- Shredded Parmesan cheese – ¼ cup
- Dried oregano – ½ tsp. crushed
- Torn romaine lettuce – 8 cups
- Artichoke hearts – 1 (14-oz.) can, drained and quartered
- Red onion slivers – 1/3 cup
- Balsamic vinegar – 3 Tbsp.
- Olive oil – 1 Tbsp.

Directions:
1. Preheat the oven to 400F.
2. Season the meat with salt and pepper and rub. Let stand for 20 minutes at room temperature.
3. Arrange tomato halves on a baking sheet (cut side down).
4. Heat 2 tsps. Oil in a skillet. Add meat and cook until well browned on all sides, about 8 minutes. Transfer meat to other side of baking sheet.
5. Roast for 8 to 10 minutes for medium (145F). Remove meat from oven. Cover with foil and let stand. Move oven rack for broiling.
6. Turn oven to broil. Turn tomatoes cut sides up. Combine oregano and Parmesan. Sprinkle over tomatoes. Broil 4 to 5 inches from heat for about 2 minutes, or until cheese is melted and golden.
7. In a bowl, combine onion, artichoke hearts, and lettuce. Drizzle with vinegar and 1 tbsp. oil. Toss to coat.
8. Arrange on plates. Slice steak and arrange over lettuce with tomato halves.

Lamb Fatteh with Asparagus

Preparation time: 10 minutes
Cooking time: 20 minutes
Servings: 4
Ingredients:
- Olive oil – 1 Tbsp.
- Medium onion – 1, sliced
- Garlic – 4 cloves, minced
- Boneless lamb leg – 12 oz. cut into smaller pieces
- 50% less sodium beef broth – 1 (14.5 oz.) can
- Whole wheat pearl couscous – 1 cup
- Dried oregano – ½ tsp. crushed
- Ground cumin – ½ tsp.
- Salt – ¼ tsp.
- Black pepper – ¼ tsp.
- Thin asparagus spears – 1 lb. sliced into 2-inch pieces
- Chopped red sweet pepper – ¾ cup
- Snipped fresh oregano and lemon wedges

Directions:
1. Heat oil in a skillet. Add onion and cook for 3 minutes.
2. Add garlic and cook for 1 minute.
3. Add lamb and cook until browned on all sides, about 3 to 5 minutes.
4. Stir in the next six Ingredients: (through black pepper). Bring to a boil. Lower heat and simmer, covered, for 10 minutes. Stirring occasionally.
5. Stir in sweet pepper and asparagus. Cover and simmer until vegetables are crisp-tender, about 3 to 5 minutes.
6. Fluff lamb mixture lightly with a fork. Top with fresh oregano.
7. Serve with lemon wedges.

Oven-Baked Slow Baked Pork Shoulder

Servings: 4
Preparation Time: 10 minutes
Cooking Time: 9-10 hours 20 minutes
Ingredients:
- 4 pounds of pork shoulder
- 2 teaspoons oregano
- 1 teaspoon garlic powder
- 1 teaspoon onion powder
- Salt and pepper to taste

Directions:
1. Preheat your oven to 250 degrees F
2. Rinse meat and wash well; rub the meat with seasoning
3. Take a roasting pan and cover with aluminum foil
4. Transfer meat to the pan
5. Cover with another foil and transfer to the oven
6. Bake for 9-10 hours

7. Remove meat, increase oven temperature to 500 degrees F
8. Return meat and bake for 15-20 minutes more
9. Let it cool, slice, and enjoy!

Onion And Bacon Pork Chops

Servings: 4
Preparation Time: 10 minutes
Cooking Time: 45 minutes
Ingredients:
- 2 onions, peeled and chopped
- 6 bacon slices, chopped
- ½ cup chicken stock
- Salt and pepper to taste
- 4 pork chops

Directions:
1. Heat up a pan over medium heat and add bacon
2. Stir and cook until crispy
3. Transfer to bowl
4. Return pan to medium heat and add onions, season with salt and pepper
5. Stir and cook for 15 minutes
6. Transfer to the same bowl with bacon
7. Return the pan to heat (medium-high) and add pork chops
8. Season with salt and pepper and brown for 3 minutes
9. Flip and lower heat to medium
10. Cook for 7 minutes more
11. Add stock and stir. Cook for 2 minutes
12. Return the bacon and onions to the pan and stir. Cook for 1 minute
13. Serve and enjoy!

The Classical Medi Pork

Servings: 4
Preparation Time: 10 minutes
Cooking Time: 35 minutes
Ingredients:
- 4 pork chops, bone-in
- Salt and pepper to taste
- 1 teaspoon dried rosemary
- 3 garlic cloves, peeled and minced

Directions:
1. Season pork chops with salt and pepper
2. Place in roasting pan
3. Add rosemary and garlic to a pan
4. Preheat your oven to 425-degree F
5. Bake for 10 minutes
6. Lower heat to 350-degree F
7. Roast for 25 minutes more
8. Slice pork and divide on plates
9. Drizzle pan juice all over
10. Serve and enjoy!

Awesome Asian Beef Steak

Servings: 3
Preparation Time: 10 minutes
Cooking Time: 5 minutes
Ingredients:
- 2 tablespoons of sriracha sauce
- 1 tablespoon of garlic, minced
- 1 tablespoon of ginger, freshly grated
- 1 yellow bell pepper, cut into strips
- 1 red bell pepper cut into thin strips
- 1 tablespoon of sesame oil, garlic flavored
- 1 tablespoon of stevia
- ½ a teaspoon of curry powder
- ½ a teaspoon of rice wine vinegar
- 8 ounces of beef sirloin cut into strips
- 2 cups of baby spinach, stemmed
- ½ head of butter of lettuce, torn

Directions:
1. Add garlic, sriracha sauce, 1 teaspoon of sesame oil, rice wine vinegar, and stevia bowl
2. Mix well
3. Pour half of the mix into a zip bag and add steak; allow it to marinade
4. Assemble the brightly colored salad by layer the vegetables in two bowls in the following order: baby spinach, butter lettuce, two peppers on top
5. Remove the steak from the marinade and discard the liquid
6. Heat up sesame oil in a skillet over medium heat and add steak; stir fry for 3 minutes
7. Transfer your cooker steak on top of the salad
8. Drizzle the other half of your marinade mix
9. Sprinkle sriracha sauce on top and serve!

Healthy Avocado Beef Patties

Servings: 2
Preparation Time: 15 minutes
Cooking Time: 10 minutes
Ingredients:
- 1 pound of 85% lean ground beef
- 1 small avocado, pitted and peeled
- 2 slices of yellow cheddar cheese
- Salt as needed
- Fresh ground black pepper as needed

Directions:
1. Preheat and prepare your broiler to be high
2. Divide beef into two equal-sized patties
3. Season the patties with salt and pepper accordingly
4. Broil the patties for 5 minutes per side
5. Transfer the patties to a platter and add cheese
6. Slice avocado into strips and place them on top of the patties
7. Serve and enjoy!

The Fresh Thai Beef

Servings: 4
Preparation Time: 10 minutes
Cooking Time: 10 minutes
Ingredients:
- 1 cup beef stock
- 4 tablespoons peanut butter
- ¼ teaspoon garlic powder
- ¼ teaspoon onion powder
- 1 tablespoon coconut aminos
- 1 and ½ teaspoons lemon pepper
- 1 pound beef steak, cut into strips
- Salt and pepper to taste
- 1 green bell pepper, seeded and chopped
- 3 green onions, chopped

Directions:
1. Take a bowl and add peanut butter, stock, aminos, lemon pepper, and stir
2. Keep the mixture on the side
3. Take a pan and place it over medium-high heat
4. Add beef, and season with salt, pepper, onion, and garlic powder
5. Cook for 7 minutes
6. Add green pepper, stir cook for 3 minutes
7. Add peanut sauce and green onions
8. Stir cook for 1 minute
9. Divide between platters and serve
10. Enjoy!

Beef Zucchini Chips

Servings: 4
Preparation Time: 10 minutes
Cooking Time: 35 minutes
Ingredients:
- 2 garlic cloves, peeled and minced
- 1 teaspoon cumin
- 1 tablespoon coconut oil
- 1 pound of ground beef
- ½ cup onion, chopped
- 1 teaspoon smoked paprika
- Salt and pepper to taste
- 3 zucchini, sliced lengthwise, insides scooped out
- ¼ cup fresh cilantro, chopped
- ½ cup cheddar cheese, shredded
- 1 and ½ cups keto-friendly enchilada sauce
- Avocado, chopped
- Green onions, chopped
- Tomatoes, cored and chopped

Directions:
1. Take a pan and place it over medium-high heat
2. Add oil and heat it up
3. Add onions and stir. Cook for 2 minutes
4. Add beef and stir for a few minutes
5. Add paprika, salt, pepper, cumin, and garlic and stir cook for 2 minutes
6. Transfer zucchini halves to a baking pan
7. Stuff each with the beef mix, and pour enchilada sauce on top
8. Sprinkle cheddar
9. Bake (covered) for 20 minutes at 350-degree F
10. Uncover and sprinkle cilantro
11. Bake for 5 minutes or more
12. Sprinkle avocado, green onions, and tomatoes on top
13. Serve and enjoy!

Juicy Ground Beef Casserole

Servings: 6
Preparation Time: 10 minutes
Cooking Time: 35 minutes
Ingredients:
- 2 teaspoons onion flakes
- 1 tablespoon gluten-free Worcestershire sauce
- 2 pounds of ground beef
- 2 garlic cloves, peeled and minced
- Salt and pepper to taste
- 1 cup mozzarella cheese, shredded
- 2 cups cheddar cheese, shredded
- 1 cup of Russian dressing
- 2 tablespoons sesame seeds, toasted
- 20 dill pickle slices
- 1 romaine lettuce head, torn

Directions:
1. Take a pan and place it over medium heat
2. Add beef, onion flakes, Worcestershire sauce, salt, pepper, and garlic
3. Stir for 5 minutes
4. Transfer to a baking dish and add a 1 cup of cheddar, mozzarella cheese, half of the dressing
5. Stir and spread evenly
6. Arrange pickle slices on top
7. Sprinkle remaining cheddar and sesame seeds
8. Transfer to oven and bake for 20 minutes at 350-degree F
9. Turn oven to broil and broil for 5 minutes
10. Divide lettuce between serving platters and top with remaining dressing
11. Enjoy!

Majestic Beef And Tomato Squash

Servings: 4
Preparation Time: 10 minutes
Cooking Time: 60 minutes
Ingredients:
- 2 pounds acorn squash, pricked with a fork
- Salt and pepper to taste
- 3 garlic cloves, peeled and minced
- 1 onion, peeled and chopped
- 1 portobello mushroom, sliced
- 28 ounces canned tomatoes, diced
- 1 teaspoon dried oregano
- ¼ teaspoon cayenne pepper
- ½ teaspoon dried thyme
- 1 pound of ground beef
- 1 green bell pepper, seeded and chopped

Directions:
1. Preheat your oven to 400 degrees F
2. Take acorn squash and transfer to lined baking sheet, bake for 40 minutes
3. Cut in half and let it cool
4. Deseed them
5. Take a pan and place it over medium-high heat; add meat, garlic, onion, and mushroom, stir cook until brown
6. Add salt, pepper, thyme, oregano, cayenne, tomatoes, and green pepper, and stir
7. Cook for 10 minutes
8. Stuff squash halves with beef mix
9. Transfer to oven and bake for 10 minutes more
10. Serve and enjoy!

Tamari Steak Salad

Servings: 4
Preparation Time: 15 minutes
Cooking Time: 10 minutes
Ingredients:
- 2 large bunches of salad greens
- 8-9 ounces beef steak

- ½ red bell pepper, sliced
- 6-8 cherry tomatoes, cut into halves
- 4 radishes, sliced
- 4 tablespoons olive oil
- ½ tablespoon fresh lemon juice
- 2 ounces gluten-free tamari sauce
- Salt as needed

Directions:
1. Marinate steak in tamari sauce
2. Make the salad by adding bell pepper, tomatoes, radishes, salad green, oil, salt, and lemon juice to a bowl, and toss them well
3. Grill the steak to your desired doneness and transfer the steak on top of the salad platter
4. Let it sit for 1 minute and cut it crosswise
5. Serve and enjoy!

Ravaging Beef Pot Roast

Servings: 4
Preparation Time: 10 minutes
Cooking Time: 75 minutes
Ingredients:
- 3 and ½ pounds beef roast
- 4 ounces mushrooms, sliced
- 12 ounces of beef stock
- 1-ounce onion soup mix
- ½ cup Italian dressing

Directions:
1. Take a bowl and add stock, onion soup mix, and Italian dressing
2. Stir
3. Put beef roast in pan
4. Add mushrooms, stock mix to the pan and cover with foil
5. Preheat your oven to 300 degrees F
6. Bake for 1 hour and 15 minutes
7. Let the roast cool
8. Slice and serve
9. Enjoy with the gravy on top!

Juicy Glazed Beef Meatloaf

Servings: 6
Preparation Time: 10 minutes
Cooking Time: 1 hour 10 minutes
Ingredients:
- 1 cup white mushrooms, chopped
- 3 pounds of ground beef
- 2 tablespoons fresh parsley, chopped
- 2 garlic cloves, peeled and minced
- ½ cup onion, chopped
- ¼ cup red bell pepper, seeded and chopped
- ½ cup almond flour
- 1/3 cup parmesan cheese, grated
- 3 whole eggs
- Salt and pepper to taste
- 1 teaspoon balsamic vinegar

For Glaze
- 1 tablespoon swerve
- 2 tablespoons sugar-free ketchup
- 2 cups balsamic vinegar

Directions:
1. Take a bowl and add beef, salt, pepper, mushrooms, garlic, onion, bell pepper, parsley, almond flour, cheese, 1 teaspoon vinegar, salt, pepper, and eggs and stir well
2. Transfer mixture to loaf pan and bake for 30 minutes at 375 degrees F
3. Take a small pan and heat over medium heat
4. Add ketchup, swerve, 2 cups vinegar, and stir. Cook for 20 minutes
5. Take the meatloaf out of the oven and spread glaze over the meatloaf
6. Place in oven and bake for 20 minutes more
7. Let it cool, slice and serve!

Zucchini Beef Sauté With Coriander Greens

Servings: 4
Preparation Time: 10 minutes
Cooking Time: 10 minutes
Ingredients:
- 10 ounces beef, sliced into 1-2 inch strips
- 1 zucchini, cut into 2-inch strips
- ¼ cup parsley, chopped
- 3 garlic cloves, minced
- 2 tablespoons tamari sauce
- 4 tablespoons avocado oil

Directions:
1. Add 2 tablespoons avocado oil to a frying pan over high heat
2. Place strips of beef and brown for a few minutes on high heat
3. Once the meat is brown, add zucchini strips and Saute until tender
4. Once tender, add tamari sauce, garlic, and parsley, and let them sit for a few minutes more
5. Serve immediately and enjoy!

Pure Broccoli Rib Eye

Servings: 4
Preparation Time: 5 minutes
Cooking Time: 15 minutes
Ingredients:
- 4 ounces butter
- ¾ pound Ribeye steak, sliced
- 9 ounces broccoli, chopped
- 1 yellow onion, sliced
- 1 tablespoon coconut aminos
- 1 tablespoon pumpkin seeds
- Salt and pepper to taste

Directions:
1. Slice steak and the onions
2. Chop broccoli, including the stem parts
3. Take a frying pan and place it over medium heat; add butter and let it melt
4. Add meat and season accordingly with salt and pepper
5. Cook until both sides are browned
6. Transfer meat to a platter
7. Add broccoli and onion to the frying pan, and add more butter if needed
8. Brown
9. Add coconut aminos and return the meat

10. Stir and season again
11. Serve with a dollop of butter with a sprinkle of pumpkin seeds
12. Enjoy!

Mushroom And Olive "Mediterranean" Steak

Servings: 4
Preparation Time: 10 minutes
Cooking Time: 14 minutes
Ingredients:
- 1 pound boneless beef sirloin steak, ¾ inch thick, cut into 4 pieces
- 1 large red onion, chopped
- 1 cup mushrooms
- 4 garlic cloves, thinly sliced
- 4 tablespoons olive oil
- ½ cup green olives, coarsely chopped
- 1 cup parsley leaves, finely cut

Directions:
1. Take a large-sized skillet and place it over medium-high heat
2. Add oil and let it heat p
3. Add beef and cook until both sides are browned; remove beef and drain fat
4. Add the rest of the oil to the skillet and heat it up
5. Add onions, garlic and cook for 2-3 minutes
6. Stir well
7. Add mushrooms and olives and cook until mushrooms are thoroughly done
8. Return beef to skillet and lower heat to medium
9. Cook for 3-4 minutes (covered_
10. Stir in parsley
11. Serve and enjoy!

Satisfying Low-Carb Beef Liver Salad

Servings: 3
Preparation Time: 10 minutes
Cooking Time: Nil
Ingredients:
- 3-4 ounces beef liver, cooked
- 1 egg, hard-boiled
- 1 ounce dried mushroom
- 1 whole onion, minced
- 2 ounces mayonnaise
- 2 ounces olive oil
- Salt and pepper to taste
- Dill for serving
- ½ a red bell pepper, sliced

Directions:
1. Cut mushroom and livers into strips and transfer to a bowl
2. Peel the egg and, slice it, transfer it to a bowl
3. Add remaining ingredients and toss well
4. Sprinkle with dill, and serve!

Perfect Aromatic Beef Roast

Servings: 4
Preparation Time: 10 minutes
Cooking Time: 50 minutes
Ingredients:
- 1 lb of beef sirloin or similar lean cut for roast
- 2 tbsp of mustard
- 2 tbsp of olive oil
- 2 tbsp of garlic salt
- 1 spring of fresh rosemary

Directions:
1. Combine the mustard, olive oil, and garlic salt in a small bowl.
2. Take the roast beef, remove excess fat and make small incisions lengthwise to let the mixture penetrate more easily.
3. Brush the mustard mixture over the beef, ensuring it is nicely coated.
4. Place on a baking dish and arrange the rosemary leaves on the sides for extra aroma.
5. Cook in a preheated oven at 380F/180 C for 50 minutes (for a medium cook inside).
6. Serve with mashed sweet potatoes and/or salad

Beef Packed Zucchini Boats

Servings: 4
Preparation Time: 10 minutes
Cooking Time: 30 minutes
Ingredients:
- 1 lb of ground beef with around 80% meat and 20% fat ratio
- 1 cup of red Mexican salsa
- 4 medium zucchinis
- 1/2 shredded cheddar cheese
- 1 tbsp of olive oil

Directions:
1. Take the zucchinis, cut them in half lengthwise, and scoop the middle flesh inside (leaving enough flesh to make a boat on the sides). Take a form and pinch the insides slightly.
2. Heat the pan with olive oil and add the ground beef.
3. Sauté for 7-8 minutes or until most of the juices have evaporated.
4. Add the salsa and cook for another couple of minutes
5. Distribute the ground beef and salsa over the zucchini boats
6. Sprinkle with the cheese on top of each.
7. Bake in the oven for 15 minutes and serve

Spicy Chipotle Steak

Servings: 4
Preparation Time: 10 minutes
Cooking Time: 10-20 minutes
Ingredients:
- 2 sirloin steaks, cut into thin strips
- 1 tbsp of chipotle seasoning powder
- 2 tbsp of olive oil
- 1/4 cup tomato paste
- Salt to taste

Directions:
1. Combine the tomato paste, olive oil, and chipotle seasoning with salt to make a marinade.
2. Brush the mixture onto the steaks.
3. Heat a grilling pan and cook the steaks for 2-3 minutes on each side for medium inside or depending on how cooked you want them to be

Beef Cheeseburger Wraps

Servings: 4
Preparation Time: 10 minutes
Cooking Time: 50 minutes
Ingredients:
- 8 oz. of ground beef with 20% fat
- 1/4 cup chopped onion
- 4 small low-carb tortillas
- 2 slices of mild cheddar cheese
- 2 tbsp of salsa

Directions:
1. Lightly grease a pan, add the onion, and saute for a couple of minutes until almost transparent.
2. Add the ground beef and sauté for 4-5 minutes or until the juices have evaporated.
3. Add the salsa and toss.
4. Distribute the ground beef mixture onto the tortilla chips and top with parmesan cheese.
5. Serve optionally with a bit of sour cream

Cheddar Jalapeno Meatloaf

Servings: 4
Preparation Time: 10 minutes
Cooking Time: 35-40 minutes
Ingredients:
- 2 lb ground beef
- ½ tsp cumin
- 2 jalapenos, sliced
- 1 1/2 tbsp of garlic salt
- 1 1/2 cups of cheddar cheese

Directions:
1. Preheat the oven to 375F/180C.
2. Combine all the ingredients together except the jalapenos and cheese.
3. Fill a deep baking dish (around 8X8 inches) with the ground beef and spice mixture, top with the jalapenos, and finish with the layer of cheddar cheese.
4. Bake in the oven for 35-40 minutes. Let rest for 5 minutes before serving and cut ideally into squares or triangles before serving

Perfect Philly Cheesesteak Stuffed Peppers

Servings: 4
Preparation Time: 10 minutes
Cooking Time: 20 minutes
Ingredients:
- 2 large bell peppers cut in half lengthwise
- 8 oz. of thinly sliced roast beef or pastrami beef
- 6 oz. of baby mushrooms, sliced
- 8 slices of provolone or cheddar cheese
- 2 tbsp of salted butter

Directions:
1. Make sure the bell peppers are cut lengthwise into halves and contain no seeds.
2. In a pan, melt the butter and add the mushrooms. Saute for 3-4 minutes and remove from the heat.
3. Take the bell pepper halves and start arranging one slice of cheese over the bottom layer of the pepper, then 2 slices of pastrami on each, and then a few mushrooms. Finish off each pepper boat with an extra slice of cheese on top.
4. In a preheated oven (around 400F/200C), pop the peppers and cook for 18-20 minutes so that the peppers are cooked and the cheese is melted.
5. Let cool for 5 minutes and serve

Grilled Beef Short Loin

Servings: 4
Preparation Time: 10 minutes
Cooking Time: 15-20 minutes
Ingredients:
- 1 1/2 pounds beef short loin
- 2 thyme sprigs, chopped
- 1 rosemary sprig, chopped
- 1 teaspoon garlic powder
- Sea salt and ground black pepper to taste

Directions:
1. Place all of the above ingredients in a re-sealable zipper bag. Shake until the short beef loin is well coated on all sides.
2. Cook on a preheated grill for 15 to 20 minutes, flipping once or twice during the cooking time.
3. Let it stand for 5 minutes before slicing and serving.

Hearty Beef Bourguignon

Servings: 4
Preparation Time: 10 minutes
Cooking Time: 60-70 minutes
Ingredients:
- 1 1/2 pounds shoulder steak, cut into cubes
- 1 tablespoon Herbs de Provence
- 1 onion, chopped
- 1 celery stalk, chopped
- 1 cup red Burgundy wine

Directions:
1. Heat up a lightly greased soup pot over a medium-high flame. Now brown the beef in batches until no longer pink.
2. Add a splash of wine to deglaze your pan.
3. Add the Herbs de Provence, onion, celery, and wine to the pot; pour 3 cups of water and stir to combine well. Bring to a rapid boil; then, turn the heat to medium-low.
4. Cover and let it simmer for 1 hour and 10 minutes. Serve over hot cauliflower rice if desired. Enjoy!

Zucchini And Cheddar Beef Mugs

Servings: 4
Preparation Time: 10 minutes
Cooking Time: 5 minutes
Ingredients:
- 4 oz roast beef deli slices, torn apart
- 3 tbsp sour cream
- 1 small zucchini, chopped
- 2 tbsp chopped green chilies
- 3 oz shredded cheddar cheese

Directions:
1. Divide the beef slices at the bottom of 2 wide mugs and spread 1 tbsp of sour cream.

2. Top with 2 zucchini slices, season with salt and pepper, add green chilies, top with the remaining sour cream, and then cheddar cheese.
3. Place the mugs in the microwave for 1-2 minutes until the cheese melts.
4. Remove the mugs, let cool for 1 minute, and serve.

Beef Stuffed Peppers

Servings: 4
Preparation Time: 10 minutes
Cooking Time: 50 minutes
Ingredients:
- 1 /2-pound ground beef
- 1 garlic clove, minced
- Sea salt and ground black pepper to taste
- 1/4 cup cream of onion soup
- 1/2 teaspoon paprika

Directions:
1. Heat the olive oil in a saute pan over moderate heat. Once hot, sear the ground beef for 5 to 6 minutes, turning once or twice to ensure even cooking.
2. Add in the cream of onion soup, paprika, salt, and black pepper. Cook for a further 3 minutes until heated through. The meat thermometer should register 145 degrees F.
3. Serve in individual plates garnished with freshly snipped chives if desired. Enjoy!

Fine Filet Mignon In Dijon Sauce

Servings: 4
Preparation Time: 10 minutes
Cooking Time: 10-15 minutes
Ingredients:
- 2 teaspoons lard, at room temperature
- 2 pounds beef filet mignon, cut into bite-sized chunks
- Flaky salt and ground black pepper to season
- 1 tablespoon Dijon mustard
- 1 cup double cream

Directions:
1. Melt the lard in a saucepan over moderate heat; now, sear the filet mignon for 2 to 3 minutes per side—season with salt and pepper to taste.
2. Fold in the Dijon mustard and cream. Reduce the heat to medium-low and cook for 6 minutes or until the sauce has reduced slightly.
3. Serve in individual plates, garnished with cauli rice if desired. Enjoy!

Shitake Butter Beef Dish

Servings: 4
Preparation Time: 10 minutes
Cooking Time: 5-10 minutes
Ingredients:
- 2 cups shitake mushrooms, sliced
- 4 ribeye steaks
- 2 tbsp butter
- 2 tsp olive oil
- Salt and black pepper to taste

Directions:

1. Heat olive oil in a pan over medium heat. Rub the steaks with salt and pepper and cook for 4 minutes per side. Set aside.
2. Melt butter in the pan and cook the shitakes for 4 minutes.
3. Pour the butter and mushrooms over the steak.

Crazy Beef Meatballs

Servings: 4
Preparation Time: 10 minutes
Cooking Time: 18-20 minutes
Ingredients:
- 1 lb ground beef
- 1/2 cup grated parmesan cheese
- 1 tbsp minced garlic (or paste)
- 1/2 cup mozzarella cheese
- 1 tsp freshly ground pepper

Directions:
1. Preheat your oven to 400°F/200°C.
2. In a bowl, mix all the ingredients together.
3. Roll the meat mixture into 6 generous meatballs.
4. Bake inside your oven at 170°F/80°C for about 18 minutes.
5. Serve with sauce!

Delicious Beef Casserole

Servings: 4
Preparation Time: 10 minutes
Cooking Time: 30-40 minutes
Ingredients:
- 1/2 lb. ground beef
- 1/2 cup chopped onion
- 1/2 bag coleslaw mix
- 1-1/2 cups tomato sauce
- 1 tbsp lemon juice

Directions:
1. In a skillet, cook the ground beef until browned and to the side.
2. Mix the onion and cabbage to the skillet and sauté until soft.
3. Add the ground beef back in along with the tomato sauce and lemon juice.
4. Bring the mixture to a boil, then cover and simmer for 30 minutes.
5. Enjoy!

Ground Beef Hamburger Patties

Servings: 4
Preparation Time: 10 minutes
Cooking Time: 5-10 minutes
Ingredients:
- ½ an egg
- 12 oz. ground beef
- 1 and 1/2 oz. crumbled feta cheese
- 1 oz. butter
- Salt & Black pepper

Directions:
1. Add the feta cheese, ground beef, black pepper, egg, and salt to a mixing bowl, then combine well.
2. Shape the mixture into equal patties.
3. Put a pan on fire to melt the butter.

4. Cook the patties for 4 minutes on each side on medium-low heat.
5. Serve!

Ultimate Mediterranean Lamb Chops

Serving: 4
Preparation Time: 10 minutes
Cooking Time: 10 minute
Ingredients
- 4 lamb shoulder chops, 8 ounces each
- 2 tablespoons Dijon mustard
- 2 tablespoons Balsamic vinegar
- 1 tablespoon garlic, chopped
- ½ cup olive oil
- 2 tablespoons shredded fresh basil

Directions:
1. Pat your lamb chop dry using a kitchen towel and arrange them on a shallow glass baking dish
2. Take a bowl and a whisk in Dijon mustard, balsamic vinegar, garlic, and pepper, and mix them well
3. Whisk in the oil very slowly into the marinade until the mixture is smooth
4. Stir in basil
5. Pour the marinade over the lamb chops and stir to coat both sides well
6. Cover the chops and allow them to marinate for 1-4 hours (chilled)
7. Take the chops out and leave them for 30 minutes to allow the temperature to reach a normal level
8. Preheat your grill to medium heat and add oil to the grate
9. Grill the lamb chops for 5-10 minutes per side until both sides are browned
10. Once the center reads 145 degrees Fahrenheit, the chops are ready, serve and enjoy!

Herbed Lamb Cutlets

Serving: 6
Preparation Time: 15 minutes
Cooking Time: 45 minute
Ingredients
- 2 peppers, deseeded and cut into chunky pieces
- 1 large sweet potato, peeled and cut into chunky pieces
- 2 courgettes, sliced into chunks
- 1 red onion, cut into wedges
- 1 tablespoon olive oil
- 8 lean lamb cutlets
- 1 tablespoon thyme leaf, chopped
- 2 tablespoon mint leaves, chopped

Directions:
1. Preheat your oven to a temperature of 392 degrees Fahrenheit
2. Take a large-sized baking dish and add peppers, courgettes, sweet potatoes, and onion
3. Drizzle oil all over
4. Season with some ground pepper
5. Roast for about 25 minutes
6. Trim off any fat from lamb cutlets (if present)
7. Mix in herbs with a few twists of ground black pepper and pat it all over
8. Take the veggies out of the oven and shove them to one side of your tray using a spatula
9. Place your lamb cutlets on one side and roast for another 10 minutes
10. Turn the cutlets over and cook for another 10 minutes until the veggies are ready (lightly charred and tender)
11. Mix everything on the tray and enjoy!

Pork Chops And Wild Mushrooms

Serving: 4
Preparation Time: 10 minutes
Cooking Time: 25 minute
Ingredients
- 4 (5 ounces) bone-in-center pork chops
- ¼ teaspoon sea salt
- ¼ teaspoon freshly ground black pepper
- 1 tablespoon extra-virgin olive oil
- 1 sweet onion, chopped
- 2 teaspoons garlic, minced
- 1 pound mixed wild mushrooms, sliced
- 1 teaspoon fresh thyme, chopped
- ½ cup sodium-free chicken stock

Directions:
1. Pat pork chops dry with a kitchen towel and season with salt and pepper
2. Take a large skillet and place it over medium-high heat
3. Add olive oil and heat it up
4. Add pork chops and cook for 6 minutes, brown both sides
5. Transfer meat to a platter and keep it on the side
6. Add onion and garlic and Saute for 3 minutes
7. Stir in mushrooms and thyme and Saute for 6 minutes until the mushrooms are caramelized
8. Return pork chops to the skillet and pour chicken stock
9. Cover and bring the liquid to boil
10. Lower the heat to low and simmer for 10 minutes
11. Serve and enjoy!

Herbed Pork Tenderloin

Serving: 8
Preparation Time: 10 minutes
Cooking Time: 30 minute
Ingredients
- ¼ cup extra virgin olive oil
- ¼ cup fresh oregano, chopped
- 1/ cup parsley, chopped
- 1 tablespoon fresh rosemary, chopped
- 2 teaspoons garlic, minced
- ½ teaspoon red pepper flakes
- ½ teaspoon sea salt
- ½ teaspoon fresh ground black pepper
- 2 pounds of pork tenderloin, trimmed of visible fat and silver skin

Directions:
1. Preheat your oven to 400 degrees Fahrenheit
2. Take a food processor and add ¼ cup olive oil, parsley, oregano, rosemary, garlic, red pepper flakes, sea salt, and pepper, and blend until you have a thick paste
3. Scrape down the sides of the bowl

4. Rub herb mix all over tenderloin
5. Take a medium ovenproof skillet over medium-high heat
6. Heat up 1 tablespoon olive oil
7. Add pork and sear on all sides, turning every 3 meat until the meat is browned
8. Place skillet in your oven and roast for 20 minutes until the internal temperature reaches 120-145 degrees Fahrenheit
9. Remove from oven and let it rest
10. Slice and serve
11. Enjoy!

Mushroom Beef Risotto

Serving: 4
Preparation Time: 5 minutes
Cooking Time: 10 minutes
Ingredients
- 2 cups low-sodium beef stock
- 2 cups water
- 2 tablespoon olive oil
- ½ cup scallions, chopped
- 1 cup Arborio rice
- ¼ cup dry white wine
- 1 cup roast beef, thinly stripped
- 1 cup button mushrooms
- ½ cup canned cream of mushrooms
- Salt and pepper as needed
- Oregano, chopped
- Parsley, chopped

Directions:
1. Take a stock pot and put it over medium heat
2. Add water and beef stock to it
3. Bring the mixture to boil and remove the heat
4. Take another heavy-bottomed saucepan and put it over medium heat
5. Add in the scallions and stir fry them for 1 minute
6. Add in the rice then and cook it for at least 2 minutes, occasionally stirring it to ensure that it is finely coated with oil
7. In the rice mixture, keep adding your beef stock ½ a cup at a time, making sure to stir it often
8. Once all the stock has been added, cook the rice for another 2 minutes
9. During the last 5 minutes of your cooking, make sure to add the beef, cream of mushroom, and beef while stirring it nicely
10. Transfer the whole mix to a serving dish
11. Garnish with some chopped-up parsley and oregano
12. Serve hot

Chapter 10

Soups and Stews

Asparagus and Chicken Soup

Preparation time: 30 minutes
Cooking time: 20 minutes
Servings: 4
Ingredients:
- 2 chicken breast fillets, cooked and diced
- 2-3 leeks, finely cut
- 1 bunch asparagus, trimmed and cut
- 4 cups chicken broth
- 2 tbsp. extra virgin olive oil
- 1/2 cup fresh parsley, finely chopped
- Salt and black pepper, to taste
- Lemon juice, to serve

Directions:
1. Heat the olive oil in a large soup pot. Add in the leeks and gently sauté, stirring, for 2-3 minutes. Add chicken broth, the diced chicken, and bring to a boil. Reduce heat and simmer for 15 minutes.
2. Add in asparagus, parsley, salt and black pepper, and cook for 5 minutes more. Serve with lemon juice.

Mediterranean Fish and Quinoa Soup

Preparation time: 30 minutes
Cooking time: 20 minutes
Servings: 4-5
Ingredients:
- 1 lb. cod fillets, cubed
- 1 onion, chopped
- 3 tomatoes, chopped
- 1/2 cup quinoa, rinsed
- 1 red pepper, chopped
- 1 carrot, chopped
- 1/2 cup black olives, pitted and sliced
- 1 garlic clove, crushed
- 3 tbsp. extra virgin olive oil
- A pinch of cayenne pepper
- 1 bay leaf
- 1 tsp dried thyme
- 1 tsp dried dill
- ½ tsp pepper
- ½ cup white wine
- 4 cups water
- Salt and black pepper, to taste
- 1/2 cup fresh parsley, finely cut

Directions:
1. Heat the olive oil over medium heat and sauté the onion, red pepper, garlic and carrot until tender.
2. Stir in the cayenne pepper, bay leaf, herbs, salt and pepper. Add the white wine, water, quinoa and tomatoes and bring to a boil.
3. Reduce heat, cover, and cook for 10 minutes. Stir in olives and the fish and cook for another 10 minutes. Stir in parsley and serve hot.

Alkalizing Green Soup

Preparation time: 20 minutes
Cooking time: 20 minutes
Servings: 4-5
Ingredients:
- 2 cups broccoli, cut into florets and chopped
- 2 zucchinis, peeled and chopped
- 2 cups chopped kale
- 1 small onion, chopped
- 2-3 garlic cloves, chopped
- 4 cups vegetable broth
- 2 tbsp. extra virgin olive oil
- 1/2 tsp ground ginger
- 1/2 tsp ground coriander
- 1 lime, juiced, to serve

Directions:
1. Gently heat olive oil in a large saucepan over medium-high heat. Cook onion and garlic for 3-4 minutes until tender. Add ginger and coriander and stir to coat well.
2. Add in broccoli, zucchinis, kale and vegetable broth. Bring to the boil, then reduce heat and simmer for 15 minutes, stirring from time to time. Set aside to cool and blend until smooth. Return to pan and cook until heated through. Serve with lime juice.

Lentil, Ground Beef and Quinoa Soup

Preparation Time: 45 minutes
Cooking time: 40 minutes
Servings: 4-5
Ingredients:
- 1 lb. ground beef
- 1/2 cup quinoa
- 1/1 cup green lentils
- 1 carrot, chopped
- 1 onion, chopped
- 1 small potato, peeled and diced
- 2-3 garlic cloves, chopped
- 2 tomatoes, grated or pureed
- 5 cups water

- 1 tsp summer savory or dried mint
- 1 tsp paprika
- 2 tbsp. olive oil
- 1 tsp salt
- Ground black pepper, to taste

Directions:
1. Heat olive oil in a large soup pot. Brown the ground beef, breaking it up with a spoon. Add in paprika and garlic and stir. Add lentils, washed quinoa, remaining vegetables, water and spice.
2. Bring the soup to a boil. Reduce heat to low and simmer, covered, for about 40 minutes, or until the lentils are tender. Stir occasionally.

Hearty Lamb and Root Vegetables Soup

Preparation Time: 45 minutes
Cooking time: 20 minutes
Servings: 6-7
Ingredients:
- 2 cups roasted lamb, shredded
- 3 cups chicken or vegetable broth
- 1 cup water
- 1 cup canned tomatoes, diced, undrained
- 1 onion, chopped
- 1 large carrot, chopped
- 1 medium parsnip, peeled and chopped
- 1 small turnip, chopped
- 1 celery rib
- 3 tbsp. olive oil
- Salt and black pepper, to taste

Directions:
1. Gently heat olive oil in a large saucepan and sauté onion, carrot, parsnip, celery and turnip, stirring, for 5 minutes, or until softened.
2. Add in lamb, broth, tomatoes, and a cup of water. Bring to the boil then reduce heat and simmer for 20 minutes, or until vegetables are tender. Season with salt and black pepper to taste.

Spicy Red Pepper and Potato Soup

Preparation time: 30 minutes
Cooking time: 20 minutes
Servings: 4
Ingredients:
- 1 onion, chopped
- 2 garlic cloves, minced
- 2 carrots, chopped
- 2 red bell peppers, chopped
- 2 cups, diced potatoes
- 4 cups vegetable broth
- 3 tbsp. extra virgin olive oil
- 1/2 tsp smoked paprika
- 1/4 tsp ginger
- 1/2 tsp dried sage
- 1/2 tsp cinnamon
- 1/2 tsp nutmeg
- Salt, to taste
- Black pepper, to taste

Directions:
1. Gently heat olive oil in a large saucepan over medium-high heat. Cook onion, garlic, carrot and the peppers together with all the spices for 3-4 minutes, stirring.
2. Add in potatoes and the broth. Season with salt and black pepper to taste. Cover and simmer for 20 minutes or until the potatoes and carrots are tender.

Creamy Brussels Sprout Soup

Preparation time: 30 minutes
Cooking time: 25 minutes
Servings: 4-5
Ingredients:
- 1 lb. frozen Brussels sprouts, thawed
- 2 potatoes, peeled and chopped
- 1 large onion, chopped
- 3 garlic cloves, minced
- 1 cup raw cashews
- 4 cups vegetable broth
- 3 tbsp. extra virgin olive oil
- 1/2 tsp curry powder
- Salt and black pepper, to taste

Directions:
1. Soak cashews in a bowl covered with water for at least 4 hours. Drain water and blend cashews with 1 cup of vegetable broth until smooth. Set aside.
2. Gently heat olive oil in a large saucepan over medium-high heat. Cook onion and garlic and for 3-4 minutes until tender. Add in Brussels sprouts, potato, curry and vegetable broth.
3. Cover and bring to a boil, then reduce heat and simmer for 20 minutes, stirring from time to time. Remove from heat and stir in cashew mixture. Blend until smooth, return to pan and cook until heated through.

Tuscan Chicken Stew

Preparation time: 15 minutes
Cooking time: 6 hours
Servings: 6
Ingredients:
- 1 medium eggplant, cubed
- 3 zucchinis, cubed
- 1 cup chopped onion
- 2 cans great northern beans
- 2 cans diced tomatoes (no salt added)
- 1 tsp sugar
- 2 tbsp. Italian seasoning
- 1 tsp garlic powder
- Salt and pepper to taste
- 2 lbs. of chicken breasts (boneless, skinless)
- 3 cups chicken stock

Directions:
1. Put tomatoes, chicken, broth seasonings and sugar into the slow cooker. Cook on low for 6 hours or 8 if using frozen chicken breasts.
2. During the last 1 1/2 hours, add eggplant, zucchini and beans in, and stir.

Zucchini Vegetable Stew

Preparation time: 15 minutes

Cooking time: 10-15 minutes
Servings: 6
Ingredients:
- 1 (1 lb.) eggplant, peeled, cubed
- 1 zucchini, sliced
- 1/2 cup reduced-sodium pasta sauce
- 1 package (12 oz.) frozen mixed stew vegetables (celery, onion, peppers)

Directions:
1. Combine eggplant, vegetable blend, zucchini and 2 tablespoons water in large heavy pan. Heat until mixture boils, then reduce heat to low and cover.
2. Cook for about 10 to 15 minutes or until vegetables are tender and drain.
3. Return eggplant mixture to pan. Add pasta sauce and stir until sauce heats through.

Creamy Chicken Soup

Preparation time: 35 minutes
Cooking time: 30 minutes
Servings: 4
Ingredients:
- 4 chicken breasts
- 1 carrot, chopped
- 1 cup zucchini, peeled and chopped
- 2 cups cauliflower, broken into florets
- 1 celery rib, chopped
- 1 small onion, chopped
- 5 cups water
- 1/2 tsp salt
- Black pepper, to taste

Directions:
1. Place chicken breasts, onion, carrot, celery, cauliflower and zucchini in a deep soup pot. Add in salt, black pepper and 5 cups of water. Stir and bring to a boil.
2. Simmer for 30 minutes then remove chicken from the pot and let it cool slightly.
3. Blend soup until completely smooth. Shred or dice the chicken meat, return it back to the pot, stir, and serve.

Broccoli and Chicken Soup

Preparation time: 35 minutes
Cooking time: 30 minutes
Servings: 4
Ingredients:
- 4 boneless chicken thighs, diced
- 1 small carrot, chopped
- 1 broccoli head, broken into florets
- 1 garlic clove, chopped
- 1 small onion, chopped
- 4 cups water
- 3 tbsp. extra virgin olive oil
- 1/2 tsp salt
- Black pepper, to taste

Directions:
1. In a deep soup pot, heat olive oil and gently sauté broccoli for 2-3 minutes, stirring occasionally. Add in onion, carrot, chicken and cook, stirring, for 2-3 minutes. Stir in salt, black pepper and water.

2. Bring to a boil. Simmer for 30 minutes then remove from heat and set aside to cool.
3. In a blender or food processor, blend soup until completely smooth. Serve and enjoy!

Warm Chicken and Avocado Soup

Preparation time: 6-7 minutes
Cooking time: 25 minutes
Servings: 4
Ingredients:
- 2 ripe avocados, peeled and chopped
- 1 cooked chicken breast, shredded
- 1 garlic clove, chopped
- 3 cups chicken broth
- Salt and black pepper, to taste
- Fresh coriander leaves, finely cut, to serve
- 1/2 cup sour cream, to serve

Directions:
1. Combine avocados, garlic, and chicken broth in a blender. Process until smooth and transfer to a saucepan.
2. Add in chicken and cook, stirring, over medium heat until the mixture is hot. Serve topped with sour cream and finely cut coriander leaves.

Quick Clam Chowder

Preparation time: 10 minutes
Cooking time: 15 minutes
Servings: 4
Ingredients:
- 2 tablespoons extra-virgin olive oil
- 3 slices pepper bacon, chopped
- 1 onion, chopped
- 1 red bell pepper, seeded and chopped
- 1 fennel bulb, chopped
- 3 tablespoons flour
- 5 cups low-sodium or unsalted chicken broth
- 6 ounces (170 g) chopped canned clams, undrained
- ½ teaspoon sea salt
- ½ cup milk

Directions:
1. In a large pot over medium-high heat, heat the olive oil until it shimmers. Add the bacon and cook, stirring, until browned, about 4 minutes. Remove the bacon from the fat with a slotted spoon, and set it aside on a plate.
2. Add the onion, bell pepper, and fennel to the fat in the pot. Cook, stirring occasionally, until the vegetables are soft, about 5 minutes. Add the flour and cook, stirring constantly, for 1 minute. Add the broth, clams, and salt. Bring to a simmer. Cook, stirring, until the soup thickens, about 5 minutes more.
3. Stir in the milk and return the bacon to the pot. Cook, stirring, 1 minute more.

Beef Barley Soup

Preparation time: 20 minutes
Cooking time: 30 minutes
Servings: 4
Ingredients:
- 2 teaspoons extra-virgin olive oil
- 1 sweet onion, chopped
- 1 tablespoon minced garlic

- 4 celery stalks, with greens, chopped
- 2 carrots, peeled, diced
- 1 sweet potato, peeled, diced
- 8 cups low-sodium beef broth
- 1 cup cooked pearl barley
- 2 cups diced cooked beef
- 2 bay leaves
- 2 teaspoons hot sauce
- 2 teaspoons chopped fresh thyme
- 1 cup shredded kale
- Sea salt and freshly ground black pepper, to taste

Directions:
1. Place a large stockpot over medium-high heat and add the oil.
2. Sauté the onion and garlic until softened and translucent, about 3 minutes.
3. Stir in the celery, carrot, and sweet potato, and sauté for a further 5 minutes.
4. Stir in the beef broth, barley, beef, bay leaves, and hot sauce.
5. Bring the soup to a boil, then reduce the heat to low.
6. Simmer until the vegetables are tender, about 15 minutes.
7. Remove the bay leaves and stir in the thyme and kale.
8. Simmer for 5 minutes, and season with salt and pepper.

Seafood Stew

Preparation time: 20 minutes
Cooking time: 30 minutes
Servings: 6
Ingredients:
- 1 tablespoon extra-virgin olive oil
- 1 sweet onion, chopped
- 2 teaspoons minced garlic
- 3 celery stalks, chopped
- 2 carrots, peeled and chopped
- 1 (28-ounce / 794-g) can sodium-free diced tomatoes, undrained
- 3 cups low-sodium chicken broth
- ½ cup clam juice
- ¼ cup dry white wine
- 2 teaspoons chopped fresh basil
- 2 teaspoons chopped fresh oregano
- 2 (4-ounce / 113-g) haddock fillets, cut into 1-inch chunks

Directions:
1-pound (454 g) mussels, scrubbed, debearded
8 ounces (227 g) shrimp, peeled, deveined, quartered
Sea salt and freshly ground black pepper, to taste
2 tablespoons chopped fresh parsley

Directions:
1. Place a large saucepan over medium-high heat and add the olive oil.
2. Sauté the onion and garlic until softened and translucent, about 3 minutes.
3. Stir in the celery and carrots and sauté for 4 minutes.
4. Stir in the tomatoes, chicken broth, clam juice, white wine, basil, and oregano.
5. Bring the sauce to a boil, then reduce the heat to low. Simmer for 15 minutes.
6. Add the fish and mussels, cover, and cook until the mussels open, about 5 minutes.
7. Discard any unopened mussels. Add the shrimp to the pan and cook until the shrimp are opaque, about 2 minutes.
8. Season with salt and pepper. Serve garnished with the chopped parsley.

Potlikker Soup

Preparation time: 15 minutes
Cooking time: 20 minutes
Servings: 6
Ingredients:
- 3 cups chicken broth, divided
- 1 medium onion, chopped
- 3 garlic cloves, minced
- 1 bunch collard greens or mustard greens including stems, roughly chopped
- 1 fresh ham bone
- 5 carrots, peeled and cut into 1-inch rounds
- 2 fresh thyme sprigs
- 3 bay leaves
- Freshly ground black pepper, to taste

Directions:
1. Select the Sauté setting on an electric pressure cooker, and combine ½ cup of chicken broth, the onion, and garlic and cook for 3 to 5 minutes, or until the onion and garlic are translucent.
2. Add the collard greens, ham bone, carrots, remaining 2½ cups of broth, the thyme, and bay leaves.
3. Close and lock the lid and set the pressure valve to sealing.
4. Change to the Manual setting, and cook for 15 minutes.
5. Once cooking is complete, quick-release the pressure. Carefully remove the lid. Discard the bay leaves.
6. Serve with Skillet Bivalves.

Roasted Carrot Soup with Basil

Preparation Time: 10 minutes
Cooking Time: 10 minutes
Servings: 8
Ingredients:
- 3 pounds' carrots, peeled and cut into 2- to 3-inch pieces
- 2 onions, peeled and quartered
- 6 cloves garlic, unpeeled
- 1 (1 inch) piece fresh ginger, peeled and sliced
- 2 tablespoons coconut oil
- 3 cups unsweetened coconut milk
- 1-1/2 cups low-sodium vegetable broth
- 1 teaspoon coarsely ground black pepper
- 1-1/2 cups water
- 1 teaspoon Shredded carrot
- 2 Fresh basil leaves

Directions:
1. Preheat the oven to 400 degrees. In a large bowl, combine the carrot pieces, onions, garlic and ginger. Drizzle with coconut oil; toss to coat. Place vegetables in a 15 x 10 x 1-inch baking dish in a single layer. Bake for 50 to 60 minutes or until carrots are very tender. Let cool slightly.
2. In a food processor or blender, press the garlic cloves out of the skin. Add the grilled carrots, onions and ginger; Cover and

process or turn on / off in several turns until vegetables are chopped. Add the coconut milk, broth and pepper. Cover and mix or stir until smooth.
3. Transfer to a medium saucepan. Add the water. Cook and stir until heated through. Garnish with grated carrots and basil leaves if desired.

Asparagus Carrot Soup
Preparation Time: 10 minutes
Cooking Time: 10 minutes
Servings: 6
Ingredients:
- ½ tablespoon butter
- ½ tablespoon olive oil
- 1 pounds' fresh asparagus, trimmed and cut into 1-inch pieces
- ½ medium onion, chopped
- ½ medium carrot, thinly sliced
- ¼ teaspoon salt
- 1/8 teaspoon pepper
- 1/8 teaspoon dried thyme
- 2/3 cup uncooked long grain brown rice
- 3 cups vegetable broth
- Reduced-fat sour cream, optional

Directions:
1. Heat the pot, Add butter and oil over medium heat. Add vegetables and spices; cook until vegetables are tender, 8 to 10 minutes, stirring occasionally.
2. Add the brown rice and broth; bring to a boil. Reduce the heat; Cook, covered, over low heat for 40 to 45 minutes, stirring occasionally, until the rice is tender.
3. Puree the soup with a hand blender or allow it to cool slightly and puree the soup in batches in a blender. Return to the pot and heat. Serve with sour cream and croutons if desired.

Meatball and Chickpea Soup
Preparation Time: 30 minutes
Cooking time: 30 minutes
Servings: 4-5
Ingredients:
- 1 lb. lean ground beef
- 3-4 tbsp. flour
- 1 small onion, chopped
- 1 garlic clove, chopped
- 1 can tomatoes, diced and undrained
- 1 can chickpeas, drained
- 1 green pepper, chopped
- 4 cups water
- ½ bunch of parsley, finely cut
- 3 tbsp. olive oil
- ½ tsp black pepper
- 1 tsp dried mint
- 1 tsp paprika - 1 tsp salt

Directions:
1. Combine ground meat, paprika, black pepper and salt in a large bowl. Mix well with hands and roll teaspoonfuls of the mixture into balls. Put flour in a small bowl and roll each meatball in the flour, coating entire surface then set aside on a large plate.
2. Heat olive oil into a large soup pot and gently sauté onion, garlic and pepper until tender. Add water and tomatoes and bring to the boil over high heat. Add in meatballs and chickpeas.
3. Reduce heat to low and simmer, uncovered, for 25 minutes. Add mint and stir. Serve with lemon juice.

Beef Noodle Soup
Preparation Time: 30 minutes
Cooking time: 15 minutes
Servings: 7-8
Ingredients:
- 8 oz. fillet steak, thinly sliced
- 6 oz. rice stick noodles
- 2 carrots, peeled, halved, sliced diagonally
- 1 red pepper, deseeded, thinly sliced diagonally
- 7-8 spring onions, chopped
- 8 oz. green beans, sliced diagonally
- 3 tbsp. sweet chili sauce
- 4 cups beef broth
- 1 tbsp. olive oil

Directions:
1. In a skillet, heat olive oil and cook beef, stirring, until medium rare.
2. Place broth and half the onions in a saucepan over high heat. Bring to the boil, cover, reduce heat to low. Simmer for 5 minutes then add carrots, pepper and beans. Bring to the boil, uncovered. Cook for 2 minutes or until vegetables are tender. Remove from heat.
3. Stir in remaining onions and sweet chili sauce.
4. Place noodles in a heatproof bowl. Cover with boiling water. Stand for 5 minutes or until tender. Drain. Divide noodles between bowls. Top with beef. Ladle over boiling soup mixture. Serve.

Cabbage, Beef and Buckwheat Soup
Preparation Time: 30 minutes
Cooking time: 35 minutes
Servings: 7-8
Ingredients:
- 3/4 – 1 lb. beef, chuck (boneless, cut into 1-inch cubes)
- 1 cup buckwheat
- 2 cups chopped cabbage
- 1 small onion, chopped
- 2 carrots, peeled, halved, sliced diagonally
- 1 red pepper, deseeded, thinly sliced diagonally
- 1 tbsp. paprika
- 4 cups beef broth
- 1 tbsp. olive oil
- 1/2 cup sour cream, to serve, optional
- Salt and black pepper, to taste

Directions:
1. In a deep soup pot, heat olive oil and cook beef, stirring, until lightly browned.
2. Add broth, paprika, onion and carrot and bring to the boil. Cover, reduce heat to low and simmer for 20 minutes then add the pepper, cabbage and buckwheat.

3. Bring to the boil and cook for 15 minutes or until vegetables are tender. Remove from heat.
4. Season with salt and pepper to taste and serve with sour cream.

Italian Wedding Soup

Preparation Time: 30 minutes
Cooking time: 40 minutes
Servings: 4-5
Ingredients:
- 1 lb. lean ground beef
- 1/3 cup breadcrumbs
- 1 egg, lightly beaten
- 1 onion, grated
- 2 carrots, chopped
- 1 small head escarole, trimmed and cut into 1/2-inch strips
- 1 cup baby spinach leaves
- 1 cup small pasta
- 2 tbsp. Parmesan cheese, grated
- 2 tbsp. parsley, finely cut
- 1 tsp salt
- 1 tsp ground black pepper
- 3 tbsp. olive oil
- 3 cups chicken broth
- 3 cups water
- 1 tsp dried oregano

Directions:
1. Combine ground beef, egg, onion, breadcrumbs, cheese, parsley, 1/2 teaspoon of the salt and 1/2 teaspoon of the black pepper. Mix well with hands. Using a tablespoon, make walnut sized meatballs. Heat olive oil in a large skillet and brown meatballs in batches. Place aside on a plate.
2. In a large soup pot boil broth and water together with carrots, oregano, and the remaining salt and pepper. Gently add meatballs. Reduce heat and simmer for 30 minutes. Add pasta, spinach and escarole and simmer 10 minutes more.

Italian Meatball Soup

Preparation Time: 5 minutes
Cooking time: 15 minutes
Servings: 6-7
Ingredients:
- 1 lb. lean ground beef
- 1 small onion, grated
- 1 onion, chopped
- 2 garlic cloves, crushed
- ½ cup breadcrumbs
- 3-4 basil leaves, finely chopped
- 1/3 cup Parmesan cheese, grated
- 1 egg, lightly beaten
- 2 cups tomato sauce with basil
- 3 cups water
- ½ cup small pasta
- 1 zucchini, diced
- ½ cup green beans, trimmed, cut into thirds
- 2 tbsp. olive oil

Directions:
1. Combine ground meat, grated onion, garlic, breadcrumbs, basil, Parmesan and egg in a large bowl. Season with salt and pepper. Mix well with hands and roll tablespoonfuls of the mixture into balls. Place on a large plate.
2. Heat olive oil into a large deep saucepan and sauté onion and garlic until transparent. Add tomato sauce, water, and bring to the boil over high heat. Add meatballs.
3. Reduce heat to medium-low and simmer, uncovered, for 10 minutes. Add in pasta and cook for 5 more minutes. Add the zucchini and beans. Cook until pasta and vegetables are tender. Serve sprinkled with Parmesan.

Spicy Chick Pea Stew

Preparation time: 15 minutes
Cooking time: 3-4 hours
Servings: 6
Ingredients:
- 1 tablespoon vegetable oil
- 2 onions, peeled and finely chopped
- 4 garlic cloves, finely chopped
- 2 tablespoons minced fresh gingerrcot
- 2 teaspoons ground coriander
- 1 teaspoon cumin seed
- 1 teaspoon salt
- 1/2 teaspoon fresh ground black pepper
- 1/2 teaspoon cayenne pepper
- 2 teaspoons balsamic vinegar
- 2 cups coarsely chopped tomatoes (canned or fresh)
- 2 (19 ounce) cans chickpeas, rinsed and drained

Directions:
1. In a skillet over medium heat, cook onions, stirring, just until they begin to brown; then add garlic and all spices and cook, stirring, for 1 minute.
2. Add vinegar and tomatoes and bring to a boil, then place mixture in your slow cooker; add chickpeas and combine well.
3. Cover and cook on Low for 6 to 8 hours or on High for 3 to 4 hours, or until the mixture is hot and bubbling.

Easy Salsa Chicken Stew

Preparation time: 15 minutes
Cooking time: 6-8 hours
Servings: 6
Ingredients:
- 4 boneless skinless chicken breasts
- 32 ounces salsa
- 1 (14 1/2 ounce) can corn, drained
- 1 (14 1/2 ounce) can black beans, drained

Directions:
1. Place Ingredients: in slow cooker and cook on low 6-8 hours.
2. 30-60 minutes prior to serving, remove chicken, shred, and return to slow cooker.

Moroccan Eggplant Stew

Preparation time: 20 minutes
Cooking time: 3 minutes
Servings: 4
Ingredients:
- 2 tablespoons avocado oil
- 1 large onion, minced
- 2 garlic cloves, minced

- 1 teaspoon ras el hanout spice blend or curry powder
- ¼ teaspoon cayenne pepper
- 1 teaspoon kosher salt
- 1 cup vegetable broth or water
- 1 tablespoon tomato paste
- 2 cups chopped eggplant
- 2 medium gold potatoes, peeled and chopped
- 4 ounces (113 g) tomatillos, husks removed, chopped
- 1 (14-ounce / 397-g) can diced tomatoes

Directions:
1. Set the electric pressure cooker to the Sauté setting. When the pot is hot, pour in the avocado oil.
2. Sauté the onion for 3 to 5 minutes, until it begins to soften. Add the garlic, ras el hanout, cayenne, and salt. Cook and stir for about 30 seconds. Hit Cancel.
3. Stir in the broth and tomato paste. Add the eggplant, potatoes, tomatillos, and tomatoes with their juices.
4. Close and lock the lid of the pressure cooker. Set the valve to sealing.
5. Cook on high pressure for 3 minutes.
6. When the cooking is complete, hit Cancel and allow the pressure to release naturally.
7. Once the pin drops, unlock and remove the lid.
8. Stir well and spoon into serving bowls.

Cheeseburger Soup

Preparation time: 5 minutes
Cooking time: 25 minutes
Servings: 4
Ingredients:
- Avocado oil cooking spray
- ½ cup diced white onion
- ½ cup diced celery
- ½ cup sliced portobello mushrooms
- 1 pound (454 g) 93% lean ground beef
- 1 (15-ounce / 425-g) can no-salt-added diced tomatoes
- 2 cups low-sodium beef broth
- 1/3 cup half-and-half
- ¾ cup shredded sharp Cheddar cheese

Directions:
1. Heat a large stockpot over medium-low heat. When hot, coat the cooking surface with cooking spray. Put the onion, celery, and mushrooms into the pot. Cook for 7 minutes, stirring occasionally.
2. Add the ground beef and cook for 5 minutes, stirring and breaking apart as needed.
3. Add the diced tomatoes with their juices and the broth. Increase the heat to medium-high and simmer for 10 minutes.
4. Remove the pot from the heat and stir in the half-and-half.
5. Serve topped with the cheese.

Taco Soup

Preparation time: 5 minutes
Cooking time: 20 minutes
Servings: 4
Ingredients:
- Avocado oil cooking spray
- 1 medium red bell pepper, chopped
- ½ cup chopped yellow onion
- 1 pound (454 g) 93% lean ground beef
- 1 teaspoon ground cumin
- ½ teaspoon salt
- ½ teaspoon chili powder
- ½ teaspoon garlic powder
- 2 cups low-sodium beef broth
- 1 (15-ounce / 425-g) can no-salt-added diced tomatoes
- 1½ cups frozen corn
- 1/3 cup half-and-half

Directions:
1. Heat a large stockpot over medium-low heat. When hot, coat the cooking surface with cooking spray. Put the pepper and onion in the pan and cook for 5 minutes.
2. Add the ground beef, cumin, salt, chili powder, and garlic powder. Cook for 5 to 7 minutes, stirring and breaking apart the beef as needed.
3. Add the broth, diced tomatoes with their juices, and corn. Increase the heat to medium-high and simmer for 10 minutes.
4. Remove from the heat and stir in the half-and-half.

Lentil Vegetable Soup

Preparation time: 10 minutes
Cooking time: 15 minutes
Servings: 4
Ingredients:
- 2 tablespoons extra-virgin olive oil
- 1 onion, finely chopped
- 1 carrot, chopped
- 1 cup chopped kale (stems removed)
- 3 garlic cloves, minced
- 1 cup canned lentils, drained and rinsed
- 5 cups unsalted vegetable broth
- 2 teaspoons dried rosemary (or 1 tablespoon chopped fresh rosemary)
- ½ teaspoon sea salt
- ¼ teaspoon freshly ground black pepper

Directions:
1. In a large pot over medium-high heat, heat the olive oil until it shimmers. Add the onion and carrot and cook, stirring, until the vegetables begin to soften, about 3 minutes. Add the kale and cook for 3 minutes more. Add the garlic and cook, stirring constantly, for 30 seconds.
2. Stir in the lentils, vegetable broth, rosemary, salt, and pepper. Bring to a simmer. Simmer, stirring occasionally, for 5 minutes more.

Broccoli Soup

Preparation time: 15 minutes
Cooking time: 7 minutes
Servings: 6
Ingredients:
- 1-pound fresh broccoli (1 medium-sized head)
- 14 ounces low-sodium fat free chicken broth
- 2 tablespoons margarine
- 2 tablespoons all-purpose flour
- 2 cups skim milk
- 1/4 teaspoon pepper

- 1 cup reduced-fat shredded cheddar cheese

Directions:
1. Clean the broccoli, then chop the florets and thinly slice the stems.
2. In a medium-sized saucepan, combine the broccoli and chicken broth; heat to a boil. Reduce heat and simmer, covered, for about 7 minutes or until the broccoli is fork-tender.
3. Transfer to a food processor or blender. Process until fairly smooth.
4. In the same saucepan, melt the margarine over medium heat; add the flour. Cook, stirring constantly, until it starts to bubble. Add the milk and pepper; heat to a boil, stirring constantly.
5. Reduce heat to medium and add the broccoli purée. Stir in the cheese; heat just until the cheese melts - do not boil, keep stirring constantly.

Chicken and Potato Stew

Preparation time: 15 minutes
Cooking time: 6 hours
Servings: 6
Ingredients:
- 1 1/2 cups russet potatoes, peeled cut into bite-size pieces, and washed
- 1 1/2 cups carrots, peeled, cut into bite-size pieces, and washed
- 1/2 cup finely chopped onion
- 1/4 teaspoon garlic powder (to taste)
- 1/2 teaspoon salt (to taste)
- 3/4 teaspoon ground black pepper (to taste)
- 1/2 teaspoon sage (to taste)
- 1/4 teaspoon thyme (to taste)
- 2 boneless skinless chicken breast halves
- 1 (10 3/4 ounce) can cream of chicken soup

Directions:
1. Place vegetables in the bottom of a 2 1/2-quart slow cooker. Sprinkle seasonings evenly over the vegetables.
2. Top with chicken, then cover with soup. Cook on low for 6 hours.

Mediterranean Spinach and Tomato Pasta

Preparation time: 3 minutes
Cooking time: 20 minutes
Servings: 6
Ingredients:
- 1 cup vegetable broth
- 12 dehydrated sun-dried tomatoes
- 1 (8 ounce) package uncooked penne pasta
- 2 tablespoons pine nuts
- 1 tablespoon olive oil
- 1/4 teaspoon crushed red pepper flakes
- 1 clove garlic, minced
- 1 bunch fresh spinach, rinsed and torn into bite-size pieces
- 1/4 cup grated Parmesan cheese

Directions:
1. In a small saucepan, bring the broth to a boil. Remove from heat. Place the sun-dried tomatoes in the broth 15 minutes, or until softened. Drain, reserving broth, and coarsely chop.
2. Bring a large pot of lightly salted water to a boil. Place penne pasta in the pot, cook 9 to 12 minutes, until al dente, and drain.
3. Place the pine nuts in a skillet over medium heat. Cook and stir until lightly toasted.
4. Heat the olive oil and red pepper flakes in a skillet over medium heat, and sauté the garlic 1 minute, until tender. Mix in the spinach, and cook until almost wilted. Pour in the reserved broth, and stir in the chopped sun-dried tomatoes. Continue cooking 2 minutes, or until heated through.
5. In a large bowl, toss the cooked pasta with the spinach and tomato mixture and pine nuts. Serve with Parmesan cheese.

Butternut Squash Stew

Preparation time: 15 minutes
Cooking time: 8-10 hours
Servings: 6
Ingredients:
- 1 butternut squash - peeled, seeded, and cubed
- 2 cups cubed eggplant, with peel
- 2 cups cubed zucchini
- 1 (10 ounce) package frozen okra, thawed
- 1 (8 ounce) can tomato sauce
- 1 cup chopped onion
- 1 ripe tomato, chopped
- 1 carrot, sliced thin
- 1/2 cup vegetable broth
- 1/3 cup raisins
- 1 clove garlic, chopped
- 1/2 teaspoon ground cumin
- 1/2 teaspoon ground turmeric
- 1/4 teaspoon crushed red pepper
- 1/4 teaspoon ground cinnamon
- 1/4 teaspoon paprika

Directions:
1. In a slow cooker, combine butternut squash, eggplant, zucchini, okra, tomato sauce, onion, tomato, carrot, broth, raisins, and garlic. Season with cumin, turmeric, red pepper, cinnamon, and paprika.
2. Cover, and cook on Low for 8 to 10 hours, or until vegetables are tender.

Fish and Noodle Soup

Preparation Time: 30 minutes
Cooking time: 10 minutes
Servings: 4-5
Ingredients:
- 14 oz. firm white fish, cut into strips
- 2 carrots, cut into ribbons
- 1 zucchini, cut into thin ribbons
- 7 oz. white button mushrooms, sliced
- 1 celery rib, finely cut
- 1 cup baby spinach
- 7 oz. fresh noodles
- 3 cups chicken broth
- 2 cups water
- 2 tbsp. soy sauce
- 1/2 tsp ground ginger
- Black pepper, to taste

Directions:

1. Place chicken broth, water and soy sauce in a large saucepan. Bring to a boil and add in carrots, celery, zucchini, mushrooms, ginger and noodles.
2. Cook, partially covered, for 3-4 minutes then add in fish and simmer for 3 minutes or until the fish is cooked through. Add baby spinach and simmer, stirring, for 1 minute, or until it wilts. Season with black pepper and serve.

Lime Chicken Tortilla Soup

Preparation time: 10 minutes
Cooking time: 35 minutes
Servings: 4
Ingredients:

- 1 tablespoon extra-virgin olive oil
- 1 onion, thinly sliced
- 1 garlic clove, minced
- 1 jalapeño pepper, diced
- 2 boneless, skinless chicken breasts
- 4 cups low-sodium chicken broth
- 1 Roma tomato, diced
- ½ teaspoon salt
- 2 (6-inch) corn tortillas, cut into thin strips
- Nonstick cooking spray
- Juice of 1 lime
- Minced fresh cilantro, for garnish
- ¼ cup shredded Cheddar cheese, for garnish

Directions:
1. In a medium pot, heat the oil over medium-high heat. Add the onion and cook for 3 to 5 minutes until it begins to soften. Add the garlic and jalapeño, and cook until fragrant, about 1 minute more.
2. Add the chicken, chicken broth, tomato, and salt to the pot and bring to a boil. Reduce the heat to medium and simmer gently for 20 to 25 minutes until the chicken breasts are cooked through. Remove the chicken from the pot and set aside.
3. Preheat a broiler to high.
4. Spray the tortilla strips with nonstick cooking spray and toss to coat. Spread in a single layer on a baking sheet and broil for 3 to 5 minutes, flipping once, until crisp.
5. When the chicken is cool enough to handle, shred it with two forks and return to the pot.
6. Season the soup with the lime juice. Serve hot, garnished with cilantro, cheese, and tortilla strips.

Beef Barley Mushroom Soup

Preparation time: 10 minutes
Cooking time: 1 hour 20 minutes
Servings: 6
Ingredients:

- 1-pound (454 g) beef stew meat, cubed
- ¼ teaspoon salt
- ¼ teaspoon freshly ground black pepper
- 1 tablespoon extra-virgin olive oil
- 8 ounces (227 g) sliced mushrooms
- 1 onion, chopped
- 2 carrots, chopped
- 3 celery stalks, chopped
- 6 garlic cloves, minced
- ½ teaspoon dried thyme
- 4 cups low-sodium beef broth
- 1 cup water
- ½ cup pearl barley

Directions:
1. Season the meat with the salt and pepper.
2. In an Instant Pot, heat the oil over high heat. Add the meat and brown on all sides. Remove the meat from the pot and set aside.
3. Add the mushrooms to the pot and cook for 1 to 2 minutes, until they begin to soften. Remove the mushrooms and set aside with the meat.
4. Add the onion, carrots, and celery to the pot. Sauté for 3 to 4 minutes until the vegetables begin to soften. Add the garlic and continue to cook until fragrant, about 30 seconds longer.
5. Return the meat and mushrooms to the pot, then add the thyme, beef broth, and water. Set the pressure to high and cook for 15 minutes. Let the pressure release naturally.
6. Open the Instant Pot and add the barley. Use the slow cooker function on the Instant Pot, affix the lid (vent open), and continue to cook for 1 hour until the barley is cooked through and tender. Serve.

Split Pea Soup with Carrots

Preparation time: 8 minutes
Cooking time: 15 minutes
Servings: 4
Ingredients:

- 1½ cups dried green split peas, rinsed and drained
- 4 cups vegetable broth or water
- 2 celery stalks, chopped
- 1 medium onion, chopped
- 2 carrots, chopped
- 3 garlic cloves, minced
- 1 teaspoon herbs de Provence
- 1 teaspoon liquid smoke
- Kosher salt and freshly ground black pepper, to taste
- Shredded carrot, for garnish (optional)

Directions:
1. In the electric pressure cooker, combine the peas, broth, celery, onion, carrots, garlic, herbs de Provence, and liquid smoke.
2. Close and lock the lid of the pressure cooker. Set the valve to sealing.
3. Cook on high pressure for 15 minutes.
4. When the cooking is complete, hit Cancel and allow the pressure to release naturally for 10 minutes, then quick release any remaining pressure.
5. Once the pin drops, unlock and remove the lid.
6. Stir the soup and season with salt and pepper.
7. Spoon into serving bowls and sprinkle shredded carrots on top (if using).

Buttercup Squash Soup

Preparation time: 15 minutes
Cooking time: 10 minutes
Servings: 6
Ingredients:

- 2 tablespoons extra-virgin olive oil
- 1 medium onion, chopped
- 4 to 5 cups vegetable broth or chicken bone broth

- 1½ pounds (680 g) buttercup squash, peeled, seeded, and cut into 1-inch chunks
- ½ teaspoon kosher salt
- ¼ teaspoon ground white pepper
- Whole nutmeg, for grating

Directions:
1. Set the electric pressure cooker to the Sauté setting. When the pot is hot, pour in the olive oil.
2. Add the onion and sauté for 3 to 5 minutes, until it begins to soften. Hit Cancel.
3. Add the broth, squash, salt, and pepper to the pot and stir. (If you want a thicker soup, use 4 cups of broth. If you want a thinner, drinkable soup, use 5 cups.)
4. Close and lock the lid of the pressure cooker. Set the valve to sealing.
5. Cook on high pressure for 10 minutes.
6. When the cooking is complete, hit Cancel and allow the pressure to release naturally.
7. Once the pin drops, unlock and remove the lid.
8. Use an immersion blender to purée the soup right in the pot. If you don't have an immersion blender, transfer the soup to a blender or food processor and purée. (Follow the instructions that came with your machine for blending hot foods.)
9. Pour the soup into serving bowls and grate nutmeg on top.

Creamy Sweet Potato Soup

Preparation time: 15 minutes
Cooking time: 10 minutes
Servings: 6
Ingredients:
- 2 tablespoons avocado oil
- 1 small onion, chopped
- 2 celery stalks, chopped
- 2 teaspoons minced garlic
- 1 teaspoon kosher salt
- ½ teaspoon freshly ground black pepper
- 1 teaspoon ground turmeric
- ½ teaspoon ground cinnamon
- 2 pounds (907 g) sweet potatoes, peeled and cut into 1-inch cubes
- 3 cups vegetable broth or chicken bone broth
- Plain Greek yogurt, to garnish (optional)
- Chopped fresh parsley, to garnish (optional)
- Pumpkin seeds (pepitas), to garnish (optional)

Directions:
1. Set the electric pressure cooker to the Sauté setting. When the pot is hot, pour in the avocado oil.
2. Sauté the onion and celery for 3 to 5 minutes or until the vegetables begin to soften.
3. Stir in the garlic, salt, pepper, turmeric, and cinnamon. Hit Cancel.
4. Stir in the sweet potatoes and broth.
5. Close and lock the lid of the pressure cooker. Set the valve to sealing.
6. Cook on high pressure for 10 minutes.
7. When the cooking is complete, hit Cancel and allow the pressure to release naturally.
8. Once the pin drops, unlock and remove the lid.
9. Use an immersion blender to purée the soup right in the pot. If you don't have an immersion blender, transfer the soup to a blender or food processor and purée. (Follow the instructions that came with your machine for blending hot foods.)
10. Spoon into bowls and serve topped with Greek yogurt, parsley, and/or pumpkin seeds (if using).

Bean Soup with Lime-Yogurt Drizzle

Preparation time: 10 minutes
Cooking time: 40 minutes
Servings: 8
Ingredients:
- 2 tablespoons avocado oil
- 1 medium onion, chopped
- 3 garlic cloves, minced
- 1 teaspoon ground cumin
- 1 (10-ounce / 283-g) can diced tomatoes and green chilies
- 6 cups chicken bone broth, vegetable broth, or water
- 1 pound (454 g) dried black beans, rinsed
- Kosher salt, to taste
- ¼ cup plain Greek yogurt or sour cream
- 1 tablespoon freshly squeezed lime juice

Directions:
1. Set the electric pressure cooker to the Sauté setting. When the pot is hot, pour in the avocado oil.
2. Sauté the onion for 3 to 5 minutes, until it begins to soften. Hit Cancel.
3. Stir in the garlic, cumin, tomatoes and their juices, broth, and beans.
4. Close and lock the lid of the pressure cooker. Set the valve to sealing.
5. Cook on high pressure for 40 minutes.
6. While the soup is cooking, combine the yogurt and lime juice in a small bowl.
7. When the cooking is complete, hit Cancel. Allow the pressure to release naturally for 15 minutes, then quick release any remaining pressure.
8. Once the pin drops, unlock and remove the lid.
9. (Optional) for a thicker soup, remove 1½ cups of beans from the pot using a slotted spoon. Use an immersion blender to blend the beans that remain in the pot. If you don't have an immersion blender, transfer the soup left in the pot to a blender or food processor and purée. (Follow the instructions that came with your machine for blending hot foods.) Stir in the reserved beans. Season with salt, if desired.
10. Spoon into serving bowls and drizzle with lime-yogurt sauce.

Roasted Brussels sprouts and Cauliflower Soup

Preparation Time: 25 minutes
Cooking time: 40 minutes
Servings: 4
Ingredients:
- 1 onion, finely chopped
- 2 garlic cloves, crushed
- 16 oz. cauliflower florets
- 16 oz. Brussels sprouts, halved
- 4 cups vegetable broth

- 6 tbsp. olive oil
- Salt and pepper, to taste
- Parmesan cheese, to serve

Directions:
1. Preheat oven to 450F.
2. Line a large baking sheet and place the cauliflower and Brussels sprouts on it. Drizzle with half the olive oil and roast on the bottom third of the oven for 30 minutes, or until slightly browned.
3. Heat the remaining oil in a saucepan over medium heat and sauté the onion and garlic, stirring, for 2-3 minutes or until soft.
4. Add in vegetable broth and bring to the boil then simmer 3-4 minutes. Stir in roasted vegetables and cook for 5 minutes more.
5. Set aside to cool then blend in batches and reheat. Serve sprinkled with Parmesan cheese.

Beetroot and Carrot Soup

Preparation Time: 20 minutes
Cooking time: 40 minutes
Servings: 6
Ingredients:
- 4 beets, washed and peeled
- 2 carrots, peeled, chopped
- 2 potatoes, peeled, chopped
- 1 medium onion, chopped
- 2 cups vegetable broth
- 3 cups water
- 2 tbsp. yogurt
- 2 tbsp. olive oil
- Salt and pepper, to taste
- A bunch or spring onions, finely cut, to serve

Directions:
1. Peel and chop the beets. Heat the olive oil in a saucepan over medium high heat and sauté the onion and carrot until tender.
2. Add in beets, potatoes, broth and water. Bring to the boil.
3. Reduce heat to medium and simmer, partially covered, for 30-40 minutes, or until the beets are tender.
4. set aside to cool slightly.
5. Blend the soup in batches until smooth. Return it to pan over low heat and cook, stirring, for 4-5 minutes or until heated through. Season with salt and pepper to taste. Serve topped with yogurt and sprinkled with spring onions.

Baked Beet and Apple Soup

Preparation Time: 10 minutes
Cooking time: 1-2 hours
Servings: 8
Ingredients:
- 1.5 lb. fresh beets, peeled and grated
- 2 carrots, chopped
- 1 onion, chopped
- 2 apples, peeled and chopped
- 1 tbsp. sugar
- 1 bay leaf
- 2 tbsp. lemon juice
- 3 cups vegetable broth
- 3 tbsp. olive oil
- 1 cup heavy cream
- A bunch of fresh parsley, chopped, to serve
- Salt and black pepper, to taste

Directions:
1. Preheat the oven to 350 F. Toss the beets, apples, onion and carrots in olive oil and arrange in a casserole dish.
2. Add in the bay leaf and vegetable broth. Season with salt and pepper, cover with foil and bake for 1-2 hours. Discard the bay leaf and set aside to cool.
3. Blend everything in a blender, in batches, until smooth, then transfer to a large saucepan.
4. Season with salt and pepper to taste, stir in the cream and reheat without boiling. Serve the soup with a dollop of extra cream and sprinkled with chopped parsley.

Vegetarian Borscht

Preparation Time: 45 minutes
Cooking time: 1 hour 30 minutes
Servings: 6
Ingredients:
- 4 beets, peeled, quartered
- 1 carrot, peeled, chopped
- 1 parsnip, peeled, cut into chunks
- 1 leek, white part only, sliced
- 1 onion, chopped
- 1/3 cup lemon juice
- ½ tsp nutmeg
- 3 bay leaves
- 6 cups vegetable broth
- 1 cup sour cream
- 2-3 dill springs, chopped

Directions:
1. Place the beets, carrot, parsnip, leek, onion, lemon juice, spices and bay leaves in a large saucepan with the vegetable broth.
2. Bring to the boil, then reduce the heat to low and simmer, partially covered, for 1 ½ hours.
3. Cool slightly, then blend in batches and season well with salt and pepper. Return to the saucepan and gently heat through. Place in bowls and garnish with sour cream and dill.

Ingenious Eggplant Soup

Servings: 8
Preparation Time: 20 minutes
Cooking Time: 15 minutes
Ingredients:
- 1 large eggplant, washed and cubed
- 1 tomato, seeded and chopped
- 1 small onion, diced
- 2 tablespoons parsley, chopped
- 2 tablespoons extra virgin olive oil
- 2 tablespoons distilled white vinegar
- ½ cup parmesan cheese, crumbled
- Salt as needed

Directions:
1. Preheat your outdoor grill to medium-high
2. Pierce the eggplant a few times using a knife/fork
3. Cook the eggplants on your grill for about 15 minutes until they are charred
4. Keep it on the side and allow them to cool

5. Remove the skin from the eggplant and dice the pulp
6. Transfer the pulp to a mixing bowl and add parsley, onion, tomato, olive oil, feta cheese, and vinegar
7. Mix well and chill for 1 hour
8. Season with salt, and enjoy!

Amazing Roasted Carrot Soup

Servings: 4
Preparation Time: 10 minutes
Cooking Time: 50 minutes
Ingredients:
- 8 large carrots,s washed and peeled
- 6 tablespoons olive oil
- 1-quart broth
- Cayenne pepper to taste
- Salt and pepper to taste

Directions:
1. Preheat your oven to 425 degrees F
2. Take a baking sheet and add carrots, drizzle olive oil, and roast for 30-45 minutes
3. Put roasted carrots into a blender and add broth, puree
4. Pour into saucepan and heat soup
5. Season with salt, pepper, and cayenne
6. Drizzle olive oil
7. Serve and enjoy!

The Brussels's Fever

Servings: 4
Preparation Time: 10 minutes
Cooking Time: 20 minutes
Ingredients:
- 2 tablespoons olive oil
- 1 yellow onion, chopped
- 2 pounds Brussels sprouts, trimmed and halved
- 4 cups chicken stock
- ¼ cup coconut cream

Directions:
1. Take a pot and place it over medium heat
2. Add oil and let it heat up
3. Add onion and stir. Cook for 3 minutes
4. Add Brussels sprouts and stir; cook for 2 minutes
5. Add stock and black pepper, stir and bring to a simmer
6. Cook for 20 minutes more
7. Use an immersion blender to make the soup creamy
8. Add coconut cream and stir well
9. Ladle into soup bowls and serve
10. Enjoy!

Curious Roasted Garlic Soup

Servings: 10
Preparation Time: 10 minutes
Cooking Time: 60 minutes
Ingredients:
- 1 tablespoon olive oil
- 2 bulbs garlic, peeled
- 3 shallots, chopped
- 1 large head cauliflower, chopped
- 6 cups vegetable broth
- Salt and pepper to taste

Directions:
1. Preheat your oven to 400 degrees F
2. Slice ¼ inch top of the garlic bulb and place it in an aluminum foil
3. Grease with olive oil and roast in the oven for 35 minutes
4. Squeeze flesh out of the roasted garlic
5. Heat oil in a saucepan and add shallots; saute for 6 minutes
6. Add garlic and remaining ingredients
7. Cover the pan and lower the heat to low
8. Let it cook for 15-20 minutes
9. Use an immersion blender to puree the mixture
10. Season soup with salt and pepper
11. Serve and enjoy!

Beef And Onion Stew

Servings: 4
Preparation Time: 10 minutes
Cook Time 1-2 hours
Ingredients:
- 2 pounds lean beef, cubed
- 3 pounds shallots, peeled
- 5 garlic cloves, peeled, whole
- 3 tablespoons tomato paste
- 1 bay leaves
- ¼ cup olive oil
- 3 tablespoons lemon juice
- 1 teaspoon salt

Directions:
1. Take a stew pot and place it over medium heat
2. Add olive oil and let it heat up
3. Add meat and brown
4. Add remaining ingredients and cover with water
5. Bring the whole mix to a boil
6. Lower heat to low and cover the pot
7. Simmer for 1-2 hours until beef is cooked thoroughly
8. Serve hot!

Healthy Cucumber Soup

Servings: 4
Preparation Time: 14 minutes
Cooking Time: Nil
Ingredients:
- 2 tablespoons garlic, minced
- 4 cups English cucumbers, peeled and diced
- ½ cup onions, diced
- 1 tablespoon lemon juice
- 1 and ½ cups vegetable broth
- ½ teaspoon salt
- ¼ teaspoon red pepper flakes
- ¼ cup parsley, diced
- ½ cup Greek yogurt, plain

Directions:
1. Add the listed ingredients to a blender and emulsify by blending them (except ½ cup of chopped cucumbers)
2. Blend until smooth
3. Divide the soup among 4 servings and top with extra cucumbers and chili/pepper flakes if you want
4. Enjoy chilled!

Dreamy Zucchini Bowl

Servings: 4

Preparation Time: 10 minutes
Cooking Time: 20 minutes
Ingredients:
- 1 onion, chopped
- 3 zucchinis, cut into medium chunks
- 2 tablespoons coconut milk
- 2 garlic cloves, minced
- 4 cups chicken stock
- 2 tablespoons coconut oil
- Pinch of salt
- Black pepper to taste

Directions:
1. Take a pot and place it over medium heat
2. Add oil and let it heat up
3. Add zucchini, garlic, and onion, and stir
4. Cook for 5 minutes
5. Add stock, salt, pepper, and stir
6. Bring to a boil and lower the heat
7. Simmer for 20 minutes. Remove heat and add coconut milk
8. Use an immersion blender until smooth
9. Ladle into soup bowls and serve
10. Enjoy!

Wild Mushroom Soup

Servings: 4
Preparation Time: 10 minutes
Cooking Time: 30 minutes
Ingredients:
- 10 oz of wild mushrooms
- 1/4 cup salted butter
- 1 tbsp of garlic, minced
- 5 cups of vegetable broth
- 1/2 cup of fresh cream

Directions:
1. Heat a pan with the butter and saute the mushrooms with the garlic for 3-4 minutes.
2. Transfer to a large saucepan and add the vegetable broth. Bring to a boil and reduce the heat to simmer for 20 minutes.
3. Add the creme fresh towards the last two minutes of cooking.
4. Let the soup cool for 5 minutes and use an immersion blender, blend until the soup is silky smooth with no visible parts of mushrooms. You should end up with a grayish-brown sort of color.
5. Transfer into soup bowls and add extra doses of cream or parsley on top optionally, for garnish

Pumpkin And Coconut Cream Soup

Servings: 4
Preparation Time: 10 minutes
Cooking Time: 50 minutes
Ingredients:
- 2 cups of pumpkin chunks
- 2 cups of vegetable stock
- 1 cup of coconut cream
- 1 tbsp of butter
- 1 tsp of ginger powder

Directions:
1. Heat a cooking pot and add the butter and the pumpkin chunks. Saute for 3-4 minutes.
2. Add the vegetable stock and the ginger powder and bring to a boil. Reduce the heat to simmer for 20-25 minutes.
3. Add the coconut cream last and cook for another 2-3 minutes.
4. Blend the soup with an immersion blender until creamy and smooth. Serve with a drizzle of coconut cream (optionally) on top

Fish Packed White Chowder

Servings: 4
Preparation Time: 10 minutes
Cooking Time: 5-10 minutes
Ingredients:
- 2 teaspoons butter, at room temperature
- 1/2 white onion, chopped
- 1 tablespoon Old Bay seasoning
- 3/4 pound sea bass, broken into chunks
- 1 cup double cream

Directions:
1. Melt the butter in a soup pot over a moderate flame. Now, sweat the white onion until tender and translucent.
2. Then, add in the Old Bay seasoning and 3 cups of water; bring to a rapid boil. Reduce the heat to medium-low and let it simmer for 9 to 12 minutes.
3. Fold in the sea bass and double cream; continue to cook until everything is thoroughly heated or about 5 minutes. Serve warm, and enjoy!

Awesome Fish Curry

Servings: 4
Preparation Time: 10 minutes
Cooking Time: 12-20 minutes
Ingredients:
- 1 tablespoon butter, at room temperature
- 1 shallot, chopped
- 1 teaspoon curry paste
- 1 cup tomatoes, pureed
- 3/4 pound sole fillets, cut into 1-inch pieces

Directions:
1. Melt the butter in a stockpot over a medium-high flame. Sauté the shallot until softened.
2. Add the curry paste, pureed tomatoes, and 2 cups of water to the pot; bring to a rolling boil.
3. Immediately reduce the heat to medium-low and continue to simmer, covered, for 12 minutes longer; make sure to stir periodically
4. Fold in the chopped sole fillets; cook for 8 minutes or until the fish flakes easily with a fork. Enjoy!

Honorable Mahi Mahi Stew

Servings: 4
Preparation Time: 10 minutes
Cooking Time: 30-40 minutes
Ingredients:
- 1 1/2 tablespoons butter
- 3/4-pound cubed Mahi Mahi fillets
- 1/2 chopped onion
- Salt & Black pepper

- ¾ cup homemade fish broth

Directions:
1. Sprinkle the Mahi Mahi fillets with some seasonings.
2. Put the butter in a pressure cooker to melt, then add the onions
3. Cook the onions for 3 minutes, then add the fish broth and mahi-mahi fillets
4. Cook for 30 minutes with the lid sealed at high pressure
5. Release the pressure naturally.
6. Serve!

Hearty Crab Soup

Servings: 4
Preparation Time: 20 minutes
Cook Time: 6-7 hours
Ingredients
- 1 cup crab meat, cubed
- 1 tablespoon garlic, minced
- Red chili flakes as needed
- 3 cups vegetable broth
- 1 teaspoon salt

Directions:
1. Coat the crab cubes in lime juice and let them sit for a while
2. Add the all ingredients (including marinated crab meat) to your Slow Cooker and put the lid
3. Cook on MEDIUM for 3 hours
4. Let it sit for a while
5. Remove the lid and simmer the soup for 5 minutes more on LOW
6. Stir and check to season
7. Enjoy!

Mexican Chicken Soup

Servings: 4
Preparation Time: 10 minutes
Cooking Time: 5 minutes
Ingredients:
- 1 and ½ pounds chicken pieces, boneless, skinless
- 8 ounces Pepper Jack cheese, cubed
- 2 cups chicken broth
- 15 ounces of chunky salsa

Directions:
1. Take a crockpot and put the chicken pieces on the bottom of it.
2. Add the remaining ingredients.
3. Cook for 8 hours on low.
4. Remove chicken pieces and shred, and return to the pot.
5. Serve hot, and enjoy!

Delicious Turkey Stew

Servings: 12
Preparation Time: 10 minutes
Cooking Time: 25 minutes
Ingredients:
- 15 ounces can eat vegetables, mixed
- 2 cups turkey, cooked and cubed
- 14 ounces can chicken broth
- 3 tablespoon butter

Directions:
1. Take a saucepan and put all the ingredients into it.
2. Bring it to a boil.
3. Reduce the heat to low.
4. Simmer for about 25 minutes.
5. Dish out and serve hot.
6. Enjoy!

Turkey, Kale, And Sausage Delight

Servings: 4
Preparation Time: 10 minutes
Cooking Time: 40 minutes
Ingredients:
- 1 broccoli head, cut into florets
- 2 cloves garlic, chopped
- 4 cups vegetable broth
- 1 cup heavy cream
- 4 slices of beef bacon, chopped

Directions:
1. Add all the ingredients except salt and black pepper into a stockpot.
2. Let it bring to a boil.
3. Reduce heat to simmer.
4. Cook for 40 minutes.
5. Warm the heavy cream, and then add to the soup.
6. Season with salt and black pepper.
7. Serve and enjoy!

Awesome Egg Drop Soup

Servings: 4
Preparation Time: 10 minutes
Cooking Time: 10 minutes
Ingredients:
- ½ cup chicken breast, cooked, boneless, and skinless
- 1 egg, lightly beaten
- ½ teaspoon coconut aminos + 4 cups low sodium chicken broth
- ½ cup green beans, frozen
- ¼ cup green onion, sliced

Directions:
1. Add chicken stock and soy sauce to a saucepan.
2. Place it over medium heat.
3. Bring the mix to a boil and add green onions, peas, and chicken.
4. Stir it and bring the mix to boil once again.
5. Remove the heat and slowly drizzle in the egg.
6. Set it aside for a few minutes.
7. Stir and transfer into a serving bowl, then ladle the soup.
8. Serve and enjoy!

Cheesy Broccoli Soup

Servings: 4
Preparation Time: 10 minutes
Cooking Time: 30 minutes
Ingredients:
- 3 cans of 14 and ½ ounces of chicken broth
- 10-ounce Velveeta low-fat cheese
- 2 bags of frozen broccoli
- 1 can of 10 and ½ ounce tomatoes and green chili pepper

Directions:

1. Add frozen broccoli, tomatoes, broth, and chili to a pot.
2. Mix them well and place the pot over medium heat.
3. Bring it to a boil.
4. Then reduce the heat and simmer for 25 minutes.
5. Add cubed Velveeta into the soup.
6. Simmer until the cheese melts.
7. Serve hot, and enjoy!

Chicken Liver Stew

Servings: 4
Preparation Time: 10 minutes
Cooking Time: 20 minutes
Ingredients:
- 10 ounces of chicken livers
- 2 ounces sour cream
- Salt, to taste
- 1-ounce onion, chopped
- 1 tablespoon olive oil

Directions:
1. Place a pan over medium heat.
2. Add oil and let it heat up.
3. Add onions and fry until it turns brown.
4. Put livers and season with salt.
5. Cook till the livers become half-cooked.
6. Take a stew pot and transfer the mix.
7. Add sour cream and cook for 20 minutes.
8. Serve hot and enjoy!

Chicken And Mushroom Stew

Servings: 4
Preparation Time: 10 minutes
Cooking Time: 30 minutes
Ingredients:
- 4 chicken breast halves, cut into bite-sized pieces
- 4 tablespoons olive oil
- 1 teaspoon thyme
- 1 pound mushrooms, sliced (5-6 cups)
- 1 bunch of spring onion, chopped

Directions:
1. Take a large deep frying pan and place it over medium-high heat.
2. Add oil to it and let it heat up.
3. Put chicken and cook for 4-5 minutes for each side.
4. Add spring mushrooms and onions and season with salt and pepper.
5. Stir it well, and then cover the lid.
6. Bring the mix to a boil.
7. Reduce the heat and simmer for 25 minutes.
8. Serve and enjoy!

Garlic Chicken Soup

Servings: 4
Preparation Time: 10 minutes
Cooking Time: 5-10 minutes
Ingredients:
- 2 tablespoons butter
- 4 ounces cream cheese, cubed
- 14.5-ounce chicken broth
- 2 cups chicken, shredded
- ¼ cup heavy cream
- 2 tablespoons Stacey Hawkins Garlic Gusto Seasoning
- Salt, to taste

Directions:
1. Take a saucepan and place it over medium heat.
2. Add butter into the saucepan and melt the butter.
3. Put the shredded chicken in the pan and coat it with melted butter.
4. Add cream cheese and Stacey Hawkins garlic gusto seasoning when the chicken is warm.
5. Mix to blend the ingredients.
6. Add chicken broth, heavy cream, and evenly distributed cream cheese.
7. Bring them to boil, then reduce the heat to low.
8. Simmer for 3-4 minutes.
9. Add salt to taste and serve.
10. Enjoy!

Spicy Fish Stew

Servings: 4
Preparation Time: 10 minutes
Cooking Time: 20 minutes
Ingredients:
- 6 white fish fillets
- 1 cup vegetable stock
- 1 red and 1 green bell pepper, sliced
- 1 cup Marinara Tomato Sauce, low carb
- 1 green onion, sliced

Directions:
1. Add vegetable stock, red bell pepper, green onion, sliced bell pepper, and green onion into your crockpot.
2. Mix them well.
3. Pour the tomato sauce.
4. Season it with salt and pepper.
5. Place the fish fillets and fill them with hot sauce carefully.
6. Cook for 6 hours on low heat.
7. Serve hot, and enjoy!

Chilled Minty Avocado Soup

Servings: 4
Preparation Time: 10 minutes + Chill Time
Cooking Time: Nil
Ingredients:
- 1 avocado, ripe
- 1 cup coconut milk, chilled
- 2 romaine lettuce leaves
- 20 mint leaves, fresh
- 1 tablespoon lime juice

Directions:
1. Turn on your slow cooker and add all the ingredients to it.
2. Mix them in a food processor.
3. Make a smooth mixture.
4. Let it chill for 10 minutes.
5. Serve and enjoy!

Original Guacamole Soup

Servings: 4
Preparation Time: 10 minutes
Cooking Time: Nil

Ingredients:
- 4 cups vegetable broth
- 2 ripe avocados, pitted
- ½ cup cilantro, freshly chopped
- 1 tomato, chopped
- ½ cup heavy cream

Directions:
1. Add all the ingredients into a blender.
2. Blend until creamy by using an immersion blender.
3. Let it chill for 1 hour.
4. Serve and enjoy!

Awesome Zucchini Soup

Servings: 4
Preparation Time: 10 minutes
Cooking Time: 6-8 Hours
Ingredients:
- 2 cups vegetable broth
- 2 zucchinis, cut into chunks
- 2 tablespoons sour cream, low fat
- 2 cloves garlic, minced
- *Salt, pepper, thyme, and pepper, to taste*

Directions:
1. Add all the ingredients except sour cream to a crockpot.
2. Close the lid.
3. Cook for 6-8 hours on low.
4. Add sour cream.
5. Make a smooth puree by using a blender.
6. Serve hot with parmesan cheese if you want.
7. Enjoy!

Spring Soup With Poached Egg

Servings: 4
Preparation Time: 10 minutes
Cooking Time: 15 minutes
Ingredients:
- 2 eggs
- 32 ounces of chicken broth
- 1 head of romaine lettuce, chopped
- Salt, to taste

Directions:
1. Bring the chicken broth to a boil.
2. Reduce the heat and poach the 2 eggs in the broth for 5 minutes.
3. Take two bowls and transfer the eggs into a separate bowl.
4. Add chopped romaine lettuce into the broth and cook for a few minutes.
5. Serve the broth with lettuce in the bowls.
6. Enjoy!

Spanish Soup

Servings: 4
Preparation Time: 10 minutes + Chill Time
Cooking Time: 5 minutes
Ingredients:
- 1 and ½ tomatoes, chopped
- 1 cucumber, peeled, seeded, and chopped
- ¼ white onion, chopped
- ½ green bell pepper, seeded and chopped
- tablespoons olive oil, garlic-flavored

Directions:
1. Add all the ingredients and mix them in a blender.
2. Blend until you get a smooth mixture.
3. Close the lid and cook for 5 minutes.
4. Let it refrigerate for 1 hour.
5. Garnish with bell pepper and chopped tomato.
6. Serve and enjoy!

Butternut Garlic Soup

Servings: 4
Preparation Time: 10 minutes
Cooking Time: 5 minutes
Ingredients:
- 4 cups butternut squash, cubed
- 4 cups vegetable broth, stock
- ½ cup full-fat cream
- 2 garlic cloves, finely chopped
- Salt and pepper

Directions:
1. Add butternut squash, garlic cloves, broth, salt, and pepper to a large pot.
2. Place the pot over medium heat and cover the lid.
3. Bring it to a boil, and then reduce the temperature.
4. Let it simmer for sometimes
5. Blend the soup for 1-2 minutes until you get a smooth mixture.
6. Stir the cream through the soup.
7. Serve and enjoy!

The Brussels's Fever

Serving: 4
Preparation Time: 5 minutes
Cooking Time: 20 minutes
Ingredients
- 2 tablespoons olive oil
- 1 yellow onion, chopped
- 2 pounds Brussels sprouts, trimmed and halved
- 4 cups chicken stock
- ¼ cup coconut cream

Directions:
1. Take a pot and place it over medium heat
2. Add oil and let it heat up
3. Add onion and stir. Cook for 3 minutes
4. Add Brussels sprouts and stir; cook for 2 minutes
5. Add stock and black pepper, stir and bring to a simmer
6. Cook for 20 minutes more
7. Use an immersion blender to make the soup creamy
8. Add coconut cream and stir well
9. Ladle into soup bowls and serve
10. Enjoy!

Dreamy Zucchini Bowl

Serving: 4
Preparation Time: 5 minutes
Cooking Time: 20 minutes
Ingredients
- 1 onion, chopped
- 3 zucchinis, cut into medium chunks
- 2 tablespoons coconut milk
- 2 garlic cloves, minced
- 4 cups chicken stock

- 2 tablespoons coconut oil
- Pinch of salt
- Black pepper to taste

Directions:
1. Take a pot and place it over medium heat
2. Add oil and let it heat up
3. Add zucchini, garlic, and onion and stir
4. Cook for 5 minutes
5. Add stock, salt, pepper, and stir
6. Bring to a boil and lower the heat
7. Simmer for 20 minutes. Remove heat and add coconut milk
8. Use an immersion blender until smooth
9. Ladle into soup bowls and serve
10. Enjoy!

Garlic Tomato Soup

Serving: 4
Preparation Time: 10 minutes
Cooking Time: 15 minutes
Ingredients

- 8 Roma tomatoes, chopped
- 1 cup tomatoes, sundried
- 2 tablespoons coconut oil
- 5 garlic cloves, chopped
- 14 ounces of coconut milk
- 1 cup vegetable broth
- Pepper to taste
- Basil, for garnish

Directions:
1. Take a pot, and heat oil into it.
2. Sauté the garlic in it for ½ minute.
3. Mix in the Roma tomatoes and cook for 8-10 minutes.
4. Stir occasionally.
5. Add in the rest of the ingredients except the basil and stir well.
6. Cover the lid and cook for 5 minutes.
7. Let it cool.
8. Blend the soup until smooth by using an immersion blender.
9. Garnish with basil.
10. Serve and enjoy!

Melon Soup

Serving: 4
Prep Time: 6 minutes
Cooking Time: Nil
Ingredients

- 4 cups casaba melon, seeded and cubed
- 1 tablespoon fresh ginger, grated
- ¾ cup of coconut milk
- Juice of 2 lime

Directions:
1. Add the lime juice, coconut milk, casaba melon, ginger, and salt into your blender.
2. Blend it for 1-2 minutes until you get a smooth mixture.
3. Serve and enjoy!

Healthy Ginger Soup

Serving: 4
Preparation Time: 9 minutes
Cooking Time: 9 minutes
Ingredients

- 3 cups of green onions, diced
- 2 cups of mushrooms, sliced
- 3 teaspoon of fresh ginger, grated
- 3 teaspoon of garlic, minced
- 2 cups of bok choy, chopped
- 1 tablespoon of cilantro, chopped
- 3 tablespoons of carrot, grated
- 1 can of each diced tomatoes and peppers (or freshly prepared)
- 6 cups of vegetable broth

Directions:
1. Add the listed ingredients (except green onions and carrot) to a saucepan and bring the mix to a boil over medium-high heat
2. Lower heat to medium-low and cook for 6 minutes
3. Stir in green onions and carrots and cook for 2 minutes
4. Sprinkle cilantro and serve
5. Enjoy!

Cucumber Soup

Serving: 4
Preparation Time: 14 minutes
Cooking Time: nil
Ingredients

- 2 tablespoons garlic, minced
- 4 cups English cucumbers, peeled and diced
- ½ cup onion, diced
- 1 tablespoon lemon juice
- 1 and ½ cups vegetable broth
- ½ teaspoon salt
- 1 whole avocado, diced
- ¼ teaspoon dried pepper flakes
- ¼ cup parsley, diced
- ½ cup cashew cream

Directions:
1. Add the listed ingredients to a blender and emulsify by blending them (except ½ a cup of chopped cucumbers)
2. Blend well until smooth
3. Pour into 4 servings and top with remaining cucumbers
4. Enjoy!

Tasty Tofu and Mushroom Soup

Serving: 8
Preparation Time: 10 minutes
Cooking Time: 10 minutes
Ingredients

- 3 cups prepared dashi stock
- ¼ cup shiitake mushrooms, sliced
- 1 tablespoon miso paste
- 1 tablespoon coconut aminos
- 1/8 cup cubed soft tofu
- 1 green onion, diced

Directions:
1. Take a saucepan and add the stock; bring to a boil
2. Add mushrooms, cook for 4 minutes
3. Take a bowl and add coconut aminos and miso paste and mix well
4. Pour the mixture into stock and let it cook for 6 minutes on simmer

5. Add diced green onions, and enjoy!

Mushroom Cream Soup

Serving: 4
Preparation Time: 5 minutes
Cooking Time: 25 minutes
Ingredients
- 1 tablespoon olive oil
- ½ large onion, diced
- 20 ounces mushrooms, sliced
- 6 garlic cloves, minced
- 2 cups vegetable broth
- 1 cup coconut cream
- ¾ teaspoon sunflower seeds
- ¼ teaspoon black pepper

Directions:
1. Take a large-sized pot and place it over medium heat
2. Add onion and mushrooms in olive oil and Sauté for 5 minutes
3. Make sure to keep stirring it from time to time until it browned evenly
4. Add garlic and Sauté for 5 minutes more
5. Add vegetable broth, coconut cream, coconut almond milk, black pepper, and sunflower seeds
6. Bring it to a boil and lower the temperature to low
7. Simmer for 15 minutes
8. Use an immersion blender to puree the mixture
9. Enjoy!

Pumpkin, Coconut, and Sage Soup

Serving: 3
Preparation Time: 10 minutes
Cooking Time: 20 minutes
Ingredients
- 1 cup pumpkin, canned
- 6 cups chicken broth
- 1 cup low-fat coconut almond milk
- 1 teaspoon sage, chopped
- 3 garlic cloves, peeled
- Sunflower seeds and pepper to taste

Directions:
1. Take a stockpot and add all the ingredients except coconut almond milk.
2. Place stockpot over medium heat.
3. Let's bring it to a boil.
4. Reduce heat to simmer for 20 minutes.
5. Add the coconut almond milk and stir.
6. Serve bacon, and enjoy!

Fine Black Bean Soup

Serving: 4
Preparation Time: 5 minutes
Cooking Time: 25 minutes
Ingredients
- 1 teaspoon olive oil
- 1 onion, chopped
- 6 garlic cloves, minced
- 1 teaspoon chili powder
- ½ teaspoon ground cinnamon
- ½ teaspoon salt
- 1 can (15 ounces) of black beans, drained
- 1 (28 ounces) can of crushed tomatoes, undrained
- 3 cups of water
- 3 celery water, chopped
- 2 cups collard greens, chopped
- 2 tablespoons freshly squeezed lime juice

Directions:
1. Take a large soup pot and place it over medium heat, add oil and let it heat up
2. Add onion, garlic, and Sauté for 5 minutes
3. Stir in chili powder, cinnamon, salt, beans, tomato with juice, and water, and bring the mix to a boil
4. Lower heat to low and simmer for 10-15 minutes
5. Use a hand blender to puree the mixture until smooth
6. Stir in greens, cover, and let it cook for 10 minutes more
7. Stir in lime juice and serve!

Chapter 11

Poultry

Stuffed Chicken Breasts Greek-style

Preparation time: 10 minutes
Cooking Time: 20 Minutes
Servings: 4
Ingredients:
- 4 oz. chicken breasts, skinless and boneless
- ¼ cup onion, minced
- 4 artichoke hearts, minced
- 1 teaspoon oregano, crushed
- 4 lemon slices
- What you will need from the store cupboard:
- cup canned chicken broth, fat-free
- 1-1/2 lemon juice
- 2 tablespoon olive oil
- 2 teaspoons of cornstarch
- Ground pepper Salt, optional

Directions:
1. Take out all the fat from the chicken. Wash and pat dry. Season your chicken with pepper and salt.
2. Pound the chicken to make it flat and thin. Bring together the oregano, onion, and artichoke hearts.
3. Now spoon equal amounts of the mix at the center of your chicken.
4. Roll up the log and secure using a skewer or toothpick. Heat oil in your skillet over medium temperature.
5. Add the chicken. Brown all sides evenly.
6. Pour the lemon juice and broth.
7. Add lemon slices on top of the chicken.
8. Simmer covered for 10 minutes.
9. Transfer to a platter.
10. Remove the skewers or toothpick.
11. Mix cornstarch with a fork. Transfer to skillet and stir over high temperature. Put lemon sauce on the chicken.

Chicken & Tofu

Preparation Time: 1 hour and 15 minutes
Cooking Time: 25 minutes
Servings: 6
Ingredients:
- 2 tablespoons olive oil, divided
- 2 tablespoons orange juice
- 1 tablespoon Worcestershire sauce
- 1 tablespoon low-sodium soy sauce
- 1 teaspoon ground turmeric
- 1 teaspoon dry mustard
- 8 oz. chicken breast, cooked and sliced into cubes
- 8 oz. extra-firm tofu, drained and sliced into cubed
- 2 carrots, sliced into thin strips
- 1 cup mushroom, sliced
- 2 cups fresh bean sprouts
- 3 green onions, sliced
- Red sweet pepper, sliced into strips

Directions:
1. In a bowl, mix half of the oil with the orange juice, Worcestershire sauce, soy sauce, turmeric and mustard.
2. Coat all sides of chicken and tofu with the sauce.
3. Marinate for 1 hour. In a pan over medium heat, add 1 tablespoon oil.
4. Add carrot and cook for 2 minutes.
5. Add mushroom and cook for another 2 minutes.
6. Add bean sprouts, green onion and sweet pepper.
7. Cook for two to three minutes. Stir in the chicken and heat through.

Jerk Style Chicken Wings

Preparation time: 10 minutes
Cooking time: 30 minutes
Servings: 2-3
Ingredients:
- 1g ground thyme
- 1g dried rosemary
- 2g allspice
- 4g ground ginger
- 3 g garlic powder
- 2g onion powder
- 1g of cinnamon
- 2g of paprika
- 2g chili powder
- 1g nutmeg
- Salt to taste
- 30 ml of vegetable oil
- 0.5 - 1 kg of chicken wings
- 1 lime, juice

Directions:
1. Select Preheat, set the temperature to 200°C and press Start/Pause.
2. Combine all spices and oil in a bowl to create a marinade.
3. Mix the chicken wings in the marinade until they are well covered.
4. Place the chicken wings in the preheated air fryer.
5. Select Chicken and press Start/Pause. Be sure to shake the baskets in the middle of cooking.
6. Remove the wings and place them on a serving plate.
7. Squeeze fresh lemon juice over the wings and serve.

Italian Chicken

Preparation time: 10 minutes
Cooking time: 30 minutes
Servings: 4
Ingredients:
- 5 chicken thighs
- 1 tbsp. olive oil
- 1/4 cup parmesan; grated
- 1/2 cup sun dried tomatoes
- 2 garlic cloves; minced
- 1 tbsp. thyme; chopped.
- 1/2 cup heavy cream
- 3/4 cup chicken stock
- 1 tsp. red pepper flakes; crushed
- 2 tbsp. basil; chopped
- Salt and black pepper to the taste

Directions:
1. Season chicken with salt and pepper, rub with half of the oil, place in your preheated air fryer at 350 °F and cook for 4 minutes.
2. Meanwhile; heat up a pan with the rest of the oil over medium high heat, add thyme garlic, pepper flakes, sun dried tomatoes, heavy cream, stock, parmesan, salt and pepper; stir, bring to a simmer, take off heat and transfer to a dish that fits your air fryer.
3. Add chicken thighs on top, introduce in your air fryer and cook at 320 °F, for 12 minutes. Divide among plates and serve with basil sprinkled on top.

Coconut Chicken

Preparation time: 10 minutes
Cooking time: 30 minutes
Servings: 6
Ingredients:
- 2 garlic cloves, minced
- Fresh cilantro, minced
- 1/2 cup light coconut milk
- 6 tablespoons sweetened coconut, shredded and toasted
- 2 tablespoons brown sugar
- 6 (about 1-1/2 pounds) boneless skinless chicken thighs
- 2 tablespoons reduced-sodium soy sauce
- 1/8 teaspoon ground cloves

Directions:
1. Mix brown sugar, 1/2 cup light coconut milk, 2 tablespoons soy sauce, 1/8 teaspoon ground cloves and 2 minced cloves of garlic in a bowl.
2. Add 6 chicken boneless thighs into a Crockpot.
3. Now pour the mixture of coconut milk over chicken thighs. Cover the cooker and cook for about 4-5 hours on low.
4. Serve coconut chicken with cilantro and coconut; enjoy!

Spicy Lime Chicken

Preparation time: 10 minutes
Cooking time: 30 minutes
Servings: 6
Ingredients:
- 3 tablespoons lime juice
- Fresh cilantro leaves
- 1-1/2 pounds (about 4) boneless skinless chicken breast halves
- 1 teaspoon lime zest, grated
- 2 cups chicken broth
- 1 tablespoon chili powder

Directions:
1. Add chicken breast halves into a slow cooker.
2. Add 1 tablespoon chili powder, 3 tablespoons lime juice and 2 cups chicken broth in a small bowl; mix well and pour over chicken.
3. Cover the cooker and cook for about 3 hours on low. Once done, take chicken out from the cooker and let it cool.
4. Once cooled, shred chicken by using forks and transfer back to the Crockpot.
5. Stir in 1 teaspoon grated lime zest. Serve spicy lime chicken with cilantro and enjoy!

Chicken & Peanut Stir-Fry

Preparation Time: 15 minutes
Cooking Time: 15 minutes
Servings: 4
Ingredients:
- 3 tablespoons lime juice
- ½ teaspoon lime zest
- 4 cloves garlic, minced
- 2 teaspoons chili bean sauce
- ½ tablespoon fish sauce
- 1 tablespoon water
- 2 tablespoons peanut butter
- 3 teaspoons oil, divided
- 1 lb. chicken breast, sliced into strips
- Red sweet pepper, sliced into strips
- 3 green onions, sliced thinly
- 2 cups broccoli, shredded
- 2 tablespoons peanuts, chopped

Directions:
1. In a bowl, mix the lime juice, lime zest, garlic, chili bean sauce, fish sauce, water and peanut butter.
2. Mix well. In a pan over medium high heat, add 2 teaspoons of oil.
3. Cook the chicken until golden on both sides.
4. Pour in the remaining oil. Add the pepper and green onions.
5. Add the chicken, broccoli and sauce. Cook for 2 minutes. Top with peanuts before serving.

Honey Mustard Chicken

Preparation Time: 15 minutes
Cooking Time: 12 minutes
Servings: 4
Ingredients:
- 2 tablespoons honey mustard
- 2 teaspoons olive oil
- Salt to taste 1 lb. chicken tenders
- Baby carrots, steamed - Chopped parsley

Directions:
1. Preheat your oven to 450 degrees F.
2. Mix honey mustard, olive oil and salt.
3. Coat the chicken tenders with the mixture. Place the chicken on a single layer on the baking pan.
4. Bake for 10 to 12 minutes. Serve with steamed carrots and garnish with parsley.

Chicken Chili

Preparation Time: 15 minutes
Cooking Time: 40 minutes
Servings: 6
Ingredients:
- 4 cups low-sodium chicken broth, divided
- 3 cups boiled black beans, divided
- 1 tablespoon extra-virgin olive oil
- 1 large onion, chopped
- 1 jalapeño pepper, seeded and chopped
- 4 garlic cloves, minced
- 1 teaspoon dried thyme, crushed
- 1½ tablespoons ground coriander
- 1 tablespoon ground cumin
- ½ tablespoon red chili powder
- 4 cups cooked chicken, shredded
- ½ tablespoon fresh lime juice
- ¼ cup fresh cilantro, chopped

Directions:
1. In a food processor, add 1 cup of broth and 1 can of black beans and pulse until smooth. Transfer the beans puree into a bowl and set aside.
2. In a large pan, heat the oil over medium heat and sauté the onion and jalapeño for about 4-5 minutes.
3. Add the garlic, spices and sea salt and sauté for about 1 minute.
4. Add the beans puree and remaining broth and bring to a boil. Now, reduce the heat to low and simmer for about 20 minutes.
5. Stir in the remaining can of beans, chicken and lime juice and bring to a boil.
6. Now, reduce the heat to low and simmer for about 5-10 minutes.
7. Serve hot with the garnishing of cilantro.

Meal Prep Tip: Transfer the chili into a large bowl and set aside to cool.
Divide the chili into 6 containers evenly. Cover the containers and refrigerate for 1-2 days.
Reheat in the microwave before serving.

Chicken with Chickpeas

Preparation Time: 15 minutes
Cooking Time: 36 minutes
Servings: 4
Ingredients:
- 2 tablespoons olive oil
- 1 pound skinless, boneless chicken breast, cubed
- 2 carrots, peeled and sliced
- 1 onion, chopped
- 2 celery stalks, chopped 2 garlic cloves, chopped
- ½ tablespoon fresh ginger root, minced
- ½ teaspoon dried oregano, crushed
- ¾ teaspoon ground cumin
- ½ teaspoon paprika
- ¼-13 teaspoon cayenne pepper
- ¼ teaspoon ground turmeric
- 1 cup tomatoes, crushed
- 1½ cups low-sodium chicken broth
- Zucchini, sliced
- cup boiled chickpeas, drained
- 1 tablespoon fresh lemon juice

Directions:
1. In a large nonstick pan, heat the oil over medium heat and cook the chicken cubes for about 4-5 minutes.
2. With a slotted spoon, transfer the chicken cubes onto a plate.
3. In the same pan, add the carrot, onion, celery and garlic and sauté for about 4-5 minutes.
4. Add the ginger, oregano and spices and sauté for about 1 minute.
5. Add the chicken, tomato and broth and bring to a boil. Now, reduce the heat to low and simmer for about 10 minutes.
6. Add the zucchini and chickpeas and simmer, covered for about 15 minutes. Stir in the lemon juice and serve hot.

Chicken, Oats & Chickpeas Meatloaf

Preparation Time: 20 minutes
Cooking Time: 1¼ hours
Servings: 4
Ingredients:
- ½ cup cooked chickpeas - 2 egg whites
- 2½ teaspoons poultry seasoning
- Ground black pepper, as required
- 10-ounce lean ground chicken
- 1 cup red bell pepper, seeded and minced
- 1 cup celery stalk, minced
- 1/3 cup steel-cut oats
- 1 cup tomato puree, divided
- 2 tablespoons dried onion flakes, crushed
- 1 tablespoon prepared mustard

Directions:
1. Preheat the oven to 350 degrees F. Grease a 9x5-inch loaf pan. In a food processor, add chickpeas, egg whites, poultry seasoning and black pepper and pulse until smooth.
2. Transfer the mixture into a large bowl. Add the chicken, veggies oats, ½ cup of tomato puree and onion flakes and mix until well combined. Transfer the mixture into prepared loaf pan evenly.
3. With your hands, press, down the mixture slightly. In another bowl mix together mustard and remaining tomato puree. Place the mustard mixture over loaf pan evenly.
4. Bake for about 1-1¼ hours or until desired doneness. Remove from the oven and set aside for about 5 minutes before slicing.
5. Cut into desired sized slices and serve.

Herbed Turkey Breast

Preparation Time: 15 minutes
Cooking Time: 1 hour 50 minutes
Servings: 6
Ingredients:
- ½ cup olive oil
- 2 tablespoons fresh lemon juice
- 1 tablespoon scallion, chopped
- ½ teaspoon dried marjoram, crushed
- ½ teaspoon dried sage, crushed
- ½ teaspoon dried thyme, crushed
- Salt and ground black pepper, as required
- (2-pound) boneless, skinless turkey breast half

Directions:
1. Preheat the oven to 325 degrees F. Arrange a rack into a greased shallow roasting pan. In a small pan, all the Ingredients: except turkey breast over medium heat and bring to a boil, stirring frequently.
2. Remove from the heat and set aside to cool. Place turkey breast into the prepared roasting pan. Place some of the herb mixture over the top of turkey breast.
3. Cover the roasting pan and bake for about 1¼-1¾ hours, basting with the remaining herb mixture occasionally.
4. Remove from the oven and set aside for about 10-15 minutes before slicing.
5. With a sharp knife, cut into desired slices and serve.

Turkey with Lentils

Preparation Time: 15 minutes
Cooking Time: 51 minutes
Servings: 7
Ingredients:
- 3 tablespoons olive oil, divided
- 1 onion, chopped
- 1 tablespoon fresh ginger, minced
- 4 garlic cloves, minced
- 3 plum tomatoes, chopped finely
- 2 cups dried red lentils, soaked for 30 minutes and drained
- 2 cups filtered water
- 2 teaspoons cumin seeds
- ½ teaspoon cayenne pepper
- 1 pound lean ground turkey
- Jalapeño pepper, seeded and chopped
- 2 scallions, chopped
- ¼ cup fresh cilantro, chopped

Directions:
1. In a Dutch oven, heat 1 tablespoon of oil over medium heat and sauté the onion, ginger and garlic for about 5 minutes.
2. Stir in tomatoes, lentils and water and bring to a boil now, reduce the heat to medium-low and simmer, covered for about 30 minutes.
3. Meanwhile, in a skillet, heat remaining oil over medium heat and sauté the cumin seeds and cayenne pepper for about 1 minute.
4. Transfer the mixture into a small bowl and set aside. In the same skillet, add turkey and cook for about 4-5 minutes
5. Add the jalapeño and scallion and cook for about 4-5 minutes. Add the spiced oil mixture and stir to combine well.
6. Transfer the turkey mixture in simmering lentils and simmer for about 10-15 minutes or until desired doneness. Serve hot.

Lemon Garlic Turkey

Preparation Time: 1 hour and 10 minutes
Cooking Time: 5 minutes
Servings: 4
Ingredients:
- 4 turkey breasts fillet - 2 cloves garlic, minced - 1 tablespoon olive oil
- 3 tablespoons lemon juice
- 1 oz. Parmesan cheese, shredded
- Pepper to taste
- 1 tablespoon fresh sage, snipped
- 1 teaspoon lemon zest

Directions:
1. Pound the turkey breast until flat. In a bowl, mix the olive oil, garlic and lemon juice.
2. Add the turkey to the bowl. Marinate for 1 hour.
3. Broil for 5 minutes until turkey is fully cooked. Sprinkle cheese on top on the last minute of cooking. In a bowl, mix the pepper, sage and lemon zest.
4. Sprinkle this mixture on top of the turkey before serving.

Crockpot Slow Cooker Ranch Chicken

Preparation time: 10 minutes
Cooking time: 30 minutes
Servings: 4
Ingredients:
- 1 cup chive and onion cream cheese spread
- ½ teaspoon freshly ground black pepper
- 4 boneless chicken breasts
- 1 1-oz package ranch dressing and seasoning mix
- ½ cup low sodium chicken stock

Directions:
1. Spray the Crock-Pot slow cooker with cooking spray and preheat it.
2. Dry chicken with paper towel and transfer it to the Crock-Pot slow cooker.
3. Cook each side, until chicken is browned, for about 4-5 minutes.
4. Add ½ cup low sodium chicken stock, 1 1-oz. package ranch dressing and seasoning mix, 1 cup chive and onion cream cheese spread and ½ teaspoon freshly ground black pepper. Cover the Crock-Pot slow cooker and cook for about 4 hours on Low or until the internal temperature reaches 165 F. Once cooked, take it out from the Crock-Pot slow cooker.
5. Whisk the sauce present in the Crock-Pot slow cooker until smooth. If you need thick sauce, then cook for about 5-10 minutes, with frequent stirring.

6. Garnish chicken with sliced onions and bacon and serve.

Chicken Wings

Preparation time: 10 Minutes
Cooking time: 1 hour and 30 minutes
Servings: 4
Ingredients:
- 3 pounds chicken wing parts, pastured
- 1 tablespoon old bay seasoning
- 1 teaspoon lemon zest
- 3/4 cup potato starch
- 1/2 cup butter, unsalted, melted

Directions:
1. Switch on the air fryer, insert fryer basket, grease it with olive oil, then shut with its lid, set the fryer at 360 degrees F and preheat for 5 minutes.
2. Meanwhile, pat dry chicken wings and then place them in a bowl.
3. Stir together seasoning and starch, add to chicken wings and stir well until evenly coated.
4. Open the fryer, add chicken wings in it in a single layer, close with its lid and cook for 35 minutes, shaking every 10 minutes.
5. Then switch the temperature of air fryer to 400 degrees F and continue air frying the chicken wings for 10 minutes or until nicely golden brown and cooked, shaking every 3 minutes. When air fryer beeps, open its lid, transfer chicken wings onto a serving plate and cook the remaining wings in the same manner. Whisk together melted butter and lemon zest until blended and serve it with the chicken wings.

Chicken Tenders

Preparation time: 5 Minutes
Cooking time: 10 minutes
Servings: 2
Ingredients:
- 1/8 cup almond flour
- 12 ounces chicken breasts, pastured
- ½ teaspoon ground black pepper
- ¾ teaspoon salt
- 1.2 ounces panko bread crumbs
- 1 egg white, pastured

Directions:
1. Switch on the air fryer, insert fryer basket, grease it with olive oil, then shut with its lid, set the fryer at 350 degrees F and preheat for 5 minutes.
2. Meanwhile, season the chicken with salt and black pepper on both sides and then evenly coat with flour.
3. Crack the egg, whisk until blended, dip the coated chicken in it and then coat with bread crumbs. Open the fryer, add chicken in it, close with its lid and cook for 10 minutes until nicely golden and cooked, turning the chicken halfway through the frying. When air fryer beeps, open its lid, transfer chicken onto a serving plate and serve.

Chicken Meatballs

Preparation time: 5 Minutes
Cooking time: 26 minutes
Servings: 4
Ingredients:
- 1-pound ground chicken
- 2 green onions, chopped
- ¾ teaspoon ground black pepper
- 1/4 cup shredded coconut, unsweetened
- 1 teaspoon salt
- 1 tablespoon hoisin sauce
- 1 tablespoon soy sauce
- 1/2 cup cilantro, chopped
- 1 teaspoon Sriracha sauce
- 1 teaspoon sesame oil

Directions:
1. Switch on the air fryer, insert fryer basket, grease it with olive oil, then shut with its lid, set the fryer at 350 degrees F and preheat for 5 minutes.
2. Meanwhile, place all the Ingredients: in a bowl, stir until well mixed and then shape the mixture into meatballs, 1 teaspoon of chicken mixture per meatball.
3. Open the fryer, add chicken meatballs in it in a single layer, close with its lid and then spray with oil.
4. Cook the chicken meatballs for 10 minutes, flipping the meatballs halfway through, and then continue cooking for 3 minutes until golden.
5. When air fryer beeps, open its lid, transfer chicken meatballs onto a serving plate and then cook the remaining meatballs in the same manner.
6. Serve straight away.

Chicken & Spinach

Preparation Time: 15 minutes
Cooking Time: 13 minutes
Servings: 4
Ingredients:
- 2 tablespoons olive oil
- 2 chicken breast fillets, sliced into small pieces
- Salt and pepper to taste
- 4 cloves garlic, minced
- 1 tablespoon lemon juice
- ½ cup dry white wine
- 1 teaspoon lemon zest
- 10 cups fresh spinach, chopped
- 4 tablespoons Parmesan cheese, grated

Directions:
1. Pour oil in a pan over medium heat. Season chicken with salt and pepper.
2. Cook in the pan for 7 minutes until golden on both sides.
3. Add the garlic and cook for 1 minute. Stir in the lemon juice and wine.
4. Sprinkle lemon zest on top. Simmer for 5 minutes.
5. Add the spinach and cook until wilted.
6. Serve with Parmesan cheese.

Balsamic Chicken

Preparation Time: 15 minutes
Cooking Time: 5 hours
Servings: 6

Ingredients:
- 6 chicken breast halves, skin removed
- 1 onion, sliced into wedges
- 1 tablespoon tapioca (quick cooking), crushed
- Salt and pepper to taste
- 1 teaspoon dried thyme, crushed
- 1 teaspoon dried rosemary, crushed
- ¼ cup balsamic vinegar
- 2 tablespoons chicken broth
- 9 oz. frozen Italian green beans
- Red sweet pepper, sliced into strips

Directions:
1. Put the chicken, onion and tapioca inside a slow cooker. Season with the salt, pepper, thyme and rosemary.
2. Seal the pot and cook on low setting for 4 hours and 30 minutes.
3. Add the sweet pepper and green beans.
4. Cook for 30 more minutes.
5. Pour sauce over the chicken and vegetables before serving.

Mustard Chicken with Basil

Preparation time: 10 minutes
Cooking time: 30 minutes
Servings: 4
Ingredients:
- 1 tsp Chicken stock
- 2 Chicken breasts; skinless and boneless chicken breasts: halved
- 1 tbsp. Chopped basil
- What you'll need from the store cupboard:
- Salt and black pepper
- 1 tbsp. Olive oil
- ½ tsp Garlic powder
- ½ tsp Onion powder
- 1 tsp Dijon mustard

Directions:
1. Press 'Sauté' on the instant pot and add the oil. When it is hot, brown the chicken in it for 2-3 minutes.
2. Mix in the remaining Ingredients: and seal the lid to cook for 12 minutes at high pressure. Natural release the pressure for 10 minutes, share into plates and serve.

Chicken with Cashew Nuts

Preparation time: 10 minutes
Cooking time: 30 minutes
Servings: 4
Ingredients:
- 1 lb. chicken cubes
- 2 tbsp. soy sauce
- 1 tbsp. corn flour
- 2 ½ onion cubes
- 1 carrot, chopped
- 1/3 cup cashew nuts, fried
- 1 capsicum, cut
- 2 tbsp. garlic, crushed
- Salt and white pepper

Directions:
1. Marinate the chicken cubes with ½ tbsp. of white pepper, ½ tsp salt, 2 tbsp. soya sauce, and add 1 tbsp. corn flour.
2. Set aside for 25 minutes. Preheat the Air Fryer to 380 F and transfer the marinated chicken. Add the garlic, the onion, the capsicum, and the carrot; fry for 5-6 minutes. Roll it in the cashew nuts before serving.

Chicken & Broccoli Bake

Preparation time: 10 minutes
Cooking time: 30 minutes
Servings: 6
Ingredients:
- 6 (6-ounce) boneless, skinless chicken breasts
- 3 broccoli heads, cut into florets
- 4 garlic cloves, minced
- ¼ cup olive oil
- 1 teaspoon dried oregano, crushed
- 1 teaspoon dried rosemary, crushed
- Sea Salt and ground black pepper, as required

Directions:
1. Preheat the oven to 375 degrees F. Grease a large baking dish.
2. In a large bowl, add all the ingredients: and toss to coat well.
3. In the bottom of prepared baking dish, arrange the broccoli florets and top with chicken breasts in a single layer.
4. Bake for about 45 minutes.
5. Remove from the oven and set aside for about 5 minutes before serving.

Zucchini with Tomatoes

Preparation time: 10 minutes
Cooking time: 30 minutes
Servings: 8
Ingredients:
- 6 medium zucchinis, chopped roughly
- 1 pound cherry tomatoes
- 2 small onions, chopped roughly
- 2 tablespoons fresh basil, chopped
- 1 cup water
- 1 tablespoon olive oil
- 2 garlic cloves, minced
- Salt and ground black pepper, as required

Directions:
1. In the Instant Pot, place oil and press "Sauté". Now add the onion, garlic, ginger, and spices and cook for about 3-4 minutes.
2. Add the zucchinis and tomatoes and cook for about 1-2 minutes.
3. Press "Cancel" and stir in the remaining Ingredients: except basil.
4. Close the lid and place the pressure valve to "Seal" position.
5. Press "Manual" and cook under "High Pressure" for about 5 minutes.
6. Press "Cancel" and allow a "Natural" release.

7. Open the lid and transfer the vegetable mixture onto a serving platter.
8. Garnish with basil and serve.

Chicken Liver Curry

Preparation time: 10 minutes
Cooking time: 30 minutes
Servings: 2
Ingredients:
- 1lb diced chicken breast
- 0.5lb diced chicken liver
- 1lb chopped vegetables
- 1 cup broth
- 3tbsp curry paste

Directions:
1. Mix all the Ingredients: in your Instant Pot.
2. Cook on Stew for 35 minutes.
3. Release the pressure naturally.

Chicken Stuffed Potatoes

Preparation time: 10 minutes
Cooking time: 30 minutes
Servings: 4
Ingredients:
- 6-ounce chicken sausage links
- 4 medium potatoes, each about 8-ounce
- 1 medium zucchini, chopped
- 1 cup chopped green onion
- 1/8 teaspoon salt
- ¼ teaspoon ground black pepper
- ½ teaspoon dried oregano
- 1 teaspoon hot sauce
- 2 tablespoons olive oil, divided
- 2 cups water
- 2 tablespoons crumbled blue cheese, reduced fat

Directions:
1. Plugin instant pot, insert the inner pot, press sauté/simmer button, add 1 tablespoon oil and when hot, add chicken sausage and cook for 3 minutes or until edges are nicely golden brown.
2. Add zucchini and ¾ cup green onion, sprinkle with oregano, pour in 1/3 cup water and cook for 3 minutes or until tender-crisp.
3. Then transfer vegetables from the instant pot to a bowl, drizzle with remaining oil and hot sauce, toss until mixed and keep warm by covering the bowl.
4. Press the cancel button, pour in the remaining water, then insert steamer basket and place potatoes on it.
5. Shut the instant pot with its lid, turn the pressure knob to seal the pot, press the 'manual' button, then press the 'timer' to set the cooking time to 18 minutes and cook at high pressure, instant pot will take 5 minutes or more for building its inner pressure.
6. When the timer beeps, press 'cancel' button and do quick pressure release until pressure nob drops down.
7. Open the instant pot, transfer potatoes to a plate, let cool for 5 minutes, then cut each potato in half.
8. Use fork to fluff potatoes, then season with salt and black pepper and evenly top with prepared sausage and zucchini mixture.

9. Sprinkle remaining green onions and cheese on loaded potatoes and serve straight away.

Greek Chicken Lettuce Wraps

Preparation Time: 1 hour and 15 minutes
Cooking Time: 8 minutes
Servings: 4
Ingredients:
- 2 tablespoons freshly squeezed lemon juice
- 1 teaspoon lemon zest
- 5 teaspoons olive oil, divided
- 3 teaspoons garlic, minced and divided
- 1 teaspoon dried oregano
- ¼ teaspoon red pepper, crushed
- 1 lb. chicken tenders
- 1 cucumber, sliced in half and grated
- Salt and pepper to taste
- ¾ cup non-fat Greek yogurt
- 2 teaspoons fresh mint, chopped
- 2 teaspoons fresh dill, chopped
- 4 lettuce leaves
- ½ cup red onion, sliced
- 1 cup tomatoes, chopped

Directions:
1. In a bowl, mix the lemon juice, lemon zest, half of oil, half of garlic, and red pepper. Coat the chicken with the marinade.
2. Marinate it for 1 hour. Toss grated cucumber in salt. Squeeze to release liquid.
3. Add the yogurt, dill, salt, pepper, remaining garlic and remaining oil.
4. Grill the chicken for 4 minutes per side.
5. Shred the chicken and put on top of the lettuce leaves.
6. Top with the yogurt mixture, onion and tomatoes.
7. Wrap the lettuce leaves and secure with a toothpick.

Lemon Chicken with Kale

Preparation Time: 10 minutes
Cooking Time: 19 minutes
Servings: 4
Ingredients:
- ½ tablespoon olive oil
- 1 lb. chicken thighs, trimmed
- Salt and pepper to taste
- ½ cup low-sodium chicken stock
- 1 lemon, sliced
- 1 tablespoon fresh tarragon, chopped
- 4 cloves garlic, minced
- 6 cups baby kale

Directions:
1. Pour olive oil in a pan over medium heat. Season chicken with salt and pepper.
2. Cook until golden brown on both sides.
3. Pour in the stock. Add the lemon, tarragon and garlic. Simmer for 15 minutes.
4. Add the kale and cook for 4 minutes.

Amazing Buffalo Lettuce Wraps

Servings: 2
Preparation Time: 35 minutes

Cooking Time: 10 minutes
Ingredients:
- 3 chicken breast, boneless and cubed
- 20 slices of butter lettuce leaves
- ¾ cup cherry tomatoes halved
- 1 avocado, chopped
- ¼ cup green onions, diced
- ½ a cup of ranch dressing
- ¾ cup hot sauce

Directions:
1. Take a mixing bowl and add chicken cubes and hot sauce, mix
2. Place in fridge and let it marinate for 30 minutes
3. Preheat your oven to 400 degrees Fahrenheit
4. Place coated chicken on cookie pan and bake for 9 minutes
5. Assemble lettuce serving cups with equal amounts of lettuce, green onions, tomatoes, ranch dressing, and cubed chicken
6. Serve and enjoy!

Balsamic Chicken

Servings: 6
Preparation Time: 10 minutes
Cooking Time: 25 minutes
Ingredients:
- 6 chicken breast halves, skinless and boneless
- 1 teaspoon garlic salt
- Ground black pepper
- 2 tablespoons olive oil
- 1 onion, thinly sliced
- 14 and ½ ounces tomatoes, diced
- ½ cup balsamic vinegar
- 1 teaspoon dried basil
- 1 teaspoon dried oregano
- 1 teaspoon dried rosemary
- ½ teaspoon dried thyme

Directions:
1. Season both sides of your chicken breasts thoroughly with pepper and garlic salt
2. Take a skillet and place it over medium heat
3. Add some oil and cook your seasoned chicken for 3-4 minutes per side until the breasts are nicely browned
4. Add some onion and cook for another 3-4 minutes until the onions are browned
5. Pour the diced-up tomatoes and balsamic vinegar over your chicken and season with some rosemary, basil, thyme, and rosemary
6. Simmer the chicken for about 15 minutes until they are no longer pink
7. Take an instant-read thermometer and check if the internal temperature gives a reading of 165 degrees Fahrenheit
8. If yes, then you are good to go!

Low-Carb Butternut Chicken

Servings: 4
Preparation Time: 15 minutes
Cooking Time: 30 minutes
Ingredients:
- ½ pound Nitrate free bacon
- 6 chicken thighs, boneless and skinless
- 2-3 cups butternut squash, cubed
- Extra virgin olive oil
- Fresh chopped sage
- Salt and pepper as needed

Directions:
1. Prepare your oven by preheating it to 425 degrees F
2. Take a large skillet and place it over medium-high heat; add bacon and fry until crispy
3. Take bacon and place it on the side; crumble the bacon
4. Add cubed butternut squash to the bacon grease and Saute; season with salt and pepper
5. Once the squash is tender, remove the skillet and transfer it to the plate
6. Add coconut oil to the skillet and add chicken thigh; cook for 10 minutes
7. Season with salt and pepper
8. Remove skillet from the stove and transfer to oven
9. Bake for 12-15 minutes, top with crumbled bacon and sage
10. Enjoy!

The Original Greek Chicken Breast

Servings: 4
Preparation Time: 10 minutes
Cooking Time: 25 minutes
Ingredients:
- 4 chicken breast halves, skinless and boneless
- 1 cup extra virgin olive oil
- 1 lemon, juiced
- 2 teaspoons garlic, crushed
- 1 and ½ teaspoons black pepper
- 1/3 teaspoon paprika

Directions:
1. Cut 3 slits in the chicken breast
2. Take a small bowl and whisk in olive oil, salt, lemon juice, garlic, paprika, and pepper, and whisk for 30 seconds
3. Place chicken in a large bowl and pour marinade
4. Rub the marinade all over using your hand
5. Refrigerate overnight
6. Preheat grill to medium heat and oil the grate
7. Cook chicken on the grill until the center is no longer pink
8. Serve and enjoy!

Chicken Ham And Turnip Pasta

Servings: 4
Preparation Time: 10 minutes
Cooking Time: 10 minutes
Ingredients:
- 6 slices of chicken ham, chopped
- 1 lb turnips, spiralized
- 1 tbsp smoked paprika
- Salt and black pepper to taste
- 4 tbsp olive oil

Directions:
1. Preheat oven to 450 F. Pour turnips into a bowl; add paprika, salt, and pepper; toss to coat.
2. Spread the mixture on a greased baking sheet, scatter ham on top, and drizzle with olive oil.
3. Bake for 10 minutes until golden brown

Turkey Bacon Garlic Knots

Servings: 4

Preparation Time: 10 minutes
Cooking Time: 10-15 minutes
Ingredients:
- 4 slices of turkey bacon
- 1 tsp garlic powder
- 1/4 tsp red pepper flakes
- 1/4 tsp Italian seasoning
- 2 tbsp grated parmesan cheese

Directions:
1. Turn on the oven, set it to 425 degrees F, and let preheat.
2. Working on a slice of bacon at a time, tie it into a double knot, and then place it on a baking sheet.
3. Prepare remaining bacon knots in the same manner, season evenly with garlic powder, red pepper, and Italian seasoning, and then bake for 7 to 10 minutes until almost crisp.
4. Then sprinkle cheese over bacon knots and continue baking for 3 to 4 minutes until cheese has melted.
5. Serve.

Chinese Duck Breast

Servings: 4
Preparation Time: 10 minutes
Cooking Time: 10-15 minutes
Ingredients:
- 1- and 1/2-pounds duck breast
- 1 tablespoon sesame oil
- 1 white onion, chopped
- 1/4 cup rice wine
- teaspoons soy sauce

Directions:
1. Gently score the duck breast skin in a tight crosshatch pattern using a sharp knife.
2. Heat the sesame oil in a skillet over moderate heat.
3. Now, sauté the onion until tender and translucent.
4. Add in the duck breasts; sear the duck breasts for 10 to 13 minutes or until the skin looks crispy with golden brown color; drain off the duck fat from the skillet.
5. Serve and enjoy once done!

The Perfect Winter Turkey Goulash

Servings: 4
Preparation Time: 10 minutes
Cooking Time: 40-50 minutes
Ingredients:
- 2 tablespoons olive oil
- 1 large-sized leek, chopped
- 2 cloves garlic, minced
- 2 pounds turkey thighs, skinless, boneless, and chopped
- 2 celery stalks, chopped

Directions:
1. Heat the olive oil in a soup pot over a moderate flame. Then, sweat the leeks until just tender and fragrant.
2. Then, cook the garlic until aromatic.
3. Add in the turkey thighs and celery; add 4 cups of water, and bring to a boil. Immediately reduce the heat and allow it to simmer for 35 to 40 minutes.
4. Ladle into individual bowls and serve hot.

Classic Teriyaki Chicken

Servings: 4
Preparation Time: 10 minutes
Cooking Time: 50 minutes
Ingredients:
- 2 chicken thighs, boneless
- 2 tbsp soy sauce
- 1 tbsp swerve sweetener
- 1 tbsp avocado oil

Directions:
1. Take a skillet pan, place it over medium heat, add oil and when hot, add chicken thighs and cook for 5 minutes per side until seared.
2. Then sprinkle sugar over chicken thighs, drizzle with soy sauce and bring the sauce to boil.
3. Switch heat to medium-low level, continue cooking for 3 minutes until chicken is evenly glazed, and then transfer to a plate.
4. Serve chicken with cauliflower rice.

Juicy Italian Chicken Basil Pizza

Servings: 4
Preparation Time: 10 minutes
Cooking Time: 15-20 minutes
Ingredients:
- 1 1/2 cups grated mozzarella cheese
- 1 lb ground chicken
- 1 tsp Italian seasoning
- 1 cup tomato sauce
- 1/2 cup fresh basil leaves

Directions:
1. Preheat the oven to 390 F and line a round pizza pan with parchment paper.
2. Mix ground chicken, Italian seasoning, and 1 cup of mozzarella cheese in a bowl.
3. Spread the pizza "dough" on the pizza pan and bake for 18 minutes—spread tomato sauce on top.
4. Scatter the mozzarella cheese and basil all over and bake for 15 minutes.
5. Slice and serve.

Cocktail-Styled Meatball

Servings: 4
Preparation Time: 10 minutes
Cooking Time: 15-25 minutes
Ingredients:
- 1 pound ground turkey
- 1 tablespoon Italian seasoning blend
- 2 cloves garlic, minced
- 1/2 cup leeks, minced
- 1 egg

Directions:
1. Throw all ingredients into a mixing bowl; mix to combine well.
2. Form the mixture into bite-sized balls and arrange them on a parchment-lined baking pan.

3. Spritz the meatballs with cooking spray.
4. Bake in the preheated oven at 395 degrees F for 18 to 22 minutes.
5. Serve with cocktail sticks, and enjoy!

Zucchini And Duck Meal
Servings: 4
Preparation Time: 10 minutes
Cooking Time: 35 minutes
Ingredients:
- 1 pound duck breasts, skinless, boneless, and roughly cubed
- 2 zucchinis, sliced
- 1 tablespoon avocado oil
- 2 shallots, chopped'/2 teaspoon chili powder
- 1 cup chicken stock
- A pinch of salt and black pepper

Directions:
1. Heat up a pan with the oil over medium-high heat, add the shallots, stir and saute for 5 minutes.
2. Add the meat and the other ingredients, toss, bring to a simmer and cook over medium heat for 30 minutes.
3. Divide the mix into bowls and serve.

Feisty Tikka Chicken And Butter
Servings: 4
Preparation Time: 10 minutes
Cooking Time: 15 minutes
Ingredients:
- 3 boneless chicken thighs, sliced
- 1/2 cup Tikka Masala Paste
- 1 cup of coconut cream
- 2 tbsp of butter or ghee
- 1 tbsp of garlic salt

Directions:
1. In a small bowl, combine the pasta with coconut cream.
2. Season the chicken thighs with garlic salt, heat the butter and add to the skillet. Cook the thighs for 4-5 minutes.
3. Add the tikka masala paste and coconut cream mixture, stir to cover the chicken thighs, and cook for another minute.
4. Serve on a deep dish or bowl over a bed of basmati rice

Creamy Chicken Cajun
Servings: 4
Preparation Time: 10 minutes
Cooking Time: 15 minutes
Ingredients:
- 4 boneless chicken thighs, skin on
- 1 tbsp of cajun seasoning mix
- 1 tbsp of garlic salt
- 1/2 cup heavy cream
- 1 full tbsp of butter or ghee

Directions:
1. Cut the chicken thighs into thick slices and season with the Cajun seasoning mix, ensuring that it covers all the pieces evenly.
2. Melt the butter on a skillet and add the chicken thighs. Shallow fry for 3 minutes on each side. (They should look white and opaque but still be juicy).
3. Add the heavy cream, toss and cook for a minute or so before turning off the heat.
4. Serve with cauliflower rice

Crispy Chicken Tenders
Servings: 4
Preparation Time: 10 minutes
Cooking Time: 20 minutes
Ingredients:
- 1 lb. or 4 pieces of chicken breast
- ¾ cup flaxseed flour
- 3 eggs beaten
- 1 tbsp of parmesan cheese
- 1 tbsp of garlic salt

Directions:
1. In a bowl, combine the flaxseed flour and parmesan cheese with the garlic salt and set aside.
2. In another bowl, beat two eggs.
3. Cut the chicken breasts into two thick stripes or bite-sized squares.
4. Dip each chicken piece into the egg and then into the dry mixture, ensuring that everything is coated evenly.
5. Grease a skillet with a bit of oil or butter and shallow fry for 3-4 minutes on each side until golden brown.
6. Remove from the heat and serve on a dish with paper and a small bowl of marinara sauce

Easy-Going Chicken Lettuce Wraps
Servings: 4
Preparation Time: 10 minutes
Cooking Time: Nil
Ingredients:
- 9 oz. of cooked chicken bites (roasted or boiled)
- 4 slices of fried beef bacon, chopped
- 1/2 cup of mayonnaise
- 4 large romaine lettuce leaves
- 1 large tomato seeded and cubed

Directions:
1. Combine all the ingredients together except the lettuce leaves in a bowl.
2. Distribute the mixture into each lettuce leaf, as if you are filling a boat, and serve

Beautiful Tarragon Chicken Roast
Servings: 4
Preparation Time: 10 minutes
Cooking Time: 45 minutes
Ingredients:
- 2 bone-in chicken thighs
- 2 tbsp of fresh tarragon leaves, chopped
- 2-3 shallots, thoroughly chopped
- 1 tbsp of garlic salt
- 2 tbsp of olive oil

Directions:
1. Preheat the oven to 380F/180 C.
2. In a small bowl, combine the olive oil, garlic salt, and tarragon with the shallots.
3. Brush the mixture over the chicken pieces.

4. Bake in a greased baking dish for 40 minutes, and switch on the broiler for the last five minutes to form a light crust.
5. Serve with salad or cauliflower rice

Cauliflower Rice And Chicken Curry

Servings: 4
Preparation Time: 10 minutes
Cooking Time: 7-15 minutes
Ingredients:
- 2 lb chicken (4 breasts)
- 1 packet curry paste
- 3 tbsp ghee (can substitute with butter)
- 1/2 cup heavy cream
- 1 head cauliflower (around 1 kg/2.2 lb)

Directions:
1. Melt the ghee in a pot. Mix in the curry paste.
2. Add the water and simmer for 5 minutes.
3. Add the chicken, cover, and simmer on medium heat for 20 minutes or until the chicken is cooked.
4. Shred the cauliflower florets in a food processor to resemble rice.
5. Once the chicken is cooked, uncover, and incorporate the cream.
6. Cook for 7 minutes and serve over the cauliflower.

Juicy Chicken Blanket

Servings: 4
Preparation Time: 10 minutes
Cooking Time: 50 minutes
Ingredients:
- 3 boneless chicken breasts
- 1 package of beef bacon
- 1 8-oz package of cream cheese
- 3 jalapeno peppers
- Salt, pepper, garlic powder, or other seasonings

Directions:
1. Cut the chicken breast in half lengthwise to create two pieces.
2. Cut the jalapenos in half lengthwise and remove the seeds.
3. Dress each breast with a half-inch slice of cream cheese and half a slice of jalapeno. Sprinkle with garlic powder, salt, and pepper.
4. Roll the chicken and wrap 2 to 3 pieces of bacon around it—secure with toothpicks.
5. Bake in a preheated 375°F/190°C oven for 50 minutes.
6. Serve!

The Duck Eye Ribeye

Servings: 4
Preparation Time: 10 minutes
Cooking Time: 10-20 minutes
Ingredients:
- One 16-oz ribeye steak (1 - 1 1/14 inches thick)
- 1 tbsp duck fat (or other high smoke point oil like peanut oil)
- 1/2 tbsp butter
- 1/2 tsp thyme, chopped
- Salt and pepper to taste

Directions:
1. Preheat a skillet in your oven at 400°F/200°C.
2. Season the steaks with oil, salt, and pepper. Remove the skillet from the oven once pre-heated.
3. Put the skillet on your stovetop burner on medium heat and drizzle in the oil.
4. Sear the steak for 1-4 minutes, depending on if you like it rare, medium, or well done.
5. Turn over the steak and place it in your oven for 6 minutes.
6. Take the steak from your oven and place it on the stovetop on low heat.
7. Toss in the butter and thyme and cook for 3 minutes, basting as you go along.
8. Rest for 5 minutes and serve.

Everyone's Favorite Turkey Avocado Rolls

Servings: 4
Preparation Time: 10 minutes
Cooking Time: 5 minutes
Ingredients:
- 12 slices (12 oz) of turkey breast
- 12 slices of Swiss cheese
- 2 cups baby spinach
- 1 large avocado, cut into
- 12 slices
- 1 cup homemade mayonnaise

Directions:
1. Lay the slices of turkey breast flat and place a slice of Swiss cheese on top.
2. Top each slice with 1 cup of baby spinach and 3 slices of avocado.
3. Drizzle the mayonnaise on top.
4. Sprinkle each "sandwich" with lemon pepper.
5. Roll up the sandwiches and secure them with toothpicks.
6. Serve immediately or refrigerate until ready to serve.

Sweet And Savory Grilled Chicken

Servings: 4
Preparation Time: 10 minutes
Cooking Time: 12-15 minutes
Ingredients:
- 1 teaspoon dry mustard
- 1 teaspoon light brown sugar
- 1 and 1/2 teaspoon onion powder
- 3/4 pound skinless chicken breast
- Kosher salt & White pepper

Directions:
1. Set the grill to preheat at medium-high temperatures as you add some greasing
2. In a small bowl, add onion powder, dry mustard, salt, brown sugar, and white pepper and mix well
3. Pass the chicken meat through the mixture to coat evenly.
4. Grill the chicken for 6 minutes on each side
5. Serve!

The Perfect Mediterranean Turkey Cutlets

Servings: 4
Preparation Time: 10 minutes
Cooking Time: 12-15 minutes
Ingredients:
- 1 tablespoon olive oil
- *1 and 1/2 pound* turkey cutlets
- 1/4 cup low-carb flour mix
- 1/2 teaspoon Greek seasoning
- 1/2 teaspoon turmeric powder

Directions:
1. In a medium bowl, mix the turkey cutlets with turmeric powder, low-carb flour mix, and Greek seasoning
2. Put a frying pan on fire, then add the oil to heat.
3. Add the cutlets and cook for 5 minutes on each side under medium-low heat.
4. Serve!

Burnt Fried Chicken

Servings: 4
Preparation Time: 10 minutes
Cooking Time: 20 minutes
Ingredients:
- 1/2 teaspoon cayenne pepper
- 1/2 teaspoon onion powder
- 1/2 teaspoon black pepper
- 2 teaspoons paprika
- 1 teaspoon ground thyme
- 1 teaspoon cumin
- 1/4 teaspoon salt
- 2 (12-ounce / 340-g) skinless, boneless chicken breasts
- 2 teaspoons olive oil

Directions:
1. Mix the cayenne pepper, onion powder, black pepper, paprika, thyme, cumin, and salt in a bowl.
2. Rub the chicken breasts with the olive oil, then put them in the spice mixture. Ensure they are coated with the spices, then set aside to marinate for 5 minutes.
3. Preheat the air fryer to 375°F (190°C).
4. Put the chicken in the air fryer basket and cook for 10 minutes. Flip it over and cook for another 10 minutes.
5. Remove the chicken from the basket to a plate and let it rest for 5 minutes before serving.

Crunched Up Chicken Taco Wings

Servings: 4
Preparation Time: 10 minutes
Cooking Time: 15 minutes
Ingredients:
- 3 pounds (1.4 kg) of chicken wings
- 1 tablespoon taco seasoning mix
- 2 teaspoons olive oil

Directions:
1. Put the chicken wings in a Ziploc bag, then add the taco seasoning and olive oil.
2. Seal the bag and shake well until the chicken is coated thoroughly.
3. Preheat the air fryer to 350°F (180°C).
4. Put the chicken in the air fryer basket and cook for 6 minutes on each side until crispy.
5. Remove the chicken from the basket and serve on a plate.

Tarragon Creamy Chicken

Servings: 4
Preparation Time: 10 minutes
Cooking Time: 30 minutes
Ingredients:
- 1 tablespoon butter
- 1 tablespoon olive oil
- 4 skinless, boneless chicken breasts
- Salt and freshly ground black pepper, to taste 1/2 cup heavy cream
- 1 tablespoon Dijon mustard
- 2 teaspoons chopped fresh tarragon

Directions:
1. Melt the butter in a pan over medium-high heat, then add the olive oil.
2. Season the chicken with salt and pepper, then put it in the pan to fry for 15 minutes on both sides until the juices are clear. Remove them from the pan and set them aside.
3. Pour the heavy cream into the pan and use a wooden spoon to scrape the parts stuck to the pan, then add the mustard and the tarragon. Mix well and let it simmer for 5 minutes.
4. Put the chicken back into the pan and cover it with the creamy sauce.
5. Serve the chicken drizzled with the sauce on a plate.

Spicy And Sour Chicken Breast

Servings: 4
Preparation Time: 10 minutes
Cooking Time: 10 minutes
Ingredients:
- 4 skinless, boneless chicken breast halves 1/8 cup extra virgin olive oil
- 1 lemon, juiced
- 2 teaspoons crushed garlic
- 1 teaspoon salt
- 1 1/2 teaspoons black pepper
- 1/3 teaspoon paprika
- 2 tablespoons olive oil, divided

Directions:
1. Combine the olive oil, lemon, garlic, salt, pepper, and paprika in a bowl, then set aside.
2. Cut 3 slits into the chicken breasts to allow the marinade to soak in. Put the chicken in a separate bowl and pour the marinade over it.
3. Cover the bowl with plastic wrap and put it in the refrigerator to marinate overnight.
4. Preheat the grill to medium heat and brush the grill grates with 1 tablespoon of olive oil.
5. Remove the chicken from the marinade and place it on the grill to cook for about 5 minutes until the juices are clear. Flip the chicken over and brush with the remaining olive oil. Grill for 3 minutes more.
6. Remove the chicken from the grill and serve on plates.

Spicy Grilled Chicken

Servings: 4
Preparation Time: 10 minutes
Cooking Time: 20 minutes
Ingredients:
- 1 teaspoon garlic powder
- 1 teaspoon ground paprika
- 1 teaspoon poultry seasoning
- 1 cup of olive oil
- 1/2 cup apple cider vinegar
- 1 tablespoon salt
- 1 teaspoon black pepper
- 10 skinless chicken thighs

Directions:
1. Pour the garlic powder, paprika, poultry seasoning, oil, vinegar, salt, and black pepper into a lid. Cover the jar and shake it well to combine.
2. Put the chicken thighs on a baking dish and pour three-quarters of the powder mixture over them. Cover the dish with plastic wrap and put it in the refrigerator to marinate for 8 hours, preferably overnight.
3. Preheat the grill to high heat.
4. Place the chicken on the grill to cook for 10 minutes on each side.
5. Transfer the chicken to a plate, brush with the remaining powder mixture, and serve.

Michigan Turkey Meal

Servings: 4
Preparation Time: 10 minutes
Cooking Time: 4 Hours
Ingredients:
- 1 (12-pound / 5.4-kg) whole turkey
- 6 tablespoons butter, divided
- 3 tablespoons chicken broth
- 4 cups of warm water
- 2 tablespoons dried onion, minced
- 2 tablespoons dried parsley
- 2 tablespoons seasoning salt

Directions:
1. Start by preheating the oven to 350 °F (180 °C).
2. Rinse the turkey and pat dry with paper towels.
3. Put the turkey on a roasting pan, then separate the skin over the breast to make pockets.
4. Put 3 tablespoons of butter into each pocket.
5. Mix the broth and water in a medium bowl.
6. Add the minced onion and parsley, then pour over the turkey. Sprinkle some salt on the turkey, then cover with aluminum foil.
7. Bake in the preheated oven until the turkey's internal temperature reads 180°F (80 °C) for about 4 hours.
8. When 45 minutes remain, remove the foil, so the turkey browns well.
9. Remove from the oven and serve warm.

Bacon-Wrapped Chicken Breast With Spinach

Servings: 4
Preparation Time: 10 minutes
Cooking Time: 10 minutes
Ingredients:
- 1 (10-ounce / 284-g) package frozen chopped spinach, thawed and drained
- 1/2 cup mayonnaise, keto-friendly
- 1/2 cup feta cheese, shredded
- 2 cloves garlic, chopped
- 4 skinless, boneless chicken breasts 4 slices of bacon

Directions:
1. Preheat the oven to 375²F (190²C).
2. Combine the spinach, mayo, feta cheese, and garlic in a bowl, then set aside.
3. Cut the chicken crosswise to butterfly the chicken breasts (butterfly cutting technique: not to cut the chicken breast through, leave a 1-inch space uncut at the end of the chicken. So when flipping open the halved chicken breast, it resembles a butterfly.)
4. Unfold the chicken breasts like a book. Divide and arrange the spinach mixture over each breast, then wrap each breast with a slice of bacon and secure with a toothpick.
5. Arrange them in a baking dish, and cover a piece of aluminum foil. Place the dish in the oven and bake for 1 hour or until the bacon is crispy and the chicken breasts' juice runs clear.
6. Remove the baking dish from the oven and serve warm.

Fancy Roast Chicken

Serving: 6
Preparation Time: 60 minutes
Cooking Time: 30 minute
Ingredients
- 1 large orange, juiced
- ¼ cup Dijon mustard
- ¼ cup olive oil
- 4 teaspoon dried Greek Oregano
- Salt as needed
- Ground black pepper
- 12 potatoes, cubed and peeled
- 5 garlic cloves, minced
- 1 whole chicken

Directions:
1. Preheat your oven to 375 degrees Fahrenheit
2. Take a bowl and whisk in orange juice, Dijon mustard, Greek oregano, salt, and pepper; give it a nice mix
3. Add potatoes to the bowl and mix to coat them with the mixture
4. Transfer the potatoes to a large-sized baking dish
5. Stuff the garlic cloves into the chicken (under the skin)
6. Transfer the chicken to the bowl with the orange and mix well
7. Transfer the coated chicken to your baking dish and place it on top of the potatoes
8. Pour any remaining juice on top of the chicken and potato
9. Bake for 60-90 minutes until the juices run clear
10. Remove the chicken and cover with an aluminum foil; allow it to rest for 10 minutes
11. Slice and serve!

Ravaging Oven Roasted Garlic Chicken Thigh

Serving: 4
Preparation Time:10 minutes
Cooking Time: 55 minute
Ingredients

- 8 chicken thighs
- Salt and pepper as needed
- 1 tablespoon extra-virgin olive oil
- 6 cloves garlic, peeled and crushed
- 1 jar (10 ounces) roasted red peppers, drained and chopped
- 1 and1/2 pounds potatoes, diced
- 2 cups cherry tomatoes, halved
- 1/3 cup capers, sliced
- 1 teaspoon dried Italian seasoning
- 1 tablespoon fresh basil

Directions:
1. Season chicken with kosher salt and black pepper
2. Take a cast-iron skillet over medium-high heat and heat up olive oil
3. Sear the chicken on both sides
4. Add remaining ingredients except for basil and stir well
5. Remove heat and place cast iron skillet in the oven
6. Bake for 45 minutes at 400 degrees Fahrenheit until the internal temperature reaches 165 degrees Fahrenheit
7. Serve and enjoy!

Loving Honey Lemon Chicken

Serving: 4
Preparation Time:10 minutes
Cooking Time: 55 minute
Ingredients

- 8 chicken thighs
- Salt and pepper as needed
- 1 tablespoon extra-virgin olive oil
- 6 cloves garlic, peeled and crushed
- 1 jar (10 ounces) roasted red peppers, drained and chopped
- 1 and1/2 pounds potatoes, diced
- 2 cups cherry tomatoes, halved
- 1/3 cup capers, sliced
- 1 teaspoon dried Italian seasoning
- 1 tablespoon fresh basil

Directions:
1. Mix flour, salt, and pepper in a bowl and dredge chicken in the seasoned flour
2. Heat oil in a large skillet and pan-fry the chicken for 3-5 minutes per side, making sure to season with pepper
3. Remove chicken from pan and add asparagus
4. Saute until the color brightens and the asparagus is tender
5. Transfer to plate
6. Add lemon slices and brown them; transfer them to a plate as well
7. Take a bowl and mix lemon zest, honey, and 2 tablespoons butter; whisk well
8. Pour the sauce into the skillet and whisk until the butter melts and the sauce is ready
9. Serve chicken and asparagus by topping with lemon slices and drizzling butter sauce on top
10. Enjoy!

Gnocchi Turkey Ham And Olives

Serving: 4
Preparation Time:5 minutes
Cooking Time: 15 minute
Ingredients

- 2 tablespoons olive oil
- 1 medium onion, chopped
- 3 garlic cloves, minced
- 1 medium red bell pepper, deseeded and chopped
- 1 cup tomato puree
- 1 pound gnocchi
- 1 cup turkey ham, coarsely chopped
- ½ cup olives, pitted and sliced
- Salt and pepper as needed
- Bunch of fresh basil leaves

Directions:
1. Take a medium-sized saucepan and heat it over medium-high heat
2. Add olive oil and let it heat up
3. Add bell pepper, garlic, and onion, and Saute for 2 minutes
4. Pour tomato puree, gnocchi, tomato paste, turkey ham, Italian seasoning, and olives
5. Lower the heat to low and simmer for 15 minutes, making sure to stir from time to time
6. Season with salt and pepper
7. Transfer mix to serving dish and garnish with basil leaves
8. Serve and enjoy!

Chicken And Parmesan Veggie

Serving: 4
Preparation Time:5 minutes
Cooking Time: 0 minute
Ingredients

- 3 cups cooked shell pasta
- 2 cups baby spinach, torn
- 1 cup roasted cherry tomatoes, halved
- 8 ounces roasted chicken breast, cut into strips
- ¼ cup parmesan cheese, grated
- Lemon vinaigrette dressing
- 1/3 cup extra-virgin olive oil
- 2 tablespoons lemon juice
- 1 teaspoon lemon zest, finely grated
- ½ teaspoon dried rosemary
- Salt and pepper as needed

Directions:
1. Take a glass bowl and whisk in oil, zest, lemon juice, and rosemary
2. Keep the mixture on the side
3. Take another large bowl and add spinach, pasta, cherry tomatoes, and chicken, and drizzle the dressing on top
4. Season with salt and pepper
5. Toss until coated well
6. Divide the salad among serving plates and sprinkle cheese on top
7. Serve and enjoy!

Awesome Chicken Cacciatore

Serving: 8
Preparation Time: 5 minutes
Cooking Time: 37 minute
Ingredients
- 2 tablespoons extra virgin olive oil
- 1 medium onion, chopped
- 3 tablespoons garlic, chopped
- 1 whole chicken, cut into 8 pieces
- 1 medium carrot, cubed
- 1 medium potato, cubed
- 1 red bell pepper, sliced
- 2 cups stewed tomatoes
- 1 cup tomato sauce
- ½ cup green peas
- 1 teaspoon dried thyme
- Salt and pepper as needed

Directions:
1. Take a large saucepan and place it over medium-high heat
2. Add olive oil and heat up
3. Stir in onion and garlic and cook for 2 minutes
4. Add chicken and cook for 7 minutes
5. Add carrots, bell pepper, stewed tomatoes, potato, green peas, tomato sauce, and thyme
6. Bring to a simmer and lower down heat; simmer for 30 minutes
7. Season with salt and pepper
8. Transfer to a serving platter
9. Enjoy!

Chapter 12

Salads

Cabbage Slaw Salad

Preparation Time: 20 minutes
Cooking Time: 0 minutes
Servings: 6
Ingredients:
- 2 cups finely chopped green cabbage
- 2 cups finely chopped red cabbage
- 2 cups grated carrots
- 3 scallions, both white and green parts, sliced
- 2 tbsp. extra-virgin olive oil
- 2 tbsp. rice vinegar
- 1 tsp. honey
- 1 garlic clove, minced
- ¼ tsp. salt

Directions:
1. In a large bowl, toss together the green and red cabbage, carrots, and scallions.
2. In a small bowl, whisk together the oil, vinegar, honey, garlic, and salt.
3. Pour the dressing over the veggies and mix to thoroughly combine.
4. Serve immediately, or cover and chill for several hours before serving.

Green Salad with Blackberries, Goat Cheese, and Sweet Potatoes

Preparation Time: 20 minutes
Cooking Time: 15 minutes
Servings: 4
Ingredients:
For The Vinaigrette:
- 1-pint blackberries
- 2 tbsp. red wine vinegar
- 1 tbsp. honey
- 3 tbsp. extra-virgin olive oil
- ¼ tsp. salt
- Freshly ground black pepper

For The Salad:
- 1 sweet potato, cubed
- 1 tsp. extra-virgin olive oil
- 8 cups salad greens (baby spinach, spicy greens, romaine)
- ½ red onion, sliced
- ¼ cup crumbled goat cheese

Directions:
To Make the Vinaigrette:
1. In a blender jar, combine the blackberries, vinegar, honey, oil, salt, and pepper, and process until smooth. Set aside.

To Make the Salad:
2. Preheat the oven to 425°F.
3. Line a baking sheet with parchment paper.
4. In a medium mixing bowl, toss the sweet potato with the olive oil. Transfer to the prepared baking sheet and roast for 20 minutes, stirring once halfway through, until tender.
5. Remove and cool for a few minutes.
6. In a large bowl, toss the greens with the red onion and cooled sweet potato, and drizzle with the vinaigrette.
7. Serve topped with 1 tbsp. goat cheese per serving.

Pomegranate & Brussels Sprouts Salad

Preparation Time: 8 minutes
Cooking Time: 12 minutes
Servings: 6
Ingredients:
- 3 slices bacon, cooked crisp and crumbled
- 3 cup Brussels sprouts, shredded
- 3 cup kale, shredded
- 1 ½ cup pomegranate seeds
- ½ cup almonds, toasted and chopped
- ¼ cup reduced-fat parmesan cheese, grated
- Citrus Vinaigrette

Directions:
1. Combine all Ingredients: in a large bowl.
2. Drizzle vinaigrette over salad, and toss to coat well. Serve garnished with more cheese if desired.

Strawberry & Avocado Salad

Preparation Time: 6 minutes
Cooking Time: 9 minutes
Servings: 6
Ingredients:
- 6 oz. baby spinach
- 2 avocados, chopped
- 1 cup strawberries, sliced
- ¼ cup feta cheese, crumbled
- Creamy Poppy Seed Dressing

¼ cup almonds, sliced
Direction:
1. Add spinach, berries, avocado, nuts, and cheese to a large bowl and toss to combine.
2. Pour ½ recipe of Creamy Poppy Seed Dressing over salad and toss to coat. Add more dressing if desired. Serve.

Shrimp & Avocado Salad

Preparation Time: 11 minutes
Cooking Time: 5 minutes
Servings: 4

Ingredients:
- ½ lb. raw shrimp, peeled and deveined
- 3 cups romaine lettuce, chopped
- 1 cup Napa cabbage, chopped
- 1 avocado, pit removed, and sliced
- ¼ cup red cabbage, chopped
- ¼ cucumber, julienned
- 2 tbsp. green onions, diced fine
- 2 tbsp. fresh cilantro, diced
- 1 tsp. fresh ginger, diced fine
- 2 tbsp. coconut oil
- 1 tbsp. sesame seeds
- 1 tsp. Chinese 5 spice
- Fat-free Ranch dressing

Directions:
1. Toast sesame seeds in a medium skillet over medium heat. Shake the skillet to prevent them from burning. Cook until they start to brown, about 2 minutes. Set aside.
2. Add the coconut oil to the skillet. Pat the shrimp dry and sprinkle with the 5 spices. Add to hot oil. Cook 2 minutes per side, or until they turn pink. Set aside.
3. Arrange lettuce and cabbage on a serving platter. Top with green onions, cucumber, and cilantro. Add shrimp and avocado.
4. Drizzle with the desired amount of dressing and sprinkle sesame seeds over top. Serve.

Kale Salad with Avocado Dressing

Preparation Time: 10 minutes
Cooking Time: 0 minutes
Servings: 6
Ingredients:
- 6 cups chopped kale
- 1 cup finely chopped red bell pepper
- 1 bunch scallions, white and green parts, finely chopped
- 1 avocado, pitted and peeled
- ½ cup raw cashews
- 3 garlic cloves, peeled
- ½ lemon, juiced
- ¼ cup extra-virgin olive oil
- Salt
- Freshly ground black pepper

Directions:
1. In a large bowl, toss together the kale, red bell pepper, and scallions.
2. In a high-speed blender or food processor, combine the avocado, cashews, garlic, lemon juice, and olive oil, and process until smooth. Add up to ½ cup water as needed to create a pourable dressing. Season with salt and pepper. Pour the dressing over the kale, mix well, and serve.

Asian Noodle Salad

Preparation Time: 20 minutes
Cooking Time: 15 minutes
Servings: 4
Ingredients:
- 2 carrots, sliced thin
- 2 radishes, sliced thin
- 1 English cucumber, sliced thin
- 1 mango, julienned
- 1 bell pepper, julienned
- 1 small serrano pepper, seeded and sliced thin
- 1 bag tofu Shirataki Fettuccini noodles
- ¼ cup lime juice
- ¼ cup fresh basil, chopped
- ¼ cup fresh cilantro, chopped
- 2 tbsp. fresh mint, chopped
- 2 tbsp. rice vinegar
- 2 tbsp. sweet chili sauce
- 2 tbsp. roasted peanuts finely chopped
- 1 tbsp. Splenda
- ½ tsp. sesame oil

Directions:
1. Pickle the vegetables: In a large bowl, place radish, cucumbers, and carrots.
2. Add vinegar, coconut sugar, and lime juice and stir to coat the vegetables. Cover and chill for 15–20 minutes.
3. Prep the noodles: remove the noodles from the package and rinse under cold water.
4. Cut into smaller pieces. Pat dry with paper towels.
5. To assemble the salad. Remove the vegetables from the marinade, reserving marinade, and place them in a large mixing bowl.
6. Add noodles, mango, bell pepper, chili, and herbs.
7. In a small bowl, combine 2 tbsp. marinade with the chili sauce and sesame oil.
8. Pour over salad and toss to coat.
9. Top with peanuts and serve.

Avocado & Citrus Shrimp Salad

Preparation Time: 11 minutes
Cooking Time: 5 minutes
Servings: 4
Ingredients:
- 1 lb. medium shrimp, peeled and deveined, remove tails
- 8 cup salad greens
- 1 lemon
- 1 avocado, diced
- 1 shallot, diced fine
- ½ cup almonds, sliced and toasted
- 1 tbsp. olive oil
- Salt and freshly ground black pepper

Directions:
1. Cut the lemon in half and squeeze the juice, from both halves, into a small bowl, set aside. Slice the lemon into thin wedges.
2. Heat the oil in a skillet over medium heat. Add lemon wedges and let cook, about 1 minute, to infuse the oil with the lemons.
3. Add the shrimp and cook, stirring frequently, until shrimp turn pink. Discard the lemon wedges and let cool.
4. Place the salad greens in a large bowl. Add the shrimp, with the juices from the pan, and toss to coat. Add remaining Ingredients: and toss to combine. Serve.

Healthy Taco Salad

Preparation Time: 20 minutes
Cooking Time: 9 minutes

Servings: 4
Ingredients:
- 2 whole Romaine hearts, chopped
- 1 lb. lean ground beef
- 1 whole avocado, cubed
- 3 oz. grape tomatoes, halved
- ½ cup cheddar cheese, cubed
- 2 tbsp. sliced red onion
- ½ batch Tangy Mexican Salad Dressing
- 1 tsp. ground cumin
- Salt and pepper to taste

Directions:
1. Cook ground beef in a skillet over medium heat. Break the beef up into little pieces as it cooks. Add seasonings and stir to combine. Drain grease and let cool for about 5 minutes.
2. To assemble the salad, place all Ingredients: into a large bowl. Toss to mix then add dressing and toss. Top with reduced-fat sour cream and/or salsa if desired.

Chicken Guacamole Salad

Preparation Time: 6 minutes
Cooking Time: 25 minutes
Servings: 6
Ingredients:
- 1 lb. chicken breast, boneless and skinless
- 2 avocados
- 1–2 jalapeno peppers, seeded and diced
- 1/3 cup onion, diced
- 3 tbsp. cilantro, diced
- 2 tbsp. fresh lime juice
- 2 garlic cloves, diced
- 1 tbsp. olive oil
- Salt and pepper, to taste

Directions:
1. Heat oven to 400°F. Line a baking sheet with foil.
2. Season chicken with salt and pepper and place on prepared pan. Bake 20 minutes, or until chicken is cooked through. Let cool completely.
3. Once the chicken has cooled, shred or dice and add to a large bowl. Add the remaining Ingredients: and mix well, mashing the avocado as you mix it in. Taste and season with salt and pepper as desired. Serve immediately.

Warm Portobello Salad

Preparation Time: 20 minutes
Cooking Time: 9 minutes
Servings: 4
Ingredients:
- 6 cup mixed salad greens
- 1 cup Portobello mushrooms, sliced
- 1 green onion, sliced
- Walnut or Warm Bacon Vinaigrette
- 1 tbsp. olive oil
- 1/8 tsp. ground black pepper

Directions:
1. Heat oil in a nonstick skillet over med-high heat. Add mushrooms and cook, stirring occasionally, 10 minutes, or until they are tender. Stir in onions and reduce heat to low.
2. Place salad greens on serving plates, top with mushrooms, and sprinkle with pepper. Drizzle lightly with your choice of vinaigrette.

Cucumber Salad

Preparation Time: 10 minutes
Cooking Time: 0 minutes
Servings: 4
Ingredients:
- 2 medium cucumbers, peeled and chopped
- 1 cup cherry tomatoes, halved
- ½ red onion, thinly sliced
- 2 tbsp. red wine vinegar
- 2 tbsp. extra-virgin olive oil
- ¼ tsp. dried oregano
- ¼ tsp. salt, plus more as needed
- Freshly ground black pepper

Directions:
1. In a medium bowl, combine the cucumbers, tomatoes, and red onion.
2. In a small bowl, whisk the vinegar, olive oil, oregano, salt, and some pepper. Pour the vinaigrette over the vegetables, and toss to coat. Taste and season with more salt and pepper, if desired. Serve immediately, or refrigerate in an airtight container for 2 to 3 days.

Green Power Salad

Preparation time: 5 minutes
Cooking time: 10 minutes
Servings: 3-4
Ingredients:
- 2 cups mixed green salad leaves
- 1 cup broccoli or sunflower sprouts
- 1 small cucumber, chopped
- 1 avocado, peeled and cubed
- 5-6 radishes, sliced
- 1 tbsp. chia seeds
- 1 tbsp. pumpkin seeds

For the dressing:
- 1 tbsp. lemon juice
- 1 tbsp. red wine vinegar
- 2 tbsp. extra virgin olive oil
- 1 tbsp. Dijon mustard
- Salt and pepper, to taste

Directions:
1. Place all Ingredients: in a large salad bowl and toss until combined.
2. In a medium bowl, whisk Ingredients: for the dressing until smooth. Pour over salad, toss thoroughly and serve.

Spinach and Green Bean Salad

Preparation time: 7 minutes
Cooking time: 20-30 minutes
Servings: 4-5
Ingredients:
- 12 oz. green beans, halved diagonally
- 1 bag baby spinach leaves
- 1 cup walnuts, halved and toasted
- 1 cup sun-dried tomatoes

- 2 tbsp. pumpkin seeds

For the dressing:
- 3 tbsp. extra virgin olive oil
- 2 tbsp. red wine vinegar
- 2 garlic cloves, crushed

Directions:
1. Cook beans in a large saucepan of boiling salted water for one minute or until bright green. Rinse under cold running water, drain, pat dry and set aside.
2. Whisk oil, vinegar, garlic, salt and pepper in a small glass bowl until well combined.
3. Place spinach, walnuts, cooked beans and sun-dried tomatoes in a salad bowl and toss to combine. Drizzle with dressing and serve.

Mediterranean Spinach Salad

Preparation time: 15 minutes
Cooking time: 20 minutes
Servings: 4
Ingredients:
- 1 bag baby spinach, washed and dried
- 4-5 spring onions, finely chopped
- 1 cucumber, peeled and cut
- 1/2 cup walnuts, halved and roasted
- 1/3 cup yogurt
- 2 tbsp. red wine vinegar
- 3 tbsp. extra virgin olive oil
- Salt and black pepper, to taste

Directions:
1. Whisk yogurt, olive oil and vinegar in a small bowl. Place the baby spinach leaves in a large salad bowl.
2. Add the onions, cucumber and walnuts. Season with black pepper and salt, stir, and toss with the dressing.

Arugula and Avocado Salad

Preparation time: 5 minutes
Cooking time: 15-20 minutes
Servings: 4
Ingredients:
- 1 bunch arugula leaves
- 2 avocados, peeled and sliced
- 1 cup strawberries, halved
- 1/2 cup corn kernels, cooked
- 1 tbsp. poppy seeds
- 1 tbsp. lemon juice
- 2 tbsp. extra virgin olive oil

Directions:
1. Combine all Ingredients: in a salad bowl and gently toss. Sprinkle with lemon juice and olive oil, stir, top with poppy seeds and serve.

Arugula, Radicchio and Pomegranate Salad

Preparation time: 5 minutes
Cooking time: 10 minutes
Servings: 4
Ingredients:
- 1 bunch arugula leaves
- 1 small head radicchio, chopped
- 1 avocado, peeled and cubed
- 1/2 cup pomegranate seeds, from 1 medium pomegranate
- 1/3 cup hazelnuts

For the dressing:
- 1 tbsp. honey
- 1 tbsp. balsamic vinegar
- 2 tbsp. extra virgin olive oil
- 1/2 tsp salt

Directions:
1. Place arugula, radicchio, avocado, hazelnuts and pomegranate seeds in a large salad bowl and gently toss to combine.
2. Whisk dressing Ingredients: until smooth, pour over the salad, serve and enjoy!

Roasted Beet Salad

Preparation Time: 20 minutes
Cooking Time: 70 minutes
Servings: 4
Ingredients:
- 6 medium beets, scrubbed, tops removed
- ¼ cup balsamic vinegar
- ¼ cup extra-virgin olive oil
- 1 tsp. Dijon mustard
- Salt
- Freshly ground black pepper
- ¼ cup walnuts
- 6 oz. baby arugula
- 2 oz. feta cheese, crumbled

Directions:
1. Preheat the oven to 400°F.
2. Wrap each beet tightly in aluminum foil, and arrange it on a baking sheet. Roast for 45 to 60 minutes, depending on their size, until tender when pierced with a knife. Remove from the oven, carefully unwrap each beet, and let cool for 10 minutes.
3. Reduce the oven temperature to 350°F. Meanwhile, in a medium bowl, whisk the vinegar, olive oil, and mustard. Season with salt and pepper.
4. On the same baking sheet, spread the walnuts in a single layer. Toast for 5 to 7 minutes, until lightly browned.
5. Using a small knife, peel and slice the beets, and place them in another medium bowl. Add half of the vinaigrette, and toss to coat. Add the arugula to the remaining vinaigrette, and toss to coat. On a serving platter, arrange the arugula and top with the beets.
6. Sprinkle the toasted walnuts and feta cheese over the top and serve.

Black Bean and Corn Salad

Preparation Time: 20 minutes
Cooking Time: 0 minutes
Servings: 5
Ingredients:
- 2 (15 oz.) cans reduced-sodium black beans, rinsed and drained
- 1 red bell pepper, chopped
- 1 cucumber, chopped
- 1 avocado, peeled, seeded, and chopped

- 1 cup fresh, frozen and thawed, or canned and drained corn
- ½ cup minced red onion
- 1 jalapeño pepper, seeded and minced
- ¼ cup chopped fresh cilantro
- ¼ cup extra-virgin olive oil
- 3 tbsp. freshly squeezed lime juice
- 1 tsp. honey
- 1 tsp. ground cumin
- Salt
- Freshly ground black pepper

Directions:
1. In a large bowl, stir together the black beans, red bell pepper, cucumber, avocado, corn, red onion, jalapeño, and cilantro.
2. In a small bowl, whisk the olive oil, lime juice, honey, and cumin. Season with salt and pepper. Pour the dressing over the salad, mix well to coat, and serve.

Perfect Quinoa Salad

Preparation Time: 16 minutes
Cooking Time: 14 minutes
Servings: 6
Ingredients:
- 1 cup quinoa, rinsed
- 1½ cups water
- 1 cucumber, finely chopped
- 1 red bell pepper, finely chopped
- ½ red onion, chopped
- ½ cup fresh flat-leaf parsley
- ¼ cup extra-virgin olive oil
- 2 lemons, juiced
- 3 garlic cloves, minced
- ½ tsp. salt
- ¼ tsp. freshly ground black pepper

Directions:
1. In a small saucepan over high heat, combine the quinoa and water. Bring to a boil, reduce the heat to low, cover the pot, and cook for 10 to 15 minutes, until the water is absorbed. Turn off the heat, fluff with a fork, re-cover, and let rest for about 5 minutes.
2. Meanwhile, in a large bowl, toss the cucumber, red bell pepper, red onion, and parsley.
3. In a small bowl, whisk the olive oil, lemon juice, garlic, salt, and pepper. Pour the dressing over the vegetables, and toss well to coat. Fold in the quinoa and serve.

Tropical Fruit Salad with Coconut Milk

Preparation Time: 10 minutes
Cooking Time: 0 minutes
Servings: 8
Ingredients:
- 2 cups pineapple chunks
- 2 kiwi fruits, peeled and sliced
- 1 mango, peeled and chopped
- ¼ cup canned light coconut milk
- 1 tbsp. freshly squeezed lime juice
- 1 tbsp. honey

Directions:
1. In a medium bowl, toss together the pineapple, kiwi, and mango.
2. In a small bowl, combine the coconut milk, lime juice, and honey, stirring until the honey dissolves. Pour the mixture over the fruits, and toss to coat. Serve immediately or refrigerate in an airtight container for up to 3 days.

Cucumber, Tomato, and Avocado Salad

Preparation Time: 10 minutes
Cooking Time: 0 minutes
Servings: 4
Ingredients:
- 1 cup cherry tomatoes, halved
- 1 large cucumber, chopped
- 1 small red onion, thinly sliced
- 1 avocado, diced
- 2 tbsp. chopped fresh dill
- 2 tbsp. extra-virgin olive oil
- 1 lemon, juiced
- ¼ tsp. salt

¼ tsp. freshly ground black pepper
Directions:
1. In a large mixing bowl, combine the tomatoes, cucumber, onion, avocado, and dill.
2. In a small bowl, combine the oil, lemon juice, salt, and pepper, and mix well.
3. Drizzle the dressing over the vegetables and toss to combine. Serve.

Layered Salad

Preparation Time: 9 minutes
Cooking Time: 15 minutes
Servings: 10
Ingredients:
- 6 slices bacon, chopped and cooked crisp
- 2 tomatoes, diced
- 2 stalks celery, sliced
- 1 head romaine lettuce, diced
- 1 red bell pepper, diced
- 1 cup frozen peas, thawed
- 1 cup sharp cheddar cheese, grated
- ¼ cup red onion, fine diced
- What you'll need from the store cupboard
- 1 cup fat-free ranch dressing

Directions:
1. Use a 9x13-inch glass baking dish and layer half the lettuce, pepper, celery, tomatoes, peas, onion, cheese, bacon, and dressing. Repeat. Serve or cover and chill until ready to serve.

Baked "Potato" Salad

Preparation Time: 6 minutes
Cooking Time: 15 minutes
Servings: 8
Ingredients:
- 2 lb. cauliflower, separated into small florets
- 6-8 slices bacon, chopped and fried crisp
- 6 boiled eggs, cooled, peeled, and chopped

- 1 cup sharp cheddar cheese, grated
- ½ cup green onion, sliced
- 1 cup reduced-fat mayonnaise
- 2 tsp. yellow mustard
- 1 ½ tsp. onion powder, divided
- Salt and fresh-ground black pepper to taste

Directions:
1. Place cauliflower in a vegetable steamer, or a pot with a steamer insert, and steam for 5–6 minutes.
2. Drain the cauliflower and set it aside.
3. In a small bowl, whisk together mayonnaise, mustard, 1 tsp. onion powder, salt, and pepper.
4. Pat cauliflower dries with paper towels and place in a large mixing bowl. Add eggs, salt, pepper, remaining ½ tsp. onion powder, then dressing. Mix gently to combine Ingredients: together.
5. Fold in the bacon, cheese, and green onion. Serve warm or cover and chill before serving.

Caprese Salad

Preparation Time: 6 minutes
Cooking Time: 15 minutes
Servings: 4
Ingredients:
- 3 medium tomatoes, cut into 8 slices
- 2 (1 oz.) slices mozzarella cheese, cut into strips
- ¼ cup fresh basil, sliced thin
- 2 tsp. extra-virgin olive oil
- 1/8 tsp. salt
- Pinch black pepper

Directions:
1. Place tomatoes and cheese on serving plates. Sprinkle with salt and pepper. Drizzle oil over and top with basil. Serve.

Chopped Veggie Salad

Preparation Time: 4 minutes
Cooking Time: 15 minutes
Servings: 4
Ingredients:
- 1 cucumber, chopped
- 1-pint cherry tomatoes, cut in half
- 3 radishes, chopped
- 1 yellow bell pepper chopped
- ½ cup fresh parsley, chopped

What you'll need from the store cupboard:
- 3 tbsp. lemon juice
- 1 tbsp. olive oil
- Salt to taste

Directions:
1. Place all Ingredients: in a large bowl and toss to combine. Serve immediately, or cover and chill until ready to serve.

Tofu Salad Sandwiches

Preparation Time: 9 minutes
Cooking Time: 16 minutes
Servings: 4
Ingredients:
- 1 pkg. silken firm tofu, pressed
- 4 lettuce leaves
- 2 green onions, diced
- ¼ cup celery, diced
- 8 slices bread
- ¼ cup lite mayonnaise
- 2 tbsp. sweet pickle relish
- 1 tbsp. Dijon mustard
- ¼ tsp. turmeric - ¼ tsp. salt
- 1/8 tsp. cayenne pepper

Directions:
1. Press tofu between layers of paper towels for 15 minutes to remove excess moisture. Cut into small cubes.
2. In a medium bowl, stir together the remaining Ingredients. Fold in tofu. Spread over 4 slices of bread. Top with a lettuce leaf and another slice of bread. Serve.

Lobster Roll Salad with Bacon Vinaigrette

Preparation Time: 20 minutes
Cooking Time: 15 minutes
Servings: 6
Ingredients:
- 6 slices bacon
- 2 whole-grain ciabatta rolls, halved horizontally
- 3 medium tomatoes, cut into wedges
- 2 (8 oz.) spiny lobster tails, fresh or frozen (thawed)
- 2 cups fresh baby spinach
- 2 cups romaine lettuce, torn
- 1 cup seeded cucumber, diced
- 1 cup red sweet peppers, diced
- 2 tbsp. shallot, diced fine
- 2 tbsp. fresh chives, diced fine

What you'll need from the store cupboard:
- 2 garlic cloves, diced fine
- 3 tbsp. white wine vinegar
- 3 tbsp. olive oil, divided

Directions:
1. Heat a grill to medium heat, or medium heat charcoals.
2. Rinse lobster and pat dry. Butterfly lobster tails. Place on the grill, cover, and cook 25–30 minutes, or until meat is opaque.
3. Remove lobster and let cool.
4. In a small bowl, whisk together 2 tbsp. olive oil and garlic. Brush the cut sides of the rolls with the oil mixture. Place on grill, cut side down, and cook until crisp, about 2 minutes. Transfer to cutting board.
5. While lobster is cooking, chop bacon and cook in a medium skillet until crisp. Transfer to paper towels. Reserve 1 tbsp. bacon grease.
6. To make the vinaigrette: combine reserved bacon grease, vinegar, shallot, remaining 1 tbsp. oil and chives in a glass jar with an air-tight lid. Screw on the lid and shake to combine.
7. Remove the lobster from the shells and cut it into 1 ½-inch pieces. Cut rolls into 1-inch cubes.
8. To assemble salad: In a large bowl, combine spinach, romaine, tomatoes, cucumber, peppers, lobster, and bread cubes. Toss to combine. Transfer to serving platter and drizzle with vinaigrette. Sprinkle bacon over top and serve.

Bean and Basil Salad

Preparation Time: 20 minutes
Cooking Time: 0 minutes

Servings: 8
Ingredients:
- 1 (15 oz.) can low-sodium chickpeas, drained and rinsed
- 1 (15 oz.) can low-sodium kidney beans, drained and rinsed
- 1 (15 oz.) can low-sodium white beans, drained and rinsed
- 1 red bell pepper, seeded and finely chopped
- ¼ cup chopped scallions, both white and green parts
- ¼ cup finely chopped fresh basil
- 3 garlic cloves, minced
- 2 tbsp. extra-virgin olive oil
- 1 tbsp. red wine vinegar
- 1 tsp. Dijon mustard
- ¼ tsp. freshly ground black pepper

Directions:
1. In a large mixing bowl, combine the chickpeas, kidney beans, white beans, bell pepper, scallions, basil, and garlic. Toss gently to combine.
2. In a small bowl, combine the olive oil, vinegar, mustard, and pepper. Toss with the salad.
3. Cover and refrigerate for an hour before serving, to allow the flavors to mix.
4. Substitution tip: Feel free to substitute home-cooked beans in place of canned, using about 1½ cups per variety.

Tenderloin Grilled Salad
Preparation Time: 10 minutes
Cooking Time: 20 minutes
Servings: 5
Ingredients:
- 1 lb. pork tenderloin
- 10 cups mixed salad greens
- 2 oranges, seedless, cut into bite-sized pieces
- 1 tbsp. orange zest, grated
- 2 tbsp. cider vinegar
- 2 tbsp. olive oil
- 2 tsp. Dijon mustard
- ½ cup orange juice
- 2 tsp. honey
- ½ tsp. ground pepper

Directions:
1. Bring together all the dressing Ingredients: in a bowl.
2. Grill each side of the pork covered over medium heat for 9 minutes.
3. Slice after 5 minutes.
4. Slice the tenderloin thinly.
5. Keep the greens on your serving plate.
6. Top with the pork and oranges.
7. Sprinkle nuts (optional).

Barley Veggie Salad
Preparation Time: 10 minutes
Cooking Time: 20 minutes
Servings: 6
Ingredients:
- 1 tomato, seeded and chopped
- 2 tbsp. parsley, minced
- 1 yellow pepper, chopped
- 1 tbsp. basil, minced
- ¼ cup almonds, toasted
- 1-¼ cups vegetable broth
- 1 cup barley
- 1 tbsp. lemon juice
- 2 tbsp. white wine vinegar
- 3 tbsp. olive oil
- ¼ tsp. pepper
- ½ tsp. salt
- 1 cup water

Directions:
1. Boil the broth, barley, and water in a saucepan.
2. Reduce heat. Cover and let it simmer for 10 minutes.
3. Take out from the heat.
4. In the meantime, bring together the parsley, yellow pepper, and tomato in a bowl.
5. Stir the barley in.
6. Whisk the vinegar, oil, basil, lemon juice, water, pepper, and salt in a bowl.
7. Pour this over your barley mix. Toss to coat well.
8. Stir the almonds in before serving.

Spinach Shrimp Salad
Preparation Time: 10 minutes
Cooking Time: 10 minutes
Servings: 4
Ingredients:
- 1 lb. uncooked shrimp, peeled and deveined
- 2 tbsp. parsley, minced
- ¾ cup halved cherry tomatoes
- 1 medium lemon
- 4 cups baby spinach
- 2 tbsp. butter
- 3 minced garlic cloves
- ¼ tsp. pepper
- ¼ tsp. salt

Directions:
1. Melt the butter over a medium temperature in a nonstick skillet.
2. Add the shrimp.
3. Now cook the shrimp for 3 minutes until your shrimp becomes pink.
4. Add the parsley and garlic.
5. Cook for another minute. Take out from the heat.
6. Keep the spinach in your salad bowl.
7. Top with the shrimp mix and tomatoes.
8. Drizzle lemon juice on the salad.
9. Sprinkle pepper and salt.

Sweet Potato and Roasted Beet Salad
Preparation Time: 10 minutes
Cooking Time: 10 minutes
Servings: 4
Ingredients:
- 2 beets
- 1 sweet potato, peeled and cubed
- 1 garlic clove, minced

- 2 tbsp. walnuts, chopped and toasted
- 1 cup fennel bulb, sliced
- 3 tbsp. balsamic vinegar
- 1 tsp. Dijon mustard
- 1 tbsp. honey
- 3 tbsp. olive oil
- ¼ tsp. pepper
- ¼ tsp. salt
- 3 tbsp. water

Directions:
1. Scrub the beets. Trim the tops to 1 inch.
2. Wrap in foil and keep on a baking sheet.
3. Bake until tender. Take off the foil. Combine water and sweet potato in a bowl.
4. Cover. Microwave for 5 minutes. Drain off.
5. Now peel the beets. Cut into small wedges.
6. Arrange the fennel, sweet potato, and beets on 4 salad plates.
7. Sprinkle nuts.
8. Whisk the honey, mustard, vinegar, water, garlic, pepper, and salt.
9. Whisk in oil gradually. Drizzle over the salad.

Harvest Salad

Preparation Time: 9 minutes
Cooking Time: 25 minutes
Servings: 6
Ingredients:
- 10 oz. kale, deboned and chopped
- 1 ½ cup blackberries
- ½ butternut squash, cubed
- ¼ cup goat cheese, crumbled

What you'll need from the store cupboard:
- Maple Mustard Salad Dressing
- 1 cup raw pecans
- 1/3 cup raw pumpkin seeds
- ¼ cup dried cranberries
- 3 ½ tbsp. olive oil
- 1 ½ tbsp. sugar-free maple syrup
- 3/8 tsp. salt, divided
- Pepper, to taste
- Nonstick cooking spray

Directions:
1. Heat oven to 400°F.
2. Spray a baking sheet with cooking spray.
3. Spread squash on the prepared pan, add 1 ½ tbsp. oil, 1/8 tsp. salt, and pepper to squash, and stir to coat the squash evenly. Bake 20–25 minutes.
4. Place kale in a large bowl. Add 2 tbsp. oil and ½ tsp. salt and massage it into the kale with your hands for 3–4 minutes.
5. Spray a clean baking sheet with cooking spray.
6. In a medium bowl, stir together pecans, pumpkin seeds, and maple syrup until nuts are coated. Pour onto prepared pan and bake 8–10 minutes, these can be baked at the same time as the squash.
7. To assemble the salad: place all of the Ingredients: in a large bowl. Pour dressing over and toss to coat.
8. Serve.

Rainbow Black Bean Salad

Preparation Time: 16 minutes
Cooking Time: 0 minutes
Servings: 5
Ingredients:
- 1 (15 oz.) can low-sodium black beans, drained and rinsed
- 1 avocado, diced
- 1 cup cherry tomatoes, halved
- 1 cup chopped baby spinach
- ½ cup finely chopped red bell pepper
- ¼ cup finely chopped jicama
- ½ cup chopped scallions, both white and green parts
- ¼ cup chopped fresh cilantro
- 2 tbsp. freshly squeezed lime juice
- 1 tbsp. extra-virgin olive oil
- 2 garlic cloves, minced
- 1 tsp. honey
- ¼ tsp. salt
- ¼ tsp. freshly ground black pepper

Directions:
1. In a large bowl, combine the black beans, avocado, tomatoes, spinach, bell pepper, jicama, scallions, and cilantro.
2. In a small bowl, mix the lime juice, oil, garlic, honey, salt, and pepper. Add to the salad and toss.
3. Chill for 1 hour before serving.

Warm Barley and Squash Salad with Balsamic Vinaigrette

Preparation Time: 20 minutes
Cooking Time: 41 minutes
Servings: 8
Ingredients:
- 1 small butternut squash
- 3 tsp. plus 2 tbsp. extra-virgin olive oil, divided
- 2 cups broccoli florets
- 1 cup pearl barley
- 1 cup toasted chopped walnuts
- 2 cups baby kale
- ½ red onion, sliced
- 2 tbsp. balsamic vinegar
- 2 garlic cloves, minced
- ½ tsp. salt
- ¼ tsp. freshly ground black pepper

Directions:
1. Preheat the oven to 400°F.
2. Line a baking sheet with parchment paper.
3. Peel and seed the squash, and cut it into dice. In a large bowl, toss the squash with 2 tsp. of olive oil.
4. Transfer to the prepared baking sheet and roast for 20 minutes.
5. While the squash is roasting, toss the broccoli in the same bowl with 1 tsp. of olive oil. After 20 minutes, flip the squash and push it to one side of the baking sheet.
6. Add the broccoli to the other side and continue to roast for 20 more minutes until tender.
7. While the veggies are roasting, in a medium pot, cover the barley with several inches of water.

8. Bring to a boil, then reduce the heat, cover, and simmer for 30 minutes until tender. Drain and rinse.
9. Transfer the barley to a large bowl, and toss with the cooked squash and broccoli, walnuts, kale, and onion.
10. In a small bowl, mix the remaining 2 tbsp. olive oil, balsamic vinegar, garlic, salt, and pepper. Toss the salad with the dressing and serve.

Winter Chicken and Citrus Salad

Preparation Time: 20 minutes
Cooking Time: 0 minutes
Servings: 4
Ingredients:
- 4 cups baby spinach
- 2 tbsp. extra-virgin olive oil
- 1 tbsp. freshly squeezed lemon juice
- 1/8 tsp. salt
- Freshly ground black pepper
- 2 cups chopped cooked chicken
- 2 mandarin oranges, peeled and sectioned
- ½ peeled grapefruit, sectioned
- ¼ cup sliced almonds

Directions:
1. In a large mixing bowl, toss the spinach with the olive oil, lemon juice, salt, and pepper.
2. Add the chicken, oranges, grapefruit, and almonds to the bowl. Toss gently.
3. Arrange on 4 plates and serve.

Hearty Brussels Salad

Serving: 2
Preparation Time: 5 minutes
Cooking Time: 10-15 minutes
Ingredients
- ¼ cup hazelnuts, whole and skinless
- 1 tablespoon olive oil
- 1 pound Brussels sprouts
- Salt to taste

Directions:
1. Preheat your oven to 350 degrees F
2. Line a baking sheet with parchment paper and trim the bottom of the Brussels
3. Put leaves in a medium-sized bowl, making sure that they are broken
4. Toss leaves with olive oil and season with salt
5. Spread leaves on a baking sheet
6. Roast for 10-15 minutes until crispy
7. Divide between bowls and toss with remaining ingredients
8. Serve and enjoy!

Broccoli Salad With Almond

Serving: 4
Preparation Time: 5 minutes
Cooking Time: 5 minutes
Ingredients
- 1 large head of broccoli, cut into florets
- ¼ cup slivered almonds
- 2 tablespoons olive oil
- Salt and pepper to taste
- Juice of ½ lemon

Directions:
1. Steam broccoli in the microwave
2. Place cooked broccoli in a large bowl and add slivered almonds, salt, pepper, olive oil, and lemon juice
3. Stir well to combined
4. Serve and enjoy!

Great Tomato Platter

Serving: 8
Preparation Time: 10 minutes + Chill time
Cooking Time: Nil
Ingredients
- 1/3 cup olive oil
- 1 teaspoon salt
- 2 tablespoons onion, chopped
- ¼ teaspoon pepper
- ½ a garlic, minced
- 1 tablespoon fresh parsley, minced
- 3 large fresh tomatoes, sliced
- 1 teaspoon dried basil
- ¼ cup red wine vinegar

Directions:
1. Take a shallow dish and arrange tomatoes in the dish
2. Add the rest of the ingredients to a mason jar, cover the jar and shake it well
3. Pour mix over tomato slices
4. Let it chill for 2-3 hours
5. Serve!

Supreme Avocado and Cilantro Medley

Serving: 2
Preparation Time: 10 minutes
Cooking Time: nil
Ingredients
- 2 avocados, peeled, pitted, and diced
- 1 sweet onion, chopped
- 1 green bell pepper, chopped
- 1 large ripe tomato, chopped
- ¼ cup of fresh cilantro, chopped
- ½ a lime, juiced
- Salt and pepper as needed

Directions:
1. Take a medium-sized bowl and add onion, tomato, avocados, bell pepper, lime, and cilantro
2. Give the whole mixture a toss
3. Season accordingly and serve chilled
4. Enjoy!

Hearty Orange and Onion Salad

Serving: 2
Preparation Time: 10 minutes
Cooking Time: nil
Ingredients
- 6 large orange
- 3 tablespoons of red wine vinegar
- 6 tablespoons of olive oil
- 1 teaspoon of dried oregano
- 1 red onion, thinly sliced

- 1 cup olive oil
- ¼ cup of fresh chives, chopped
- Ground black pepper

Directions:
1. Peel orange and cut into 4-5 crosswise slices
2. Transfer orange to a shallow dish
3. Drizzle vinegar and olive oil on top
4. Sprinkle oregano
5. Toss well to mix
6. Chill for 30 minutes and arrange sliced onion and black olives on top
7. Sprinkle more chives and pepper
8. Serve and enjoy!

Healthy Cauliflower Salad
Serving: 4
Preparation Time: 10 minutes
Cooking Time: nil
Ingredients
- 1 head of cauliflower, broken into florets
- 1 small onion, chopped
- 1/8 cup of extra virgin olive oil
- ¼ cup of apple cider vinegar
- ½ a teaspoon of sea salt
- ½ a teaspoon of black pepper
- ¼ cup of dried cranberries
- ¼ cup of pumpkin seeds

Directions:
1. Wash the cauliflower thoroughly and break them down into florets
2. Transfer the florets to a bowl
3. Take another bowl and whisk in oil, salt, pepper, and vinegar
4. Add pumpkin seeds and cranberries to the bowl with dressing
5. Mix well and pour dressing over cauliflower florets
6. Toss well
7. Add onions and toss
8. Chill and serve
9. Enjoy!

Lovely Japanese Cabbage Dish
Serving: 6
Preparation Time: 25 minutes
Cooking Time: Nil
Ingredients
- 3 tablespoons sesame oil
- 3 tablespoons rice vinegar
- 1 garlic clove, minced
- 1 teaspoon fresh ginger root, grated
- 1 teaspoon sunflower seeds
- 1 teaspoon pepper
- ½ large head cabbage, cored and shredded
- 1 bunch of green onions, thinly sliced
- 1 cup almond slivers
- ¼ cup toasted sesame seeds

Directions:
1. Add all listed ingredients to a large bowl, making sure to add the wet ingredients first, followed by the dried ones
2. Toss well to ensure that the cabbages are coated well
3. Let it chill and enjoy it!

Southern Salad
Serving: 2
Preparation Time: 10 minutes
Cooking Time: nil
Ingredients
- 5 cups of Romaine lettuce
- ½ a cup of sprouted black beans
- 1 cup cherry tomatoes, halved
- 1 avocado, diced
- ¼ cup almonds, chopped
- ½ a cup of fresh cilantro
- ½ a cup of Salsa Fresca

Directions:
1. Take a large-sized bowl and add lettuce, tomatoes, beans, almonds, cilantro, avocado, Salsa Fresco
2. Toss everything well and mix them
3. Divide the salad into serving bowls and serve!
4. Enjoy!

A Turtle Friend Salad
Serving: 6
Preparation Time: 5 minutes
Cooking Time: 5 minutes
Ingredients
- 1 Romaine lettuce, chopped
- 3 Roma tomatoes, diced
- 1 English cucumber, diced
- 1 small red onion, diced
- ½ cup parsley, chopped
- 2 tablespoons virgin olive oil
- ½ large lemon, juiced
- 1 teaspoon garlic powder
- Sunflower seeds and pepper to taste

Directions:
1. Wash the vegetables thoroughly under cold water
2. Prepare them by chopping, dicing, or mincing as needed
3. Take a large salad bowl and transfer the prepped veggies
4. Add vegetable oil, olive oil, lemon juice, and spice
5. Toss well to coat
6. Serve chilled if preferred
7. Enjoy!

Quinoa Been Salad
Serving: 6
Preparation Time: 5 minutes
Cooking Time: 15 minutes
Ingredients
- 1 cup of uncooked quinoa
- 1 can of 15-ounce black beans, drained and rinsed
- 1/3 cup of cilantro, chopped
- 1 tablespoon of olive oil
- 1 clove of garlic, minced
- Juice from 1 lime
- Salt and pepper as needed

Directions:
1. Cook quinoa according to the package instructions
2. Transfer quinoa to a medium bowl and let it cool for 10 minutes

3. Add remaining ingredients and toss well
4. Serve and enjoy!

Exceptional Watercress and Melon Salad

Serving: 4
Preparation Time: 10 minutes
Cooking Time: Nil
Ingredients

- 3 tablespoons lime juice
- 1 teaspoon date paste
- 1 teaspoon fresh ginger root, minced
- ¼ cup of vegetable oil
- 2 bunch watercress, chopped
- 2 and ½ cups watermelon, cubed
- 2 and ½ cups cantaloupe, cubed
- 1/3 cup almonds, toasted and sliced

Directions:
1. Take a large-sized bowl and add lime juice, ginger, date paste
2. Whisk well and add oil
3. Season with pepper and sunflower seeds
4. Add watercress, watermelon
5. Toss well
6. Transfer to a serving bowl and garnish with sliced almonds
7. Enjoy!

Hearty and Quinoa and Fruit Salad

Serving: 5
Preparation Time: 5 minutes
Cooking Time: 10 minutes
Ingredients

- 3 and ½ ounces Quinoa
- 3 peaches, diced
- 1 and ½ ounces toasted hazelnuts, chopped
- A handful of mint, chopped
- A handful of parsley, chopped
- 2 tablespoons olive oil
- Zest of 1 lemon
- Juice of 1 lemon

Directions:
1. Take a medium-sized saucepan and add quinoa
2. Add 1 and ¼ cups of water and bring it to a boil over medium-high heat
3. Lower the heat to low and simmer for 20 minutes
4. Drain any excess liquid
5. Add fruits, herbs, and Hazelnuts to the quinoa
6. Allow it to cool and season
7. Take a bowl and add olive oil, lemon zest, and lemon juice
8. Pour the mixture over the salad and give it a mix
9. Enjoy!

Red Cabbage Coleslaw With Vinegar Dressing

Serving: 4
Preparation Time: 10 minutes
Ingredients:

- 4 cups red cabbage, shredded
- 2 cups Napa cabbage, sliced
- 1 cup daikon radish, shredded
- ¼ cup fresh orange juice
- 2 tablespoons Chinese black vinegar
- 1 tablespoon soy sauce
- 1 tablespoon toasted sesame oil
- 1 teaspoon fresh ginger, grated
- ½ teaspoon ground Schezuan peppercorns
- 1 tablespoon black sesame seeds, garnish

Directions:
1. Take a large bowl and add red cabbage, napa, and daikon and keep it on the side
2. Take a small bowl and add orange juice, vinegar, soy sauce, grapeseed oil, sesame oil, ginger, peppercorns
3. Blend well
4. Pour dressing onto slaw, stir well
5. Taste accordingly
6. Serve and enjoy!

Balsamic Grilled Zucchini

Serving: 4
Preparation Time: 10 minutes
Cooking Time: 10-15 minutes
Ingredients

- 1 zucchini, sliced lengthwise 1/3 tsp garlic powder
- 1 tsp Italian seasoning
- 2 tbsp balsamic vinegar 2 tsp avocado oil
- Seasoning:
- ¼ tsp salt

Directions:
1. Take a griddle pan, place it over medium-low heat, brush it with oil and let it preheat.
2. Meanwhile, brush zucchini slices with oil and sprinkle with garlic powder, Italian seasoning, and salt.
3. Place zucchini slices on the griddle pan and cook for 2 to 3 minutes per side. Then brush zucchini with vinegar and cook for another minute.
4. Serve and enjoy!

Fancy Eggplant Salad

Serving: 8
Preparation Time: 20 minutes
Cooking Time: 15 minutes
Ingredients

- 1 large eggplant, washed and cubed
- 1 tomato, seeded and chopped
- 1 small onion, diced
- 2 tablespoons parsley, chopped
- 2 tablespoons extra virgin olive oil
- 2 tablespoons distilled white vinegar
- ½ cup feta cheese, crumbled
- Salt as needed

Directions:
1. Preheat your outdoor grill to medium-high
2. Pierce the eggplant a few times using a knife/fork
3. Cook the eggplants on your grill for about 15 minutes until they are charred
4. Keep it on the side and allow them to cool
5. Remove the skin from the eggplant and dice the pulp

6. Transfer the pulp to a mixing bowl and add parsley, onion, tomato, olive oil, feta cheese, and vinegar
7. Mix well and chill for 1 hour
8. Season with salt, and enjoy!

Great Pepper Soup

Serving: 6
Preparation Time:5 minutes
Cooking Time: 30 minutes
Ingredients
- 1 pound lean ground beef
- 1 onion, chopped
- 1 large green pepper, chopped
- 2 garlic cloves, minced
- 1 large tomato, chopped
- 2 tablespoons tomato paste
- 2 tablespoons all-purpose flour
- ¼ cup uncooked rice
- 2 tablespoons fresh parsley, chopped
- 4 cups beef broth
- 2 tablespoons olive oil
- Salt and pepper as needed

Directions:
1. Take a large-sized pot and place it over medium heat
2. Add oil and allow the oil to heat up
3. Add flour and keep whisking until you have a thick paste
4. Keep whisking for 3-4 minutes more while it bubbles and begins to thin
5. Add chopped onion and Saute for 3-4 minutes
6. Stir in tomato paste and beef
7. Take a wooden spoon and stir to break the ground beef
8. Cook for 5 minutes
9. Add garlic, pepper, and chopped tomatoes
10. Mix well and combine
11. Add broth and bring the mix to a light boil; lower the heat to low, and simmer for 30 minutes
12. Add rice, parsley and cook for 15 minutes
13. Once it has a nice soup-like consistency, serve with a garnish of parsley
14. Enjoy!

Watermelon, Radish, And Beet Salad

Serving: 4
Preparation Time:15 minutes
Cooking Time: 25 minutes
Ingredients
- 10 medium beets, peeled and cut into 1-inch chunks
- 1 teaspoon extra virgin olive oil
- 4 cups seedless watermelon, diced
- 5 large radishes, quartered
- 1 cup kale, shredded
- 1 tablespoon fresh thyme, chopped
- 1 lemon juice
- Sea salt
- Freshly ground black pepper

Directions:
1. Preheat your oven to 350 degrees Fahrenheit
2. Take a small bowl, add beets olive oil, and toss well to coat the beets
3. Roast beets for 25 minutes until tender
4. Transfer to a large bowl and cool them
5. Add watermelon, kale, radishes, thyme, and lemon juice, and toss
6. Season sea salt and pepper
7. Serve and enjoy!

A Very "Medi" Tomato Soup

Serving: 6
Preparation Time:5 minutes
Cooking Time: 25 minutes
Ingredients
- 4 tablespoons olive oil
- 2 medium yellow onions, thinly sliced
- 1 teaspoon salt
- 2 teaspoons curry powder
- 1 teaspoon red curry powder
- 1 teaspoon ground coriander
- 1 teaspoon ground cumin
- 1 can (15 ounces) Roma tomatoes, diced
- 1 can (28 ounces) plum tomatoes, diced
- 5 and ½ cups of water
- 1 can (14 ounces) of coconut milk
- Coconut brown rice, lemon wedges, fresh thyme, etc. as extra mix-ins

Directions:
1. Take a medium-sized pan and add oil
2. Place it over medium heat and allow it to heat up
3. Add onions and salt and cook for about 10-12 minutes until browned
4. Stir in curry powder, coriander, red pepper flakes, and cumin, and cook for 30 seconds
5. Make sure to keep stirring it well
6. Add tomatoes alongside the juice and 5 and a ½ cups of water (or broth if you prefer)
7. Simmer the mixture for 15 minutes
8. Take an immersion blender and puree the mixture until a soupy consistency is achieved
9. Enjoy as it is, or add some extra add-ins for a more flavorful experience

Cucumber And Yogurt Salad

Serving: 4
Preparation Time:10 minutes
Cooking Time: nil
Ingredients
- 5-6 small cucumbers, peeled and diced
- 1 (8 ounces) container of plain Greek yogurt
- 2 garlic cloves, minced
- 1 tablespoon fresh mint, minced
- 1 teaspoon dried oregano
- Sea salt and fresh black pepper

Directions:
1. Take a large bowl and add cucumbers, garlic, yogurt, mint, and oregano
2. Season with salt and pepper
3. Refrigerate the salad for 1 hour and serve
4. Enjoy!

Summer Veggie Chicken Wraps

Serving: 4
Preparation Time: 15 minutes
Cooking Time: nil
Ingredients
- 2 cups cooked chicken, chopped
- ½ English cucumbers, diced
- ½ red bell pepper, diced
- ½ cup carrot, shredded
- 1 scallion, white and green parts, chopped
- ¼ cup plain Greek yogurt
- 1 tablespoon freshly squeezed lemon juice
- ½ teaspoon fresh thyme, chopped
- Pinch of salt
- Pinch of ground black pepper
- 4 multigrain tortillas

Directions:
1. Take a medium bowl and mix in chicken, red bell pepper, cucumber, carrot, yogurt, scallion, lemon juice, thyme, sea salt, and pepper
2. Mix well
3. Spoon one-quarter of the chicken mixture into the middle of the tortilla and fold opposite ends of the tortilla over the filling
4. Roll tortilla from side to create a snug pocket
5. Repeat with the remaining ingredients and serve
6. Enjoy!

Chilled Chicken Artichoke And Zucchini Salad

Serving: 4
Preparation Time: 10 minutes
Cooking Time: 5 minutes
Ingredients
- 2 medium chicken breasts, cooked and cut into 1-inch cubes
- ¼ cup extra virgin olive oil
- 2 cups artichoke hearts, drained and roughly chopped
- 3 large zucchini, diced/cut into small rounds
- 1 can (15 ounces) of chickpeas
- 1 cup Kalamata olives
- ½ teaspoon Fresh ground black pepper
- ½ teaspoon Italian seasoning
- ¼ cup parmesan, grated

Directions:
1. Take a large skillet and place it over medium heat; heat up olive oil
2. Add zucchini and Saute for 5 minutes; season with salt and pepper
3. Remove from heat and add all the listed ingredients to the skillet
4. Stir until combined
5. Transfer to glass container and store
6. Serve and enjoy!

White Bean Soup And Swiss Chard

Serving: 4
Preparation Time: 15 minutes
Cooking Time: 30 minutes
Ingredients
- 1 teaspoon extra virgin olive oil
- 2 celery stalks, diced
- 1 sweet onion, peeled and chopped
- 2 teaspoons garlic, minced
- 6 cups vegetable broth
- 1 can (15 ounces) sodium-free Great Northern beans, drained and rinsed
- 1 cup tomato, diced
- 2 carrots, peeled and diced
- 2 cups Swiss chard, shredded
- 1 cup green beans, cut into 1-inch piece
- ¼ teaspoon red pepper flakes
- Sea salt
- Freshly ground black pepper

Directions:
1. Take a medium stock and place it over medium-high heat
2. Add olive oil and heat it up
3. Add celery, onion, and garlic
4. Saute for 5 minutes
5. Stir in stock, tomato, beans, and carrots, and bring to a boil
6. Reduce heat to low and simmer for 15 minutes until the carrots are tender
7. Add Swiss chard, red pepper flakes, and green beans
8. Simmer for 5 minutes
9. Season the soup with sea salt, pepper and serve
10. Enjoy!

Pure Kidney Beans And Cilantro Salad

Serving: 6
Preparation Time: 5 minutes
Cooking Time: nil
Ingredients
- 1 can (15 ounces) of kidney beans, drained and rinsed
- ½ English Cucumber, chopped
- 1 medium heirloom tomato chopped
- 1 bunch fresh cilantro, stems removed and chopped
- 1 red onion, chopped
- Juice of 1 large lime
- 3 tablespoons Dijon mustard
- ½ teaspoon fresh garlic paste
- 1 teaspoon Sumac
- Salt and pepper as needed

Directions:
1. Take a medium-sized bowl and add Kidney beans, chopped-up veggies, and cilantro
2. Take a small bowl and make the vinaigrette by adding lime juice, oil, fresh garlic, pepper, mustard, and sumac
3. Pour the vinaigrette over the salad and give it a gentle stir
4. Add some salt and pepper
5. Cover it up and allow it to chill for half an hour
6. Serve!

Chapter 13

Dinner

Cauliflower Mash
Preparation time: 30 minutes
Cooking time: 5 minutes
Servings: 4
Ingredients:
- 2 tbsp. butter
- 1/4 c. milk
- 10 oz. cauliflower florets
- 3/4 tsp. salt

Directions:
1. Add water to the saucepan and bring to boil.
2. Reduce the heat and simmer for 10 minutes.
3. Drain the vegetables well. Transfer vegetables, butter, milk, and salt to a blender and blend until smooth.
4. Serve and enjoy.

French toast in Sticks
Preparation time: 5 minutes
Cooking time: 10 minutes
Servings: 4
Ingredients:
- 4 slices of white bread, 38 mm. thick, preferably hard
- 2 eggs
- 60 ml of milk
- 15 ml maple sauce
- 2 ml vanilla extract
- Nonstick spray oil
- 38 g of sugar
- 3 g. ground cinnamon
- Maple syrup, to serve
- Powdered sugar to sprinkle

Directions:
1. Cut each slice of bread into thirds making 12 pieces. Place sideways
2. Beat the eggs, milk, maple syrup, and vanilla.
3. Preheat the air fryer, set it to 175 °C.
4. Dip the sliced bread into the egg mixture and place it in the preheated air fryer. Sprinkle French toast generously with oil spray.
5. Cook French toast for 10 minutes at 175 °C. Turn the toast halfway through cooking.
6. Mix the sugar and cinnamon in a bowl.
7. Cover the French toast with the sugar and cinnamon mixture when you have finished cooking.
8. Serve with maple syrup and sprinkle with powdered sugar

Misto Quente
Preparation time: 5 minutes
Cooking time: 10 minutes
Servings: 4
Ingredients:
- 4 slices of bread without shell
- 4 slices of turkey breast
- 4 slices of cheese
- 2 tbsp. cream cheese
- 2 spoons of butter

Directions:
1. Preheat the air fryer. Set the timer of 5 minutes and the temperature to 200 °C.
2. Pass the butter on one side of the slice of bread, and on the other side of the slice, the cream cheese.
3. Mount the sandwiches placing 2 slices of turkey breast and 2 slices of cheese between the bread, with the cream cheese inside and the side with butter.
4. Place the sandwiches in the basket of the air fryer. Set the timer of the air fryer for 5 minutes and press the power button.

Seared Tuna Steak
Preparation time: 10 minutes
Cooking time: 10 minutes
Servings: 2
Ingredients:
- 1 tsp. sesame seeds
- 1 tbsp. sesame oil
- 2 tbsp. soya sauce
- Salt and pepper, to taste
- 2 (6 oz.) ahi tuna steaks

Directions:
1. Seasoning the tuna steaks with salt and pepper. Keep it aside on a shallow bowl.
2. In another bowl, mix soya sauce and sesame oil.
3. Pour the sauce over the salmon and coat them generously with the sauce.
4. Keep it aside for 10–15 minutes and then heat a large skillet over medium heat.
5. Once hot, keep the tuna steaks and cook them for 3 minutes or until seared underneath.
6. Flip the fillets and cook them for a further 3 minutes.
7. Transfer the seared tuna steaks to the serving plate and slice them into 1/2-in. slices. Top with sesame seeds.

Vegetable Soup
Preparation time: 10 minutes
Cooking time: 30 minutes
Servings: 5
Ingredients:
- 8 c. vegetable broth
- 2 tbsp. olive oil
- 1 tbsp. Italian seasoning
- 1 onion, large and diced

- 2 bay leaves, dried
- 2 bell peppers, large and diced
- Sea salt and black pepper, as needed
- 4 cloves of garlic, minced
- 28 oz. tomatoes, diced
- 1 cauliflower head, medium and torn into florets
- 2 c. green beans, trimmed and chopped

Directions:
1. Heat oil in a Dutch oven over medium heat.
2. Once the oil becomes hot, stir in the onions and pepper.
3. Cook for 10 minutes or until the onion is softened and browned.
4. Spoon in the garlic and sauté for a minute or until fragrant.
5. Add all the remaining Ingredients: to it. Mix until everything comes together.
6. Bring the mixture to a boil. Lower the heat and cook for further 20 minutes or until the vegetables have softened.
7. Serve hot.

Pork Chop Diane

Preparation time: 10 minutes
Cooking time: 20 minutes
Servings: 4
Ingredients:
- 1/4 c. low-sodium chicken broth
- 1 tbsp. freshly squeezed lemon juice
- 2 tsps. Worcestershire sauce
- 2 tsps. Dijon mustard
- 4 (5-oz.) boneless pork top loin chops
- 1 tsp. extra-virgin olive oil
- 1 tsp. lemon zest
- 1 tsp. butter
- 2 tsps. Chopped fresh chives

Directions:
1. Blend together the chicken broth, lemon juice, Worcestershire sauce, and Dijon mustard and set it aside.
2. Season the pork chops lightly.
3. Situate a large skillet over medium-high heat and add the olive oil.
4. Cook the pork chops, turning once, until they are no longer pink, about 8 minutes per side.
5. Put aside the chops.
6. Pour the broth mixture into the skillet and cook until warmed through and thickened, about 2 minutes. Blend lemon zest, butter, and chives.
7. Garnish with a generous spoonful of sauce.

Autumn Pork Chops with Red Cabbage and Apples

Preparation time: 15 minutes
Cooking time: 30 minutes
Servings: 4
Ingredients:
- 1/4 c. apple cider vinegar
- 2 tbsps. Granulated sweetener
- 4 (4-oz.) pork chops, about 1 in. thick
- 1 tbsp. extra-virgin olive oil
- 1/2 red cabbage, finely shredded
- 1 sweet onion, thinly sliced
- 1 apple, peeled, cored, and sliced
- 1 tsp. chopped fresh thyme
- Salt and pepper, to taste

Directions:
1. Mix vinegar and sweetener. Set it aside.
2. Season the pork with salt and pepper.
3. Position a big skillet over medium-high heat and add the olive oil.
4. Cook the pork chops until no longer pink, turning once, about 8 minutes per side.
5. Put chops aside.
6. Add the cabbage and onion to the skillet and sauté until the vegetables have softened, for about 5 minutes.
7. Add the vinegar mixture and the apple slices to the skillet and bring the mixture to a boil.
8. Adjust heat to low and simmer, covered, for 5 additional minutes.
9. Return the pork chops to the skillet, along with any accumulated juices and thyme, cover, and cook for 5 more minutes.

Chipotle Chili Pork Chops

Preparation time: 4 hours
Cooking time: 20 minutes
Servings: 4
Ingredients:
- Juice and zest of 1 lime
- 1 tbsp. extra-virgin olive oil
- 1 tbsp. chipotle chili powder
- 2 tsps. Minced garlic
- 1 tsp. ground cinnamon
- Pinch sea salt
- 4 (5-oz.) pork chops
- Lime wedges

Directions:
1. Combine the lime juice and zest, oil, chipotle chili powder, garlic, cinnamon, and salt in a resealable plastic bag. Add the pork chops. Remove as much air as possible and seal the bag.
2. Marinate the chops in the refrigerator for at least 4 hours, and up to 24 hours, turning them several times.
3. Ready the oven to 400 °F and set a rack on a baking sheet. Let the chops rest at room temperature for 15 minutes, then arrange them on the rack and discard the remaining marinade.
4. Roast the chops until cooked through, turning once, about 10 minutes per side.
5. Serve with lime wedges.

Orange-Marinated Pork Tenderloin

Preparation time: 2 hours
Cooking time: 30 minutes
Servings: 4
Ingredients:
- 1/4 c. freshly squeezed orange juice
- 2 tsps. Orange zest
- 2 tsps. Minced garlic
- 1 tsp. low-sodium soy sauce
- 1 tsp. grated fresh ginger
- 1 tsp. honey
- 1 1/2 lbs. pork tenderloin roast
- 1 tbsp. extra-virgin olive oil

Directions:
1. Blend together the orange juice, zest, garlic, soy sauce, ginger, and honey.
2. Pour the marinade into a resealable plastic bag and add the pork tenderloin.
3. Remove as much air as possible and seal the bag. Marinate the pork in the refrigerator, turning the bag a few times, for 2 hours.
4. Preheat the oven to 400 °F.
5. Pull out tenderloin from the marinade and discard the marinade.
6. Position big ovenproof skillet over medium-high heat and add the oil.
7. Sear the pork tenderloin on all sides, about 5 minutes in total.
8. Position skillet to the oven and roast for 25 minutes.
9. Put aside for 10 minutes before serving.

Homestyle Herb Meatballs

Preparation time: 10 minutes
Cooking time: 15 minutes
Servings: 4
Ingredients:
- 1/2-lb. lean ground pork
- 1/2-lb. lean ground beef
- 1 sweet onion, finely chopped
- 1/4 c. bread crumbs
- 2 tbsps. Chopped fresh basil
- 2 tsps. Minced garlic
- 1 egg
- Salt and pepper, to taste

Directions:
1. Preheat the oven to 350 °F.
2. Prepare a baking tray with parchment paper and set it aside.
3. In a large bowl, mix together the pork, beef, onion, bread crumbs, basil, garlic, egg, salt, and pepper until very well mixed.
4. Roll the meat mixture into 2-in. meatballs.
5. Transfer the meatballs to the baking sheet and bake until they are browned and cooked through, about 15 minutes.
6. Serve the meatballs with your favorite marinara sauce and some steamed green beans.

Lime-Parsley Lamb Cutlets

Preparation time: 4 hours
Cooking time: 10 minutes
Servings: 4
Ingredients:
- 1/4 c. extra-virgin olive oil
- 1/4 c. freshly squeezed lime juice
- 2 tbsps. Lime zest
- 2 tbsps. Chopped fresh parsley
- 12 lamb cutlets (about 1 1/2 lbs. total)
- Salt and pepper, to taste

Directions:
1. Scourge the oil, lime juice, zest, parsley, salt, and pepper.
2. Pour the marinade into a resealable plastic bag.
3. Add the cutlets to the bag and remove as much air as possible before sealing.
4. Marinate the lamb in the refrigerator for about 4 hours, turning the bag several times.
5. Preheat the oven to broil.
6. Remove the chops from the bag and arrange them on an aluminum foil-lined baking sheet. Discard the marinade.
7. Broil the chops for 4 minutes per side for medium doneness. Let the chops rest for 5 minutes before serving.

Beef Chili

Preparation time: 10 minutes
Cooking time: 20 minutes
Servings: 4
Ingredients:
- 1/2 tsp. garlic powder
- 1 tsp. coriander, grounded
- 1 lb. beef, grounded
- 1/2 tsp. sea salt
- 1/2 tsp. cayenne pepper
- 1 tsp. cumin, grounded
- 1/2 tsp. pepper, grounded
- 1/2 c. salsa, low-carb and no-sugar

Directions:
1. Heat a large-sized pan over medium-high heat and cook the beef in it until browned.
2. Stir in all the spices and cook them for 7 minutes or until everything is combined.
3. When the beef gets cooked, spoon in the salsa.
4. Bring the mixture to a simmer and cook for another 8 minutes or until everything comes together.
5. Take it from heat and transfer it to a serving bowl.

Greek Broccoli Salad

Preparation time: 10 minutes
Cooking time: 15 minutes
Servings: 4
Ingredients:
- 1 1/4 lb. broccoli, sliced into small bites
- 1/4 c. almonds, sliced
- 1/3 c. sun-dried tomatoes
- 1/4 c. feta cheese, crumbled
- 1/4 c. red onion, sliced

For the Dressing
- 1/4 c. olive oil
- Dash of red pepper flakes
- 1 garlic clove, minced
- 1/4 tsp. salt
- 2 tbsp. lemon juice
- 1/2 tsp. Dijon mustard
- 1 tsp. low carb sweetener syrup
- 1/2 tsp. oregano, dried

Directions:
1. Mix broccoli, onion, cheese, almonds, and sun-dried tomatoes in a large mixing bowl.
2. In another small-sized bowl, combine all the dressing Ingredients: until emulsified.
3. Spoon the dressing over the broccoli salad.
4. Allow the salad to rest for half an hour before serving.

Mediterranean Steak Sandwiches

Preparation time: 1 hour
Cooking time: 10 minutes
Servings: 4

Ingredients:
- 2 tbsps. Extra-virgin olive oil
- 2 tbsps. Balsamic vinegar
- 2 tsps. Garlic
- 2 tsps. Lemon juice
- 2 tsps. Fresh oregano
- 1 tsp. fresh parsley
- 1-pound flank steak
- 4 whole-wheat pitas
- 2 c. shredded lettuce
- 1 red onion, thinly sliced
- 1 tomato, chopped
- 1 oz. low-sodium feta cheese

Directions:
1. Scourge olive oil, balsamic vinegar, garlic, lemon juice, oregano, and parsley.
2. Add the steak to the bowl, turning to coat it completely.
3. Marinate the steak for 1 hour in the refrigerator, turning it over several times.
4. Preheat the broiler. Line a baking sheet with aluminum foil.
5. Put the steak out of the bowl and discard the marinade. . Situate the steak on the baking sheet and broil for 5 minutes per side for medium. Set aside for 10 minutes before slicing. Stuff the pitas with the sliced steak, lettuce, onion, tomato, and feta.

Roasted Beef with Peppercorn Sauce

Preparation time: 10 minutes
Cooking time: 90 minutes
Servings: 4
Ingredients:
- 1 1/2 lbs. top rump beef roast
- 3 tsps. Extra-virgin olive oil
- 3 shallots, minced
- 2 tsps. Minced garlic
- 1 tbsp. green peppercorns
- 2 tbsps. Dry sherry
- 2 tbsps. All-purpose flour
- 1 c. sodium-free beef broth
- Salt and pepper, to taste

Directions:
1. Heat the oven to 300 °F.
2. Season the roast with salt and pepper.
3. Position a big skillet over medium-high heat and add 2 tsps. Of olive oil.
4. Brown the beef on all sides, about 10 minutes in total, and transfer the roast to a baking dish.
5. Roast until desired doneness, about 1 1/2 hours for medium. When the roast has been in the oven for 1 hour, start the sauce.
6. In a medium saucepan over medium-high heat, sauté the shallots in the remaining 1 tsp of olive oil until translucent, about 4 minutes.
7. Stir in the garlic and peppercorns, and cook for another minute. Whisk in the sherry to deglaze the pan.
8. Whisk in the flour to form a thick paste, cooking for 1 minute and stirring constantly.
9. Fill in the beef broth and whisk for 4 minutes. Season the sauce.
10. Serve the beef with a generous spoonful of sauce.

Coffee-and-Herb-Marinated Steak

Preparation time: 2 hours
Cooking time: 10 minutes
Servings: 3
Ingredients:
- 1/4 c. whole coffee beans
- 2 tsps. Garlic
- 2 tsps. Rosemary
- 2 tsps. Thyme
- 1 tsp. black pepper
- 2 tbsps. Apple cider vinegar
- 2 tbsps. Extra-virgin olive oil
- 1-pound flank steak, trimmed of visible fat

Directions:
1. Place the coffee beans, garlic, rosemary, thyme, and black pepper in a coffee grinder or food processor and pulse until coarsely ground.
2. Transfer the coffee mixture to a resealable plastic bag and add the vinegar and oil. Shake to combine.
3. Add the flank steak and squeeze the excess air out of the bag. Seal it. Marinate the steak in the refrigerator for at least 2 hours, occasionally turning the bag over.
4. Preheat the broiler. Line a baking sheet with aluminum foil.
5. Pull the steak out and discard the marinade.
6. Position steak on the baking sheet and broil until it is done to your liking.
7. Put aside for 10 minutes before cutting it.
8. Serve with your favorite side dish. .

Traditional Beef Stroganoff

Preparation time: 10 minutes
Cooking time: 30 minutes
Servings: 4
Ingredients:
- 1 tsp. extra-virgin olive oil
- 1-lb. top sirloin, cut into thin strips
- 1 c. sliced button mushrooms
- 1/2 sweet onion, finely chopped
- 1 tsp. minced garlic
- 1 tbsp. whole-wheat flour
- 1/2 c. low-sodium beef broth
- 1/4 c. dry sherry
- 1/2 c. fat-free sour cream
- 1 tbsp. chopped fresh parsley
- Salt and pepper, to taste

Directions:
1. Position the skillet over medium-high heat and add the oil.
2. Sauté the beef until browned, about 10 minutes, then remove the beef with a slotted spoon to a plate and set it aside.
3. Add the mushrooms, onion, and garlic to the skillet and sauté until lightly browned, for about 5 minutes.
4. Whisk in the flour and then whisk in the beef broth and sherry.
5. Return the sirloin to the skillet and bring the mixture to a boil.
6. Reduce the heat to low and simmer until the beef is tender, about 10 minutes.

7. Stir in the sour cream and parsley. Season with salt and pepper.

Chicken and Roasted Vegetable Wraps

Preparation time: 10 minutes
Cooking time: 20 minutes
Servings: 4
Ingredients:
- 1/2 small eggplant
- 1 red bell pepper
- 1 medium zucchini
- 1/2 small red onion, sliced
- 1 tbsp. extra-virgin olive oil
- 2 (8-oz.) cooked chicken breasts, sliced
- 4 whole-wheat tortilla wraps
- Salt and pepper, to taste

Directions:
1. Preheat the oven to 400 °F.
2. Wrap a baking sheet with foil and set it aside.
3. In a large bowl, toss the eggplant, bell pepper, zucchini, and red onion with olive oil.
4. Transfer the vegetables to the baking sheet and lightly season with salt and pepper.
5. Roast the vegetables until soft and slightly charred, about 20 minutes.
6. Divide the vegetables and chicken into four portions.
7. Wrap 1 tortilla around each portion of chicken and grilled vegetables, and serve.

Spicy Chicken Cacciatore

Preparation time: 20 minutes
Cooking time: 1 hour
Servings: 6
Ingredients:
- 1 (2-lb.) chicken
- 1/4 c. all-purpose flour
- 2 tbsps. Extra-virgin olive oil
- 3 slices bacon
- 1 sweet onion
- 2 tsps. Minced garlic
- 4 oz. button mushrooms, halved
- 1 (28-oz.) can of low-sodium stewed tomatoes
- 1/2 c. red wine
- 2 tsps. Chopped fresh oregano
- 2 tsps. Red pepper flakes
- Salt and pepper, to taste

Directions:
1. Cut the chicken into pieces 2 drumsticks, 2 thighs, 2 wings, and 4 breast pieces.
2. Dredge the chicken pieces in the flour and season each piece with salt and pepper.
3. Place a large skillet over medium-high heat and add the olive oil.
4. Brown the chicken pieces on all sides, about 20 minutes in total. Transfer the chicken to a plate.
5. Cook the chopped bacon in the skillet for 5 minutes. With a slotted spoon, transfer the cooked bacon to the same plate as the chicken.
6. Pour off most of the oil from the skillet, leaving just a light coating. Sauté the onion, garlic, and mushrooms in the skillet until tender, about 4 minutes.
7. Stir in the tomatoes, wine, oregano, and red pepper flakes.
8. Bring the sauce to a boil. Return the chicken and bacon, plus any accumulated juices from the plate, to the skillet.
9. Reduce the heat to low and simmer until the chicken is tender, about 30 minutes.

Scallion Sandwich

Preparation time: 10 minutes
Cooking time: 10 minutes
Servings: 1
Ingredients:
- 2 slices wheat bread
- 2 tsps. Butter, low-fat
- 2 scallions, sliced thinly
- 1 tbsp. of parmesan cheese, grated
- 3/4 c of cheddar cheese, reduced-fat, grated

Directions:
1. Preheat the Air fryer to 356 °F.
2. Spread butter on a slice of bread. Place inside the cooking basket with the butter side facing down.
3. Place cheese and scallions on top. Spread the rest of the butter on the other slice of bread Put it on top of the sandwich and sprinkle it with parmesan cheese.
4. Cook for 10 minutes.

Cheesy Cauliflower Gratin

Preparation time: 5 minutes
Cooking time: 25 minutes
Servings: 6
Ingredients:
- 6 deli slices pepper jack cheese
- 4 c. cauliflower florets
- Salt and pepper, as needed
- 4 tbsp. butter
- 1/3 c. heavy whipping cream

Directions:
1. Mix the cauliflower, cream, butter, salt, and pepper in a safe microwave bowl and combine well.
2. Microwave the cauliflower mixture for 25 minutes on high until it becomes soft and tender.
3. Remove the Ingredients: from the bowl and mash with the help of a fork.
4. Taste for seasonings and spoon in salt and pepper as required.
5. Arrange the slices of Pepper Jack cheese on top of the cauliflower mixture and microwave for 3 minutes until the cheese starts melting.
6. Serve warm.

Strawberry Spinach Salad

Preparation time: 5 minutes
Cooking time: 10 minutes
Servings: 4
Ingredients:
- 4 oz. feta cheese, crumbled
- 8 strawberries, sliced
- 2 oz. almonds
- 6 slices bacon, thick-cut, crispy, and crumbled

- 10 oz. spinach leaves, fresh
- 2 Roma tomatoes, diced
- 2 oz. red onion, sliced thinly

Directions:
1. For making this healthy salad, mix all the Ingredients: needed to make the salad in a large-sized bowl and toss them well.

Garlic Bread

Preparation time: 10 minutes
Cooking time: 15 minutes
Servings: 4–5
Ingredients:
- 2 stale French rolls
- 4 tbsp. crushed or crumpled garlic
- 1 c of mayonnaise
- Powdered grated Parmesan
- 1 tbsp. olive oil

Directions:
1. Preheat the air fryer. Set the time of 5 minutes and the temperature to 200 °C.
2. Mix mayonnaise with garlic and set aside.
3. Cut the French rolls into slices, but without separating them completely.
4. Fill the cavities of equals. Brush with olive oil and sprinkle with grated cheese.
5. Place in the basket of the air fryer. Set the timer to 10 minutes, adjust the temperature to 180 °C, and press the power button.

Bruschetta

Preparation time: 5 minutes
Cooking time: 10 minutes
Servings: 2
Ingredients:
- 4 slices of Italian bread
- 1 c. chopped tomato tea
- 1 c. grated mozzarella tea
- Olive oil
- Oregano, salt, and pepper
- 4 fresh basil leaves

Directions:
1. Preheat the air fryer. Set the timer of 5 minutes and the temperature to 200 °C.
2. Sprinkle the slices of Italian bread with olive oil. Divide the chopped tomatoes and mozzarella between the slices. Season with salt, pepper, and oregano.
3. Put oil in the filling. Place a basil leaf on top of each slice.
4. Put the bruschetta in the basket of the air fryer being careful not to spill the filling. Set the timer of 5 minutes, set the temperature to 180 °C, and press the power button.
5. Transfer the bruschetta to a plate and serve.

Cream Buns with Strawberries

Preparation time: 10 minutes
Cooking time: 12 minutes
Servings: 6
Ingredients:
- 240 g. all-purpose flour
- 50 g. granulated sugar
- 8 g. baking powder
- 1 g of salt
- 85 g. chopped cold butter
- 84 g. chopped fresh strawberries
- 120 ml whipping cream
- 2 large eggs
- 10 ml vanilla extract
- 5 ml of water

Directions:
1. Sift flour, sugar, baking powder, and salt in a large bowl. Put the butter with the flour with the use of a blender or your hands until the mixture resembles thick crumbs.
2. Mix the strawberries in the flour mixture. Set aside for the mixture to stand. Beat the whipping cream, 1 egg, and the vanilla extract in a separate bowl.
3. Put the cream mixture in the flour mixture until they are homogeneous, and then spread the mixture to a thickness of 38 mm.
4. Use a round cookie cutter to cut the buns. Spread the buns with a combination of egg and water. Set aside
5. Preheat the air fryer, set it to 180 °C.
6. Place baking paper in the preheated inner basket.
7. Place the buns on top of the baking paper and cook for 12 minutes at 180 °C, until golden brown.

Blueberry Buns

Preparation time: 10 minutes
Cooking time: 12 minutes
Servings: 6
Ingredients:
- 240 g. all-purpose flour
- 50 g. granulated sugar
- 8 g. baking powder
- 2 g of salt
- 85 g. chopped cold butter
- 85 g of fresh blueberries
- 3 g. grated fresh ginger
- 113 ml whipping cream
- 2 large eggs
- 4 ml vanilla extract
- 5 ml of water

Directions:
1. Put sugar, flour, baking powder, and salt in a large bowl.
2. Put the butter with the flour using a blender or your hands until the mixture resembles thick crumbs.
3. Mix the blueberries and ginger in the flour mixture and set aside
4. Mix the whipping cream, 1 egg, and the vanilla extract in a different container.
5. Put the cream mixture with the flour mixture until combined.
6. Shape the dough until it reaches a thickness of approximately 38 mm and cut it into eighths.
7. Spread the buns with a combination of egg and water. Set aside.
8. Preheat the air fryer to 180 °C.
9. Place baking paper in the preheated inner basket and place the buns on top of the paper. Cook for 12 minutes at 180 °C, until golden brown

Lean Lamb and Turkey Meatballs with Yogurt

Preparation time: 10 minutes
Servings: 4
Cooking time: 8 minutes
Ingredients:
For the Meatballs
- 1 egg white
- 4 oz. ground lean turkey
- 1 lb. of ground lean lamb
- 1 tsp. each of cayenne pepper, ground coriander, red chili pastes, salt, and ground cumin
- 2 garlic cloves, minced
- 1 1/2 tbsps. Parsley, chopped
- 1 tbsp. mint, chopped
- 1/4 c of olive oil

For the Yogurt
- 2 tbsps. Of buttermilk
- 1 garlic clove, minced
- 1/4 c. mint, chopped
- 1/2 c of Greek yogurt, non-fat
- Salt to taste

Directions:
1. Set the air fryer to 390 °F.
2. Mix all the Ingredients: for the meatballs in a bowl. Roll and mold them into golf-size round pieces. Arrange in the cooking basket. Cook for 8 minutes.
3. While waiting, combine all the ingredients: for the mint yogurt in a bowl. Mix well.
4. Serve the meatballs with mint yogurt. Top with olives and fresh mint.

Air Fried Section and Tomato

Preparation time: 10 minutes
Cooking time: 5 minutes
Servings: 2
Ingredients:
- 1 aubergine, sliced thickly into 4 disks
- 1 tomato, sliced into 2 thick disks
- 2 tsp. feta cheese, reduced fat
- 2 fresh basil leaves, minced
- 2 balls, small buffalo mozzarella, reduced fat, torn
- Pinch of salt
- Pinch of black pepper

Directions:
1. Preheat air fryer to 330 °F.
2. Spray a small amount of oil into the air fryer basket. Fry the aubergine slices for 5 minutes or until golden brown on both sides. Transfer to a plate.
3. Fry tomato slices in batches for 5 minutes or until seared on both sides.
4. To serve, stack salad starting with an aborigine base, buffalo mozzarella, basil leaves, tomato slice, and 1/2-teaspoon feta cheese.
5. Top of with another slice of aborigine and 1/2 tsp. feta cheese. Serve.

Cheesy Salmon Fillets

Preparation time: 15 minutes
Cooking time: 20 minutes
Servings: 2–3
Ingredients:
For the Salmon Fillets
- 2 pieces, 4 oz. each salmon fillets, choose even cuts
- 1/2 c. sour cream, reduced fat
- 1/4 c. cottage cheese, reduced fat
- 1/4 c. Parmigiano-Reggiano cheese, freshly grated

For the Garnish
- Spanish paprika
- 1/2-piece lemon, cut into wedges

Directions:
1. Preheat the air fryer to 330 °F.
2. To make the salmon fillets, mix sour cream, cottage cheese, and Parmigiano-Reggiano cheese in a bowl.
3. Layer salmon fillets in the Air fryer basket. Fry for 20 minutes or until cheese turns golden brown.
4. To assemble, place a salmon fillet and sprinkle paprika. Garnish with lemon wedges and squeeze lemon juice on top. Serve.

Salmon with Asparagus

Preparation time: 5 minutes
Cooking time: 10 minutes
Servings: 3
Ingredients:
- 1 lb. salmon, sliced into fillets
- 1 tbsp. olive oil
- Salt and pepper, as needed
- 2 cloves of garlic, minced
- Zest and juice of 1/2 lemon
- 1 tbsp. butter, salted

Directions:
1. Spoon in the butter and olive oil into a large pan and heat it over medium-high heat.
2. Once it becomes hot, place the salmon and season it with salt and pepper.
3. Cook for 4 minutes per side and then cook the other side.
4. Stir in the garlic and lemon zest to it.
5. Cook for further 2 minutes or until slightly browned.
6. Off the heat and squeeze the lemon juice over it.
7. Serve it hot.

Shrimp in Garlic Butter

Preparation time: 5 minutes
Cooking time: 20 minutes
Servings: 4
Ingredients:
- 1 lb. shrimp, peeled and deveined
- 1/4 tsp. red pepper flakes
- 6 tbsp. butter, divided
- 1/2 c. chicken stock
- Salt and pepper, as needed
- 2 tbsp. parsley, minced
- 5 cloves of garlic, minced
- 2 tbsp. lemon juice

Directions:
1. Heat a large, bottomed skillet over medium-high heat.
2. Spoon in 2 tbsps. Of the butter and melt it. Add the shrimp.

3. Season it with salt and pepper. Sear for 4 minutes or until shrimp gets cooked.
4. Transfer the shrimp to a plate and stir in the garlic.
5. Sauté for 30 seconds or until aromatic.
6. Pour the chicken stock and whisk it well. Allow it to simmer for 5–10 minutes or until it has reduced to half.
7. Spoon the remaining butter, red pepper, and lemon juice into the sauce. Mix.
8. Continue cooking for another 2 minutes.
9. Take off the pan from the heat and add the cooked shrimp to it.
10. Garnish with parsley and transfer to the serving bowl.
11. Enjoy.

Cauliflower Mac and Cheese

Preparation time: 5 minutes
Cooking time: 25 minutes
Servings: 4
Ingredients:
- 1 cauliflower head, torn into florets
- Salt and black pepper, as needed
- 1/4 c. almond milk, unsweetened
- 1/4 c. heavy cream
- 3 tbsp. butter, preferably grass-fed
- 1 c. cheddar cheese, shredded

Directions:
1. Preheat the oven to 450 °F.
2. Melt the butter in a small microwave-safe bowl and heat it for 30 seconds.
3. Pour the melted butter over the cauliflower florets along with salt and pepper. Toss them well.
4. Place the cauliflower florets in a parchment paper-covered large baking sheet.
5. Bake them for 15 minutes or until the cauliflower is crisp-tender.
6. Once baked, mix the heavy cream, cheddar cheese, almond milk, and the remaining butter in a large microwave-safe bowl and heat it on high heat for 2 minutes or until the cheese mixture is smooth. Repeat the procedure until the cheese has melted.
7. Finally, stir in the cauliflower to the sauce mixture and coat well.

Easy Egg Salad

Preparation time: 5 minutes
Cooking time: 15–20 minutes
Servings: 4
Ingredients:
- 6 eggs, preferably free-range
- 1/4 tsp. salt
- 2 tbsp. mayonnaise
- 1 tsp. lemon juice
- 1 tsp. Dijon mustard
- Pepper, to taste
- Lettuce leaves, to serve

Directions:
1. Keep the eggs in a saucepan of water and pour cold water until it covers the egg by another 1 in.
2. Bring to a boil and then remove the eggs from heat.
3. Peel the eggs under cold running water.
4. Transfer the cooked eggs into a food processor and pulse them until chopped.
5. Stir in the mayonnaise, lemon juice, salt, Dijon mustard, pepper and mix them well.
6. Taste for seasoning and add more if required.
7. Serve in the lettuce leaves.

Baked Chicken Legs

Preparation time: 10 minutes
Cooking time: 40 minutes
Servings: 6
Ingredients:
- 6 chicken legs
- 1/4 tsp. black pepper
- 1/4 c. butter
- 1/2 tsp. sea salt
- 1/2 tsp. smoked paprika
- 1/2 tsp. garlic powder

Directions:
1. Preheat the oven to 425 °F.
2. Pat the chicken legs with a paper towel to absorb any excess moisture.
3. Marinate the chicken pieces by first applying the butter over them and then with the seasoning. Set it aside for a few minutes.
4. Bake them for 25 minutes. Turnover and bake for further 10 minutes or until the internal temperature reaches 165 °F.
5. Serve them hot.

Creamed Spinach

Preparation time: 5 minutes
Cooking time: 10 minutes
Servings: 4
Ingredients:
- 3 tbsp. butter
- 1/4 tsp. black pepper
- 4 cloves of garlic, minced
- 1/4 tsp. sea salt
- 10 oz. baby spinach, chopped
- 1 tsp. Italian seasoning
- 1/2 c. heavy cream
- 3 oz. cream cheese

Directions:
1. Melt butter in a large sauté pan over medium heat.
2. Once the butter has melted, spoon in the garlic and sauté for 30 seconds or until aromatic.
3. Spoon in the spinach and cook for 3–4 minutes or until wilted.
4. Add all the remaining Ingredients: to it and continuously stir until the cream cheese melts and the mixture gets thickened. Serve hot.

Stuffed Mushrooms

Preparation time: 10 minutes
Cooking time: 20 minutes
Servings: 4
Ingredients:
- 4 portobello mushrooms, large
- 1/2 c. mozzarella cheese, shredded
- 1/2 c. marinara, low sugar
- Olive oil spray

Directions:
1. Preheat the oven to 375 °F.
2. Take out the dark gills from the mushrooms with the help of a spoon.
3. Keep the mushroom stem upside down and spoon it with 2 tbsps. Of marinara sauce and mozzarella cheese.
4. Bake for 18 minutes or until the cheese is bubbly.

Cobb Salad

Preparation time: 5 minutes
Cooking time: 5 minutes
Servings: 1
Ingredients:
- 4 cherry tomatoes, chopped
- 1/4 c. bacon, cooked and crumbled
- 1/2 of 1 avocado, chopped
- 2 oz. chicken breast, shredded
- 1 egg, hardboiled
- 2 c. mixed green salad
- 1 oz. feta cheese, crumbled

Directions:
1. Toss all the Ingredients: for the cobb salad in a large mixing bowl and toss well.
2. Serve and enjoy it.

Muffins Sandwich

Preparation time: 2 minutes
Cooking time: 10 minutes
Servings: 1
Ingredients:
- Nonstick spray oil
- 1 slice of white cheddar cheese
- 1 slice of Canadian bacon
- 1 English muffin, divided
- 15 ml. hot water
- 1 large egg
- Salt and pepper to taste

Directions:
1. Spray the inside of an 85 g. mold with oil spray and place it in the air fryer.
2. Preheat the air fryer, set it to 160 °C.
3. Add the cheese and Canadian bacon to the preheated air fryer.
4. Pour the hot water and the egg into the hot pan and season with salt and pepper.
5. Select Bread, set to 10 minutes.
6. Take out the English muffins after 7 minutes, leaving the egg for the full time.
7. Build your sandwich by placing the cooked egg on top of the English muffing and serve

Bacon BBQ

Preparation time: 2 minutes
Cooking time: 8 minutes
Servings: 2
Ingredients:
- 13 g. dark brown sugar
- 5 g. chili powder
- 1 g. ground cumin
- 1 g. cayenne pepper
- 4 slices of bacon, cut in half

Directions:
1. Mix seasonings until well combined.
2. Dip the bacon in the dressing until it is completely covered. Leave aside.
3. Preheat the air fryer, set it to 160 °C.
4. Place the bacon in the preheated air fryer
5. Select Bacon and press Start/Pause.

The All-Time Favorite Tomato And Basil Soup

Servings: 4
Preparation Time: 10 minutes
Cooking Time: 15 minutes
Ingredients:
- 14.5 ounces tomatoes, diced
- 2 ounces cream cheese
- ¼ cup heavy whipping cream
- ¼ cup basil, fresh and chopped
- 4 tablespoons butter

Directions:
1. Add tomatoes into a blender, alongside juices, and puree until smooth
2. Take a saucepan and place it over medium heat; add tomato puree, heavy cream, butter, and cream cheese, and cook for 10 minutes
3. Add basil, season as desired, and cook for 5 minutes more
4. Use an immersion blender to blend the mixture
5. Serve and enjoy!

Healthy Lamb Stew

Servings: 4
Preparation Time: 10 minutes
Cooking Time: 3 hours
Ingredients:
- 1 onion, peeled and chopped
- 3 carrots, peeled and chopped
- 2 pounds lamb, cubed
- 1 tomato, cored and chopped
- 1 garlic clove, peeled and minced
- 2 tablespoons butter
- 1 cup beef stock
- 1 cup white wine
- Salt and pepper to taste
- 2 rosemary sprigs
- 1 teaspoon fresh thyme, chopped

Directions:
1. Heat up the Dutch oven over medium-high heat
2. Add oil and let it heat up
3. Add lamb, salt, pepper, and brown all sides
4. Transfer to plate
5. Add onion to Dutch oven and cook for 2 minutes
6. Add carrots, tomato, garlic, butter stick, wine, salt, pepper, rosemary, and thyme, and stir for a few minutes
7. Return lamb to Dutch Oven and cook for 4 hours
8. Discard rosemary sprigs
9. Add more salt and pepper, and stir
10. Divide between bowls

11. Serve and enjoy!

Hearty Chicken Liver Stew

Servings: 2
Preparation Time: 10 minutes
Cooking Time: Nil
Ingredients:
- 10 ounces of chicken livers
- 1-ounce onion, chopped
- 2 ounces sour cream
- 1 tablespoon olive oil
- Salt to taste

Directions:
1. Take a pan and place it over medium heat
2. Add oil and let it heat up
3. Add onions and fry until just browned
4. Add livers and season with salt
5. Cook until livers are half cooked
6. Transfer the mix to a stew pot
7. Add sour cream and cook for 20 minutes
8. Serve and enjoy!

Tender Slow Cooked Ham Stew

Servings: 4
Preparation Time: 10 minutes
Cooking Time: 4 hours
Ingredients:
- 8 ounces cheddar cheese, grated
- 14 ounces of chicken stock
- ½ teaspoon garlic powder
- Salt and pepper to taste
- 4 garlic cloves, peeled and minced
- ¼ cup heavy cream
- 3 cups ham, chopped
- 16 ounces cauliflower florets
- 1 cup carrot, sliced into thin rings

Directions:
1. Add ham, stock, cheese, cauliflower, garlic powder, onion powder, salt, pepper, garlic, carrot, and heavy cream to Slow Cooker
2. Stir well
3. Place lid and cook on HIGH for 4 hours
4. Stir and divide between bowls
5. Serve and enjoy!

Loving Cauliflower Soup

Servings: 6
Preparation Time: 10 minutes
Cooking Time: 10 minutes
Ingredients:
- 4 cups vegetable stock
- 1 pound cauliflower, trimmed and chopped
- 7 ounces cream cheese
- 4 ounces butter
- Salt and pepper to taste

Directions:
1. Take a skillet and place it over medium heat
2. Add butter and melt
3. Add cauliflower and Saute for 2 minutes
4. Add stock and bring the mix to a boil
5. Cook until Cauliflower is Al-Dente
6. Stir in cream cheese, salt, and pepper
7. Puree the mix using an immersion blender
8. Serve and enjoy!

Pork Sausage And Pepper Stew

Servings: 2
Preparation Time: 10 minutes
Cooking Time: 45 minutes
Ingredients:
- 32-ounce pork sausages
- 1 tablespoon olive oil
- 10-ounce raw spinach
- 1 medium Green Bell Pepper
- 1 can of jalapenos with tomatoes
- 4 cup beef stock
- 1 tablespoon of chili powder
- 1 tablespoon of cumin
- 1 teaspoon of garlic powder
- 1 teaspoon of Italian seasoning
- ¾ teaspoon of salt

Directions:
1. Take a large-sized pot and place it over medium heat
2. Add olive oil and allow the oil to heat up
3. Add sausages and cook until seared all around
4. Slice the green pepper into small pieces and add to the pot
5. Season with pepper and salt
6. Add tomatoes and jalapenos and stir
7. Add spinach on top and cover with a lid; wait until the spinach has wilted
8. Add the remaining spice and broth
9. Allow it to cook for 30 minutes over medium-low heat
10. Remove the lid and simmer for 15 minutes
11. Serve and enjoy!

Simple Garlic And Lemon Soup

Servings: 3
Preparation Time: 10 minutes
Cooking Time: nil
Ingredients:
- 1 avocado, pitted and chopped
- 1 cucumber, chopped
- 2 bunches spinach
- 1 and ½ cups watermelon, chopped
- 1 bunch of cilantro, roughly chopped
- Juice from 2 lemons
- ½ cup coconut aminos
- ½ cup lime juice

Directions:
1. Add cucumber and avocado to your blender and pulse well
2. Add cilantro, spinach, and watermelon and blend
3. Add lemon, lime juice, and coconut amino
4. Pulse a few more times
5. Transfer to a soup bowl and enjoy!

Hearty Parmesan Baked Chicken

Servings: 2
Preparation Time: 5 minutes
Cooking Time: 20 minutes
Ingredients:

- 2 tablespoons ghee
- 2 boneless chicken breasts, skinless
- Pink salt
- Freshly ground black pepper
- ½ cup mayonnaise
- ¼ cup parmesan cheese, grated
- 1 tablespoon dried Italian seasoning
- ¼ cup crushed pork rinds

Directions:
1. Preheat your oven to 425 degrees F
2. Take a large baking dish and coat with ghee
3. Pat chicken breasts dry and wrap with a towel
4. Season with salt and pepper
5. Place in baking dish
6. Take a small bowl and add mayonnaise, parmesan cheese, Italian seasoning
7. Slather mayo mix evenly over chicken breast
8. Sprinkle crushed pork rinds on top
9. Bake for 20 minutes until topping is browned
10. Serve and enjoy!

The Almond Breaded Chicken Goodness

Servings: 3
Preparation Time: 15 minutes
Cooking Time: 15 minutes
Ingredients:
- 2 large chicken breasts, boneless and skinless
- 1/3 cup lemon juice
- 1 and ½ cups seasoned almond meal
- 2 tablespoons coconut oil
- Lemon pepper, to taste
- Parsley for decoration

Directions:
1. Slice chicken breast in half
2. Pound out each half until ¼ inch thick
3. Take a pan and place it over medium heat, add oil, and heat it up
4. Dip each chicken breast slice into lemon juice and let it sit for 2 minutes
5. Turnover and the let the other side sit for 2 minutes as well
6. Transfer to almond meal and coat both sides
7. Add coated chicken to the oil and fry for 4 minutes per side, making sure to sprinkle lemon pepper liberally
8. Transfer to a paper-lined sheet and repeat until all chicken is fried
9. Garnish with parsley, and enjoy!

Brown Butter Duck Breast

Servings: 3
Preparation Time: 5 minutes
Cooking Time: 25 minutes
Ingredients:
- 1 whole 6 ounces duck breast, skin on
- Salt and pepper to taste
- 1 head radicchio, 4 ounces, core removed
- ¼ cup unsalted butter
- 6 fresh sage leaves, sliced

Directions:
1. Preheat your oven to 400 degrees F
2. Pat duck breast dry with a paper towel
3. Season with salt and pepper
4. Place duck breast in skillet and place it over medium heat, sear for 3-4 minutes on each side
5. Turn the breast over and transfer the skillet to the oven
6. Roast for 10 minutes (uncovered)
7. Cut radicchio in half
8. Remove and discard the woody white core and thinly slice the leaves
9. Keep them on the side
10. Remove skillet from oven
11. Transfer duck breast, fat side up, to cutting board and let it rest
12. Re-heat your skillet over medium heat
13. Add Unsalted butter, sage and cook for 3-4 minutes
14. Cut the duck into 6 equal slices
15. Divide radicchio between 2 plates, top with slices of duck breast, and drizzle browned butter and sage
16. Enjoy!

Healthy Chicken Cream Salad

Servings: 3
Preparation Time: 5 minutes
Cooking Time: 50 minutes
Ingredients:
- 2 chicken breasts
- 1 and ½ cups heavy cream
- 3 ounces celery
- 2-ounce green pepper, chopped
- ½ ounce green onion, chopped
- ½ cup Keto-Friendly mayo
- 3 hard-boiled eggs, chopped

Directions:
1. Preheat your oven to 350 degrees F
2. Take a baking sheet and place chicken, cover with cream
3. Bake for 30-40 minutes
4. Take a bowl and mix in chopped celery, peppers, onions
5. Shred the baked chicken
6. Peel and chop hard-boiled eggs
7. Take a large salad bowl and mix in eggs, veggies, and chicken
8. Toss well and serve
9. Enjoy!

BlackBerry Chicken Wings

Servings: 4
Preparation Time: 35 minutes
Cooking Time: 50minutes
Ingredients:
- 3 pounds of chicken wings, about 20 pieces
- ½ cup blackberry chipotle jam
- Salt and pepper to taste
- ½ cup water

Directions:
1. Add water and jam to a bowl and mix well
2. Place chicken wings in a zip bag and add two-thirds of the marinade
3. Season with salt and pepper
4. Let it marinate for 30 minutes
5. Preheat your oven to 400 degrees F

6. Prepare a baking sheet and wire rack, place chicken wings in the wire rack and bake for 15 minutes
7. Brush remaining marinade and bake for 30 minutes more
8. Enjoy!

Hearty Chicken Keto Nuggets

Servings: 2
Preparation Time: 5 minutes
Cooking Time: 10 minutes
Ingredients:
- 1 chicken breast, pre-cooked
- ½ ounce parmesan, grated
- 2 tablespoons almond flour
- ½ teaspoon baking powder
- 1 whole egg
- 1 tablespoon water

Directions:
1. Cut the breast into bite-sized portions
2. Take a bowl and add parmesan, flour, baking powder, water
3. Mix well
4. Cover chicken pieces in the batter
5. Take a skillet and place it over medium heat, add oil and let it heat up
6. Add chicken nuggets and fry until golden brown
7. Serve and enjoy!

Zucchini Zoodles With Chicken and Basil

Servings: 3
Preparation Time: 10 minutes
Cooking Time: 10 minutes
Ingredients:
- 2 chicken fillets, cubed
- 2 tablespoons ghee
- 1 pound of tomatoes, diced
- ½ cup basil, chopped
- ¼ cup coconut milk
- 1 garlic clove, peeled, minced
- 1 zucchini, shredded

Directions:
1. Sauté cubed chicken in ghee until no longer pink
2. Add tomatoes and season with salt
3. Simmer and reduce liquid
4. Prepare your zucchini Zoodles by shredding zucchini in a food processor
5. Add basil, garlic, and coconut milk to the chicken and cook for a few minutes
6. Add half of the zucchini Zoodles to a bowl and top with creamy tomato basil chicken
7. Enjoy!

Salsa Chicken

Servings: 4
Preparation Time: 4 minutes
Cooking Time: 14 minutes
Ingredients:
- 2 chicken breast
- 1 cup salsa
- 1 taco seasoning mix
- 1 cup plain Greek Yogurt
- ½ a cup of cheddar cheese, cubed

Directions:
1. Take a skillet and place it over medium heat
2. Add chicken breast, ½ cup of salsa, and taco seasoning
3. Mix well and cook for 12-15 minutes until the chicken is done
4. Take the chicken out and cube them
5. Place the cubes on a toothpick and top with cheddar
6. Place yogurt and remaining salsa in cups and use as dips
7. Enjoy!

Bacon And Chicken Garlic Wrap

Servings: 4
Preparation Time: 15 minutes
Cooking Time: 10 minutes
Ingredients:
- 1 chicken fillet, cut into small cubes
- 8-9 thin slices of bacon, cut to fit cubes
- 6 garlic cloves, minced

Directions:
1. Preheat your oven to 400 degrees F
2. Line a baking tray with aluminum foil
3. Add minced garlic to a bowl and rub each chicken piece with it
4. Wrap bacon piece around each garlic chicken bite
5. Secure with toothpick
6. Transfer bites to a baking sheet, keeping a little bit of space between them
7. Bake for about 15-20 minutes until crispy
8. Serve and enjoy!

Cheesy Grilled Chicken Platter

Servings: 6
Preparation Time: 5 minutes
Cooking Time: 10 minutes
Ingredients:
- 3 large chicken breast, sliced half lengthwise
- 10-ounce spinach, frozen and drained
- 3-ounce mozzarella cheese, part-skim
- ½ a cup of roasted red peppers, cut into long strips
- 1 teaspoon of olive oil
- 2 garlic cloves, minced
- Salt and pepper as needed

Directions:
1. Preheat your oven to 400 degrees Fahrenheit
2. Slice 3 chicken breasts lengthwise
3. Take a non-stick pan and grease it with cooking spray
4. Bake for 2-3 minutes on each side
5. Take another skillet and cook spinach and garlic in oil for 3 minutes
6. Place chicken on an oven pan and top with spinach, roasted peppers, and mozzarella
7. Bake until the cheese melted
8. Enjoy!

Chicken Parmesan Fingers

Servings: 6
Preparation Time: 15 minutes
Cooking Time: 30 minutes
Ingredients:
- 2 pounds of chicken breast, boneless and skinless

- 4 garlic cloves, peeled and chopped
- 4 ounces clarified butter
- 1 cup fresh parmesan cheese, grated
- 2 tablespoons fresh thyme, chopped
- 1 teaspoon chili pepper flakes
- Salt and pepper to taste

Directions:
1. Preheat your oven to 350 degrees F
2. Coat baking sheet with non-stick cooking spray
3. Take a saucepan and place it over medium heat
4. Add butter and let it melt; swirl the pan well to coat it
5. Stir in garlic and Saute for 15 minutes until fragrant; keep it on the side
6. Take another bowl and add thyme chili pepper, pepper, parmesan, and stir
7. Rinse breast thoroughly and blot it dry with a kitchen towel
8. Slice into 24 fingers and coat in the garlic and butter mix
9. Dredge the fingers in the cheese mix and arrange them on your baking sheet
10. Bake for 25-30 minutes until the fingers are golden brown
11. Transfer them to a cooling rack and allow them to cool

Clean Parsley And Chicken Breast

Servings: 4
Preparation Time: 10 minutes
Cooking Time: 40 minutes
Ingredients:
- 1 tablespoon dry parsley
- 1 tablespoon dry basil
- 4 chicken breast halves, boneless and skinless
- ½ teaspoon salt
- ½ teaspoon red pepper flakes, crushed
- 2 tomatoes, sliced

Directions:
1. Preheat your oven to 350 degrees F
2. Take a 9x13 inch baking dish and grease it up with cooking spray
3. Sprinkle 1 tablespoon of parsley and 1 teaspoon of basil, and spread the mixture over your baking dish
4. Arrange the chicken breast halves over the dish and sprinkle garlic slices on top
5. Add 1 teaspoon parsley, 1 teaspoon of basil, salt, and red pepper, and mix well. Pour the mixture over the chicken breast
6. Top with tomato slices and cover; bake for 25 minutes
7. Remove the cover and bake for 15 minutes more
8. Serve and enjoy!

Creative Lamb Chops

Servings: 3
Preparation Time: 35 minutes
Cooking Time: 5 minutes
Ingredients:
- ¼ cup olive oil
- ¼ cup mint, fresh and chopped
- 8 lamb rib chops
- 1 tablespoon garlic, minced
- 1 tablespoon rosemary, fresh and chopped

Directions:
1. Add rosemary, garlic, mint, and olive oil into a bowl and mix well
2. Keep a tablespoon of the mixture on the side for later use
3. Toss lamb chops into the marinade, letting them marinate for 30 minutes
4. Take a cast-iron skillet and place it over medium-high heat
5. Add lamb and cook for 2 minutes per side for medium-rare
6. Let the lamb rest for a few minutes and drizzle the remaining marinade
7. Serve and enjoy!

Crazy Lamb Salad

Servings: 4
Preparation Time: 10 minutes
Cooking Time: 35 minutes
Ingredients:
- 1 tablespoon olive oil
- 3 pounds leg of lamb, bone removed, leg butterflied
- Salt and pepper to taste
- 1 teaspoon cumin
- Pinch of dried thyme
- 2 garlic cloves, peeled and minced

For Salad
- 4 ounces feta cheese, crumbled
- ½ cup pecans
- 2 cups spinach
- 1 and ½ tablespoons lemon juice
- ¼ cup olive oil
- 1 cup fresh mint, chopped

Directions:
1. Rub lamb with salt and pepper, 1 tablespoon oil, thyme, cumin, minced garlic
2. Preheat your grill to medium-high h and transfer lamb
3. Cook for 40 minutes, making sure to flip it once
4. Take a lined baking sheet and spread pecans
5. Toast in the oven for 10 minutes at 350 degrees F
6. Transfer grilled lamb to cutting board and let it cool
7. Slice
8. Take a salad bowl and add spinach, 1 cup mint, feta cheese, ¼ cup olive oil, lemon juice, toasted pecans, salt, and pepper, and toss well
9. Add lamb slices on top
10. Serve and enjoy!

Healthy Slow-Cooker Lamb Leg

Servings: 6
Preparation Time: 10 minutes
Cooking Time: 8 hours
Ingredients:
- 2 pounds of lamb leg
- Salt and pepper to taste
- 1 tablespoon vanilla bean extract
- 2 tablespoons mustard
- ¼ cup olive oil
- 4 thyme sprigs
- 6 mint leaves
- 1 teaspoon garlic, minced
- Pinch of dried rosemary

Directions:
1. Add oil to your Slow Cooker

2. Add lamb, salt, pepper, vanilla bean extract, mustard, rosemary, and garlic to your Slow Cooker and rub the mixture well
3. Place lid and cook on LOW for 7 hours
4. Add mint and thyme
5. Cook for 1 hour more
6. Let it cool and slice
7. Serve with pan juices
8. Enjoy!

Spicy Paprika Lamb Chops

Servings: 4
Preparation Time: 10 minutes
Cooking Time: 15 minutes
Ingredients:
- 2 lamb racks, cut into chops
- Salt and pepper to taste
- 3 tablespoons paprika
- ¾ cup cumin powder
- 1 teaspoon chili powder

Directions:
1. Take a bowl and add paprika, cumin, chili, salt, pepper, and stir
2. Add lamb chops and rub the mixture
3. Heat grill over medium temperature and add lamb chops; cook for 5 minutes
4. Flip and cook for 5 minutes more; flip again
5. Cook for 2 minutes, flip and cook for 2 minutes more
6. Serve and enjoy!

Simple Lamb Riblets And Mini Pesto

Servings: 4
Preparation Time: 60 minutes
Cooking Time: 120 minutes
Ingredients:
- 1 cup parsley
- 1 cup mint
- 1 and ½ onions, peeled and chopped
- 1/3 cup pistachios
- 1 teaspoon lemon zest
- 5 tablespoons avocado oil
- Salt, to taste
- 2 pounds lamb riblets
- 5 garlic cloves, peeled and minced
- Juice of 1 orange

Directions:
1. Add parsley, mint, 1 onion, pistachios, lemon zest, salt, and avocado oil to the Food processor
2. Rub lamb with a mix
3. Transfer to a bowl and let it refrigerate for 1 hour
4. Transfer lamb to baking dish
5. Add garlic and ½ onion, and drizzle orange juice
6. Bake for 2 hours at 250-degree F
7. Divide between plates and serve
8. Enjoy!

Terrific Jalapeno Bacon Bombs

Servings: 2
Preparation Time: 15 minutes
Cooking Time: 10 minutes
Ingredients:
- 12 large jalapeno peppers
- 16 bacon strips
- 6 ounces of full-fat cream cheese
- 2 teaspoons of garlic powder
- 1 teaspoon of chili powder

Directions:
1. Preheat your oven to 350-degree Fahrenheit
2. Place a wire rack over a roasting pan and keep it on the side
3. Make a slit lengthways across jalapeno pepper and scrape out the seeds, discard them
4. Place a nonstick skillet over high heat and add half of your bacon strip; cook until crispy
5. Drain them
6. Chop the cooked bacon strips and transfer them to a large bowl
7. Add cream cheese and mix
8. Season the cream cheese and bacon mixture with garlic and chili powder
9. Mix well
10. Stuff the mix into the jalapeno peppers and wrap raw bacon strips all around
11. Arrange the stuffed wrapped jalapeno on a prepared wire rack
12. Roast for 10 minutes
13. Transfer to a cooling rack and serve!

Elegant Mushroom Pork Chops

Servings: 3
Preparation Time: 10 minutes
Cooking Time: 40 minutes
Ingredients:
- 8 ounces mushrooms, sliced
- 1 teaspoon garlic
- 1 onion, peeled and chopped
- 1 cup Keto-Friendly Mayonnaise
- 3 pork chops, boneless
- 1 teaspoon ground nutmeg
- 1 tablespoon balsamic vinegar
- ½ cup coconut oil

Directions:
1. Take a pan and place it over medium heat
2. Add oil and let it heat up
3. Add mushrooms and onions and stir
4. Cook for 4 minutes
5. Add pork chops, season with nutmeg and garlic powder, and brown both sides
6. Transfer the pan to the oven and bake for 30 minutes at 350-degree F
7. Transfer pork chops to plates and keep them warm
8. Take a pan and place it over medium heat
9. Add vinegar and mayonnaise over the mushroom mixture and stir for a few minutes
10. Drizzle sauce over pork chops
11. Enjoy!

Lemon And Garlic Pork Platter

Servings: 4
Preparation Time: 10 minutes

Cooking Time: 30 minutes
Ingredients:
- 3 tablespoons butter
- 4 pork steak, bone-in
- 1 cup chicken stock
- Salt and pepper to taste
- Pinch of lemon pepper
- 3 tablespoons coconut oil
- 6 garlic cloves, peeled and minced
- 2 tablespoons fresh parsley, chopped
- 8 ounces mushrooms, chopped
- 1 lemon, sliced

Directions:
1. Take a pan and place it over medium medium-high heat
2. Add 2 tablespoons butter and 2 tablespoons oil, and let it heat up
3. Add pork steaks and season with salt and pepper
4. Cook until browned on both sides
5. Transfer to plate
6. Return the pan to medium heat and add the remaining butter, oil, and half of stock
7. Stir well and cook for 1 minute
8. Add mushrooms, garlic, stir cook for 4 minutes
9. Add lemon slices, remaining stock, salt, pepper, and lemon pepper
10. Stir cook for 5 minutes
11. Return steaks to pan and cook for 10 minutes
12. Divide steak and sauce between serving platters
13. Enjoy!

The Herbal Buttery Pork Chops

Servings: 3
Preparation Time: 5 minutes
Cooking Time: 25 minutes
Ingredients:
- 1 tablespoon butter, divided
- 2 boneless pork chops
- Salt and pepper to taste
- 1 tablespoon dried Italian seasoning
- 1 tablespoon olive oil

Directions:
1. Preheat your oven to 350-degree F
2. Pat pork chops dry with a paper towel and place them in a baking dish
3. Season with salt, pepper, and Italian seasoning
4. Drizzle olive oil over pork chops
5. Top each chop with ½ tablespoon of butter
6. Bake for 25 minutes
7. Transfer pork chops to two plates and top with butter juice
8. Serve and enjoy!

Italian Pork Chops

Servings: 4
Preparation Time: 10 minutes
Cooking Time: 40 minutes
Ingredients:
- 4 pork chops
- 1 tablespoon fresh oregano, chopped
- 2 garlic cloves, peeled and minced
- 1 tablespoon canola oil
- 15 ounces canned tomatoes, diced
- 1 tablespoon tomato paste
- Salt and pepper to taste
- ¼ cup tomato juice

Directions:
1. Heat up a pan with oil over medium-high heat
2. Add pork chops, season with salt and pepper
3. Cook for 3 minutes
4. Flip and cook for 3 minutes more
5. Return the pan to medium heat
6. Add garlic and stir. Cook for 10 seconds
7. Add tomato juice, tomato paste, and tomatoes, bring to a boil, and lower heat to medium-low
8. Add pork chops, stir and cover pan
9. Simmer for 30 minutes
10. Transfer chops to a platter and adds oregano to the pan. Stir cook for 2 minutes
11. Pour over pork chops
12. Serve and enjoy!

Gentle Cheesy Pork Chops

Servings: 4
Preparation Time: 10 minutes
Cooking Time: 20 minutes
Ingredients:
- 3 ounces parmesan cheese
- ½ cup almond flour
- 7 center-cut pork chops
- 1 whole egg
- Bacon grease for frying
- Salt and pepper to taste

Directions:
1. Preheat your oven to 400-degree F
2. Take a bowl and mix in cheese, flour, and seasoning
3. Take another bowl and mix in the egg
4. Dip pork chops in eggs, followed by a dip in the flour/cheese mix
5. Fry in oil for 1-2 minutes on each side (on medium heat)
6. Transfer to a baking dish and bake in the oven until golden brown
7. Enjoy!

Original Caramelized Pork Chops

Servings: 4
Preparation Time: 5 minutes
Cooking Time: 30 minutes
Ingredients:
- 4 pounds chuck roast
- 4 ounces green chili, chopped
- 2 tablespoons chili powder
- ½ teaspoon dried oregano
- ½ teaspoon ground cumin
- 2 garlic cloves, minced
- Salt as needed

Directions:
1. Rub up your chop with 1 teaspoon of pepper and 2 teaspoons of seasoning salt
2. Take a skillet and heat some oil over medium heat
3. Brown your pork chops on each side
4. Add water and onions to the pan

5. Cover it up and lower down the heat; simmer it for about 20 minutes
6. Turn your chops over and add the rest of the pepper and salt
7. Cover it up and cook until the water evaporates and the onions turn to a medium brown texture
8. Remove the chops from your pan and serve with some onions on top!

Simple Pork Stuffed Bell Peppers

Servings: 4
Preparation Time: 10 minutes
Cooking Time: 26 minutes
Ingredients:
- 1 teaspoon Cajun spice
- 1 pound pork, ground
- 1 tablespoon tomato paste
- 6 garlic cloves, minced
- 1 yellow onion, chopped
- 4 big bell peppers, tops cut off and deseeded
- Pinch of salt
- Black pepper as needed
- 1 cup cheddar cheese

Directions:
1. Take a pan and place it over medium-high heat
2. Add oil and let the oil heat up
3. Add garlic and onion and cook for 4 minutes
4. Add meat and gently stir. Cook for 10 minutes
5. Season with salt and pepper according to your desire
6. Add Cajun seasoning and tomato paste
7. Stir cook for 3 minutes more
8. Stuff bell peppers with the mix and transfer to a pre-heated grill; top with cheese
9. Grill for 3 minutes (each side)
10. Divide between plates and serve
11. Enjoy!

Parmesan Pork Steak

Servings: 4
Preparation Time: 10 minutes
Cooking Time: 15 minutes
Ingredients:
- ½ pound pork steak
- Salt and pepper to taste
- 1-ounce parmesan, grated/melted
- 1 tablespoon lemon juice
- 2 tablespoons olive oil

Directions:
1. Beat the pork steak with a kitchen mallet to flatten it a bit
2. Season with salt and pepper
3. Let it rest for a few minutes
4. Take a frying pan and grease it with oil; place it over high heat
5. Once the oil is hot, add steak and cook for 7-8 minutes per side
6. Transfer cooked steak to a plate and drizzle lemon juice
7. Cover with grated parmesan/melted parmesan
8. Serve and enjoy!

Curious Slow-Cooked Cranberry And Pork Roast

Servings: 4
Preparation Time: 10 minutes
Cooking Time: 8 hours
Ingredients:
- 1 tablespoon coconut flour
- Salt and pepper to taste
- 1 and ½ pound pork loin
- Pinch of dry mustard
- ½ teaspoon ginger
- 2 tablespoons stevia
- ½ cup cranberries
- 2 garlic cloves, peeled and minced
- ½ lemon, sliced
- ¼ cup water

Directions:
1. Take an owl and add ginger, mustard, pepper, and flour
2. Stir well
3. Add roast and toss well to coat it
4. Transfer meat to a Slow Cooker and add stevia, cranberries, garlic, water, and lemon slices
5. Place lid and cook on LOW for 8 hours
6. Drizzle the pan juice on top and serve!

Satisfyingly Spicy Pork Chops

Servings: 4
Preparation Time: 4 hours 10 minutes
Cooking Time: 15 minutes
Ingredients:
- ¼ cup lime juice
- 4 pork rib chops
- 1 tablespoon coconut oil, melted
- 2 garlic cloves, peeled and minced
- 1 tablespoon chili powder
- 1 teaspoon ground cinnamon
- 2 teaspoons cumin
- Salt and pepper to taste
- ½ teaspoon hot pepper sauce
- Mango, sliced

Directions:
1. Take a bowl and mix in lime juice, oil, garlic, cumin, cinnamon, chili powder, salt, pepper, hot pepper sauce
2. Whisk well
3. Add pork chops and toss
4. Keep it on the side and let it refrigerate for 4 hours
5. Preheat your grill to medium and transfer pork chops to a pre-heated grill
6. Grill for 7 minutes, flip and cook for 7 minutes more
7. Divide between serving platters and serve with mango slices
8. Enjoy!

Chapter 14

Snacks and Appetizers

Crispy Parmesan Cauliflower

Preparation Time: 12 minutes
Cooking Time: 14 to 17 minutes
Servings: 20 cauliflower bites
Ingredients:
- 4 cups of cauliflower florets
- 1 cup of whole-wheat breadcrumbs
- 1 teaspoon of coarse sea salt or kosher salt
- 1/4 cup of grated Parmesan cheese
- 1/4 cup of butter
- 1/4 cup of mild hot sauce
- Olive oil spray

Directions:
1. Place a parchment liner in the Air Fryer basket.
2. Cut the cauliflower florets in half and set aside.
3. In a small bowl, mix the breadcrumbs, salt, and Parmesan; set aside.
4. In a small microwave-safe bowl, combine the butter and hot sauce. Heat in the microwave until the butter is melted, about 15 seconds. Whisk.
5. Holding the stems of the cauliflower florets, dip them in the butter mixture to coat. Shake off any excess mixture.
6. Dredge the dipped florets with the bread crumb mixture, then put them in the Air Fryer basket. There's no need for a single layer; just toss them all in there.
7. Spray the cauliflower lightly with olive oil and air fry at 350 °F (177 °C) for 14 to 17 minutes, shaking the basket a few times throughout the cooking process. The florets are done when they are lightly browned and crispy. Serve warm.

Cream Cheese Stuffed Jalapeños

Preparation Time: 12 minutes
Cooking Time: 6-8 minutes
Servings: 10 poppers
Ingredients:
- 8 ounces (227 g) of cream cheese, at room temperature
- 1 cup of whole-wheat breadcrumbs, divided
- 2 tablespoons of fresh parsley, minced
- 1 teaspoon of chili powder
- 10 jalapeño peppers, halved and seeded

Directions:
1. In a small bowl, combine the cream cheese, 1/2 cup of breadcrumbs, the parsley, and the chili powder. Whisk to combine.
2. Stuff the cheese mixture into the jalapeños.
3. Sprinkle the tops of the stuffed jalapeños with the remaining 1/2 cup of breadcrumbs.
4. Place in the Air Fryer basket and air fry at 360 °F (182 °C) for 6 to 8 minutes, until the peppers are softened, and the cheese is melted. Serve warm.

Honeydew & Ginger Smoothies

Preparation Time: 10 minutes
Cooking Time: 3 Minutes
Servings: 3
Ingredients:
- 1 1/2 cup honeydew melon, cubed
- 1/2 cup banana
- 1/2 cup nonfat vanilla yogurt
- 1/4 tsp fresh ginger, grated

What you'll need from store cupboard:
- 1/2 cup ice cubes

Directions:
1. Place all Ingredients: in a blender and pulse until smooth. Pour into glasses and serve immediately.

Pea Soup

Preparation time: 10 minutes
Cooking Time: 20 minutes
Servings: 2
Ingredients:
- 1 1/2 spring onions
- 250 g potatoes - 375 g peas (frozen)
- 1/2 vegetable broth
- 1 tbsp. rapeseed oil
- 1 tbsp. sour cream

Directions:
1. Clean the spring onions and cut into rings.
2. Peel the potatoes and cut into cubes.
3. Fill 1 cup with peas and arrange.
4. Heat a saucepan with the rapeseed oil and fry the onions until golden.
5. Put the potatoes and peas in the pot and sauté. Stir well every now and then.
6. Deglaze with the broth and cook everything for about 20 minutes over a low flame.
7. Puree the soup. Add sour cream. Stir. Season with salt and pepper. Bring everything to the boil briefly and then serve.

Potato Curry Soup

Preparation time: 10 minutes
Cooking Time: 20 minutes
Servings: 2
Ingredients:
- 400 g potatoes

- 2 onions
- 1 teaspoon butter
- 400 ml vegetable broth
- 3 tbsp. heavy cream
- Coriander

Directions:
1. Wash, peel and cut the potatoes into small cubes. Peel the onion and cut it into small cubes.
2. Heat the butter in a saucepan. Add onion and sauté until translucent. Add the potatoes, season with curry, and sweat.
3. Prepare the vegetable stock and use it to deglaze the potatoes. Stir and cook for about 15 minutes.
4. Take out some potato pieces and set them aside. Puree the soup. Add the cream. Season with salt and pepper. Add the potato pieces again. The soup can now be served on a plate.

Asparagus Salad

Preparation time: 15 minutes
Cooking Time: 10 minutes
Servings: 2
Ingredients:
- 2 potatoes (50 g)
- 200 g frisée salad
- 200 g carrots
- 250 g carrots
- 250 g asparagus
- 2 tbsp. vinegar
- 2 tablespoons oil
- 1 teaspoon pink berries

Directions:
1. Peel the potatoes, cook them in salted boiling water and drain them. Then place in a bowl and mash with a fork.
2. Wash the frisée salad, spin dry.
3. Cook the asparagus in salted water for about 8 minutes, remove, and drain and set aside.
4. Peel the carrots, cut into small pieces, and cook in the asparagus water for about 2 minutes.
5. Add asparagus and carrots to the potatoes, let cool down a bit and add the salad.
6. Mix vinegar with salt, pepper, sugar, and asparagus water. Add oil. Put everything in the bowl and mix well.
7. Sprinkle the lettuce with the pink berries.

Zucchini Salmon Salad

Preparation time: 15 minutes
Cooking Time: 0 minutes
Servings: 2
Ingredients:
- 400 g zucchini
- 100 g smoked salmon
- 2 tbsp. olive oil
- 2 tbsp. lemon juice

Directions:
1. Wash and peel the zucchini and cut thin strips. If you have one, use a spiral cutter to do this. Lightly fry the zucchini strips with a little olive oil, allow to cool and pat dry with kitchen paper. Then put the strips in a salad bowl.
2. Cut the smoked salmon into slices (or you can use cut salmon or have it cut at a specialist store).
3. Wash, drain and finely chop the basil. Add the basil and salmon to the zucchini. Add lemon juice, salt, and pepper. Stir the salad well. Season a little if necessary.

Cheesy Onion Dip

Preparation Time: 10 minutes
Cooking Time: 5 Minutes
Servings: 8
Ingredients:
- 8 oz. low fat cream cheese, soft
- 1 cup onions, grated
- 1 cup low fat Swiss cheese, grated
- What you'll need from store cupboard:
- 1 cup lite mayonnaise

Directions:
1. Heat oven to broil.
2. Combine all Ingredients: in a small casserole dish. Microwave on high, stirring every 30 seconds, until cheese is melted and Ingredients: are combined.
3. Place under the broiler for 1-2 minutes until the top is nicely browned. Serve warm with vegetables for dipping.

Almond Coconut Biscotti

Preparation Time: 10 minutes
Cooking Time: 50 Minutes
Servings: 16
Ingredients:
- 1 egg, room temperature
- 1 egg white, room temperature
- 1/2 cup margarine, melted

What you'll need from store cupboard:
- 2 1/2 cup flour
- 1 1/3 cup unsweetened coconut, grated
- 3/4 cup almonds, sliced
- 2/3 cup Splenda
- 2 tsp. baking powder
- 1 tsp. vanilla
- 1/2 tsp. salt

Directions:
1. Heat oven to 350 °F. Line a baking sheet with parchment paper.
2. In a large bowl, combine dry Ingredients.
3. In a separate mixing bowl, beat other Ingredients: together. Add to dry Ingredients: and mix until thoroughly combined.
4. Divide dough in half. Shape each half into a loaf measuring 8x2 3/4-inches. Place loaves on pan 3 inches apart.
5. Bake 25-30 minutes or until set and golden brown. Cool on wire rack 10 minutes.
6. With a serrated knife, cut loaf diagonally into 1/2-inch slices. Place the cookies, cut side down, back on the pan and bake another 20 minutes, or until firm and nicely browned. Store in airtight container

Margarita Chicken Dip

Preparation Time: 10 minutes
Cooking Time: 1 Hour
Servings: 12
Ingredients:
- 2 1/2 cup Monterrey jack cheese, grated
- 1 1/2 cup chicken, cooked and shredded
- 1 1/2 blocks cream cheese, soft, cut into cubes
- 1/4 cup fresh lime juice
- 2 tbsp. fresh orange juice
- 2 tbsp. Pico de Gallo
- 1 tbsp. lime zest

What you'll need from store cupboard:
- 1/4 cup tequila
- 2 cloves garlic, diced fine
- 1 tsp cumin
- 1 tsp salt

Directions:
1. Place the cream cheese on bottom of crock pot. Top with chicken, then grated cheese. Add remaining Ingredients, except the Pico de Gallo.
2. Cover and cook on low 60 minutes. Stir the dip occasionally to combine Ingredients.
3. When dip is done transfer to serving bowl. Top with Pico de Gallo and serve with tortilla chips.

Parmesan Truffle Chips

Preparation Time: 10 minutes
Cooking Time: 20 Minutes
Servings: 4
Ingredients:
- 4 egg whites
- 1/2 tsp fresh parsley, diced fine
- What you'll need from store cupboard:
- 3 tbsp. reduced fat parmesan cheese, divided
- 2 tsp water
- 1/2 tsp salt
- Truffle oil to taste
- Nonstick cooking spray

Directions:
1. Heat oven to 400 °F. Spray two muffin pans with cooking spray.
2. In a small bowl, whisk together egg whites, water, and salt until combined.
3. Spoon just enough egg white mixture into each muffin cup to barely cover the bottom. Sprinkle a small pinch of parmesan on each egg white.
4. Bake 10-15 minutes or until the edges are dark brown, be careful not to burn them.
5. Let cool in the pans 3-4 minutes then transfer to a small bowl and drizzle lightly with truffle oil. Add parsley and 1/2 tablespoon parmesan and toss to coat. Serve.

Filled Mushrooms

Preparation time: 30 minutes
Cooking Time: 20 minutes
Servings: 2
Ingredients:
- 6 mushrooms
- 1 small onion
- 1 clove of garlic
- 1 piece of ginger
- 1 small zucchini
- 2 tomatoes
- 1 tbsp. rapeseed oil
- Coriander

Directions:
1. Clean the mushrooms. Peel the garlic, onion, ginger and cut everything into small pieces.
2. Peel the zucchini. Remove the case and cut them into small pieces.
3. Wash the tomatoes. Remove the stem and pulp. Cut the tomato into small pieces.
4. Heat the pan with canola oil. Add the mushroom stalks, zucchini, onion, ginger, and garlic and braise everything. Add the tomato pieces. Add salt and pepper.
5. Grease a baking dish. Put in the mushroom heads. Add the fried vegetables. Sprinkle cheese on top. Cook everything in the oven for 20 minutes.

Mango and Avocado Salad

Preparation time: 10 min
Cooking Time: 0 minutes
Servings: 2
Ingredients:
- 1/2 mango
- 1 avocado
- 2 tbsp. lemon juice
- 175 g tomatoes
- 125 g rocket
- 2 tbsp. orange juice
- 1 tbsp. mustard
- 2 tbsp. olive oil

Directions:
1. Peel the mango. Cut the pulp into small cubes.
2. Cut the avocado open. Remove the core, cut the meat into pieces and sprinkle with 1 tablespoon of lemon.
3. Wash the tomatoes and cut them in half.
4. Wash the rocket, shake dry and cut into small pieces.
5. Mix all Ingredients: in a bowl.
6. Mix lemon and orange juice with mustard in a small bowl or cup. Add pepper and stir in the olive oil.
7. Serve the salad on plates. Add the dressing.

Salad with Strips of Ham

Preparation time: 15 min
Cooking Time: 0 minutes
Servings: 2
Ingredients:
- 150 g cooked ham
- 1 yellow and 1 red pepper each
- 40 g peas (frozen)
- 1/4 bunch of spring onions
- 1 clove of garlic
- 3 pickles
- 1/2 tbsp. mustard
- 3 tbsp. mayonnaise

Directions:
1. Wash the peppers, cut into small strips and place in a bowl.
2. Cut the ham and the pickles into small cubes and add to the pepper.
3. Finely chop the spring onions and garlic and place in the bowl. Add the peas.
4. Add mayonnaise, some cucumber water, and the mustard. Stir everything well. Season with salt, pepper, and season to taste.

Pointed Cabbage Pot

Preparation time: 10 minutes
Cooking Time: 1 hour 5 minutes
Servings: 2
Ingredients:
- 300 g potatoes
- 240 g carrots
- 400 g pointed cabbage
- 1cl. onion
- 500 ml vegetable broth
- 20 g sour cream
- 2 bunches of chives

Directions:
1. Peel the potatoes and cut into small cubes.
2. Peel the carrots. Wash the cabbage and shake dry. Cut both into small pieces.
3. Peel the onion and cut into small cubes.
4. Skip the bacon. In the interim fry EBELN. Add potatoes and carrots and fry briefly. Deglaze with the vegetable stock. Put a lid on the pot and cook everything for a quarter of an hour. After about 5 minutes, add the cabbage. Mix well.
5. Pour the cream into the stew and stir in
6. Season with salt and pepper.
7. Cut the chives into small pieces.
8. Serve on a deep plate. Sprinkle the chives.

Rustic Pear Pie with Nuts

Preparation Time: 10 minutes
Cooking Time: 45 Minutes
Servings: 4
Ingredients:
- Cake
- 100g all-purpose flour
- 1g of salt
- 12g granulated sugar
- 84g unsalted butter, cold, cut into 13 mm pieces
- 30 ml of water, frozen
- 1 egg, beaten
- 12g turbinated sugar
- Nonstick Spray Oil
- 20g of honey
- 5 ml of water
- Roasted nuts, chopped, to decorate

Filling:
- 1 large pear, peeled, finely sliced
- 5g cornstarch
- 24g brown sugar
- 1g ground cinnamon
- A pinch salt

Directions:
1. Mix 90 g of flour, salt, and granulated sugar in a large bowl until well combined. Join the butter in the mixture using a pastry mixer or food processor until thick crumbs form. Add cold water and mix until it joins. Shape the dough into a bowl, cover with plastic and let cool in the refrigerator for 1 hour.
2. Mix the stuffing Ingredients: in a bowl until they are combined. Roll a roll through your cooled dough until it is 216 mm in diameter. Add 10 g of flour on top of the dough leaving 38 mm without flour. Place the pear slices in decorative circles superimposed on the floured part of the crust. Remove any remaining pear juice on the slices. Fold the edge over the filling.
3. Cover the edges with beaten eggs and sprinkle the sugar over the whole cake. Set aside
4. Preheat the air fryer set the temperature to 320 °F (160 °C). Spray the preheated air fryer with oil spray and place the cake inside. Set the time to 45 minutes at 320 °F (160 °C). Mix the honey and water and pass the mixture through the cake when you finish cooking.
5. Garnish with toasted chopped nuts.

Apricot Soufflé

Preparation Time: 10 minutes
Cooking Time: 30 Minutes
Servings: 6
Ingredients:
- 4 egg whites
- 3 egg yolks, beaten
- 3 tbsp. margarine

What you'll need from store cupboard
- 3/4 cup sugar free apricot fruit spread
- 1/3 cup dried apricots, diced fine
- 1/4 cup warm water
- 2 tbsp. flour
- 1/4 tsp. cream of tartar
- 1/8 tsp. salt

Directions:
1. Heat oven to 325 °F.
2. In a medium saucepan, over medium heat, melt margarine. Stir in flour and cook, stirring, until bubbly.
3. Stir together the fruit spread and water in a small bowl and add it to the saucepan with the apricots. Cook, stirring, 3 minutes or until mixture thickens.
4. Remove from heat and whisk in egg yolks. Let cool to room temperature, stirring occasionally.
5. In a medium bowl, beat egg whites, salt, and cream of tartar on high speed until stiff peaks form. Gently fold into cooled apricot mixture.
6. Spoon into a 1 1/2-quart soufflé dish. Bake 30 minutes, or until puffed and golden brown. Serve immediately.

Cinnamon Apple Popcorn

Preparation Time: 10 minutes
Cooking Time: 50 Minutes
Servings: 11

Ingredients:
- 4 tbsp. margarine, melted
- What you'll need from store cupboard
- 10 cup plain popcorn
- 2 cup dried apple rings, unsweetened and chopped
- 1/2 cup walnuts, chopped
- 2 tbsp. Splenda brown sugar
- 1 tsp. cinnamon
- 1/2 tsp. vanilla

Directions:
1. Heat oven to 250 °F.
2. Place chopped apples in a 9x13-inch baking dish and bake 20 minutes. Remove from oven and stir in popcorn and nuts.
3. In a small bowl, whisk together margarine, vanilla, Splenda, and cinnamon. Drizzle evenly over popcorn and toss to coat.
4. Bake 30 minutes, stirring quickly every 10 minutes. If apples start to turn a dark brown, remove immediately.
5. Pout onto waxed paper to cool at least 30 minutes. Store in an airtight container. Servings is 1 cup.

Blackberry Crostata

Preparation Time: 10 minutes
Cooking Time: 20 Minutes
Servings: 6
Ingredients:
- 1 9-inch pie crust, unbaked
- 2 cup fresh blackberries
- Juice and zest of 1 lemon
- 2 tbsp. butter, soft
- What you'll need from store cupboard:
- 3 tbsp. Splenda, divided
- 2 tbsp. cornstarch

Directions:
1. Heat oven to 425 °F. Line a large baking sheet with parchment paper and unroll pie crust in pan.
2. In a medium bowl, combine blackberries, 2 tablespoons Splenda, lemon juice and zest, and cornstarch. Spoon onto crust leaving a 2-inch edge. Fold and crimp the edges.
3. Dot the berries with 1 tablespoon butter. Brush the crust edge with remaining butter and sprinkle crust and fruit with remaining Splenda.
4. Bake 20-22 minutes or until golden brown. Cool before cutting and serving.

Ratatouille Salat

Preparation time: 10 minutes
Cooking Time: 15 minutes
Servings: 2
Ingredients:
- 2 peppers
- 1 small zucchini
- 1 onion & 1 clove of garlic
- 1 sprig of rosemary
- 10 g parmesan cheese
- 150 g tomatoes
- 2 sprigs of basil
- 2 tbsp. balsamic vinegar

Directions:
1. Heat the oven to 200 °F. Wash the vegetables and herbs. Cut the peppers into strips.
2. Peel the zucchini and cut into large pieces.
3. Peel and slice the onion. Put everything in an oven-safe bowl. Cut the tomatoes into small pieces.
4. Peel and squeeze the garlic with a press and add it to the vegetables.
5. Chop the rosemary and add to the vegetables. Add salt, pepper, and olive oil. Mix everything well and then cooks in the oven for about a quarter of an hour.
6. Chop the basil.
7. Put the oven vegetables in a bowl. Add tomatoes, basil, and vinegar. Mix everything well. Slice the parmesan on top of the salad.

Brussels sprouts

Preparation Time: 5 minutes
Cooking Time: 3 minutes
Servings: 5
Ingredients:
- 1 tsp. extra-virgin olive oil
- 1 lb. halved Brussels sprouts
- 3 tbsps. Apple cider vinegar
- 3 tbsps. Gluten-free tamari soy sauce
- 3 tbsps. Chopped sun-dried tomatoes

Directions:
1. Select the "Sauté" function on your Instant Pot, add oil and allow the pot to get hot.
2. Cancel the "Sauté" function and add the Brussels sprouts.
3. Stir well and allow the sprouts to cook in the residual heat for 2-3 minutes.
4. Add the tamari soy sauce and vinegar, and then stir.
5. Cover the Instant Pot, sealing the pressure valve by pointing it to "Sealing."
6. Select the "Manual, High Pressure" setting and cook for 3 minutes.
7. Once the cook cycle is done, do a quick pressure release, and then stir in the chopped sun-dried tomatoes.
8. Serve immediately.

Garlic and Herb Carrots

Preparation Time: 2 minutes
Cooking Time: 18 minutes
Servings: 3
Ingredients:
- 2 tbsps. Butter
- 1 lb. baby carrots
- 1 cup water
- 1 tsp. fresh thyme or oregano
- 1 tsp. minced garlic
- Black pepper
- Coarse sea salt

Directions:
1. Add water to the inner pot of the Instant Pot, and then put in a steamer basket.

2. Layer the carrots into the steamer basket.
3. Close and seal the lid, with the pressure vent in the "Sealing" position.
4. Select the "Steam" setting and cook for 2 minutes on high pressure.
5. Quick release the pressure and then carefully remove the steamer basket with the steamed carrots, discarding the water.
6. Add butter to the inner pot of the Instant Pot and allow it to melt on the "Sauté" function.
7. Add garlic and sauté for 30 seconds, and then add the carrots. Mix well.
8. Stir in the fresh herbs and cook for 2-3 minutes.
9. Season with salt and black pepper, and the transfer to a serving bowl.
10. Serve warm and enjoy!

Mushroom and Leek Soup

Preparation time: 5 min
Cooking Time: 15 minutes
Servings: 2
Ingredients:
- 1 leek
- 1/2 tbsp. rapeseed oil
- 400 ml vegetable stock
- 150g mushrooms
- 100 ml of milk
- Parsley

Directions:
1. Wash the leek sticks and cut them into small strips. Put the leek in a saucepan and sauté lightly over a low heat while adding the rapeseed oil.
2. Add vegetable stock
3. Clean the mushrooms and cut them into small pieces. Put a few mushrooms aside. Add the rest of the leek and let everything stand for about 12 minutes.
4. Now add the milk. Puree everything now.
5. Clean and chop the parsley. Add the parsley to the soup. Add salt, pepper, and the remaining mushrooms.

Pistachio Cookies

Preparation Time: 5 minutes
Cooking Time: 15 Minutes
Servings: 13-14
Ingredients:
- 2 eggs, beaten
- What you'll need from store cupboard:
- 1 2/3 cup almond flour
- 1 cup + 2 tbsp. Splenda
- 3/4 cup + 50 pistachio nuts, shelled

Directions:
1. Add the 3/4 cup nuts and 2 tablespoons Splenda to a food processor. Process until nuts are ground fine.
2. Pour the ground nuts into a large bowl and stir in flour and remaining Splenda until combined.
3. Add eggs and mix Ingredients: thoroughly. Wrap dough with plastic wrap and chill at least 8 hours or overnight.
4. Heat oven 325 °F. Line a cookie sheet with parchment paper.
5. Roll teaspoonful of dough into small balls, about 1-inch in diameter. Place on prepared sheet.
6. Smash cookie slightly then presses a pistachio in the center. Bake 12-15 minutes or until the edges are lightly browned.
7. Transfer to wire rack to cool completely. Store in airtight container. Servings is 3 cookies.

Crispy Apple Chips

Preparation Time: 3 minutes
Cooking Time: 2 Hours
Servings: 4
Ingredients:
- 2 medium apples, sliced
- 1 teaspoon ground cinnamon

Directions:
1. Preheat the oven to 200 °F (93 °C). Line a baking sheet with parchment paper.
2. Arrange the apple slices on the prepared baking sheet, then sprinkle with cinnamon.
3. Bake in the preheated oven for 2 hours or until crispy. Flip the apple chips halfway through the cooking time.
4. Allow to cool for 10 minutes and serve warm.

Chili Lime Tortilla Chips

Preparation Time: 5 minutes
Cooking Time: 15 Minutes
Servings: 10
Ingredients:
- 12 6-inch corn tortillas cut into 8 triangles
- 3 tbsp. lime juice

What you'll need from store cupboard:
- 1 tsp. cumin
- 1 tsp. chili powder

Directions:
1. Heat oven to 350 °F.
2. Place tortilla triangles in a single layer on a large baking sheet.
3. In a small bowl stir together spices.
4. Sprinkle half the lime juice over tortillas, followed by 1/2 the spice mixture. Bake 7 minutes.
5. Remove from oven and turn tortillas over. Sprinkle with remaining lime juice and spices. Bake another 8 minutes or until crisp, but not brown. Serve with your favorite salsa, Servings is 10 chips.

Palm Trees Holder

Preparation Time: 3 minutes
Cooking Time: 15 Minutes
Servings: 2
Ingredients:
- 1 Sheet of puff pastry
- Sugar

Directions:
1. Stretch the puff pastry sheet.
2. Pour the sugar over and fold the puff pastry sheet in half.
3. Put a thin layer of sugar on top and fold the puff pastry in half again.
4. Roll the puff pastry sheet from both ends towards the center (creating the shape of the palm tree).
5. Cut into sheets 5-8 mm thick.

6. Preheat the air fryer to 356 °F (180 °C) and put the palm trees in the basket.
7. Set the timer about 10 minutes at 356 °F (180 °C).

Homemade Cheetos

Preparation Time: 10 minutes
Cooking Time: 30 Minutes
Servings: 6
Ingredients:
- 3 egg whites
- 1/2 cup cheddar cheese, grated and frozen
- What you'll need from store cupboard:
- 1/4 cup reduced fat parmesan cheese
- 1/8 tsp cream of tartar

Directions:
1. Heat oven to 300 °F. Line a baking sheet with parchment paper.
2. Put the frozen cheese in a food processor/blender and pulse, until it's in tiny little pieces.
3. In a large mixing bowl, beat egg whites and cream of tartar until very stiff peaks from. Gently fold in chopped cheese. Spoon mixture into a piping bag with 1/2-inch hole. Gently pipe "cheeto" shapes onto prepared pan. Sprinkle with parmesan cheese.
4. Bake 20-30 minutes. Turn off oven and leave the puffs inside another 30 minutes. Let cool completely and store in an airtight container.

Butternut Cream Soup

Preparation time: 10 min
Cooking Time: 36 minutes
Servings: 2
Ingredients:
- 1 small Butternut squash
- 2 tbsp. rapeseed oil
- 1 onion
- 1 piece of ginger (the size of a thumb)
- 1-2 cloves - 600 ml vegetable stock
- 100 g sour cream

Directions:
1. Peel the pumpkin. Remove the cores. Cut 3 cm pieces from the pumpkin flesh.
2. Peel the onion. Cut them up small. Stew them with the rapeseed oil.
3. Put the pumpkin pieces in the pot and sauté them for about 6 minutes.
4. Peel the ginger. Cut it up.
5. Prepare the vegetable stock. Add these, the ginger, and the cloves to the pumpkin. Bring the mixture to the boil briefly and then cook over a low heat for half an hour.
6. Take out the cloves. Add the cream and puree the mixture. Serve with pumpkin seed oil.

The Cheesy Mug

Servings: 1
Preparation Time: 4 minutes
Cooking Time: 1-2 minutes
Ingredients:
- 2 ounces roast beef slices
- 1 and ½ tablespoons green chilies, diced
- 1 and ½ ounces pepper jack cheese, shredded
- 1 tablespoon sour cream

Directions:
1. Layer roast beef on the bottom of your mug, making sure to break it down into small pieces
2. Add half a tablespoon of sour cream, add half a tablespoon of green Chile, and half an ounce of pepper jack cheese
3. Keep layering until all ingredients are used
4. Microwave for 2 minutes
5. Server warm and enjoy!

Cashew And Almond Butter

Servings: 1 and ½ cups
Preparation Time: 5 minutes
Cooking Time: Nil
Ingredients:
- 1 cup almonds, blanched
- 1/3 cup cashew nuts
- 2 tablespoons coconut oil
- Salt as needed
- ½ teaspoon cinnamon

Directions:
1. Preheat your oven to 350 degrees F
2. Bake almonds and cashews for 12 minutes
3. Let them cool
4. Transfer to a food processor and add the remaining ingredients
5. Add oil and keep blending until smooth
6. Serve and enjoy!

Crispy Walnut Crumbles

Servings: 10
Preparation Time: 10 minutes
Cooking Time: 8 minutes
Ingredients:
- 6 ounces parmesan cheese, grated
- 2 tablespoons walnuts, chopped
- 1 tablespoon unsalted butter
- ½ tablespoon fresh thyme chopped

Directions:
1. Preheat your oven to 350 degrees F
2. Take two large rimmed baking sheets and line them with parchment
3. Add cheese and butter to the food processor and blend
4. Add walnuts to the mix and pulse
5. Take a tablespoon and scoop the mix onto a baking sheet
6. Top with chopped thymes
7. Bake for 8 minutes, transfer to a cooling rack
8. Let it cool for 30 minutes
9. Serve and enjoy!

Keto Kohlslaw

Servings: 4
Preparation Time: 10 minutes
Cooking Time: 0 minutes
Ingredients:
- 1 pound kohlrabi, peeled and shredded
- Fresh parsley
- 1 cup mayonnaise (Keto-Friendly)
- Salt, to taste

- Ground black pepper to taste

Directions:
1. Take a bowl and all the remaining ingredients
2. Mix it well until well combined
3. Adjust seasoning with salt and pepper
4. Serve and enjoy!

Stuffed Mushrooms

Servings: 4
Preparation Time: 10 minutes
Cooking Time: 15 minutes
Ingredients:
- 4 Portobello mushroom
- 1 cup crumbled blue cheese
- 2 teaspoons extra virgin olive oil
- Salt, to taste
- Fresh thyme

Directions:
1. Preheat your oven to 350 degrees Fahrenheit
2. Put out the stems from the mushrooms
3. Chop them into small pieces
4. Take a bowl and mix stem pieces with thyme, salt, and blue cheese and mix well
5. Fill up the mushroom with the prepared cheese
6. Top them with some oil
7. Take a baking sheet and place the mushrooms
8. Bake for 15 minutes to 20 minutes
9. Serve warm, and enjoy!

Flax And Almond Crunchies

Servings: 20 Crackers
Preparation Time: 15 minutes
Cooking Time: 60 minutes
Ingredients:
- ½ cup ground flax seeds
- ½ cup almond flour
- 1 tablespoon coconut flour
- 2 tablespoons shelled hemp seeds
- ¼ teaspoon sea salt, plus more to sprinkle on top
- 1 egg white
- 2 tablespoons unsalted butter, melted

Directions:
1. Preheat your oven to 300 degrees F
2. Take a baking sheet and line it with parchment paper; keep the prepared sheet on the side
3. Add flax, coconut flour, almond, salt, and hemp seed to a bowl and mix well
4. Add egg and melted butter, mix well
5. Transfer dough to a sheet of parchment paper and cover with another sheet of paper
6. Roll out dough
7. Cut into crackers and bake for 60 minutes
8. Cool and serve!

Juicy Salmon Fat Bombs

Servings: 12
Preparation Time: 5 minutes
Cooking Time: 10 minutes
Ingredients:
- ½ cup goat cheese, at room temperature
- 2 teaspoons lemon juice, fresh
- ½ cup butter, at room temperature
- 2 ounces smoked salmon
- Black pepper to taste

Directions:
1. Place a parchment paper over a baking sheet
2. Take a medium bowl and stir in goat cheese, smoked salmon, pepper, and lemon juice together
3. Scoop it out into 12 mounds
4. Chill for 2-3 hours
5. Serve when needed, and enjoy!

Roasted Herb Crackers

Servings: 75 Crackers
Preparation Time: 10 minutes
Cooking Time: 120 minutes
Ingredients:
- ¼ cup avocado oil
- 10 celery sticks
- 1 sprig of fresh rosemary, stem discarded
- 2 sprigs of fresh thyme, stems discarded
- 2 tablespoons apple cider vinegar
- 1 teaspoon Himalayan salt
- 3 cups ground flax seeds

Directions:
1. Preheat your oven to 225 degrees F
2. Line a baking sheet with parchment paper and keep it on the side
3. Add oil, herbs, celery, vinegar, and salt to a food processor and pulse until you have an even mixture
4. Add flax and puree
5. Let it sit for 2-3 minutes
6. Transfer batter to your prepared baking sheet and spread evenly, cut into cracker shapes
7. Bake for 60 minutes, flip and bake for 60 minutes more
8. Enjoy!

Crunchy Garlic Bread Stick

Servings: 8 breadsticks
Preparation Time: 15 minutes
Cooking Time: 15 minutes
Ingredients:
- ¼ cup butter softened
- 1 teaspoon garlic powder
- 2 cups almond flour
- ½ tablespoon baking powder
- 1 tablespoon Psyllium husk powder
- ¼ teaspoon salt
- 3 tablespoons butter, melted
- 1 egg
- ¼ cup boiling water

Directions:
1. Preheat your oven to 400-degree F
2. Line the baking sheet with parchment paper and keep it on the side
3. Beat butter with garlic powder and keep it on the side
4. Add almond flour, baking powder, husk, and salt in a bowl and mix in butter and egg; mix well
5. Pour boiling water into the mix and stir until you have a nice dough
6. Divide the dough into 8 balls and roll it into breadsticks

7. Place on a baking sheet and bake for 15 minutes
8. Brush each stick with garlic butter and bake for 5 minutes more
9. Serve and enjoy!

Magnificent Camembert Mushrooms

Servings: 4
Preparation Time: 5 minutes
Cooking Time: 13 minutes
Ingredients:
- 2 tablespoons butter
- 4 ounces Camembert cheese, diced
- 2 teaspoons garlic, minced
- 1 pound button mushrooms, halved
- Black pepper to taste

Directions:
1. Place a skillet over medium-high heat
2. Add butter and let it melt
3. Once the butter has melted, add garlic and Saute until translucent, it should take 3 minutes
4. Add mushrooms and cook for 10 minutes
5. Season with pepper and serve
6. Enjoy!

Golden Eggplant Fries

Servings: 8
Preparation Time: 10 minutes
Cooking Time: 15 minutes
Ingredients:
- 2 eggs
- 2 cups almond flour
- 2 tablespoons coconut oil, spray
- 2 eggplant, peeled and cut thinly
- Salt and pepper

Directions:
1. Preheat your oven to 400 degrees Fahrenheit
2. Take a bowl and mix with salt and black pepper in it
3. Take another bowl and beat eggs until frothy
4. Dip the eggplant pieces into eggs
5. Then coat them with a flour mixture
6. Add another layer of flour and egg
7. Then, take a baking sheet and grease it with coconut oil on top
8. Bake for about 15 minutes
9. Serve and enjoy!

Cheesy Mozzarella Sticks

Servings: 8 breadsticks
Preparation Time: 10 minutes
Cooking Time: 20 minutes
Ingredients:
- 2 cups shredded mozzarella cheese
- 2 tablespoons coconut flour
- 2 whole eggs
- 1 pinch of salt

Toppings
- ½ cup shredded parmesan cheese
- 1 tablespoon Italian seasoning
- ½ teaspoon garlic powder

Directions:
1. Preheat your oven to 350 degrees F
2. Line a baking sheet with parchment paper
3. Take your food processor and add cheese, flour, eggs, salt, and process
4. Scoop the mix onto your lined baking sheet and flatten to 1-inch thickness, forming a square
5. Bake for 15 minutes
6. Remove from oven and sprinkle parmesan cheese, Italian seasoning, and garlic powder
7. Bake for 5 minutes
8. Remove from oven and let it cool
9. Serve and enjoy!

Salt And Rosemary Cracker

Servings: 36 Crackers
Preparation Time: 10 minutes
Cooking Time: 10-15 minutes
Ingredients:
- 1 and ½ cups almond flour
- ½ teaspoon Celtic salt
- 1 egg, at room temp
- 2 tablespoons coconut oil
- ¼ teaspoon pepper
- 1 tablespoon rosemary, chopped

Directions:
1. Preheat oven to 350 degrees F
2. Take a baking tray and line it with parchment paper
3. Take a bowl and add almond flour, salt and keep it on the side
4. Take another bowl and add coconut oil, pepper, rosemary
5. Add almond mixture to the bowl
6. Mix well until you have an even dough
7. Transfer dough to a piece of parchment paper, cover with another parchment paper piece, and roll it out into a thin layer
8. Cut into crackers, arrange them on prepped baking sheet
9. Bake for 10-15 minutes
10. Let them cool
11. Serve and enjoy!

Premium Goat Cheese Salad

Servings: 2
Preparation Time: 4 minutes
Cooking Time: 10 minutes
Ingredients:
- 1 and ½ cups Hard Goat cheese, grated
- 4 cups spinach, fresh
- 4 strawberries, garnish
- ½ cup flaked almonds, toasted
- 4 tablespoons Raspberry vinaigrette, check for Keto-Friendliness

Directions:
1. Preheat your oven to 400 degrees F
2. Line a baking sheet using parchment paper and cut the parchment paper in half
3. Grate goat cheese onto each half
4. Form two circles using the grated cheese
5. Bake for 10 minutes
6. Transfer to a bowl and let it cool in the bowl shape
7. Peel the cheese off
8. Add remaining ingredients into the cheese and toss well

9. Serve immediately and enjoy!

Grilled Avocado And Melted Cheese

Servings: 6
Preparation Time: 5 minutes
Cooking Time: 4 minutes
Ingredients:

- 1 whole avocado
- 1 tablespoon chipotle sauce
- 1 tablespoon lime juice
- ¼ cup parmesan cheese
- Salt and pepper to taste

Directions:
1. Prepare avocado by slicing half lengthwise, and discard the seed
2. Gently prick the skin of the avocado with a fork
3. Set your avocado halves, skin down on the small baking sheet lined with aluminum foil
4. Top with sauce and drizzle lime juice
5. Season with salt and pepper
6. Sprinkle half parmesan cheese in each cavity, and set your broiler to high for 2 minutes
7. Add rest of the cheese and return to your broiler until the cheese melts and the avocado slightly browns
8. Serve hot, and enjoy!

Mozzarella And Bacon Bites

Servings: 4
Preparation Time: 10 minutes
Cooking Time: 5 minutes
Ingredients:

- 8 bacon strips
- 4 mozzarella string cheese pieces
- Olive oil, as needed

Directions:
1. Take a heavy-duty skillet and place it over medium heat
2. Add 2 inches of oil, and let it heat up to 350 degrees F (check using a thermometer)
3. Cut the string cheese into 8 pieces
4. Wrap each piece of string cheese with a strip of bacon and secure using a toothpick
5. Cook the sticks in hot oil for 2 minutes until the slices of bacon are browned
6. Transfer to a serving platter and drain with a kitchen towel
7. Serve!

Brazilian Butter Macadamia

Servings: 1 and ½ cups
Preparation Time: 5 minutes
Cooking Time: Nil
Ingredients:

- 2 tablespoons chives, fresh and chopped
- 1 tablespoon lemon juice, fresh
- ¼ cup Keto-Friendly mayonnaise
- ½ avocado, large
- 3 egg yolks, large and cooked

Directions:
1. Add listed ingredients to a food processor and blend until smooth

2. Scrap the sides and transfer to a mason jar
3. Serve when needed!

Tasty Roasted Broccoli

Servings: 4
Preparation Time: 5 minutes
Cooking Time: 20 minutes
Ingredients:

- 4 cups broccoli florets
- 1 tablespoon olive oil
- Salt and pepper to taste

Directions:
1. Preheat your oven to 400 degrees F
2. Add broccoli in a zip bag alongside oil and shake until coated
3. Add seasoning and shake again
4. Spread broccoli out on the baking sheet, bake for 20 minutes
5. Let it cool and serve
6. Enjoy!

Spicy Pimento Cheese Dip

Servings: 10
Preparation Time: 5 minutes
Cooking Time: 5 minutes
Ingredients:

- 1 brick cream cheese
- 10 cherry peppers, chopped
- 1 and ½ cups cheddar cheese, shredded
- 1 tablespoon garlic, minced
- Black pepper to taste

Directions:
1. Heat up garlic in a pan over medium heat
2. Drop cream cheese and let it soft; stir consistently
3. Mix in cheddar, add chopped peppers
4. Stir and enjoy with your desired dippers!

Bacon Smoky Doodles

Servings: 4
Preparation Time: 5 minutes
Cooking Time: 25 minutes
Ingredients:

- 24 little Smokies (Sausages)
- 3 tablespoons BBQ sauce, check for Keto Friendliness
- Salt and pepper to taste
- 6 slices bacon

Directions:
1. Preheat your oven to 375 degrees F
2. Cut bacon into quarter pieces
3. Put sausage on each one and roll bacon over them; use a toothpick to secure it properly
4. Bake for 25 minutes and baste with BBQ sauce
5. Bake for 10 minutes or more
6. Serve and enjoy!

Tantalizing Butter Beans

Servings: 4
Preparation Time: 5 minutes
Cooking Time: 12 minutes
Ingredients:

- 2 garlic cloves, minced
- Red pepper flakes to taste

- Salt to taste
- 2 tablespoons clarified butter
- 4 cups green beans, trimmed

Directions:
1. Bring a pot of salted water to boil
2. Once the water starts to boil, add beans and cook for 3 minutes
3. Take a bowl of ice water and drain beans, plunge them in the ice water
4. Once cooled, keep them on the side
5. Take a medium skillet and place it over medium heat; add ghee and melt
6. Add red pepper, salt, garlic
7. Cook for 1 minute
8. Add beans and toss until coated well; cook for 3 minutes
9. Serve and enjoy!

Walnuts And Asparagus Delight

Servings: 4
Preparation Time: 5 minutes
Cooking Time: 5 minutes
Ingredients:
- 1 and ½ tablespoons olive oil
- ¾ pound asparagus, trimmed
- ¼ cup walnuts, chopped
- Salt and pepper to taste

Directions:
1. Place a skillet over medium heat, add olive oil and let it heat up
2. Add asparagus; saute for 5 minutes until browned
3. Season with salt and pepper
4. Remove heat
5. Add walnuts and toss
6. Serve warm!

Spicy Chili Crackers

Servings: 30 crackers
Preparation Time: 15 minutes
Cooking Time: 60 minutes
Ingredients:
- ¾ cup almond flour
- ¼ cup coconut four
- ¼ cup coconut flour
- ½ teaspoon paprika
- ½ teaspoon cumin
- 1 and ½ teaspoons chili pepper spice
- 1 teaspoon onion powder
- ½ teaspoon salt
- 1 whole egg
- ¼ cup unsalted butter

Directions:
1. Preheat your oven to 350 degrees F
2. Take a baking sheet and line it up with parchment paper; keep it on the side
3. Add listed ingredients to the food processor and process until you have a nice and firm dough
4. Divide dough into two equal parts
5. Place one ball on a sheet of parchment paper and cover it with another paper
6. Roll it out
7. Cut into crackers and do the same with the other ball
8. Transfer dough to your prepared baking dish and bake for 8-10 minutes
9. Remove from oven and serve
10. Enjoy!

Faux Mac And Cheese

Servings: 4
Preparation Time: 15 minutes
Cooking Time: 45 minutes
Ingredients:
- 5 cups cauliflower florets
- Salt and pepper to taste
- 1 cup coconut milk
- ½ cup vegetable broth
- 2 tablespoon coconut flour, sifted
- 1 organic egg, beaten
- 2 cups cheddar cheese

Directions:
1. Preheat your oven to 350 degrees F
2. Season florets with salt and steam until firm
3. Place florets in a greased oven-proof dish
4. Heat coconut milk over medium heat in a skillet; make sure to season the oil with salt and pepper
5. Stir in broth and add coconut flour to the mix, stir
6. Cook until the sauce begins to bubble
7. Remove heat and add beaten egg
8. Pour the thick sauce over cauliflower and mix in cheese
9. Bake for 30-45 minutes
10. Serve and enjoy!

Hearty Roasted Cauliflower

Servings: 8
Preparation Time: 5 minutes
Cooking Time: 30 minutes
Ingredients:
- 1 large cauliflower head
- 2 tablespoons melted coconut oil
- 2 tablespoons fresh thyme
- 1 teaspoon Celtic sea salt
- 1 teaspoon fresh ground pepper
- 1 head of roasted garlic
- 8 ounces burrata cheese, for garnish
- 2 tablespoons fresh thyme for garnish

Directions:
1. Preheat your oven to 425 degrees F
2. Rinse cauliflower and trim, core, and slice
3. Lay cauliflower evenly on a rimmed baking tray
4. Drizzle coconut oil evenly over cauliflower, sprinkle thyme leaves
5. Season with a pinch of salt and pepper
6. Squeeze roasted garlic
7. Roast cauliflower until slightly caramelize for about 30 minutes, making sure to turn once
8. Garnish with fresh thyme leaves and burrata
9. Enjoy!

Sausage And Shrimp Skewers

Servings: 6
Preparation Time: 20 minutes
Cooking Time: 10 minutes

Ingredients:
- 3 large smoked sausages cut into 30-35 slices in total
- 2 medium-sized zucchinis, cut into 35-40 slices
- 40 shrimps, peeled with tail on
- 1 batch of low-carb barbeque sauce

Directions:
1. Take each skewer and thread 2 pieces of shrimp, two zucchini, and two sausages (one ingredient, then another to make a pattern).
2. Brush the barbeque sauce over the shrimp and zucchini and cook over a grill pan for 3-4 minutes on each side.
3. Serve optionally with chopped lettuce and some extra barbeque sauce

Fancy Grilled Halloumi Bruschetta

Servings: 4
Preparation Time: 10 minutes
Cooking Time: 10 minutes
Ingredients:
- 2 medium tomatoes, chopped
- 2 packages of halloumi cheese (Cyprus grilling cheese), cut into 1-inch thick slices lengthwise
- 2 tbsp of olive oil
- 1 tbsp of chopped fresh basil leaves, chopped

Directions:
1. In a bowl, combine the tomatoes with the basil and 1 tbsp of olive oil.
2. Heat the remaining tsp of olive oil in a grilling pan and add the halloumi cheese slices to grill for around 2 minutes on each side.
3. Serve the halloumi slices with the tomato mixture on top, as if you are making a bruschetta

Broccoli And Dill Salad

Servings: 4
Preparation Time: 10 minutes
Cooking Time: 5 minutes
Ingredients:
- 1 pound (454 g) broccoli, cut into florets and stems
- 3/4 cup fresh dill
- 1 cup keto-friendly mayonnaise
- 1/2 teaspoon ground pepper
- 1/2 teaspoon salt

Directions:
1. Boil the broccoli florets and stems in a pot of lightly salted water for about 5 minutes, until it becomes fork-tender but firm and greenish.
2. Drain the broccoli using a colander, then put it in a medium bowl. Add the fresh dill and mayonnaise and mix gently. Lightly season with pepper and salt before serving.

Cheddar Biscuits

Servings: 4
Preparation Time: 10 minutes
Cooking Time: 30 minutes
Ingredients:
- 2 1/2 cups almond flour
- 2 tsp baking powder
- 2 eggs beaten
- 3 tbsp melted butter
- 3/4 cup grated cheddar cheese

Directions:
1. Preheat the oven to 350 F; line a baking sheet with parchment paper. Mix flour, baking powder, and eggs until smooth in a bowl.
2. Whisk in the melted butter and cheddar cheese until well combined.
3. Mold 12 balls out of the mixture and arrange them on the sheet at 2-inch intervals.
4. Bake for 25 minutes until golden brown. Remove, let cool and serve

The Faux Cinnamon Rice Pudding

Servings: 4
Preparation Time: 15 minutes
Cooking Time: Nil
Ingredients:
- 1 1/4 cups coconut cream
- 1 tsp vanilla extract
- 1 tsp cinnamon powder
- 1 cup mashed tofu
- 2 oz fresh strawberries

Directions:
1. Pour coconut cream into a bowl and whisk until a soft peak forms. Mix in vanilla and cinnamon.
2. Lightly fold in tofu and refrigerate for 10-15 minutes to set. Spoon into served glasses, top with the strawberries, and serve

Almond Flour English Cake

Servings: 4
Preparation Time: 10 minutes
Cooking Time: 10-15 minutes
Ingredients:
- 2 tbsp flax seed powder + 6 tbsp water
- 2 tbsp almond flour
- 1/2 tsp baking powder
- 1 pinch salt
- 3 tbsp vegan butter

Directions:
1. In a bowl, mix flax seed with water until evenly combined, and leave to soak for 5 minutes.
2. In another bowl, combine almond flour, baking powder, and salt. Then, pour in the flax egg and whisk again.
3. Let the batter sit for 5 minutes to set. Melt the vegan butter in a frying pan over medium heat, and add the mixture in four dollops.
4. Fry until golden brown on one side, flip the bread with a spatula and fry until golden brown.
5. Serve with tea

Bacon And Avocado Fat Bombs

Servings: 4
Preparation Time: 10 minutes
Cooking Time: 50 minutes
Ingredients:
- 1 avocado, halved, pitted
- 4 slices of bacon
- 2 tbsp grated parmesan cheese

Directions:

1. Turn on the oven and broiler and let it preheat. Meanwhile, prepare the avocado, cut it in half, remove its pit, and peel the skin.
2. Cover one half of the avocado with cheese, replace it with the other half and then wrap the avocado with bacon slices.
3. Take a baking sheet, line it with aluminum foil, place wrapped avocado on it, and broil for 5 minutes per side, flipping carefully with a tong halfway.
4. When done, cut each avocado in half crosswise and serve

Green Olives With Deviled Eggs

Servings: 2
Preparation Time: 10 minutes
Cooking Time: Nil
Ingredients:
- 2 eggs, boiled
- 1 tbsp chopped green olives
- 1/4 tsp paprika
- 2 tbsp mayonnaise
- 1 tbsp cream cheese, softened

Directions:
1. Peel the boiled eggs, then slice in half lengthwise and transfer egg yolks to a medium bowl using a spoon.
2. Mash the egg yolk, add the remaining ingredients and stir until well combined.
3. Spoon the egg yolk mixture into egg whites and then serve.

Spinach And Bacon Salad

Servings: 2
Preparation Time: 10 minutes
Cooking Time: 5 minutes
Ingredients:
- 4 oz spinach
- 4 sliced of bacon, chopped
- 2 eggs, boiled, sliced
- 1/a cup mayonnaise

Directions:
1. Take a skillet pan, place it over medium heat, add bacon, and cook for 5 minutes until browned.
2. Meanwhile, take a salad bowl, add spinach
3. Top with bacon and eggs, and drizzle with mayonnaise.
4. Toss until well mixed, and then serve.

Cool Bacon And Cheese Rolls

Servings: 4
Preparation Time: 10 minutes
Cooking Time: 50 minutes
Ingredients:
- 2 oz mozzarella cheese, sliced, full-fat
- 4 slices of bacon

Directions:
1. Take a skillet pan, place it over medium heat and when hot, add bacon slices and cook for 3 minutes per side until crisp.
2. Transfer bacon to the cutting board, cool for 5 minutes and then chop.
3. Cut cheese into thin slices, top with chopped bacon, and then roll the cheese.
4. Serve.

Roasted Brussels And Bacon

Servings: 4
Preparation Time: 10 minutes
Cooking Time: 35-40 minutes
Ingredients:
- 24 oz brussels sprouts
- 1/4 cup fish sauce
- 1/4 cup bacon grease
- 6 strips of bacon Pepper to taste

Directions:
1. De-stem and quarter the brussels sprouts.
2. Mix them with the bacon grease and fish sauce.
3. Slice the bacon into small strips and cook.
4. Add the bacon and pepper to the sprouts.
5. Spread onto a greased pan and cook at 450°F/230°C for 35 minutes.
6. Stir every 5 minutes or so.
7. Broil for a few more minutes and serve.

Parmesan Garlic Cauliflower

Servings: 4
Preparation Time: 10 minutes
Cooking Time: 50 minutes
Ingredients:
- 3/4 cup cauliflower florets 2 tbsp butter
- 1 clove of garlic, sliced thinly
- 2 tbsp shredded parmesan 1 pinch of salt

Directions:
1. Preheat your oven to 350°F/175°C.
2. Melt the butter with the garlic on low heat for 5-10 minutes.
3. Strain the garlic in a sieve.
4. Add the cauliflower, parmesan, and salt.
5. Bake for 20 minutes or until golden.
6. Serve and enjoy once done!

Flaxy Cheese Chips

Servings: 4
Preparation Time: 10 minutes
Cooking Time: 10-15 minutes
Ingredients:
- 1 1/2 cup cheddar cheese
- 4 tbsp ground flaxseed meal
- Seasonings of your choice

Directions:
1. Preheat your oven to 425°F/220°C.
2. Spoon 2 tablespoons of cheddar cheese into a mound onto a non-stick pad.
3. Spread out a pinch of flaxseed on each chip.
4. Season and bake for 10-15 minutes.
5. Serve and enjoy!

Handy Baked Tortillas

Servings: 4
Preparation Time: 10 minutes
Cooking Time: 20-30 minutes
Ingredients:
- 1 large head of cauliflower, divided into florets. 4 large eggs
- 2 garlic cloves (minced)

- 1 1/2 tsp herbs (whatever your favorite is - basil, oregano, thyme)
- 1/2 tsp salt

Directions:
1. Preheat your oven to 375°F/190°C.
2. Put parchment paper on two baking sheets.
3. In a food processor, break down the cauliflower into rice.
4. Add 1/4 cup water and the riced cauliflower to a saucepan.
5. Cook on medium-high heat until tender for 10 minutes. Drain.
6. Dry with a clean kitchen towel.
7. Mix the cauliflower, eggs, garlic, herbs, and salt.
8. Make 4 thin circles on the parchment paper.
9. Bake for 20 minutes, until dry.
10. Serve and enjoy!

Fine Jarlsberg Omelet

Servings: 4
Preparation Time: 10 minutes
Cooking Time: 5 minutes
Ingredients:
- 4 medium mushrooms, sliced, 2 oz
- 1 green onion, sliced
- 2 eggs, beaten
- 1 oz Jarlsberg or Swiss cheese, shredded 1 oz ham, diced

Directions:
1. In a skillet, cook the mushrooms and green onion until tender.
2. Add the eggs and mix well.
3. Sprinkle with salt and top with the mushroom mixture, cheese, and ham.
4. When the egg is set, fold the plain side of the omelet on the filled side.
5. Turn off the heat and let it stand until the cheese has melted.
6. Serve!

Asparagus And Baked Pork

Servings: 4
Preparation Time: 10 minutes
Cooking Time: 20 minutes
Ingredients:
- 1 pound (454 g) asparagus, tough ends removed
- *1/2 cup* roughly ground pork rinds
- 1 cup ranch dressing Pinch of sea salt

Directions:
1. Arrange the asparagus spears in a casserole dish. Spread the pork rinds and ranch dressing over the asparagus, then season with sea salt.
2. Place the casserole dish in the oven and bake for 18 minutes or until lightly browned.
3. Transfer them onto a platter and serve warm.

Spicy Fired Up Jalapeno Poppers

Servings: 4
Preparation Time: 10 minutes
Cooking Time: 30 minutes
Ingredients:
- 5 oz cream cheese
- 1/4 cup mozzarella cheese
- 8 medium jalapeno peppers
- 1/2 tsp Mrs. Dash Table Blend
- 8 slices bacon

Directions:
1. Preheat your oven to 400°F/200°C.
2. Cut the jalapenos in half.
3. Use a spoon to scrape out the insides of the peppers.
4. Add the cream cheese, mozzarella cheese, and spices of your choice to a bowl.
5. Pack the cream cheese mixture into the jalapenos and place the peppers on top.
6. Wrap each pepper in 1 slice of bacon, starting from the bottom and working up.
7. Bake for 30 minutes. Broil for an additional 3 minutes.
8. Serve!

Bacon And Chicken Patties

Servings: 4
Preparation Time: 10 minutes
Cooking Time: 10-15 minutes
Ingredients:
- 12 oz can chicken breast
- 4 slices bacon
- 1/4 cup parmesan cheese
- 1 large egg
- 3 tbsp keto coconut flour

Directions:
1. Cook the bacon until crispy.
2. Chop the chicken and bacon together in a food processor until fine.
3. Add in the parmesan, egg, and coconut flour, and mix.
4. Make the patties by hand and fry on medium heat in a pan with some oil.
5. Once browned, flip over, continue cooking, and lie them to drain.
6. Serve!

Juicy Grilled Ham And Cheese

Servings: 4
Preparation Time: 10 minutes
Cooking Time: 20-30 minutes
Ingredients:
- 3 low-carb keto buns
- 4 slices medium-cut deli ham 1 tbsp salted butter
- 3 slices cheddar cheese, 1/2 cup almond flour
- 1 tsp. baking powder
- 2 eggs. Scrambled
- 1 and 1/2 tablespoon coconut flour

Directions:
1. Preheat your oven to 350°F/175°C.
2. Mix the almond flour, salt, and baking powder in a bowl. Put to the side.
3. Add the butter and coconut oil to a skillet.
4. Melt for 20 seconds and pour into another bowl.
5. In this bowl, mix in the dough.
6. Scramble two eggs. Add to the dough.

7. Add 1/2 tablespoon coconut flour to thicken, and place evenly into a cupcake tray. Fill about 3/4 inch.
8. Bake for 20 minutes until browned.
9. Allow to cool for 15 minutes, and cut each in half for the buns.
10. Sandwich:
11. Fry the deli meat in a skillet on high heat.
12. Put the ham and cheese between the buns.
13. Heat the butter on medium-high.
14. When brown, turn too low and add the dough to the pan.
15. Press down with weight until you smell burning, then flip to crisp both sides.
16. Enjoy!

Prosciutto Spinach Salad

Servings: 4
Preparation Time: 10 minutes
Cooking Time: Ni
Ingredients:
- 2 cups baby spinach
- 1/3 lb prosciutto
- 1 cantaloupe
- 1 avocado
- 1/4 cup diced red onion handful of raw, unsalted walnuts

Directions:
1. Put a cup of spinach on each plate.
2. Top with the diced prosciutto, cubes of balls of melon, slices of avocado, a handful of red onion, and a few walnuts.
3. Add some freshly ground pepper, if you like.
4. Serve!

Lasagna Spaghetti Squash

Servings: 4
Preparation Time: 10 minutes
Cooking Time: 60-80 minutes
Ingredients:
- 25 slices of mozzarella cheese
- 1 large jar (40 oz) Rao's Marinara sauce
- 30 oz whole-milk ricotta cheese
- 2 large spaghetti squash, cooked (44 oz)
- 4 lbs ground beef

Directions:
1. Preheat your oven to 375°F/190°C.
2. Slice the spaghetti squash and place it face down inside an oven-proof dish. Fill with water until covered.
3. Bake for 45 minutes until the skin is soft.
4. Sear the meat until browned.
5. In a large skillet, heat the browned meat and marinara sauce. Set aside when warm.
6. Scrape the flesh off the cooked squash to resemble strands of spaghetti.
7. Layer the lasagna in a large greased pan in alternating layers of spaghetti squash, meat sauce, mozzarella, and ricotta. Repeat until all increases have been used.
8. Bake for another 30 minutes and serve!

Blue Cheese Chicken Wedges

Servings: 4
Preparation Time: 10 minutes
Cooking Time: 30 minutes
Ingredients:
- 2 tbsp crumbled blue cheese
- 4 strips of bacon
- 2 chicken breasts (boneless)
- 3/4 cup of your favorite buffalo sauce

Directions:
1. Boil a large pot of salted water.
2. Add two chicken breasts to the pot and cook for 28 minutes.
3. Turn off the heat and let the chicken rest for 10 minutes. Using a fork, pull the chicken apart into strips.
4. Cook and cool the bacon strips and put them to the side.
5. On medium heat, combine the chicken and buffalo sauce. Stir until hot.
6. Add the blue cheese and buffalo pulled chicken. Top with the cooked bacon crumbles.
7. Serve and enjoy.

Feisty Bacon Snack

Servings: 4
Preparation Time: 10 minutes
Cooking Time: 60 minutes
Ingredients:
- 30 slices of thick-cut bacon
- 12 oz steak
- 10 oz beef sausage
- 4 oz cheddar cheese, shredded

Directions:
1. Lay out 5 x 6 slices of bacon in a woven pattern and bake at 400°F/200°C for 20 minutes until crisp.
2. Combine the steak, bacon, and sausage to form a meaty mixture.
3. Lay out the meat in a rectangle similar to the bacon strips. Season with salt/pepper.
4. Place the bacon weave on top of the meat mixture.
5. Place the cheese in the center of the bacon.
6. Roll the meat into a tight roll and refrigerate.
7. Make a 7 x 7 bacon weave and roll the bacon weave over the meat diagonally.
8. Bake at 400°F/200°C for 60 minutes or 165°F/75°C internally.
9. Let rest for 5 minutes before serving.

Bacon And Scallops Snack

Servings: 4
Preparation Time: 10 minutes
Cooking Time: 6 minutes
Ingredients:
- 12 scallops
- 12 thin bacon slices
- 12 toothpicks
- Salt and pepper to taste
- 1/2 tbsp oil

Directions:
1. Heat a skillet on high heat while drizzling in the oil.

2. Wrap each scallop with a piece of thinly cut bacon—secure with a toothpick.
3. Season to taste.
4. Cook for 3 minutes per side.
5. Serve!

Perfect Gluten-Free Gratin

Servings: 4
Preparation Time: 10 minutes
Cooking Time: 20-25 minutes
Ingredients:
- 4 cups raw cauliflower florets
- 4 tbsp butter
- 1/3 cup heavy whipping cream
- Salt and pepper to taste
- 5 deli slices pepper jack cheese

Directions:
1. Combine the cauliflower, butter, cream, salt, and pepper and microwave on medium for 20 minutes, or until tender.
2. Mash with a fork—season to your liking.
3. Lay the slices of cheese across the top of the cauliflower.
4. Cook inside your microwave for an additional 3 minutes, depending on the power of your microwave.
5. Serve!

Cheesed Up Bacon Butternut Squash

Servings: 4
Preparation Time: 10 minutes
Cooking Time: 25-30 minutes
Ingredients:
- 1 tablespoon olive oil
- 1 and 1/2 pound sliced butternut squash
- Kosher salt & Black pepper
- 1 and 1/2 cup grated Parmesan cheese
- 2 oz. chopped bacon

Directions:
1. Set the oven to 4250F to preheat, then grease the baking tray
2. Add the olive oil to a medium skillet to heat to sauté the bacon, butternut squash, and the seasonings for 2 minutes.
3. After 2 minutes, pour everything on the baking tray to bake for 25 minutes
4. Remove from the oven, sprinkle the parmesan cheese on top, then bake for 10 more minutes
5. Serve the meal while still warm.

Great Nutty Lion

Serving: 2
Preparation Time: 5 minutes
Ingredients
- 1 tablespoon almond butter
- 1 tablespoon chia seeds
- 4 ice cubes
- ¾ cup plain low-fat Greek yogurt
- 1 cup baby spinach
- 1 cup unsweetened almond milk
- 2 fresh bananas

Directions
1. Add all the ingredients except vegetables/fruits first
2. Blend until smooth
3. Add the vegetable/fruits
4. Blend until smooth
5. Add a few ice cubes and serve the smoothie
6. Enjoy!

A Whole Melon Surprise

Serving: 2
Preparation Time: 5 minutes
Ingredients
- 1 tablespoon chia seeds
- 4 ice cubes
- 1 fresh banana
- 1 cup cantaloupe
- 1 cup honeydew
- 1 cup plain coconut yogurt
- 1 cup unsweetened coconut milk

Directions
1. Add all the ingredients except vegetables/fruits first
2. Blend until smooth
3. Add the vegetable/fruits
4. Blend until smooth
5. Add a few ice cubes and serve the smoothie
6. Enjoy!

Muscular Macho Green

Serving: 2
Preparation Time: 5 minutes
Ingredients
- 2 teaspoons matcha powder
- 1 tablespoon chia seeds
- ¾ cup plain coconut yogurt
- 1 fresh banana
- 1 cup baby spinach
- 1 cup of frozen mango
- 1 cup unsweetened coconut milk

Directions
1. Add all the ingredients except vegetables/fruits first
2. Blend until smooth
3. Add the vegetable/fruits
4. Blend until smooth
5. Add a few ice cubes and serve the smoothie
6. Enjoy!

Buddha's Banana Berry

Serving: 2
Preparation Time: 5 minutes
Ingredients
- 1 tablespoon hemp seeds
- ¾ cup plain low-fat Greek yogurt
- 1 fresh banana
- 1 cup baby spinach
- 1 cup frozen raspberries
- 1 cup unsweetened vanilla almond milk

Directions
1. Add all the ingredients except vegetables/fruits first
2. Blend until smooth

3. Add the vegetable/fruits
4. Blend until smooth
5. Add a few ice cubes and serve the smoothie
6. Enjoy!

Brain Nutrition-Analyzer

Serving: 2
Preparation Time: 5 minutes
Ingredients

- 4 large ice cubes
- ¾ cup plain-low-fat Greek yogurt
- 1 cup baby spinach
- 1 cup unsweetened vanilla almond milk
- 2 fresh bananas
- 1 tablespoon almond butter
- 1 tablespoon peanut butter

Directions
1. Add all the ingredients except vegetables/fruits first
2. Blend until smooth
3. Add the vegetable/fruits
4. Blend until smooth
5. Add a few ice cubes and serve the smoothie
6. Enjoy!

Complete Banana Meal

Serving: 2
Preparation Time: 5 minutes
Ingredients

- 1 tablespoon cacao powder
- 4 tablespoons chocolate hemp protein powder
- 1 fresh banana
- 1 cup baby spinach
- 1 cup of frozen coconut pieces
- 1 cup unsweetened vanilla almond milk

Directions
1. Add all the ingredients except vegetables/fruits first
2. Blend until smooth
3. Add the vegetable/fruits
4. Blend until smooth
5. Add a few ice cubes and serve the smoothie
6. Enjoy!

Smoothie Vegetable Blast

Serving: 2
Preparation Time: 5 minutes
Ingredients

- 1 cucumber, peeled and sliced
- 4 tomatoes, peeled
- 1 garlic cloves
- ½ onion
- ½ cup rosemary infusion cooled
- Pepper and salt to taste
- 1 tablespoon virgin olive oil
- 1 cup kale
- 1 lemon, juiced

Directions
1. Add all the ingredients except vegetables/fruits first
2. Blend until smooth
3. Add the vegetable/fruits
4. Blend until smooth

5. Add a few ice cubes and serve the smoothie
6. Enjoy!

Strawberry Banana Yogurt Smoothie

Serving: 2
Preparation Time: 5 minutes
Ingredients

- 4 large strawberries
- ½ banana, sliced
- ½ cup blueberries
- 3 ounces soy yogurt
- 1 cup unsweetened soy milk
- 12 raw almonds
- 3 ice cubes

Directions
1. Add all the ingredients except vegetables/fruits first
2. Blend until smooth
3. Add the vegetable/fruits
4. Blend until smooth
5. Add a few ice cubes and serve the smoothie
6. Enjoy!

Cantaloupe Lettuce Smoothie

Serving: 2
Preparation Time: 5 minutes
Ingredients

- 10 large romaine lettuce leaves
- 2 cups cantaloupe slice, chopped
- 1 cup strawberries, frozen
- 6 ice cubes

Directions
1. Add all the ingredients except vegetables/fruits first
2. Blend until smooth
3. Add the vegetable/fruits
4. Blend until smooth
5. Add a few ice cubes and serve the smoothie
6. Enjoy!

Powerful Alkaline Smoothie

Serving: 2
Preparation Time: 5 minutes
Ingredients

- 1 cup full-fat coconut milk
- 1 avocado, diced
- ½ cucumber, sliced
- 1 handful shake, chopped
- ½ inch ginger knob
- 1 tablespoon almond butter
- 1 tablespoon flaxseed
- 1 tablespoon coconut oil

Directions
1. Add all the ingredients except vegetables/fruits first
2. Blend until smooth
3. Add the vegetable/fruits
4. Blend until smooth
5. Add a few ice cubes and serve the smoothie
6. Enjoy!

Alkaline Breakfast Breaker

Serving: 2
Preparation Time: 5 minutes
Ingredients
- 1 cup of coconut milk
- ¾ cup of filtered water
- 1 tablespoon coconut oil
- 1 handful of almonds
- 1 handful cashews
- 1 handful flaxseeds
- ½ avocado, diced
- 1 cucumber, sliced
- 1 handful kale, chopped

Directions
1. Add all the ingredients except vegetables/fruits first
2. Blend until smooth
3. Add the vegetable/fruits
4. Blend until smooth
5. Add a few ice cubes and serve the smoothie
6. Enjoy!

Mixed Berry Smoothie

Serving: 2
Preparation Time: 5 minutes
Ingredients
- 2 cups of filtered water
- 1 teaspoon organic stevia powder
- 1 handful of wild arugula
- ½ cup organic Greek yogurt, non-fat
- 1 banana, in frozen chunks
- 2 cups mixed berries

Directions
1. Add all the ingredients except vegetables/fruits first
2. Blend until smooth
3. Add the vegetable/fruits
4. Blend until smooth
5. Add a few ice cubes and serve the smoothie
6. Enjoy!

Sweet Kale Smoothie

Serving: 2
Preparation Time: 5 minutes
Ingredients
- 2 cups kale leaves
- 1 ripe pear, peeled, cored, and chopped
- 15 green grapes
- 6 ounces fat-free plain Greek yogurt
- 2 tablespoons avocado, chopped
- 1-2 tablespoons fresh lime juice

Directions
1. Add all the ingredients except vegetables/fruits first
2. Blend until smooth
3. Add the vegetable/fruits
4. Blend until smooth
5. Add a few ice cubes and serve the smoothie
6. Enjoy!

Almond Butter Berry Smoothie

Serving: 2
Preparation Time: 5 minutes
Ingredients
- 2 cups kale, chopped
- 2 cups almond milk, unsweetened
- 1 cup grapes, mixed
- 1 banana, peeled and frozen
- 4 tablespoons almond butter, raw
- 1 tablespoon chia

Directions
1. Add all the ingredients except vegetables/fruits first
2. Blend until smooth
3. Add the vegetable/fruits
4. Blend until smooth
5. Add a few ice cubes and serve the smoothie
6. Enjoy!

Green Smoothie Bowl

Serving: 2
Preparation Time: 5 minutes
Ingredients
- 1 ripe avocado, peeled and cut into cubes
- 1 cup of coconut water
- 1 small cucumber, cut into cubes
- 1 cup collard greens
- 1 small bunch of fresh parsley
- 1 lime, juiced only
- 1 teaspoon chia seeds
- 1 tablespoon unsweetened coconut
- 1 tablespoon almond flakes

Directions
1. Add all the ingredients except vegetables/fruits first
2. Blend until smooth
3. Add the vegetable/fruits
4. Blend until smooth
5. Add a few ice cubes and serve the smoothie
6. Enjoy!

The Flat Belly Smoothie

Serving: 2
Preparation Time: 5 minutes
Ingredients
- 3 ounces vanilla nonfat Greek yogurt
- 1 tablespoon almond butter
- ½ cup frozen blueberries
- ½ cup frozen pineapple
- 1 cup kale
- ¾ cup of water

Directions
1. Add all the ingredients except vegetables/fruits first
2. Blend until smooth
3. Add the vegetable/fruits
4. Blend until smooth
5. Add a few ice cubes and serve the smoothie
6. Enjoy!

Mango And Blueberry Bean Smoothie

Serving: 2
Preparation Time: 5 minutes
Ingredients
- 1 teaspoon ground flaxseed

- 2 tablespoons almonds
- ¼ cup kidney beans
- ½ frozen bananas, sliced into rounds
- ½ cup of frozen mango
- ½ cup frozen blueberries
- 1 cup baby spinach
- ½ cup Greek yogurt
- ¾ cup of water
- 1 cup ice

Directions
1. Add all the ingredients except vegetables/fruits first
2. Blend until smooth
3. Add the vegetable/fruits
4. Blend until smooth
5. Add a few ice cubes and serve the smoothie
6. Enjoy!

Pineapple Green Anti-Ager
Serving: 2
Preparation Time: 5 minutes
Ingredients

- ½ teaspoon fresh ginger, grated
- ¼ teaspoon turmeric
- 1 cup romaine lettuce
- ¼ cup avocado, chopped
- ½ frozen banana, sliced
- 1 cup frozen pineapple, chunks
- 1 cup unsweetened vanilla almond milk
- ½ tablespoon lime juice
- 2 tablespoons Brazil nuts
- 1 Medjool date, pitted
- 1 cup of water

Directions
1. Add all the ingredients except vegetables/fruits first
2. Blend until smooth
3. Add the vegetable/fruits
4. Blend until smooth
5. Add a few ice cubes and serve the smoothie
6. Enjoy!

Apple Cherry Pumpkin Tea
Serving: 2
Preparation Time: 5 minutes
Ingredients

- ¼ cup almonds
- ¼ cup canned pumpkin
- 1 red apple, cored, peel on
- 1 cup frozen cherries
- 1 cup brewed and chilled rooibos tea
- 1 tablespoon coconut flour
- 1 serving pea protein
- ¼ teaspoon cinnamon
- 1 pitted Medjool date
- 1 cup ice

Directions
1. Add all the ingredients except vegetables/fruits first
2. Blend until smooth
3. Add the vegetable/fruits
4. Blend until smooth
5. Add a few ice cubes and serve the smoothie
6. Enjoy!

Beets And Berry Beauty Enhancer
Serving: 2
Preparation Time: 5 minutes
Ingredients

- 1 teaspoon ginger, grated
- 2 tablespoons pumpkin seeds
- ¼ cup avocado, chopped
- ¼ cup beet, steamed and peeled
- 1/3 cup frozen strawberries
- 1/3 cup frozen raspberries
- 1/3 cup frozen blueberries
- ½ cup Greek yogurt
- ½ cup unsweetened almond milk

Directions
1. Add all the ingredients except vegetables/fruits first
2. Blend until smooth
3. Add the vegetable/fruits
4. Blend until smooth
5. Add a few ice cubes and serve the smoothie
6. Enjoy!

Hot Buffalo Wings
Servings: 8
Preparation Time: 10 minutes
Cook Time: 6 hours
Ingredients

- 1 bottle of (12 ounces) hot pepper sauce
- ½ cup melted ghee
- 1 tablespoon dried oregano + onion powder
- 2 teaspoons garlic powder
- 5 pounds of chicken wing sections

Directions:
1. Take a large bowl and mix in hot sauce, ghee, garlic powder, oregano, and onion powder, and mix well
2. Add chicken wings and toss to coat
3. Pour mix into Slow Cooker and cook on LOW for 6 hours
4. Serve and enjoy!

A Jar Full Of Pecans
Servings: 4
Preparation Time: 10 minutes
Cook Time: 2 hours
Ingredients

- 3 cups of raw pecans
- ¼ cup of date paste
- 2 teaspoons of vanilla bean extract
- 1 teaspoon of sea salt
- 1 tablespoon of coconut oil

Directions:
1. Add all of the listed ingredients to your pot
2. Cook on LOW for about 3 hours, making sure to stir it from time to time
3. Once done, allow it to cool and serve!

The Exquisite Spaghetti Squash
Servings: 6
Preparation Time: 5 minutes

Cook Time: 7-8 hours
Ingredients
- 1 spaghetti squash
- 2 cups water

Directions:
1. Wash squash carefully with water and rinse it well
2. Puncture 5-6 holes in the squash using a fork
3. Place squash in a Slow Cooker
4. Place lid and cook on LOW for 7-8 hours
5. Remove squash to a cutting board and let it cool
6. Cut squash in half and discard seeds
7. Use two forks and scrape out squash strands and transfer them to the bowl
8. Serve and enjoy!

Worthy Bacon-Wrapped Drumsticks

Servings: 6
Preparation Time: 10 minutes
Cook Time: 8 hours
Ingredients
- 12 chicken drumsticks
- 12 slices of thin-cut bacon

Directions:
1. Wrap each chicken drumstick in bacon
2. Place drumsticks in your Slow Cooker
3. Place lid and cook on LOW for 8 hours
4. Serve and enjoy!

Coconut Chocolate Cookie

Servings: 4
Preparation Time: 10 minutes
Cooking Time: Nil
Ingredients:
- 4 cups unsweetened coconut, shredded
- ½ cup coconut milk
- ¼ cup sugar-free maple syrup
- ¼ teaspoon almond extract

Directions:
1. Blend coconut in your food processor until you have a nice texture.
2. Add coconut milk and syrup; keep blending until you have a nice batter.
3. Add more milk if the batter is a bit too crumbly.
4. Transfer the mixture to the mixing bowl.
5. Use your hand to form small balls.
6. Line a baking tray with parchment paper and transfer the balls, flatten them lightly to form a cookie shape.
7. Sprinkle coconut on top and chill for 2-3 hours until firm
8. Enjoy!

Keto Shortbread

Servings: 4
Preparation Time: 10 minutes
Cooking Time: 15 minutes
Ingredients:
- ½ cup Erythritol
- 1 teaspoon vanilla extract
- 2 and ½ cups almond flour
- 6 tablespoons butter

Directions:
1. Preheat your oven to 350 degrees F.
2. Line cookie sheet with parchment paper.
3. Take a bowl, beat in butter and Erythritol, and mix until it is fluffy.
4. Beat in vanilla extract, beat in almond flour ½ cup at a time.
5. Use a tablespoon to transfer the dough to a cookie sheet.
6. Flatten each cookie to about 1/3 inch thick.
7. Bake for 12-15 minutes until golden.
8. Let them cool and serve
9. Enjoy!

1 Minute Keto Muffin

Servings: 4
Preparation Time: 10 minutes
Cooking Time: 1 minute
Ingredients:
- 1 whole egg
- 2 teaspoon coconut flour
- A pinch of baking soda
- A pinch salt
- Coconut oil, for grease

Directions:
1. Grease the ramekin dish with coconut oil.
2. Keep it aside.
3. Take a bowl and add ingredients and mix well.
4. Pour batter into a ramekin.
5. Place into microwave for 1 minute on HIGH.
6. Serve and enjoy!

Chilled No-Bake Lemon Cheesecake

Servings: 4
Preparation Time: 10 minutes + 60 minutes Chill Time
Cooking Time: Nil
Ingredients:
- 6-8 ounces cream cheese
- 2 ounces full-fat cream
- 1 tablespoon lemon juice
- Few drops of vanilla extract
- Peel ½ lemon, grated

Directions:
1. Add cream and cream cheese, and mix well.
2. Add the remaining ingredients.
3. Transfer the mixture to your fridge.
4. Keep it for 1 hour in the fridge.
5. Serve and enjoy!

Fancy Rutabaga Cakes

Servings: 4
Preparation Time: 10 minutes
Cooking Time: 25-30 minutes
Ingredients:
- 2 rutabagas, thinly sliced
- ½ stick butter, melted
- 2 tablespoons fresh thyme, chopped
- 2 teaspoons salt

Directions:

1. Place a saucepan over medium heat.
2. Add butter and let it melt.
3. Add thyme and stir for 2 minutes.
4. Take a bowl and add rutabaga slices into it and pour the mix.
5. Layer rutabaga slices in muffin tins and top with butter on top.
6. Take a foil and cover muffin tins.
7. Preheat your oven to 350 degrees F.
8. Bake for 25-30 minutes.
9. Serve and enjoy!

Eggplant Fries

Servings: 4
Preparation Time: 10 minutes
Cooking Time: 15 minutes
Ingredients:
- 2 whole eggs
- 2 cups almond flour
- 2 tablespoons coconut oil, spray
- 2 eggplant, peeled and cut thinly
- Salt and pepper to taste

Directions:
1. Preheat your oven to 400 degrees Fahrenheit.
2. Take a bowl and mix with salt and black pepper in it.
3. Take another bowl and beat eggs until frothy.
4. Dip the eggplant pieces into eggs.
5. Then coat them with a flour mixture.
6. Add another layer of flour and egg.
7. Then, take a baking sheet and grease it with coconut oil.
8. Bake for about 15 minutes.
9. Serve and enjoy!

Stuffed Parmesan Cheese Avocado

Servings: 4
Preparation Time: 10 minutes
Cooking Time: 15 minutes
Ingredients:
- 1 whole avocado
- 1 tablespoon chipotle sauce
- 1 tablespoon lime juice
- ¼ cup parmesan cheese
- Salt and pepper to taste

Directions:
1. Prepare avocado by slicing half lengthwise and discarding the seed.
2. Gently prick the skin of the avocado with a fork.
3. Set your avocado halves and skin on the small baking sheet lined with aluminum foil.
4. Top with sauce and drizzle lime juice.
5. Season with salt and pepper.
6. Sprinkle half parmesan cheese in each cavity, and set your broiler to high for 2 minutes.
7. Add the rest of the cheese and return to your broiler until the cheese melts and the avocado slightly browns.
8. Serve hot, and enjoy!

Orange And Coconut Creamsicles

Servings: 4
Preparation Time: 10 minutes + 3 Hours Chill Time
Cooking Time: Nil
Ingredients:
- A ½ cup of coconut oil
- ½ cup heavy whipping cream
- 4 ounces cream cheese
- 1 teaspoon orange mix
- 10 drops of liquid stevia

Directions:
1. Add the listed ingredients to a bowl.
2. Use an immersion blender and blend the mixture well.
3. Take a silicone tray and add the mixture.
4. Keep in the refrigerator for 2-3 hours.
5. Serve and enjoy!

Coffee Popsicles

Servings: 4
Preparation Time: 10 minutes
Cooking Time: Nil
Ingredients:
- 2 tablespoons chocolate chips, sugar-free
- 2 cups coffee, brewed and cold
- ¾ cup heavy whip cream
- 2 teaspoons natural sweetener

Directions:
1. Blend in heavy whip cream, sweetened, and coffee in your blender.
2. Mix them well.
3. Pour the mix into popsicle molds.
4. Add a few chocolate chips.
5. Keep in the fridge for 2 hours.
6. Serve and enjoy!

Tantalizing Butter Beans

Serving: 4
Preparation Time: 5 minutes
Cooking Time: 12 minutes
Ingredients
- 2 garlic cloves, minced
- Red pepper flakes to taste
- Salt to taste
- 2 tablespoons coconut butter
- 4 cups green beans, trimmed

Directions:
1. Bring a pot of salted water to boil
2. Once the water starts to boil, add beans and cook for 3 minutes
3. Take a bowl of ice water and drain beans, plunge them in the ice water
4. Once cooled, keep them on the side
5. Take a medium skillet and place it over medium heat; add ghee and melt
6. Add red pepper, salt, garlic
7. Cook for 1 minute
8. Add beans and toss until coated well; cook for 3 minutes
9. Serve and enjoy!

Healthy Carrot Chips

Serving: 4
Preparation Time: 10 minutes

Cooking Time:10 minutes
Ingredients
- 3 cups carrots, sliced paper-thin rounds
- 2 tablespoons olive oil
- 2 teaspoons ground cumin
- ½ teaspoon smoked paprika
- Pinch of salt

Directions:
1. Preheat your oven to 400 degrees Fahrenheit
2. Slice carrot into paper-thin shaped coins using a peeler
3. Place slices in a bowl and toss with oil and spices
4. Layout the slices on a parchment paper-lined baking sheet in a single layer
5. Sprinkle salt
6. Transfer to oven and bake for 8-10 minutes
7. Remove and serve
8. Enjoy!

Hearty Brussels and Pistachio
Serving: 4
Preparation Time: 15 minutes
Cooking Time:15 minutes
Ingredients
- 1 pound Brussels sprouts, tough bottom trimmed and halved lengthwise
- 4 shallots, peeled and quartered
- 1 tablespoon extra-virgin olive oil
- Sea salt
- Freshly ground black pepper
- ½ cup roasted pistachios, chopped
- Zest of ½ lemon
- Juice of ½ lemon

Directions:
1. Preheat your oven to 400 degrees F
2. Take a baking sheet and line it with aluminum foil
3. Keep it on the side
4. Take a large bowl and add Brussels, shallots and dress them with olive oil
5. Season with salt, pepper and spread veggies on a sheet
6. Bake for 15 minutes until slightly caramelized
7. Remove the oven and transfer to a serving bowl
8. Toss with lemon zest, lemon juice, and pistachios
9. Serve and enjoy!

Morning Peach
Serving: 4
Preparation Time: 10 minutes
Cooking Time:5 minutes
Ingredients
- 6 small peaches, cored and cut into wedges
- ¼ cup of coconut sugar
- 2 tablespoons almond butter
- ¼ teaspoon almond extract

Directions:
1. Take a small pan and add peaches, sugar, butter, and almond extract
2. Toss well
3. Cook over medium-high heat for 5 minutes, divide the mix into bowls and serve
4. Enjoy!

Sticky Mango Rice
Serving: 4
Preparation Time: 5 minutes
Cooking Time:20-25 minutes
Ingredients
- 1/2 cup sugar
- 1 mango, sliced
- 14 ounces coconut milk, canned
- 1/2 cup basmati rice

Directions:
1. Cook the rice according to package instructions and add half of the sugar. Make sure to substitute half of the required water with coconut milk
2. Take another skillet and boil the remaining coconut milk with sugar; once the mixture is thick, add rice and gently stir
3. Add mango slices and serve
4. Enjoy!

Pecan and Blueberry Crumble
Serving: 4
Preparation Time: 5 minutes
Cooking Time:20-25 minutes
Ingredients
- 14 ounces blueberries
- 1 tablespoon lemon juice, fresh
- 1 and ½ teaspoon stevia powder
- 3 tablespoons chia seeds
- 2 cups almond flour, blanched
- ¼ cup pecans, chopped
- 5 tablespoons coconut oil
- 2 tablespoons cinnamon

Directions:
1. Take a bowl and mix in blueberries, stevia, chia seeds, and lemon juice, and stir
2. Take an iron skillet and place it overheat; add mixture and stir
3. Take a bowl and mix in the remaining ingredients; spread the mixture over blueberries
4. Preheat your oven to 400 degrees F
5. Transfer the baking dish to your oven, bake for 25 minutes
6. Serve and enjoy!

Oatmeal Cookies
Serving: 4
Preparation Time: 10 minutes
Cooking Time:15 minutes
Ingredients
- 1/4 cup applesauce
- 1/2 teaspoon cinnamon
- 1/3 cup raisins
- 1/2 teaspoon vanilla extract, pure
- 1 cup ripe banana, mashed
- 2 cups oatmeal

Directions:
1. Preheat your oven to 350 degrees F
2. Take a bowl and mix in everything until you have a gooey mixture
3. Pour batter into an ungreased baking sheet drop by drop and flatten them using a tablespoon

4. Transfer to your oven, bake for 15 minutes
5. Serve once ready!

Cherry Tomatoes and Linguine
Serving: 4
Preparation Time: 10 minutes
Cooking Time:15 minutes
Ingredients
- 2 pounds of cherry tomatoes
- 3 tablespoons extra virgin olive oil
- 2 tablespoons balsamic vinegar
- 2 teaspoons garlic, minced
- Pinch of fresh ground black pepper
- ¾ pound whole-wheat linguine pasta
- 1 tablespoon fresh oregano, chopped
- ¼ cup feta cheese, crumbled

Directions:
1. Preheat your oven to 350-degree Fahrenheit
2. Line the baking sheet with parchment paper and keep it on the side
3. Take a large bowl and add cherry tomatoes, 2 tablespoons olive oil, balsamic vinegar, garlic, and pepper, and toss
4. Spread tomatoes evenly on a baking sheet and roast for 15 minutes
5. While the tomatoes are roasting, cook the pasta according to package instructions and drain the pasta into a large bowl
6. Toss pasta with 1 tablespoon olive oil
7. Add roasted tomatoes (with juice) and toss
8. Serve with a topping of oregano
9. Enjoy!

Apple Slices
Serving: 4
Preparation Time: 10 minutes
Cooking Time:10 minutes
Ingredients
- 1 cup of coconut oil
- ¼ cup date paste
- 2 tablespoons ground cinnamon
- 4 granny smith apples, peeled and sliced, cored

Directions:
1. Take a large-sized skillet and place it over medium heat
2. Add oil and allow the oil to heat up
3. Stir in cinnamon and date paste into the oil
4. Add cut-up apples and cook for 5-8 minutes until crispy
5. Serve and enjoy!

Vegetable and Red Pepper Hummus
Serving: 4
Preparation Time: 5 minutes
Cooking Time: Nil
Ingredients
- 1 can (15 ounces) of chickpeas
- ¼ cup tahini
- 2 tablespoons extra virgin olive oil
- ¼ cup fresh squeezed lemon juice
- 2 garlic cloves, minced
- 2 tablespoons extra virgin olive oil
- ½ teaspoon ground cumin
- ¾ cup fire-roasted red peppers
- Pinch of cayenne pepper
- Assorted selection of veggies such as cauliflower, broccoli florets, carrot sticks, snow peas, celery)

Directions:
1. Add all of the listed ingredients (except veggies) and blend until you have a nice consistency
2. Serve the hummus with raw veggies
3. Enjoy!

Cocoa Mejdool Balls
Serving: 4
Preparation Time: 5 minutes + 20 minutes chill time
Cooking Time:2-3 minutes
Ingredients
- 3 cups Medjool dates, chopped
- 12 ounces brewed coffee
- 1 cup pecan, chopped
- ½ cup coconut, shredded
- ½ cup of cocoa powder

Directions:
1. Soak dates in warm coffee for 5 minutes
2. Remove dates from the coffee and mash them, making a fine smooth mixture
3. Stir in the remaining ingredients (except cocoa powder) and form small balls out of the mixture
4. Coat with cocoa powder, serve and enjoy!

Succulent Cheesy Cauliflowers
Serving: 3
Preparation Time: 5 minutes
Cooking Time:25 minutes
Ingredients
- 1 cauliflower head
- ¼ cup vegan butter, cut into small pieces
- 1 teaspoon Vegan-Friendly Mayo
- 1 tablespoon Mustard
- ½ cup vegan cheese, grated

Directions:
1. Preheat your oven to 390 degrees F
2. Add mayo and mustard to a bowl
3. Add cauliflower to mayo mix and toss
4. Spread cauliflower in a baking dish and top with butter
5. Sprinkle cheese on top
6. Bake for 25 minutes
7. Serve and enjoy!

Creamy Leeks Platter
Serving: 6
Preparation Time: 5 minutes
Cooking Time:25 minutes
Ingredients
- 1 and ½ pound leeks, trimmed and chopped into 4-inch pieces
- 2 ounces vegan butter
- 1 cup coconut cream
- 3 and ½ ounces vegan cheese
- Salt and pepper to taste

Directions:
1. Preheat your oven to 400 degrees F

2. Take a skillet and place it over medium heat, add butter and let it heat up
3. Add leeks and Saute for 5 minutes
4. Spread leeks in greased baking dish
5. Boil cream in a saucepan and lower heat to low
6. Stir in cheese, salt, and pepper
7. Pour sauce over leeks
8. Bake for 15-20 minutes and serve warm
9. Enjoy!

Tender Coconut And Cauliflower Rice With Chili

Serving: 4
Preparation Time: 20 minutes
Cooking Time: 20 minutes
Ingredients
- 3 cups cauliflower, riced
- 2/3 cup full-fat coconut milk
- 1-2 teaspoons sriracha paste
- ¼- ½ teaspoon onion powder
- Salt as needed
- Fresh basil for garnish

Directions:
1. Take a pan and place it over medium-low heat
2. Add all of the ingredients and stir them until fully combined
3. Cook for about 5-10 minutes, making sure that the lid is on
4. Remove the lid and keep cooking until any excess liquid goes away
5. Once the rice is soft and creamy, enjoy!

Perfect Smoked Peaches

Serving: 4
Preparation Time: 10 minutes
Cooking Time: 20-30 minutes
Ingredients
- 6 fresh peaches

Directions:
1. Preheat your smoker to 200 degrees F
2. Transfer peaches directly onto your smoker and smoke for 30 minutes; the first 20 minutes should be skin side down while the final 10 should be skin side up
3. Remove from smoker and serve, enjoy!

Simple Apple Pie

Serving: 4
Preparation Time: 10 minutes
Cooking Time: 20-30 minutes
Ingredients
- 5 apples
- ¼ cup sugar
- 1 tablespoon cornstarch
- Flour as needed
- 1 refrigerated pie crust
- ¼ cup peach preserve

Directions:
1. Preheat your smoker to 275 degrees F
2. Take a medium-sized bowl and add apples, sugar, and cornstarch and stir well until combined thoroughly
3. Transfer to one side
4. Dust a work surface with flour and roll out your pie crust
5. Transfer pie crust into pie pan (no greasing)
6. Spread preserve on bottom of pan and top with apple slices
7. Transfer into smoker and smoke for 30-40 minutes
8. Serve and enjoy!

Awesome Baba Ganoush

Serving: 4
Preparation Time: 10 minutes
Cooking Time: 60-90 minutes
Ingredients
- 1 eggplant halved lengthwise
- 1 tablespoon of olive oil
- 2 and a ½ teaspoons of salt
- 2 and a ½ tablespoons of tahini
- Juice of 1 lemon
- 1 garlic clove minced
- 2 tablespoons of chopped fresh parsley
- Pita chips

Directions:
1. Preheat your smoker to 200 degrees Fahrenheit
2. Rub eggplant halves with olive oil and sprinkle 2 teaspoons of salt
3. Place the halves o the smoker rack and smoker for about 1 and a ½ hours
4. Remove and peel off the skin, discard it
5. Transfer eggplant flesh to a food processor
6. Add tahini, garlic, lemon juice, 1/ a teaspoon of salt, and blend well
7. Transfer to a storage
8. Stir in parsley and serve with pita chips
9. Enjoy!

The Great Yellow Rice

Serving: 4
Preparation Time: 5 minutes
Cooking Time: 3 minutes
Ingredients
- 2 cups stock, chicken
- ½ tablespoon turmeric
- 1 bay leaf
- 1 cup rice, long grain
- 1 tablespoon coconut butter, unsalted

Directions:
1. Rinse long-grain rice until water runs clear
2. Add rice to Instant Pot except for butter, stir
3. Stir
4. Lock lid and cook on HIGH pressure for 3 minutes
5. Naturally, release the pressure over 10 minutes
6. Remove lid and add butter
7. Fluff up and serve

Brown Rice

Serving: 4
Preparation Time: 5 minutes
Cooking Time: 22 minutes
Ingredients
- 2 cups brown rice
- 2 and ½ cups of water

Directions:
1. Add rice to the Pot
2. Add water and lock up the lid

3. Cook on HIGH pressure for 22 minutes
4. Release the pressure naturally and enjoy your favorite dish!

Israeli Couscous Dish

Serving: 4
Preparation Time: 10 minutes
Cooking Time: 5 minutes
Ingredients
- 2 and ½ cups chicken stock
- 2 tablespoons almond butter
- 16 ounces harvest grains blend
- Parsley Leaves, chopped and served
- Salt and black pepper to taste
- Sliced tomatoes and lemon as garnish

Directions:
1. Set your Instant Pot on Sauté mode.
2. Add butter and melt it; once it is hot, add grains, blend and gently mix it well.
3. Add chicken stock and seal the lid.
4. Cook for 5 minutes at high pressure.
5. Once cooked, quick release of the pressure.
6. Fluff couscous with a fork, and season with salt and pepper to taste.
7. Take a plate, divide among plates, sprinkle with parsley on top, and add sliced tomato and lemon.
8. Serve and enjoy!

Roasted Cauliflower with Ginger and Mint

Serving: 4
Preparation Time: 5 minutes
Cooking Time: 30 minutes
Ingredients
- 1 head cauliflower, cut into florets
- 2 tablespoons fresh mint, chopped
- 1 tablespoon ginger, grated
- 2 cloves garlic, minced
- 2 tablespoons fresh mint, chopped
- 1 tablespoon fresh lime juice
- ½ teaspoon salt

Directions:
1. Preheat your oven to 375 degrees F
2. Take a bowl and add cauliflower, ginger, oil, and garlic
3. Season with salt
4. Place on a baking sheet
5. Roast for 30 minutes
6. Garnish with mint and lemon juice
7. Serve and enjoy!

Spicy Sautéed Kale and Chickpeas

Serving: 4
Preparation Time: 5 minutes
Cooking Time: 5 minutes
Ingredients
- 2 cups chickpeas, rinsed and drained
- 1 pound of kale leaves
- 3 clove garlic, minced
- ¼ cup olive oil
- Pinch of red pepper flakes
- Salt to taste

Directions:
1. Take a large skillet over medium heat
2. Sauté the garlic until fragrant
3. Add in the kale leaves and chickpeas
4. Season with salt to taste
5. Allow the kale leaves to wilt for 5 minutes
6. Serve with red pepper flakes on top
7. Enjoy!

Roasted Fennel and Artichoke Hearts

Serving: 4
Preparation Time: 5 minutes
Cooking Time: 25 minutes
Ingredients
- 1 can of whole artichoke hearts in water, drained, and cut in half
- 1 fennel bulb, cut into wedges
- 2 tablespoons parsley, chopped
- 1 lemon juice
- 3 tablespoons extra virgin olive oil
- Salt and pepper to taste

Directions:
1. Preheat your oven to 425 degrees F
2. Take a bowl and place all ingredients
3. Toss to coat well
4. Arrange the vegetable on a baking sheet
5. Lined with aluminum foil
6. Roast for 25 minutes
7. Serve and enjoy!

Lovely Japanese Cabbage Dish

Serving: 6
Preparation Time: 25 minutes
Cooking Time: 0 minute
Ingredients
- ½ large head cabbage, cored and shredded
- 3 tablespoons sesame oil
- 1 teaspoon fresh ginger root, grated
- 1 teaspoon sunflower seeds
- 3 tablespoons rice vinegar
- 1 garlic clove, minced
- 1 bunch of green onions, thinly sliced
- 1 cup almond slivers
- ¼ cup toasted sesame seeds
- 1 teaspoon pepper

Directions
4. Add all listed ingredients to a large bowl
5. Add the wet ingredients first, followed by the dried ones
6. Toss well to ensure that the cabbages are coated well
7. Let it chill
8. Serve and enjoy!

Herbal Roasted Baby Potatoes

Serving: 4
Preparation Time: 10 minutes
Cooking Time: 35 minutes
Ingredients
- 2 pounds of new yellow potatoes, scrubbed and cut into wedges

- 2 tablespoons extra virgin olive oil
- 2 teaspoons fresh rosemary, chopped
- 1 teaspoon garlic powder
- 1 teaspoon sweet paprika
- ½ teaspoon sea salt
- ½ teaspoon freshly ground black pepper

Directions:
6. Preheat your oven to 400 degrees Fahrenheit
7. Line the baking sheet with aluminum foil and set it aside
8. Take a large bowl and add potatoes, olive oil, garlic, rosemary, paprika, sea salt, and pepper
9. Spread potatoes in a single layer on a baking sheet and bake for 35 minutes
10. Serve and enjoy!

Brussels Sprouts And Pistachios
Serving: 4
Preparation Time:15 minutes
Cooking Time: 15 minutes
Ingredients
- 1 pound Brussels sprouts, tough bottom trimmed and halved lengthwise
- 4 shallots, peeled and quartered
- 1 tablespoon extra-virgin olive oil
- Sea salt
- Freshly ground black pepper
- ½ cup roasted pistachios, chopped
- Zest of ½ lemon
- Juice of ½ lemon

Directions:
1. Preheat your oven to 400 degrees Fahrenheit
2. Line a baking sheet with aluminum foil and keep it on the side
3. Take a large bowl and add Brussels sprouts and shallots with olive oil and coat well
4. Season sea salt and pepper, and spread veggies evenly on a sheet
5. Bake for 15 minutes until lightly caramelized
6. Remove the oven and transfer to a serving bowl
7. Toss with lemon zest, pistachios, and lemon juice
8. Serve warm, and enjoy!

Pesto Vegetable Pizza
Serving: 4
Preparation Time:25 minutes
Cooking Time: 20 minutes
Ingredients
- 1 (10 inches) pizza crust, homemade/premade
- ½ cup sun-dried tomato pesto
- 1 cup button mushrooms, sliced
- 1 red bell pepper, chopped
- 1 cup zucchini, sliced
- 12 cup red onion, thinly sliced
- ½ cup black olives, sliced
- ½ cup parmesan cheese, grated

Directions:
1. Preheat your oven to 400 degrees Fahrenheit
2. Line a baking sheet with parchment paper and keep it on the side
3. Dust the work surface with flour and roll our pizza dough into a 10-inch circle
4. Transfer dough to a baking sheet
5. Spread pesto over dough (leaving 1 inch from the edge)
6. Arrange mushrooms, red bell pepper, zucchini, onion, and olives on pizza
7. Top with cheese
8. Bake for 20 minutes until golden and crispy

Chili Kale Chips
Serving: 4
Preparation Time:10 minutes
Cooking Time: 25 minutes
Ingredients
- 3 cups kale, stemmed and thoroughly washed, torn into 2-inch pieces
- 1 tablespoon extra-virgin olive oil
- ½ teaspoon chili powder
- ¼ teaspoon sea salt

Directions:
1. Preheat your oven to 300 degrees Fahrenheit
2. Line 2 baking sheets with parchment paper and keep it on the side
3. Dry kale entirely and transfer to a large bowl
4. Add olive oil and toss
5. Make sure each leaf is covered
6. Season kale with chili powder and salt, and toss again
7. Divide kale between baking sheets and spread into a single layer
8. Bake for 25 minutes until crispy
9. Cool the chips for 5 minutes and serve
10. Enjoy!

Cherry Tomatoes And Linguine
Serving: 4
Preparation Time:10 minutes
Cooking Time: 15 minutes
Ingredients
- 2 pounds of cherry tomatoes
- 3 tablespoons extra virgin olive oil
- 2 tablespoons balsamic vinegar
- 2 teaspoons garlic, minced
- Pinch of fresh ground black pepper
- ¾ pound whole-wheat linguine pasta
- 1 tablespoon fresh oregano, chopped
- ¼ cup feta cheese, crumbled

Directions:
1. Preheat your oven to 350 degrees Fahrenheit
2. Line the baking sheet with parchment paper and keep it on the side
3. Take a large bowl and add cherry tomatoes, 2 tablespoons olive oil, balsamic vinegar, garlic, pepper, and toss
4. Spread tomatoes evenly on a baking sheet and roast for 15 minutes
5. While the tomatoes are roasting, cook the pasta according to package instructions and drain the pasta into a large bowl
6. Toss pasta with 1 tablespoon olive oil
7. Add roasted tomatoes (with juice) and toss
8. Serve with a topping of oregano cheese and feta cheese
9. Enjoy!

Caramelized Onion And Fennel Pizza

Serving: 4
Preparation Time: 15 minutes
Cooking Time: 35 minutes
Ingredients
- 1 (10 inches) pizza crust, homemade/premade
- 1 tablespoon extra-virgin olive oil, divided
- 4 cups sweet onion, sliced
- 4 cups fennel, sliced
- 1 teaspoon fresh oregano, chopped
- 1 teaspoon dried thyme
- ¼ teaspoon freshly ground black pepper
- ¼ teaspoon sea salt
- ½ cup parmesan cheese, grated

Directions:
1. Preheat your oven to 450 degrees Fahrenheit
2. Place pizza crust on a baking sheet and brush edges with 1 tablespoon olive oil
3. Take a large skillet and place it over medium-high heat
4. Heat the remaining olive oil in the skillet
5. Add onions, fennel, thyme, oregano, pepper, salt, and Saute for 25 minutes
6. Spread veggies over pizza crust about ½ inch from the edge
7. Sprinkle vegetables with parmesan cheese
8. Bake for 10-12 minutes until crust is crispy
9. Cut pizza into 8 pieces and serve
10. Enjoy!

Linguine Dredged In Tomato Clam Sauce

Serving: 4
Preparation Time: 10 minutes
Cooking Time: 10 minutes
Ingredients
- 1 pound linguine
- Salt and black pepper as needed
- 1 teaspoon extra virgin olive oil
- 1 tablespoon garlic, minced
- 1 teaspoon fresh thyme, chopped
- ½ teaspoon red pepper flakes
- 1 can (15 ounces) sodium-free tomatoes, diced and drained
- 1 can (15 0unce) can whole baby clams, with juice

Directions:
1. Cook the linguine accordingly
2. While linguine cooks, heat olive oil in a large skillet over medium heat
3. Add garlic, thyme, and red pepper flakes, and Saute for 3 minutes
4. Stir in tomatoes and clams
5. Bring sauce to boil and lower heat to low
6. Simmer for 5 minutes
7. Season with salt and pepper
8. Drain cooked pasta and toss with sauce
9. Garnish with parsley and serve
10. Enjoy!

A Honeydew And Cucumber Medley

Serving: 2
Preparation Time: 5 minutes
Ingredients
- 1 cup ice
- 1 Medjool date, pitted
- 1 tablespoon ground flaxseed
- 1 tablespoon coconut flour
- ½ lime, juiced
- 1 tablespoon fresh mint, chopped
- 1 cup honeydew
- 1 cup cucumber, chopped
- ¾ cup Greek yogurt

Directions
1. Add all the ingredients except vegetables/fruits first
2. Blend until smooth
3. Add the vegetable/fruits
4. Blend until smooth
5. Add a few ice cubes and serve the smoothie
6. Enjoy!

Natural Nectarine

Serving: 2
Preparation Time: 5 minutes
Ingredients
- 1 cup ice
- Pinch of turmeric
- 1 teaspoon vanilla extract
- 1 tablespoon coconut flour
- ¼ cup brazil nuts
- 2 cups baby spinach
- 1 nectarine, pit removed
- 1 cup seedless red grapes
- 1 cup of coconut water

Directions
1. Add all the ingredients except vegetables/fruits first
2. Blend until smooth
3. Add the vegetable/fruits
4. Blend until smooth
5. Add a few ice cubes and serve the smoothie
6. Enjoy!

Fine Tea Toner

Serving: 2
Preparation Time: 5 minutes
Ingredients
- ½ cup edamame shelled
- 1 cup dandelion greens
- 1 green apple, cored and peeled on
- ½ frozen banana, sliced
- 1 cup brewed and chilled green tea
- 2 tablespoons walnuts
- 1-2 pitted Medjool dates
- 1 cup ice

Directions
1. Add all the ingredients except vegetables/fruits first
2. Blend until smooth

3. Add the vegetable/fruits
4. Blend until smooth
5. Add a few ice cubes and serve the smoothie
6. Enjoy!

The Grapefruit Glow

Serving: 2
Preparation Time: 5 minutes
Ingredients
- 1 cup ice
- 2 tablespoons hemp seeds
- Pinch of cinnamon
- 1 teaspoon vanilla extract
- ½ lime, peeled
- ½ cup fresh cilantro, chopped
- 1 small cucumber, sliced
- ½ cup frozen pineapple
- 1 pink grapefruit, peeled
- ½ cup silken tofu
- ½ cup 100% orange juice

Directions
1. Add all the ingredients except vegetables/fruits first
2. Blend until smooth
3. Add the vegetable/fruits
4. Blend until smooth
5. Add a few ice cubes and serve the smoothie
6. Enjoy!

The Anti-Aging Avocado

Serving: 2
Preparation Time: 5 minutes
Ingredients
- 1 cup ice
- 1 teaspoon vanilla extract
- 1 teaspoon grapeseed oil
- ½ cup avocado, chopped
- ½ cup of frozen strawberries
- ½ cup frozen peaches, chopped
- ½ cup plain Greek yogurt
- ¼ cup 100% pomegranate juice

Directions
1. Add all the ingredients except vegetables/fruits first
2. Blend until smooth
3. Add the vegetable/fruits
4. Blend until smooth
5. Add a few ice cubes and serve the smoothie
6. Enjoy!

A Green Grape Shake

Serving: 2
Preparation Time: 5 minutes
Ingredients
- 1 cup ice
- 2 tablespoons chia seeds
- 1 orange, peeled and quartered
- 1 pear, cored and chopped
- 1 cup green seedless grapes
- 2 cups baby kale
- ½ frozen banana, sliced
- ½ cup silken tofu
- ½ cup of water

Directions
1. Add all the ingredients except vegetables/fruits first
2. Blend until smooth
3. Add the vegetable/fruits
4. Blend until smooth
5. Add a few ice cubes and serve the smoothie
6. Enjoy!

Berry-Licious Anti-Oxidant Banana Smoothie

Serving: 2
Preparation Time: 5 minutes
Ingredients
- 4 ice cubes
- 1 tablespoon protein powder
- 1 banana, cut in rounds
- 1 and ½ cups mixed berries of your choice
- 1 cup of coconut water, organic

Directions
1. Add all the ingredients except vegetables/fruits first
2. Blend until smooth
3. Add the vegetable/fruits
4. Blend until smooth
5. Add a few ice cubes and serve the smoothie
6. Enjoy!

Protein-Packed Anti-Oxidizer

Serving: 2
Preparation Time: 5 minutes
Ingredients
- 2/3 scoop protein powder
- 1 tablespoon chia seeds
- 1 tablespoon flaxseeds, ground
- ½ cup baby spinach
- ¼ banana, sliced
- 1 black plum
- 5 strawberries, frozen
- 1/3 cup blackberries, frozen
- 1/3 cup raspberries, frozen
- 1/3 cup blueberries, frozen
- 2/3 cup almond milk

Directions
1. Add all the ingredients except vegetables/fruits first
2. Blend until smooth
3. Add the vegetable/fruits
4. Blend until smooth
5. Add a few ice cubes and serve the smoothie
6. Enjoy!

Triple Berry Supreme

Serving: 2
Preparation Time: 5 minutes
Ingredients
- ½ cup almond milk
- ½ cup Greek yogurt, plain
- 1 tablespoon almond butter
- 1 tablespoon flaxseed meal

- 2 cups organic spinach
- 1 banana, frozen
- ¼ cup blueberries, frozen
- ½ cup raspberries, frozen
- ½ cup blackberries, frozen

Directions
1. Add all the ingredients except vegetables/fruits first
2. Blend until smooth
3. Add the vegetable/fruits
4. Blend until smooth
5. Add a few ice cubes and serve the smoothie
6. Enjoy!

A Green Grape Shake

Serving: 2
Preparation Time: 5 minutes
Ingredients
- 1 cup ice
- 2 tablespoons chia seeds
- 1 orange, peeled and quartered
- 1 pear, cored and chopped
- 1 cup green seedless grapes
- 2 cups baby kale
- ½ frozen banana, sliced
- ½ cup silken tofu
- ½ cup of water

Directions
1. Add all the ingredients except vegetables/fruits first
2. Blend until smooth
3. Add the vegetable/fruits
4. Blend until smooth
5. Add a few ice cubes and serve the smoothie
6. Enjoy!

The Flaxseed Anti-Oxidizer

Serving: 2
Preparation Time: 5 minutes
Ingredients
- 1 small banana
- 2 cups of berries of your choice
- 2 packed cups of leafy greens of your choice
- 1 date, dried
- 1 teaspoon of cinnamon
- 2 ounces of green tea, brewed
- ¼ cup aloe vera gel
- 1 tablespoon of flaxseed
- ¼ teaspoon of pepper
- ¼ teaspoon of turmeric
- 1 tablespoon of Indian gooseberries, powdered
- 1 and ½ cup of almond milk

Directions
1. Add all the ingredients except vegetables/fruits first
2. Blend until smooth
3. Add the vegetable/fruits
4. Blend until smooth
5. Add a few ice cubes and serve the smoothie
6. Enjoy!

Mixed Berry And Kiwi Medley

Serving: 2
Preparation Time: 5 minutes
Ingredients
- 1 small banana, cut into rounds
- 1 cup of orange juice
- 1 kiwi, skin removed
- 1 and ½ cups frozen berries, mixed

Directions
1. Add all the ingredients except vegetables/fruits first
2. Blend until smooth
3. Add the vegetable/fruits
4. Blend until smooth
5. Add a few ice cubes and serve the smoothie
6. Enjoy!

Supreme Green Tea Glass

Serving: 2
Preparation Time: 5 minutes
Ingredients
- ½ teaspoon matcha powder
- 1 vanilla protein powder
- ¾ cup ice
- 1 cup strawberries, hulled
- 1 cup spinach leaves, loosely packed
- ½ banana, peeled
- 1 cup unsweetened almond milk

Directions
1. Add all the ingredients except vegetables/fruits first
2. Blend until smooth
3. Add the vegetable/fruits
4. Blend until smooth
5. Add a few ice cubes and serve the smoothie
6. Enjoy!

Pomegranate Anti-Oxidizer

Serving: 2
Preparation Time: 5 minutes
Ingredients
- 1 cup of water
- 1 cup unsweetened pomegranate juice
- 2 cups mixed berries, frozen

Directions
1. Add all the ingredients except vegetables/fruits first
2. Blend until smooth
3. Add the vegetable/fruits
4. Blend until smooth
5. Add a few ice cubes and serve the smoothie
6. Enjoy!

Anti-Oxi Boosting Rolled Oats Smoothie

Serving: 2
Preparation Time: 5 minutes
Ingredients
- 2 teaspoons LSA
- 2 tablespoons rolled oats
- 1 cup low-fat almond milk
- ½ a small banana, sliced into rounds
- ½ cup mixed berries

Directions

1. Add all the ingredients except vegetables/fruits first
2. Blend until smooth
3. Add the vegetable/fruits
4. Blend until smooth
5. Add a few ice cubes and serve the smoothie
6. Enjoy!

Anti-Oxi Rich Almond Flavored Smoothie

Serving: 2
Preparation Time: 5 minutes
Ingredients
- Just a pinch of cinnamon
- ½ cup berries, frozen
- 1 banana, frozen
- 1 cup almond milk

Directions
1. Add all the ingredients except vegetables/fruits first
2. Blend until smooth
3. Add the vegetable/fruits
4. Blend until smooth
5. Add a few ice cubes and serve the smoothie
6. Enjoy!

A Melon Cucumber Medley

Serving: 2
Preparation Time: 5 minutes
Ingredients
- ¾ cup honeydew melon, peeled and chopped
- 2 cups kale, chopped
- 1 medium cucumber, cubed

Directions
1. Add all the ingredients except vegetables/fruits first
2. Blend until smooth
3. Add the vegetable/fruits
4. Blend until smooth
5. Add a few ice cubes and serve the smoothie
6. Enjoy!

Kale And Beet 2021 Fusion

Serving: 2
Preparation Time: 5 minutes
Ingredients
- ¼ teaspoon cinnamon
- ¼ lemon, juiced
- 1 medium cucumber, cubed
- 4 cups kale, chopped
- 2 medium beets, scrubbed, halved

Directions
1. Add all the ingredients except vegetables/fruits first
2. Blend until smooth
3. Add the vegetable/fruits
4. Blend until smooth
5. Add a few ice cubes and serve the smoothie
6. Enjoy!

Strawberry And Watermelon Medley

Serving: 2
Preparation Time: 5 minutes
Ingredients
- 1 cup ice
- 1 tablespoon fresh basil
- 1 cup watermelon, cubed
- 1 cup frozen strawberries, cubed
- 1 cup unsweetened almond milk

Directions
1. Add all the ingredients except vegetables/fruits first
2. Blend until smooth
3. Add the vegetable/fruits
4. Blend until smooth
5. Add a few ice cubes and serve the smoothie
6. Enjoy!

Punch Watermelon

Serving: 2
Preparation Time: 5 minutes
Ingredients
- 1 large cucumber, cubed
- 1 cup kale, chopped
- 1 cup baby spinach, chopped
- 4 cups watermelon, chopped

Directions
1. Add all the ingredients except vegetables/fruits first
2. Blend until smooth
3. Add the vegetable/fruits
4. Blend until smooth
5. Add a few ice cubes and serve the smoothie
6. Enjoy!

Hearty Cucumber Quencher

Serving: 2
Preparation Time: 5 minutes
Ingredients
- 2 cups kale, chopped
- 1 fuji apple, quartered
- 1 large cucumber, cubed

Directions
1. Add all the ingredients except vegetables/fruits first
2. Blend until smooth
3. Add the vegetable/fruits
4. Blend until smooth
5. Add a few ice cubes and serve the smoothie
6. Enjoy!

Dandelion Aloha

Serving: 2
Preparation Time: 5 minutes
Ingredients
- 1 cup ice
- 1 cup pineapple, chopped
- 2 cups dandelion greens
- 1 cup unsweetened almond milk

Directions
1. Add all the ingredients except vegetables/fruits first
2. Blend until smooth
3. Add the vegetable/fruits
4. Blend until smooth
5. Add a few ice cubes and serve the smoothie
6. Enjoy!

Blueberry Detox Drink

Serving: 2
Preparation Time: 5 minutes
Ingredients
- 1 cup ice
- 2 tablespoons spirulina
- ½ frozen banana, sliced
- 2 cups blueberries, frozen
- 2 cups baby spinach
- 2 cups of coconut water

Directions
1. Add all the ingredients except vegetables/fruits first
2. Blend until smooth
3. Add the vegetable/fruits
4. Blend until smooth
5. Add a few ice cubes and serve the smoothie
6. Enjoy!

Chapter 15

Dessert

Sticky Ginger Cake
Preparation Time: 10 minutes
Cooking Time: 30 minutes
Servings: 16
Ingredients:
- 2 eggs, beaten
- 1 cup buttermilk
- 2 tbsps. butter
- 2 tsps. fresh ginger, grated
- 1 cup flour
- ¼ cup + 1 tbsp. honey
- ¼ cup + 1 tbsp. molasses
- ¼ cup Splenda brown sugar
- 1 tbsp. water
- 1 tsp. baking soda
- 1 tsp. ginger
- 1 tsp. cinnamon
- ½ tsp. allspice
- ¼ tsp. salt
- Nonstick cooking spray
- Swerve confections sugar, for dusting

Directions:
1. Heat the oven to 400°F. Spray an 8-inch square pan with cooking spray.
2. In a saucepan over medium heat, stir together ¼ of honey, ¼ cup of molasses, Splenda, butter, and grated ginger until the butter is melted. Remove from heat and let cool for 5 minutes.
3. In a medium bowl, stir together the dry Ingredients.
4. In a small bowl, beat the eggs and buttermilk together. Whisk into the molasses mixture until combined. Add to the dry Ingredients: and mix well. Pour into the prepared pan.
5. Bake for 25 minutes. Use a skewer to poke holes every inch across the top of the cake.
6. In a small bowl, mix the remaining honey, molasses, and water together. Brush over the hot cake. Cool completely and dust lightly with the confectioner's sugar before serving.

Tiramisu
Preparation Time: 20 minutes
Cooking Time: 4 Hours
Servings: 15
Ingredients:
- 2 (8 oz.) pkgs. reduced-fat cream cheese, soft
- 2 cups fat-free sour cream
- 2 (3 oz.) pkgs. ladyfingers, split
- ¼ cup skim milk
- 2 tbsps. Coffee liqueur
- 2/3 cup Splenda
- ½ cup strong brewed coffee
- 2 tbsps. Unsweetened cocoa powder, sifted
- ½ tsp. vanilla

Directions:
1. In a large bowl, combine the sour cream, cream cheese, sugar substitute, milk, and vanilla. Beat on high until smooth.
2. In a small bowl, stir together the coffee and liqueur.
3. Place one package of ladyfingers, cut side up, in a 2-quart baking dish. Brush with ½ of the coffee mixture. Spread ½ of the cheese mixture over the top. Repeat the layers.
4. Sprinkle the cocoa powder over top. Cover and chill for 4 hours or overnight. Cut into squares to serve.

Toffee Apple Mini Pies
Preparation Time: 20 minutes
Cooking Time: 25 minutes
Servings: 12
Ingredients:
- 2 9-inch pie crusts, soft
- 2 cups Gala apples, diced fine
- 1 egg, beaten
- 1 tbsp. butter, cut in 12 cubes
- 1½ tsp. fresh lemon juice
- 2 tbsps. Toffee bits
- 1 tbsp. Splenda
- ½ tsp. cinnamon
- Nonstick cooking spray

Directions:
1. Heat the oven to 375°F. Spray a cookie sheet with cooking spray.
2. In a medium bowl, stir together the apples, toffee, Splenda, lemon juice, and cinnamon.
3. Roll pie crusts, one at a time, out on a lightly floured surface. Use a 3-inch round cookie cutter to cut 12 circles from each crust. Place 12 on the prepared pan.
4. Brush the dough with half the egg. Spoon 1 tbsp. of the apple mixture on each round, leaving ½- inch edge. Top with a pat of butter. Place the second dough round on top and seal edges closed with a fork. Brush with the remaining egg.
5. Bake for 25 minutes, or until golden brown. Serve warm.

Pineapple Frozen Yogurt
Preparation Time: 5 minutes
Cooking Time: 1 Hour
Servings: 4
Ingredients:
- ½ cup half-and-half
- ½ cup plain reduced-fat yogurt
- ¼ cup egg substitute
- ¾ cup crushed pineapple, in juice

- ¼ cup Splenda

Directions:
1. In a medium bowl, beat the egg substitute until thick and cream-colored. Add the remaining Ingredients: and mix to thoroughly combine. Cover and chill completely, if using an ice cream maker. Once chilled, add to the ice cream maker and freeze according to the manufacturer's directions.
2. Or, you can pour the mixture into a shallow glass baking dish and freeze. Stir and scrape the mixture, every 10 minutes, with a rubber spatula until it reaches the desired consistency, about 1 hour.

Pomegranate Panna Cotta

Preparation Time: 15 minutes
Cooking Time: 4 Hours
Servings: 8
Ingredients:
- 2 ½ cup heavy cream
- ½ cup skim milk
- 8 tbsps. Pomegranate seeds
- ½ vanilla pod
- 1 envelope plain gelatin
- ¼ cup Splenda

Directions:
1. Pour the milk in a small, wide bowl and sprinkle gelatin over. Let it sit for 10 minutes.
2. Scrape the seeds from the vanilla pod into a heavy-bottomed saucepan, add the pod, too. Add the cream and Splenda and bring to a simmer over medium heat, stirring frequently. Remove from heat and stir in the gelatin mixture.
3. Pour the mixture through a fine-mesh sieve, then divide evenly between 8 4-oz. ramekins or jars. Cover and refrigerate it for at least 4 hours or overnight.
4. Serve it topped with 1 tbsp. of pomegranate seeds.

Coconutty Pudding Clouds

Preparation Time: 5 minutes
Cooking Time: 10 minutes
Servings: 4
Ingredients:
- 2 cups of heavy whipping cream
- ½ cup of reduced-fat cream cheese, soft
- ½ cup hazelnuts, ground
- 4 tbsps. Unsweetened coconut flakes, toasted
- 2 tbsps. Stevia, divided
- ½ tsp. of vanilla
- ½ tsp. of hazelnut extract
- ½ tsp. of cacao powder, unsweetened

Directions:
1. In a medium bowl, beat the cream, vanilla, and 1 tbsp. of stevia until soft peaks form.
2. In another mixing bowl, beat the cream cheese, cocoa, remaining stevia, and hazelnut extract until smooth.
3. In 4 glasses, place the ground nuts on the bottom, add a layer of the cream cheese mixture, then the whip cream, and top with toasted coconut.

Cream Cheese Pound Cake

Preparation Time: 10 minutes
Cooking Time: 35 minutes
Servings: 14
Ingredients:
- 4 eggs
- 3 ½ oz. cream cheese, soft
- 4 tbsps. Butter, soft
- 1 ¼ cup almond flour
- ¾ cup Splenda
- 1 tsp. baking powder
- 1 tsp. of vanilla
- ¼ tsp. of salt
- Butter flavored cooking spray

Directions:
1. Heat the oven to 350°F. Spray an 8-inch loaf pan with cooking spray.
2. In a medium bowl, combine flour, baking powder, and salt.
3. In a large bowl, beat the butter and Splenda until light and fluffy. And the cream cheese and vanilla and beat well.
4. Add the eggs, one at a time, beating after each one. Stir in the dry the ingredients: until thoroughly combined.
5. Pour it into the prepared pan and bake for 30-40 minutes or until the cake passes the toothpick test. Let it cool for 10 minutes in the pan, then invert it onto a serving plate. Slice and serve.

Dark Chocolate Coffee Cupcakes

Preparation Time: 10 minutes
Cooking Time: 20 minutes
Servings: 24
Ingredients:
- 2 eggs
- ½ cup fat-free sour cream
- ½ cup butter, melted
- 2 cups Splenda
- 1 cup almond flour, sifted
- 1 cup strong coffee, room temperature
- 4 oz. unsweetened chocolate
- ½ cup coconut flour
- 3 tsps. Of baking powder
- ½ tsp salt

Directions:
1. Heat the oven to 350°F. Line two 12-cups muffin tins with cupcake liners.
2. Melt the chocolate in a double broiler, set it aside, and allow it to cool.
3. Combine the Splenda, almond, and coconut flours, baking powder, and sea salt.
4. In a small bowl, combine the coffee, sour cream, and butter.
5. Add the butter mixture to the dry Ingredients: and beat on low speed until thoroughly combined.
6. Add the eggs, one at a time, beating after each one. Fold in the chocolate until well blended.
7. Spoon into the prepared pans and bake for 20-25 minutes or until they pass the toothpick test. Cool completely before serving.

German Chocolate Cake Bars

Preparation Time: 10 minutes
Cooking Time: 5 minutes
Servings: 20
Ingredients:
- 2 cups unsweetened coconut flakes

- 1 cup coconut milk, divided
- ¾ cup chopped pecans
- ¾ cup dark baking chocolate, chopped
- 1½ cup almond flour cracker crumbs
- ½ cup + 2 tbsps. Powdered sugar substitute
- ½ cup coconut oil
- Nonstick cooking spray

Directions:
1. Spray an 8x8-inch baking dish with cooking spray.
2. In a large bowl, combine the coconut, ½ cup sugar substitute, cracker crumbs, and pecan, stir to combine.
3. In a medium saucepan, combine ½ cup of milk and oil, cook over medium heat until the oil is melted, and the mixture is heated through. Pour over the coconut mixture and stir to combine. Press evenly in the prepared baking dish and chill for 1-2 hours.
4. In a clean saucepan, place the chocolate and remaining milk over med-low heat. Cook, stirring constantly until chocolate is melted and the mixture is smooth. Add the 2 tbsps. Of sugar substitute and stir to combine.
5. Pour the chocolate over the coconut layer and chill for 1 hour, or until set. Cut into squares to serve.

Gingerbread Soufflés

Preparation Time: 15 minutes
Cooking Time: 25 minutes
Servings: 10
Ingredients:
- 6 eggs, separated
- 1 cup skim milk
- 1 cup fat-free whipped topping
- 2 tbsps. Butter, soft
- ½ cup Splenda
- 1/3 cup molasses
- ¼ cup flour
- 2 tsps. Pumpkin pie spice
- 2 tsps. Vanilla
- 1 tsp. ginger
- ¼ tsp. salt
- 1/8 tsp. cream of tartar
- Butter flavored cooking spray

Directions:
1. Heat the oven to 350°F. Spray 10 ramekins with cooking spray and sprinkle with Splenda to coat, shaking out excess. Place on a large baking sheet.
2. In a large saucepan, over medium heat, whisk together the milk, Splenda, flour, and salt until smooth. Bring to a boil, whisking constantly. Pour it into a large bowl and whisk in molasses, butter, vanilla, and spices. Let it cool for 15 minutes.
3. Once the spiced mixture has cooled, whisk in the egg yolks.
4. In a large bowl, beat the egg whites and cream of tartar on high speed until stiff peaks form. Fold into the spiced mixture, a third at a time, until blended completely. Spoon into ramekins.
5. Bake for 25 minutes until puffed and set. Serve immediately with a dollop of whipped topping.

Lemon Meringue Ice Cream

Preparation Time: 5 minutes
Cooking Time: 15 minutes
Servings: 8
Ingredients:
- 4 eggs, separated
- 2 cans coconut milk, refrigerated for 24 hours
- 6 tbsps. Fresh lemon juice
- Zest of 2 lemons
- 2 ½ tbsp. Liquid stevia
- 1 tbsp. Vanilla
- 1 tsp. Cream of tartar

Directions:
1. Heat the oven to 325°F.
2. In a medium bowl, beat the egg whites and cream of tartar on high speed until soft peaks form. Add 1½ tbsps. Of stevia and continue beating on high until stiff peaks form.
3. Spread the meringue in a small baking dish and bake for 15 minutes, or until the top is golden brown. Remove it from the oven and let it cool completely.
4. Turn the canned coconut milk upside down and open. Drain off the water, save it for another use later. Scoop the cream into a large bowl. Add the egg yolks, juice, zest, remaining tablespoon of stevia, and vanilla and beat until the Ingredients: are thoroughly combined.
5. Pour into an ice cream maker and freeze according to directions.
6. In a liter-sized plastic container, spread a layer of ice cream to cover the bottom. Top with a layer of meringue. Repeat layers. Place an airtight cover on the container and freeze at least 3 hours before serving.

Mini Bread Puddings

Preparation Time: 5 minutes
Cooking Time: 35 minutes
Servings: 12
Ingredients:
- 6 slices cinnamon bread, cut into cubes
- 1¼ cup skim milk
- ½ cup egg substitute
- 1 tbsp. margarine, melted
- 1/3 cup Splenda
- 1 tsp. vanilla
- 1/8 tsp. salt
- 1/8 tsp. nutmeg

Directions:
1. Heat the oven to 350°F. Line 12 medium-size muffin cups with paper baking cups.
2. In a large bowl, stir together milk, egg substitute, Splenda, vanilla, salt, and nutmeg until combined. Add bread cubes and stir until moistened. Let it rest for 15 minutes.
3. Spoon evenly into the prepared baking cups. Drizzle margarine evenly over the tops. Bake for 30-35 minutes or until puffed and golden brown. Remove it from the oven and let cool completely.

Pumpkin Ice Cream with Candied Pecans

Preparation Time: 20 minutes
Cooking Time: 1 Hour
Servings: 8
Ingredients:
- 2 eggs

- 2 cups almond milk, unsweetened, divided
- 1 cup half-n-half
- 1 cup pumpkin
- 1 envelope unflavored gelatin
- ¾ cup Splenda
- ¾ cup Candied Pecans
- 2 tsps. Pumpkin pie spice

Directions:
1. Pour 1 cup of almond milk into a small bowl. Sprinkle the gelatin on top. Allow sitting for about 5 minutes.
2. In a medium saucepan, whisk together the Splenda and the eggs. Whisk in the pumpkin and pumpkin spice. Whisk in the gelatin.
3. Bring the mixture just to a simmer, then remove it from the heat. Allow it to cool for about 5 minutes at room temperature, then refrigerate, uncovered for 45 minutes, stirring occasionally. Do not cool too long or the mixture will set.
4. Remove the pumpkin mixture from the refrigerator and whisk in half-n-half and the remaining cup of almond milk. Pour into an ice-cream freezer and freeze according to the manufacturer's instructions.
5. When the ice cream reaches the desired consistency, transfer to a freezer-safe container with a lid. Stir in the candied pecans, cover, and place the container in the freezer to further harden the ice cream.

Raspberry Almond Clafoutis

Preparation Time: 10 minutes
Cooking Time: 1 Hour
Servings: 8
Ingredients:

- 1-pint raspberries, rinse, and pat dry
- 3 eggs
- ¾ cup almond milk, unsweetened
- ¼ cup half-n-half
- 4 tbsps. Margarine
- ½ cup almond flour
- 1/3 cup Splenda
- ¼ cup almonds, sliced
- 1 tbsp. coconut flour
- 1½ tsp. vanilla
- ½ tsp. baking powder
- ¼ tsp. allspice
- ¼ tsp. almond extract
- Nonstick cooking spray

Directions:
1. Heat the oven to 350°F. Spray a 9-inch pie dish with cooking spray and place it on a baking sheet.
2. Place the berries, in a single layer, in the pie dish.
3. In a medium bowl, stir together the flours, baking powder, and allspice.
4. Add the margarine to a small saucepan and melt over low heat. Once melted, remove from heat and whisk in Splenda until smooth.
5. Pour the margarine into a large bowl and whisk in eggs, one at a time. Add the extracts and dry Ingredients. Stir in the almond milk and half-n-half, the batter will be thin.
6. Pour over the raspberries and top with almonds. Bake for 50-60 minutes, or until the center is set and the top is lightly browned. Cool to room temperature before serving.

Blackberry Soufflés

Preparation Time: 15 minutes
Cooking Time: 30 minutes
Servings: 4
Ingredients:

- 12 oz. blackberries
- 4 egg whites
- 1/3 cup Splenda
- 1 tbsp. water
- 1 tbsp. Swerve powdered sugar
- Nonstick cooking spray

Directions:
1. Heat the oven to 375°F. Spray 4 1-cup ramekins with cooking spray.
2. In a small saucepan, over med-high heat, combine the blackberries and 1 tbsp. of water, bring to a boil. Reduce the heat and simmer until the berries are soft. Add the Splenda and stir it over medium heat until it dissolves, without boiling.
3. Bring back to boiling, reduce the heat and simmer for 5 minutes. Remove from the heat and cool for 5 minutes.
4. Place a fine-meshed sieve over a small bowl and push the berry mixture through it using the back of a spoon. Discard the seeds. Cover and chill for 15 minutes.
5. In a large bowl, beat the egg whites until soft peaks form. Gently fold in the berry mixture. Spoon evenly into the prepared ramekins and place them on a baking sheet.
6. Bake for 12 minutes, or until puffed and light brown. Dust with the powdered Swerve and serve immediately.

Blueberry Lemon "Cup" Cakes

Preparation Time: 5 minutes
Cooking Time: 10 minutes
Servings: 5
Ingredients:

- 4 eggs
- ½ cup coconut milk
- ½ cup blueberries
- 2 tbsps. Lemon zest
- ½ cup + 1 tsp. coconut flour
- ¼ cup Splenda
- ¼ cup coconut oil, melted
- 1 tsp. baking soda
- ½ tsp. lemon extract
- ¼ tsp. stevia extract
- Pinch salt

Directions:
1. In a small bowl, toss berries in the 1 tsp. of flour.
2. In a large bowl, stir together remaining flour, Splenda, baking soda, salt, and zest.
3. Add the remaining Ingredients: and mix well. Fold in the blueberries.
4. Divide batter evenly into 5 coffee cups. Microwave, one at a time, for 90 seconds, or until they pass the toothpick test.

Blueberry No-Bake Cheesecake

Preparation Time: 5 minutes

Cooking Time: 3 Hours
Servings: 8
Ingredients:
- 16 oz. fat-free cream cheese, softened
- 1 cup sugar-free frozen whipped topping, thawed
- ¾ cup blueberries
- 1 tbsp. margarine, melted
- 8 zwieback toasts
- 1 cup boiling water
- 1/3 cup Splenda
- 1 envelope unflavored gelatin
- 1 tsp. vanilla

Directions:
1. Place the toasts and margarine in a food processor. Pulse until the mixture resembles coarse crumbs. Press on the bottom of a 9-inch springform pan.
2. Place the gelatin in a medium bowl and add the boiling water. Stir until gelatin dissolved completely.
3. In a large bowl, beat cream cheese, Splenda, and vanilla on medium speed until well blended. Beat in whipped topping. Add gelatin, in a steady stream, while beating at low speed. Increase the speed to medium and beat for 4 minutes or until smooth and creamy.
   1. Add the chicken, tomato and broth and bring to a boil. Now, reduce the heat to low and simmer for about 10 minutes.
   2. Add the zucchini and chickpeas and simmer, covered for about 15 minutes. Stir in the lemon juice and serve hot.

Broiled Stone Fruit

Preparation Time: 5 minutes
Cooking Time: 5 minutes
Servings: 2
Ingredients:
- 1 peach
- 1 nectarine
- 2 tbsps. Sugar-free whipped topping
- 1 tbsp. Splenda brown sugar
- Nonstick cooking spray

Directions:
1. Heat the oven to broil. Line a shallow baking dish with foil and spray with cooking spray.
2. Cut the peach and nectarine in half and remove pits. Place cut side down in prepared dish. Broil for 3 minutes.
3. Turn the fruit over and sprinkle with the Splenda brown sugar. Broil for another 2-3 minutes.
4. Transfer 1 of each fruit to a dessert bowl and top with 1 tbsp. of whipped topping.

Café Mocha Torte

Preparation Time: 15 minutes
Cooking Time: 25 minutes
Servings: 14
Ingredients:
- 8 eggs
- 1 cup margarine, cut into cubes
- 1 pound Bittersweet chocolate, chopped
- ¼ cup brewed coffee, room temperature
- Nonstick cooking spray

Directions:
1. Heat the oven to 325°F. Spray an 8-inch springform pan with cooking spray. Line the bottom of the sides with parchment paper and spray again. Wrap the outside with a double layer of foil and place in a 9x13-inch baking dish. Put a small saucepan of water on to boil.
2. In a large bowl, beat the eggs on med speed until doubled in volume, about 5 minutes.
3. Place the chocolate, margarine, and coffee into a microwave-safe bowl and microwave on high, until chocolate is melted and mixture is smooth, stir every 30 seconds.
4. Fold 1/3 of the eggs into the chocolate mixture until almost combined. Add the remaining eggs, 1/3 at a time, and fold until combined.
5. Pour into the prepared pan. Pour the boiling water around the springform pan until it reaches halfway up the sides. Bake 22-25 minutes, or until the cake has risen slightly and edges are just beginning to set.
6. Remove it from the water bath and let it cool completely. Cover with plastic wrap and chill for 6 hours or overnight. About 30 minutes before serving, run a knife around the edges and remove the side of the pan. Slice and serve.

Cappuccino Mousse

Preparation Time: 5 minutes
Cooking Time: 1 Hour
Servings: 8
Ingredients:
- 2 cups low fat cream cheese, soft
- 1 cup half-n-half
- ½ cup almond milk, unsweetened
- ¼ cup strong brewed coffee, cooled completely
- 1-2 tsps. Coffee extract
- 1 tsp. Vanilla liquid sweetener
- Whole coffee beans for garnish

Directions:
1. In a large bowl, beat the cream cheese and coffee on high speed until smooth. Add milk, 1 tsp. coffee extract and liquid sweetener. Beat until smooth and thoroughly combined.
2. Pour in half-n-half and continue beating until the mixture resembles the texture of mousse.
3. Spoon into dessert glasses or ramekins, cover, and chill at least 1 hour before serving. Garnish with a coffee bean and serve.

Caramel Pecan Pie

Preparation Time: 5 minutes
Cooking Time: 35 minutes
Servings: 8
Ingredients:
- 1 cup pecans, chopped
- ¾ cup almond milk, unsweetened
- 1/3 cup margarine, melted
- 1 tbsp. margarine, cold
- 2 cups almond flour
- ½ cup + 2 tbsps. Splenda for baking
- 1 tsp. vanilla
- 1 tsp. Arrowroot powder
- ¾ tsp. sea salt
- ½ tsp. vanilla

- ½ tsp. maple syrup, sugar-free
- Nonstick cooking spray

Directions:
1. Heat the oven to 350°F. Spray a 9-inch pie pan with cooking spray.
2. In a medium bowl, combine the flour, melted margarine, 2 tbsps. Of Splenda, and vanilla. Mix to thoroughly combine the ingredients. Press on the bottom and sides of a prepared pie pan. Bake for 12-15 minutes, or until the edges start to brown. Set it aside.
3. In a small saucepan, combine the milk, remaining Splenda, arrowroot, salt, ½ tsp. vanilla and syrup. Cook over medium heat until it starts to boil, stirring constantly. Keep cooking until it turns a gold color and starts to thicken for about 2-3 minutes. Remove it from the heat and let it cool. Stir in ½ the pecans.
4. Pour the filling in the crust and top with the remaining pecans. Bake for about 15 minutes, or until the filling starts to bubble. Cool completely before serving.

Carrot Cupcakes

Preparation Time: 10 minutes
Cooking Time: 35 minutes
Servings: 12
Ingredients:
- 2 cups carrots, grated
- 1 cup low fat cream cheese, soft
- 2 eggs
- 1-2 tsps. Skim milk
- ½ cup coconut oil, melted
- ¼ cup coconut flour
- ¼ cup Splenda
- ¼ cup honey
- 2 tsps. Vanilla, divided
- 1 tsp. baking powder
- 1 tsp. cinnamon
- Nonstick cooking spray

Directions:
1. Heat the oven to 350°F. Lightly spray a muffin pan with cooking spray, or use paper liners.
2. In a large bowl, stir together the flour, baking powder, and cinnamon.
3. Add the carrots, eggs, oil, Splenda, and vanilla to a food processor. Process until the Ingredients are combined but carrots still have some large chunks remaining. Add the dry Ingredients: and stir them to combine.
4. Pour evenly into the prepared pan, filling cups 2/3 full. Bake for 30-35 minutes, or until cupcakes pass the toothpick test. Remove it from the oven and let it cool.
5. In a medium bowl, beat the cream cheese, honey, and vanilla on high speed until smooth. Add milk, 1 tsp. at a time, beating after each addition, until frosting is creamy enough to spread easily.
6. Once cupcakes have cooled, spread each one with about 2 tbsps. Of frosting. Chill until ready to serve.

Raspberry and Dark Chocolate Mini Soufflés

Preparation Time: 10 minutes
Cooking Time: 10 minutes
Servings: 6
Ingredients:
- 1 cup fresh raspberries
- 4 egg whites
- ½ oz. dark chocolate, chopped
- 6 tsps. Splenda
- 1 tsp. margarine, soft

Directions:
1. Heat the oven to 400°F. Use the margarine to grease 6 small ramekins.
2. Puree the raspberries in a blender or food processor and press through a fine sieve to get all of the seeds out. Add 1 tbsp. of the Splenda and set it aside.
3. Beat the egg whites until thickened and start adding the remaining Splenda, gradually, until the mixture forms stiff glossy peaks.
4. Gently fold 1/3 of the egg whites into the raspberry puree. Once mixed, fold the raspberry puree mixture into the remaining egg whites and fold gently until there are no streaks of pink left.
5. Spoon the raspberry mixture into the ramekins filling them half full. Divide the chocolate between the ramekins and then fill to the top with soufflé mixture. Place the ramekins on a baking sheet. Bake it for 9 minutes until golden brown and puffed up. Serve immediately.

Tropical Fruit Tart

Preparation Time: 10 minutes
Cooking Time: 10 minutes
Servings: 8
Ingredients:
- 1 mango, peeled, pitted, and sliced thin
- 1 banana, sliced thin
- 2 egg whites
- 15 ¼ oz. can pineapple chunks in juice, undrained
- 3 ½ oz. can sweetened flaked coconut
- 1 cup cornflakes, crushed
- 3 tsps. Splenda
- 2 tsps. Cornstarch
- 1 tsp. coconut extract
- Nonstick cooking spray

Directions:
1. Heat the oven to 425°F. Spray a 9-inch springform pan with cooking spray.
2. In a medium bowl, combine the cornflakes, coconut, and egg whites. Toss until blended. Press firmly over the bottom and ½-inch up the sides of the prepared pan. Bake for 8 minutes or until the edges start to brown. Cool completely.
3. Drain the juice from the pineapple into a small saucepan. Add the cornstarch and stir until smooth. Bring to a boil over high heat and let it cook for 1 minute, stirring constantly. Remove from heat and cool completely. Once cooled, stir in the Splenda and coconut extract.
4. In a medium bowl, combine the pineapple, mango, and banana. Spoon over the crust and drizzle with the pineapple juice mixture. Cover and chill at least for 2 hours before serving.

Sweet Potato Crème Brule

Preparation Time: 10 minutes
Cooking Time: 1 hour 5 minutes
Servings: 12

Ingredients:
- 7 egg yolks
- 1¼ cup sweet potato, baked, peeled, and mashed
- 2 cups half-n-half
- 1 tbsp. fresh lemon juice
- ¾ cup Splenda
- ¼ cup + 1/3 cup Splenda brown sugar
- 3 tsps. Vanilla
- Butter flavored cooking spray

Directions:
1. Heat the oven to 325°F. Spray a 10-inch metal quiche dish with cooking spray.
2. In a medium bowl, combine sweet potato, ¼ cup the Splenda brown sugar, and lemon juice. Spoon into the prepared dish.
3. In a 2-quart saucepan, whisk together the half-n-half, Splenda, egg yolks, and vanilla. Cook over med-low heat for 15 minutes, stirring frequently until hot, do not boil. Pour over the sweet potato mixture.
4. Place the dish in a shallow pan and put it in the oven. Pour enough boiling water to cover halfway up the sides of the dish. Bake for 1 hour or until a knife inserted in the center comes out clean. Cool it on a rack. Cover and refrigerate for 8 hours or overnight.
5. Heat the oven to broil. Sprinkle the custard with 1/3 cup of Splenda brown sugar and place the dish on a baking sheet. Broil for 3-5 minutes or until the sugar has melted. Cool for 5 minutes before serving.

Raspberry Lemon Cheesecake Squares

Preparation Time: 5 minutes
Cooking Time: 40 minutes
Servings: 12
Ingredients:
- 2 cups raspberries
- 1 cup fat-free sour cream
- ¾ cup fat-free cream cheese, softened
- ½ cup egg substitute
- 2 tbsps. Lemon juice
- 2 tsps. Lemon zest, divided
- ½ cup + 3 tbsps. Splenda
- 1 tsp. vanilla
- Nonstick cooking spray

Directions:
1. Heat the oven to 350°F. Spray 8-inch square baking pan with cooking spray.
2. In a large bowl, beat the cream cheese, ½ cup of Splenda, and vanilla on high speed until smooth. Add juice, 1 tsp. zest and egg substitute. Beat until thoroughly combined. Pour into the prepared pan.
3. Bake for 40 minutes or until firm to the touch. Remove it from the oven and cool completely.
4. In a small bowl, stir together the sour cream and 1 tbsp. of Splenda until smooth. Spoon evenly over cooled cheesecake. Cover and refrigerate overnight.
5. 30 minutes before serving, toss the berries and the remaining 2 tbsps. Of Splenda in a small bowl. Let it sit. Just before serving, stir in the remaining zest and spoon the berry mixture over the top of the cheesecake.

Mini Key Lime Tarts

Preparation Time: 5 minutes
Cooking Time: 10 minutes
Servings: 8
Ingredients:
- 4 sheets phyllo dough
- ¾ cup skim milk
- ¾ cup fat-free whipped topping, thawed
- ½ cup egg substitute
- ½ cup fat-free sour cream
- 6 tbsps. Fresh lime juice
- 2 tbsps. Cornstarch
- ½ cup Splenda
- Butter-flavored cooking spray

Directions:
1. In a medium saucepan, combine milk, juice, and cornstarch. Cook, stirring, over medium heat for 2-3 minutes or until thickened. Remove from heat.
2. Add the egg substitute and whisk for 30 seconds to allow it to cook. Stir in the sour cream and Splenda. Cover and chill until completely cool.
3. Heat the oven to 350°F. Spray 8 muffin cups with cooking spray.
4. Lay 1 sheet of the phyllo on a cutting board and lightly spray it with cooking spray. Repeat this with the remaining sheets so they are stacked on top of each other.
5. Cut the phyllo into 8 squares and gently place them in the prepared muffin cups, pressing firmly on the bottom and sides. Bake for 8-10 minutes or until golden brown. Remove them from the pan and let them cool.
6. To serve: spoon the lime mixture evenly into the 8 cups and top with whipped topping. Garnish with the fresh lime slices if desired.

Moist Butter Cake

Preparation Time: 15 minutes
Cooking Time: 30 minutes
Servings: 14
Ingredients:
- 3 eggs
- ¾ cup margarine, divided
- ½ cup fat-free sour cream
- 2 cups almond flour, packed
- 1 cup Splenda, divided
- 1 tsp. baking powder
- 2 tbsps. Water
- 1 tbsp. + 1 tsp. vanilla, divided
- Butter flavored cooking spray

Directions:
1. Heat the oven to 350°F. Spray a Bundt cake pan generously with cooking spray.
2. In a large bowl, whisk together the flour, sour cream, ½ cup of margarine, 3 eggs, 2/3 cup of Splenda, baking powder, and 1 tsp. vanilla until thoroughly combined.
3. Pour into the prepared pan and bake for 30-35 minutes, or until it passes the toothpick test. Remove it from the oven.
4. Melt ¼ cup of margarine in a small saucepan over medium heat. Whisk in 1/3 cup of Splenda, tablespoon vanilla, and water. Continue to stir until the Splenda is completely dissolved.

5. Use a skewer to poke several small holes on top of the cake. Pour the syrup mixture evenly over the cake making sure all the holes are filled. Swirl the pan for a couple of minutes until the syrup is absorbed into the cake.

No-Bake Chocolate Swirl Cheesecake

Preparation Time: 25 minutes
Cooking Time: 10 minutes
Servings: 16
Ingredients:
- 3 (8 oz.) pkgs. fat-free cream cheese, soft
- 1 cup fat-free sour cream
- ¾ cup skim milk
- ½ cup semisweet chocolate, melted and cooled
- 2 tbsps. Margarine, melted
- ½ cup graham crackers, finely crushed
- 1/3 cup Splenda
- 1 envelope unflavored gelatin
- 2 tsps. Vanilla

Directions:
1. In a medium bowl, stir together the cracker crumbs and margarine until moistened. Press evenly on the bottom of an 8-inch springform pan. Cover and chill.
2. In a small saucepot, add the milk and sprinkle gelatin over the top, let stand for 5 minutes. Heat to low heat, and stir until the gelatin dissolves. Remove from the heat and let it cool for 15 minutes.
3. In a large bowl, beat the cream cheese until smooth. Beat in the sour cream, sugar, and vanilla. Slowly beat in the gelatin mixture.
4. Divide the cheese mixture in half. Slowly stir the melted chocolate into one half.
5. Spread half the chocolate mixture evenly over chilled crust. Spoon half the white cheese mix over the chocolate in small dollops. Using a butter knife, swirl the two layers together. Repeat with the remaining fillings. Cover and chill for 6 hours, or until set.

No-Bake Lemon Tart

Preparation Time: 10 minutes
Cooking Time: 2 Hours
Servings: 8
Ingredients:
- ½ cup margarine, soft
- 1/3 cup + 3 tbsps. Fresh lemon juice, divided
- 1/3 cup almond milk, unsweetened
- 4 ½ tbsp. margarine, melted
- 3-4 tbsps. Lemon zest, grated fine
- 1 cup almond flour
- ¾ cup coconut, grated fine
- ¼ cup + 3 tbsps. Splenda
- 2 ½ tsp. vanilla, divided
- 2 tsps. Lemon extract
- ¼ tsp. salt

Directions:
1. Spray a 9-inch tart pan with cooking spray.
2. In a medium bowl, combine the flour, coconut, 3 tbsps. Of lemon juice, 2 tbsps. Of Splenda, melted margarine, 1½ tsps. Of vanilla, and a pinch of salt until thoroughly combined. Dump into the prepared pan and press evenly on the bottom and halfway up the sides. Cover and chill until ready to use.
3. In a medium bowl, beat the soft margarine until fluffy. Add the remaining Ingredients: and beat until the mixture is smooth. Taste and add more lemon juice or Splenda if desired.
4. Pour the filling into the crust. Cover and chill until the filling are set, about 2 hours.

Chocolate Cherry Cake Roll

Preparation Time: 10 minutes
Cooking Time: 15 minutes
Servings: 10
Ingredients:
- 10 maraschino cherries, drained and patted dry
- 4 eggs, room temperature
- 1 cup sugar-free Cool Whip, thawed
- 2/3 cup maraschino cherries, chop, drain and pat dry
- ½ cup cream cheese, soft
- 1/3 cup flour
- ½ cup Splenda for baking
- ¼ cup unsweetened cocoa powder
- 1 tbsp. sugar-free hot fudge ice cream topping
- ¼ tsp. baking soda
- ¼ tsp. salt
- Unsweetened cocoa powder
- Nonstick cooking spray

Directions:
1. Heat the oven to 375°F. Spray a large sheet baking pan with cooking spray. Line bottom with parchment paper, spray and flour the paper.
2. In a small bowl, stir together the flour, ¼ cup cocoa, baking soda, and salt.
3. In a large bowl, beat the eggs at high speed for 5 minutes.
4. Gradually add the sweetener and continue beating until the mixture is thick and lemon-colored.
5. Fold in the dry Ingredients. Spread evenly into the prepared pan. Bake for 15 minutes or top springs back when touched lightly.
6. Place a clean towel on a cutting board and sprinkle with cocoa powder. Turn the cake onto a towel and carefully remove parchment paper.
7. Starting at a short end, roll up the towel. Cool on a wire rack for 1 hour.
8. Prepare the filling: In a small bowl, beat the cream cheese until smooth. Add ½ cup whipped topping, beat on low until combined. Fold in another ½ cup whipped topping. Fold in the chopped cherries.
9. Unroll the cake and remove the towel. Spread the filling to within 1 inch of the edges. Reroll the cake and trim the ends. Cover and chill for at least 2 hours or overnight.
10. To serve, warm up the fudge topping and drizzle it over the cake, garnish with whole cherries, then slice and serve.

Chocolate Orange Bread Pudding

Preparation Time: 10 minutes
Cooking Time: 35 minutes
Servings: 8
Ingredients:
- 4 cups French baguette cubes
- 1½ cups skim milk
- 3 eggs, lightly beaten
- 1-2 tsps. Orange zest, grated
- ¼ cup Splenda
- ¼ cup sugar-free chocolate ice cream topping
- 3 tbsps. Unsweetened cocoa powder
- 1 tsp. vanilla
- ¾ tsp. cinnamon

Directions:
1. Heat the oven to 350°F.
2. In a medium bowl, stir together the Splenda and cocoa. Stir in milk, eggs, zest, vanilla, and cinnamon until well blended.
3. Place bread cubes in an 8-inch square baking dish. Pour the milk mixture evenly over the top.
4. Bake for 35 minutes or until a knife inserted in the center comes out clean. Cool for 5-10 minutes.
5. Spoon into dessert dishes and drizzle lightly with ice cream topping.

Chocolate Torte

Preparation Time: 15 minutes
Cooking Time: 35 minutes
Servings: 12
Ingredients:
- 5 eggs, separated, room temperature
- ¾ cup margarine, sliced
- 1 pkg. semisweet chocolate chips
- ½ cup Splenda
- ¼ tsp. cream of tartar
- Nonstick cooking spray

Directions:
1. Heat the oven to 350°F. Spray a 6-7-inch springform pan with cooking spray.
2. In a microwave-safe bowl, melt chocolate chips and margarine, in 30-second intervals.
3. In a large bowl, beat the egg yolks till thick and lemon-colored. Beat in the chocolate.
4. In a separate large bowl, with clean beaters, beat egg whites and cream of tartar till foamy. Beat in the Splenda, 1 tbsp. at a time, till sugar is dissolved, continue beating till stiff glossy peaks form.
5. Fold ¼ of the egg whites into the chocolate mixture, then fold in the rest. Transfer to the prepared pan. Bake for 30-35 minutes, or until the center is set. Let it cool completely before removing the side of the pan and serving.

Cinnamon Bread Pudding

Preparation Time: 10 minutes
Cooking Time: 45 minutes
Servings: 6
Ingredients:
- 4 cups day-old French or Italian bread, cut into ¾-inch cubes
- 2 cups skim milk
- 2 egg whites
- 1 egg
- 4 tbsps. Margarine, sliced
- 5 tsps. Splenda
- 1½ tsp. cinnamon
- ¼ tsp. salt
- 1/8 tsp. ground cloves

Directions:
1. Heat the oven to 350°F.
2. In a medium saucepan, heat milk and margarine to simmering. Remove it from the heat and stir till the margarine is completely melted. Let it cool for 10 minutes.
3. In a large bowl, beat the egg and egg whites until foamy. Add the Splenda, spices, and salt. Beat until combined, then add in the cooled milk and bread.
4. Transfer mixture to a 1½ quart baking dish. Place on rack of roasting pan and add 1 inch of the hot water to the roaster.
5. Bake until the pudding is set and the knife inserted in the center comes out clean, about 40-45 minutes.

Coconut Cream Pie

Preparation Time: 5 minutes
Cooking Time: 10 minutes
Servings: 8
Ingredients:
- 2 cups raw coconut, grated and divided
- 2 cans coconut milk, full fat, and refrigerated for 24 hours
- ½ cup raw coconut, grated and toasted
- 2 tbsps. Margarine, melted
- 1 cup Splenda
- ½ cup macadamia nuts
- ¼ cup almond flour

Directions:
1. Heat the oven to 350°F.
2. Add the nuts to a food processor and pulse until finely ground. Add the flour, ½ cup Splenda, and 1 cup grated coconut. Pulse until the Ingredients: are finely ground and resemble cracker crumbs.
3. Add the margarine and pulse until the mixture starts to stick together. Press on the bottom and sides of a 9-inch pie pan. Bake for 10 minutes or until golden brown. Cool.
4. Turn the canned coconut upside down and open. Pour off the water and scoop the cream into a large bowl. Add the remaining ½ cup of Splenda and beat on high until stiff peaks form. Fold in the remaining 1 cup of coconut and pour it into the crust. Cover and chill at least for 2 hours. Sprinkle with toasted coconut, slice, and serve.

Coconut Milk Shakes

Preparation Time: 5 minutes
Cooking Time: 5 minutes
Servings: 2
Ingredients:
- 1½ cup vanilla ice cream
- ½ cup coconut milk, unsweetened
- 2½ tbsp. coconut flakes
- 1 tsp. unsweetened cocoa

Directions:
- Heat the oven to 350°F.

- Place the coconut on a baking sheet and bake for 2-3 minutes, stirring often, until the coconut is toasted.
- Place ice cream, milk, 2 tbsps. Of coconut, and cocoa in a blender and process them until smooth.
- Pour it into glasses and garnish it with the remaining toasted coconut. Serve immediately.

Peach Custard Tart

Preparation Time: 5 minutes
Cooking Time: 40 minutes
Servings: 8
Ingredients:
- 12 oz. frozen unsweetened peach slices, thaw, and drain
- 2 eggs, separated
- 1 cup skim milk
- 4 tbsps. Cold margarine, cut into pieces
- 1 cup flour
- 3 tbsps. Splenda
- 2-3 tbsps. Cold water
- 1 tsp. vanilla
- ¼ tsp. + 1/8 tsp. salt, divided
- ¼ tsp. nutmeg

Directions:
1. Heat the oven to 400°F.
2. In a medium bowl, stir together the flour and ¼ tsp. of salt. With a pastry blender, cut in the margarine until the mixture resembles coarse crumbs. Stir in the cold water, a tablespoon at a time, just until moistened. Shape into a disc.
3. On a lightly floured surface, roll out the dough to an 11-inch circle. Place in the bottom of a 9-inch tart pan with a removable bottom. Turn the edge under and pierce the sides and bottom with a fork.
4. In a small bowl, beat 1 egg white with a fork, discard the other or save for another use. Lightly brush crust with egg. Place the tart pan on a baking sheet and bake for 10 minutes. Cool.
5. In a large bowl, whisk together the egg yolks, Splenda, vanilla, nutmeg, and 1/8 tsp. of salt until combined.
6. Pour the milk into a glass measuring cup and microwave on high for 1 minute. Do not boil. Whisk the milk into the egg mixture until blended.
7. Arrange the peaches on the bottom of the crust and pour the egg mixture over the top. Bake for 25-30 minutes, or until set. Cool to room temperature. Cover and chill at least for 2 hours before serving.

Peach Ice Cream

Preparation Time: 15 minutes
Cooking Time: 4 Hours
Servings: 32
Ingredients:
- 4 peaches, peel, and chop
- 8 oz. fat-free whipped topping
- 2 cups skim milk
- ¼ cup fresh lemon juice
- 2-12 oz. cans fat-free evaporated milk
- 14 oz. can sweeten condensed milk
- 1 oz. pkg. sugar-free instant vanilla pudding mix
- ½ cup Splenda - 1 tsp. vanilla
- ½ tsp. almond extract
- 1/8 tsp. salt

Directions:
1. In a large bowl, beat the milk and pudding mix on low speed for 2 minutes. Beat in the remaining Ingredients, except whipped topping until thoroughly combined. Fold in whipped topping.
2. Freeze in the ice cream maker according to the manufacturer's directions, this may take 2 batches. Transfer it to freezer containers and freeze for 4 hours before serving.

Peanut Butter Pie

Preparation Time: 10 minutes
Cooking Time: 4 Hours
Servings: 8
Ingredients:
- 1½ cup skim milk
- 1½ cup frozen fat-free whipped topping, thawed and divided
- 1 small pkg. sugar-free instant vanilla pudding mix
- 1 (1½ oz.) pkg. sugar-free peanut butter cups, chopped
- 1 (9-inch) reduced-fat graham cracker pie crust
- 1/3 cup reduced-fat peanut butter
- ½ tsp. vanilla

Directions:
1. In a large bowl, whisk together the milk and pudding mix until it thickens. Whisk in the peanut butter, vanilla, and 1 cup of whip cream. Fold in the peanut butter cups.
2. Pour it into the pie crust and spread the remaining whip cream over top. Cover and chill at least 4 hours before serving.

Raspberry Peach Cobbler

Preparation Time: 15 minutes
Cooking Time: 40 minutes
Servings: 8
Ingredients:
- 1¼ pounds peaches, peeled and sliced
- 2 cups fresh raspberries
- ½ cup low-fat buttermilk
- 2 tbsps. Cold margarine, cut into pieces
- 1 tsp. lemon zest
- ¾ cup + 2 tbsps. Flour, divided
- 4 tbsps. + 2 tsps. Splenda, divided
- ½ tsp. baking powder
- ½ tsp. baking soda
- 1/8 tsp. salt
- Nonstick cooking spray

Directions:
1. Heat the oven to 425°F. Spray an 11×7-inch baking dish with cooking spray.
2. In a large bowl, stir together 2 tbsps. Of Splenda and 2 tbsps. Of flour. Add the fruit and zest and toss to coat. Pour into the prepared baking dish. Bake for 15 minutes, or until the fruit is bubbling around the edges.
3. In a medium bowl, combine the remaining flour, 2 tbsps. Of Splenda, baking powder, baking soda, and

salt. Cut in the margarine with the pastry cutter until it resembles coarse crumbs. Stir in the buttermilk just until moistened.

4. Remove the fruit from the oven and top with dollops of the buttermilk mixture. Sprinkle the remaining 2 tsps. Of Splenda over the top and bake for 18-20 minutes or the top is lightly browned. Serve warm.

Deliciously Simple Brownie Muffin
Servings: 5
Preparation Time: 10 minutes
Cooking Time: 35 minutes
Ingredients:
- 1 cup golden flaxseed meal
- ¼ cup cocoa powder
- 1 tablespoon cinnamon
- ½ tablespoon baking powder
- ½ teaspoon salt
- 1 large egg
- 2 tablespoons coconut oil
- 2 tablespoons stevia
- ½ cup pumpkin puree
- 1 teaspoon vanilla extract
- 1 teaspoon apple cider vinegar
- ¼ cup almonds, slivered

Directions:
1. Preheat your oven to 350 degrees F
2. Take a mixing bowl and add all of the listed ingredients and mix everything well
3. Take your desired number of muffin tins and line them up with paper liners
4. Scoop up the batter into the muffin tins, filling them to about 1/4rth of the liner
5. Sprinkle a bit of almond on top
6. Place them in your oven and bake for 15 minutes
7. Serve warm

The Avocado Day Stopper
Servings: 2
Preparation Time: 10 minutes
Ingredients:
- ½ avocado, cubed
- 1 cup coconut milk
- Half a lemon
- ¼ cup fresh spinach leaves
- 1 pear
- 1 tablespoon hemp. Seed powder

Toppings
- A handful of macadamia nuts
- Handful of grapes
- 2 lemon slices

Directions:
1. Add all the listed ingredients to your blender except coconut oil, salt, and chili powder
2. Blend until smooth
3. Add salt, coconut oil, and chili powder
4. Stir well and serve chilled!

Jalapeno Crisp
Servings: 20
Preparation Time: 10 minutes
Cooking Time: 1 hour 15 minutes
Ingredients:
- 1 cup sesame seeds
- 1 cup sunflower seeds
- 1 cup flaxseeds
- ½ cup hulled hemp seeds
- 3 tablespoons Psyllium husk
- 1 teaspoon salt
- 1 teaspoon baking powder
- 2 cups water

Directions:
1. Preheat your oven to a temperature of 350 degrees F
2. Take your blender and add seeds, baking powder, salt, and Psyllium husk
3. Blend well until a sand-like texture appears
4. Stir in water and mix until a batter forms
5. Allow the batter to rest for 10 minutes until a dough-like thick mixture forms
6. Pour the dough onto a cookie sheet lined up with parchment paper
7. Spread it evenly, making sure that it has a thickness of ¼ inch thick all around
8. Bake for 75 minutes in your oven
9. Remove and cut up into 20 spices
10. Allow them to cool for 30 minutes, and enjoy!

Easy Jalapeno Bread
Servings: 4
Preparation Time: 10 minutes
Cooking Time: 50 minutes
Ingredients:
- 4 ounces bacon
- 3 Jalapenos, sliced
- 6 eggs
- ½ cup Ghee, melted + more for greasing
- ¼ cup water
- ¼ teaspoon baking soda
- ½ cup coconut flour sifted
- ½ teaspoon salt

Directions:
1. Preheat your oven to 400 degrees F
2. Place bacon and sliced jalapeno on a baking tray, roast for 10 minutes, making sure to flip halfway through
3. Once done, take them out and let them cool
4. Discard seeds from roasted jalapeno
5. Add bacon and jalapeno to the food processor and pulse until combined
6. Take a bowl and add eggs, ghee, baking soda, water, coconut flour, salt
7. Add jalapeno and bacon to the batter and mix well
8. Grease your baking dish with ghee and pour batter into the pan; bake for 40 minutes at 375 degrees F
9. Let it cool, slice, and enjoy!

Spicy Popper Mug Cake
Servings: 2
Preparation Time: 5 minutes
Cooking Time: 5 minutes
Ingredients:

- 2 tablespoons almond flour
- 1 tablespoon flaxseed meal
- 1 tablespoon butter
- 1 tablespoon cream cheese
- 1 large egg
- 1 bacon, cooked and sliced
- ½ a jalapeno pepper
- ½ teaspoon baking powder
- ¼ teaspoon salt

Directions:
1. Take a frying pan and place it over medium heat
2. Add sliced bacon and cook until they have a crispy texture
3. Take a microwave-proof container and, mix all of the listed ingredients (including cooked bacon), clean the sides
4. Microwave for 75 seconds making to put your microwave to high power
5. Take out the cup and slam it against a surface to take the cake out
6. Garnish with a bit of jalapeno, and serve!

Creamy Coffee Popsicles

Servings: 4
Preparation Time: 2 hours
Cooking Time: Nil
Ingredients:
- 2 tablespoon chocolate chips, sugar-free
- 2 cups coffee, brewed and cold
- ¾ cup heavy whip cream
- 2 teaspoons natural sweetener

Directions:
1. Blend in heavy whip cream, sweetened, and coffee in a blender
2. Mix well
3. Pour mix into popsicle molds and add a few chocolate chips
4. Let it freeze for 2 hours
5. Serve and enjoy!

The Most Elegant Parsley Soufflé Ever

Servings: 5
Preparation Time: 5 minutes
Cooking Time: 6 minutes
Ingredients:
- 2 whole eggs
- 1 fresh red chili pepper, chopped
- 2 tablespoons coconut cream
- 1 tablespoon fresh parsley, chopped
- Salt to taste

Directions:
1. Preheat your oven to 390 degrees F
2. Butter 2 soufflé dishes
3. Add the ingredients to a blender and mix well
4. Divide batter into soufflé dishes and bake for 6 minutes
5. Serve and enjoy!

Almond Butter Cup Cookies

Servings: 4
Preparation Time: 10 minutes
Cooking Time: 90 minutes
Ingredients:
- 1 cup almond butter
- ½ cup coconut crystals
- 1 teaspoon vanilla bean extract
- ¼ teaspoon almond extract
- 2 whole eggs
- ½ cup almond flour, blanched
- 2 tablespoons coconut flour
- ¼ teaspoon salt
- 1 cup dark chocolate, chopped, unsweetened

Directions:
1. Preheat your oven to 350 degrees F
2. Prepare a baking sheet by lightly greasing it with coconut oil
3. Add crystal, almond butter, eggs, almond extract, and vanilla extract to a medium bowl
4. Mix well
5. Take another bowl and add flours, salt, and mix
6. Add the flour mix to the bowl with wet ingredients and stir until combined
7. Form golf ball-sized cookies and form them into peanut butter cups
8. Place cookies on a baking sheet and let them bake for 12 minutes
9. Chill for 30 minutes in refrigerators
10. Melt chocolate over medium heat in a double boiler and cool for 15 minutes; pour chocolate over chilled cookies
11. Serve and enjoy!

Lovely Pumpkin Buns

Servings: 10
Preparation Time: 10 minutes
Cooking Time: 50 minutes
Ingredients:
- ½ cup coconut flour
- 1 and ½ cups almond flour
- ½ cup ground flax seeds
- 1 teaspoon onion powder
- 1 teaspoon garlic powder
- 1 teaspoon baking soda
- 2 teaspoon cream of tartar
- 5 tablespoons sesame seeds
- 1 teaspoons salt

Wet Ingredients:
- 2 Eggs
- 6 egg whites
- 1 cup of warm water
- 1/3 cup Psyllium husk powder

Directions:
1. Preheat your oven to 350 degrees F
2. Take a baking tray and line it up with parchment paper; keep it on the side
3. Take a bowl and mix in dry ingredients; mix it well
4. Take another bowl and whisk in eggs, water, and husk
5. Mix well until smooth
6. Slowly add dry ingredients into the wet ingredients bowl
7. Keep mixing until you have an even dough
8. Knead dough until smooth and roll dough into buns, arrange them on your baking tray
9. Bake for 50 minutes

10. Once done, remove them from the oven and let them cool. Serve!

Gingerbread Keto Muffins

Servings: 6
Preparation Time: 10 minutes
Cooking Time: 10-15 minutes
Ingredients:
- 1 tablespoon ground flaxseed
- 6 tablespoons coconut milk
- 1 tablespoon apple cider vinegar
- ½ cup peanut butter
- 2 tablespoons gingerbread spice blend
- 1 teaspoon baking powder
- 1 teaspoon vanilla extract
- 2 tablespoons Swerve

Directions:
1. Preheat your oven to 350 degrees F
2. Take a bowl and add flaxseed, salt, vanilla, sweetener, spices, and non-dairy milk
3. Keep it on the side
4. Add peanut butter and baking powder and keep mixing
5. Stir well
6. Spoon batter into muffin liners and bake for 30 minutes
7. Let them cool and serve
8. Enjoy!

Sensational Lemonade Fat Bomb

Servings: 2
Preparation Time: 2 hours
Cooking Time: Nil
Ingredients:
- ½ a lemon
- 4 ounces cream cheese
- 2 ounces butter
- Salt to taste
- 2 teaspoon natural sweetener

Directions:
1. Take a fin grater and zest lemon
2. Squeeze lemon juice into the bowl with the zest
3. Add butter, and cream cheese to a bowl and add zest, juice, salt, sweetener
4. Mix well using a hand mixer until smooth
5. Spoon mixture into molds and let them freeze for 2 hours
6. Serve and enjoy!

The Easy "No-Bake" Fudge

Servings: 25
Preparation Time: 15 minutes + chill time
Cooking Time: 5 minutes
Ingredients:
- 1 and ¾ cups coconut butter
- 1 cup pumpkin puree
- 1 teaspoon ground cinnamon
- ¼ teaspoon ground nutmeg
- 1 tablespoon coconut oil

Directions:
1. Take an 8x8 inch square baking pan and line it up with aluminum foil
2. Take a spoon and scoop out coconut butter into a heated pan and allow the butter to melt
3. Keep stirring well, and remove the heat once fully melted
4. Add spices and pumpkin, and keep training until you have a grain-like texture
5. Add coconut oil and keep stirring to incorporate everything
6. Scoop the mixture into your baking pan and evenly distribute it
7. Place a wax paper on top of the mixture and press gently to straighten the top
8. Remove the paper and discard
9. Allow it to chill for 1-2 hours
10. Once chilled, take it out and slice it up into pieces
11. Enjoy!

Elegant Poppyseed Muffins

Servings: 6
Preparation Time: 10 minutes
Cooking Time: 10-15 minutes
Ingredients:
- ¾ cup blanched almond flour
- ¼ cup golden flaxseed meal
- 1/3 cup Erythritol
- 1 teaspoon baking powder
- 2 tablespoons poppy seeds
- ¼ cup melted salted butter
- ¼ cup heavy cream
- 3 large whole eggs
- Zest of 2 lemons
- 3 tablespoons lemon juice
- 1 teaspoon vanilla extract
- 25 drops of liquid stevia

Directions:
1. Preheat your oven to a temperature of 350 degrees Fahrenheit
2. Take a mixing bowl and add poppy seeds, almond flour, Erythritol
3. Add the Flaxseed meal as well and let it stir completely
4. Add the melted butter
5. Pour heavy cream alongside the egg
6. Mix everything well
7. Add baking powder, vanilla, lemon juice, stevia, and zest
8. Mix everything to incorporate them well
9. Pour the batter into cupcake molds and bake for 20 minutes until a brown texture is seen
10. Cool the muffins on a cooling rack for 10 minutes and serve!

Swirly Cinnamon Muffins

Servings: 6
Preparation Time: 10 minutes
Cooking Time: 10-15 minutes
Ingredients:
- 1 cup cauliflower, cooked and cooled
- ¾ cup Keto-Friendly Protein Powder
- ½ cup ground peanuts
- 3 egg
- 1 tablespoon coconut oil
- 4 teaspoons stevia
- 1 teaspoon baking powder

- 2 tablespoons Ghee, melted
- 1 tablespoon cinnamon

Directions:
1. Preheat your oven to 350 degrees F
2. Grease muffin tin
3. Add cauliflower, peanut butter, powder, eggs, coconut oil, baking powder, and stevia to a bowl and mix; keep it on the side
4. Pour batter into muffin tins
5. Take a bowl and add cinnamon and ghee; pour ½ teaspoon of the mix on top of each muffin and swirl using a toothpick
6. Bake for 10 minutes
7. Remove from oven and let them cool
8. Serve and enjoy!

Mesmerizing Garlic Bagels

Servings: 6
Preparation Time: 10 minutes
Cooking Time: 15 minutes
Ingredients:
- 6 whole eggs
- 1 and ½ teaspoon Garlic powder
- 1/3 cup butter, melted
- ½ teaspoon salt
- ½ cup coconut flour sifted
- ½ teaspoon baking powder

Directions:
1. Preheat your oven to 400 degrees F
2. Grease the bagel pan and keep it on the side
3. Whisk in eggs, garlic powder, butter, and salt to a bowl and keep it on the side
4. Add coconut flour and baking powder to the egg mix, mix well until incorporated, and a batter forms with no lumps
5. Pour batter into bagel pan
6. Bake for 15 minutes
7. Remove from oven and let them cool
8. Serve and enjoy!

Ravaging Blueberry Muffin

Servings: 4
Preparation Time: 10 minutes
Cooking Time: 30 minutes
Ingredients:
- 1 cup almond flour
- Pinch of salt
- 1/8 teaspoon baking soda
- 1 whole egg
- 2 tablespoons coconut oil, melted
- ½ cup coconut milk
- ¼ cup fresh blueberries

Directions:
1. Preheat your oven to 350 degrees F
2. Line a muffin tin with paper muffin cups
3. Add almond flour, salt, and baking soda to a bowl and mix; keep it on the side
4. Take another bowl and add egg, coconut oil, coconut milk, and mix
5. Add mix to flour mix and gently combine until incorporated
6. Mix in blueberries and fill the cupcakes tins with batter
7. Bake for 20-25 minutes
8. Enjoy!

No-Bake Cheesecake

Servings: 10
Preparation Time: 120 minutes
Cooking Time: Nil
Ingredients:
For Crust
- 2 tablespoons ground flaxseeds
- 2 tablespoons desiccated coconut
- 1 teaspoon cinnamon

For Filling
- 4 ounces vegan cream cheese
- 1 cup cashews, soaked
- ½ cup frozen blueberries
- 2 tablespoons coconut oil
- 1 tablespoon lemon juice
- 1 teaspoon vanilla extract
- Liquid stevia

Directions:
1. Take a container and mix in the crust ingredients; mix well
2. Flatten the mixture at the bottom to prepare the crust of your cheesecake
3. Take a blender/ food processor and add the filling ingredients; blend until smooth
4. Gently pour the batter on top of your crust and chill for 2 hours
5. Serve and enjoy!

Supreme Matcha Bomb

Servings: 10
Preparation Time: 100 minutes
Cooking Time: Nil
Ingredients:
- 3/4 cup hemp seeds
- ½ cup coconut oil
- 2 tablespoons coconut butter
- 1 teaspoon Matcha powder
- 2 tablespoons vanilla bean extract
- ½ teaspoon mint extract
- Liquid stevia

Directions:
1. Take your blender/food processor and add hemp seeds, coconut oil, Matcha, vanilla extract, and stevia
2. Blend until you have a nice batter and divide into silicon molds
3. Melt coconut butter and drizzle on top
4. Let the cups chill and enjoy!

Hearty Almond Bread

Servings: 8
Preparation Time: 15 minutes
Cooking Time: 60 minutes
Ingredients:
- 3 cups almond flour
- 1 teaspoon baking soda
- 2 teaspoons baking powder
- ¼ teaspoon salt
- ¼ cup almond milk
- ½ cup + 2 tablespoons olive oil

- 3 whole eggs

Directions:
1. Preheat your oven to 300 degrees F
2. Take a 9x5 inch loaf pan and grease it; keep it on the side
3. Add listed ingredients to a bowl and pour the batter into the loaf pan
4. Bake for 60 minutes
5. Once baked, remove it from the oven and let it cool

Great Fudge Popsicles

Servings: 4
Preparation Time: 2 hours 5 minutes
Cooking Time: Nil
Ingredients:
- 2 tablespoons cocoa powder, unsweetened
- 2 tablespoons chocolate chips, sugar-free
- 2 teaspoons of natural sweetener such as stevia
- ¾ cup heavy whip cream

Directions:
1. Blend the listed ingredients in a blender until smooth
2. Pour mix into popsicle molds and let them chill for 2 hours
3. Serve and enjoy!

Egg And Coconut Bread

Servings: 4
Preparation Time: 15 minutes
Cooking Time: 40 minutes
Ingredients:
- 4 whole eggs
- 1 cup water
- 2 tablespoons apple cider vinegar
- ¼ cup + 1 teaspoon coconut oil, melted
- ½ teaspoon garlic powder
- ½ cup coconut flour
- ½ teaspoon baking soda
- ¼ teaspoon Coarse salt

Directions:
1. Preheat your oven to 350 degrees F
2. Grease a baking tin with 1 teaspoon coconut oil; keep it on the side
3. Add eggs to blender alongside water, vinegar, and ¼ cup coconut oil, and blend for half a minute
4. Add garlic powder, baking soda, coconut flour, and salt, and blend for a minute
5. Transfer to the baking tin
6. Bake for 40 minutes
7. Serve and enjoy!

The Beasty Green Glass

Servings: 1
Preparation Time: 10 minutes
Ingredients:
- ½ cup unsweetened almond milk, vanilla
- ½ cup half and half
- ½ avocado, peeled, pitted, and sliced
- ½ cup frozen blueberries, unsweetened
- 1 cup spinach
- 1 tablespoon almond butter
- 1 scoop Zero Carb protein powder
- 2-4 ice cubes
- 1 pack stevia

Directions:
1. Add listed ingredients to a blender
2. Blend until you have a smooth and creamy texture
3. Serve chilled, and enjoy!

Spicy Bread Loaf

Servings: 4-6
Preparation Time: 15 minutes
Cooking Time: 55 minutes
Ingredients:
- 6 big whole eggs
- 3 big jalapenos
- 4 ounces turkey bacon
- ½ cup ghee
- ¼ teaspoon baking soda
- ¼ teaspoon salt
- ½ cup coconut flour

Directions:
1. Preheat your oven to 400 degrees F
2. Cut 3 big jalapenos and cut the jalapenos into slices, cut turkey bacon into thick slices
3. Place jalapenos and bacon on a baking tray, roast for 30 minutes
4. Flip ad bake for 5 minutes more
5. Remove seeds from jalapeno and add jalapeno and bacon slices to a food processor
6. Take a big bowl and add eggs, ghee, ¼ cup of water
7. Mix well and add coconut flour, baking soda, salt, and stir
8. Add jalapeno and bacon mix
9. Use a bit of ghee to grease the loaf pan
10. Pour batter into loaf pan
11. Bake for 40 minutes
12. Enjoy

Clean Sugar-Free Lemon Curd

Servings: 2
Preparation Time: 10 minutes
Cooking Time: 10 minutes
Ingredients:
- 4 unwaxed lemons (juice and zest kept)
- 1/3 cup of erythritol or stevia
- ½ cup grams of unsalted butter
- 3 whole eggs
- 1 egg yolk

Directions:
1. Get a medium bowl, squeeze the lemons, and zest half of their skin.
2. Add the stevia or erythritol and the butter.
3. Heat a pan with boiling water and add the bowl with the lemon mixture on the toe (ben-Marie method). Careful so that the water doesn't touch the bowl.
4. Stir the mixture until the butter has melted.
5. Reduce to low heat and carefully whisk in the eggs. Keep constantly stirring and cook for 10 minutes. You should end up with a thin conditioner-like texture.
6. Remove from the heat and place on a sterilized jar or jars

Fantastic Hollandaise Sauce

Servings: 4

Preparation Time: 10 minutes
Cooking Time: 1-2 minutes
Ingredients:
- 8 large emulsified egg yolks 1/2 tsp salt
- 2 tbsp fresh lemon juice 1 cup unsalted butter

Directions:
1. Combine the egg yolks, salt, and lemon juice in a blender until smooth.
2. Put the butter in your microwave for around 60 seconds until melted and hot.
3. Turn the blender lowly and slowly pour in the butter until the sauce thickens.
4. Serve!

Chilled Cheesecake Cups

Servings: 4
Preparation Time: 10 minutes + Chill Time
Cooking Time: Nil
Ingredients:
- 8 oz cream cheese, softened
- 2 oz heavy cream
- 1 tsp Stevia Glycerite
- 1 tsp Splenda
- 1 tsp vanilla flavoring (Frontier Organic)

Directions:
1. Combine all the ingredients.
2. Whip until a pudding consistency is achieved.
3. Divide into cups.
4. Refrigerate until served!

Raspberry Pudding Meal

Servings: 4
Preparation Time: 10 minutes + Chill Time
Cooking Time: Nil
Ingredients:
- 3 tbsp chia seeds
- 1/2 cup unsweetened almond milk
- 1 scoop of chocolate protein powder
- 1/4 cup raspberries, fresh or frozen
- 1 tsp honey

Directions:
1. Combine the almond milk, protein powder, and chia seeds together.
2. Let rest for 5 minutes before stirring.
3. Refrigerate for 30 minutes.
4. Top with raspberries.
5. Serve!

Dreamy Vanilla Dessert

Servings: 2
Preparation Time: 10 minutes +Chill Time
Cooking Time: Nil
Ingredients:
- 1/2 cup extra virgin coconut oil, softened
- 1/2 cup coconut butter, softened
- Juice of 1 lemon
- Seeds from 1/2 a vanilla bean

Directions:
1. Whisk the ingredients in an easy-to-pour cup.
2. Pour into a lined cupcake or loaf pan.
3. Refrigerate for 20 minutes. Top with lemon zest.
4. Serve!

Coconut Pillow

Servings: 4
Preparation Time: 10 minutes + Chill Time
Cooking Time: Nil
Ingredients:
- 1 can of unsweetened coconut milk
- Berries of choice
- Dark chocolate

Directions:
1. Refrigerate the coconut milk for 24 hours.
2. Remove it from your refrigerator and whip for 2-3 minutes.
3. Fold in the berries.
4. Season with chocolate shavings.
5. Serve!

The Brewed Coffee Surprise

Servings: 4
Preparation Time: 10 minutes
Cooking Time: Nil
Ingredients:
- 2 heaped tbsp flaxseed, ground
- 100ml cooking cream 35% fat
- 1/2 tsp cocoa powder, dark and unsweetened
- 1 tbsp goji berries
- Freshly brewed coffee

Directions:
1. Mix together the flaxseeds, cream and cocoa, and coffee.
2. Season with goji berries.
3. Serve!

Crusty Almond Roast

Servings: 4
Preparation Time: 10 minutes
Cooking Time: 30 minutes
Ingredients:
- 1 cup keto almond flour
- 4 tsp melted butter
- 2 large eggs
- 1/2 tsp salt

Directions:
1. Mix together the almond flour and butter.
2. Add in the eggs and salt and combine well to form a dough ball.
3. Place the dough between two pieces of parchment paper. Roll out to 10" by 16" and 1/4 inch thick.
4. Bake for 30 minutes at 350°F or until golden brown.
5. Serve!

Cute Macaroon Bites

Servings: 4
Preparation Time: 10 minutes
Cooking Time: 15-20 minutes
Ingredients:
- 4 egg whites
- 1/2 tsp vanilla

- ½ tsp EZ-Sweet (or the equivalent of 1 cup artificial sweetener)
- 4 and 1/2 tsp water
- 1 cup unsweetened coconut

Directions:
1. Preheat your oven to 375°F/190°C.
2. Combine the egg whites, liquids, and coconut.
3. Put into the oven and reduce the heat to 325°F/160°C.
4. Bake for 15 minutes.
5. Serve!

Simple Cinnamon Cocoa Almonds

Servings: 8
Preparation Time: 5 minutes
Cook Time: 2 hours
Ingredients
- 3 cups raw almonds
- 3 tablespoons coconut oil, melted
- ¼ cup Erythritol
- 1 tablespoon unsweetened cocoa powder
- 1 tablespoon ground cinnamon

Directions:
1. Add almonds and coconut oil to the slow cooker and stir until coated
2. Season with salt
3. Mix in Erythritol, cocoa powder, and cinnamon, and cover
4. Cook on HIGH for 2 hours, making sure to stir every 30 minutes
5. Transfer nuts to a large baking sheet and spread them out to cool
6. Serve and enjoy!

Delightful Coconut Custard

Servings: 8
Preparation Time: 12 minutes
Cook Time: 5 hours
Ingredients
- 8 large eggs, lightly beaten
- 4 cups coconut milk
- 1 cup Erythritol
- 2 teaspoons stevia powder
- 1 teaspoon coconut extract

Directions:
1. Coat the inside of your Slow Cooker with coconut oil
2. Stir in eggs, coconut milk, stevia, Erythritol, and coconut extract into your Slow Cooker
3. Stir and place the lid
4. Cook on LOW for 5 hours
5. Let it cool for 1-2 hours
6. Serve and enjoy!

Jalapeno And Bacon Fat Bomb

Servings: 4
Preparation Time: 10 minutes
Cooking Time: 10 minutes
Ingredients:
- 12 large jalapeno peppers
- 16 beef bacon strips
- 6 ounces full fat cream cheese
- 2 teaspoons garlic powder
- 1 teaspoon chili powder

Directions:
1. Preheat your oven to 350 degrees Fahrenheit.
2. Place a wire rack over a roasting pan and keep it on the side.
3. Make a slit lengthways across jalapeno pepper and scrape the seeds; discard them.
4. Place a nonstick skillet over high heat and add half of your bacon strip; cook until crispy.
5. Drain them.
6. Chop the cooked bacon strips and transfer them to a large bowl.
7. Add cream cheese and mix.
8. Season the cream cheese and bacon mixture with garlic and chili powder.
9. Mix well.
10. Stuff the mix into the jalapeno peppers and wrap raw bacon strips around.
11. Arrange the stuffed wrapped jalapeno on a prepared wire rack.
12. Roast for 10 minutes.
13. Transfer to a cooling rack and serve!

Poppy Seeds Fat Bomb

Servings: 4
Preparation Time: 10 minutes
Cooking Time: Nil
Ingredients:
- 8 ounces cream cheese, soft
- 3 tablespoons erythritol
- 1 tablespoon poppy seeds
- 1 lemon zest
- 2 tablespoons lemon juice
- 4 tablespoons sour cream

Directions:
1. Add listed ingredients to a bowl and mix using a hand mixer on low.
2. Once mixed, mix for 3 minutes on a medium-high setting.
3. Spoon mixture into mini cupcake cases and chill for 1 hour.
4. Enjoy once done!

Creative Fudgsicles

Servings: 4
Preparation Time: 10 minutes + 60 minutes chill time
Cooking Time: Nil
Ingredients:
- 2 tablespoons cocoa powder, unsweetened
- 2 tablespoons chocolate chips, sugar-free
- 2 teaspoon natural sweetener
- ¾ cup heavy whip cream

Directions:
1. Blend the listed ingredients into your blender.
2. Blend until smooth.
3. Pour the mix into popsicle molds.
4. Keep in the fridge for 2 hours.
5. Serve and enjoy!

Pink Yogurt Popsicles

Servings: 4
Preparation Time: 10 minutes + 3-5 hours chill time
Cooking Time: Nil
Ingredients:
- 8 ounces frozen mango, diced
- 8 ounces frozen strawberries
- 1 cup Greek yogurt
- 2 and ½ teaspoons heavy whip cream
- 1 teaspoon vanilla essence

Directions:
1. Blend the listed ingredients into your blender.
2. Blend until smooth.
3. Pour the mix into popsicle molds.
4. Keep in the fridge for 3-5 hours.
5. Serve and enjoy!

Almond And Chocolate Butter Dip

Serving: 14
Preparation Time:15 minutes
Cooking Time: 10 minute
Ingredients
- 1 cup Plain Greek Yogurt
- ½ cup almond butter
- 1/3 cup chocolate hazelnut spread
- 1 tablespoon honey
- 1 teaspoon vanilla
- Sliced fruits such as pears, apples, apricots, bananas, etc.

Directions:
1. Take a medium-sized bowl and add the first five listed ingredients
2. Take an immersion blender and blend well until you have a smooth dip
3. Serve with your favorite sliced fruit
4. Enjoy!

Gentle Strawberry Greek Frozen Yogurt

Serving: 4
Preparation Time:4 hours 15 minutes
Cooking Time: nil
Ingredients
- 3 cups plain Greek low-fat yogurt
- 1 cup sugar
- ¼ cup freshly squeezed lemon juice
- 2 teaspoons vanilla
- 1/8 teaspoon salt
- 1 cup strawberries, sliced

Directions:
1. Take a medium-sized bowl and add yogurt, lemon juice, sugar, vanilla, and salt
2. Whisk the whole mixture well
3. Freeze the yogurt mix in a 2-quart ice cream maker according to the given instructions
4. Make sure to add sliced strawberries during the final minute
5. Transfer the yogurt to an airtight container
6. Freeze for another 2-4 hours
7. Allow it to stand for about 5-15 minutes
8. Serve and enjoy!

Strawberry And Feta Delight

Serving: 4
Preparation Time:10 minutes
Cooking Time: nil
Ingredients
- 4 cups of baby spinach
- 6 ounces feta cheese, crumbled
- 1 cup fresh strawberries, thinly sliced
- ½ cup walnuts, chopped

Balsamic Dijon vinaigrette
- 2 tablespoon extra-virgin olive oil
- 2 tablespoons balsamic vinegar
- 1 tablespoon Dijon mustard
- 1 tablespoon honey
- Salt and pepper as needed

Directions:
1. Take a small-sized glass bowl and mix in the olive oil, Dijon mustard, balsamic vinegar, and honey
2. Season it with some pepper and salt
3. Add the spinach, strawberries, feta, walnuts, and pine nuts to a large-sized mixing bowl
4. Divide the mixture amongst serving plates and dress them with the previously prepared vinaigrette dressing
5. Serve

Cherry And Olive Bites

Serving: 30
Preparation Time:15 minutes
Cooking Time: nil
Ingredients
- 24 cherry tomatoes, halved
- 24 black olives, pitted
- 24 feta cheese cubes
- 24 toothpick/decorative skewers

Directions:
1. Use a toothpick or skewer and thread feta cheese, black olives, and cherry tomato halves in that order
2. Repeat until all the ingredients are used
3. Arrange in a serving platter
4. Serve and enjoy!

Amazing Tiramisu

Serving: 8
Preparation Time:5 hours
Cooking Time: nil
Ingredients
- 8 ounces cream cheese
- 8 ounces mascarpone
- ¼ cup amaretto liqueur
- ¼ cup powdered sugar
- ½ cup (16 ounces) pack of double sponge cake with no filling
- ½ cup cooled espresso coffee
- ¾ cup caster sugar
- 3 tablespoons unsalted melted butter
- 3 tablespoons whole milk
- Powdered cocoa
- Fresh sprigs mint

Directions:
1. Take an electric mixer and beat your cream cheese, amaretto liqueur, mascarpone, and powdered sugar first for 2 minutes to make the mixture smooth
2. Set it aside
3. Slice up the cake horizontally into thirds using a serrated knife
4. Place your base on a plate
5. Brush it up with espresso
6. Spread half of the previously made cream cheese mixture evenly
7. Top it up with the middle layer of your cake and brush up with espresso again, followed by the spreading of the cheese mix
8. Brush up the cut side of the uppermost cut layer of your sponge cake with coffee and place it on top of the middle layer with the brushed side facing down
9. Take a medium-sized bowl and mix your cocoa and caster sugar
10. Make an excellent well in the middle and gradually keep stirring in the butter, followed by milk
11. Spread the icing over the cake
12. Let it chill for about 4 hours or more
13. Sprinkle some cocoa on top and serve

Chapter 16
Sauces Dips and Dressing

Tangy Mexican Salad Dressing
Preparation time: 15 minutes
Cooking time: 5 minutes
Servings: 8
Ingredients:
- ½ cup cilantro, diced fine
- 3 tbsp. fresh lime juice

What you'll need from store cupboard:
- ½ cup sunflower oil
- 2 tbsp. water
- 1 tbsp. apple cider vinegar
- 2 tsp honey
- 1 tsp garlic salt
- ½ teaspoon Mexican oregano
- Freshly ground black pepper, to taste

Directions:
1. Add all Ingredients: to a food processor or blender. Pulse until well blended and emulsified. Taste and adjust seasonings as desired.
2. Store in an air-tight container in the refrigerator. To serve, bring to room temperature and shake well.

Sriracha Dipping Sauce
Preparation time: 1 minute
Cooking time: 2 minutes
Servings: 6
Ingredients:
- 2 tsp fresh lime juice

What you'll need from store cupboard:
- ½ cup lite mayonnaise
- 2 tbsp. Sriracha sauce
- 1 tbsp. Splenda
- 1 tsp Worcestershire sauce

Directions:
1. In a small bowl, stir all the Ingredients: together until smooth.
2. Use right away, or cover and refrigerate until ready to use. Serving size is 1 ½ tablespoons.

Spaghetti Sauce
Preparation time: 20 minutes
Cooking time: 30 minutes
Servings: 6
Ingredients:
- 1 onion, diced
- 1 carrot, grated
- 1 stalk celery, diced
- 1 zucchini, grated
- What you'll need from store cupboard:
- 1 (28 oz.) Italian-style tomatoes, in puree
- 1 (14 ½ oz.) diced tomatoes, with juice
- ½ cup water
- 2 cloves garlic, diced fine
- ½ tbsp. oregano
- 1 tsp olive oil
- 1 tsp basil
- 1 tsp thyme
- 1 tsp salt
- ¼ tsp red pepper flakes

Directions:
1. Heat oil in a large saucepan over medium heat. Add vegetables and garlic. Cook, stirring frequently, until vegetables get soft, about 5 minutes.
2. Add remaining Ingredients, use the back of a spoon to break up tomatoes. Bring to a simmer and cook, partially covered, over med-low heat 30 minutes, stirring frequently.
3. Store sauce in an air-tight container in the refrigerator up to 3 days, or in the freezer up to 3 months.

Pineapple Mango Hot Sauce
Preparation time: 10 minutes
Cooking time: 20 minutes
Servings: 16
Ingredients:
- 2 cherry peppers, diced
- 1 ghost pepper, diced
- 1 cup pineapple, diced
- ½ cup mango, diced
- 2 tbsp. cilantro, diced

What you'll need from store cupboard:
- 1 cup water
- ½ cup vinegar
- 1 tsp olive oil
- 1 tsp Splenda
- 1 tsp paprika
- Salt, to taste

Directions:
1. Heat oil in a large saucepan over medium heat. Add peppers and fruit and cook 8 minutes to soften.
2. Add remaining Ingredients: and bring to a boil. Reduce heat and simmer 20 minutes. Remove from heat and let cool.
3. Add mixture to a food processor and pulse until smooth. Pour into sterilized bottles, secure lids and refrigerate until ready to use.

Pizza Sauce

Preparation time: 5 minutes
Cooking time: 5 minutes
Servings: 8
Ingredients:
- ½ cup yellow onion, diced

What you'll need from store cupboard:
- 15 oz. tomatoes, crushed, no sugar added
- 1/3 cup + 1 tbsp. olive oil
- 3 cloves garlic, diced
- 2 tsp parsley
- 1 tsp rosemary
- 1 tsp thyme
- 1 tsp smoked paprika
- Salt, to taste

Directions:
1. Heat 1 tablespoon oil in a small skillet over medium heat. Add onion and garlic and cook until onions are translucent.
2. In a medium saucepan, over medium heat, stir all Ingredients: together, along with onions. Bring to a simmer and cook 2-3 minutes, stirring constantly.
3. Remove from heat and let cool completely. Store in a jar with an air tight lid in the refrigerator up to 2 weeks. Or in the freezer up to 6 months.

Queso Verde

Preparation time: 10 minutes
Cooking time: 30 minutes
Servings: 10
Ingredients:
- ½ package cream cheese, soft
- ½ cup white American cheese, cubed
- ½ cup white cheddar cheese, cubed
- ½ cup pepper Jack cheese, cubed
- ¼ cup skim milk

What you'll need from store cupboard
- ½ cup salsa verde
- ½ cup green chilies, diced
- Nonstick cooking spray

Directions:
1. Heat oven to 325. Spray a small baking dish with cooking spray.
2. In a medium mixing bowl, combine all Ingredients. Add to prepared baking dish.
3. Bake 30 minutes, stirring every 8-10 minutes, until cheese is melted and dip is hot and bubbly. Serve warm.

Cinnamon Blueberry Sauce

Preparation time: 5 minutes
Cooking time: 10 minutes
Servings: 16
Ingredients:
- 2 cup blueberries
- 2 tbsp. fresh lemon juice

What you'll need from store cupboard:
- ¼ cup Splenda
- ¼ cup water
- 2 tsp corn starch
- ½ tsp cinnamon

Directions:
1. In a small saucepan, over medium heat, Splenda and cornstarch. Stir in remaining Ingredients: and bring to a boil, stirring frequently.
2. Reduce heat and simmer 5 minutes, until thickened. Let cool completely.
3. Pour into a jar with an airtight lid and refrigerate until ready to use. Serving size is 1 tablespoon.

Citrus Vinaigrette

Preparation time: 5 minutes
Cooking time: 10 minutes
Servings: 6
Ingredients:
- 1 orange, zested and juiced
- 1 lemon, zested and juiced

What you'll need from store cupboard:
- ¼ cup extra virgin olive oil
- 1 tsp Dijon mustard
- 1 tsp honey
- 1 clove garlic, crushed
- Salt & pepper, to taste

Directions:
1. Place the zest and juices, mustard, honey, garlic, salt and pepper in a food processor. Pulse to combine.
2. With the machine running, slowly pour in the olive oil and process until combined.
3. Use right away, or store in a jar with an airtight lid in the refrigerator.

Cranberry Orange Compote

Preparation time: 5 minutes
Cooking time: 10 minutes
Servings: 8
Ingredients:
- 1 lb. fresh cranberries, rinsed and drained
- 1 large orange, halved

What you'll need from store cupboard:
- 1 tsp vanilla
- 1 tsp cinnamon

Directions:
1. Add cranberries to a medium saucepan and place over medium heat. Squeeze both halves of the orange, with pulp, into the berries. Stir in vanilla and cinnamon.
2. Cook, stirring frequently, until berries start to open. Reduce heat and continue cooking for 10 minutes, or until mixture starts to thicken.
3. Let cool 15 minutes, then spoon into a jar with an airtight lid. Refrigerate until ready to use.

Creamy Poppy Seed Dressing

Preparation time: 10 minutes
Cooking time: 5 minutes
Servings: 6
Ingredients:
- 1/3 cup light mayonnaise
- ¼ cup skim milk

What you'll need from store cupboard:
- 3 tbsp. Splenda

- 4 tsp cider vinegar
- 2 tsp poppy seeds

Directions:
1. In a small bowl, whisk all Ingredients: together until thoroughly combined. Store in an airtight jar in the refrigerator.

Dry Rub for Pork

Preparation time: 5 minutes
Cooking time: 5 minutes
Servings: 16
Ingredients:
What you'll need from store cupboard:
- 2 tbsp. ground coffee, extra fine ground
- 2 tbsp. chipotle powder
- 1 tbsp. smoked paprika
- 1 tbsp. Splenda brown sugar
- 1 tbsp. salt
- 1 tsp ginger
- 1 tsp mustard powder
- 1 tsp coriander

Directions:
1. Mix all Ingredients: together.
2. Store in airtight container in cool, dry place for up to 1 month.

Easy Cheesy Dipping Sauce

Preparation time: 2 minutes
Cooking time: 5 minutes
Servings: 2
Ingredients:
- ¾ cup skim milk
- ¾ cup reduced-fat cheddar cheese
- 1 tbsp. margarine

What you'll need from store cupboard:
- 1 tbsp. flour
- Pinch of cayenne
- Salt and pepper

Directions:
1. Melt margarine in a small saucepan over medium heat. Whisk in flour and cook, whisking constantly, until golden brown, about 1 minutes.
2. Slowly add milk and continue whisking until no lumps remain. Cook, whisking constantly, until mixture thickens and starts to bubble, 3-4 minutes.
3. Stir in cheese until smooth. Season with cayenne, salt and pepper to taste.

Raspberry & Basil Jam

Preparation time: 5 minutes
Cooking time: 20 minutes
Servings: 24
Ingredients:
- 2 lbs. fresh raspberries
- 1/3 cup fresh basil, diced fine
- 2 tbsp. lemon juice

What you'll need from store cupboard:
- ½ cup Splenda

Directions:
1. Add berries and lemon juice to a large saucepan and place over medium heat. Use a wooden spoon to break up the berries. Bring to a low boil and simmer 5-6 minutes, or until mixture starts to bubble.
2. Stir in Splenda and cook, stirring frequently, until Splenda is dissolved and mixture resembles syrup, about 15 minutes.
3. Remove from heat and stir in the basil. Spoon into glass jars with air tight lids. Let cool completely then add lids and refrigerate. Serving size is 1 tablespoon.

Garlic Dipping Sauce

Preparation time: 5 minutes
Cooking time: 5 minutes
Servings: 4
Ingredients:
- 1 cup Greek yogurt
- 1 tbsp. fresh dill, diced fine

What you'll need from store cupboard:
- 2 cloves garlic, diced fine

Directions:
1. In a small bowl, whisk all Ingredients: together.
2. Serve warm or cover and chill until ready to use.

Herb Vinaigrette

Preparation time: 5 minutes
Cooking time: 0 minute
Mix time: 5 minutes
Servings: 12
Ingredients:
- 2 tbsp. shallot, diced fine
- 1 tbsp. fresh basil, diced
- 1 tbsp. fresh oregano, diced
- 1 tbsp. fresh tarragon, diced

What you'll need from store cupboard:
- ¼ cup extra virgin olive oil
- ¼ cup low sodium chicken broth
- ¼ cup red-wine vinegar - ¼ teaspoon salt
- ¼ teaspoon freshly ground pepper

Directions:
1. Place all Ingredients: in a jar with an air tight lid. Secure lid and shake vigorously to combine.
2. Refrigerate until ready to use. Will keep up to 2 days. Serving size is 1 tablespoon.

Horseradish Mustard Sauce

Preparation time: 5 minutes
Cooking time: 5 minutes
Servings: 8
Ingredients:
- ¼ cup fat free sour cream

What you'll need from store cupboard:
- ¼ cup lite mayonnaise
- 1 ½ tsp lemon juice
- 1 tsp Splenda
- ½ tsp ground mustard
- ½ tsp Dijon mustard
- ½ tsp horseradish

Directions:

1. In a small bowl, combine all Ingredients: until thoroughly combined.
2. Store in an air tight jar in the refrigerator until ready to use. Serving size is 1 tablespoon.

Berry Dessert Sauce
Preparation time: 5 minutes
Cooking time: 3 hours
Servings: 12
Ingredients:
- 8 oz. strawberries, hulled and halved
- 6 oz. blackberries - 4 oz. blueberries
- What you'll need from store cupboard:
- ¼ cup Splenda

Directions:
1. Add the berries and Splenda to the crock pot. Stir to mix.
2. Cover and cook for 3 hours on a low heat.
3. Ladle the sauce into a jar with an air tight lid, and let cool completely before screwing on the lid and storing in the refrigerator. Serving size is 1 tablespoon.

Blackberry Spread
Preparation time: 5 minutes
Cooking time: 30 minutes
Servings: 16
Ingredients:
- 1 lb. blackberries
- 1 lemon, juiced

What you'll need from store cupboard:
- ¼ cup Splenda

Directions:
1. Place blackberries, Splenda and lemon juice in a medium sauce pan over med-high heat. Cook berries down, stirring occasionally, about 30 minutes, or mixture resembles a thick syrup.
2. Scoop 1/2 cup of the mixture out and place it in a bowl.
3. Place a fine mesh sieve over the bowl and strain the rest of the mixture through, pressing and scraping to get as much of the moisture out that you can.
4. Discard solids. Stir jam in bowl and place in a jar with an air-tight lid.

Blueberry Orange Dessert Sauce
Preparation time: 5 minutes
Cooking time: 10 minutes
Servings: 16
Ingredients:
- 1 ½ cup orange segments
- 1 cup blueberries
- ¼ cup orange juice

What you'll need from store cupboard:
- ¼ cup water
- 1/3 cup almonds, sliced
- 3 tbsp. Splenda
- 1 tbsp. cornstarch
- 1/8 tsp salt

Directions:
1. In a small saucepan, combine Splenda, cornstarch, and salt. Whisk in orange juice and water until smooth.
2. Bring to a boil over med-high heat, cook, stirring frequently, 1-2 minutes or until thickened.
3. Reduce heat and stir in fruit. Cook 5 minutes. Remove from heat and let cool completely.
4. Store in an airtight jar in the refrigerator until ready to use. Serving size is 1 tablespoon.

Caramel Sauce
Preparation time: 5 minutes
Cooking time: 10 minutes
Servings: 12
Ingredients:
- 2/3 cup heavy cream - 1/3 cup margarine

What you'll need from store cupboard:
- 3 tbsp. Splenda - 1 tsp vanilla

Directions:
1. Add the margarine and Splenda to a medium saucepan and place over low heat. Once the margarine melts, cook 3-4 minutes, stirring occasionally, until golden brown.
2. Stir in the cream and bring to a low boil. Reduce heat and simmer 7-10 minutes, stirring occasionally, until mixture is a caramel color and coats the back of a spoon.
3. Remove from heat and whisk in the vanilla. Cool completely and pour into a jar with an air tight lid. Store in the refrigerator. Serving size is 1 tablespoon.

Cheesy Jalapeno Dip
Preparation time: 5 minutes
Cooking time: 3 hours
Servings: 10
Ingredients:
- 4 pkgs. cream cheese, soft
- 1 ½ cups low fat cheddar cheese, grated
- 1 cup bacon, cooked and crumbled
- 1 cup fat free sour cream
- 1 fresh jalapeño, sliced

What you'll need from store cupboard
- 2 cans jalapenos, diced
- 1 packet ranch dressing mix

Directions:
1. In a large bowl, mix cream cheese, 2/3 cup bacon, diced jalapenos, 1 cup cheddar cheese, sour cream and dressing.
2. Spread in crock pot. Top with remaining bacon and cheese. Arrange sliced jalapeno across the top.
3. Cover and cook on low 3 hours. Serve warm.

Chinese Hot Mustard
Preparation time: 15 mins,
Cooking time: 15 minutes
Servings: 4
What you'll need from store cupboard:
- 1 tbsp. mustard powder
- 1½ tsp hot water
- ½ tsp vegetable oil
- ½ tsp rice vinegar

- 1/8 tsp salt
- 1/8 tsp white pepper

Directions:
1. In a small bowl, mix together the dry Ingredients. Add water and stir until mixture resembles liquid paste and dry Ingredients: are absorbed.
2. Stir in oil and vinegar until thoroughly combined. Cover and let rest 10 minutes.
3. Stir again. Taste and adjust any seasonings if desired. Cover and refrigerate until ready to use.

Italian Salad Dressing

Preparation time: 5 minutes
Cooking time: 5 minutes
Servings: 8
Ingredients:
- 2 tbsp. lemon juice

What you'll need from store cupboard:
- ¾ cup olive oil
- ¼ cup red wine vinegar
- 2 cloves of garlic, diced
- 2 tsp Italian seasoning
- 1 tsp oregano
- ½ tsp honey
- ½ tsp salt
- ¼ tsp black pepper
- ¼ tsp red pepper flakes

Directions:
1. Combine all Ingredients: in a measuring cup or jar. Whisk well.
2. Store in jar or bottle with an air tight lid for up to 1 week. Serving size is 1 tablespoon.

Italian Salsa

Preparation time: 10 minutes
Cooking time: 0 minute
Chill time: 1 hour
Servings: 16
Ingredients:
- 4 plum tomatoes, diced
- ½ red onion, diced fine
- 2 tbsp. fresh parsley, diced

What you'll need from store cupboard:
- 12 Kalamata olives, pitted and chopped
- 2 cloves garlic, diced fine
- 1 tbsp. balsamic vinegar
- 1 tbsp. olive oil
- 2 tsp capers, drained
- ¼ tsp salt
- ¼ tsp pepper

Directions:
1. In a medium bowl, combine all Ingredients: and stir to mix. Cover and chill 1 hour before using.
2. Store in a jar with an airtight lid in the refrigerator up to 7 days. Stir before using.

Alfredo Sauce

Preparation time: 5 minutes
Cooking time: 10 minutes
Servings: 6
Ingredients:
- 1 ½ cup heavy cream
- 1 tbsp. margarine

What you'll need from store cupboard:
- ½ cup reduced fat parmesan cheese
- 4 cloves garlic, diced fine
- Black pepper
- Salt
- Nutmeg

Directions:
1. Melt butter in a medium saucepan over medium heat. Add garlic and sauté for about 30 seconds, until fragrant.
2. Add the heavy cream. Bring to a gentle simmer, then continue to simmer for about 5 minutes, until it begins to thicken and sauce is reduced by about 1/3.
3. Reduce heat to low. Gradually whisk in the Parmesan cheese. Keep whisking over low heat, until smooth. Add salt, pepper, and nutmeg to taste. (If sauce is thicker than you like, thin it out with more cream.)

All Purpose Beef Marinade

Preparation time: 10 minutes
Cooking time: 10 minutes
Servings: 8
Ingredients:
- 6 limes zested
- 1 bunch cilantro, diced

What you'll need from store cupboard:
- ¼ c olive oil
- 6 cloves garlic, diced fine

Directions:
1. Mix all Ingredients: in an airtight container.
2. Keep refrigerated for up to 3 months or frozen up to 6 months. Serving size is 1 tablespoon.

All Purpose Chicken Marinade

Preparation time: 5 minutes
Cooking time: 5 minutes
Servings: 24
Ingredients:
- 1 onion, quartered - ½ lemon, with skin
- ½ orange, with skin
- 3 tbsp. rosemary, diced
- 2 tbsp. thyme, diced

What you'll need from store cupboard
- ½ cup olive oil
- 6 cloves garlic, diced fine

Directions:
1. Place all Ingredients: in a food processor and pulse until combined.
2. Store in an air tight container in the refrigerator up to 3 months. Serving size is 1 tablespoon.

Almond Vanilla Fruit Dip

Preparation time: 5 minutes
Cooking time: 10 minutes
Servings: 10
Ingredients:
- 2 ½ cup fat free half-n-half

What you'll need from store cupboard:
- 4-serving size fat-free sugar-free vanilla instant pudding mix
- 1 tbsp. Splenda
- 1 tsp vanilla
- 1 tsp almond extract

Directions:
1. Place all Ingredients: in a medium bowl, and beat on medium speed 2 minutes. Cover and chill until ready to serve. Serve with fruit for dipping. Serving size is ¼ cup.

Roasted Tomato Salsa

Preparation time: 10 minutes
Cooking time: 30 minutes
Servings: 8
Ingredients:
- 6 plum tomatoes
- 1 ¼ cup cilantro

What you'll need from store cupboard:
- 2 tsp olive oil
- 1 tsp adobo sauce
- ½ tsp salt, divided
- Nonstick cooking spray

Directions:
1. Heat oven to 425 degrees. Spray a broiler pan with cooking spray.
2. Cut tomatoes in half and remove seeds. Place, cut side up, on broiler pan. Brush with oil and sprinkle with ¼ teaspoon salt. Turn tomatoes cut side down and bake 30-40 minutes or until edges are browned.
3. Place cilantro in food processor and pulse until coarsely chopped. Add tomatoes, adobo, and remaining salt. Process until chunky. Store in jar with air tight lid and refrigerate until ready to use. Serving size is 2 tablespoons.

Spicy Asian Vinaigrette

Preparation time: 5 minutes
Cooking time: 10 minutes
Servings: 4
Ingredients:
- 1-inch piece fresh ginger, peel & quarter
- 1 tbsp. fresh lemon juice

What you'll need from store cupboard:
- ¼ cup sesame oil
- 2 cloves garlic, peeled
- 2 tbsp. rice vinegar
- 1 tbsp. Chinese hot mustard
- 1 tsp light soy sauce
- 1/8 tsp red pepper flakes

Directions:
1. Place all Ingredients: in a food processor or blender and process until smooth.
2. Store in a jar with an airtight lid. Serving size is 2 tablespoons

Maple Mustard Salad Dressing

Preparation time: 10 minutes
Cooking time: 5 minutes
Servings: 6
What you'll need from store cupboard:
- 2 tbsp. balsamic vinegar - 2 tbsp. olive oil
- 1 tbsp. sugar free maple syrup
- 1 tsp Dijon mustard
- 1/8 tsp sea salt

Directions:
1. Place all the Ingredients: in a jar with a tight-fitting lid. Screw on lid and shake to combine. Store in refrigerator until ready to use.

Maple Shallot Vinaigrette

Preparation time: 3 minutes
Cooking time: 5 minutes
Servings: 4
Ingredients:
- 1 tbsp. shallot, diced fine

What you'll need from store cupboard:
- 2 tbsp. apple cider vinegar
- 1 tbsp. spicy brown mustard
- 1 tbsp. olive oil
- 2 tsp sugar free maple syrup

Directions:
1. Place all Ingredients: in a small jar with an airtight lid. Shake well to mix. Refrigerate until ready to use. Serving size is 1 tablespoon.

Apple Cider Vinaigrette

Preparation time: 10 minutes
Cooking time: 5 minutes
Servings: 8
What you'll need from store cupboard:
- ½ cup sunflower oil
- ¼ cup apple cider vinegar
- ¼ cup apple juice, unsweetened
- 2 tbsp. honey
- 1 tbsp. lemon juice
- ½ tsp salt
- Freshly ground black pepper, to taste

Directions:
1. Place all Ingredients: in a mason jar. Screw on lid and shake until everything is thoroughly combined. Store in refrigerator until ready to use. Shake well before using.

Bacon Cheeseburger Dip

Preparation time: 5 minutes
Cooking time: 30 minutes
Servings: 8
Ingredients:
- 1 lb. lean ground beef
- 1 pkg. cream cheese, soft
- 2 cups low fat cheddar cheese, grated
- 1 cup fat free sour cream
- 2/3 cup bacon, cooked crisp and crumbled

What you'll need from store cupboard:
- 10 oz. can tomato with green chilies

Directions:
1. Heat oven to 350 degrees.

2. Place a large skillet over med-high heat and cook beef, breaking it up with a wooden spoon, until no longer pink. Drain off the fat.
3. In a large bowl, combine remaining Ingredients: until mixed well. Stir in beef.
4. Pour into a small baking dish. Bake 20-25 minutes or until mixture is hot and bubbly. Serve warm.

Basic Salsa

Preparation time: 15 minutes
Cooking time: 0 minute
Chill time: 1 hour
Servings: 8
Ingredients:
- 8 tomatoes
- 2-3 jalapeno peppers, depending on how spicy you like it
- 2 limes, juiced

What you'll need from store cupboard:
- 4 cloves garlic
- 1 tbsp. salt
- Nonstick cooking spray

Directions:
1. Heat oven to broil. Spray a baking sheet with cooking spray.
2. Place tomatoes, peppers, and garlic on prepared pan and broil 8-10 minutes, turning occasionally, until skin on the vegetables begins to char and peel way.
3. Let cool. Remove skins.
4. Place vegetables in a food processor and pulse. Add salt and lime juice and pulse until salsa reaches desired consistency.
5. Store in a jar with an airtight lid in the refrigerator up to 7 days. Serving size is ¼ cup.

BBQ Sauce

Preparation time: 5 minutes
Cooking time: 20 minutes
Servings: 20
What you'll need from store cupboard:
- 2 1/2 6 oz. cans tomato paste
- 1 ½ cup water
- ½ cup apple cider vinegar
- 1/3 cup swerve confectioners
- 2 tbsp. Worcestershire sauce
- 1 tbsp. liquid hickory smoke
- 2 tsp smoked paprika
- 1 tsp garlic powder
- ½ tsp onion powder
- ½ tsp salt
- ¼ tsp chili powder
- ¼ tsp cayenne pepper

Directions:
1. Whisk all Ingredients, but water, together in a saucepan. Add water, starting with 1 cup, whisking it in, until mixture resembles a thin barbecue sauce.
2. Bring to a low boil over med-high heat. Reduce heat to med-low and simmer, stirring frequently, 20 minutes, or sauce has thickened slightly.
3. Taste and adjust seasoning until you like it. Cool completely. Store in a jar with an airtight lid in the refrigerator. Serving size is 2 tablespoons of sauce.

Marinara Sauce

Preparation time: 10 minutes
Cooking time: 30 minutes
Servings: 6
Ingredients:
- 28 oz. can dice tomatoes, undrained
- 4–6 cloves garlic, diced fine
- 4 tbsp. extra virgin olive oil
- 2 tbsp. tomato paste
- 1 tbsp. basil,
- 1 tsp Splenda
- 1 tsp salt

Directions:
1. Heat oil in saucepan over medium heat. Add the garlic and cook 1 minute.
2. Stir in the tomato paste and cook 1 minute more. Add the tomatoes and basil and simmer 10-15 minutes, breaking up the tomatoes as they cook.
3. Stir in Splenda and salt. Use an immersion blender and process to desired consistency.
4. Let cool and store in a jar with an airtight lid in the refrigerator up to 7 days. Or use right away.

Orange Marmalade

Preparation time: 30 minutes
Cooking time: 30 minutes
Servings: 48
Ingredients:
- 4 navel oranges
- 1 lemon
- What you'll need from store cupboard:
- 2 ½ cup water
- ¼ cup warm water
- 4 tbsp. Splenda
- 1 oz. gelatin

Directions:
1. Quarter the oranges and remove all the pulp. Scrap the white part off the rind and cut it into thin 2-inch strips. Remove as much of the membrane between orange segments as you can and place the seeds in a small piece of cheesecloth, pull up the sides to make a "bag" and tie closed.
2. Repeat with the lemon but discard the seeds. Cut the lemon rind into smaller strips than the orange rind.
3. Chop the orange and lemon pulp and add it to a medium saucepan along with 2 ½ cups water. Bring to a rapid boil over med-high heat.
4. Reduce heat to med-low and add the bag of seeds. Boil gently for 30 minutes, or until the citrus fruit is soft. Remove and discard the seed bag.
5. Dissolve the gelatin in the warm water. Add it to the orange mixture with ½ the Splenda. Being careful not to burn yourself, taste the marmalade and adjust sweetener as desired.
6. Spoon the marmalade into 3 ½-pint jars with air-tight lids. Seal and chill.

Cashew And Almond Butter

Serving: 1 and ½ cups
Preparation Time: 5 minutes
Cooking Time: Nil
Ingredients
- 1 cup almonds, blanched
- 1/3 cup cashew nuts
- 2 tablespoons coconut oil
- Salt as needed
- ½ teaspoon cinnamon

Directions:
1. Preheat your oven to 350 degrees F
2. Bake almonds and cashews for 12 minutes
3. Let them cool
4. Transfer to a food processor and add the remaining ingredients
5. Add oil and keep blending until smooth
6. Serve and enjoy!

Spinach Dip

Serving: 2
Preparation Time: 4 minutes
Cooking Time: 0 minutes
Ingredients
- 5-ounce Spinach, raw
- 1 cup Greek yogurt
- 1/2 tablespoon of onion powder
- 1/4 teaspoon of garlic sunflower seeds
- Black pepper to taste
- 1/4 a teaspoon of Greek Seasoning

Directions:
1. Add the listed Ingredients to a blender.
2. Emulsify.
3. Season and serve.

Almond Milk

Serving: 2
Preparation Time: 10 minutes
Cooking Time: 0 minute
Ingredients
- 4 cups of water
- 1 cup almonds, raw, soaked in water for 5 hours

Directions:
1. Add listed ingredients to a blender, pulse well until smooth
2. Strain almond milk through cheesecloth, discard remaining pulp
3. Use as needed

Whipped Coconut Cream

Serving: 4
Preparation Time: 10 minutes
Cooking Time: 0 minute
Ingredients
- 14 ounces canned coconut cream
- 1 teaspoon vanilla

Directions:
1. Scoop coconut cream into a bowl, leave the liquid in the can
2. Add vanilla extract to the bowl and use an electric mixer to gently whip, starting from low speed and going to high
3. Once you have your desired consistency, serve and use as needed

Nutty Butter

Serving: 4
Preparation Time: 5 minutes
Cooking Time: 0 minute
Ingredients
- ½ cup mixed nuts such as peanuts, hazelnuts, cashews, etc.
- 2 tablespoons sunflower oil

Directions:
1. Add nuts to your blender and pulse well
2. Add the sunflower oil and keep pulsing until you have a butter-like consistency; use once needed

Standard Vegetable Stock

Serving: 4
Preparation Time: 15 minutes
Cooking Time: 0 minute
Ingredients
- Pinch of salt
- Pinch of pepper, ground
- 1 tablespoon extra virgin olive oil
- 2 and ½ cups of water
- 2 garlic cloves, diced
- 1 stick celery, diced
- 1 potato, diced
- 1 carrot, diced
- 1 onion, diced
- 1 bay leaf
- ½ cup fresh flat-leaf parsley
- 1 sprig of fresh thyme

Directions:
1. Take a large-sized saucepan and place it over medium heat; add olive oil and let it heat up
2. Add vegetables, excluding garlic and herbs
3. Cook for 10 minutes, making sure to keep stirring from time to time
4. Add garlic, fresh herbs, and salt, and bring to a boil
5. Simmer for 40 minutes
6. Drain stock and use as needed

Mashed Celeriac

Serving: 4
Preparation Time: 10 minutes
Cooking Time: 20 minutes
Ingredients
- 2 celeriac, washed, peeled, and diced
- 2 teaspoons extra-virgin olive oil
- 1 tablespoon honey
- ½ teaspoon ground nutmeg
- Sunflower seeds and pepper as needed

Directions:
1. Preheat your oven to 400 degrees Fahrenheit
2. Line a baking sheet with aluminum foil and keep it on the side
3. Take a large bowl and toss celeriac and olive oil

4. Spread celeriac evenly on a baking sheet
5. Roast for 20 minutes until tender
6. Transfer to a large bowl
7. Add honey and nutmeg
8. Use a potato masher to mash the mixture until fluffy
9. Season with sunflower seeds and pepper
10. Serve and enjoy!

Spiced Oily Avocado

Serving: 4
Preparation Time: 5 minutes
Cooking Time: Nil
Ingredients
- 1 medium avocado, cut into chunks
- ½ teaspoon ground cayenne pepper
- 2 tablespoons fresh cilantro
- Pinch of salt
- ¼ cup olive oil

Directions:
1. Take a food processor and add avocado, cayenne pepper, lime juice, salt, and cilantro
2. Mix until smooth
3. Slowly incorporate olive oil, add 1 tablespoon at a time and keep processing in between additions
4. Store and use as needed!

Hearty Cashew and Almond Butter

Serving: 1 and ½ cups
Preparation Time: 5 minutes
Cooking Time: 12 minutes
Ingredients
- 1 cup almonds, blanched
- 1/3 cup cashew nuts
- 2 tablespoons coconut oil
- Salt as needed
- ½ teaspoon cinnamon

Directions:
1. Preheat your oven to 350 degrees F
2. Bake almonds and cashews for 12 minutes
3. Let them cool
4. Transfer to a food processor and add the remaining ingredients
5. Add oil and keep blending until smooth
6. Serve and enjoy!

Black Bean Dip

Serving: 4
Preparation Time: 5 minutes
Cooking Time: 5 minutes
Ingredients
- 14 ounces black beans, drained and rinsed
- 1 lime, juiced and zested
- ¼ cup cilantro, fresh and chopped
- ¼ cup of water
- 1 teaspoon cumin
- 1 tablespoon tamari
- Pinch of cayenne pepper

Directions:
1. Take a bowl and add all ingredients except cilantro, a process well until you have a very smooth mixture
2. Serve with a garnish of cilantro
3. Use as needed
4. Enjoy!

Spicy Jerk Mayo

Serving: 4
Preparation Time: 30 minutes
Cooking Time: Nil
Ingredients
- 1 cup mayonnaise, homemade, egg-free
- 2 tablespoons onion powder
- 1 tablespoon dried chives
- 1 tablespoon dried thyme
- 2 teaspoons ground black pepper
- 2 teaspoons Scotch bonnet chili flakes
- 2 teaspoons garlic powder
- ½ teaspoon ground nutmeg
- ½ teaspoon ground cinnamon
- 1 tablespoons salt

Directions:
1. Take a bowl and mix everything
2. Season accordingly
3. Let it sit in the fridge for 30 minutes
4. Use as needed!

The Macadamia Dip

Serving: 1
Preparation Time: 10 minutes
Ingredients:
- 1 tablespoon chia seeds
- 2 cups of water
- 1 ounce of Macadamia Nuts
- 1-2 packets Stevia, optional
- 1-ounce Hazelnut

Directions:
1. Add all the listed ingredients to a blender.
2. Blend on high until smooth and creamy.
3. Enjoy your smoothie.

Tahini and Broccoli Slaw

Serving: 1
Preparation Time: 20 minutes
Ingredients:
- ¼ cup tahini
- 2 tablespoon white miso
- 1 tablespoon rice vinegar
- 1 tablespoon toasted sesame oil
- 2 teaspoons soy sauce
- 1 (12 ounces) bag broccoli slaw
- 2 green onions, minced
- ¼ cup toasted sesame seeds

Directions:
1. Take a large-sized bowl, whisk in tahini, miso, vinegar, oil, soy sauce
2. Add broccoli slaw, green onions, and sesame seeds, and toss well
3. Keep it on the side for 20 minutes
4. Serve and enjoy!

Chapter 17

Healthy Smoothies

Tropical Storm Glass
Serving: 2
Preparation Time: 5 minutes
Ingredients
- 1 tablespoon hemp seeds
- ¾ cup plain coconut yogurt
- 1 fresh banana
- 1 cup unsweetened coconut milk
- 1 and ½ cups frozen papaya blend (mix of papaya, mango, strawberry, and pineapple)

Directions
1. Add all the ingredients except vegetables/fruits first
2. Blend until smooth
3. Add the vegetable/fruits
4. Blend until smooth
5. Add a few ice cubes and serve the smoothie
6. Enjoy!

Cool Strawberry 365
Serving: 2
Preparation Time: 5 minutes
Ingredients
- 1 tablespoon chia seeds
- ½ cup of water
- ¾ cup Siggi's whole milk vanilla yogurt
- 1 cup frozen peaches
- 1 cup baby spinach
- 1 cup of frozen mixed berries
- 1 cup unsweetened vanilla almond milk

Directions
1. Add all the ingredients except vegetables/fruits first
2. Blend until smooth
3. Add the vegetable/fruits
4. Blend until smooth
5. Add a few ice cubes and serve the smoothie
6. Enjoy!

Noteworthy Vitamin C
Serving: 2
Preparation Time: 5 minutes
Ingredients
- 1 tablespoon chia seeds
- 1 clementine
- ¾ cup plain low-fat Greek yogurt
- 1 cup of frozen strawberries
- 1 cup cantaloupe
- 1 cup unsweetened vanilla almond milk

Directions
1. Add all the ingredients except vegetables/fruits first
2. Blend until smooth
3. Add the vegetable/fruits
4. Blend until smooth
5. Add a few ice cubes and serve the smoothie
6. Enjoy!

Hearty Papaya Drink
Serving: 2
Preparation Time: 5 minutes
Ingredients
- 1 tablespoon chia seeds
- ¾ cup plain coconut yogurt
- 1 cup baby spinach
- 1 cup frozen papaya
- 1 cup frozen tropical fruit mix
- 1 cup coconut milk, unsweetened

Directions
1. Add all the ingredients except vegetables/fruits first
2. Blend until smooth
3. Add the vegetable/fruits
4. Blend until smooth
5. Add a few ice cubes and serve the smoothie
6. Enjoy!

A Minty Drink
Serving: 2
Preparation Time: 5 minutes
Ingredients
- 1 tablespoon hemp seeds
- Fresh mint leaves
- ¾ cup plain coconut yogurt
- 1 cup of frozen mango
- 1 cup of frozen strawberries
- 1 cup unsweetened vanilla almond milk

Directions
1. Add all the ingredients except vegetables/fruits first
2. Blend until smooth
3. Add the vegetable/fruits
4. Blend until smooth
5. Add a few ice cubes and serve the smoothie
6. Enjoy!

The Baked Apple
Serving: 2
Preparation Time: 5 minutes
Ingredients
- Dash ground cinnamon
- 1 tablespoon rolled oats
- 1 tablespoon hemp seeds
- ¾ cup Siggi's Whole milk vanilla yogurt

- 1 cup pear chunks
- 1 cup apple chunks
- 1 cup unsweetened vanilla almond milk

Directions
1. Add all the ingredients except vegetables/fruits first
2. Blend until smooth
3. Add the vegetable/fruits
4. Blend until smooth
5. Add a few ice cubes and serve the smoothie
6. Enjoy!

The Amazing Acai

Serving: 2
Preparation Time: 5 minutes
Ingredients
- 1 tablespoon hemp seeds
- 1 pack of frozen acai
- 1 cup baby spinach
- ¾ cup plain coconut yogurt
- 1 fresh banana
- 1 cup unsweetened hemp milk

Directions
1. Add all the ingredients except vegetables/fruits first
2. Blend until smooth
3. Add the vegetable/fruits
4. Blend until smooth
5. Add a few ice cubes and serve the smoothie
6. Enjoy!

Fine Yo "Mama" Matcha

Serving: 2
Preparation Time: 5 minutes
Ingredients
- 2 teaspoons matcha powder
- 1 tablespoon hemp seeds
- ¾ cup of coconut yogurt
- 1 fresh banana
- 1 cup frozen pineapple
- 1 cup unsweetened almond milk

Directions
1. Add all the ingredients except vegetables/fruits first
2. Blend until smooth
3. Add the vegetable/fruits
4. Blend until smooth
5. Add a few ice cubes and serve the smoothie
6. Enjoy!

The Pumpkin Eye

Serving: 2
Preparation Time: 5 minutes
Ingredients
- Dash of ground cinnamon
- 1 tablespoon hemp seeds
- ½ cup unsweetened hemp milk
- ¾ cup Siggi's whole milk vanilla yogurt
- 1 fresh banana
- 1 cup kale
- 1 cup pure canned pumpkin

Directions
1. Add all the ingredients except vegetables/fruits first
2. Blend until smooth
3. Add the vegetable/fruits
4. Blend until smooth
5. Add a few ice cubes and serve the smoothie
6. Enjoy!

Great Green Garden

Serving: 2
Preparation Time: 5 minutes
Ingredients
- 1 teaspoon spirulina
- Few fresh mint leaves
- ½ cup cucumber, peeled
- ¾ cup plain coconut yogurt
- 1 cup pineapple, frozen
- 1 cup mango, frozen
- 1 cup unsweetened coconut milk

Directions
1. Add all the ingredients except vegetables/fruits first
2. Blend until smooth
3. Add the vegetable/fruits
4. Blend until smooth
5. Add a few ice cubes and serve the smoothie
6. Enjoy!

Generous Mango Surprise

Serving: 2
Preparation Time: 5 minutes
Ingredients
- 1 tablespoon spirulina
- 3 cups frozen mango, sliced
- 1 and ½ cups kale
- 2 and ½ cups unsweetened almond milk

Directions
1. Add all the ingredients except vegetables/fruits first
2. Blend until smooth
3. Add the vegetable/fruits
4. Blend until smooth
5. Add a few ice cubes and serve the smoothie
6. Enjoy!

Powerful Purple Smoothie

Serving: 2
Preparation Time: 5 minutes
Ingredients
- 1 tablespoon green superfood as you like
- 1 tablespoon spirulina
- 1 frozen banana, sliced
- 2 acai frozen berry packs
- 2 cups baby spinach
- 1 and ¼ cups of coconut water

Directions
1. Add all the ingredients except vegetables/fruits first
2. Blend until smooth
3. Add the vegetable/fruits
4. Blend until smooth
5. Add a few ice cubes and serve the smoothie
6. Enjoy!

Banana Apple Blast

Serving: 2

Preparation Time: 5 minutes
Ingredients
- 1 cup ice
- 1 teaspoon bee pollen
- 1 teaspoon spirulina
- 1 cup fresh pineapple, sliced
- 1 frozen banana, sliced
- 2 cups baby spinach
- 1 and ½ cups unsweetened coconut milk drink

Directions
1. Add all the ingredients except vegetables/fruits first
2. Blend until smooth
3. Add the vegetable/fruits
4. Blend until smooth
5. Add a few ice cubes and serve the smoothie
6. Enjoy!

Energizing Pineapple Kicker

Serving: 2
Preparation Time: 5 minutes
Ingredients
- 1 medium cucumber, diced
- ¾ cup fresh pineapple
- 1 tablespoon fresh ginger
- 3 cups baby spinach

Directions
1. Add all the ingredients except vegetables/fruits first
2. Blend until smooth
3. Add the vegetable/fruits
4. Blend until smooth
5. Add a few ice cubes and serve the smoothie
6. Enjoy!

Dandelion And Carrot Booster

Serving: 2
Preparation Time: 5 minutes
Ingredients
- ½ fuji apple
- 1 tablespoon fresh ginger
- ½ pound organic carrots, scrubbed
- ¾ cup dandelion greens
- 2 cups baby spinach

Directions
1. Add all the ingredients except vegetables/fruits first
2. Blend until smooth
3. Add the vegetable/fruits
4. Blend until smooth
5. Add a few ice cubes and serve the smoothie
6. Enjoy!

Green Skinny Energizer

Serving: 2
Preparation Time: 5 minutes
Ingredients
- ½ ripe mango, pitted and sliced
- 1 cup kale, chopped
- 3 cups baby spinach
- 1 cup of coconut water

Directions
1. Add all the ingredients except vegetables/fruits first
2. Blend until smooth
3. Add the vegetable/fruits
4. Blend until smooth
5. Add a few ice cubes and serve the smoothie
6. Enjoy!

Awesome Pineapple And Carrot Blend

Serving: 2
Preparation Time: 5 minutes
Ingredients
- 1/8 teaspoon cinnamon
- 1 cup fresh pineapple
- 3 organic carrots, scrubbed and sliced
- 5 cups of baby spinach
- 1 large cucumber, diced

Directions
1. Add all the ingredients except vegetables/fruits first
2. Blend until smooth
3. Add the vegetable/fruits
4. Blend until smooth
5. Add a few ice cubes and serve the smoothie
6. Enjoy!

Mango Energizer

Serving: 2
Preparation Time: 5 minutes
Ingredients
- 4 tablespoon protein powder
- 2 teaspoons spirulina
- 1 teaspoon bee pollen
- 1 frozen banana, sliced
- 1 cup of frozen mango, sliced
- 2 cups baby spinach
- 1 and ¼ cup unsweetened almond milk

Directions
1. Add all the ingredients except vegetables/fruits first
2. Blend until smooth
3. Add the vegetable/fruits
4. Blend until smooth
5. Add a few ice cubes and serve the smoothie
6. Enjoy!

Powerful Green Frenzy

Serving: 2
Preparation Time: 5 minutes
Ingredients
- 1 cup ice
- 2 tablespoons almond butter
- 1 teaspoon spirulina
- 3 teaspoon fresh ginger
- 1 and ½ frozen bananas, sliced
- 2 cups baby spinach, chopped
- 1 cup kale
- 1 and ½ cups unsweetened almond milk

Directions
1. Add all the ingredients except vegetables/fruits first
2. Blend until smooth
3. Add the vegetable/fruits

4. Blend until smooth
5. Add a few ice cubes and serve the smoothie
6. Enjoy!

The Minty Cucumber
Serving: 2
Preparation Time: 5 minutes
Ingredients
- ½ cup ice
- 1 and ½ cups swiss chard, chopped
- ¾ cup cucumber, diced
- 1 pear, roughly chopped
- ¼ cup fresh cilantro, chopped
- 4 fresh mint leaves, chopped
- ½ lemon, juiced
- ¼ cup of water

Directions
1. Add all the ingredients except vegetables/fruits first
2. Blend until smooth
3. Add the vegetable/fruits
4. Blend until smooth
5. Add a few ice cubes and serve the smoothie
6. Enjoy

Lemon Cilantro Delight
Serving: 2
Preparation Time: 5 minutes
Ingredients
- ½ cup ice
- 1 cup dandelion greens, chopped
- 2 celery stalks, roughly chopped
- 1 pear, roughly chopped
- 1 tablespoon chia seeds
- ¼ cup fresh cilantro, chopped
- Juice of ½ lemon
- ¼ cup of water

Directions
1. Add all the ingredients except vegetables/fruits first
2. Blend until smooth
3. Add the vegetable/fruits
4. Blend until smooth
5. Add a few ice cubes and serve the smoothie
6. Enjoy!

A Peachy Medley
Serving: 2
Preparation Time: 5 minutes
Ingredients
- 1 cup of coconut water
- 1 tablespoon flaxseed, ground
- 1 scoop of vanilla protein powder
- ¼ cup frozen peaches
- ½ cup frozen tart cherries
- 1 cup dandelion greens, chopped

Directions
1. Add all the ingredients except vegetables/fruits first
2. Blend until smooth
3. Add the vegetable/fruits
4. Blend until smooth
5. Add a few ice cubes and serve the smoothie
6. Enjoy!

Cilantro And Citrus Glass
Serving: 2
Preparation Time: 5 minutes
- ½ cup ice
- 2 cups arugula
- ½ cup celery, diced
- 1 grapefruit, peeled and segmented
- 1 handful of fresh cilantro leaves, chopped
- ½ lemon, juiced
- ½ cup of water

Directions
1. Add all the ingredients except vegetables/fruits first
2. Blend until smooth
3. Add the vegetable/fruits
4. Blend until smooth
5. Add a few ice cubes and serve the smoothie
6. Enjoy!

The Deep Green Lagoon
Serving: 2
Preparation Time: 5 minutes
Ingredients
- ½ cup ice
- ½ cup collard greens, chopped
- 1 cup spinach, chopped
- ½ cup fresh broccoli florets, diced
- 1 pear, roughly chopped
- 1 teaspoon spirulina powder
- ½ cup of water

Directions
1. Add all the ingredients except vegetables/fruits first
2. Blend until smooth
3. Add the vegetable/fruits
4. Blend until smooth
5. Add a few ice cubes and serve the smoothie
6. Enjoy!

The Wild Matcha Delight
Serving: 2
Preparation Time: 5 minutes
Ingredients
- 1 cup unsweetened coconut milk
- 1 teaspoon matcha powder
- ½ teaspoon cinnamon
- 1 cup baby spinach, chopped
- 1 cup wild blueberries, frozen

Directions
1. Add all the ingredients except vegetables/fruits first
2. Blend until smooth
3. Add the vegetable/fruits
4. Blend until smooth
5. Add a few ice cubes and serve the smoothie
6. Enjoy!

The Green Potato Chai
Serving: 2
Preparation Time: 5 minutes
Ingredients

- ½ cup chilled, brewed chai
- ½ cup ice
- 1 and ½ cups kale, chopped
- 1 pear, roughly chopped
- 1 scoop of unsweetened protein powder
- ¼ teaspoon cinnamon

Directions
1. Add all the ingredients except vegetables/fruits first
2. Blend until smooth
3. Add the vegetable/fruits
4. Blend until smooth
5. Add a few ice cubes and serve the smoothie
6. Enjoy!

Lemon Cilantro Delight

Serving: 2
Preparation Time: 5 minutes
Ingredients

- ½ cup ice
- 1 cup dandelion greens, chopped
- 2 celery stalks, roughly chopped
- 1 pear, roughly chopped
- 1 tablespoon chia seeds
- ¼ cup fresh cilantro, chopped
- Juice of ½ lemon
- ¼ cup of water

Directions
1. Add all the ingredients except vegetables/fruits first
2. Blend until smooth
3. Add the vegetable/fruits
4. Blend until smooth
5. Add a few ice cubes and serve the smoothie
6. Enjoy!

Lovely Green Gazpacho

Serving: 2
Preparation Time: 5 minutes
Ingredients

- ½ cup ice
- 1 cup collard greens, chopped
- ¼ cup red bell pepper, diced
- ½ cup frozen broccoli florets
- ½ cup fresh tomatoes, chopped
- 1 garlic clove
- ¼ cup fresh cilantro, chopped
- ½ a lemon, juiced
- ½ cup of water

Directions
1. Add all the ingredients except vegetables/fruits first
2. Blend until smooth
3. Add the vegetable/fruits
4. Blend until smooth
5. Add a few ice cubes and serve the smoothie
6. Enjoy!

Tropical Matcha Kale

Serving: 2
Preparation Time: 5 minutes
Ingredients

- ½ cup ice
- 1 cup kale, chopped
- ½ cup of frozen mango died
- 1 teaspoon matcha powder
- ½ cup plain kefir
- ¼ cup of cold water

Directions
1. Add all the ingredients except vegetables/fruits first
2. Blend until smooth
3. Add the vegetable/fruits
4. Blend until smooth
5. Add a few ice cubes and serve the smoothie
6. Enjoy!

The Glamorous Radiance

Serving: 2
Preparation Time: 5 minutes
Ingredients

- ½ cup ice
- 1 cup baby spinach, chopped
- ½ cucumber, diced
- 2 kiwis, peeled
- 1/3 avocado, pit, and skin removed
- 1 scoop collagen protein powder
- 1 teaspoon freshly squeezed lime juice
- 1 cup of water

Directions
1. Add all the ingredients except vegetables/fruits first
2. Blend until smooth
3. Add the vegetable/fruits
4. Blend until smooth
5. Add a few ice cubes and serve the smoothie
6. Enjoy!

Mesmerizing Strawberry And Chocolate Shake

Serving: 1
Preparation Time: 10 minutes
Ingredients

- ½ cup heavy cream, liquid
- 1 tablespoon cocoa powder
- 1 pack stevia
- ½ cup strawberry, sliced
- 1 tablespoon coconut flakes, unsweetened
- 1 and ½ cups of water

Directions
1. Add all the ingredients except vegetables/fruits first
2. Blend until smooth
3. Add the vegetable/fruits
4. Blend until smooth
5. Add a few ice cubes and serve the smoothie
6. Enjoy!

The Overloaded Berry Shake

Serving: 1
Preparation Time: 10 minutes
Ingredients

- ½ cup whole milk yogurt
- 1 pack stevia

- ¼ cup raspberries
- ¼ cup blackberry
- ¼ cup strawberries, chopped
- 1 tablespoon cocoa powder
- 1 tablespoon avocado oil
- 1 and ½ cups of water

Directions
1. Add all the ingredients except vegetables/fruits first
2. Blend until smooth
3. Add the vegetable/fruits
4. Blend until smooth
5. Add a few ice cubes and serve the smoothie
6. Enjoy!

Cool Coco-Loco Cream Shake

Serving: 1
Preparation Time: 10 minutes
Ingredients
- ½ cup of coconut milk
- 2 tablespoons Dutch-processed cocoa powder, unsweetened
- 1 cup brewed coffee, chilled
- 1-2 packs of stevia
- 1 tablespoon hemp seed

Directions
1. Add all the ingredients except vegetables/fruits first
2. Blend until smooth
3. Add the vegetable/fruits
4. Blend until smooth
5. Add a few ice cubes and serve the smoothie
6. Enjoy!

Healthy Chocolate Milkshake

Serving: 2
Preparation Time: 10 minutes
Ingredients
- 16 ounces unsweetened almond milk, vanilla
- 1 pack stevia
- 1 Scoop Whey isolate chocolate protein powder
- ½ cup crushed ice

Directions
1. Add all the ingredients except vegetables/fruits first
2. Blend until smooth
3. Add the vegetable/fruits
4. Blend until smooth
5. Add a few ice cubes and serve the smoothie
6. Enjoy!

The Cacao Super Smoothie

Serving: 1
Preparation Time: 10 minutes
Ingredients
- ½ cup unsweetened almond milk, vanilla
- ½ cup half and half
- ½ avocado, peeled, pitted, sliced
- ½ cup frozen blueberries, unsweetened
- 1 tablespoon cacao powder
- 1 scoop whey vanilla protein powder
- Liquid stevia

Directions
1. Add all the ingredients except vegetables/fruits first
2. Blend until smooth
3. Add the vegetable/fruits
4. Blend until smooth
5. Add a few ice cubes and serve the smoothie
6. Enjoy!

The Nutty Smoothie

Serving: 1
Preparation Time: 10 minutes
Ingredients
- 1 tablespoon chia seeds
- 2 cups of water
- 1 ounce of Macadamia Nuts
- 1-2 packets Stevia, optional
- 1-ounce Hazelnut

Directions
1. Add all the ingredients except vegetables/fruits first
2. Blend until smooth
3. Add the vegetable/fruits
4. Blend until smooth
5. Add a few ice cubes and serve the smoothie
6. Enjoy!

The Strawberry Almond Smoothie

Serving: 1
Preparation Time: 10 minutes
Ingredients
- 16 ounces unsweetened almond milk, vanilla
- 1 pack stevia
- 4 ounces heavy cream
- 1 scoop vanilla whey protein
- ¼ cup frozen strawberries, unsweetened

Directions
1. Add all the ingredients except vegetables/fruits first
2. Blend until smooth
3. Add the vegetable/fruits
4. Blend until smooth
5. Add a few ice cubes and serve the smoothie
6. Enjoy!

Mixed Fruit Madness

Serving: 1
Preparation Time: 10 minutes
Ingredients
- 1 cup spring mix salad blend
- 2 cups of water
- 3 medium blackberries, whole
- 1 packet Stevia, optional
- 1 tablespoon avocado oil
- 1 tablespoon coconut flakes shredded and unsweetened
- 2 tablespoons pecans, chopped
- 1 tablespoon hemp seed
- 1 tablespoon sunflower seed

Directions
1. Add all the ingredients except vegetables/fruits first
2. Blend until smooth
3. Add the vegetable/fruits

4. Blend until smooth
5. Add a few ice cubes and serve the smoothie
6. Enjoy!

The Big Blue Delight
Serving: 2
Preparation Time: 5 minutes
Ingredients
- 1 tablespoon blue spirulina powder
- 1 tablespoon hemp seeds
- ¾ cup plain low-fat Greek yogurt
- 1 fresh banana
- 1 cup frozen blueberries
- 1 cup unsweetened vanilla almond milk

Directions
1. Add all the ingredients except vegetables/fruits first
2. Blend until smooth
3. Add the vegetable/fruits
4. Blend until smooth
5. Add a few ice cubes and serve the smoothie
6. Enjoy!

The Big Bomb Pop
Serving: 2
Preparation Time: 5 minutes
Ingredients
- 1 tablespoon chia seeds
- ¾ cup plain low-fat Greek yogurt
- 1 cup of frozen strawberries
- 1 cup frozen blueberries
- 1 cup unsweetened vanilla almond milk

Directions
1. Add all the ingredients except vegetables/fruits first
2. Blend until smooth
3. Add the vegetable/fruits
4. Blend until smooth
5. Add a few ice cubes and serve the smoothie
6. Enjoy!

The Pinky Swear
Serving: 2
Preparation Time: 5 minutes
Ingredients
- 1 pack (3.5 ounces) of frozen dragon fruit
- ¾ cup low-fat Greek yogurt
- 1 cup frozen pineapple
- 1 cup unsweetened coconut milk

Directions
1. Add all the ingredients except vegetables/fruits first
2. Blend until smooth
3. Add the vegetable/fruits
4. Blend until smooth
5. Add a few ice cubes and serve the smoothie
6. Enjoy!

A Peachy Perfect Glass
Serving: 2
Preparation Time: 5 minutes
Ingredients
- 1 cup skim milk
- 1 cup frozen peaches
- 1 fresh banana
- ¾ cup Siggi's vanilla yogurt
- 1 tablespoon hemp seeds
- Dash of ground cinnamon

Directions
1. Add all the ingredients except vegetables/fruits first
2. Blend until smooth
3. Add the vegetable/fruits
4. Blend until smooth
5. Add a few ice cubes and serve the smoothie
6. Enjoy!

Slim-Jim Vanilla Latte
Serving: 2
Preparation Time: 5 minutes
Ingredients
- Dash of ground cinnamon
- 1 tablespoon chia seeds
- ½ cup unsweetened vanilla almond milk
- ½ cup of leftover coffee
- 4 ice cubes
- ¾ cup Siggi's vanilla yogurt
- 2 fresh bananas

Directions
1. Add all the ingredients except vegetables/fruits first
2. Blend until smooth
3. Add the vegetable/fruits
4. Blend until smooth
5. Add a few ice cubes and serve the smoothie
6. Enjoy!

Cauliflower Cold Glass
Serving: 2
Preparation Time: 5 minutes
Ingredients
- ½ cup frozen cauliflower, riced
- ½ cup of frozen strawberries
- ½ cup frozen blueberries
- ¾ cup plain low-fat Greek yogurt
- 1 fresh banana
- 1 cup unsweetened vanilla almond milk

Directions
1. Add all the ingredients except vegetables/fruits first
2. Blend until smooth
3. Add the vegetable/fruits
4. Blend until smooth
5. Add a few ice cubes and serve the smoothie
6. Enjoy!

A Batch Of Slimming Berries
Serving: 2
Preparation Time: 5 minutes
Ingredients
- 1 tablespoon chia seeds
- ¾ cup plain low-fat Greek yogurt
- 1 cup kale
- 1 cup of frozen mango
- 1 cup of frozen mixed berries
- 1 cup unsweetened vanilla almond milk

Directions

1. Add all the ingredients except vegetables/fruits first
2. Blend until smooth
3. Add the vegetable/fruits
4. Blend until smooth
5. Add a few ice cubes and serve the smoothie
6. Enjoy!

Fine Green Machine
Serving: 2
Preparation Time: 5 minutes
Ingredients
- ¼ cup fresh avocado
- ¾ cup plain coconut yogurt
- 1 fresh banana
- 1 cup baby spinach
- 1 cup of frozen mango
- 1 cup unsweetened coconut milk

Directions
1. Add all the ingredients except vegetables/fruits first
2. Blend until smooth
3. Add the vegetable/fruits
4. Blend until smooth
5. Add a few ice cubes and serve the smoothie
6. Enjoy!

The Summer Hearty Shake
Serving: 2
Preparation Time: 5 minutes
Ingredients
- 1 cup frozen blackberries
- ¾ cup Whole milk vanilla yogurt
- ½ cup unsweetened vanilla almond milk
- ½ cup of frozen strawberries
- ½ cup frozen peaches
- 1 tablespoon hemp seeds
- Dash of ground cinnamon

Directions
1. Add all the ingredients except vegetables/fruits first
2. Blend until smooth
3. Add the vegetable/fruits
4. Blend until smooth
5. Add a few ice cubes and serve the smoothie
6. Enjoy!

The Mocha Built
Serving: 2
Preparation Time: 5 minutes
Ingredients
- 1 tablespoon cacao powder
- ½ cup of leftover coffee
- ½ cup skim milk
- ¾ cup plain low-fat Greek yogurt
- 1 cup baby spinach
- 1 cup frozen cherries
- 1 fresh banana

Directions
1. Add all the ingredients except vegetables/fruits first
2. Blend until smooth
3. Add the vegetable/fruits
4. Blend until smooth

5. Add a few ice cubes and serve the smoothie
6. Enjoy!

Sweet Protein And Cherry Shake
Serving: 2
Preparation Time: 5 minutes
Ingredients
- 1 cup of water
- 3 cups spinach
- 2 bananas, sliced
- 2 cups frozen cherries
- 2 tablespoons cacao powder
- 4 tablespoons hemp seeds, shelled

Directions
1. Add all the ingredients except vegetables/fruits first
2. Blend until smooth
3. Add the vegetable/fruits
4. Blend until smooth
5. Add a few ice cubes and serve the smoothie
6. Enjoy!

Iron And Protein Shake
Serving: 2
Preparation Time: 5 minutes
Ingredients
- 2 tablespoons favorite sweetened
- 1 cup of water
- ¼ cup hemp seeds
- 2 large bananas, frozen
- 4 cups strawberries, sliced

Directions
1. Add all the ingredients except vegetables/fruits first
2. Blend until smooth
3. Add the vegetable/fruits
4. Blend until smooth
5. Add a few ice cubes and serve the smoothie
6. Enjoy!

Creamy Peachy Shake
Serving: 2
Preparation Time: 5 minutes
Ingredients
- 2 scoops of vanilla protein powder
- 2 cups peaches
- ¼ cup fat-free Greek yogurt
- ½ cup of orange juice

Directions
1. Add all the ingredients except vegetables/fruits first
2. Blend until smooth
3. Add the vegetable/fruits
4. Blend until smooth
5. Add a few ice cubes and serve the smoothie
6. Enjoy!

Protein-Packed Root Beer Shake
Serving: 2
Preparation Time: 5 minutes
Ingredients
- ½ cup fat-free vanilla yogurt
- 1 scoop vanilla whey protein
- 1 and ½ cups root beet

- 1 scoop vanilla casein protein

Directions
1. Add all the ingredients except vegetables/fruits first
2. Blend until smooth
3. Add the vegetable/fruits
4. Blend until smooth
5. Add a few ice cubes and serve the smoothie
6. Enjoy!

Peppermint And Dark Chocolate Shake Delight

Serving: 2
Preparation Time: 5 minutes
Ingredients
- ¼ teaspoon peppermint extract
- 1 scoop of chocolate whey protein powder
- 2 tablespoons cocoa powder
- Pinch of salt
- 1 cup almond milk
- 1 large frozen banana
- 2-3 large ice cubes

Directions
1. Add all the ingredients except vegetables/fruits first
2. Blend until smooth
3. Add the vegetable/fruits
4. Blend until smooth
5. Add a few ice cubes and serve the smoothie
6. Enjoy!

Spiced Up Banana Shake

Serving: 2
Preparation Time: 5 minutes
Ingredients
- 2 scoops of vanilla protein powder
- ½ teaspoon ground cinnamon
- 1/8 teaspoon ground nutmeg
- 2 ripe bananas
- 12 ice cubes

Directions
1. Add all the ingredients except vegetables/fruits first
2. Blend until smooth
3. Add the vegetable/fruits
4. Blend until smooth
5. Add a few ice cubes and serve the smoothie
6. Enjoy!

Mad Mocha Glass

Serving: 2
Preparation Time: 5 minutes
Ingredients
- 4 ice cubes
- 1 scoop 100% chocolate whey protein
- ½ scoop vanilla protein powder
- 6 ounces of water
- 6 ounces of cold coffee

Directions
1. Add all the ingredients except vegetables/fruits first
2. Blend until smooth
3. Add the vegetable/fruits
4. Blend until smooth
5. Add a few ice cubes and serve the smoothie
6. Enjoy!

Lemon And Cranberry Shake

Serving: 2
Preparation Time: 5 minutes
Ingredients
- 4 ice cubes
- 1 and ½ cups of vanilla frozen yogurt
- 1-2 scoops of 100% vanilla whey protein powder
- 2 cups mixed berries
- ½ teaspoon lemon zest
- 12 ounces cranberry juice
- 1 tablespoon lemon juice

Directions
1. Add all the ingredients except vegetables/fruits first
2. Blend until smooth
3. Add the vegetable/fruits
4. Blend until smooth
5. Add a few ice cubes and serve the smoothie
6. Enjoy!

Hearty Dandelion Smoothie

Serving: 2
Preparation Time: 5 minutes
Ingredients
- 1 cup crushed ice
- 1 tablespoon spirulina
- 1 orange
- ¾ avocado, cubed
- 2 bananas, diced
- 1 cup dandelion leaves, chopped

Directions
1. Add all the ingredients except vegetables/fruits first
2. Blend until smooth
3. Add the vegetable/fruits
4. Blend until smooth
5. Add a few ice cubes and serve the smoothie
6. Enjoy!

Apple And Zucchini Medley

Serving: 2
Preparation Time: 5 minutes
Ingredients
- 1 cup crushed ice
- 1 jalapeno pepper
- 2 stalk celery, diced
- ¾ avocado, cubed
- 2 apples, quartered

Directions
1. Add all the ingredients except vegetables/fruits first
2. Blend until smooth
3. Add the vegetable/fruits
4. Blend until smooth
5. Add a few ice cubes and serve the smoothie
6. Enjoy!

Flax And Kiwi Spinach Smoothie

Serving: 2
Preparation Time: 5 minutes
Ingredients

- 1 cup crushed ice
- 3 tablespoons ground flax
- 3 kiwis, diced
- 1 stalk celery, chopped
- 1 banana, chopped
- 2 apples, quartered
- 1 cup spinach, chopped

Directions
1. Add all the ingredients except vegetables/fruits first
2. Blend until smooth
3. Add the vegetable/fruits
4. Blend until smooth
5. Add a few ice cubes and serve the smoothie
6. Enjoy!

Cucumber Kale And Lime Apple Smoothie

Serving: 2

Preparation Time: 5 minutes

Ingredients
- 1 cup crushed ice
- 1 cucumber, diced
- ¼ cup raspberries, chopped
- 1 lime, juiced
- 1 avocado, diced
- 2 apples, quartered
- 1 cup kale, chopped

Directions
1. Add all the ingredients except vegetables/fruits first
2. Blend until smooth
3. Add the vegetable/fruits
4. Blend until smooth
5. Add a few ice cubes and serve the smoothie
6. Enjoy!

28 Days Meal Plan

Day	Breakfast	Lunch	Dinner	Dessert
1	Walnut and Oat Granola	Warm Chicken and Spinach Salad	Cauliflower Mash	Sticky Ginger Cake
2	Coconut and Berry Smoothie	Stuffed Chicken	French Toast in Sticks	Tiramisu
3	Crispy Pita with Canadian Bacon	Chicken Sandwich	Misto Quente	Toffee Apple Mini Pies
4	Coconut-Berry Sunrise Smoothie	Buttermilk Fried Chicken	Seared Tuna Steak	Pineapple Frozen Yogurt
5	Greek Yogurt Sundae	Zaatar Lamb Loin Chops	Vegetable Soup	Pomegranate Panna Cotta
6	Avocado and Goat Cheese Toast	Pork on a Blanket	Pork Chop Diane	Coconutty Pudding Clouds
7	Oat and Walnut Granola	Vietnamese Grilled Pork	Autumn Pork Chops with Red Cabbage and Apples	Cream Cheese Pound Cake
8	Zucchini Noodles with Creamy Avocado Pesto	Provencal Ribs	Chipotle Chili Pork Chops	Dark Chocolate Coffee Cupcakes
9	Avocado Chicken Salad	Steak	Orange-Marinated Pork Tenderloin	German Chocolate Cake Bars
10	Pancakes with Berries	Marinated Loin Potatoes	Homestyle Herb Meatballs	Gingerbread Soufflés
11	Omelette à la Margherita	Beef with Mushrooms	Lime-Parsley Lamb Cutlets	Lemon Meringue Ice Cream
12	Spanakopita Frittata	Cheesy and Crunchy Russian Steaks	Beef Chili	Mini Bread Puddings
13	Ratatouille Egg Bake	Chicken Wings	Greek Broccoli Salad	Pumpkin Ice Cream with Candied Pecans
14	Cottage Pancakes	Chicken Nuggets	Mediterranean Steak Sandwiches	Raspberry Almond Clafoutis
15	Greek Yogurt and Oat Pancakes	Pork Chops	Roasted Beef with Peppercorn Sauce	Blackberry Soufflés
16	Savory Breakfast Egg Bites	Buffalo Chicken Hot Wings	Coffee-and-Herb-Marinated Steak	Blueberry Lemon "Cup" Cakes
17	Simple Grain-Free Biscuits	Herb Chicken Thighs	Traditional Beef Stroganoff	Blueberry No-Bake Cheesecake
18	Brussels Sprout with Fried Eggs	Air Fryer Beef Steak Kabobs with Vegetables	Chicken and Roasted Vegetable Wraps	Broiled Stone Fruit
19	Vanilla Coconut Pancakes	Fried Pork Chops	Spicy Chicken Cacciatore	Café Mocha Torte

20	Cheesy Spinach and Egg Casserole	Pork Liver	Scallion Sandwich	Cappuccino Mousse
21	Chocolate-Zucchini Muffins	Air Fried Meatloaf	Cheesy Cauliflower Gratin	Caramel Pecan Pie
22	Gluten-Free Carrot and Oat Pancakes	Pork Tenderloin	Strawberry Spinach Salad	Carrot Cupcakes
23	Breakfast Egg Bites	Pork Bondiola Chop	Garlic Bread	Raspberry and Dark Chocolate Mini Soufflés
24	Tacos with Pico De Gallo	Air Fry Rib-Eye Steak	Bruschetta	Tropical Fruit Tart
25	Coconut and Chia Pudding	Lemon Pepper Chicken	Cream Buns with Strawberries	Sweet Potato Crème Brule
26	Tomato Waffles	Caribbean Spiced Chicken	Blueberry Buns	Raspberry Lemon Cheesecake Squares
27	Breakfast Homemade Poultry Sausage	Chicken Tenders	Lean Lamb and Turkey Meatballs with Yogurt	Mini Key Lime Tarts
28	Sausage and Pepper Burrito	Chicken in Tomato Juice	Air Fried Section and Tomato	Moist Butter Cake

Manufactured by Amazon.ca
Bolton, ON

28839201R00142